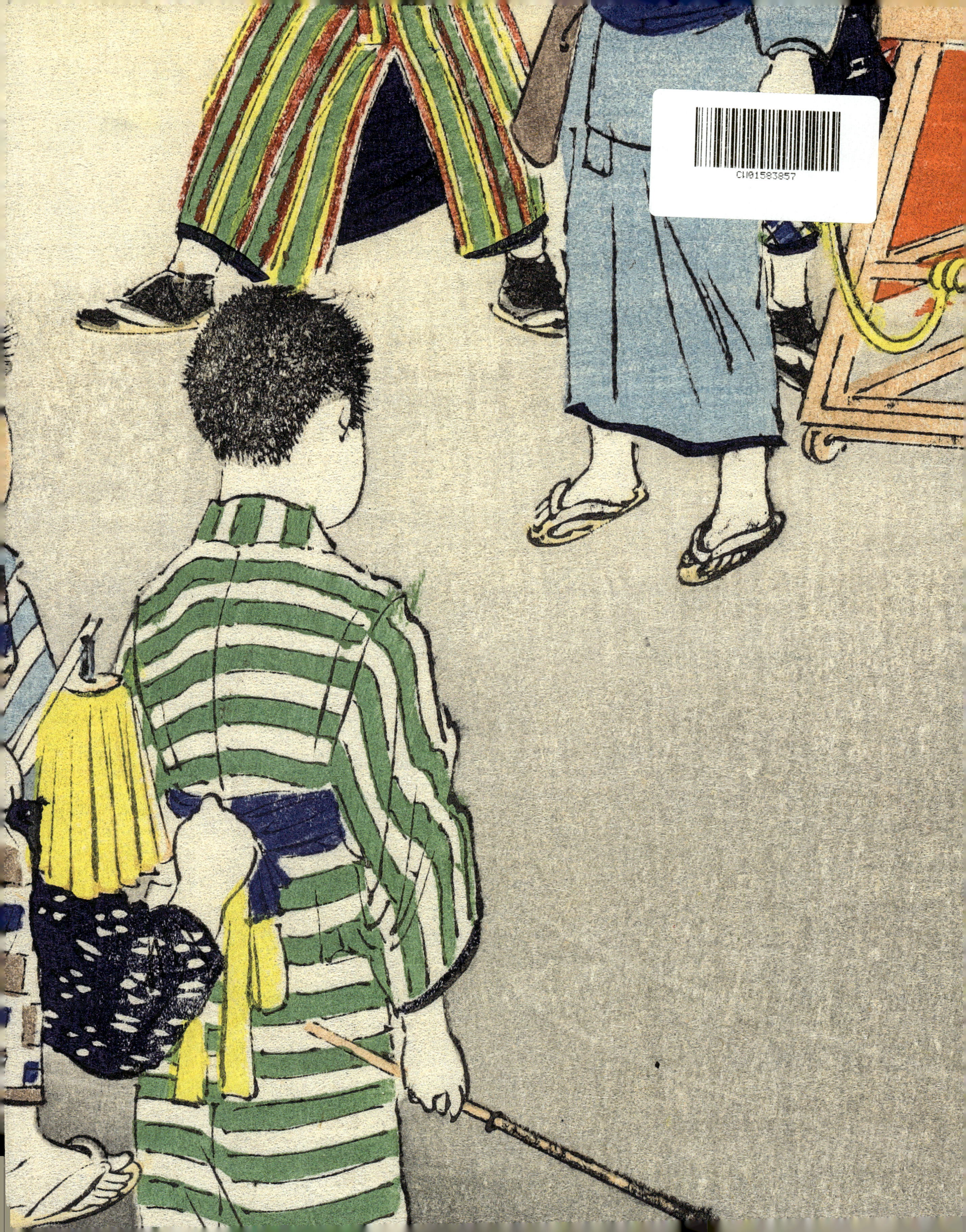

KIMONO

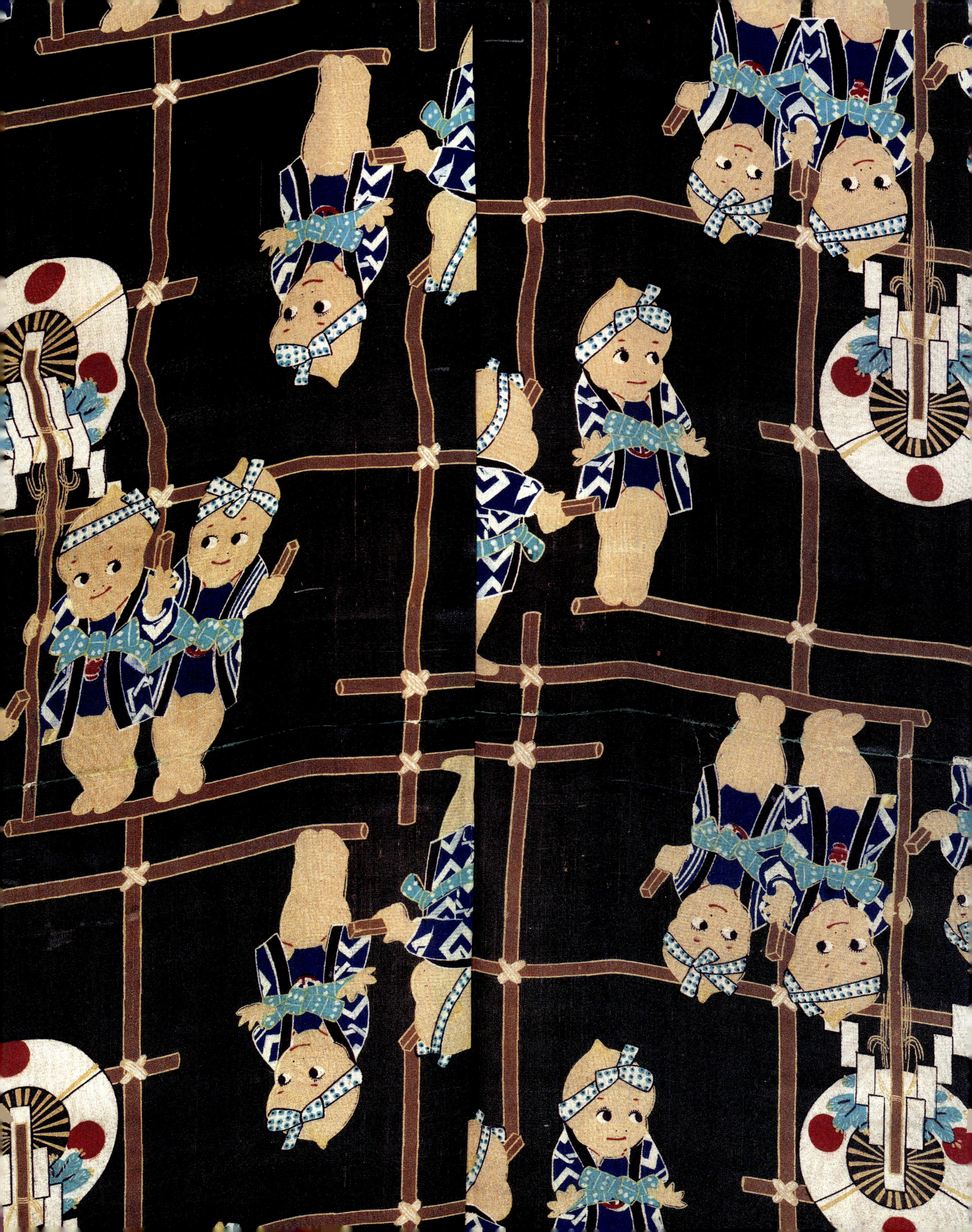

KIMONO

IMAGES OF CULTURE, 1910–1950, IN THE KHALILI COLLECTIONS

PRESTEL
MUNICH • LONDON • NEW YORK

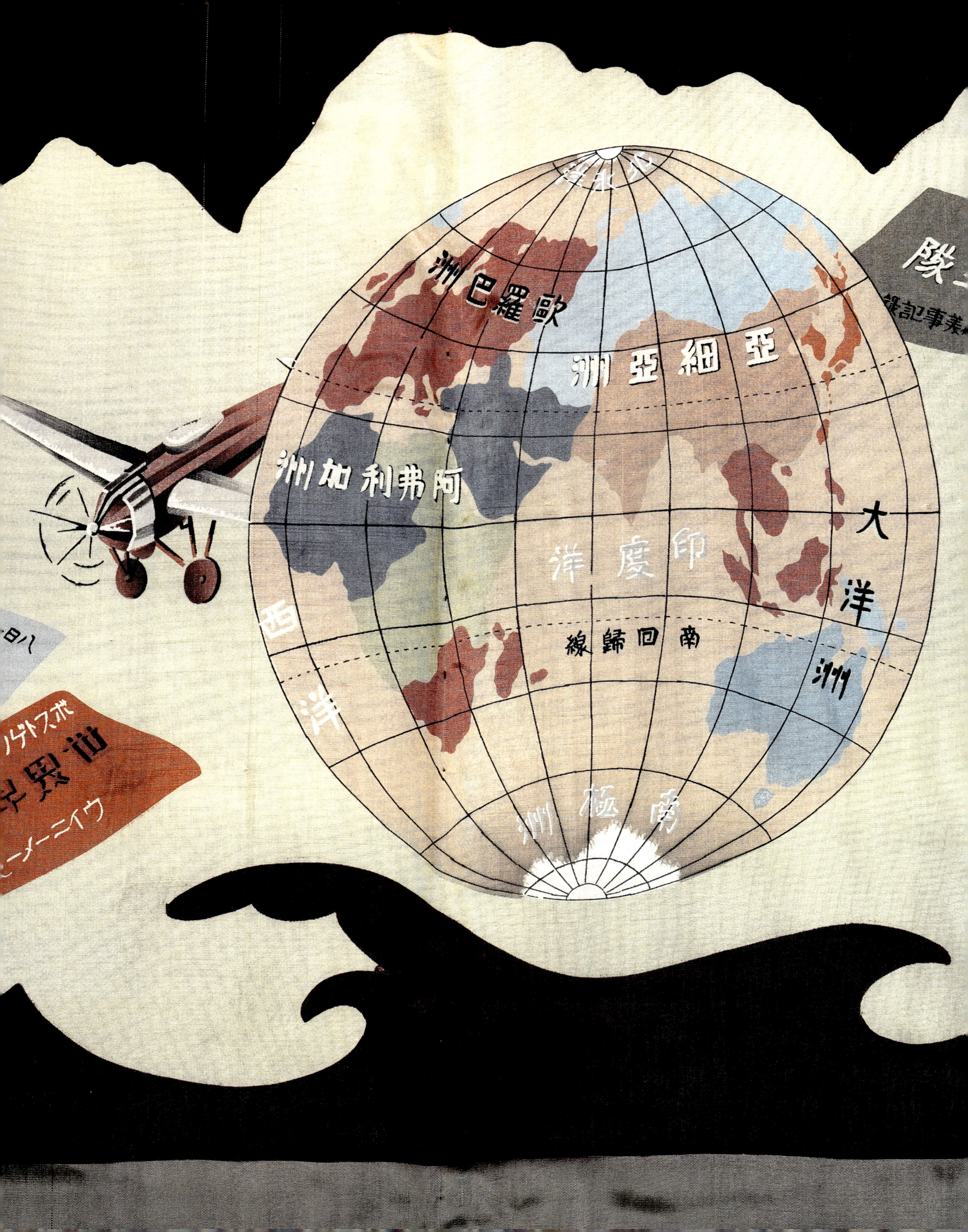

歐羅巴洲
亞細亞洲
阿弗利加洲
印度洋
南回歸線
大洋洲
西洋
南極洲

CONTENTS

PREFACE

PROFESSOR SIR NASSER DAVID KHALILI

Since childhood, my life has been filled with art that represents different facets of culture and human dreams, hopes, and imagination. I grew up with objects from far and wide that had witnessed the whole spectrum of human history, from the smallest of trends to the largest of shifts in the winds. I started forming my collections in the 1970s, and in the following 50-plus years have established eight of the world's finest and most comprehensive art collections: Islamic art (700–2000), Hajj and the arts of pilgrimage (700–2000), Aramaic documents (353–324 BC), Japanese art of the Meiji period (1868–1912), Japanese kimono (1750–2000), Swedish textiles (1700–1900), Spanish damascene metalwork (1850–1900), and enamels of the world (1700–2000). Combined, the collections span over 35,000 objects from around the globe and from ancient history to the modern age. I am immensely proud and humbled to say that each collection now stands on its own as one of the most comprehensive and significant in its field. The collections will be represented in over 100 publications, of which 90 volumes are already published, including exhibition catalogs, academic monographs, and more. By the end of 2024, we hope our dream of conserving, researching, and publishing all 35,000 objects will be fulfilled with the release of the rest of our volumes. We also constantly push to broaden accessibility to our objects, from detailed digitalization through to exhibitions, with our objects having been shown in over 126 leading museums and institutions around the world.

And yet, I always strive to find new horizons, to discover corners of knowledge that have seen little light, objects which have lain dormant and are waiting to be recognized as the fascinating testimonies to history and artistry that they are. It is my passion and my delight, and I have no intention of stopping; so much more of humanity waits to be uncovered. This publication highlights just one of these truly fascinating slices of history and artistry—the highly creative, original, and ultimately forgotten period of modernity-themed and propaganda kimono production at the turn of the 20th century and in the lead up to World War II.

In 2015, a comprehensive catalog of our kimono collection titled *Kimono: The Art and Evolution of Japanese Fashion* was published, with essays by leading scholars in the field and edited by Anna Jackson, Keeper of the Asian Department at the Victoria and Albert Museum and honorary curator here at the Khalili Collections. This was a wonderful deep dive into the history of this iconic garment and spanned the breadth of our collection of over 200 pieces, ranging from the Edo period (1603–1868) right up to the 21st century. However, we felt that the kimono that were made in that pocket period of the early 20th century deserved a more detailed approach and a more comprehensive exploration. And so, we enlisted the help of Jacqueline M. Atkins, renowned textile historian, to help us uncover the brilliant history of these unique garments in the current volume.

So much can be said, and will be said, about these items of clothing at the heart of such a turbulent period of change, doubts, and revelations. But unfortunately, other than the current publication, information has been thin on the ground regarding these beautiful relics of a period on the cusp of being forgotten. And so it is with great pride that I was able to help bring light to this corner, with the wonderful essay by my curator, Dror Elkvity, and the insightful journey offered by Jacqueline M. Atkins.

While the basic form of this T-shaped, straight-seamed, front-wrapping garment has not really changed over the centuries, the varied designs upon it, and the material and methods of its creating, have changed dramatically over time, directly reflecting the spirit of the era in which they were made. In the kimono featured in this volume, we witness the birth of a new age, filled with a fascination with airplanes, trains, cityscapes, pop culture, music, and films, as Japan turned its gaze outward to the world, and in turn inward, in a desire to figure out who it was and who it wished to be. This was a crucial crossroads for Japan, filled with elation and uncertainty, and it is my hope that by bringing you this volume, I will help to shed light on this immensely important period in Japanese artistry.

I would like to sincerely thank Jacqueline M. Atkins for her enthusiasm, expertise, and professionalism as the main author of this publication. My gratitude also to Alan Marcuson and Diane Hall for their assistance in creating this part of the kimono collections and to Dror Elkvity, curator of Japanese Meiji Art in the Khalili Collections, for his assistance in forming and managing the collection, as well as his contribution to this volume. Last but not least, I would like to sincerely thank the team at Prestel who helped bring this book to life, and, as ever, my family, who are the beating heart of all my endeavors.

Professor Sir Nasser David Khalili
2024

FOREWORD

WHO ARE WE NOW? REFLECTIONS ON *OMOSHIROGARA*

DROR ELKVITY

In Isao Takahata's 1988 animated film *Grave of the Fireflies*, based on a semi-autobiographical tale of the same name by Akiyuki Nosaka, the character of Seita—a young boy caught in the nightmare of World War II bombings in rural Japan and on a desperate, sometimes misguided journey to try and independently look after his young sister Setsuko—is allowed a moment of reprieve watching fireflies glow in the darkness of the empty bomb shelter he has adopted as a habitat for himself and his sister. To cheer his sister up, after she comments that a passing kamikaze plane looks like a firefly, he gathers a group of fireflies onto a covered bucket and sets them free in the shelter. They both rejoice at the starry night that has lighted up their small, intimate world, so punishing from without. As Setsuko falls asleep, Seita takes a moment to watch the fireflies and forget about his daily battle to survive, temporarily dousing the trauma and horror in his mind. The bright dots of light in the air remind him of a naval review he went to, watching his father standing proud in uniform onboard the *Maya* heavy cruiser, the ship decked out with lights and fireworks exploding in the sky. As the memories flood over him, he sings a war chant he once heard: "Mighty fortresses floating on the seas, defending our homeland from invaders near and far." When the memory fades, he looks back at his sleeping sister and wonders whether his father is still alive. In the following scene, when morning comes, Setsuko makes a grave for the fireflies that died, which immediately triggers the memory of their mother being thrown into a mass grave. The horrible reality comes back in stark contrast to the fantasy of the night before.

This powerful scene illustrates a very important contradiction at the heart of examining pieces such as the Japanese propaganda and modernity kimono of the interwar years presented in this book. While they fall under the category of *omoshirogara* ("amusing patterns"), which would suggest a whimsical nature, and while some do indeed depict what might be considered an apolitical celebration of a forward-looking Japan through the prism of trains, jazz, and movies, aren't they still painful relics of a period that raises very mixed emotions when faced with the historical reality and circumstances in which they were made and worn? After all, Jacqueline M. Atkins herself, whom we are honored to have write for this very publication, wrote in the introduction to her groundbreaking catalog *Wearing Propaganda* that the book was "not intended to glorify the wars discussed therein, or war in general" and emphasized the need to study them as garments which reveal "a highly personal and intimate association with war and propaganda ... [the designs on which] underscore the need to understand better the pervasive role of propaganda in garnering support for acts and aggression, today as well as in the 1930s and 1940s."[1] Indeed, the need to understand the machinations of propaganda as it applies to everyday life has never been more pressing. In the age of social media, of the self as a billboard for ideas, aspirations, and political thought, where fashions and viral videos can create shifts in opinion, and where one presents one's ideology and opinions as an ever-shifting digital avatar, the idea of wearing ideology explicitly on the body is more powerful, and relevant, than ever.

Although garments meant for adults did not often make their politics apparent in the public sphere—a large proportion of pieces in the collection are *haori*, where the illustration is on the inside, as well as *juban* and *nagajuban*, which are undergarments—they were often shared with a close circle of friends at a *zashiki-gei*

OPPOSITE FIG. 1 Kimono for a child (detail)
Children at home (see p. 202)

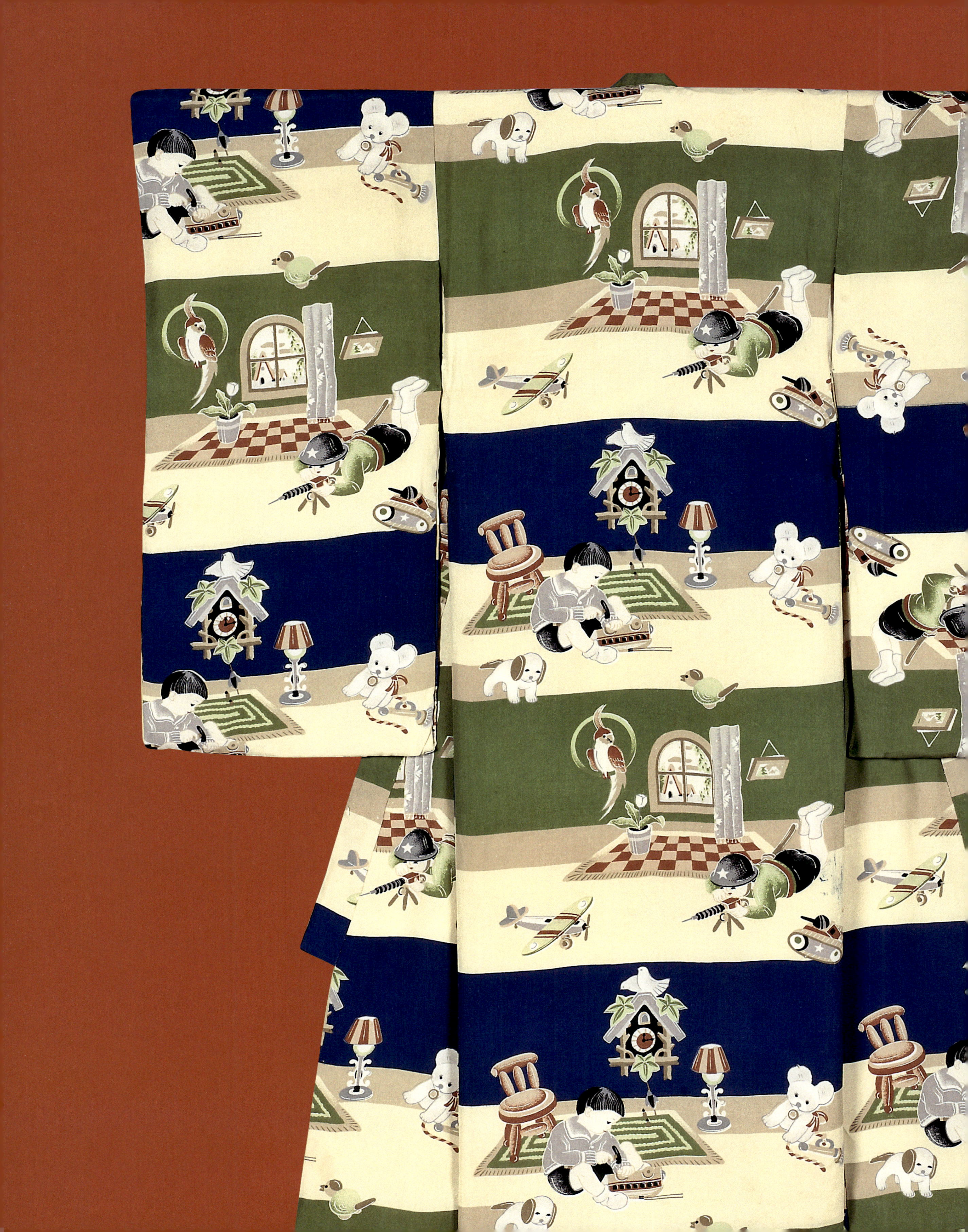

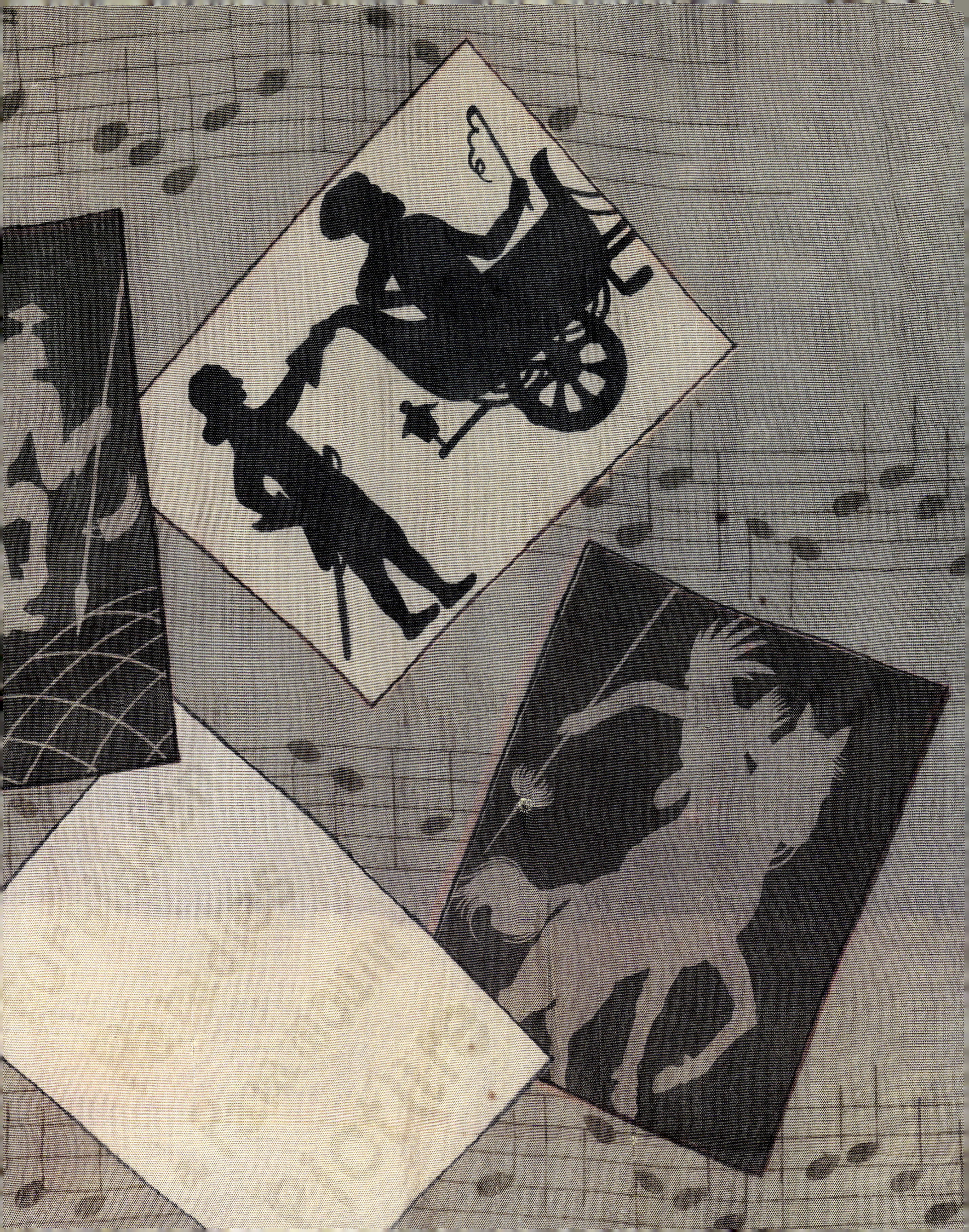

OPPOSITE FIG. 2 Man's *haori* with a decorative lining (detail)
Broadway After Dark (see p. 272)

or parlor/private room performance. As Hiroshi Kashiwagi writes in *Wearing Propaganda*, "The *zashiki-gei*, or parlor performance, is a private performance (*gei*) that takes place before a select group of friends in a small room, even a very small room, such as the four-and-a-half-mat room (270 × 270 cm or 8 feet 10 inches square) that is standard for the tea ceremony ... Conveying a message by showing off the lining of one's *haori* or the design on one's *nagajuban* can be considered part of the repertory of *zashiki-gei* performances."[2] Thus they can be conceived as the slightly less public progenitor of the political, slogan, and band T-shirts that began with the American counterculture of the 1950s and 1960s, the tendency and sensibility of which led to the more modern notion of "wearing our politics." It is interesting to note that the T-shirt itself was at first an undergarment as well, and came to be deliberately worn on the outside as a way to add to the rebellious statement. As Steve Gdula claims in *Wearing History: T-shirts from the Gay Rights Movement*, "Even as a blank slate, the humble white T-shirt carried a powerful message of its own in the 1950s and 60s. After World War II, the T-shirt had become part of the uniform of a certain segment of society, as the practice of wearing underwear as outerwear became associated with the social outsider ... What started to broaden the shirts' appeal was the potential they held as billboards—and they were readily available."[3] While the Japanese of the 1930s may have not been so bold, the articles of clothing in this book are among the first examples of political statements being printed onto and made into everyday garments that advertise the wearer's political beliefs and interests.

While *omoshirogara* kimono were often relegated to the private sphere, this was less often the case when it came to children's garments, even if these tended to be worn on special occasions or shrine visits. Wearing such garments would tell onlookers that the parents were patriotic, forward-thinking, modern people who were proud of their country and their role in society. In the build-up to World War II, motherhood was also highly elevated and prioritized. Japan had been developing programs geared at encouraging childbirth and the role of the mother had become of the utmost importance in maintaining the spirit of a prosperous Japan. Michiko Suzuki in *Reading the Kimono in Twentieth-Century Japanese Literature and Film* writes:

> From the late 1930s, images of motherhood and maternal love occupied a central place within Japanese literature and culture. Especially with the beginning of the Second Sino-Japanese War and the National Spiritual Mobilization campaign in 1937, various women's groups became a part of the war effort, and the 1937 Mother-Child Protection Act (*Boshi hogo hō*) gave assistance to financially insecure mothers and caregivers of young children, reflecting the government's emphasis on the importance of motherhood and its role on the home front. The view that a woman must "give birth and increase the population" (*umeyo fuyaseyo*) and commit to producing and supporting soldiers of the nation became part of the dominant ideology of the times. In fiction and images, this concept of the loving mother was also tied to a belief in the purity of the homeland, and highlighted the sacrifice and devotion required of all subjects for imperial Japan.[4]

It is no surprise, then, to see that a mother who celebrates Japan's achievements and who buys propaganda kimono for her children would be considered a fine example of the ideal and devoted Japanese mother. However, a closer inspection of some of these children's garments highlights that such an interpretation ignores some

RIGHT FIG. 3 Kimono for a child (detail)
Cartoon Country (see p. 267)

FAR RIGHT FIG. 4 Woman's *juban* (detail)
An orchestra seen from above (see p. 296)

meaningful context. More often than not, children's kimono bear American cartoon figures, interpreted by Japanese artists: Dumbo, Mickey Mouse, Donald Duck and others, such as Felix the Cat, or Julius the Cat, following Jacqueline M. Atkins's interpretation (fig. 3). Indeed, some of the adult pieces too depicted entertainment borrowed from the USA and Europe, including jazz, revue and cabaret, and baseball (figs 4–6) —all pieces made and worn during a time when the relationship between Japan and the West was a highly complex affair. From the strong anti-Japanese sentiments toward immigrants in California between 1900 and 1914, to being allied during World War I, to the Mukden incident (which led to the occupation of Manchuria) in 1931, Japan was highly ambivalent toward the West in the interwar years.

In fact, most of the motifs mentioned above came to inspire and sometimes be associated with counter-cultural individuals at the time and afterward. Cartoons and cartoonists such as Dōeisha and Prokino made very successful animated films at the time, which in turn inspired other artists, forming the first stepping stones for what eventually became anime. Osamu Tezuka, often dubbed "the Godfather of Manga" and a central figure in the development of modern anime sensibilities, was heavily inspired by both the work of Suihō Tagawa—who in 1931, the year of the Mukden incident, created the character of Norakuro, a black anthropomorphic dog who serves in the army—and by Disney's *Bambi*, which he reportedly saw 80 times.[5] Dōeisha, Prokino, and later Tezuka, right down to Hayao Miyazaki and Isao Takahata, director of *Grave of the Fireflies*, all included strong anti-war messages in their films. The case for the association of jazz and revue with an anti-war, left-leaning mentality is well documented and was as true for Japan as it was for the West. Seigo Matsuoka, esteemed writer and editor well known for his book review series

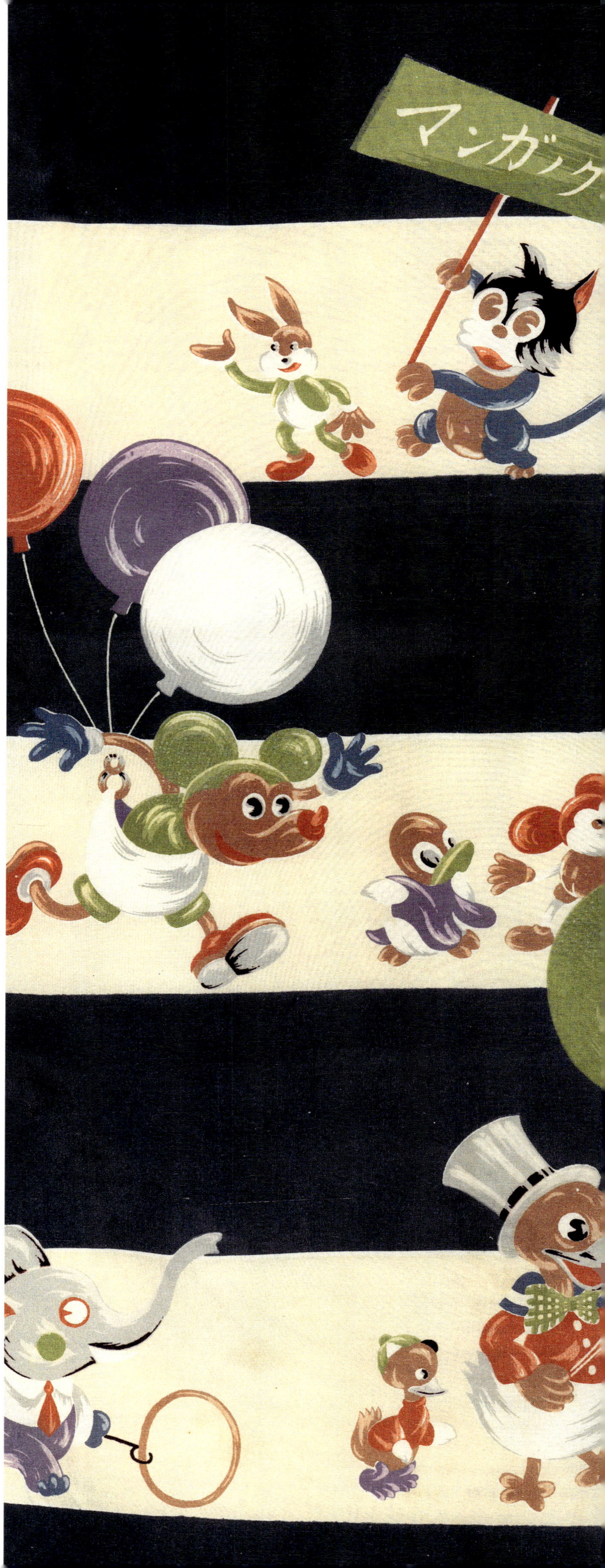

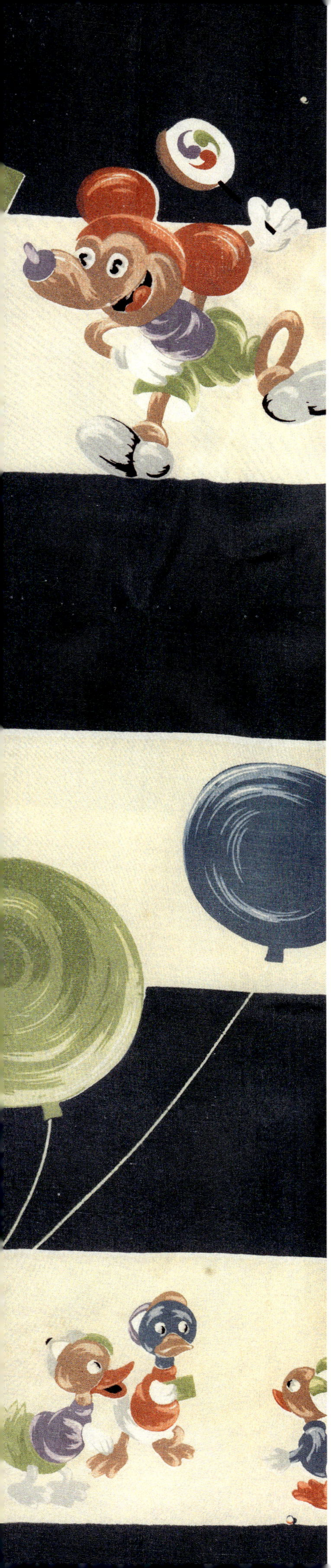

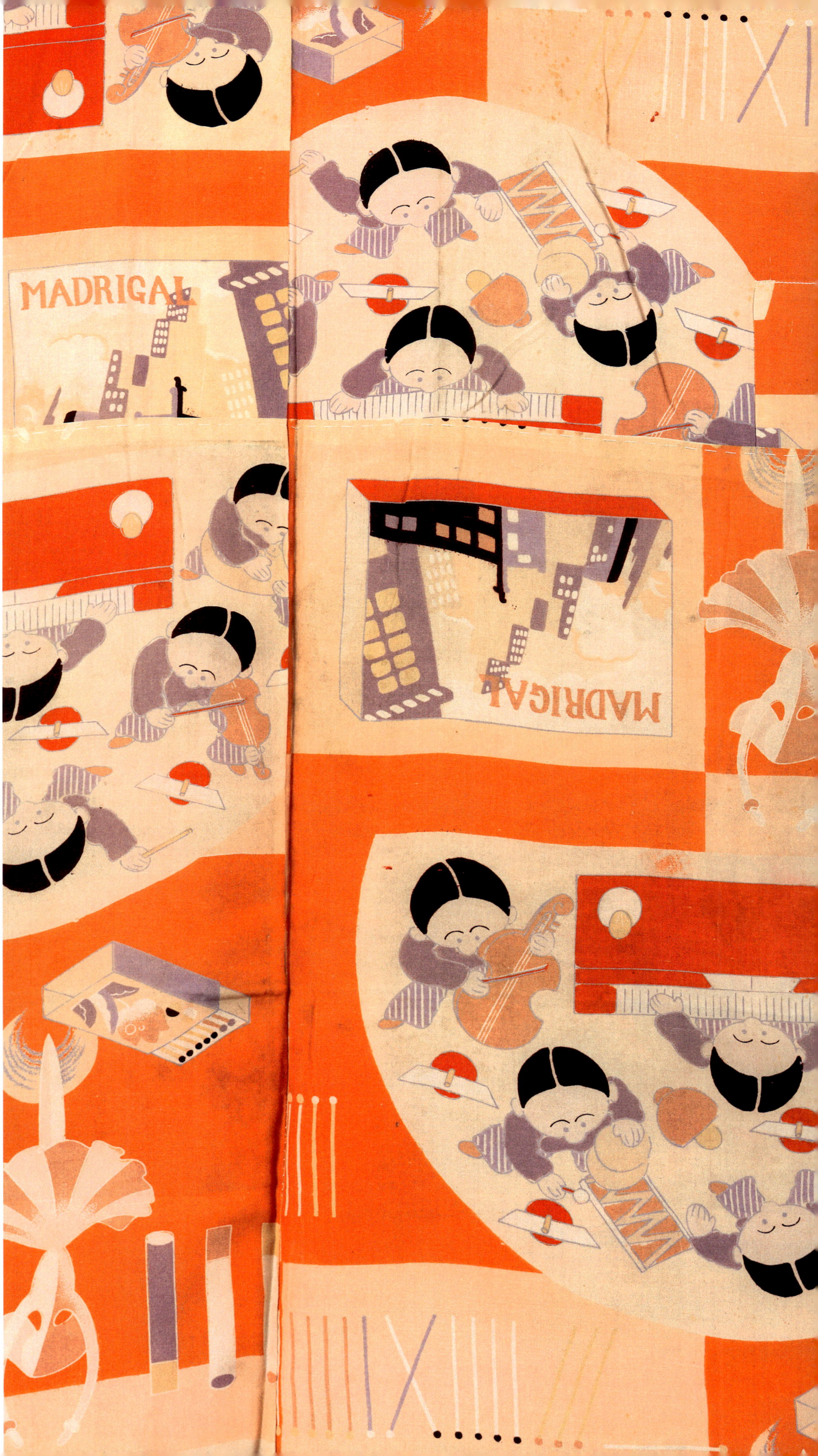
MADRIGAL
MADRIGAL

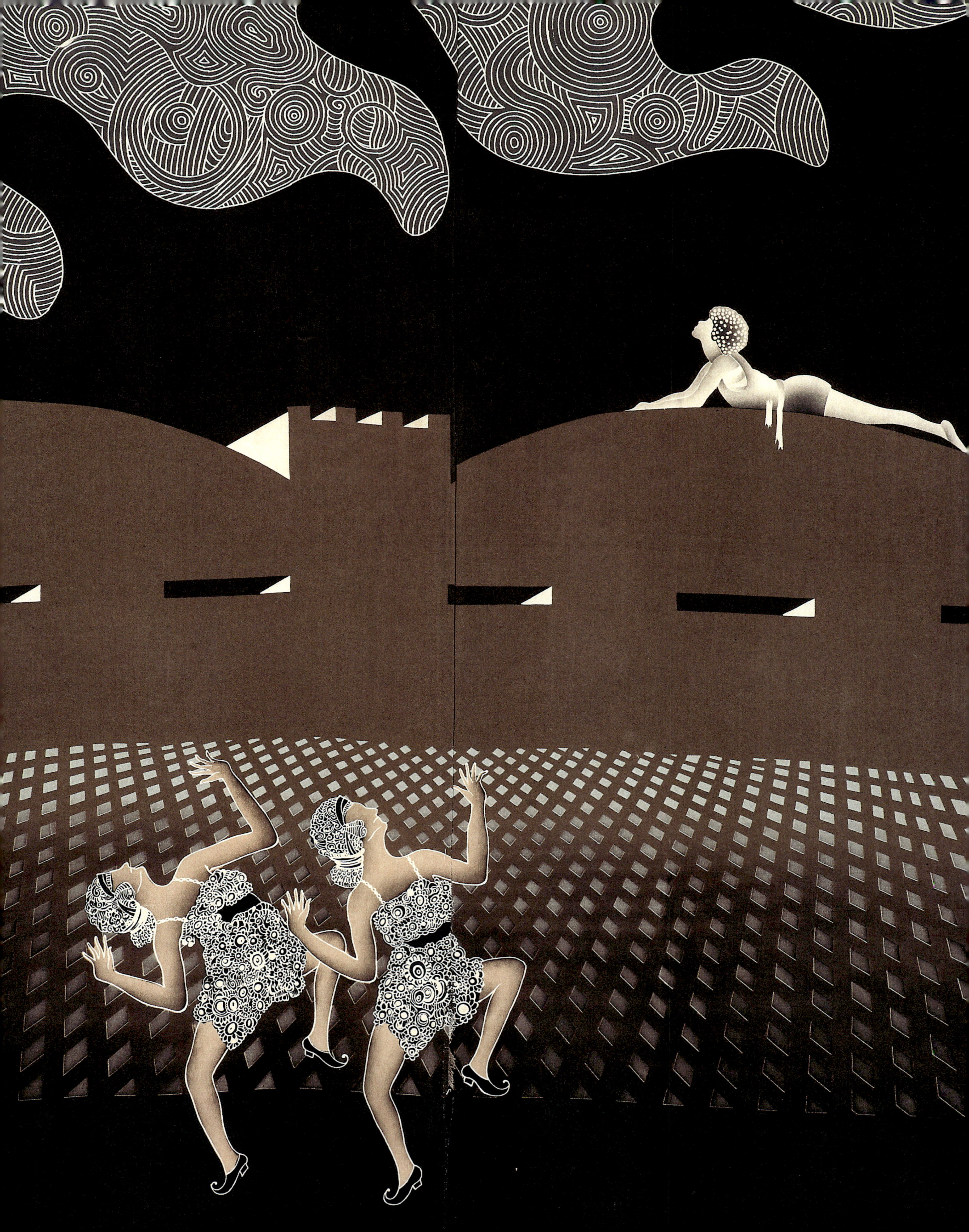

OPPOSITE FIG. 5 *Juban* for a man (detail)
Come to the cabaret (see p. 205)

BELOW FIG. 6 Man's *haori* with a decorative lining (detail)
Baseball on a pitch (see p. 233)

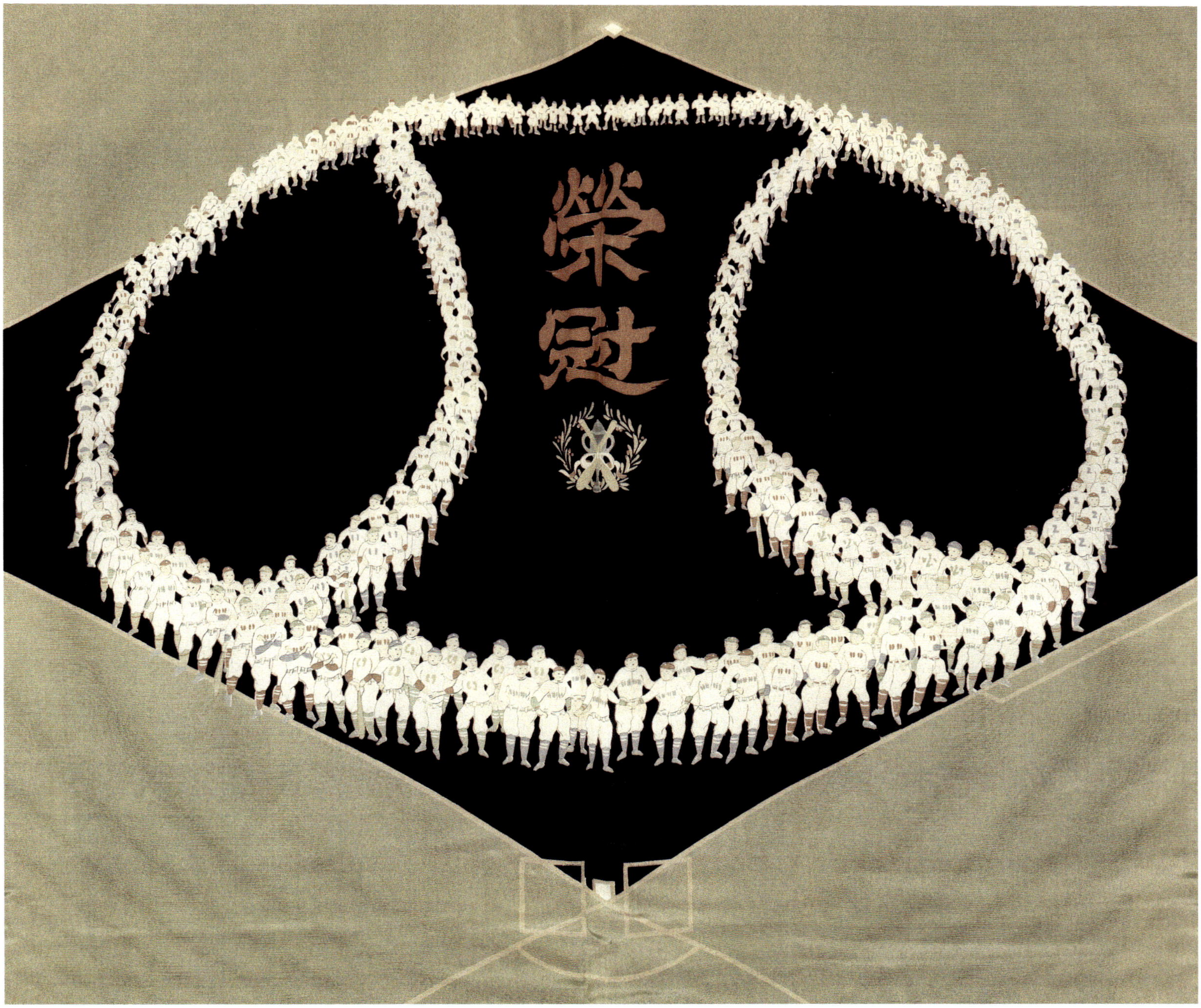

Senya Sensatsu (A thousand nights for a thousand books), which started in 2000 and is still going strong in 2024, writes that Seiichi Funahashi, one of the leading figures in Japanese modernist literature of the early 20th century, once commented: "What's wrong with turning your back on the war and sleeping with women?" and continued, "On the night of the defeat, he was so happy that he turned on all the lights in the house and played jazz, which up until then had been enemy music."[6] In 1945, Funahashi went on to write a novel about a kimono maker dealing with turbulent times and changes in taste, titled *Shikkaiya Kōkichi* (Kōkichi the Dyer).

The connection between the making and wearing of kimono and the Japanese subconscious, and wearing a kimono as a means of conveying a message, both have a long history in Japanese films and literature. The latter is not always performed by transgressive figures; in fact, it is often done by the very individuals the nation seeks to make into a symbol of the simple, patriotic individual with common sense. A fascinating example of this is explored in Michiko Suzuki's reading of a 1944 tale called "The Kasuri Kimono" by Sakae Tsuboi. Suzuki writes: "According to Sagi Tadao, the editor of *Tsuboi Sakae zenshū* (Collected works of Sakae Tsuboi), one reason Tsuboi has largely been ignored by scholars is the way her image was created at the time of her debut, as 'a good, kind-hearted auntie [obasan], who emerges smiling from the kitchen, while wiping her hands on her apron.'"[7] But this does not by any means stop her from writing the heartbreaking tale of a *kasuri* (a popular textile of rural Japan, where threads were pre-dyed prior to weaving; a form of ikat) kimono that is handed from one person to another upon their untimely death, only to end up as work pants (*monpe*) during the war. These are very similar to the pants worn by Setsuko in *Grave of the Fireflies*, a relic of a more prosperous and optimistic past. As Suzuki puts it:

> Fuyuko [the protagonist] loses her son to disease and expresses sadness over her nephew's death in action; as a protagonist seen crying through the end of the story, she is certainly not a model mother who stoically supports the war. Sagi Tadao implies that Fuyuko's maternal love is separate from nationalistic sentiments, arguing that "The *Kasuri* Kimono" expresses "the love between mother and child" (*boshi jōai*) and is not "literature following the national policy [*kokusaku shōsetsu*], complicit with war efforts and praising the war."[8]

The notions of mourning, of shattered optimism and enthusiasm, are precisely the kind of desperate feelings kimono such as *omoshirogara* bring out. They highlight the slippery slope that is the fever propaganda creates and ultimately, inevitably, shatters. In *The Brittle Decade*, Jacqueline M. Atkins herself illustrates this poignantly, saying: "How many of these designs have been lost to time, trash, or forgotten fancies or failings will never be known, but those that remain vividly convey the exuberance, the energy, the cosmopolitanism, the political dualities, and the imperialism that contributed to Japan's brittle shell of innovation, imagination, and animation—a shell that would ultimately shatter under the weight of nationalism and militarism at the end of the 1930s, bringing an end to a period of glittering modernism."[9] This is, unfortunately, the end result of the mass deception that propaganda creates before it has to be confronted by reality. Celebrating the achievements of the nation in this way, willingly eliminating oneself in the face of the collective, is what always ultimately brings about a shattering sobriety.

The ploy of propaganda lies in how it makes itself so enticing. Edward Conze states:

> Propaganda would be a poor weapon, indeed, if it had only words at its disposal—arguments

> and slogans, hymns and songs. Non-verbal propaganda—pictures, cartoons, flags, and symbols—is often more effective because it cannot be argued with. There is the propaganda of example and of the deed, which often carries more weight than mere verbiage ... The chief task of propaganda, verbal and otherwise, is to create, or maintain, unity within a social group. Propaganda is, as Lasswell put it, the "hammer and anvil of social solidarity." In this respect, all modern propaganda is a faint substitute for the tribal dance, and for tribal ceremonies. The size of modern groups renders it technically impossible to burn out dissent in the furnace of a common dance ... When we share with others in an intense and collective pleasure, we are filled with geniality and good-will towards our companions ... We do most of what we do because we are afraid to isolate ourselves from our group. Abstract reasoning has very little to do with our assent to social convictions ... The desire to maintain social unity is a force infinitely stronger than the flickering lamp of reason.[10]

Indeed, this is the only way we can rationalize how a group of people who on the one hand celebrate the enormous freedom of spirit offered through art and culture celebrate instruments of destruction and death on the other. By mixing the latter with entertainment, infantilizing them, blurring the lines of morality, the makers of *omoshirogara* kimono make everything part of a big, modern adventure for the upstanding Japanese citizen.

It is important to note, however, that the blame does not lie with the makers or the consumers: rather, a culture carefully promoted through misinformation and manufactured fashions creates the environment in which such contradictions flourish. As in the Mukden incident itself, the Japanese people were subjected to a false flag operation. Seita in *Grave of the Fireflies* does not see the contradiction and in fact clings on to the fantasy as a salve for the harsh reality, until everything around him crumbles. But that is precisely the point: such a glittering dream is so difficult to let go of. Isao Takahata mentioned that he made the film with 1980s children in mind, who would be more likely to emphasize their individualism than the "stoic" boys of the time, who would probably have adopted a more pragmatic, humbler approach.[11] But the refusal to give up the fever dream precisely and aptly illustrates the Japanese mindset of that brittle decade. The death of Seita at the end of the film is the death of that dream. Kimono such as the ones in this book are his spirit, the spirit of youthful dedication to the Japanese war effort, to its incredible might and modernity, dying away in the corner of a subway, starving, as the nation tries to pick itself up and forget such things ever existed.

Omoshirogara kimono are conspicuously absent from recorded documentation or even postwar mentions, probably due in the former case to their indoor and private nature, and in the latter to shame or a desire to forget. While not present in *Grave of the Fireflies*, it feels as though these kimonos exist in a space beside the movie. In a particularly moving part of the film, Seita is forced to sell his mother's kimono for rice, which causes his sister to cry bitterly and refuse to give up the kimono. This triggers a small flashback scene in which the family stands for a photo under cherry trees, the mother in her pink kimono and the father in uniform, while Setsuko buries her face in a fold of the fabric. The scene is full of joy, pride, and warmth, and they do not seem far from the type of family who would buy and display an *omoshirogara* kimono, though we can never be sure. Nevertheless, the

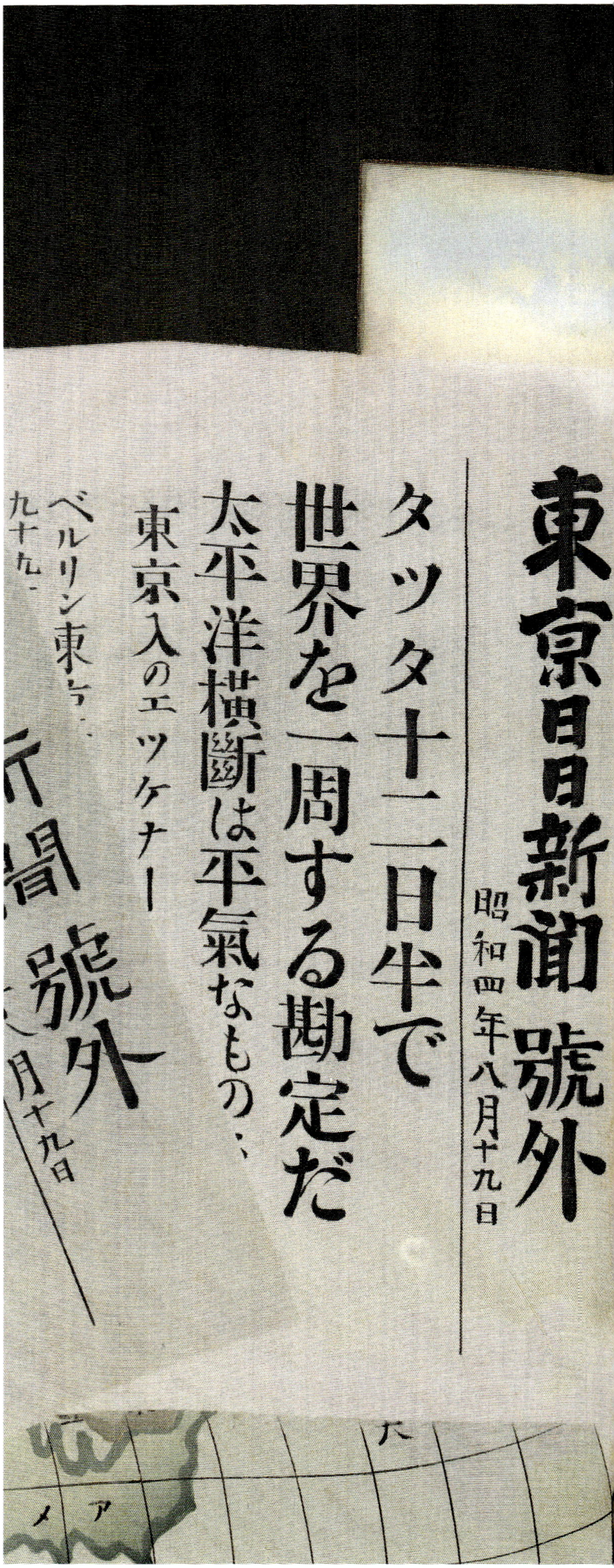

RIGHT FIG. 7 Man's *haori* with a decorative lining (detail)
Around the world with the *Graf Zeppelin* (see p. 184)

kimono's "nostalgic" role here is a powerful reminder of how these garments hold stories. In flashbacks, kimono appear as rich and resplendent; in the present day of the film, they are utilitarian, converted into work pants, or simply replaced by rudimentary Western clothing. In the interwar years, after the advent of Western clothing in the Meiji era (1868–1912), kimono were already starting to be perceived as a nostalgic symbol of the Japanese way of life, which was precisely the reason they were so useful in the hands of the Japanese propaganda machine. The kimono has been falling in and out of favor since, and its meaning and place in society are still discussed today.

What is to be made of such idiosyncratic, yet wonderful, garments? Ultimately, they should be treasured not only as wonderfully inventive textiles, their patterns and motifs brimming with originality and wit, but as reminders of how easy and tempting it is to fall into complacency, lulled by the security of entertainment and lighthearted thoughts. Now more than ever, in a post-pandemic world where entertainment and trends color a large portion of our window to the outside world, often viewed on a screen, it is vital that we remember the lesson of these kimono: that while enjoying the creativity and richness of what we are presented with, we must never forget to question, interrogate, and remain true to ourselves. While we enjoy the hazy Jazz Age dream of modernity we are presented with by these garments, and the joyous lull they invite us into, we should never forget what might be sitting just beyond the light.

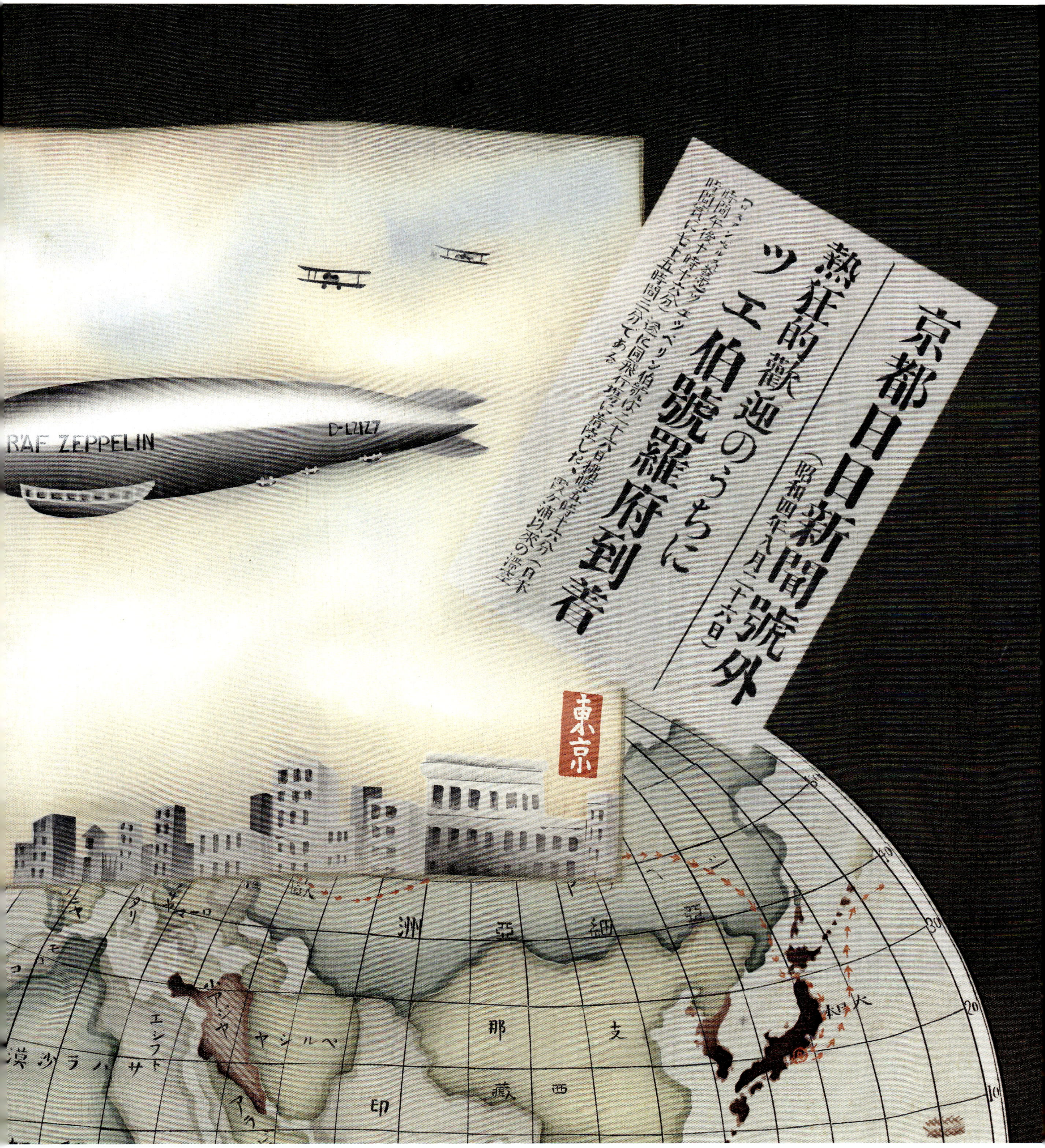
京都日日新聞號外
（昭和四年八月二十六日）
ツェ伯號羅府到着
熱狂的歡迎のうちに
【ロスアンゼルス發電】ツェッペリン伯號は二十六日拂曉五時十六分（日本時間午後十時十六分）遂に同飛行場に着陸した、霞ヶ浦以來の滯空時間實に七十五時間三分である
RAF ZEPPELIN
D-LZ127
東京

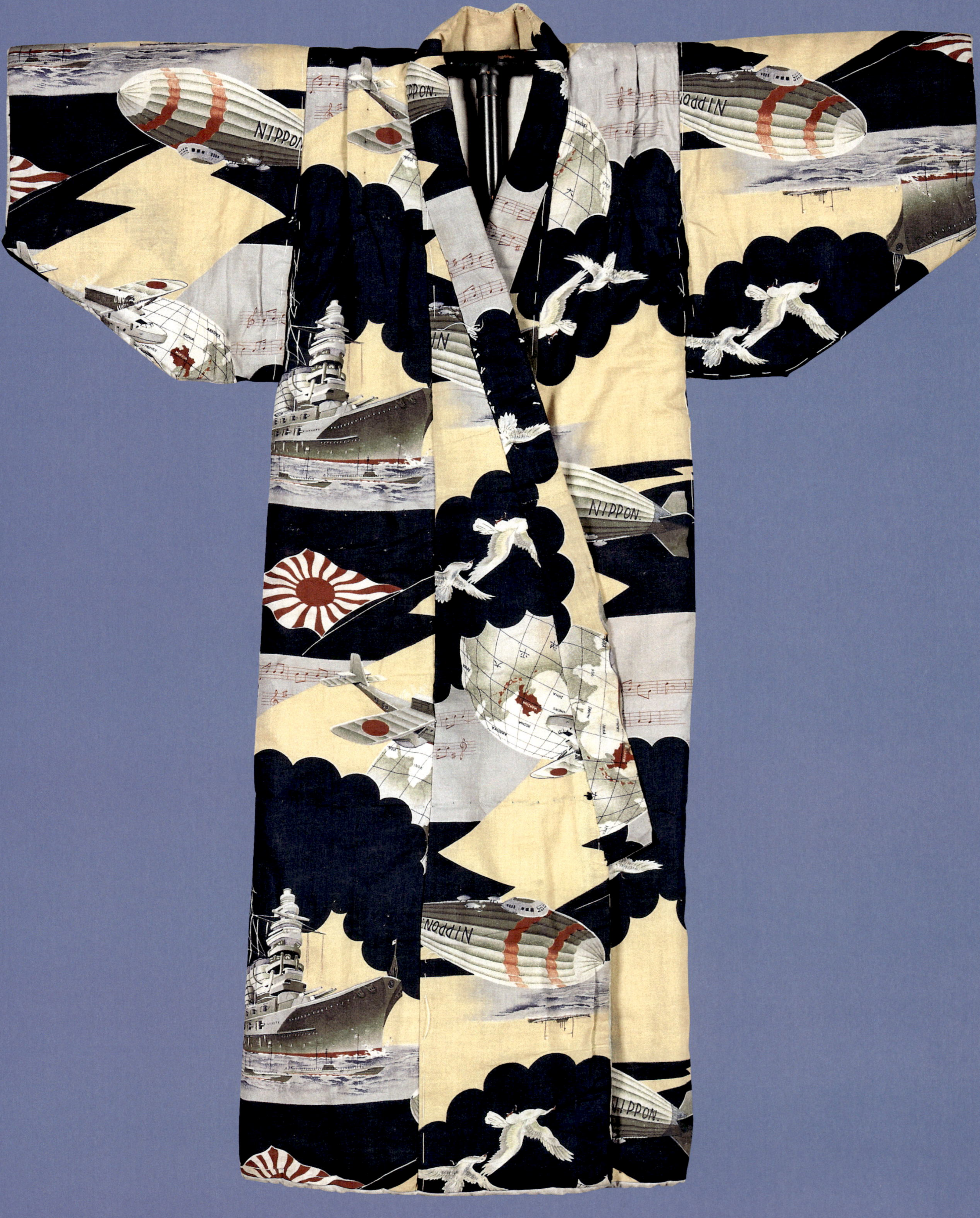

NIPPON
NIPPON.
NIPPON.

CULTURE ON CLOTH: JAPANESE KIMONO, 1910–1950

JACQUELINE M. ATKINS

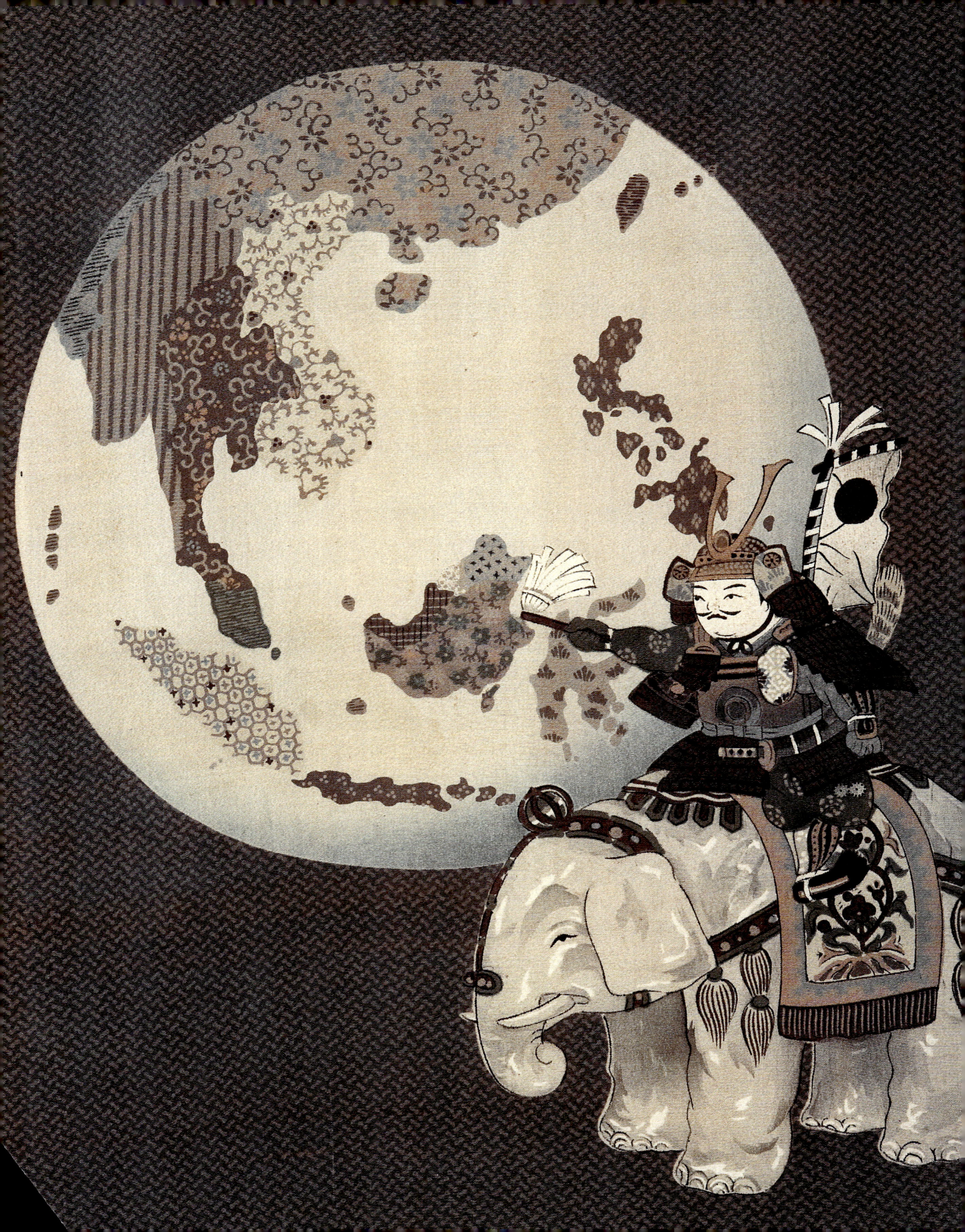

AN OVERVIEW OF 20TH-CENTURY KIMONO

This brief overview offers an illuminating window on to the social, political, and cultural concerns of the late 19th through to the mid-20th century.[1] This was a time of enormous change, and one of the most dynamic periods in the history of Japan's national dress. Changes in clothing affected the kimono, a garment worn by both men and women, who had accepted it for centuries as the standard garment for a major part of the population. In the early part of this era, kimono was still the dress of choice in Japan, worn daily by many men as well as most women. However, while some of these garments still reflected historical continuity in design and technique, many others began to show a dramatic break with aspects of the kimono tradition as Western themes and designs began to predominate over historical Japanese references.

Several elements and events contributed substantially to the changing kimono fashions of this period. Of primary importance was the introduction and rapid assimilation of new technologies, not least in the textile trade, which was one of the first industries in Japan to become fully modernized. The shift in the late 19th century to a Western-style court and military undoubtedly contributed to this, as it did not take very long for Japan to recognize that the plan for rapid modernization of the nation was not well served by importing the garments worn by the imperial court entourage from the West, as well as the uniforms demanded by the growing Japanese military. The Japanese government quickly realized the necessity to initiate its own production in this realm, and thus lost no time in developing the necessary technologies and infrastructure. Another important factor was the industry's shift to large-scale manufacture of wool and cotton fabrics, both of which were needed for military use. The availability of wool and cotton textiles from abroad likewise increased a domestic demand that was encouraged first by the male transition from traditional garments such as kimono to Western-style suits; these fabrics soon also began to be used for kimono and other indigenous garments. Silk production similarly moved to participate in the textile industry's mechanization, yet it maintained its high status—and high price. The most ambitious industrial producers of the main new textiles—*meisen*, *niko-niko*, and muslin—did not waste time, however: in the early Taishō period, their lower costs for consumers put these textiles well within reach of men and women in almost every stratum of society. Many smart, new, and affordable fabrics were also available as ready-to-wear products in Japan's new department stores, which gave them an aura of modern convenience as well as introducing novel designs and fashions. The newly developed department stores were also key players in promoting them to potential consumers.

The Asia-Pacific War, however, brought about a major change for kimono.[2] During the war years (1931–45), many men wore military uniform, business suits, or more casual Western-style clothing, while some wore *kokuminfuku* ("national civilian uniform"), an outfit much like a simplified military uniform. By the later war years, women were discouraged from wearing traditional kimono. Instead, they were encouraged to dress in more flexible Western-style garments or *monpe*, a type of pants usually worn by agricultural workers but deemed more practical for the lifestyle changes wrought by war. The kimono industry was largely gutted at the end of the war, and by the time the industry regained its strength in the postwar period, Western clothes had largely replaced kimono for everyday wear. The kimono had instead assumed a largely formal and ceremonial role.

OPPOSITE FIG. 1 Man's *juban* (detail)
Travel and treasure (see p. 97)

OPPOSITE FIG. 2 *Juban* for a man (detail)
Skyscrapers, travel, and sports (see p. 143)

In spite of this, the kimono still retains a powerful hold not only on the Japanese heart and mind but also on the Western image of the exotic "other." It provides a link to both Japan's past and its present, and though it may no longer be an everyday garment for many, it is firmly embedded in the national psyche and shows no sign of going away.

AN INTRODUCTION TO *OMOSHIROGARA*

Japan has a long and rich history in textile design, much of which has been documented extensively. Only recently, however, has attention begun to be paid to a little-recognized but ingenious genre of printed textiles that offers us a visual reference of Japanese social, cultural, and political icons, a snapshot of Japanese popular culture at a time of great change. From the late Meiji era onward, this specialty group of textile designs were called *omoshirogara*, and they were produced for kimono. They first appeared around 1900, and their peak was reached in the 1940s. They were representative of the many changes that contributed to Japan's growing modernity and signified modernity in their own right, since they carried the visual imprint of the radical cultural, political, and technological changes that the population faced as Japan progressed further down the path toward being an industrialized nation and gaining the cosmopolitan accoutrements of the modern world. These trappings included modes of transport, with trams, trains, airplanes, and ships powered by engines; skyscrapers (fig. 2) and bridges made of structural steel—designs once inconceivable for this island nation—and tracks, wires, lines, and lights standing as exemplars of a brave new world.

Design ideas and images reflected these changes as well, and new directions could be seen not only in housing, furniture, and advertising but also in textile design, demonstrating the belief that design in all ways could help to transform society. *Omoshirogara* were comparable to the fabrics known as "novelty" or "conversational" textiles in the West and served a similar function: they captured and displayed the fads, fashions, and tempo of the times as well as recognizing the changing physical and technological landscape. *Omoshirogara* were considered to be a unique genre within the larger context of modern kimono, and their designers intended them to be distinctive and dramatically different from the traditional kimono textiles that, for the most part, carried designs based on time-honored seasonal and literary motifs and themes. *Omoshirogara* were reflective of the new cosmopolitan culture (see p. 302) that was rapidly taking hold in Japan as it moved from the Victorian grasp of the Meiji into the cultural and political innovations of the Taishō and early Shōwa eras and the country found a firmer footing within the broader international community. Although *omoshirogara* were initially produced for kimono, they were intended to be very different from traditional kimono designs and, instead, be very much about contemporary life and the expanding interests of this new outward-facing Japan. Designs captured current trends and issues that ranged from the inventive to the outrageous, the frivolous to the confrontational, the humorous to the disturbing.

The ingenuity of textile designers seemed infinite as they drew their motifs and themes from wildly diverse elements of popular culture, from sports to jazz (fig. 3), cinema to art (fig. 4) and architecture, the Machine Age (fig. 5) to world travel. Designs especially reflected what was considered modern in the culture; printed and dyed textiles offer pictorial references to the times, from cosmopolitan life to the industrial and technological advances that fascinated and invigorated the public imagination. Many *omoshirogara* designs were created by using various techniques of cut-paper stencil dyeing

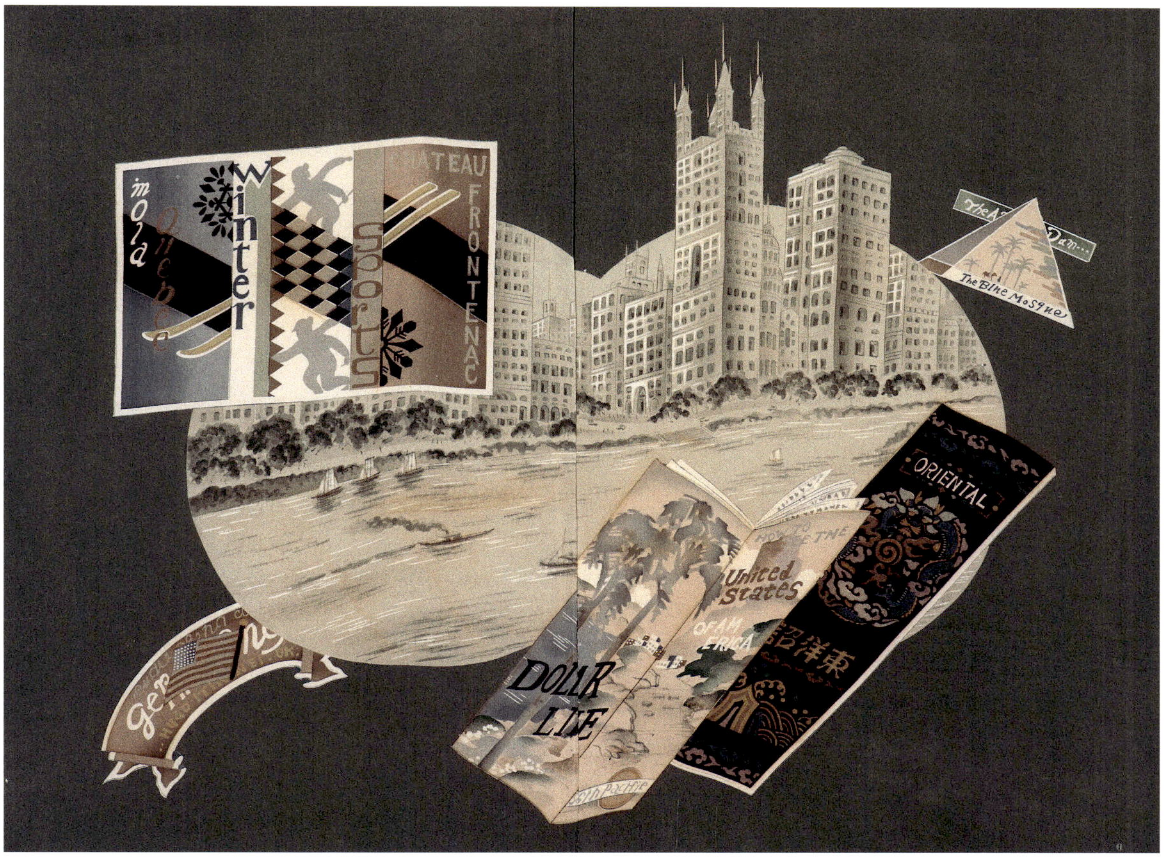
Winter
Sports
FRONTENAC
The Blue Mosque
ORIENTAL
United States
DOLLAR LINE

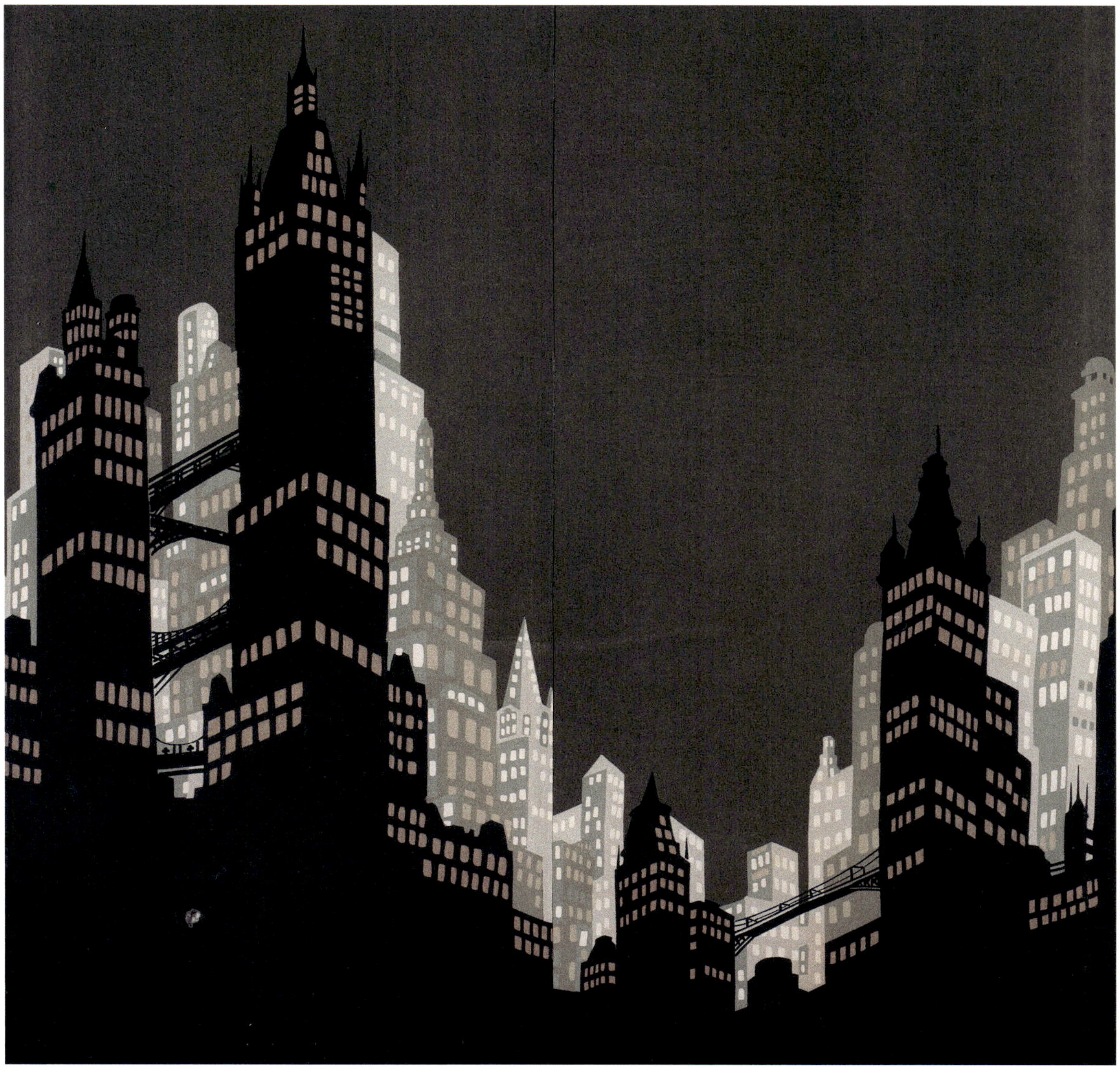

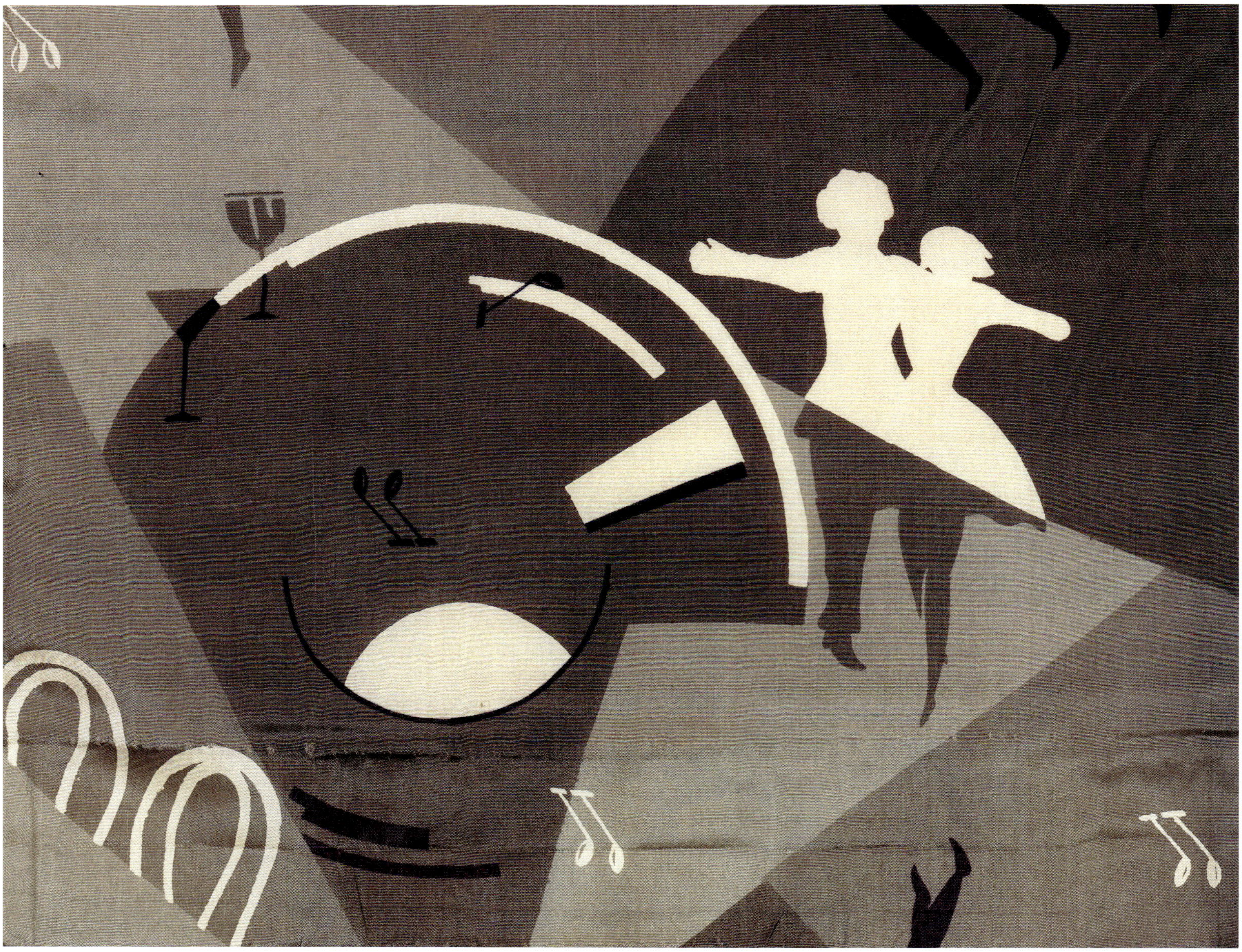

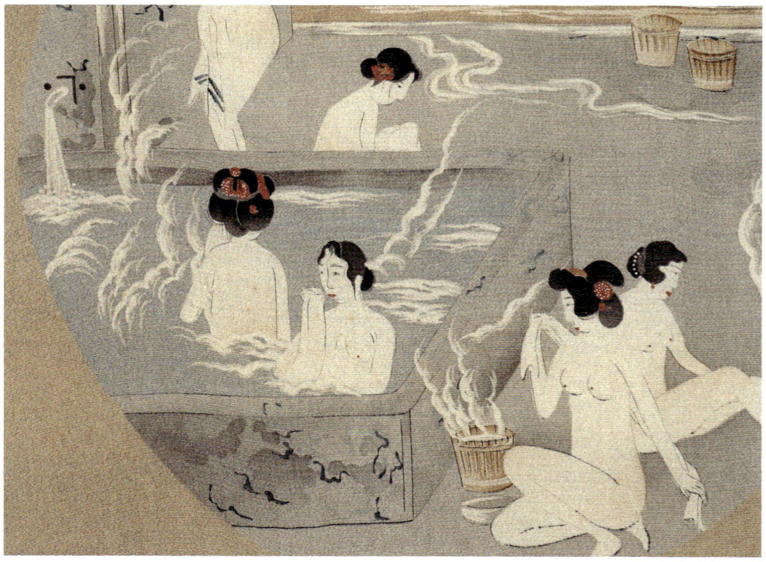

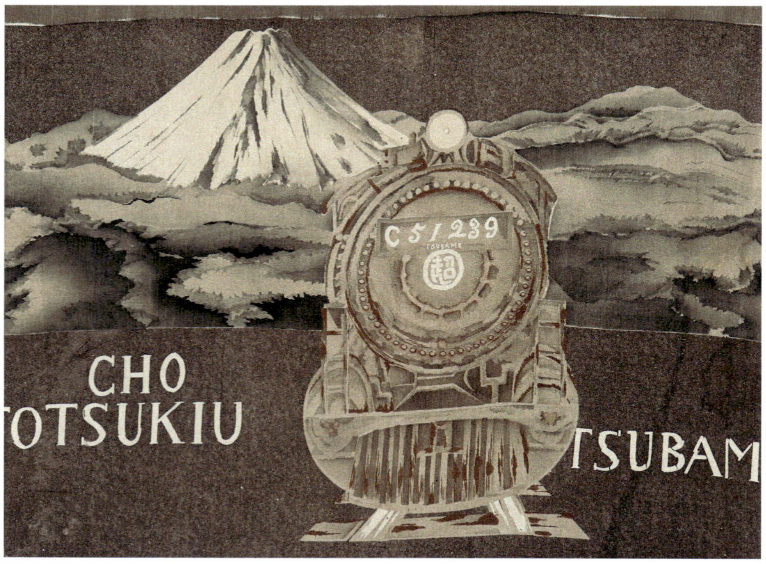
C51289
CHO
OTSUKIU
TSUBAM

OPPOSITE TOP FIG. 3 Man's *juban* (detail)
Dancing the night away (see p. 210)

OPPOSITE BELOW LEFT FIG. 4 Man's *haori* with a decorative lining (detail)
Women enjoying the bathhouse (see p. 255)

OPPOSITE BELOW RIGHT FIG. 5 Man's *haori* with a decorative lining (detail)
The *Swallow* Super Express (see p. 236)

(such as *suri-yūzen*), in which the dye-paste mixture of pigment and starch is rubbed on with a brush, or *utsushi-yūzen*, in which a spatula-like tool is used to apply the paste. As textile production technologies developed, modern fabric printing techniques that required little individual handwork were also used to make these novelty designs—and also made larger-volume production possible, which was especially useful for the less expensive textiles used for children's kimono.

One subcategory of *omoshirogara* was called *kodomogara* ("children's motifs") (see p. 158). These designs were used for children's kimono and *juban* and mirrored popular motifs in a manner that was especially designed to appeal to children. Such garments were produced and purchased until the early years of the 1970s (see p. 159). Reflecting the growing nationalism and militarism that ultimately led Japan into total war, some of the designs depicted weapons, soldiers, military flags, and other war motifs. These fell within the subcategory of the repertoire of *omoshirogara* called *sensōgara*, which will be discussed later. Overall, the subcategories and techniques of the *omoshirogara* repertoire can be placed within the larger context of "modern kimono." In essence, it could be said that *omoshirogara* stood as the sentry for the energy and vitality of the era's culture.

This array of *omoshirogara* images and patterns provides a vivid and enlightening picture of the social, cultural, economic, and political complexity of Japan from the 1923 Great Kantō Earthquake until the bombing of Pearl Harbor in 1941. The designs were not necessarily unique to these textiles: the rapid growth in mass communication allowed for constant exchange and sharing of information and images within all types of media, and what appeared one day in print or on film—or even in an art gallery—might the next find its way into advertising, postcards (fig. 6), children's literature, board games, cigarette and matchbook covers (fig. 7), or, not least, textile design.

The extensive array of designs produced for these novelty textiles not only fit well into Japanese textile culture, but also placed them within the larger context of early modern Japan, historically, culturally, and economically. The expansion of the textile industry in the late 19th century as well as the explosion of new textiles, dyes, and printing techniques in the early 20th century encouraged the move by textile artists into new styles of design, as did changing social mores and attitudes. Although World War II brought a difficult hiatus into Japan's textile production, the postwar revival and revitalization of *omoshirogara*'s presence was felt by recapturing the icons of popular culture and technology, from Walt Disney's *Bambi* (fig. 8) to the US moon landing in 1969 (fig. 9). This revival, however, lasted only until the late 1960s, when culture, fashion, and cloth went through other major upheavals that meant *omoshirogara* no longer had a place in kimono undergarments such as *juban*, *yukata*, or the carefully placed *haura* linings in *haori*. Some *kodomogara*—novelty designs for children—continued but quickly faded away as the 1970s traded them for "Hello Kitty" bags and purses, T-shirts, designer jeans, backpacks, and cat cafés, and never looked back.

NOVELTY TEXTILES AND *OMOSHIROGARA*

Textiles occupy a central position within the realm of material culture. They fulfill basic human needs for clothing and protection, and play important political, economic, and cultural functions within society. Clothing is among the most visible and public of the material arts, serving as a significant site of personal and cultural identity, yet is simultaneously intimate and private as it touches our skin. Given the nature and role of textiles and clothing, it should therefore come as no surprise to discover that they have great potential for

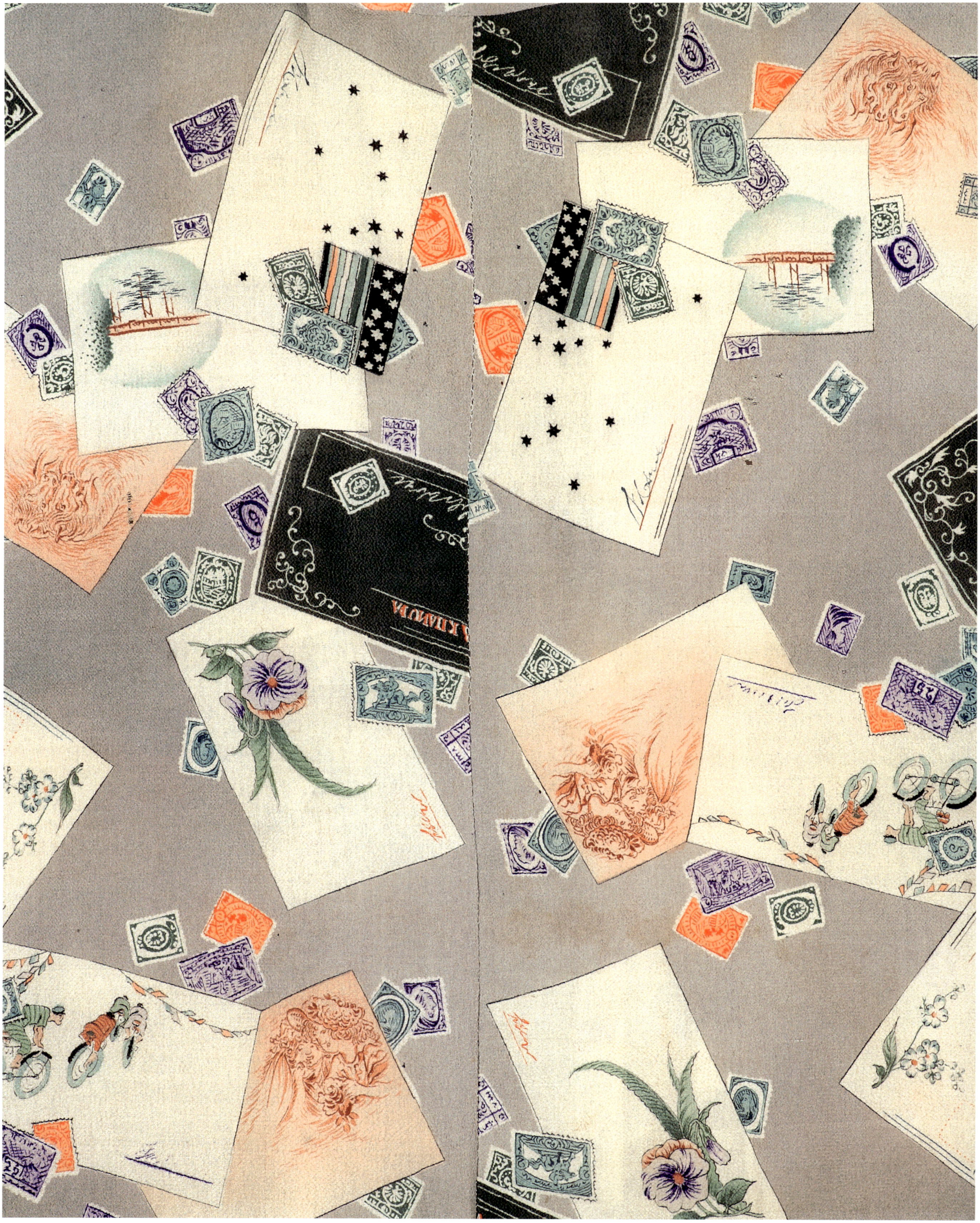

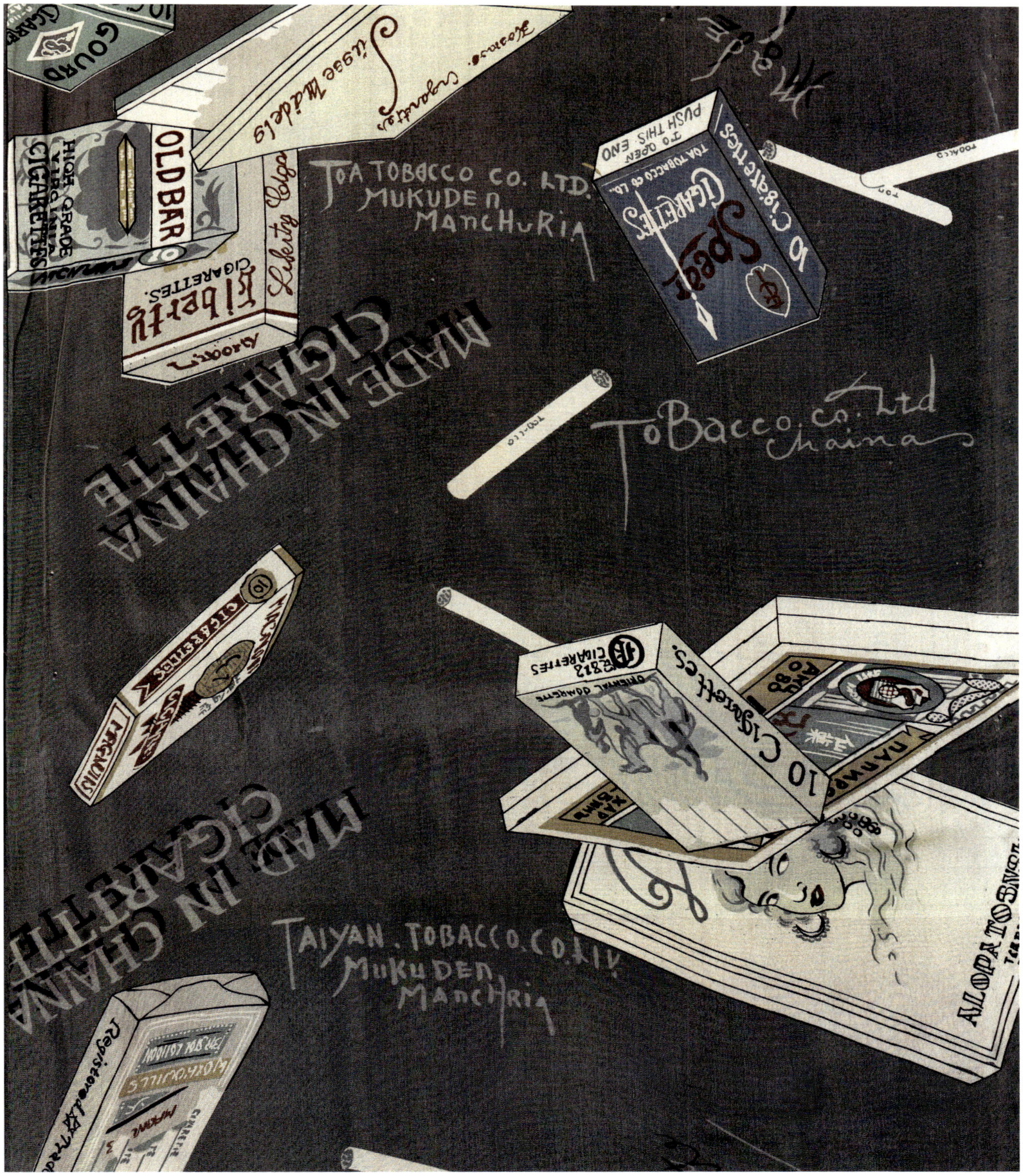

OPPOSITE FIG. 6 Woman's *juban* (detail)
Postcards and flowers (see p. 150)

ABOVE FIG. 7 Man's *haori* with a decorative lining (detail)
Cigarettes galore! (see p. 298)

OPPOSITE ABOVE FIG. 8 Kimono for a girl child (detail)
Bambi with a sled of presents (see p. 204)

OPPOSITE BELOW FIG. 9 *Juban* for a man (detail)
The first moon landing (see p. 148)

communication and can serve as potent visual vehicles for celebrations of modernity (fig. 10). While textiles have often been valued by researchers for their role in economic, political, or religious transactions, or for the technologies used in their production, until recently little attention has been paid to their importance as messengers of culture.

A primary element of artistic textile expression in Japan has been the kimono, traditionally the principal item of dress for men and women of all classes. The simple T-shaped structures of kimono and associated garments such as *nagajuban* (underkimono) and *haori* (kimono jackets) have changed little since the 16th century, and their consistent simplicity has served well in providing the canvas on which both public and personal messages can be presented, sometimes explicitly but more often as part of a visual cultural code that was widely understood. Many of the images used on kimono had complex levels of meaning, often with auspicious significance. Even as the Meiji Restoration pushed Japan into burgeoning modernity and Western fashion began to be increasingly adopted, the kimono remained a primary canvas for visual expressions of innovation and progress (see p. 182), as well as of national unity and military goals as war loomed on the horizon. Yet, while the canvas of the kimono form was retained, many of the textiles used in its construction were no longer the traditional silks, brocades, or elegantly embroidered, dyed, or hand-painted fabrics so familiar to us from earlier centuries. Instead, they were as fresh and modern as the designs they carried (fig. 11); both modernism and traditional designs could flourish as new types of fabric were produced and designs were applied to them through innovative printing processes as well as more traditional methods. Because of the whirlwind of old and new influences and forces on the cloth trade, it will be useful to provide additional background on the growing need for textile production and dyeing processes in Japan as the country moved from cottage industries to mass-market factories.

Textiles for *Omoshirogara*

Over the centuries, textiles had often been considered as measures of wealth and standing in many countries, but when the Industrial Revolution in Europe and the USA led to mass-production of fabric—and concomitant lower prices—they began to lose their mystique as well as their role as economic and social indicators. By the late 19th century, most Western countries had advanced well down this road, and a wide variety of textiles were available to the general public in a range of qualities and prices. In Japan, however, the situation was quite different. Up until the Meiji Restoration, textile production proceeded much as it had for centuries, dependent on traditional techniques and requiring skilled handwork and creative craftspeople. There was little mass-production in Japan: high-end fabrics were produced in the rarefied textile enclaves of Kyoto or in various other locales that each had their own specialty textile traditions, and many textiles were still produced in the home or by cottage industries. Fibers were limited; silk was widely available, but sumptuary laws precluded the use of the finest forms of silk except by members of the highest rank. *Asa*, or bast, made from hemp and associated fibers such as flax and ramie, provided the basis for the clothing of the common people until the late 17th century, when a type of cotton suitable for cultivation in parts of Japan was brought in from Korea. It quickly became the fiber of choice for most ordinary Japanese, although *asa* also remained in heavy use. There was no indigenous source of wool; limits on trade with the outside world meant that very little wool was imported, and that which was available was, for the most part, restricted to the upper classes.

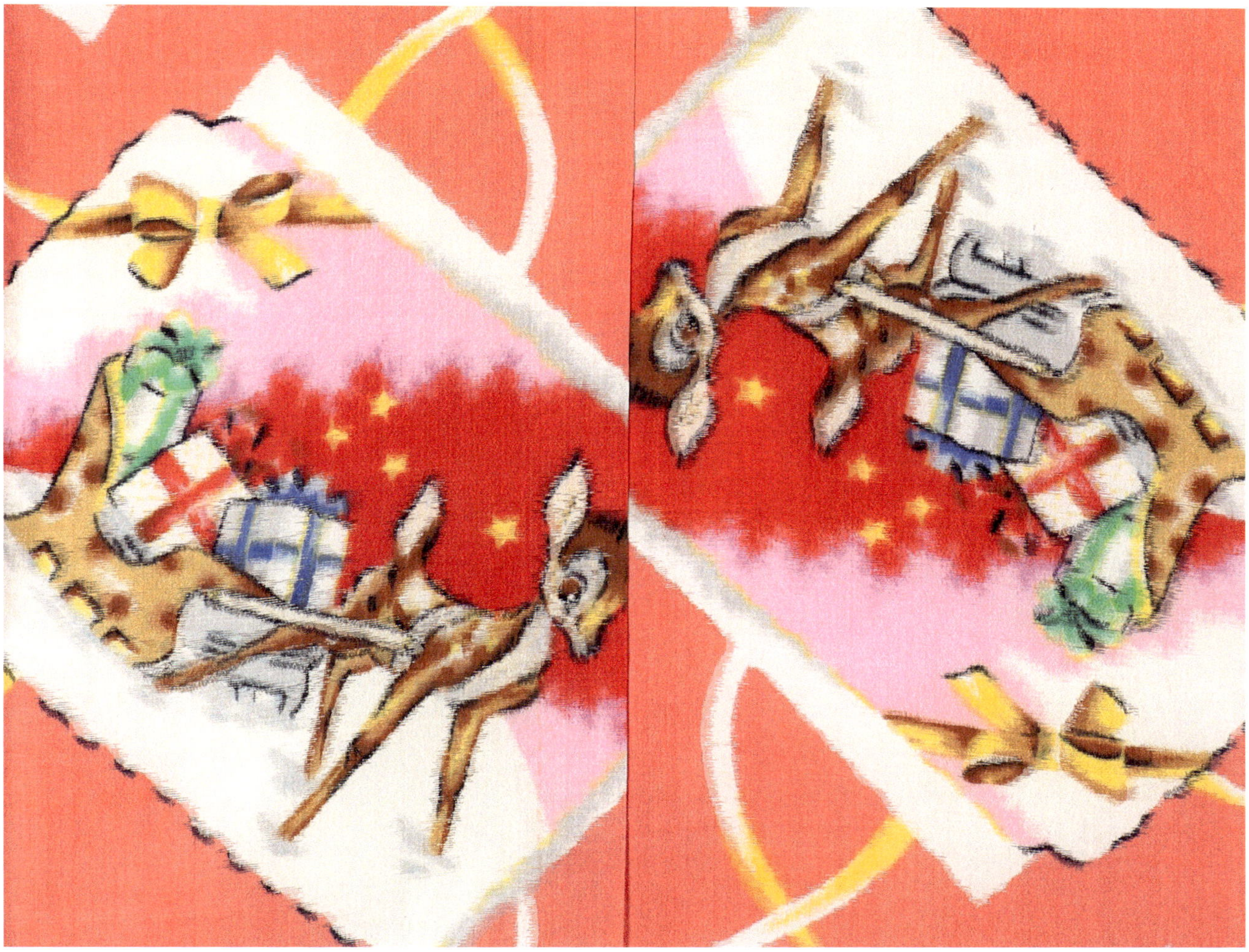

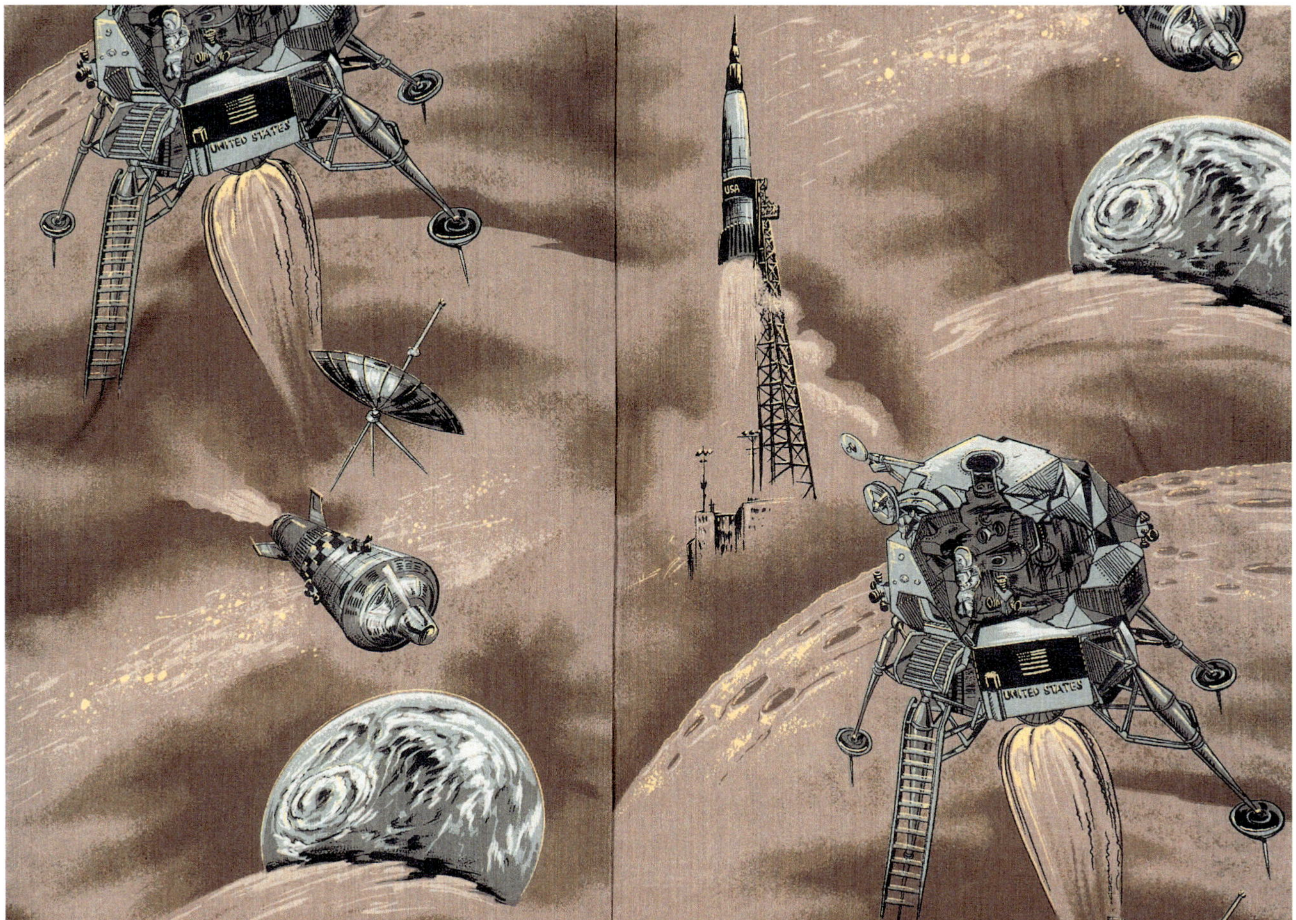
UNITED STATES
USA
UNITED STATES

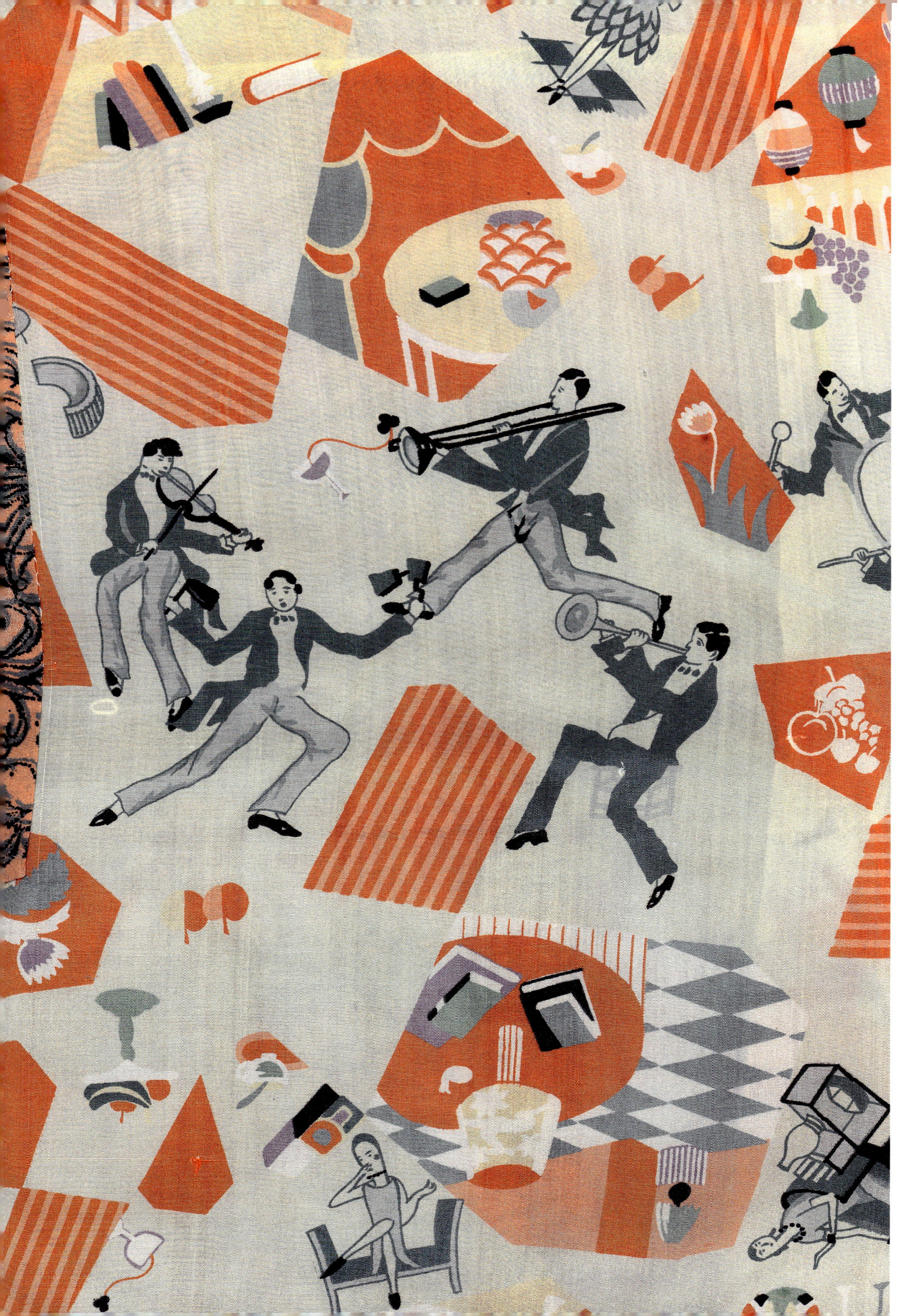

OPPOSITE FIG. 10 Woman's *haori* with a decorative lining (detail)
Living the city life (see p. 166)

LEFT FIG. 11 Kimono for a girl child (detail)
Ukeleles and accordions (see pp. 164–65)

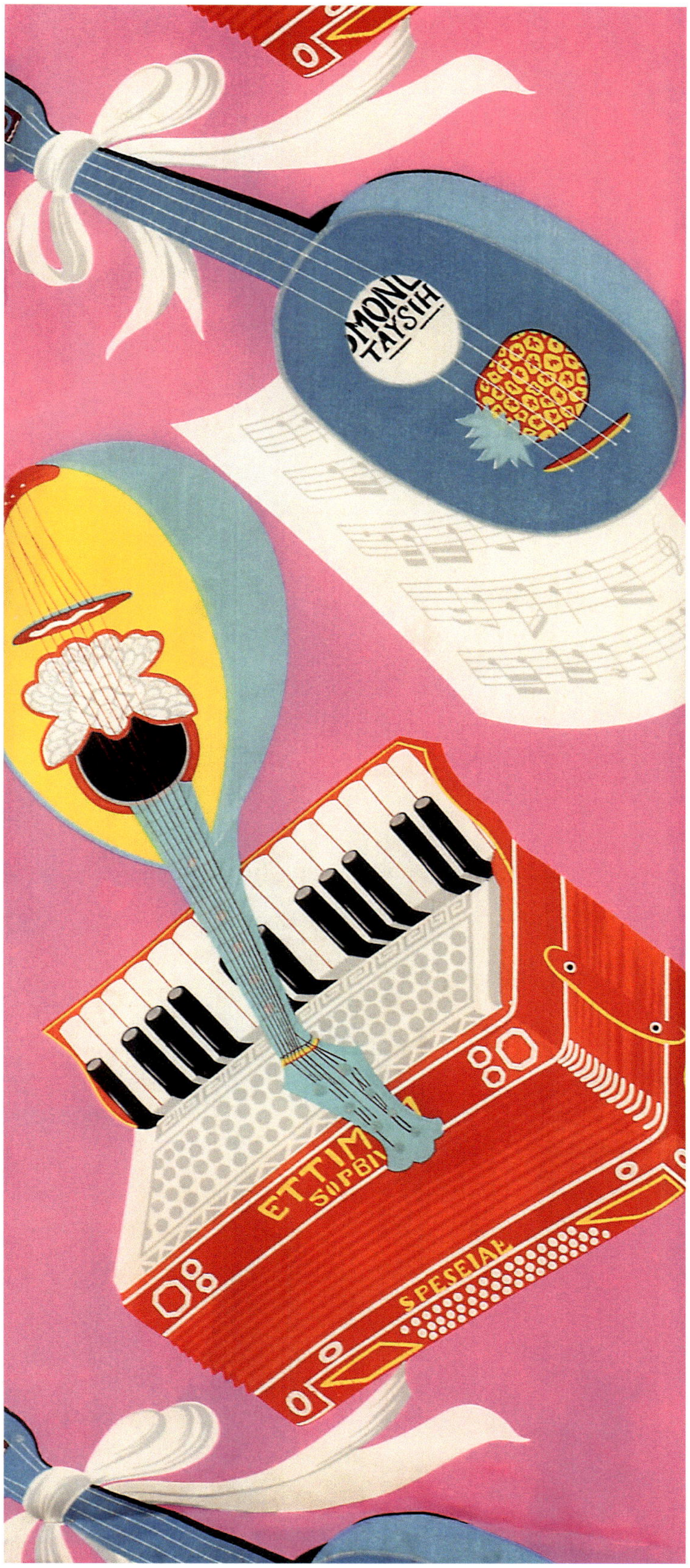

OPPOSITE FIG. 12 Woman's *juban* (detail)
Following the European style (see p. 188)

Following Commodore Matthew Perry's historic visit to Japan in 1853, Japan's expanded contact with the West began to change its situation forever. Soon after the Meiji Restoration in 1868, there began to be significant changes in the fashions worn by certain segments of society, prompted by the Meiji Emperor and his wife, who adopted Western styles for almost all formal functions and most private ones as well. Western clothing was seen as an exemplar of the cultures it came from, and the idea was to absorb attributes of foreign modernity through use of some of the West's outward symbols, such as clothing. The emperor underscored this concept with a proclamation on male dress reform: "We greatly regret that the uniform of our court has been established following the Chinese custom and it has become exceedingly effeminate in style and character ... We should no longer appear before the people in these effeminate styles. We have therefore decided to reform dress regulations entirely."[3]

As a result of this proclamation, Western-style uniforms were immediately adopted for the Japanese military, and this seemingly innocuous decision proved to be the benchmark for a major revolution in Japanese textile production.[4] The uniforms were to be made domestically in Japan, and of wool, just as European ones were, even though the wool had to be imported. Factories with modern textile equipment and manufacturing capabilities had to be built to process and produce both fabric and garments. By the turn of the century, spinning machines, mechanized looms, and jacquard attachments had changed the face of Japanese textile production dramatically.

The woolen textiles that had been used for the military were not diffused into the broader population until around 1890, when they began to be produced in the traditional narrow widths used for kimono rather than for uniforms. The success of the wool and concurrent cotton industries spurred the development of other non-traditional textiles that went well beyond what the military needed, and these textiles were then easily geared to a broad and hungry market. A wider variety of fabrics could be produced in larger quantities and at quite reasonable prices, thus putting these new textiles easily within reach of a large segment of the population as it approached the modern age. Although the manufacture of these new fabrics was based on Western technology, they were purely Japanese products and intended to be used for Japanese clothing, not for Western-style fashion. Traditional flat-weave silks and *chirimen* (a type of silk crepe) (fig. 12), however, remained mainstays for textiles that carried time-honored elegant surface designs and continued to be produced at high prices for the upper classes.

In addition to woolen textiles—now called *mosulin*, or "muslin," in Japanese[5]—these non-traditional textiles included *meisen*, which used machine-spun silk thread made from lower-grade cocoons and a printing process that mimicked traditional *kasuri*, and *niko-niko kasuri*, a printed textile made of cotton or wool (and occasionally of silk) that, like *meisen*, also mimicked *kasuri*. All three of these textiles had been developed earlier in the century and were well suited to use as traditional clothing, but as they gradually came to express the more venturesome ideas and inspirations of the early 20th century, many of their new designs were anything but traditional. When these textiles were embellished with machine- or stencil-printed designs that reflected the modern ideas and tastes of the times, they became known as *omoshirogara*—textiles with "interesting" or "novelty" designs, as was noted earlier. *Omoshirogara* quite rapidly made up a large part of the yardage produced in these textiles, manufacturers quickly found enthusiastic audiences for such eye-opening goods, and mass-production made them easily affordable.

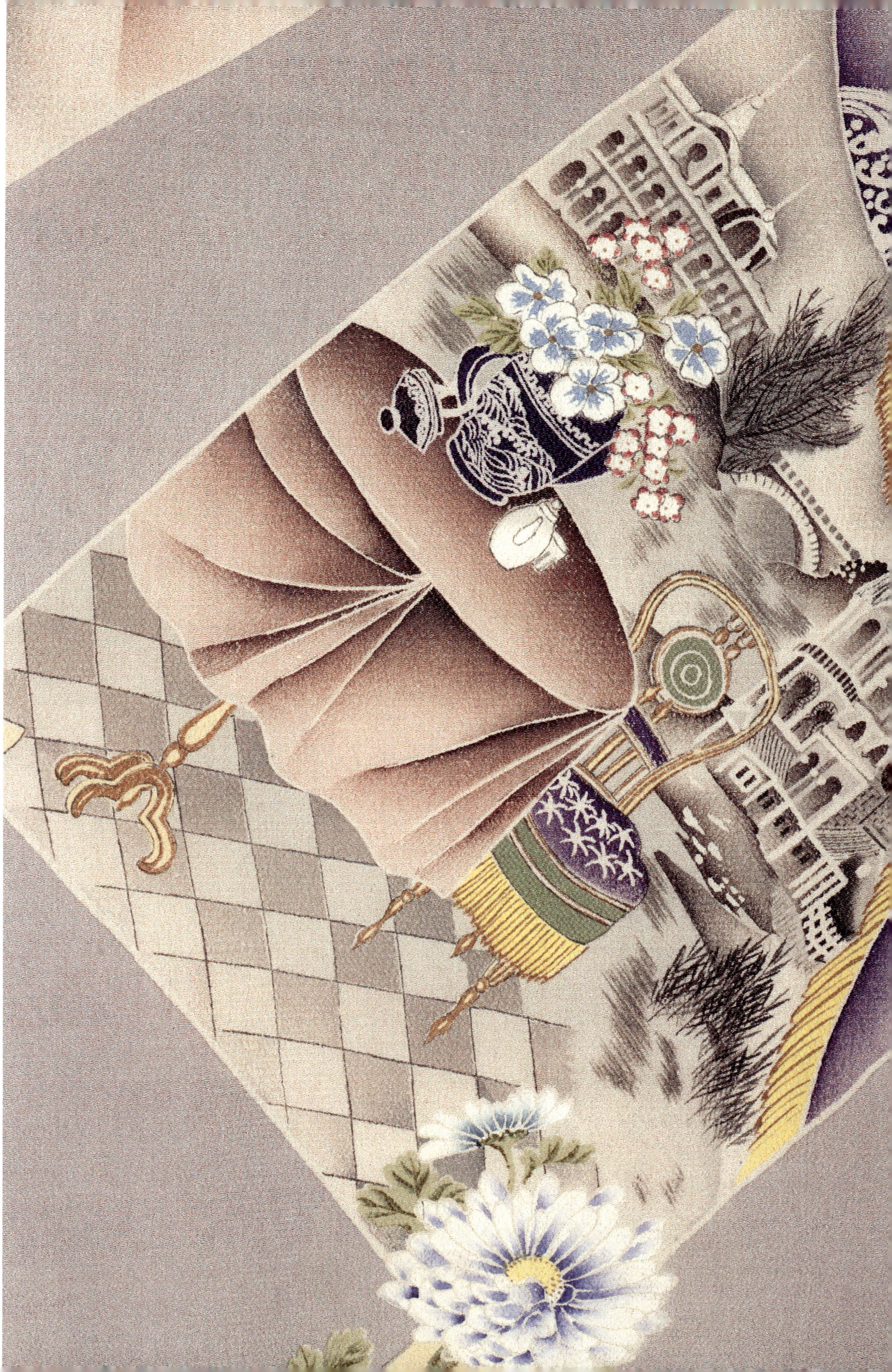

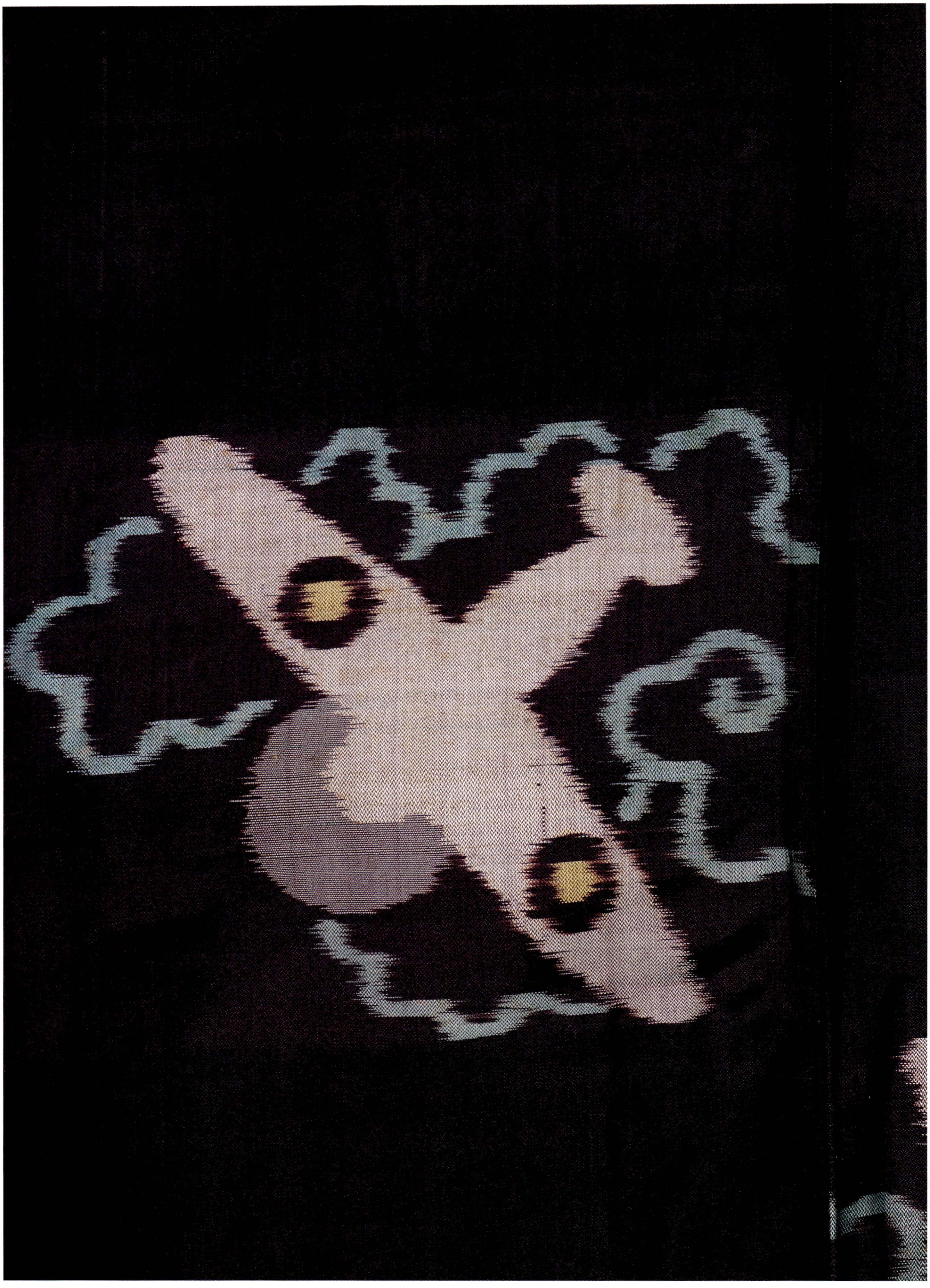

OPPOSITE FIG. 13 Kimono for a woman (detail)
Airplanes in the clouds (see p. 311)

The wide range of available designs added to their general popularity, and by 1920, *meisen*, *niko-niko*, and muslin had easily been brought well within the reach of a broad spectrum of the Japanese buying public.

Meisen

Meisen, a textile woven of machine-spun silk thread, was made from lower-grade cocoons, the most visible change in kimono fashion. Its production methods incorporated a warp-and-weft printing process that produced designs with a "blurred" look similar to the highly prized (and priced) *kasuri* (also known as ikat), a labor-intensive undertaking that requires hours of wrapping warp and weft threads by hand. It is sometimes difficult to differentiate the real *kasuri* textile from *meisen*. The economies in the *meisen* printing process, however, resulted in substantial decreases in cost for the consumer, making this new silk *kasuri* fabric widely affordable—even factory girls were able to buy it. There was an intensified demand for silk garments following World War I and the Great Kantō Earthquake, and, by the beginning of the Shōwa era (1926), both the production and the popularity of *meisen* was at its height (fig. 13). European chemical dyes (also new to Japan) worked well with the *meisen* printing process and allowed designs with intense colors and dramatic contrasts to be easily created. With these techniques now part of their standard repertoire, designers could experiment with a variety of bold and graphic patterns skewed to the predilections of their new audiences—young women who eagerly awaited each season's new *meisen* offerings. Department stores were key players in getting information to consumers by promoting new designs through their catalogs and advertising. Staff designers also created unique designs for customers, which were far more expensive than standard designs and thus ordered for special-occasion garments such as *haora* or *nagajuban*, which were frequently purchased by men to wear at "parlor" performances,[6] or *miyamairi* for recently born children.[7] Western fashions also continued to be popular, with the latest designs featured in women's high-fashion magazines.

Niko-niko kasuri

Niko-niko kasuri was another textile that gained great attention when it was first put on the market in 1912. Its name means "giggle" or "joke" *kasuri*, and purchasers were amused to play with the designs. This very durable fabric was produced primarily from wool or cotton; silk was used only very occasionally for special garments. It took dyes very well, was strong and easily washable, and, like *meisen*, it mimicked the "blurred" look characteristic of traditional *kasuri* (ikat), although it did not produce colors as bright as either *meisen* or *kasuri*. *Niko-niko* was also used for informal kimono for men who preferred a limited range of darker colors such as deep blues, browns, beiges, grays, or black, with only occasional highlights of other colors, perhaps to emphasize its similarity to the traditional indigo *kasuri*. The simplified on-loom stencil process used to print designs on *niko-niko* reduced production time substantially, allowing designers to exploit a wider range of motifs as well as to make new interpretations of traditional patterns—and giving *niko-niko* a wider appeal. Prices decreased accordingly, putting *niko-niko* fabric well within the reach of the broader buying public.

Omoshirogara were also lent to the *niko-niko* format, which, overall, retained simple and repetitive patterns that captured the spirit of the theme the artist wished to convey. If more than one image was included, each image was shown independently and kept in its own individual space, unlike the montage groupings so often found in muslin or silk *omoshirogara*. Adults wearing *niko-niko* might choose designs showing new,

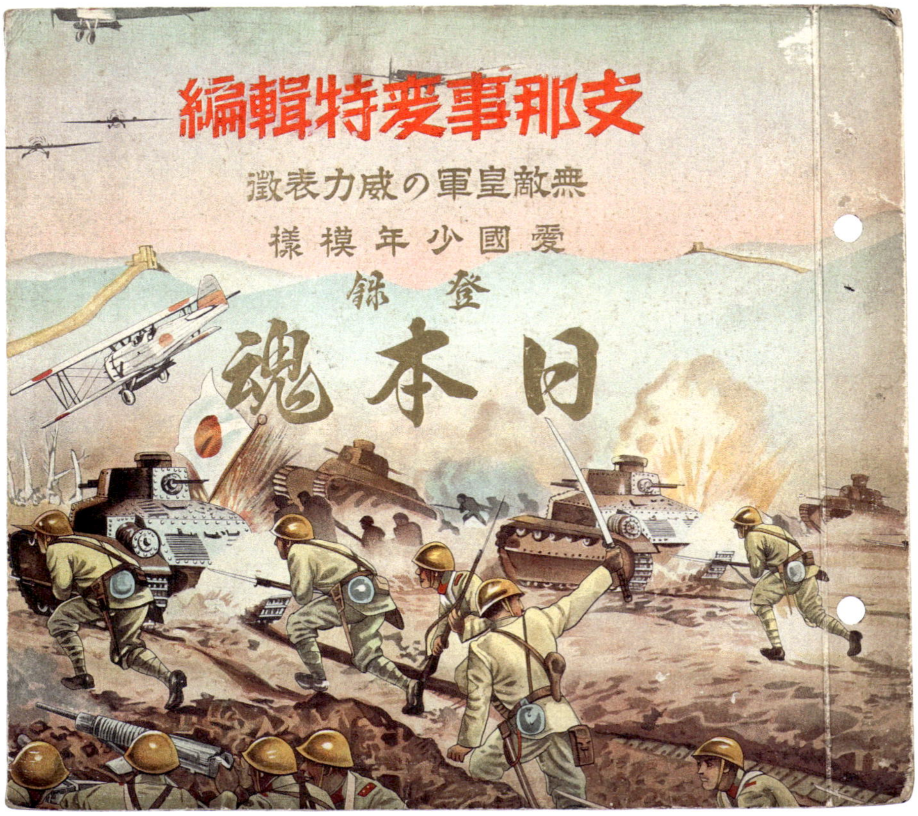

LEFT FIG. 14 *Niko-niko* sample book
Illustrated cover (see p. 132)

OPPOSITE FIG. 15 Kimono for a boy child (detail)
Flags and cities (Osaka, London, and Hōten) (see p. 110)

leisure-time sports such as baseball, skiing, and golf, or the travel ambitions of the middle class (fig. 15). *Niko-niko* was also used extensively for boys' kimono, as its durability and darker palette (which was slower to show dirt) made it ideal for everyday wear. Mothers could find pleasing motifs to play into the interests of young boys, such as cartoon characters, baseball and other sports, cars, trains, airplanes, dirigibles, ocean liners, and battlefields (fig. 14)—all of which could be found in abundance on *niko-niko* textiles.

Muslin

Muslin (*mosulin*), as noted earlier, was a lightweight, finely woven fabric made of wool or cotton; both types quickly became the initial inspiration as well as the material of choice for *omoshirogara* designers. Of all the new textiles that had gained prominence in the first quarter of the 20th century, muslin lent itself particularly well not only to Japanese designs but also to the Western chemical dyes that were then coming into common use. Textile artists also had a great deal more flexibility with designs for muslin because its printing processes were much simpler than those used for *meisen* and *niko-niko*, both of which were limited by the warp/weft printing techniques that gave them a fashionable *kasuri*-like appearance. By 1910, roller-printed muslin with designs that appeared to be as complex and vibrant as those created by the traditional *yūzen* method was being mass-produced at a fraction of the cost.[8]

Printed wool muslin soon attracted a large audience, and printed cotton muslin was equally successful. The ability to roller-print these textiles allowed the production of cheap, colorful *juban* that were bought extensively by men and women, as well as *haori*, *haura* (linings), and children's kimono. Throughout the 1920s and 1930s, these were mainstays among the manufacturers of mass-produced fabrics printed with novelty motifs typical of *omoshirogara*. Although most muslin designs during the Taishō and early Shōwa eras were conservative and based on versions of traditional themes, the real excitement was found in contemporary compositions, for which textile artists drew from the latest vocabulary of popular culture. These were *omoshirogara* at their best, with designs that reveled in popular imagery of people, events, objects, places, consumer goods (fig. 16), well-known works of art, and photo reproductions, as well as road vehicles, trains, airplanes, and ships.

Although many design compositions were used, the background patterns that seemed to dominate for *omoshirogara* played off a more structured layout that started with checkerboard patterns or alternating horizonal bands of color. These were printed in off-

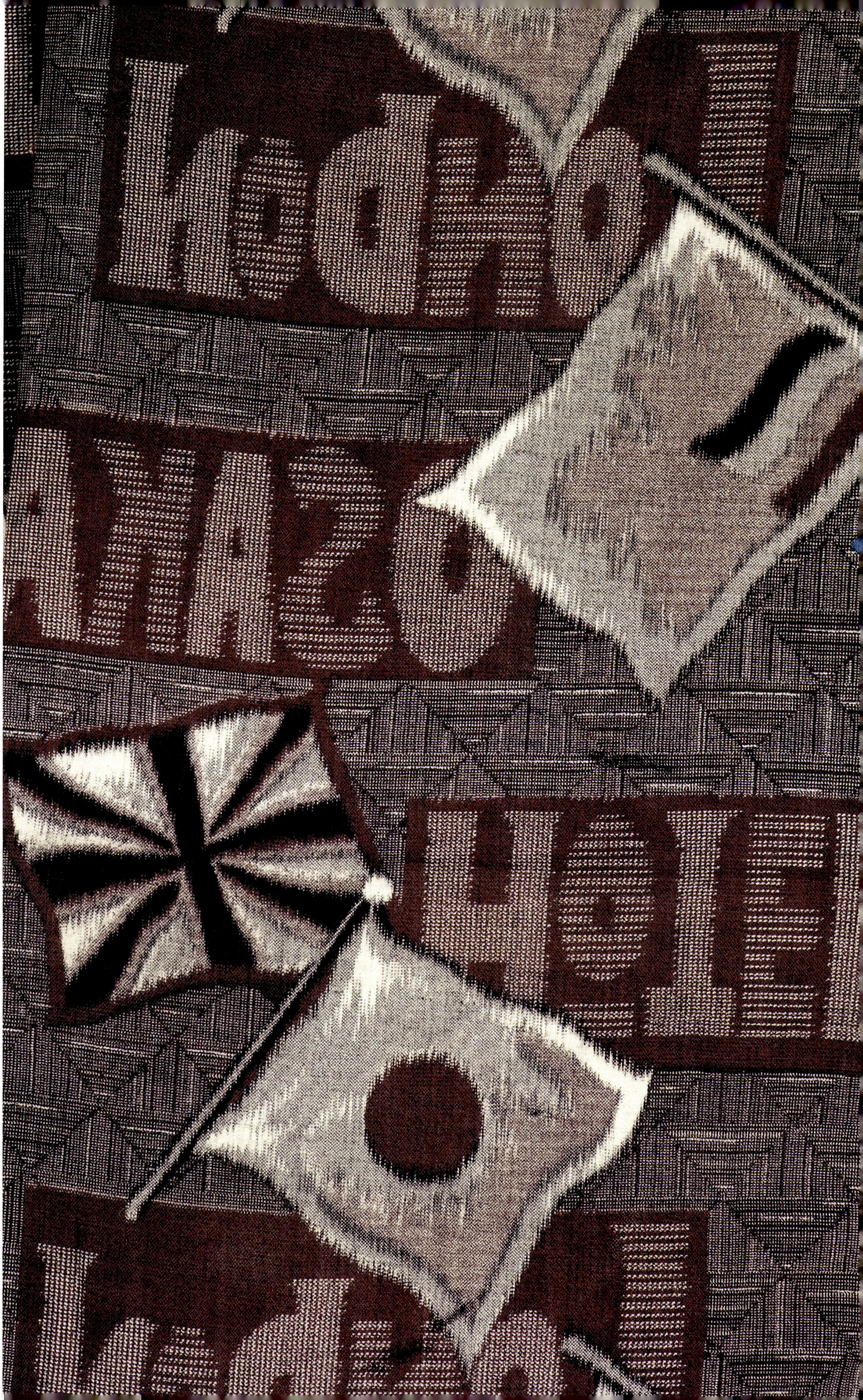

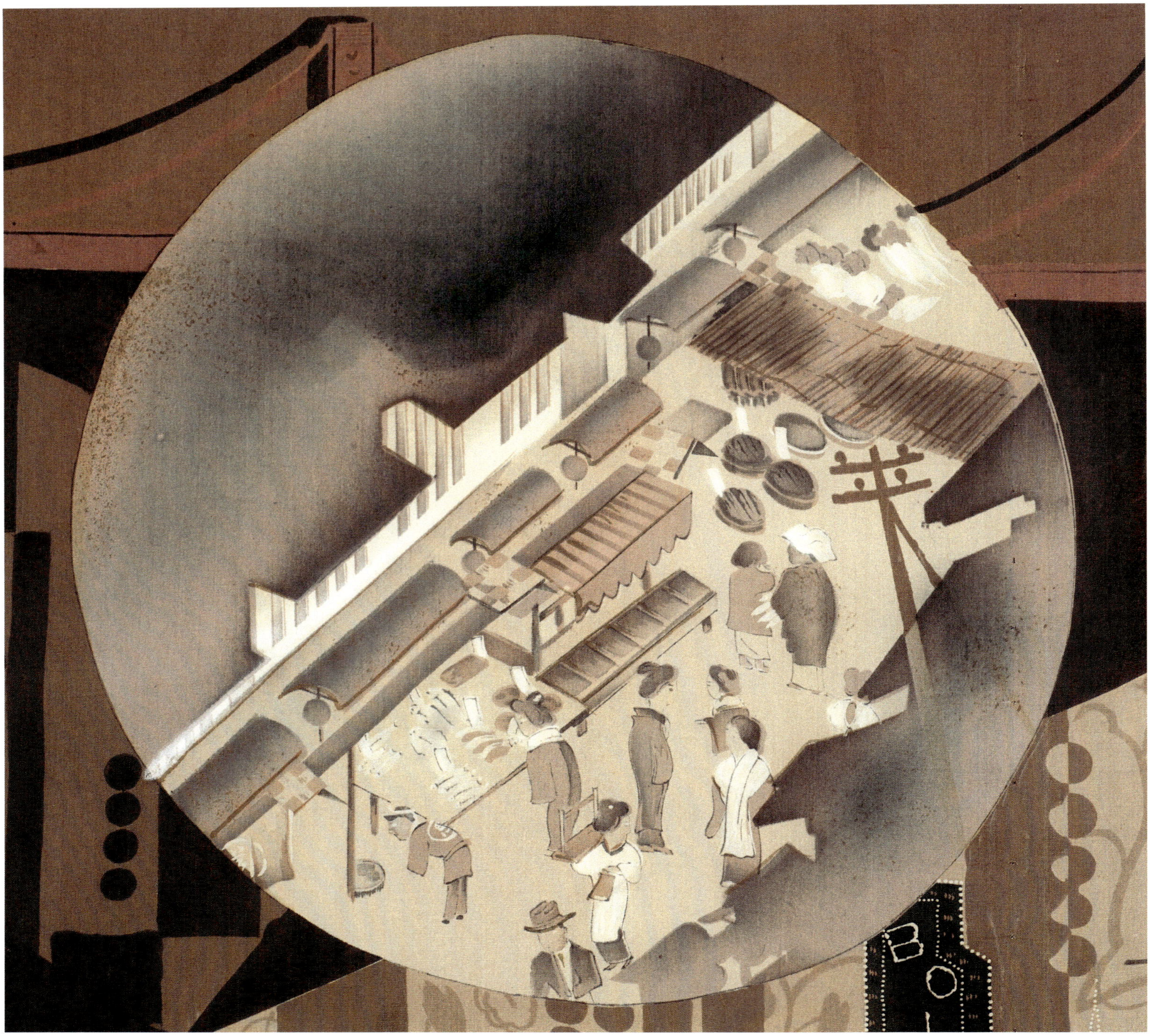

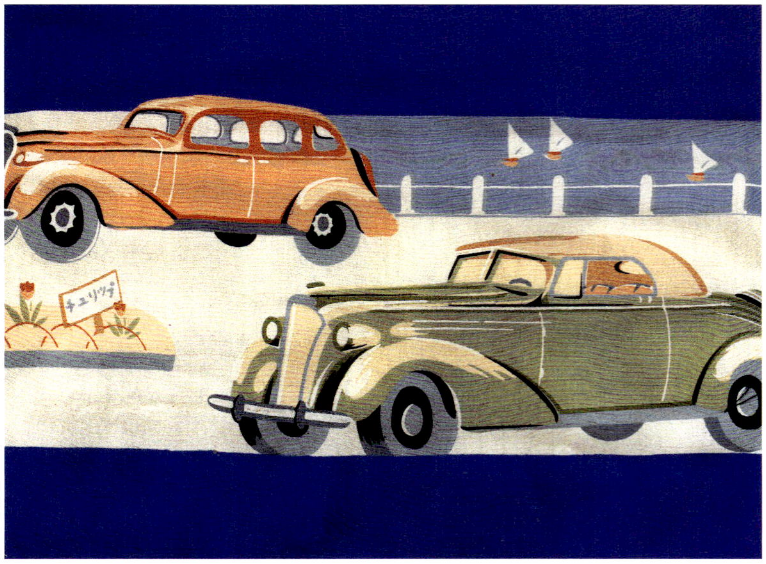

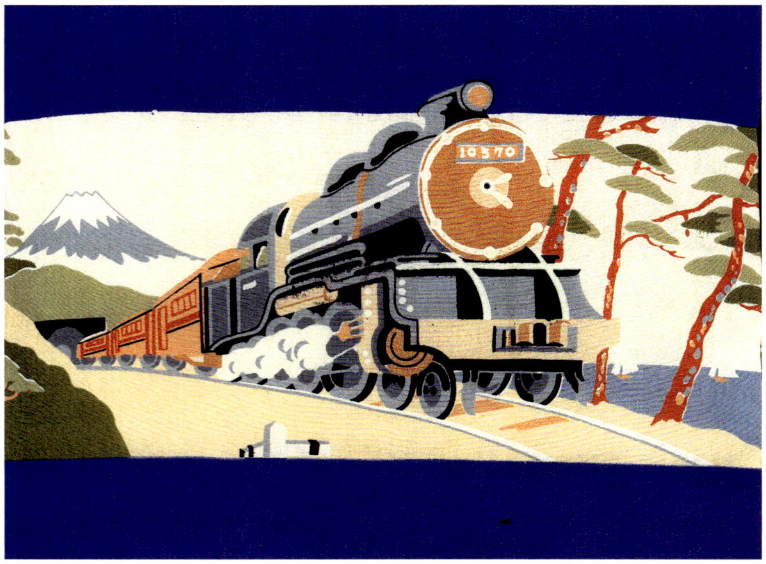

OPPOSITE TOP FIG. 16 Man's *haori* with a decorative lining (detail)
Early modern Japan vs. "The New Modern" (see p. 149)

OPPOSITE BELOW FIG. 17 Young boy's kimono (details)
Favorite things (see p. 303)

white or a light yellowish beige paired with contrasting colors such as blue, green, brown, or black; in either format, blue and yellow was the most common combination (fig. 17). Either horizontal bands or checkerboards then served as a backdrop to be overlaid with images that the artist would concoct to develop a theme, depending on the trends of the moment or the interests of the audience for whom the design was being created. The overlays used a variety of bright colors appropriate for the light-hearted atmosphere of the Taishō period that these designs were meant to convey, even when taking the most serious of subjects. Sometimes the overlays were set off from the background patterns by being partly or fully enclosed within circles (fig. 18), and at other times they were placed to float over the ground pattern. Because of the printing process that was used, muslin images were less stylized and appeared more natural in form and shape than those used in either *meisen* or *niko-niko*.

The same checkerboard or band format common to muslin was also used for printed silk *omoshirogara*. Mass-produced muslins could usually be bought directly off the shelf in department or kimono stores, but *omoshirogara* silks were still carefully treated and sold as luxury fabrics, and high-end customers were more than willing to spend more for these elegant designs. Department stores and kimono shops preferred to take special orders for *omoshirogara* silks such as *juban* (fig. 19) rather than keep a large stock of expensive products on hand.

Textiles in the War Years

As Japan moved into the years of war, raw materials for production became scarce. Stringent regulations in regard to textiles were formulated and issued in mid-1940, and ration coupons for clothing were issued in 1942. High-end luxury textiles were the most targeted under the regulations, but textiles of lesser note (such as the popular cloth-dyed patterned fabrics that included many *omoshirogara* textiles) were also restricted—in other words, many of the textiles used for everyday clothing for the general population fell within these rigorous regulations. Stringent controls on cotton were also instituted in the winter of 1939–40, as Japan did not produce raw cotton and all supplies had to be imported. Wool muslin (a favorite) was much in demand (fig. 20), especially for *juban* for men and women and for children's kimono, but in the late 1930s supply to the general public was curtailed as wool was requisitioned for military clothing; blankets and raw wool also had to be imported. Although the silk industry did not rely on imports, by the late 1930s, much of it was being channeled to the production of crucial war goods (parachutes, for example), leaving other substitutes to be found for daily wear. At the time, Japan led the world in rayon yarn production, and although its raw materials also came from abroad, most were turned into textiles for home consumption. Artificial silk (*jinken*) was the most popular product made from rayon, as it had a sheen and smooth feel like that of silk (fig. 21), but by 1940, raw materials for rayon production were also becoming scarce. By 1942, shortages of raw materials were so severe that textile companies had either turned to military production or been forced to close for lack of supplies.

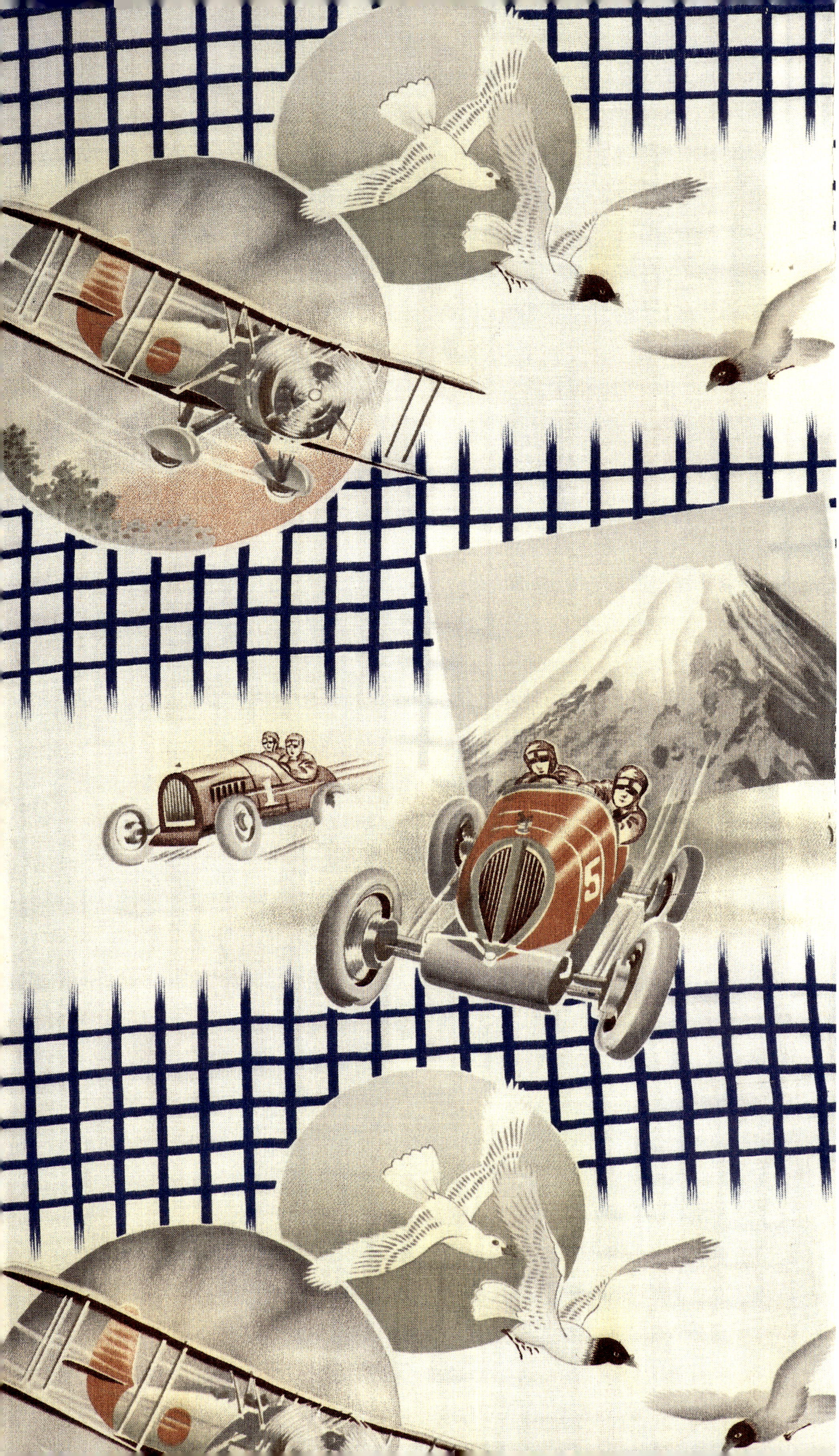

OPPOSITE FIG. 18 Man's *juban* (detail)
Racing cars and airplanes (see p. 181).

BELOW FIG. 19 Man's *juban* (detail)
On the racetrack (see p. 174)

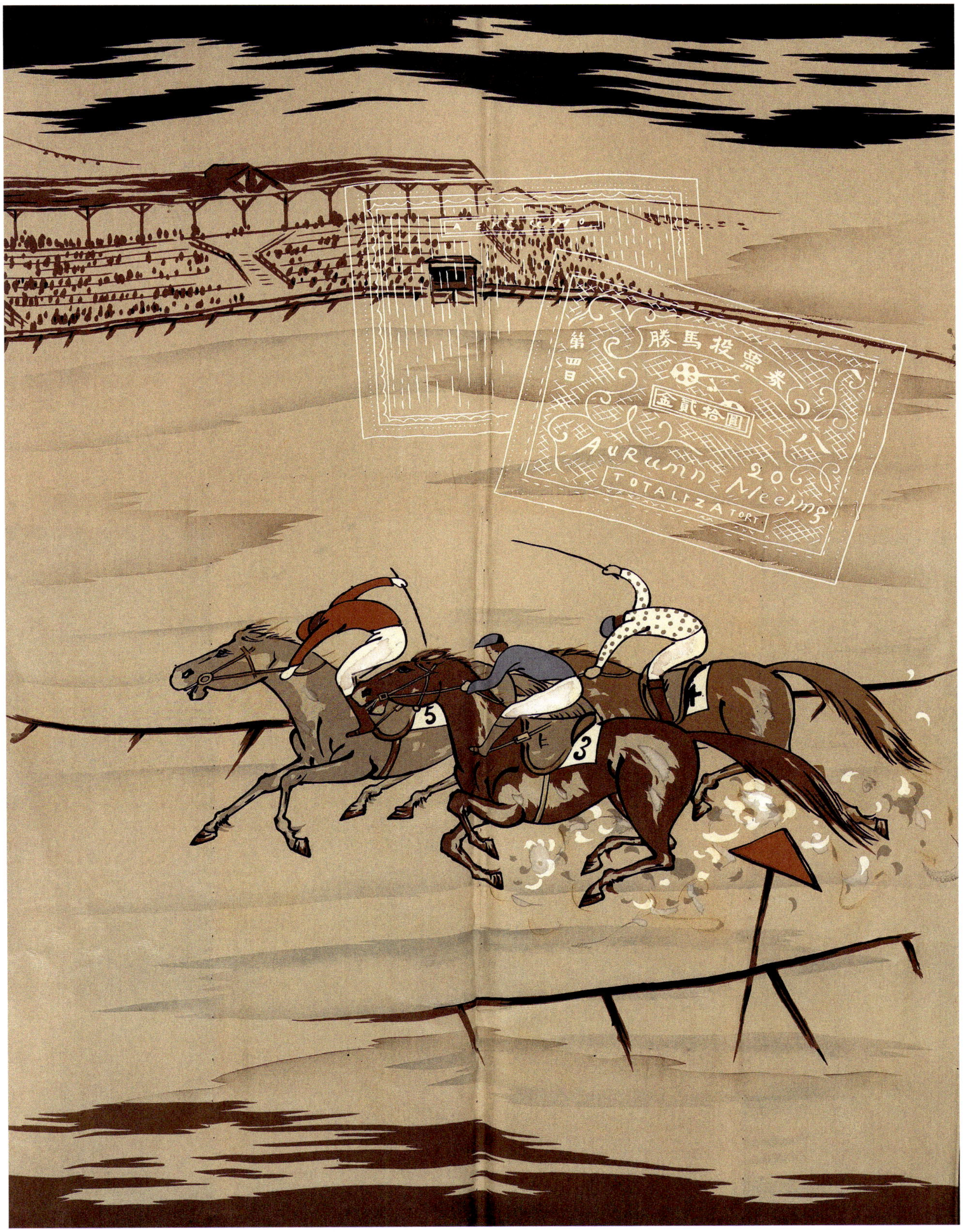

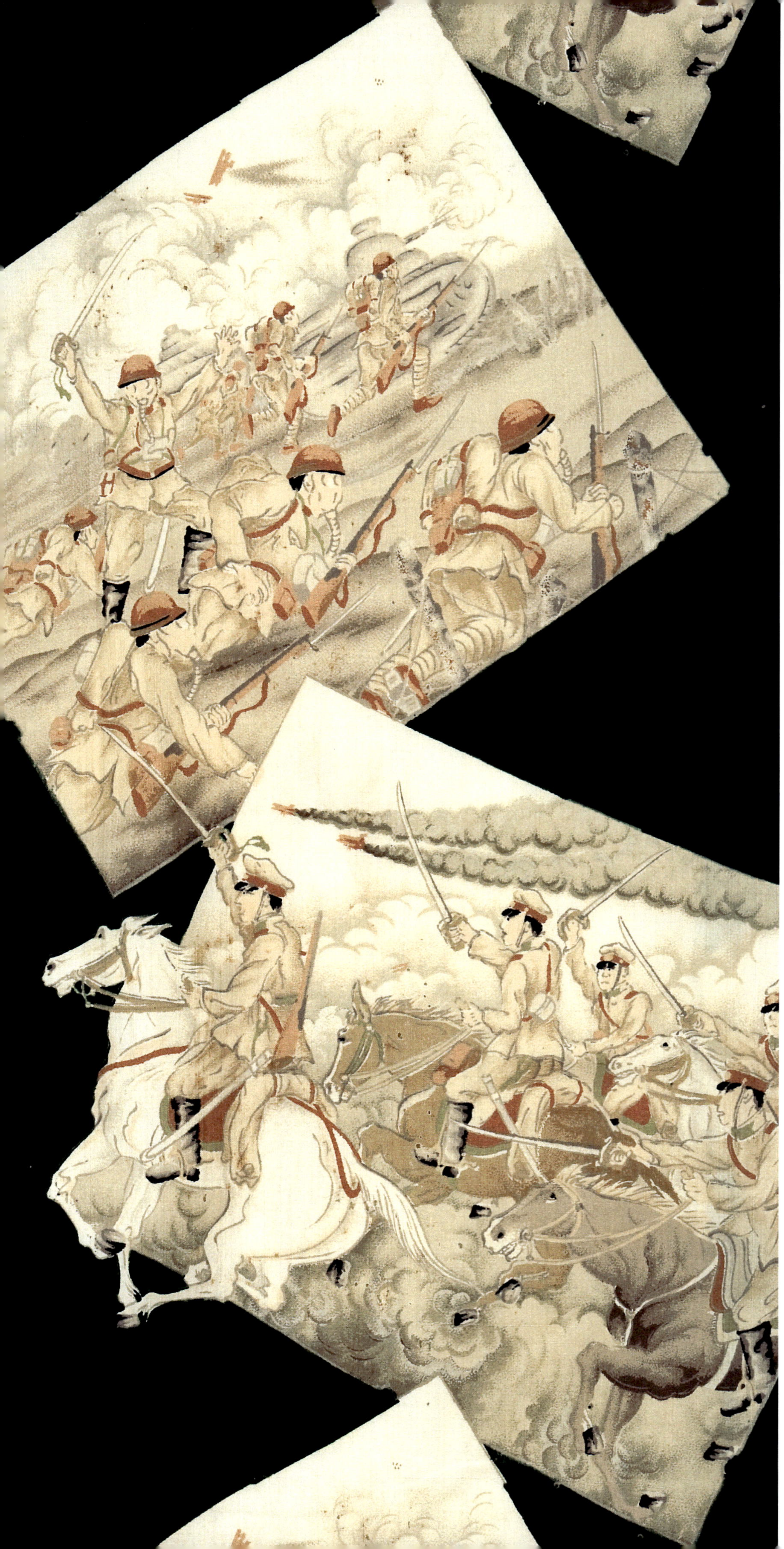

LEFT FIG. 20 Man's *juban* (detail)
Postcard illustrations of battle scenes
(see p. 96)

OPPOSITE FIG. 21 Kimono for a child (detail)
"Happy Hearts and Health" (see p. 268)

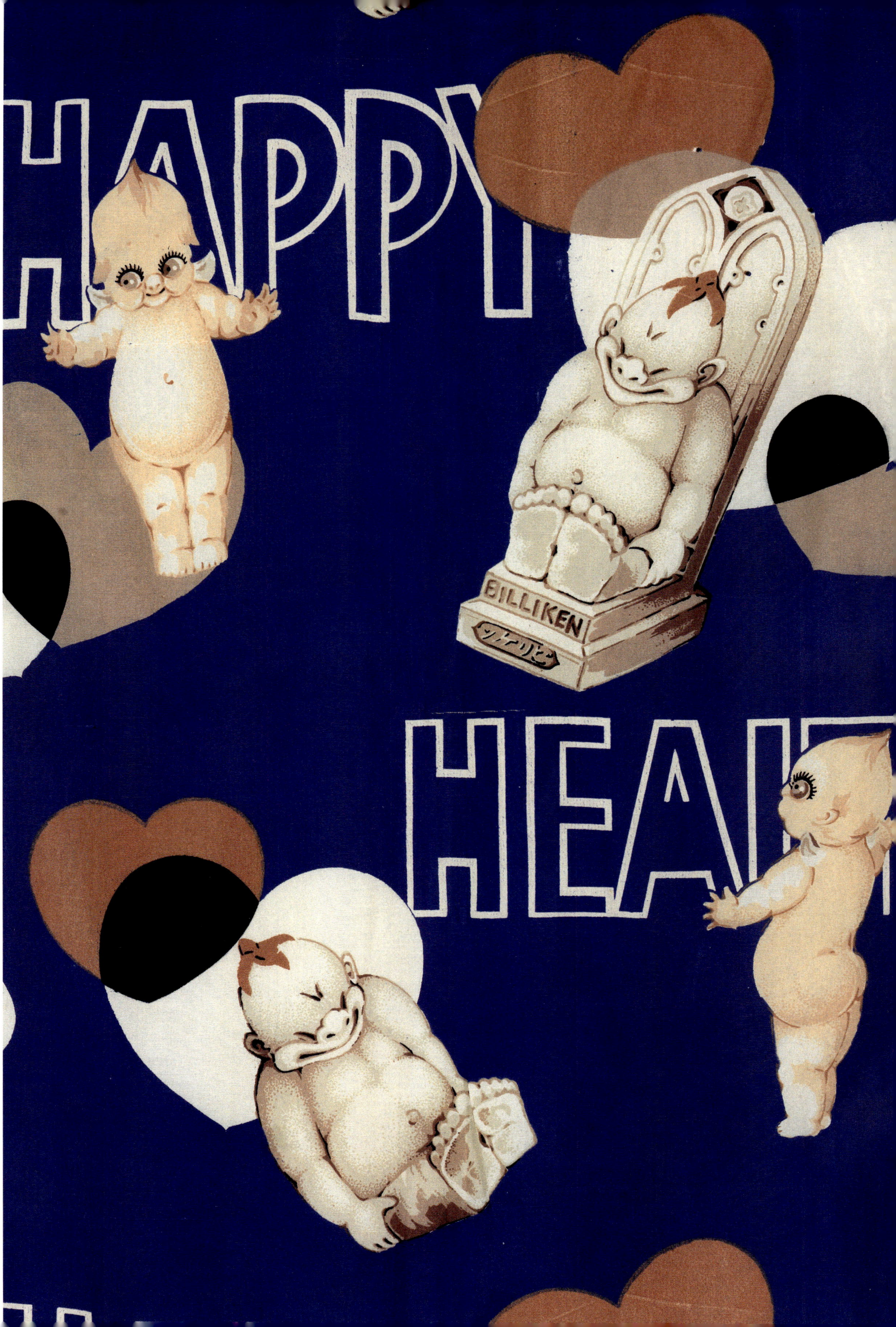
HAPPY
BILLIKEN

OPPOSITE ABOVE FIG. 22 Man's *haori* with a decorative lining (detail)
City of the Future (see p. 211)

OPPOSITE BELOW FIG. 23 Man's *juban* (detail)
From Fuji to Cairo (see p. 214)

MEN, WOMEN, FASHION, AND *OMOSHIROGARA*

And Men First

Very little attention had been paid to men's traditional garments following the Meiji Emperor's proclamation of male dress reform and the adoption of Western-style uniforms for the Japanese military. Once high-ranking military men had obtained proper Western military attire, they appeared in the imperial court in Western style, sometimes wearing elegant regimental dress and at other times frock coats or other Western garments for meetings and conferences in the court or the Imperial Diet (the House of Representatives and the House of Peers).[9] Men who were conscripted for military service found that they, too, could become quite familiar and comfortable with Western military clothing. Outside of the military, other early adaptations of Western dress began to be worn by men within the public sector. Women attached to the imperial court and a section of the upper classes quickly followed the empress's lead in wearing Western dress, as did others with pretentions to social mobility. By the turn of the 20th century, Western dress was a symbol of progress and social dignity: businessmen, bankers, doctors, and other leaders of the "new" society wore suits to work, although Western dress for workplaces and Japanese dress at home was the general rule for quite a long time.

By the middle of the Taishō period, however, Western clothing was no longer a novelty, especially in Tokyo. Although Japanese men of good standing (those with white-collar jobs, for example) continued to wear Western dress for business and work, they did not lose their appreciation for traditional Japanese garments. When invited to attend ceremonial occasions or private parties, traditional garments were often the preferred choice. Men's outer kimono tended toward the conservative on such occasions, for the most part using blacks, browns, dark blues, or other subdued colors of unpatterned silk, or textiles with small, unobtrusive woven patterns—and again, of subdued colors. The imagination could be let loose, however, with the new and innovative *omoshirogara* designs used only on men's *haura* (linings for *haori*),[10] or on their *nagajuban* (underkimono). Intimates and family members might see these hidden flights of fancy at private parties when a *haori* is removed to show the ultra-modern *haura* (lining) stitched to the interior back (fig. 22), or when the top of an outer kimono is dropped for comfort so that the exciting foreign designs on the *nagajuban* (fig. 23) become visible to observers. Otherwise, however, these rarely seen undergarments would remain hidden treasures that would be worn and shown to only a select few friends and associates. These treasures are part of the history of Japan, a unique holdover from the Edo period that once served a purpose in regard to the sumptuary laws that limited displays of wealth or luxury. After the abolishment of such laws during the Meiji period, these undergarments became fashion statements in themselves. The designs on many of these garments are quite unusual and often spectacular; they could be specially commissioned and were always carefully selected by the buyer. In this case, the man's *haura* shows an elegant ship as it leaves the dock for foreign shores, with passengers already aboard and throwing out bright streamers to the crowd on the pier (fig. 24). The pattern and motifs chosen no doubt signified information about the self-image, pride, or beliefs of the wearer.

The *haura* of men's *haori* also stand in strong contrast to the vivid coloring of women's *meisen* kimono, or the patterned silks used for women's *haori*, which often carried more feminine or traditional imagery. Male *haura* are cast almost entirely in monochromatic tones, colors associated most closely with the traditional Japan

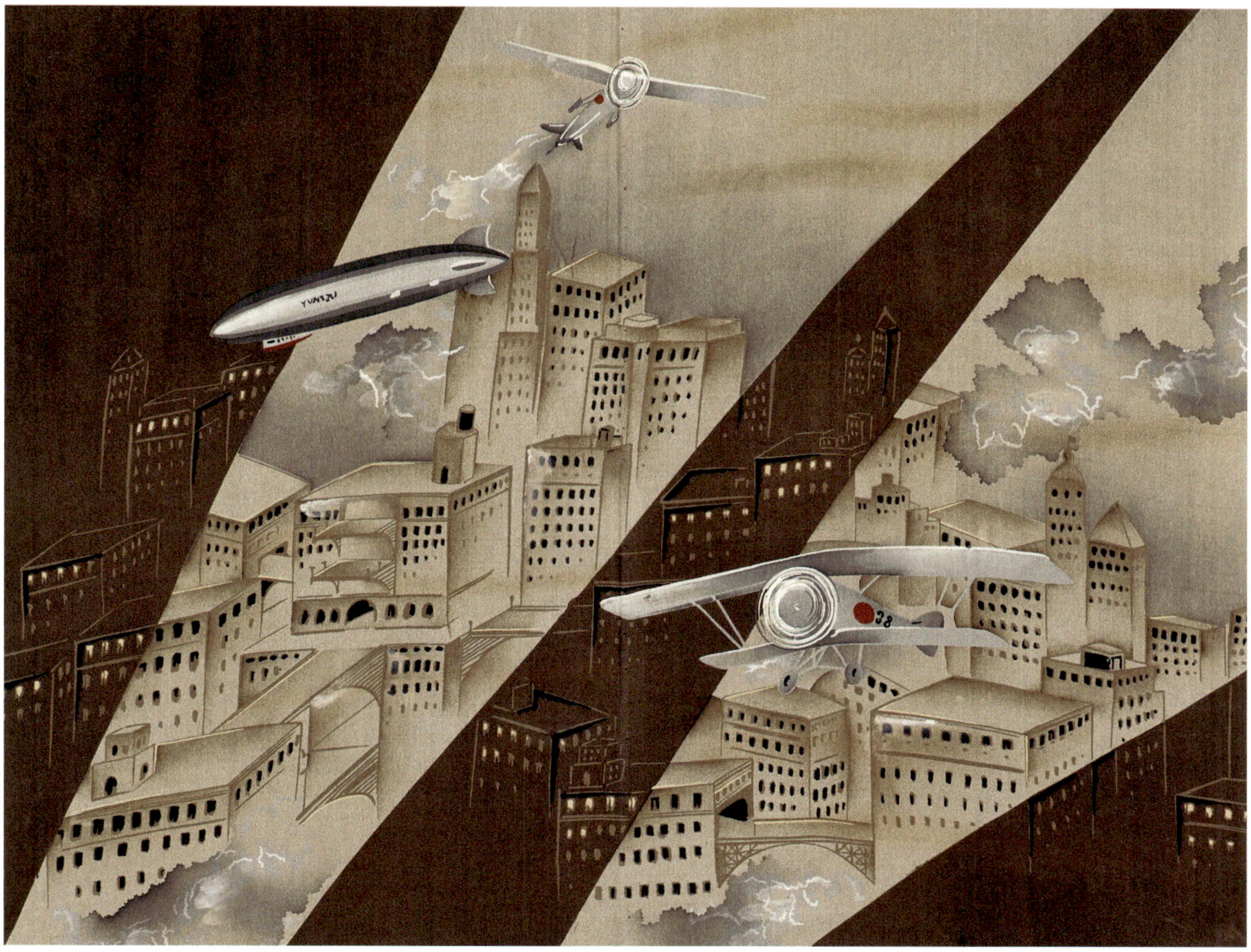

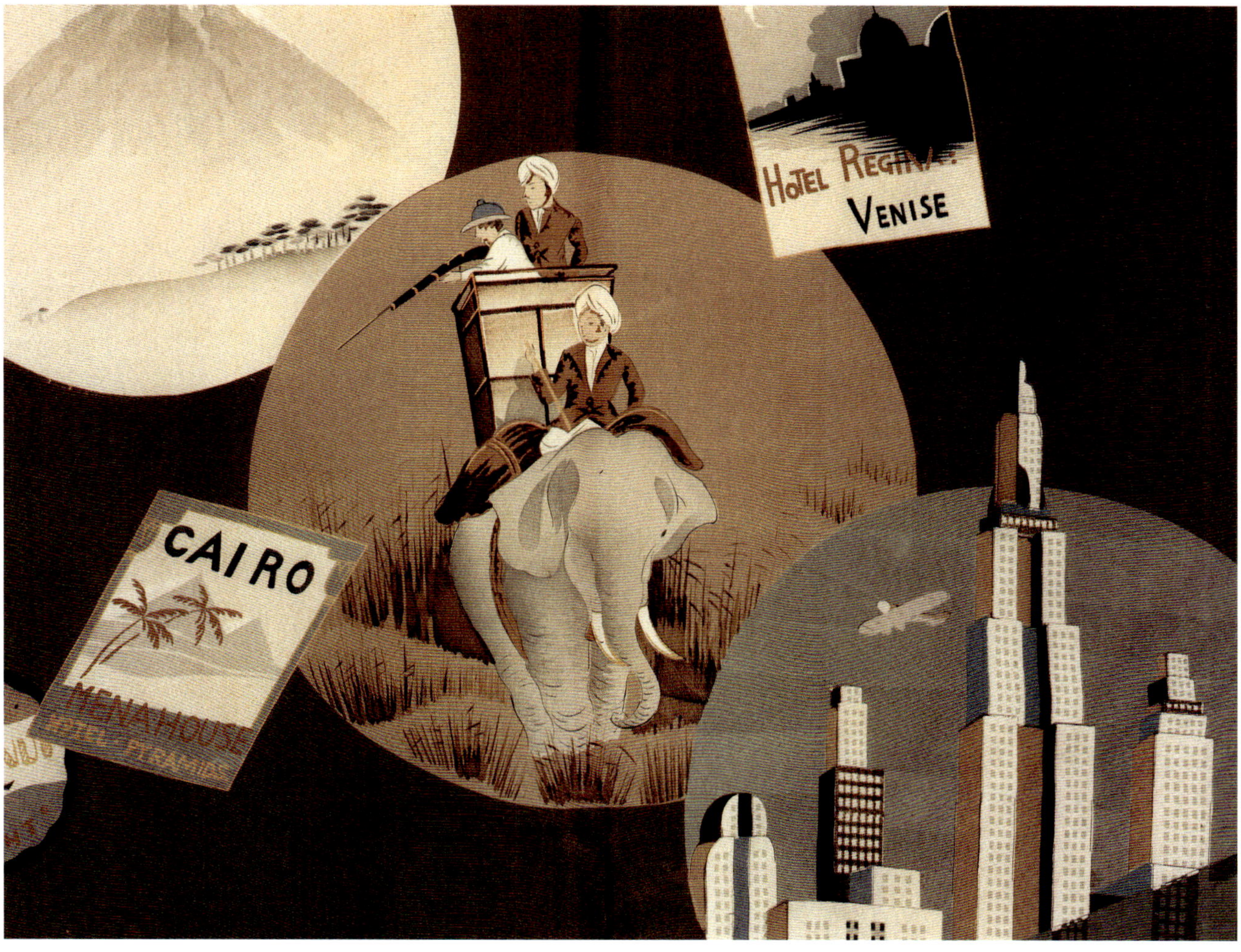
VENISE
CAIRO
MENA HOUSE
HOTEL PYRAMIDS

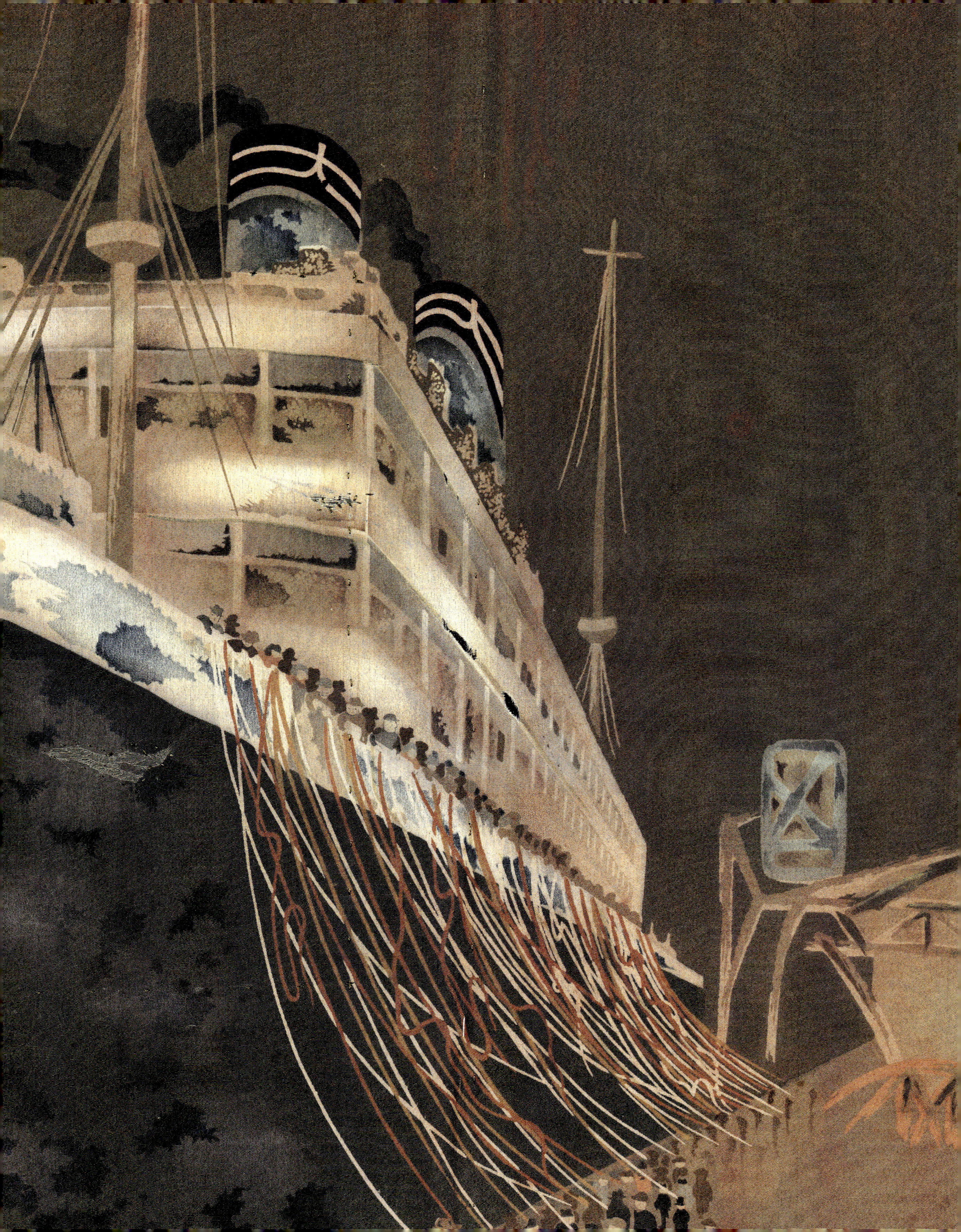

OPPOSITE FIG. 24 Man's *haori* with a decorative lining (detail)
A passenger ship ready to depart (see p. 281)

of tea ceremony and inward-looking architecture. These colors harken back to the famous 16th-century tea master Sen Rikyu, whose preferences still resonate today. Rikyu favored subdued garments of "forty-eight browns and one hundred grays," colors that would not detract from the appreciation of the tea ceremony itself, and that is what is seen in these *haura* as well.[11] The idea was to focus on the design, the content, and appreciate it as such, rather than being distracted by bright colors and busy imagery such as children or young women might wear. The subtle and complex color tones of the "forty-eight browns and one hundred grays" that developed have been drawn down through the years to these *haura*, and the tradition still continues today when it comes to men's formal kimono. Another interpretation of the subtlety of the colors may also be found in the "beauty of monochrome," and how use of a color can limit the suggestive range while less specificity in colors can expand it.[12] An occasional splash of color in a *haura* (fig. 25) exemplifies this complex and starkly stunning composition, due to the fine dyeing and delicate hand painting produced by a textile artist; the impact is made that much more powerful by the understated tones surrounding it. This may explain the use of a close-to-monochrome palette in the designs seen in men's clothing and the richness of color in textiles for boys, as adults appreciate and respond to the concept of suggestion while children, being more literal, are more responsive to sharp color contrasts rather than subtle shadings.

This restrained palette is typical of the designs used for men's formal *haura* and *nagajuban* beneath the kimono. When the textiles used for the less formal *juban* are considered, the picture changes substantively. Many of these textiles had mass-market printed designs that offered a much wider range of colors than those seen or worn in more formal garments. In some cases, however, a purchaser of *juban* might choose to engage an artist to create a one-of-a-kind dynamically hand-painted design for his garment—or perhaps even paint the design himself. Designs covered a very wide range of subjects, from cosmopolitanism to leisure activities, sports to cinema and nightclubs, modernity, art (fig. 26), and architecture to politics, and the Machine Age from electricity, radio, telephones, and skyscrapers (see p. 143) to airplanes, cars, trams, and trains.

Wool or cotton muslin, *niko-niko kasuri*, and light silks were also favored, in large part because these informal *juban* were gender- and age-interchangeable. Often these designs were of a more playful nature, and unless the design was significantly weighted toward masculine taste (fig. 27) or the lighter and more delicate images favored by women (fig. 28), either sex might find them interesting—or novel. Even designs that today might appear childish to Western eyes (fig. 29) were often worn comfortably by men or women. Kimono for young boys were often made from the same textiles that were used for adults' informal kimono or *juban*. These same textiles could easily be transformed into kimono or *juban* for boys—or even *miyamairi* for boy babies (fig. 30)—but young girls would be less likely to want to wear textiles carrying this perceived "male" imagery.

Boys' Garb

By the late 1920s and 1930s, many school-age Japanese children of middle- and upper-class families wore Western-style clothing. Younger children—usually those under six or seven years old—and those from rural or less affluent families still wore traditional garments. Once children started school, however, both boys and girls were more likely to wear school uniforms, which had become popular by the early Taishō period. Uniforms for boys were cut in a vaguely militaristic style with black jackets closed with gold buttons, stand-up collars, black pants, black caps with a gold band, and

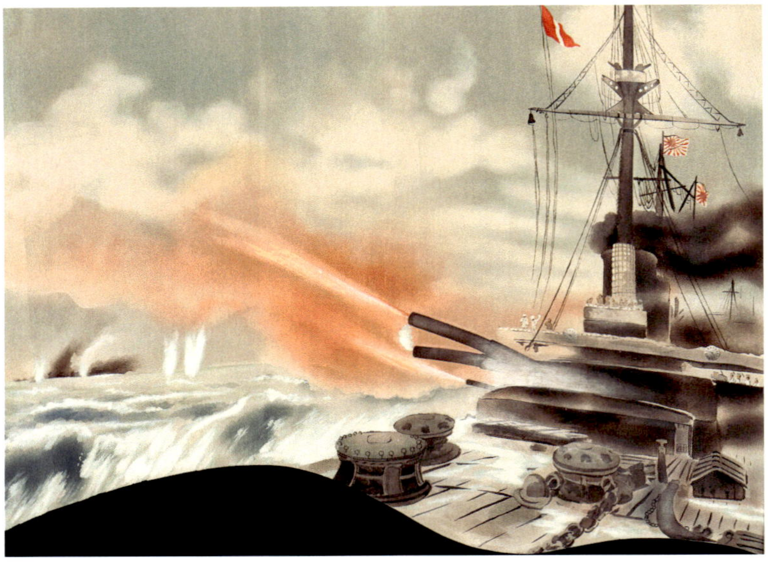

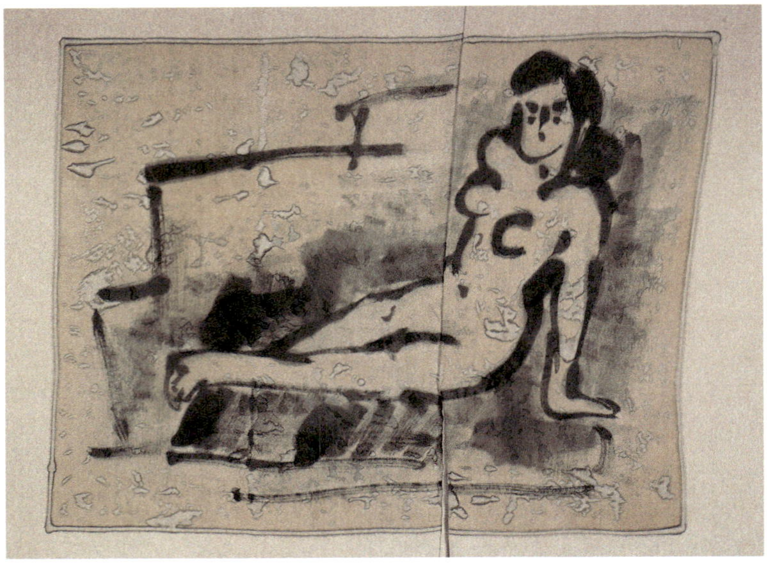

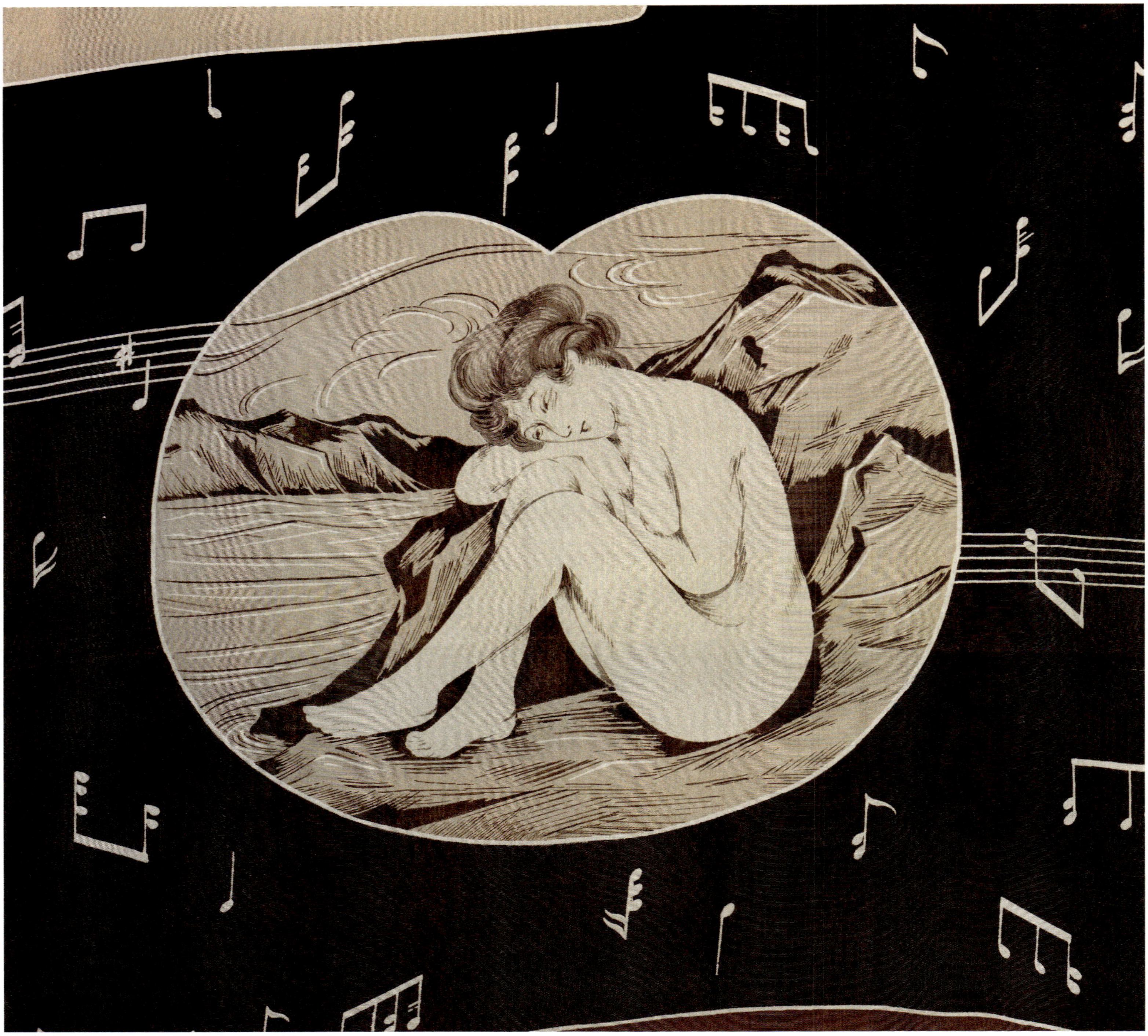

OPPOSITE
TOP LEFT FIG. 25 Man's *haori* with a decorative lining (detail)
Battleship at war in a raging sea (see p. 88)

TOP RIGHT FIG. 26 Man's *juban* (detail)
Three nude paintings (see p. 179)

BOTTOM FIG. 27 Man's *haori* with a decorative lining (detail)
Nudes posed in Western style (see p. 306)

BELOW FIG. 28 *Juban* for a woman (detail)
Happy Kewpies in Japanese dress (see p. 270)

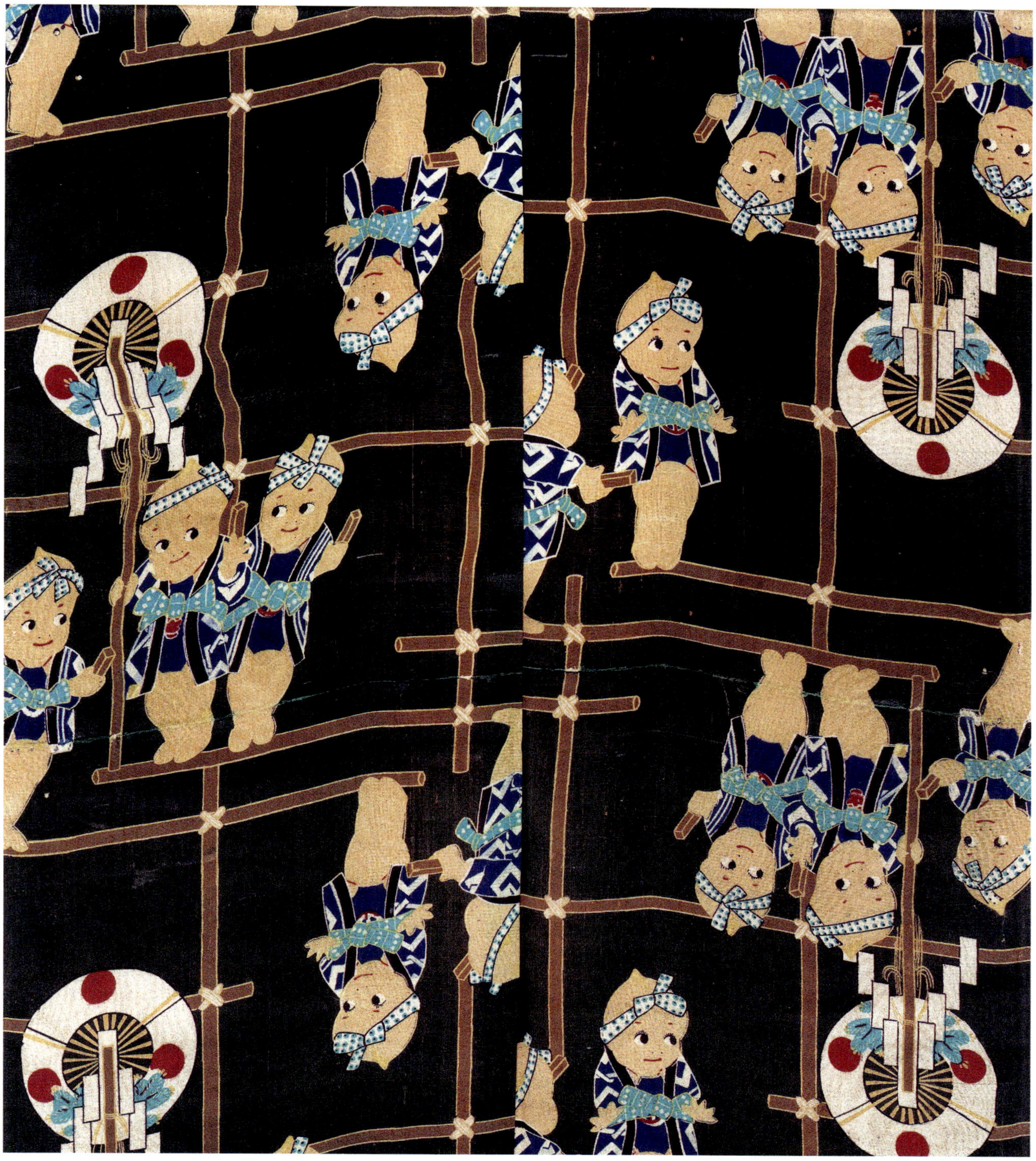

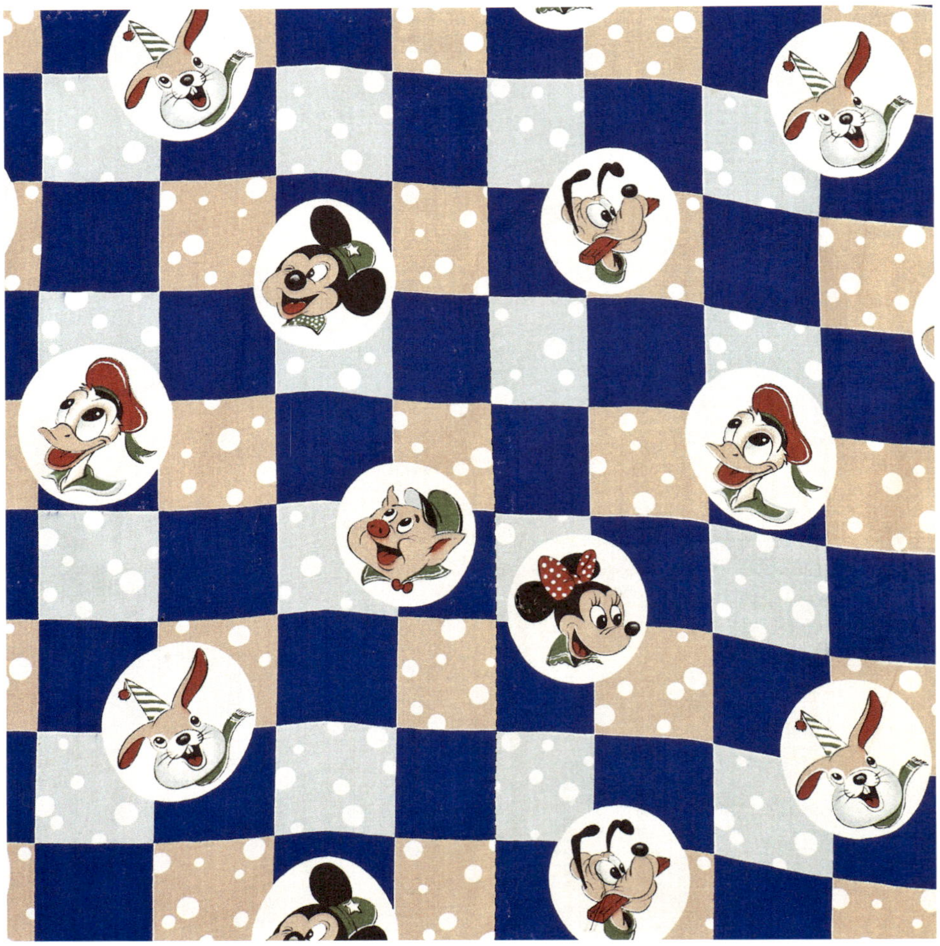

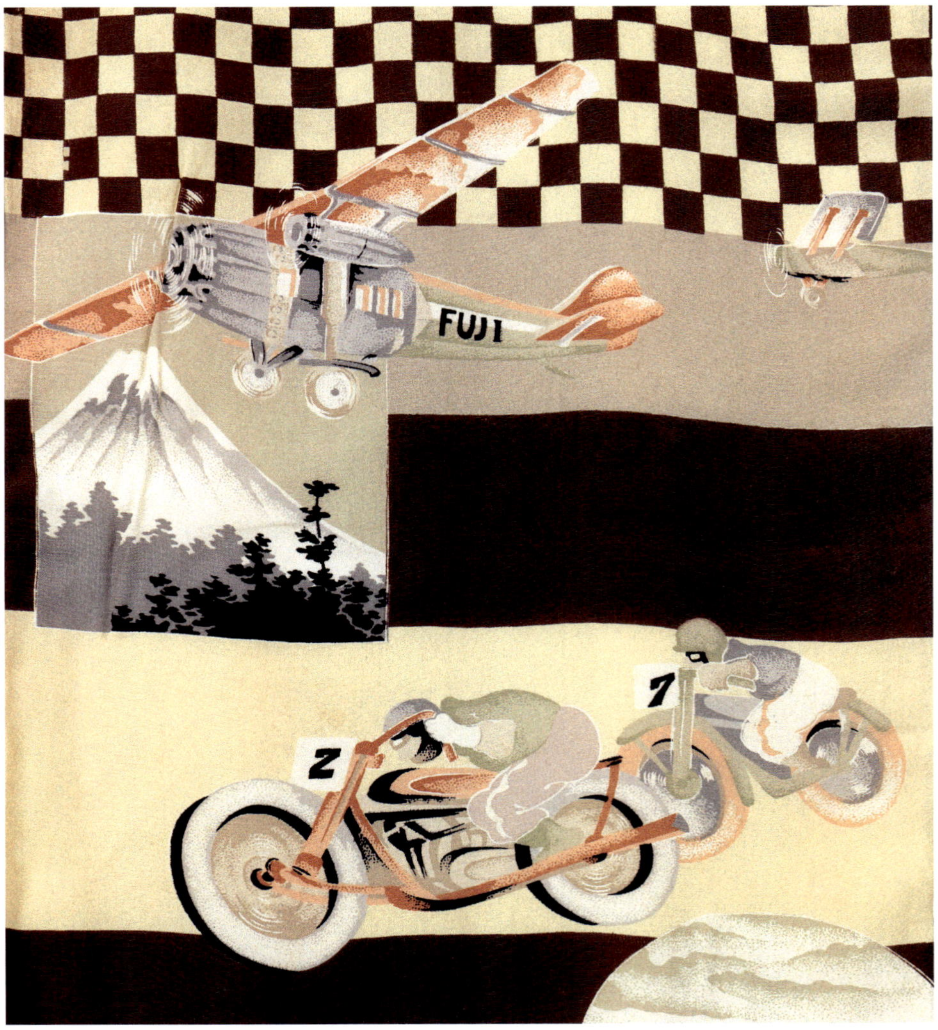

TOP FIG. 29 Woman's *juban* (detail)
Mickey Mouse and friends (see p. 240)

BOTTOM FIG. 30 *Miyamairi*
(boy child's kimono for his first
shrine visit) (detail)
Racing with cars, motorcycles,
and an airplane to Fuji (see p. 301)

black shoes (a style that has lasted a long time), and girls were given dark blue pleated skirts and blouses, with white scarves tied below the sailor-style collars.[13]

Whether their daily dress was "modern" (Western style) or traditional (kimono), however, parents would make sure that their children would wear kimono for formal or ceremonial occasions, and festivals, rather than schoolwear. For such occasions, young girls wore kimono that featured colorful images such as abundant flowers, auspicious images, Japanese court dolls, or other such designs that leaned toward the pretty, sweet, or cute rather than choosing modern new patterns. Young boys were dressed for these events in higher-end traditional garments such as *miyamairi*, *haregi* ("visiting" clothes), or festival outfits such as those worn for *Shichigosan*.[14] *Miyamairi*, of course, were not worn by school-age children, but they might well accompany parents to celebrate the new baby's health and happiness at a Shinto shrine. A boy baby's *miyamairi* might be worn only once and never again (fig. 31), but it might be lovingly cared for as a treasure piece, unless it was turned into a *Shichigosan* costume for a five-year-old boy.

Omoshirogara were extensively used in fabrics intended for boys, and there were no inhibitions about using such textiles for younger children's everyday kimono. These were mass-produced textiles made from *niko-niko kasuri* or muslin, ready for wear and tear from rough-and-tumble play. Everyday kimono for boys were usually purchased from department stores or other small shops; they were not exceptionally costly or special-order garments. They were meant to be much tougher than formal kimono, and many of these everyday garments seem to have been able to survive their years quite easily. Perhaps because Japan was a patriarchal society, an exceptionally large array of *omoshirogara* that reflected the contemporary life and interests of the Taishō/early Shōwa culture were produced especially for boys. These numerous robes feature lively and playful patterns depicting cars, modern playthings (fig. 32), aircraft, dirigibles (fig. 33), ships, sports, animals, boy soldiers (fig. 34), and much more—in other words, contemporary *omoshirogara* motifs.

Many boys' garments made from *omoshirogara* were also recycled. If their mothers tired of an *omoshirogara juban*, the design fell out of fashion, or the garment was damaged in such a way that a mother could no longer wear it, there was a very good chance that she would repurpose the garment for one of her children. It is not uncommon to come across examples where the alterations are obvious, but young boys would no doubt enjoy wearing repurposed garments as long as they carried amusing or diverting patterns and lively colors.

Women's Garments

Fewer *omoshirogara* were produced specifically for women. Images on textiles clearly meant for women's and girls' outer kimono and accessories are, for the most part, more likely to be opaque than transparent in terms of meaning. As in traditional textile design, there were many motifs and images considered appropriate for women, but there also were others that were not. The number of *omoshirogara* textiles that can be firmly identified as being for women is somewhat small, whereas men and boys clearly predominate. Of those that are ascribed to women, lightness and brightness are key, especially for young and unmarried women. *Omoshirogara* clearly meant for young women's outer kimono include the airy, almost sheer cotton used for this strikingly beautiful kimono, which was intended to be worn over a white cotton or silk *juban* to help offset summer heat (fig. 36). This kimono is stunning in design; the stenciled motif of musical notes moves from hem to collar, and, as the notes ascend, it becomes obvious that they were carefully printed to become slightly smaller as

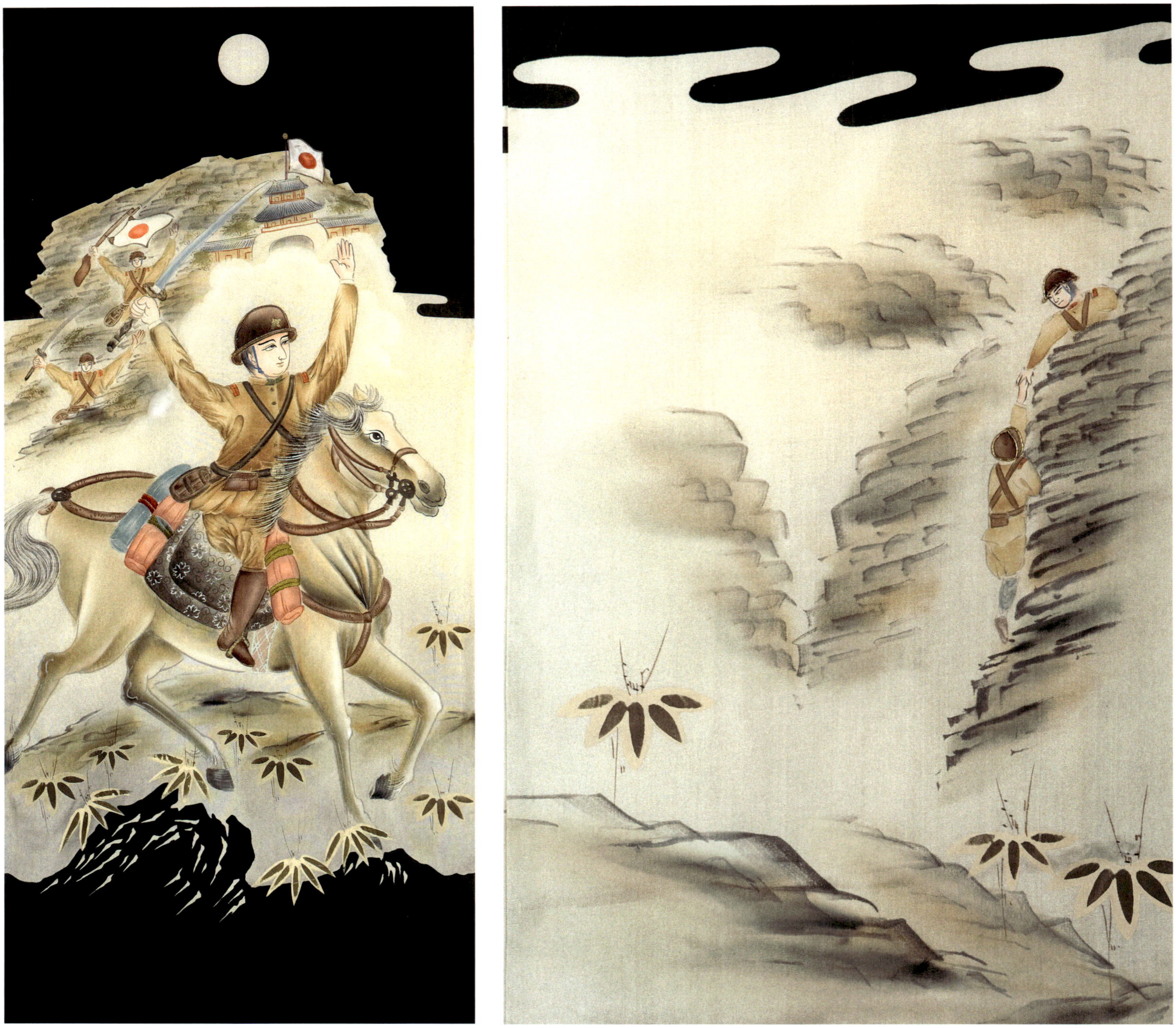

ABOVE FIG. 31 *Miyamairi* (boy child's kimono for his first shrine visit) (details)
Victory celebration (see p. 113)

OPPOSITE FIG. 32 Kimono for a boy child (detail)
Modern transportation for boys (see p. 297)

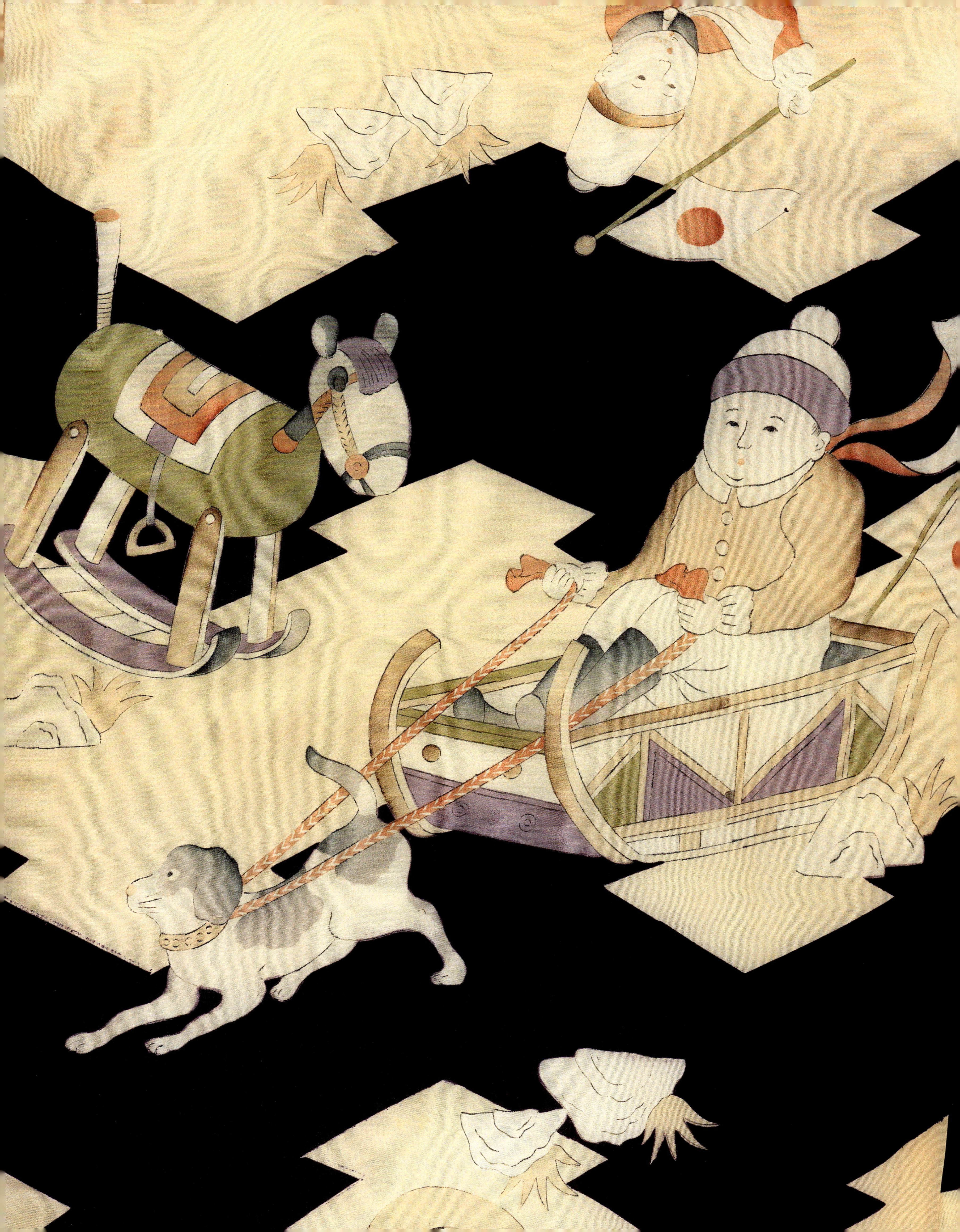

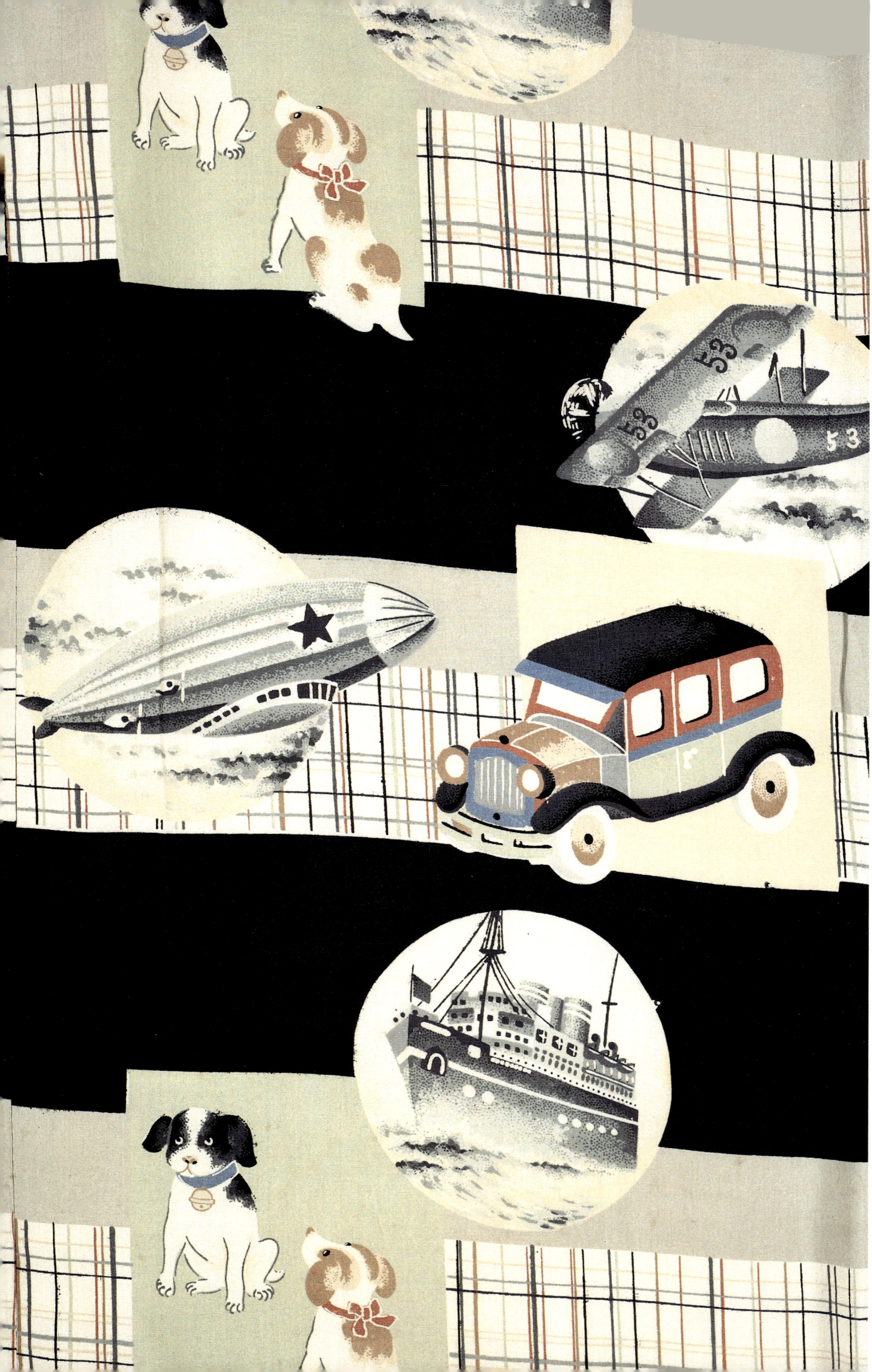

OPPOSITE FIG. 33 *Juban* for a young man (detail)
New transport for the world (see p. 223)

BELOW FIG. 34 Kimono for a young boy (detail)
Boys playing at war (see p. 75)

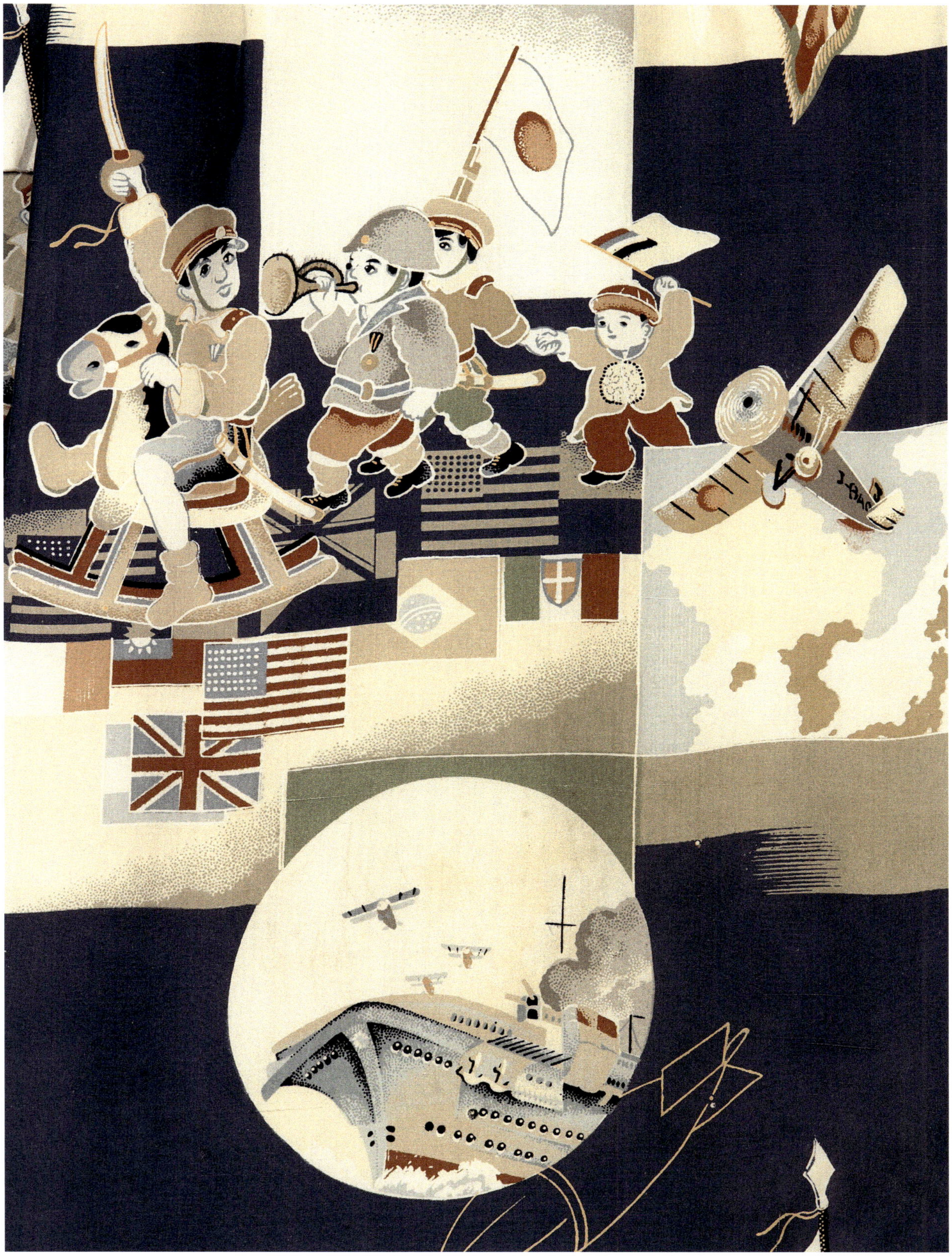

each note climbs higher. The fabric panels are also mirror-images, and the owner of such a garment was quite likely to be recognized as a leader of modern fashion. Other kimono, such as this simple *meisen* kimono decorated with planes in flight (see p. 311), may not be as extraordinary as the cotton kimono above, but this garment, too, gives a sense of lively playfulness.

When women wore *omoshirogara* as outer kimono, they would also wear *haori* and *juban* associated with the kimono style. Unlike male *haori*, which showed designs only on the inside of the jacket, *haori* for women carried designs to be shown off on the outside. Female *haori* designs might be specifically coordinated with the kimono, but many other patterns and motifs could look as good (or sometimes even better) (fig. 35). Neither does the inside of the woman's *haori* always necessarily follow the outer: the *haori* may sport a lightweight lining with a bit of color or design (fig. 37), or a slightly heavier lining may produce a very different but still elegant choice (see p. 257). The obi, too, plays a part for the wearer. This spectacular obi encompasses elements of contemporary graphic design with the modernity of aircraft. The brilliant colors of the three planes shimmer against the blue of the clouds and provide a heady sense of speed and the beauty of flight (fig. 38). When worn, this obi would surely provide a dazzling statement to enhance the wearer's kimono.

Wartime Imagery for Women

Examples of wartime imagery in *omoshirogara* textiles for women's outerwear are somewhat unusual. For the most part, fewer examples of such textiles can be definitively identified as being for women's use. Although women's outer clothing of much of the wartime period (1932–45) carried a great deal of contemporary imagery, very little of it was actually related to war; designs depicting elements of popular culture and modernity, or more traditional floral and literary designs, were much more common. Some women occasionally wore kimono, obi, and *juban* (fig. 39) that carried wartime designs, although it seemed that allowances were made for women to sport wartime imagery on undergarments rather than on outerwear. For those garments, there were a number of idealized depictions of subjects such as empire, territorial expansion, bombers, battleships, cannon, and tanks (see p. 82); occasionally heroic folk figures such as Momotaro ("Peach Boy") were used as metaphors for contemporary times. While some obi carried wartime imagery, textiles that were sewn to the backs of obi would rarely be shown publicly.

A Taste of Fashion Catalogs for Men, Women, and Children

Several major department stores in Japan, such as Mitsukoshi, Matsuzakaya, and Takashimaya, offered textiles for sale both in-house and through catalogs. Higher-end goods were sold in-house via seasonal showings, where clients could come to review the new designs and place orders; customers also had the option of requesting one-of-a-kind designs or designs modified according to color and taste. These textiles would not be produced until orders for them had been taken, thus saving the producer the trouble of making goods that did not sell. Less expensive textiles were sold through catalogs and off-the-shelf stock was also kept on hand in limited quantities; if a design proved popular, it could be rerun on an as-needed basis rather than keeping a large inventory on hand. Japanese factories were more geared to this on-demand system than were Western ones, and customers found nothing unusual in waiting for a short period for their merchandise.

The promotional fashion catalogs that Mitsukoshi Department Store—one of the largest such stores in Japan at the time (the 1920s and 1930s)—produced

TOP FIG. 35 *Haori* for a woman (detail)
Playing cards (see pp. 226–27)

BOTTOM LEFT FIG. 36 Kimono for a young girl (detail)
Musical notes (see p. 248)

BOTTOM RIGHT FIG. 37 Woman's *haori* with a decorative lining (detail)
Skyscrapers and musical programs (see p. 154)

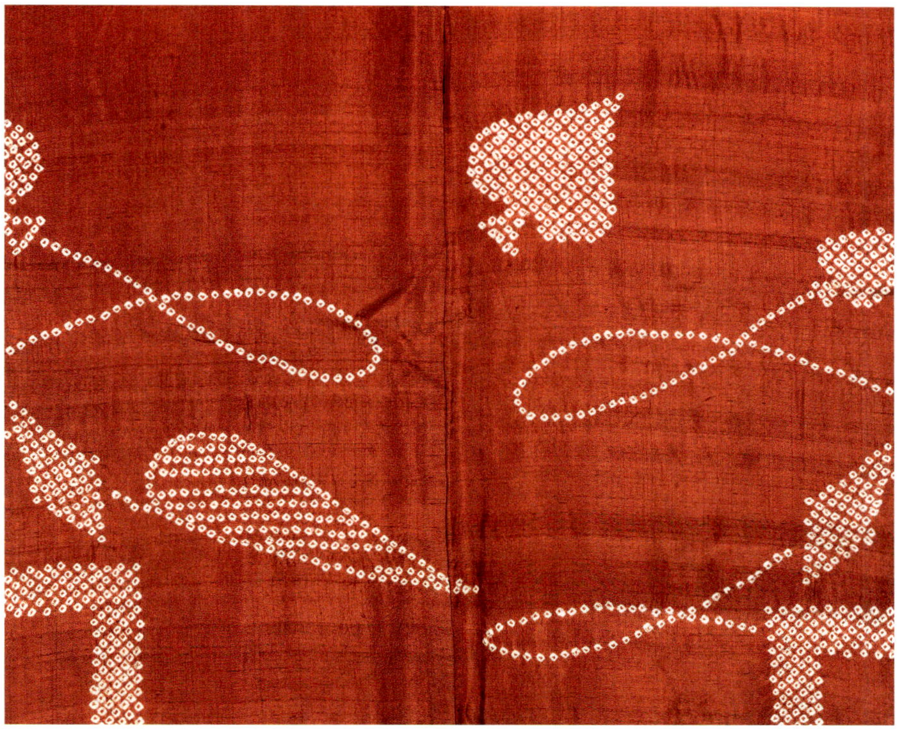

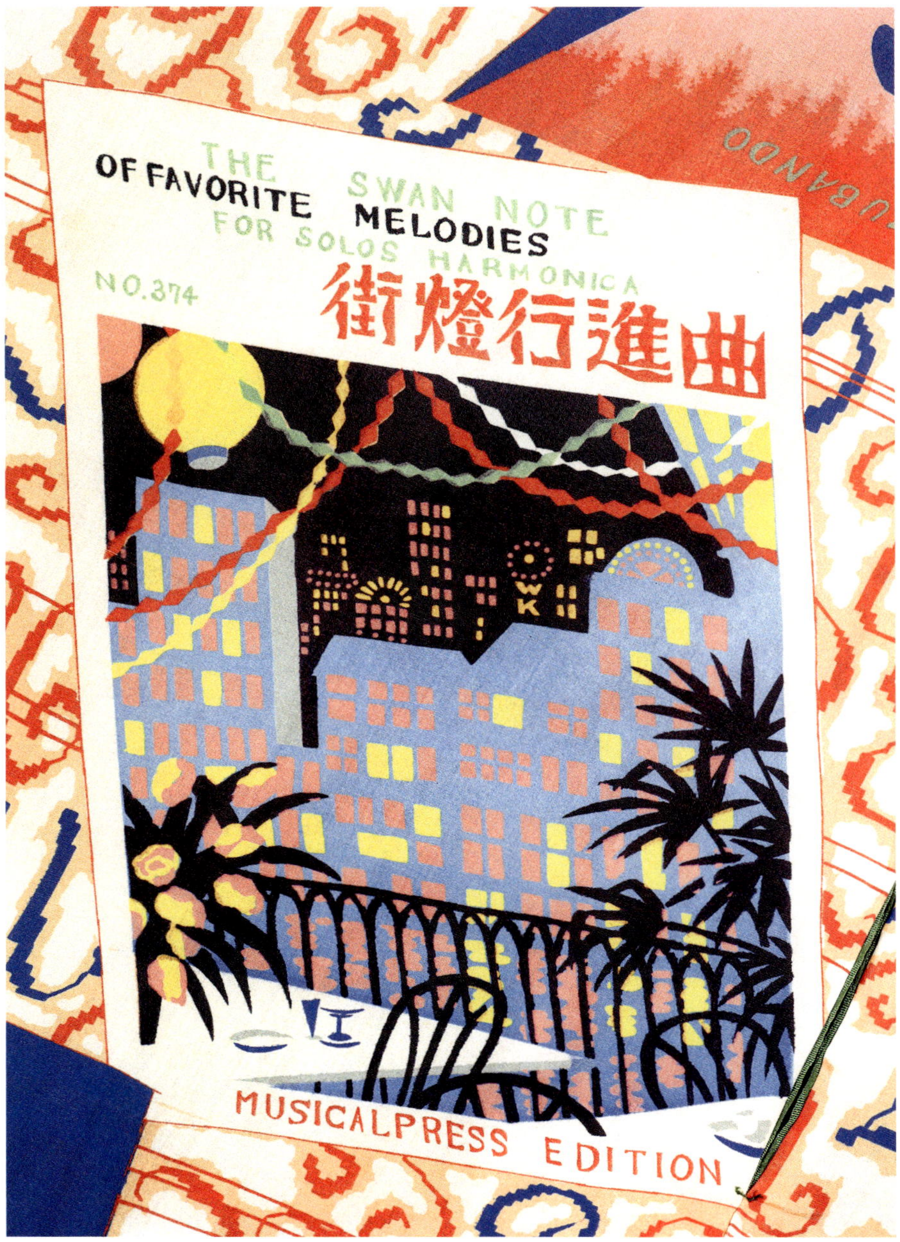

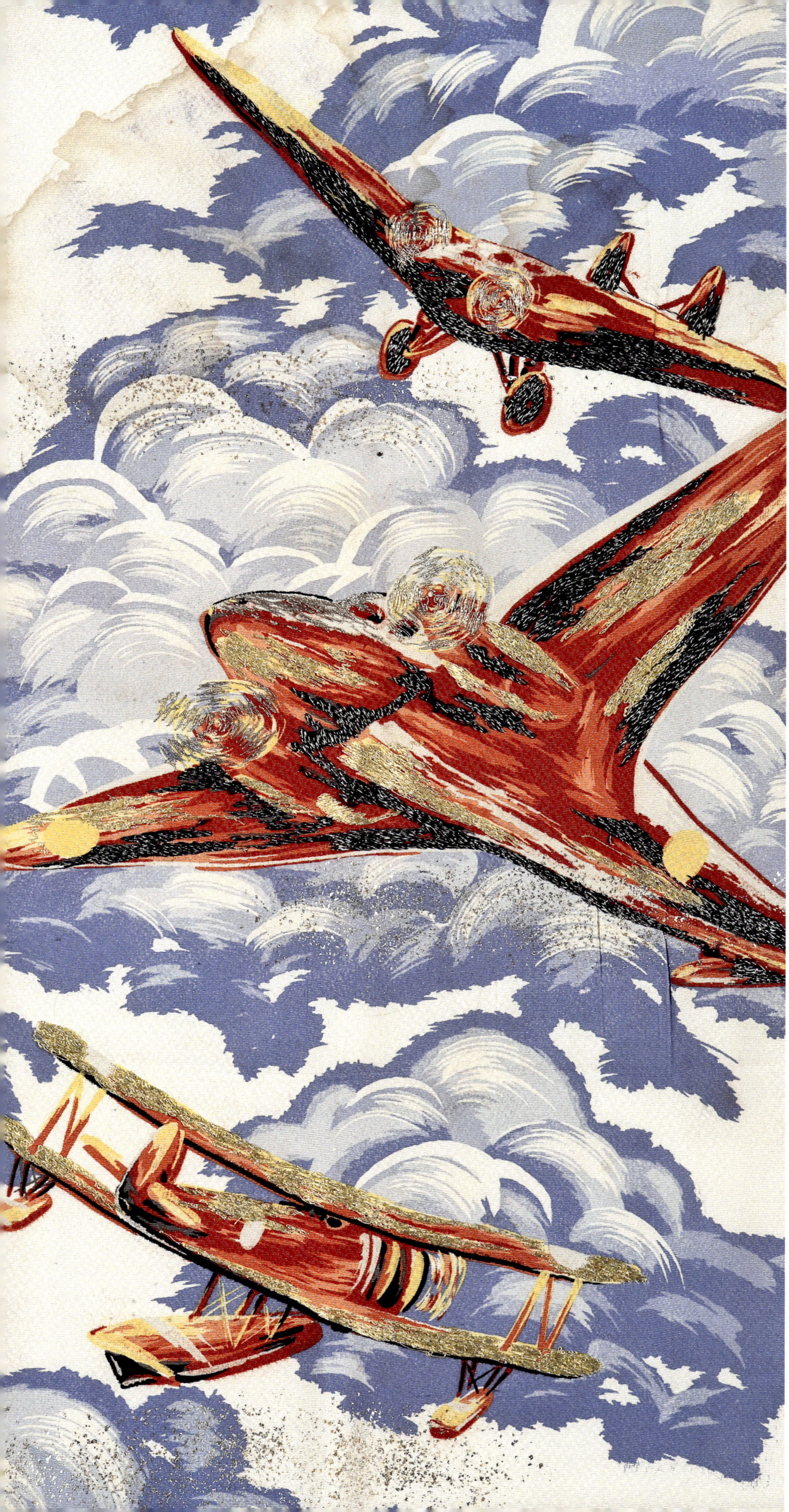

LEFT FIG. 38 Woman's obi (detail)
The beauty of flight (see p. 131)

OPPOSITE FIG. 39 Woman's *nagajuban* (detail)
Anchors and flowers (see p. 94)

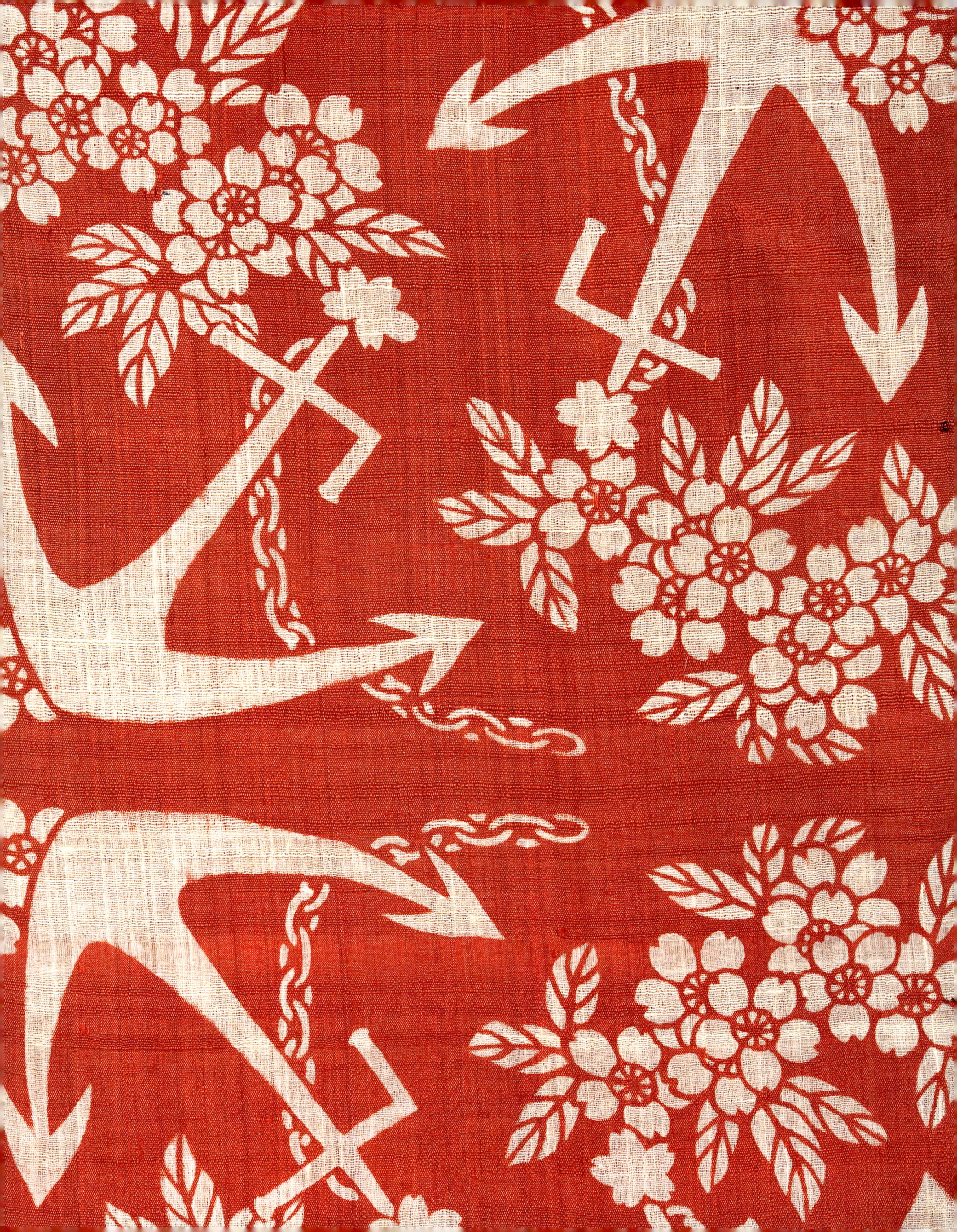

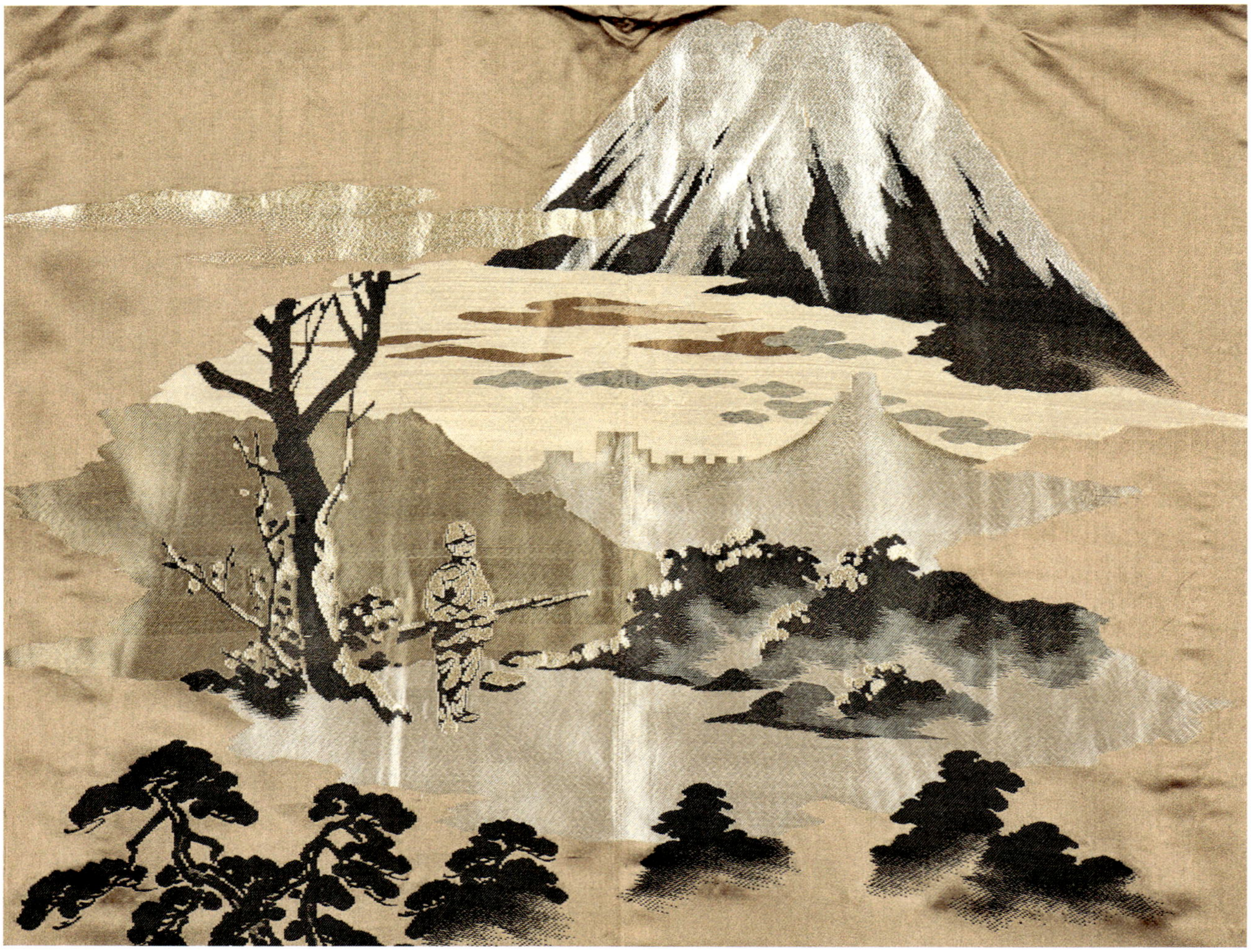

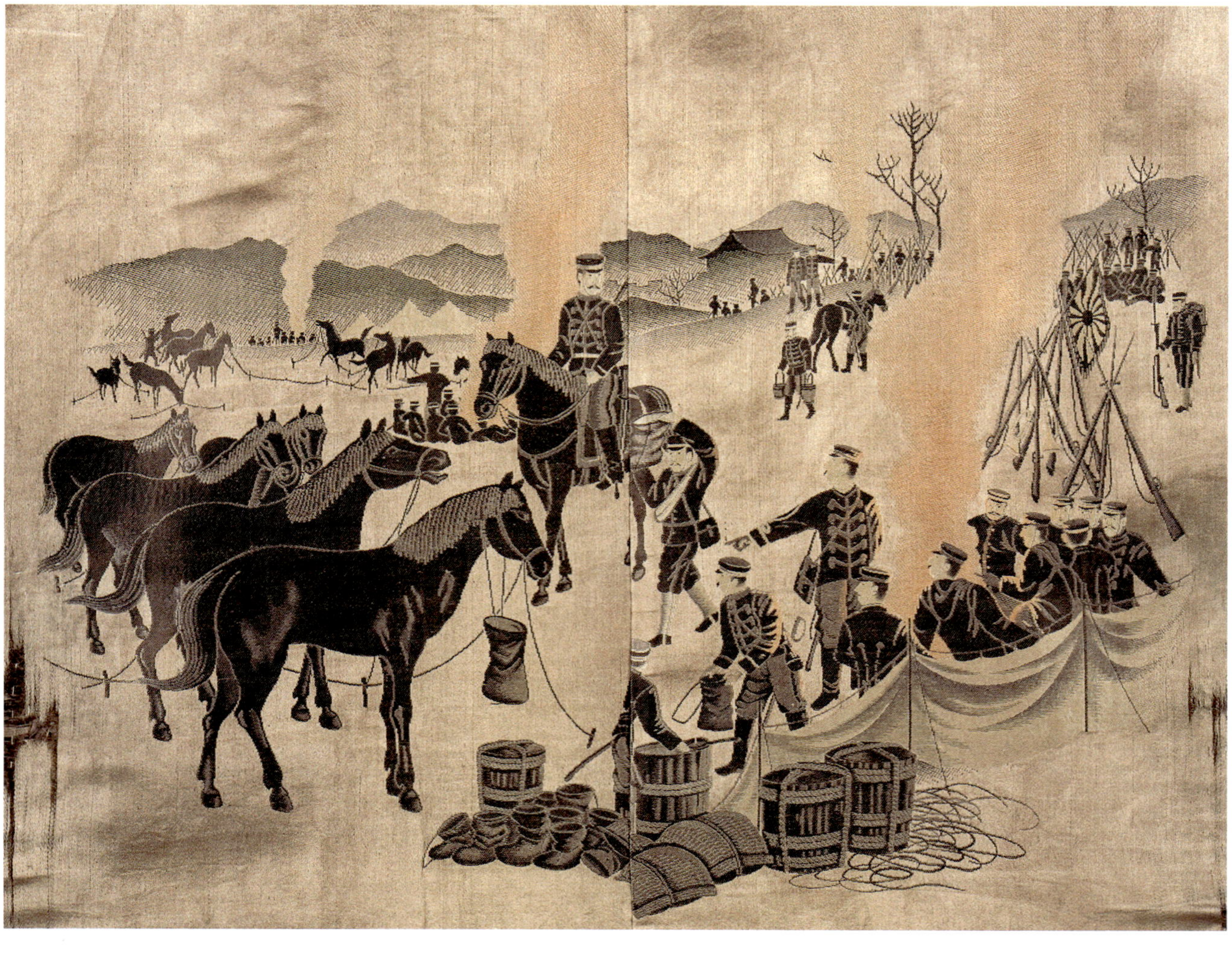

OPPOSITE ABOVE FIG. 40 Man's *haori* with a decorative lining (detail)
Lonely soldier dreaming of home (see p. 120)

OPPOSITE BELOW FIG. 41 Man's *haori* with a decorative lining (detail)
Soldiers and horses gathering at camp (see pp. 90–91)

occasionally showed textiles with images from popular culture, celebrations of new technology, or other changes in lifestyles. Most goods were intended for use in traditional children's kimono or *nagajuban*. Although the bulk of the fabrics were advertised in a wide variety of motifs and images, they had no modernist connotations. The catalogs seemed to be the place where the familiar and the traditional were promoted, not the new and faddish. Those who wished to be at the forefront of fashion rather than the vanguard would visit the store itself, especially during the seasonal design showings, to see what innovative and unusual designs were on offer. This may explain to some extent why *omoshirogara* textiles were often described as an urban phenomenon: city dwellers had easier access to the latest fashions and fads while those in the countryside relied more on catalogs, which emphasized the traditional. It made sense for them to do this, as the demand for these would be more consistent and thus they were worth keeping on hand in inventory, whereas each new novelty design had to prove its staying power. It was undoubtedly recognized that while iconic motifs might have a long shelf life, images of the day's pop stars would not.

SENSŌGARA: JAPAN IN THE YEARS OF WAR

The kimono that make up this portion of the Khalili Collections are representative of garments known as *sensōgara*, "wartime patterns" or "wartime things." They form a unique genre within the larger textile category of *omoshirogara* that directly reflected new technologies and inventions, contemporary political and cultural events, fashions and fads from popular culture, and modernity.

Sensōgara were little known outside of Japan, yet they served much the same purpose as the Home Front wartime textiles of the West. From the end of the Meiji period until 1945, *sensōgara* designs provided vivid showcases for Japan's vision of imperial expansion and military domination in East Asia; they also served as a subtle means of indoctrination in this national vision. Their wide range of graphically striking designs—sometimes playful, sometimes subtle, and sometimes overtly patriotic—appealed to the public's desire to show pride in their country. *Sensōgara* were not directly encouraged by the government; rather, they were market-driven, manufactured by private industry and designed to appeal to the civilian population. Retailers and manufacturers understood the value of patriotism as part of their sales and marketing arsenal and so produced *sensōgara* as specialty components of their broader *omoshirogara* novelty textile lines. *Sensōgara* thus were sold as unofficial voices of support for national objectives—and, at the same time, brought profit to textile producers. Whether those who purchased *sensōgara* bought them simply for their aesthetic appeal and perceived fashionableness or for the ideological messages they carried is difficult to determine today, but the purchase itself was a statement, recognized or not, that showed alignment with and acceptance of governmental political goals. In this regard, *sensōgara* may be considered propaganda by choice.

Sensōgara were rich with the patriotic, nationalistic, and militaristic imagery of the Asia-Pacific War (1931–45) and World War II (1941–45). The textiles produced often drew strongly on iconography already familiar to the public, with reminders of the stirring images of the battles fought during the early Sino- and Russo-Japanese Wars, the iconic Mount Fuji (fig. 40), or military materiél such as guns, Japanese war "tubas," tanks, aircraft, battleships, and destroyers. There were also mass-produced printed textiles reflecting themes and motifs such as bravery, loyalty, and sacrifice, as well as distinctive one-of-a-kind garments in which aesthetics and design were as important as the wartime messages.

RIGHT FIG. 42 *Haori* for a man (detail)
A tribute to Admiral Tōgō Heihachirō (see p. 128)

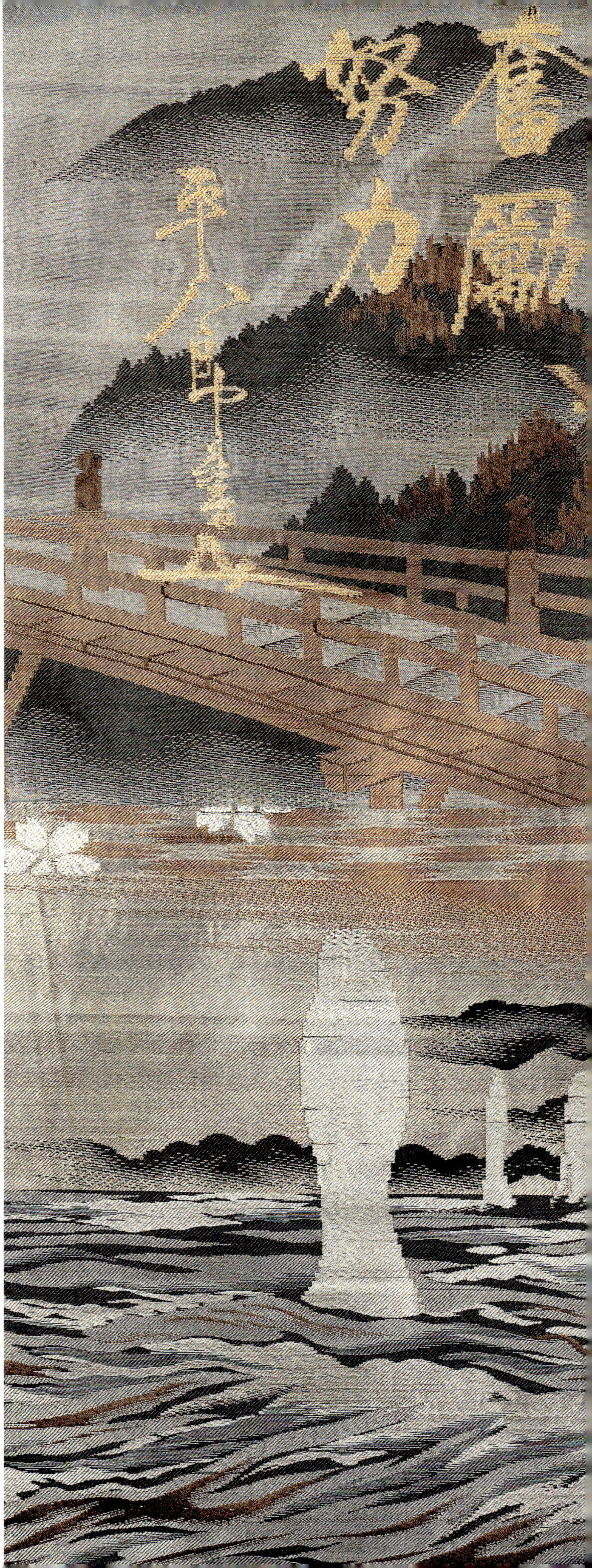

Although *sensōgara* were most prevalent after 1931, in the late Meiji, Taishō, and early Showa eras modern and traditional textile styles and motifs continued to be used to elicit loyalty to the nation, and *sensōgara* blossomed.

Sensōgara did, of course, have a longer wartime history. In the late Meiji period, Japan fought two highly successful wars, one against China (1894–95) (fig. 41), the other against Russia (1904–05) (fig. 42). These events did much to change the world's opinion of Japan from a backward country to a major new player on the world stage. The *yūzen*-dyed, woven, or stencil-printed and painted textiles from this period not only reflected the changing face of Japan as it moved from its position as a feudal agrarian society into modernity, but also carried strong memories of the stirring images of battles fought during the two early Sino-Japanese and Russo-Japanese Wars. These older textiles now offer an extraordinary glimpse of wartime impressions of the enemy, as well as early context for this *sensōgara* textile genre, which stretched over some five decades from 1894 until the close of World War II on September 2, 1945, when US General Douglas MacArthur accepted Japan's formal surrender aboard the US battleship *Missouri* in Tokyo Bay.

Textiles such as these that were tied to contemporary political or topical events are thought to have a limited life span. Once the war was over, many owners might have thought that these *sensōgara* no longer had contemporary value or meaning; they were no longer needed to boost morale or to show patriotism or support for the war effort. Some may have been packed away, thrown away, or even destroyed. Although many of these wartime designs have been lost to time, those that remain can still vividly convey a sense of the national pride and ambitions of their time (fig. 43). Their survival is due partly to Japan's long and rich textile history, which counts textile preservation almost as a national obligation. The builders of collections who

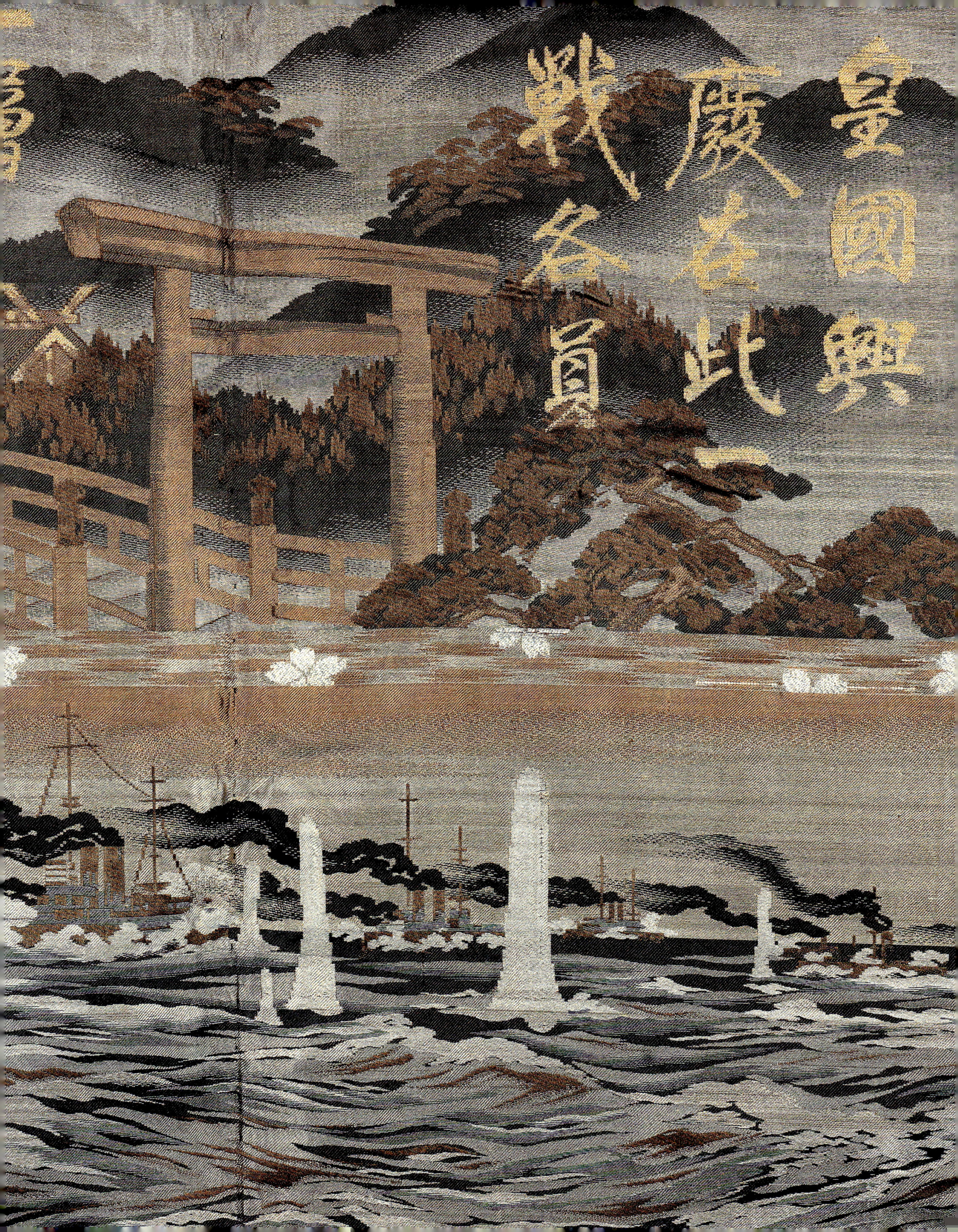
皇國興廢在此一戰各員

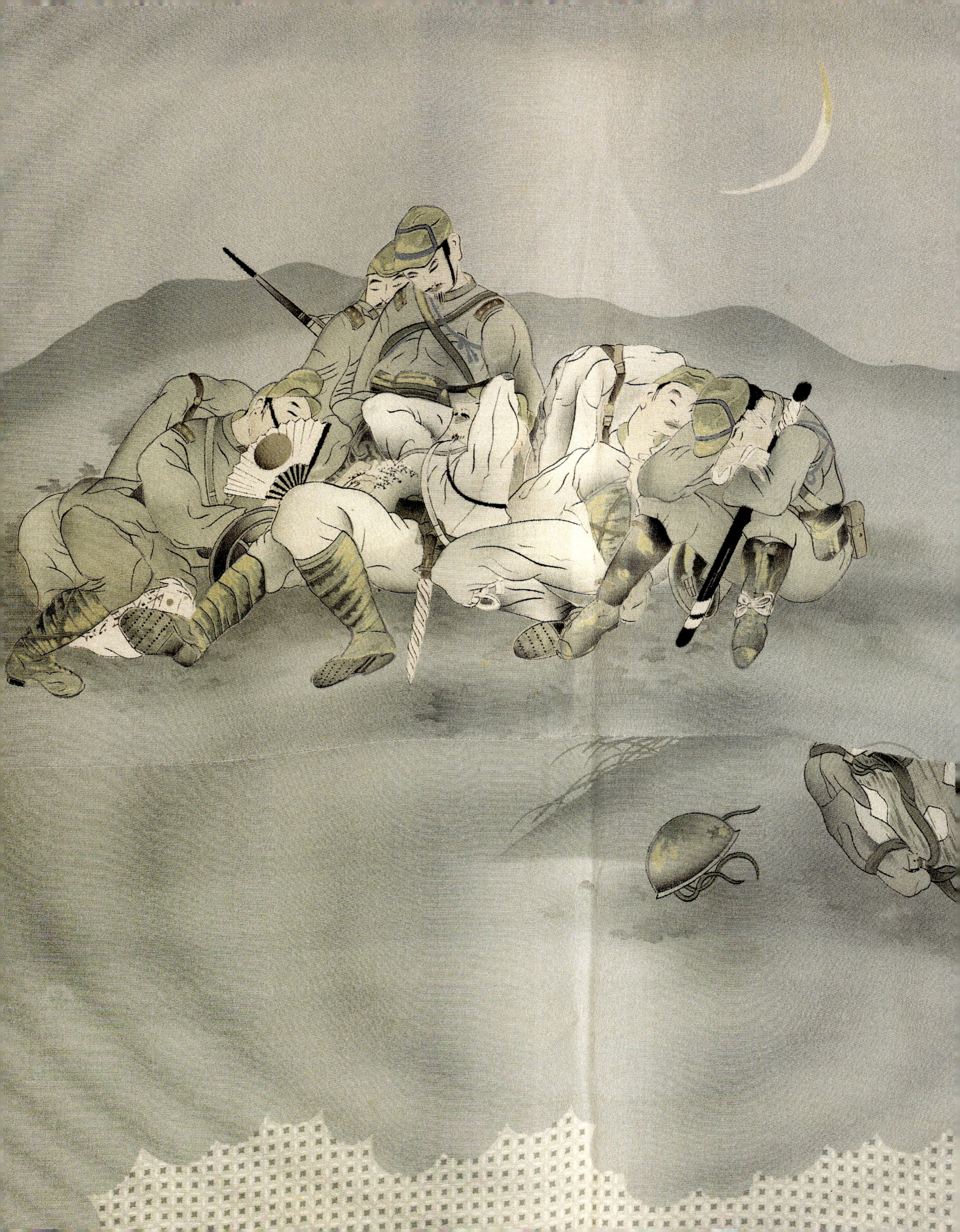

OPPOSITE FIG. 43 *Nagajuban* for a man (detail)
Sleeping soldiers (see p. 142)

have recognized the hidden cultural value of such textiles, years after their production from the 1890s to the 1940s, can provide opportunities for understanding the prevailing culture of earlier times. Likewise, this collection of *sensōgara* can offer a window on to the political, military, and even popular interests of the Japanese public from the late Meiji era and into the mid-wartime years of the 20th century. Its contents capture our attention by featuring images of war-related contemporary activities and events, providing us with an invaluable record of otherwise ephemeral moments of the past and a better understanding of how these most personal objects of everyday life—the things that people wore—helped to support the culture of war. They are narratives that should not be ignored.

THE CONTEXT OF A CHANGING WORLD

The first few decades of the 20th century in Japan produced a culturally, politically, and technologically expansive period. The Taishō era was, in general, economically prosperous, as World War I and its immediate aftermath stimulated industrial development and foreign trade, supporting a growing middle class and an increasingly literate and educated population. By the mid-1920s, nearly 100 percent of the population had achieved some degree of literacy, setting the stage for an explosion of print in the form of newspapers, magazines, and books aimed at all segments of the population. One concomitant effect was national exposure to international events, personalities, fashions, and fads, which the public, hungry for the novel, the unique, the modern, and the innovative, soaked up like a sponge. Not all of this fresh information was adopted wholesale without concern for how it fit into an already cohesive society. Rather, it was consumed, chewed over, swallowed, digested, and regurgitated in a new form, one that took the bits and pieces that most suited the Japanese personality and culture and molded them into an inventive composite of cosmopolitanism and modernism that demonstrated a sense of national energy and experimentation.

THEMES AND MOTIFS

From here we will look further at some of the popular *omoshirogara* motifs and themes that captured the spirit of the times in cloth—from the almost giddy sense of liberalism and freedom in the arts, the media, and popular culture to the concurrent emphasis on progress and supremacy in industry and technology, gaining Japan's rightful place on the international stage, and the increasing political conservatism allied to the national vision of military invincibility. These motifs, including those already discussed earlier, can be subsumed within several larger categories that offer windows into the many facets of modernity reflected in textile design: cosmopolitanism, including entertainment (cinema and music), culture, consumption, and other cultural activities; people, especially the *moga* ("modern girls"), celebrities, and national heroes; sports and the Olympics; transportation and travel; the Machine Age (new technologies, electricity, aircraft, trains, trams, and cars); internationalism (internal and external politics); nationalism; and militarism.

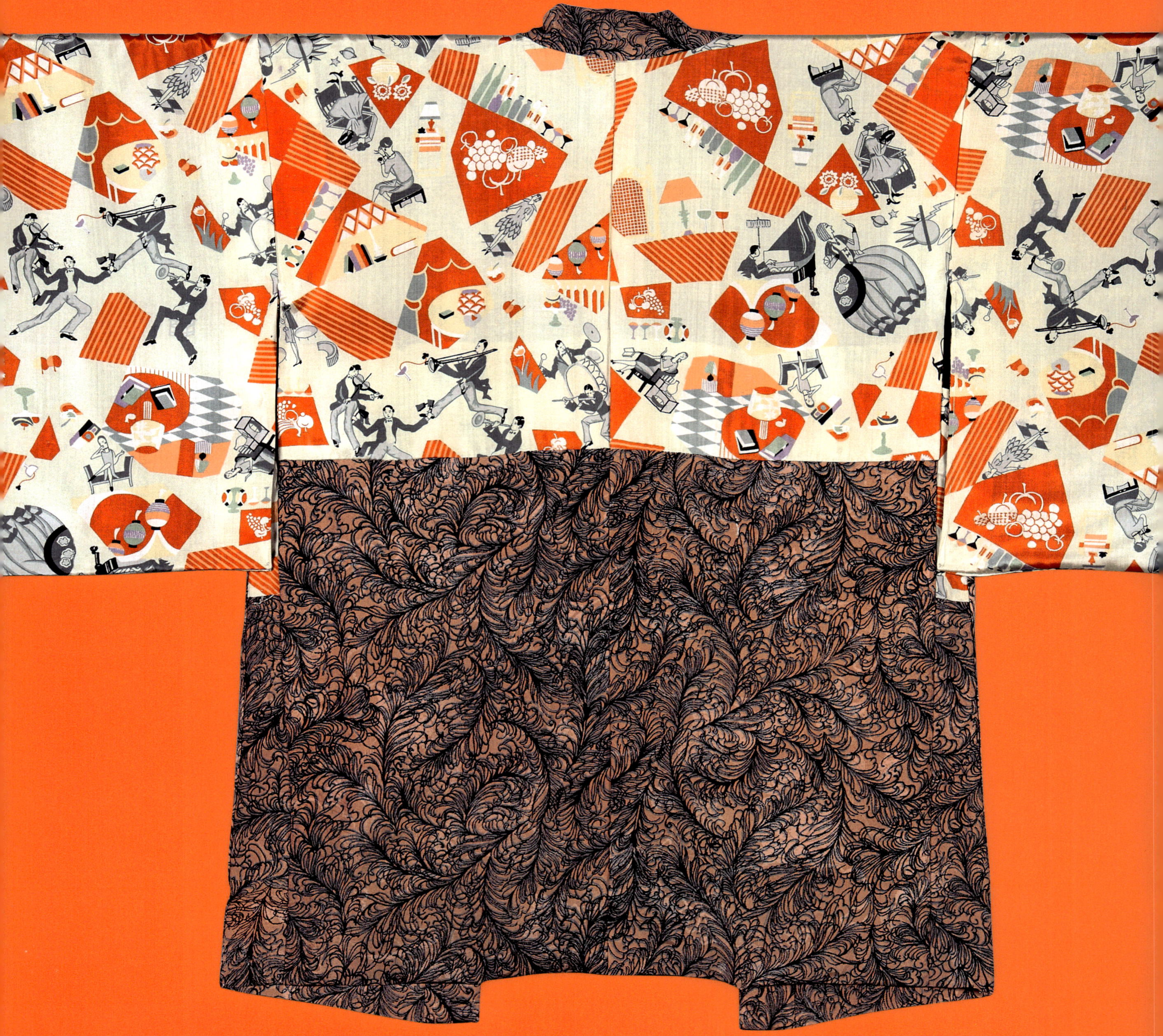

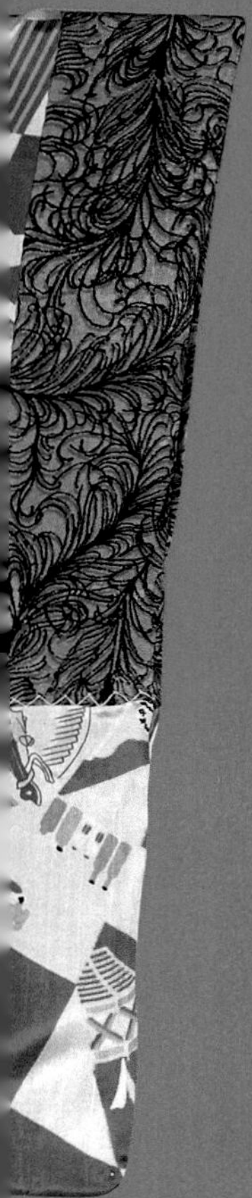

THE KIMONOS

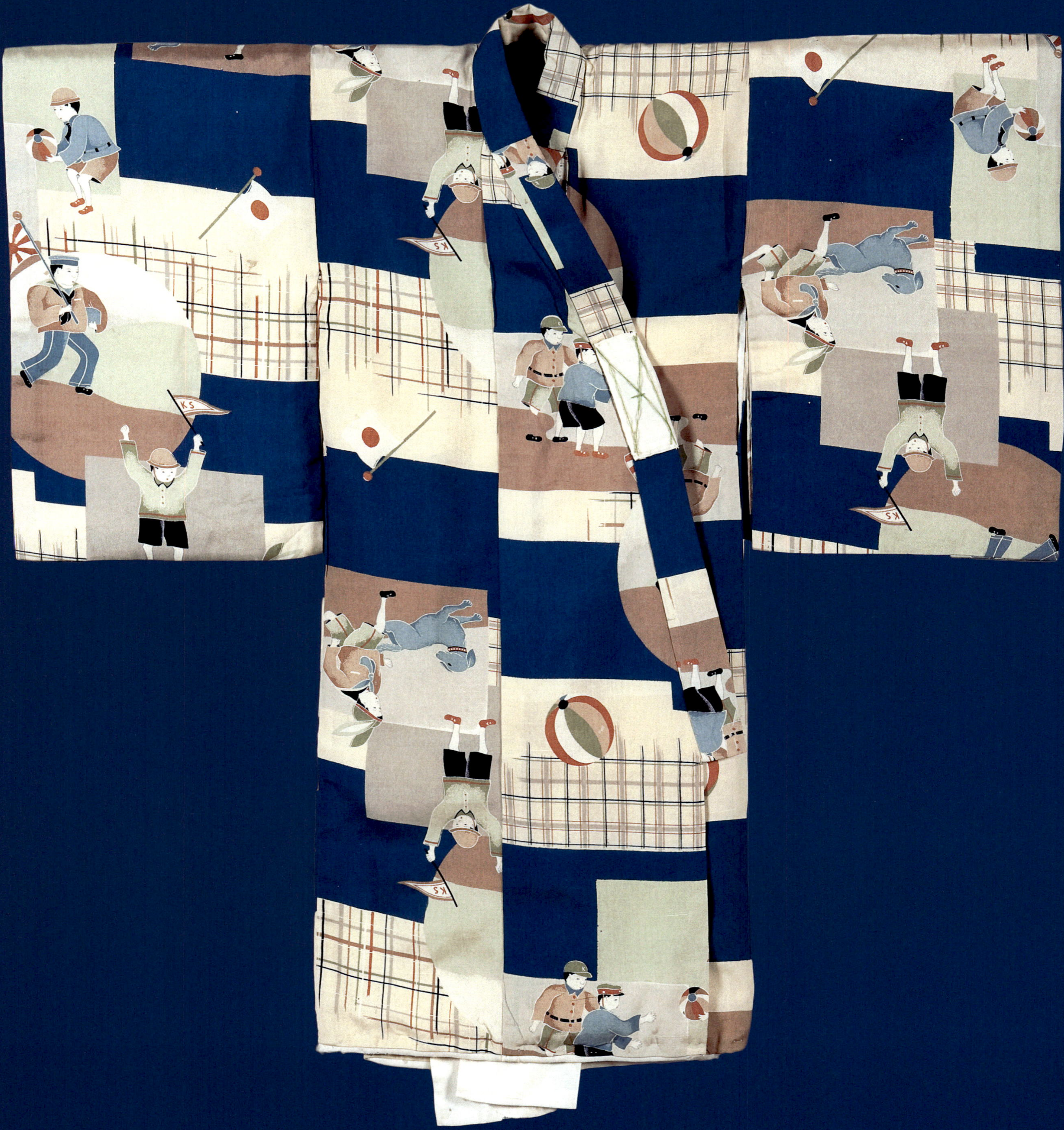

LEISURE ACTIVITIES

Kimono for a young boy
Boys at play
Taishō–Shōwa period, 1920s–1930s
Kata-yūzen dyed silk
29.5 × 29.0 inches (75 × 74 centimeters)
KM001

The lively design of this small kimono features boys playing after school. Some play ball, others race. Most wear military-style caps, while one boy's cap is trimmed with rabbit-like ears. The letters "K" on a cap and "KS" on the pennant are related to their school. A young sailor carries his military flag proudly through the field. A talisman (*semamori*) is traditionally sewn into infants' clothing and, just below the kimono collar, four intersecting embroidery threads form two pine needles. The pine tree, one of the "three friends of the cold," is a symbol of longevity and perseverance, and a fitting charm for an infant.

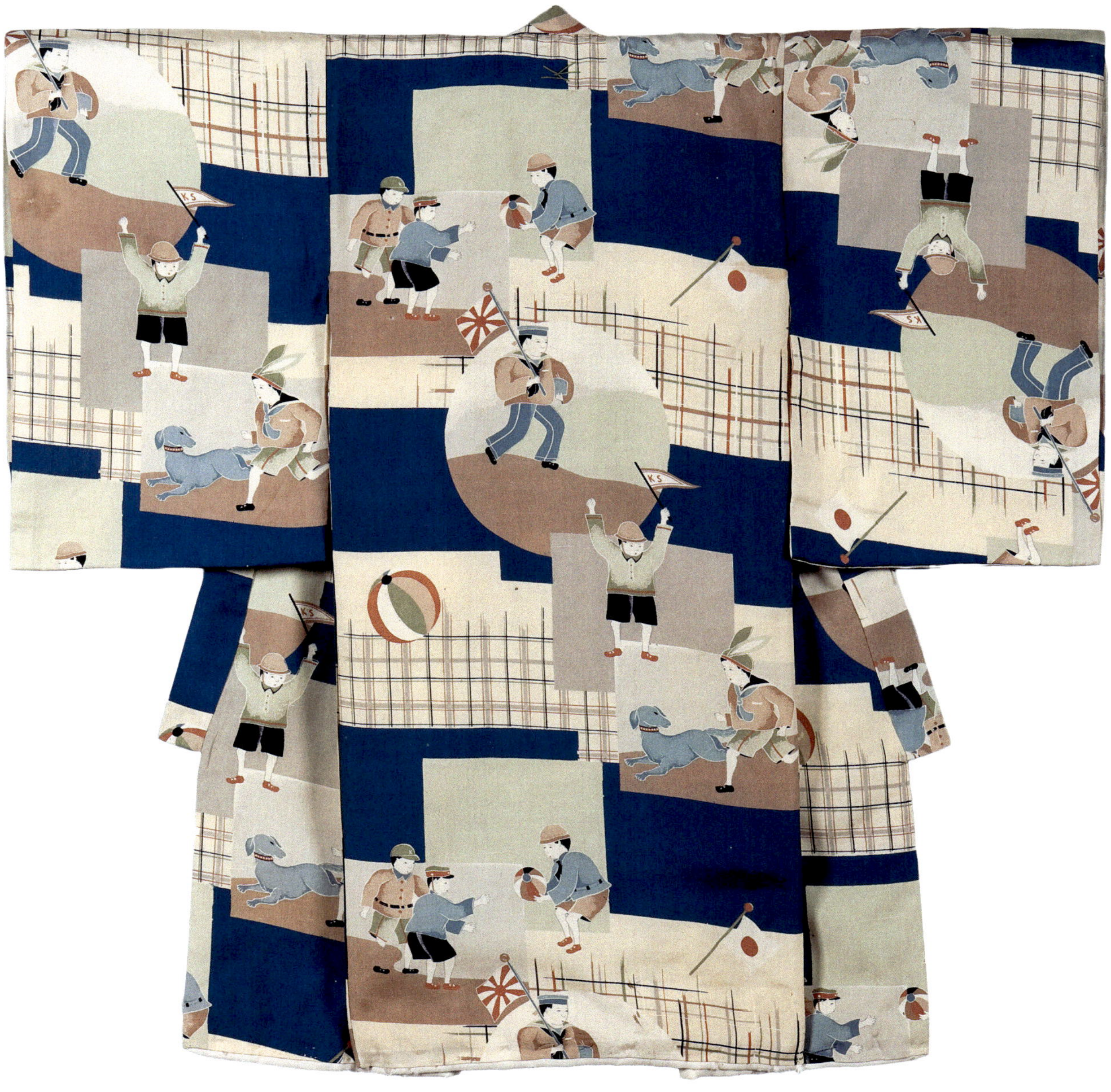

SENSŌGARA

Boy's *haregi* (kimono used for special events)
Mount Fuji and warplanes
Shōwa period, late 1930s
Printed silk
36.0 × 31.0 inches (91 × 79 centimeters)
KM002

The design of this garment takes a fresh approach to an old pattern. The standard horizontal stripes in contrasting colors have been alternately widened and narrowed so the lighter area makes an ideal canvas for the large-scale, deeply masculine design. Mount Fuji, ordinarily seen in the background in kimono, takes a dominant position here, as do the single- and twin-engine military planes. The long, undulating green forms, a long-standing design convention signifying mist (and borrowed from Chinese textile conventions), are frequently found in traditional Japanese designs. The blue and white waves have also been depicted in a traditional manner, while the mountain and the airplanes, by contrast, are portrayed with great realism.

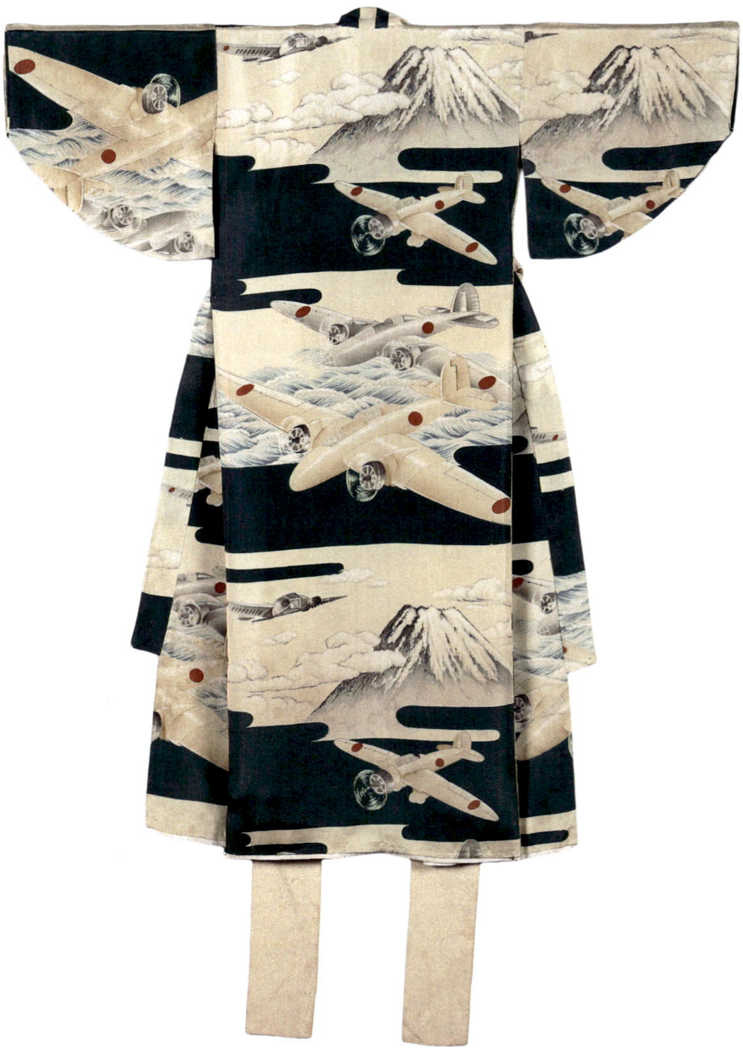

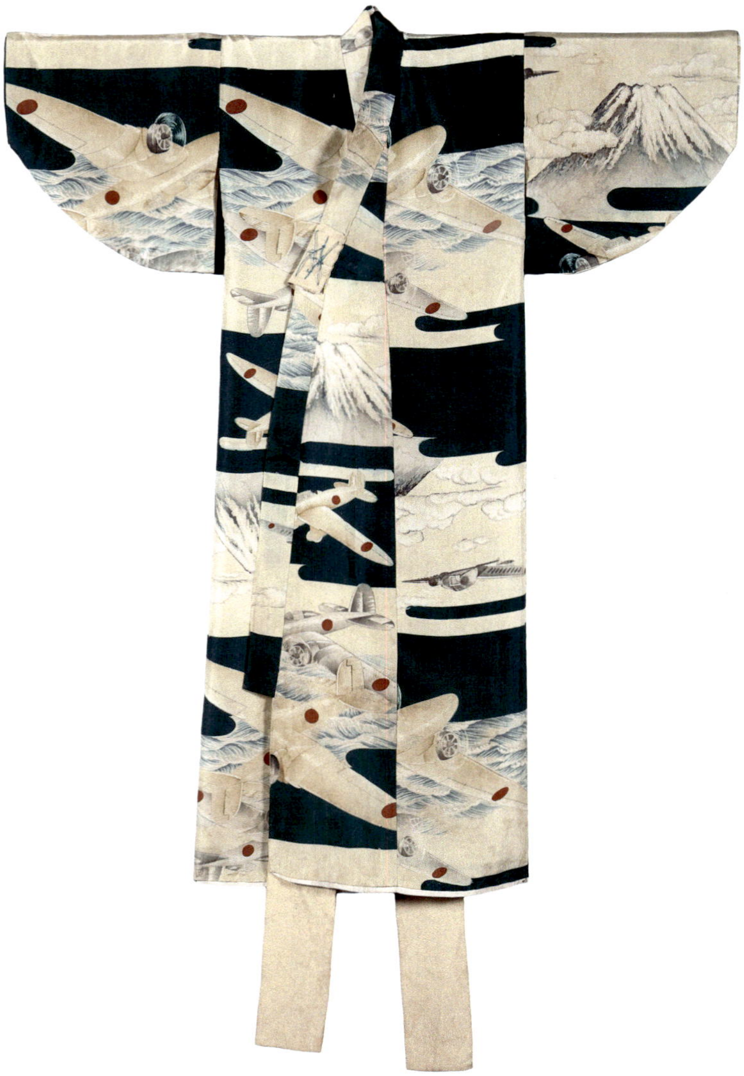

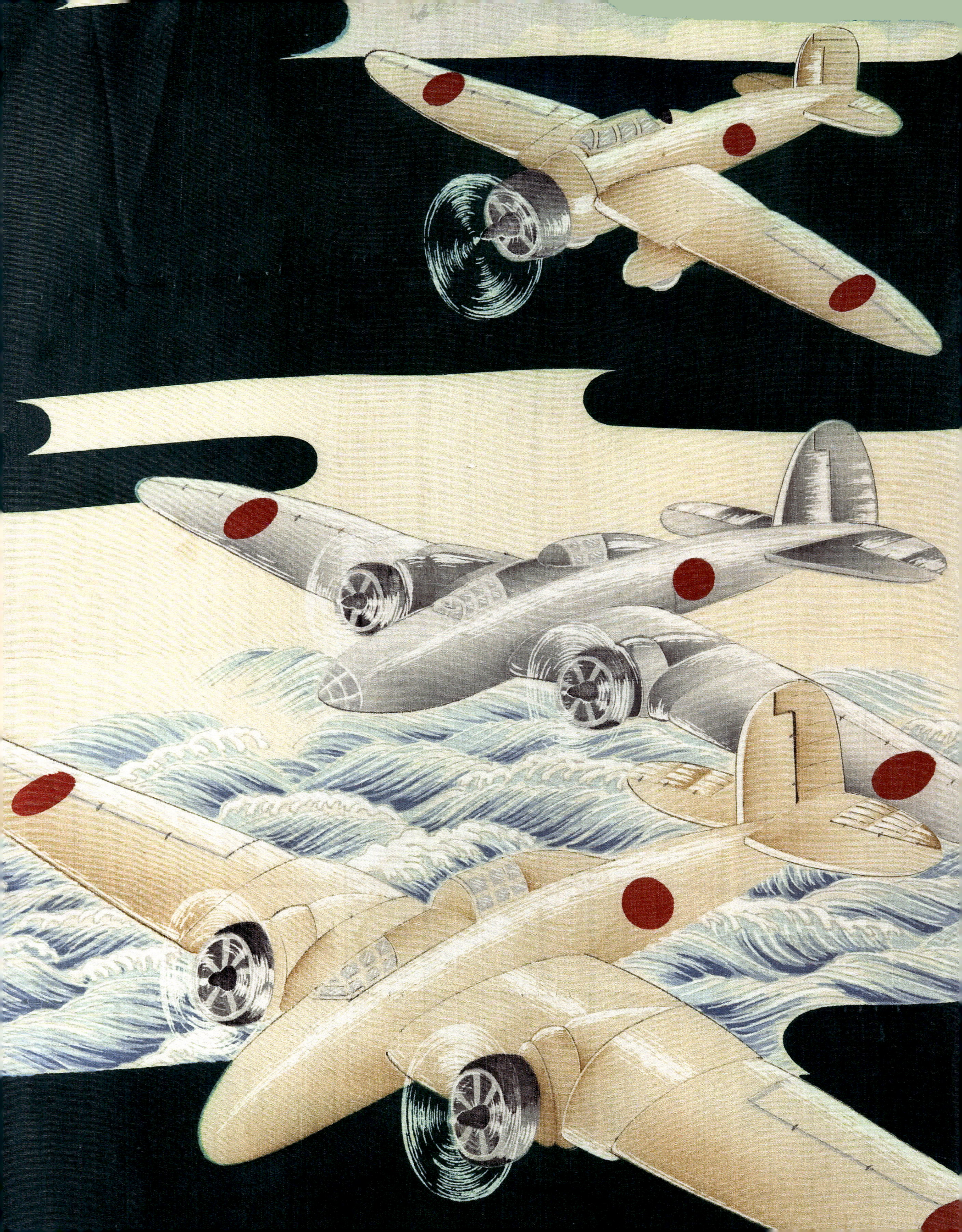

SENSŌGARA/ ENTERTAINMENT

Young child's *chanchanko* (vest)
Pretend soldiers
Taishō–Shōwa period, late 1920s–1930s
Kata-yūzen dyed silk
20.0 × 14.0 inches (51 × 36 centimeters)
KM003

Maps are frequent motifs on male kimono of the period. They supported the view that Japan, the most modernized nation in Asia, was the manifest leader of other Asian nations. Although they were less common in children's garments, the large, simplified map on this padded winter *chanchanko* would have communicated the concept to children as well. The boys wear their versions of soldiers' uniforms and carry backpacks, helmets, and weapons, inuring children to the role they would soon be expected to play. The biplanes on the front vest are each shown from a different perspective, and the clouds that decorate the hemline help to bring the front and back of the vest together. The flag at the center back was probably meant to be filled in with a family crest.

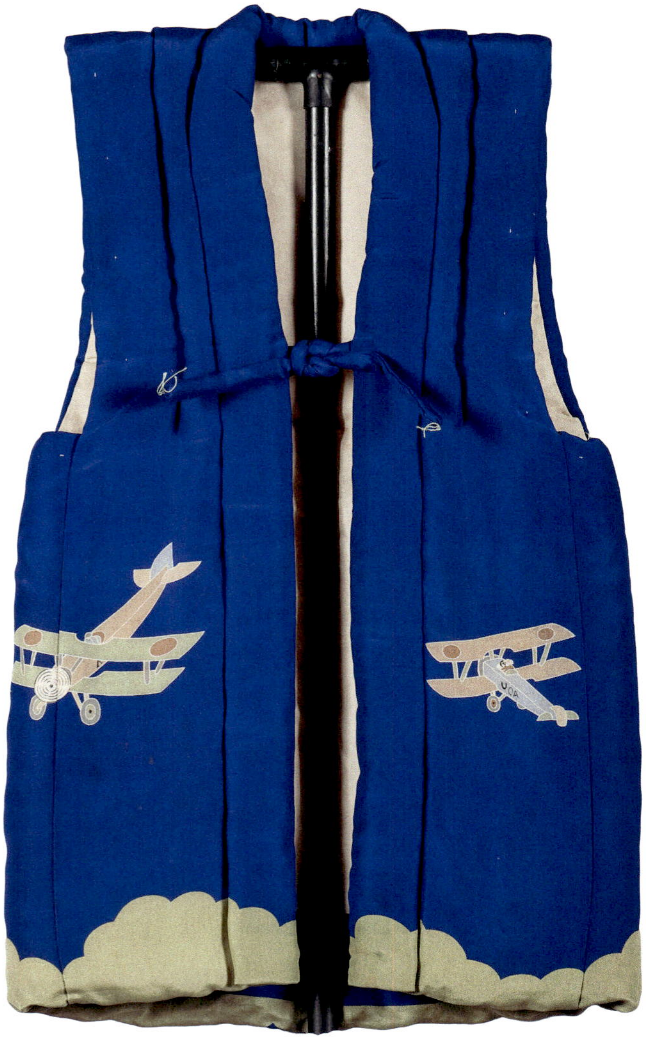

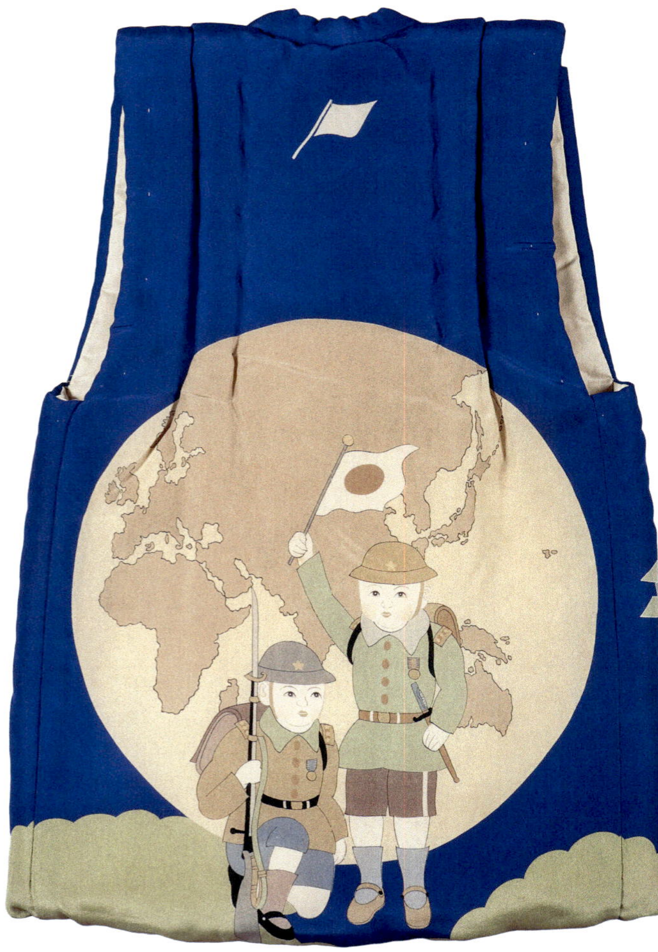

SENSŌGARA/ BOYS PLAYING AT WAR

Kimono for a young boy
Boys playing at war
Shōwa period, late 1930s–1940
Kata-yūzen dyed silk exterior, wool muslin lining
20.0 × 14.0 inches (51 × 36 centimeters)
KM004

Japanese propaganda textiles are notable for the degree to which children are shown as an integral part of the war effort, and as active participants rather than spectators. In this kimono, children take center stage against a background of flags and military machinery. A young "cavalry officer" leads the charge on his hobby horse, while behind him his bugler signals the troops, and the standard bearer holds the Japanese flag aloft. Pulling up the rear, and led by the standard bearer, is a little boy dressed in an indigenous costume and carrying a small Manchukuo flag—a reference to Japan taking the role as leader of the Asian nations.

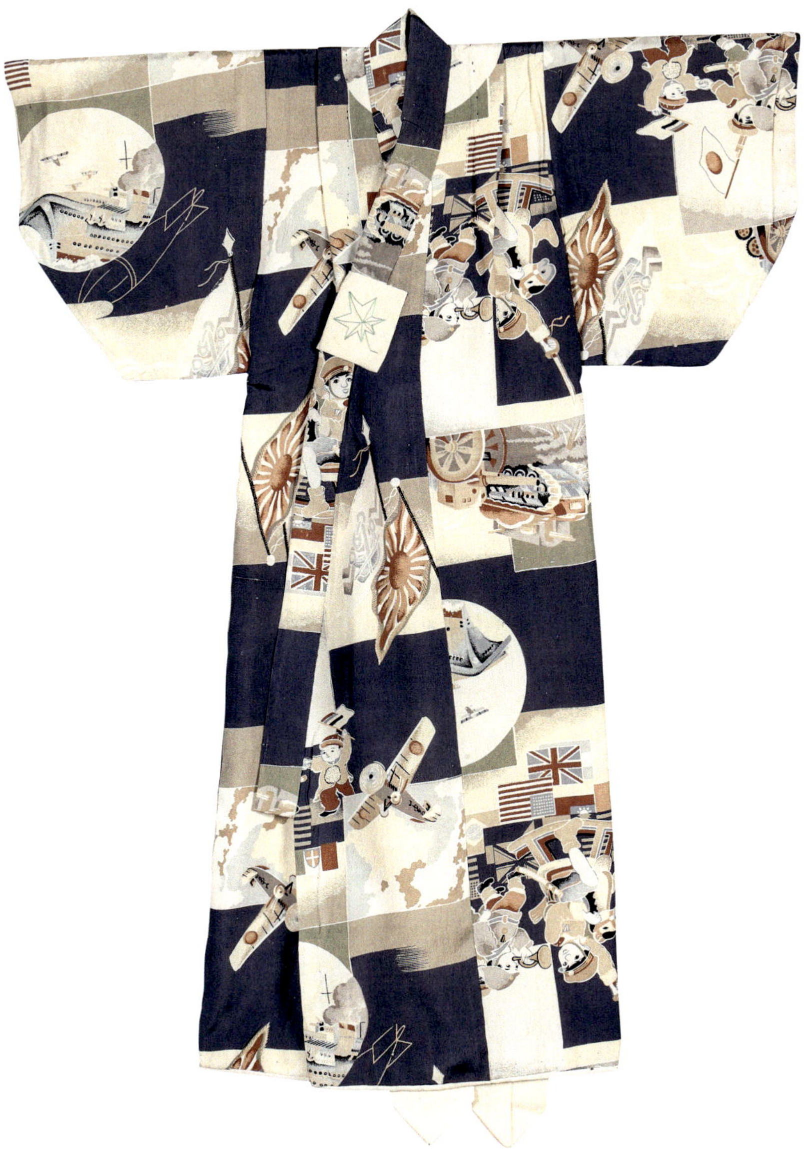

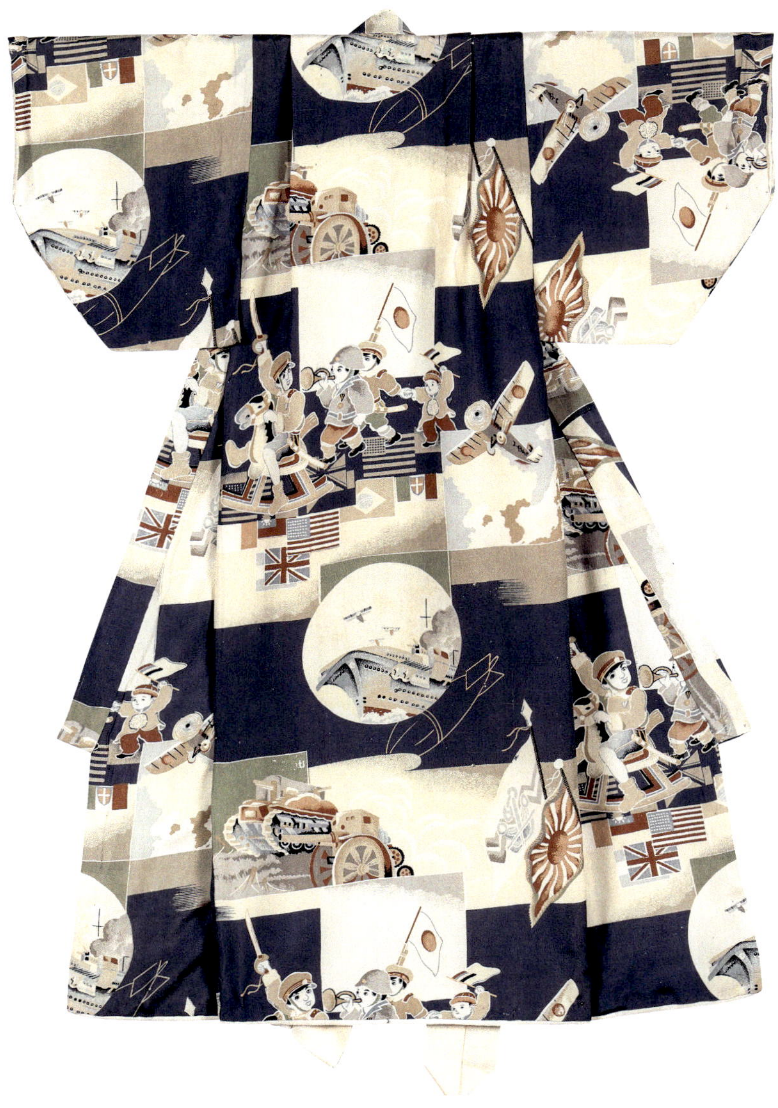

SENSŌGARA

Man's *juban*
Chevrons and helmets
Taishō–Shōwa period, 1920–1940
Stenciled silk voile
48.0 × 44.0 inches (122 × 112 centimeters)
KM005

It is unusual to see a man's *juban* worn as such a light garment, one that probably would require an additional garment—perhaps of a lightweight white or cream-colored cotton—to be worn underneath. It is clearly, however, a specially made garment. The sheer and delicate pale silk voile has carefully stenciled army helmets at top and bottom, and the *hinomaru* flag flies near the hem at lower left. The central bands look like ric-rac, but they are more likely meant to be military badges. The interesting hand-painted ideograph on the back of the garment no doubt communicates an important message, but whether it is a symbol of peace or honors a fallen comrade is not known.

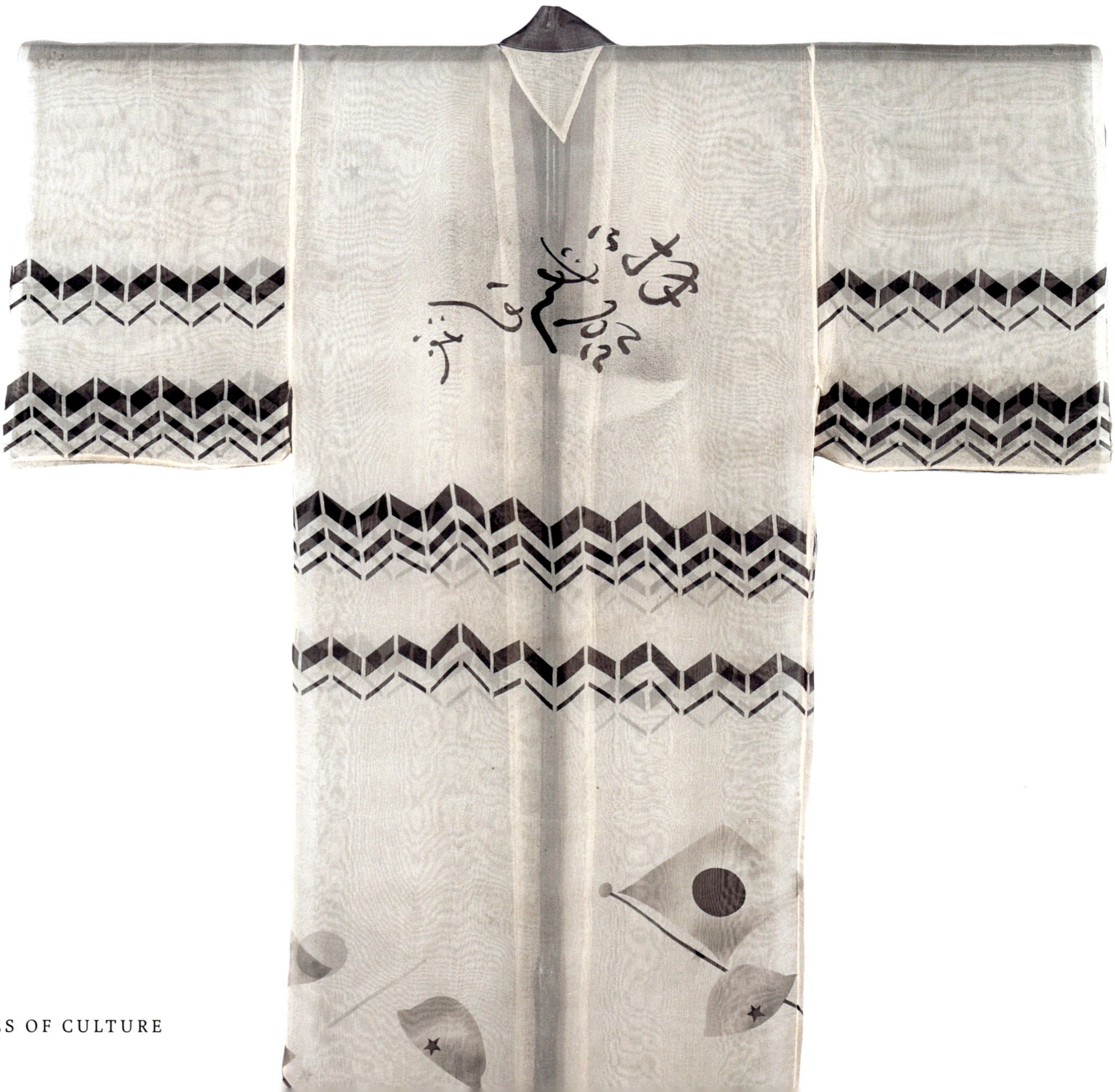

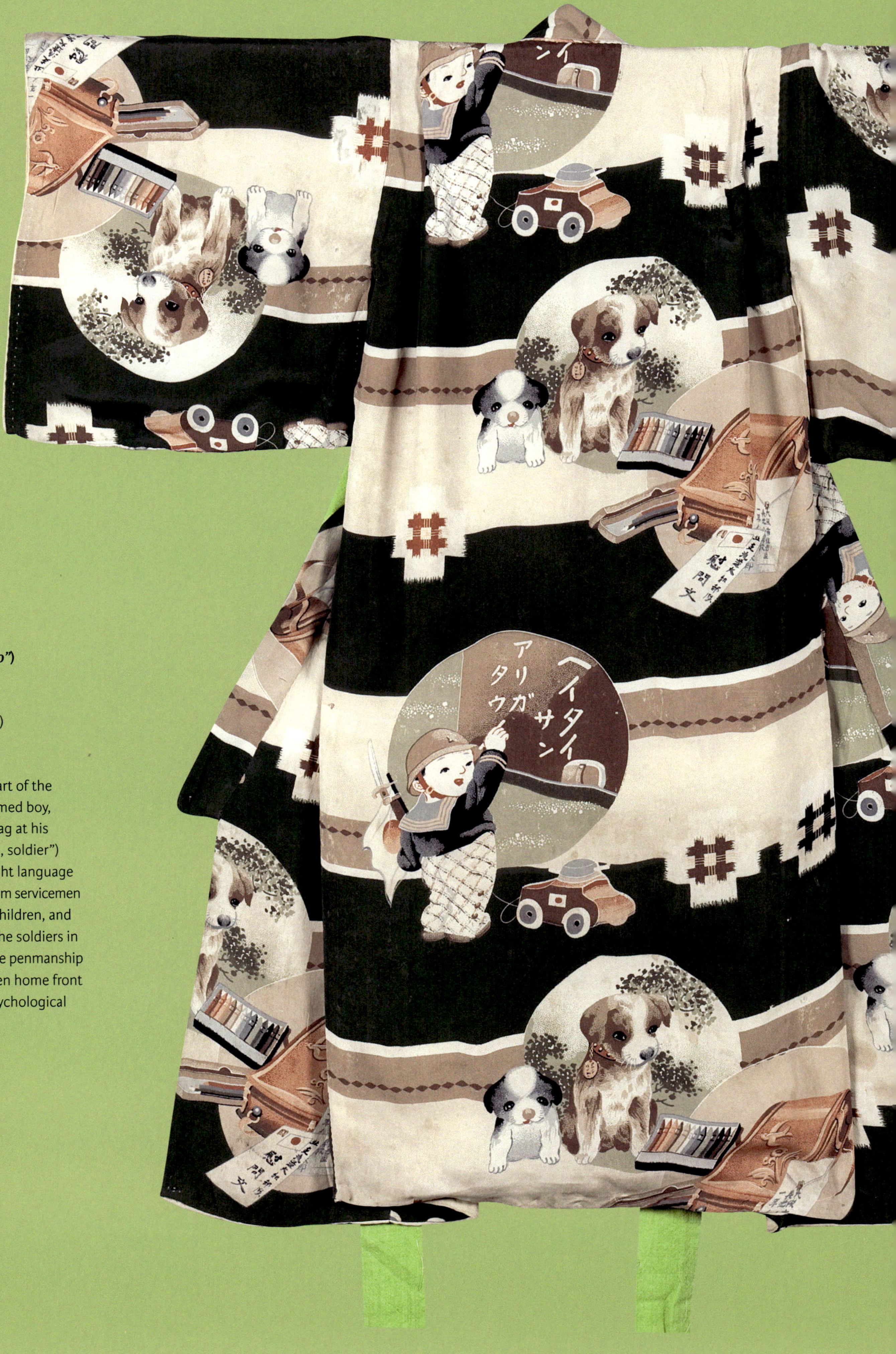

SENSŌGARA/ EDUCATION

Child's kimono for a boy
"Thank you, soldier" (*"Heitai, arigato"*)
Shōwa period, late 1930s–1940s
Printed wool muslin
29.0 × 26.0 inches (74 × 66 centimeters)
KM006

During World War II, propaganda was part of the school curriculum. Here, a small, uniformed boy, toy tank at his right side, bayonet and flag at his left, writes "Heitai, arigato" ("Thank you, soldier") on a chalkboard. The teachers who taught language classes in Japanese schools used letters from servicemen at the front as reading material for the children, and the children were expected to write to the soldiers in return. The contents of the letters and the penmanship were simple, but the connection between home front and battlefront formed an important psychological bond for both children and servicemen.

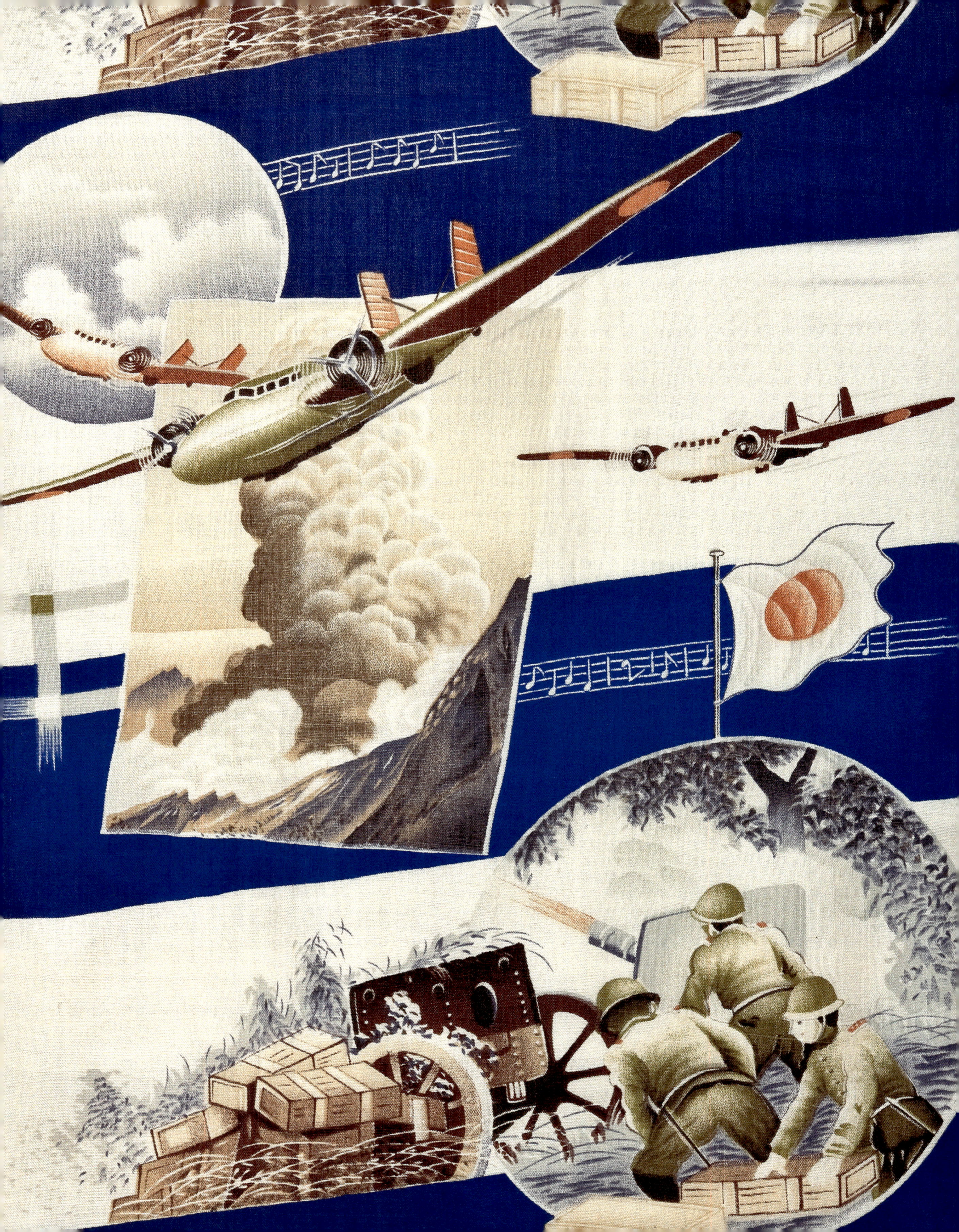

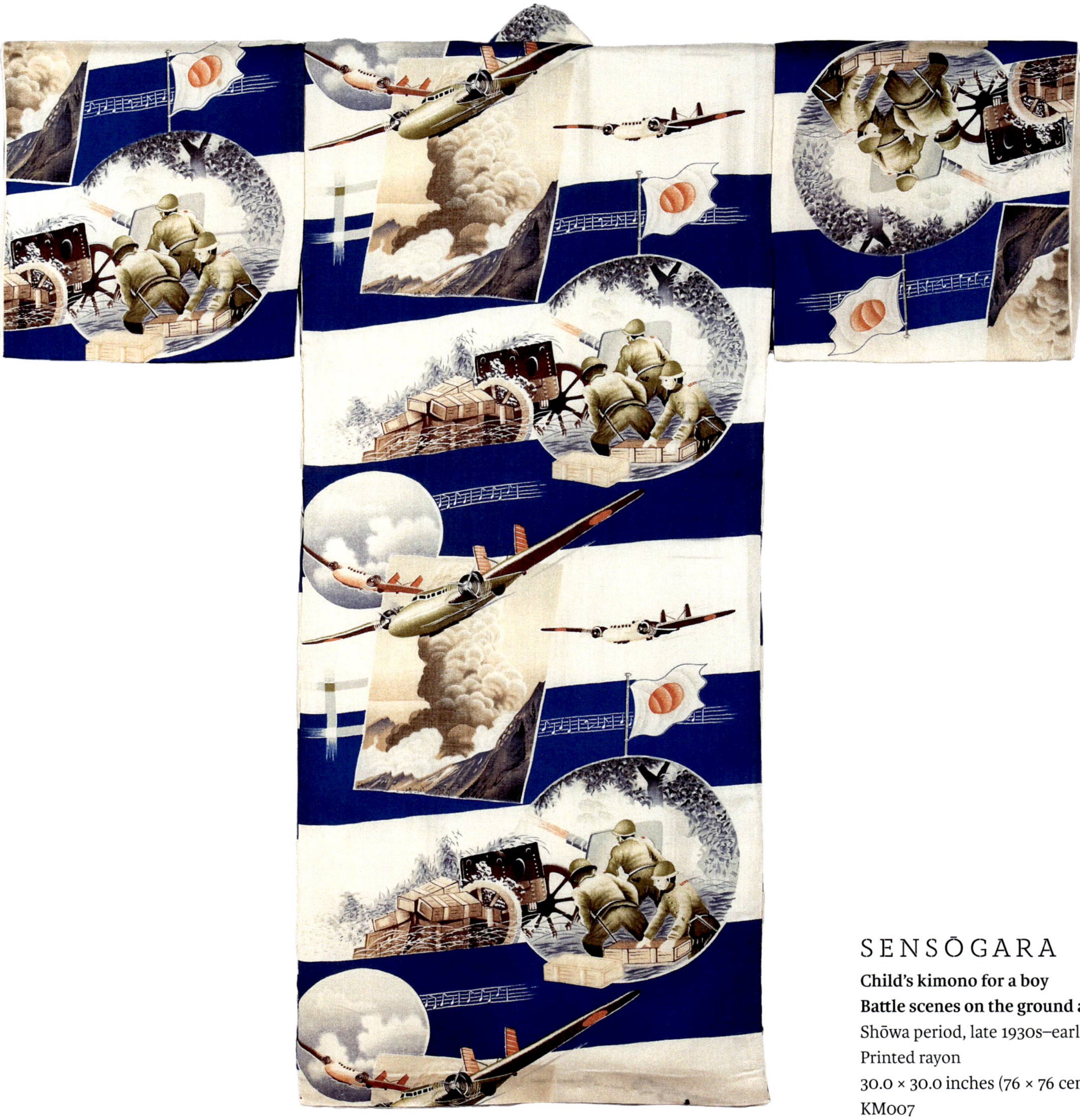

SENSŌGARA

Child's kimono for a boy
Battle scenes on the ground and in the air
Shōwa period, late 1930s–early 1940s
Printed rayon
30.0 × 30.0 inches (76 × 76 centimeters)
KM007

The Japanese textile market was very sophisticated and produced designs appropriate for children to wear as well as other designs that catered more toward adult tastes. While depictions of the symbols and activities of war were fairly commonplace on the textiles of the period, it would be unusual to produce such a realistic portrayal of a battlefield as this for a child's garment. It is more likely that the father chose this textile to be used for his *juban* and the mother took any extra fabric to use for the child.

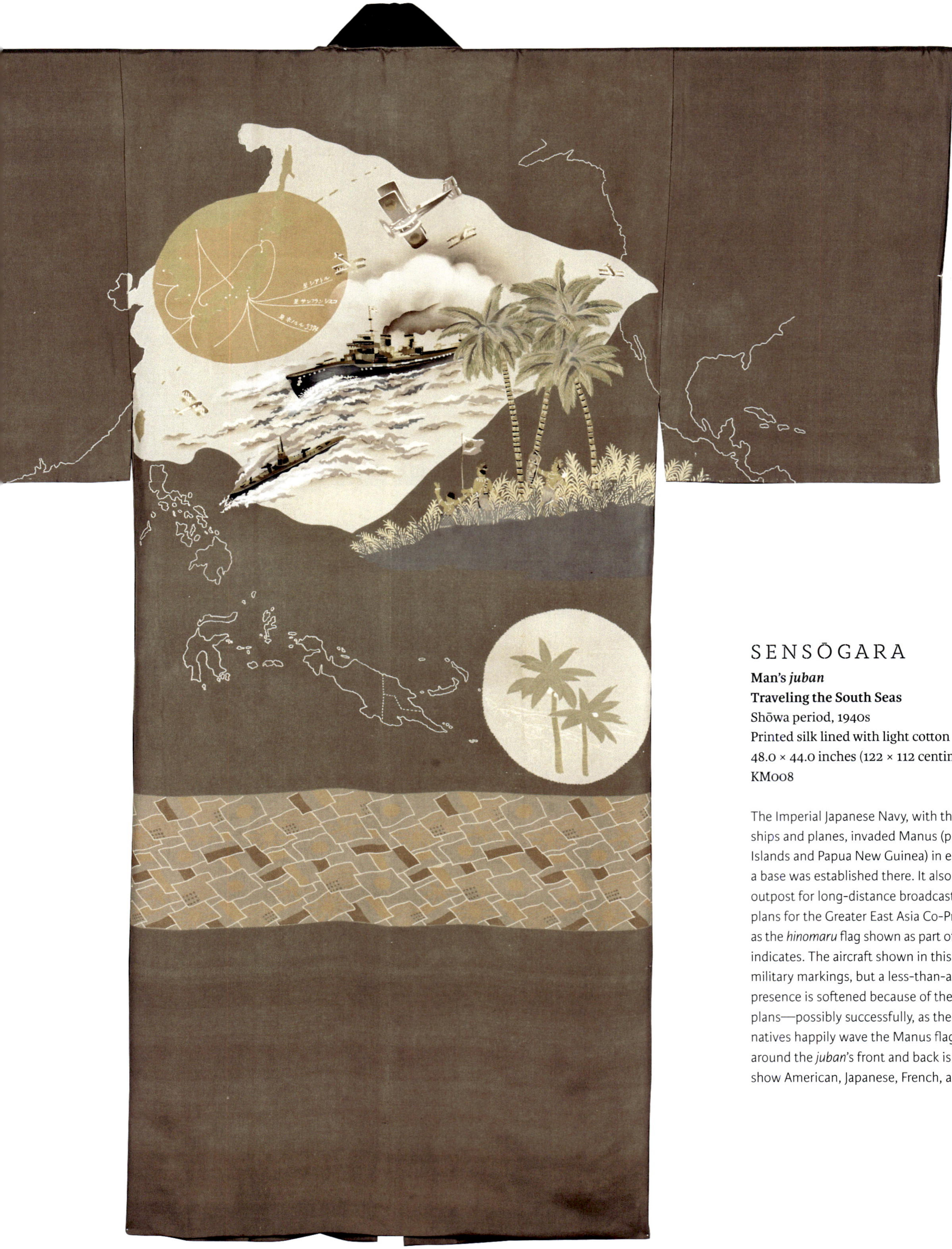

SENSŌGARA

Man's *juban*
Traveling the South Seas
Shōwa period, 1940s
Printed silk lined with light cotton
48.0 × 44.0 inches (122 × 112 centimeters)
KM008

The Imperial Japanese Navy, with the aid of several ships and planes, invaded Manus (part of the Admiral Islands and Papua New Guinea) in early 1942, and a base was established there. It also served as an outpost for long-distance broadcasting of Japan's plans for the Greater East Asia Co-Prosperity Sphere, as the *hinomaru* flag shown as part of the *juban* design indicates. The aircraft shown in this design carry military markings, but a less-than-aggressive presence is softened because of the Co-Prosperity plans—possibly successfully, as the indigenous natives happily wave the Manus flag. The panel around the *juban*'s front and back is meant to show American, Japanese, French, and other flags.

SENSŌGARA

Child's kimono for a boy
Victory celebration
Shōwa period, late 1930s–early 1940s
Printed wool muslin
30.0 × 30.0 inches (76 × 76 centimeters)
KM009

The design on this young boy's kimono celebrates a military victory in China. The two banners fluttering over one of Tokyo's tallest buildings read "Great victory" and "Long live the imperial army," and the jumble of lanterns in one roundel represents a celebratory parade marking the latest victory of the troops. The background of blue and beige stripes is a traditional theme in boys' kimono, and the many small military biplanes that dance like dragonflies through the blue background here help to increase the excitement of the day. The artist for this textile probably chose his design from the many newspaper photographs of the almost endless lines of Japanese marching soldiers and cavalry during their takeover of parts of eastern China.

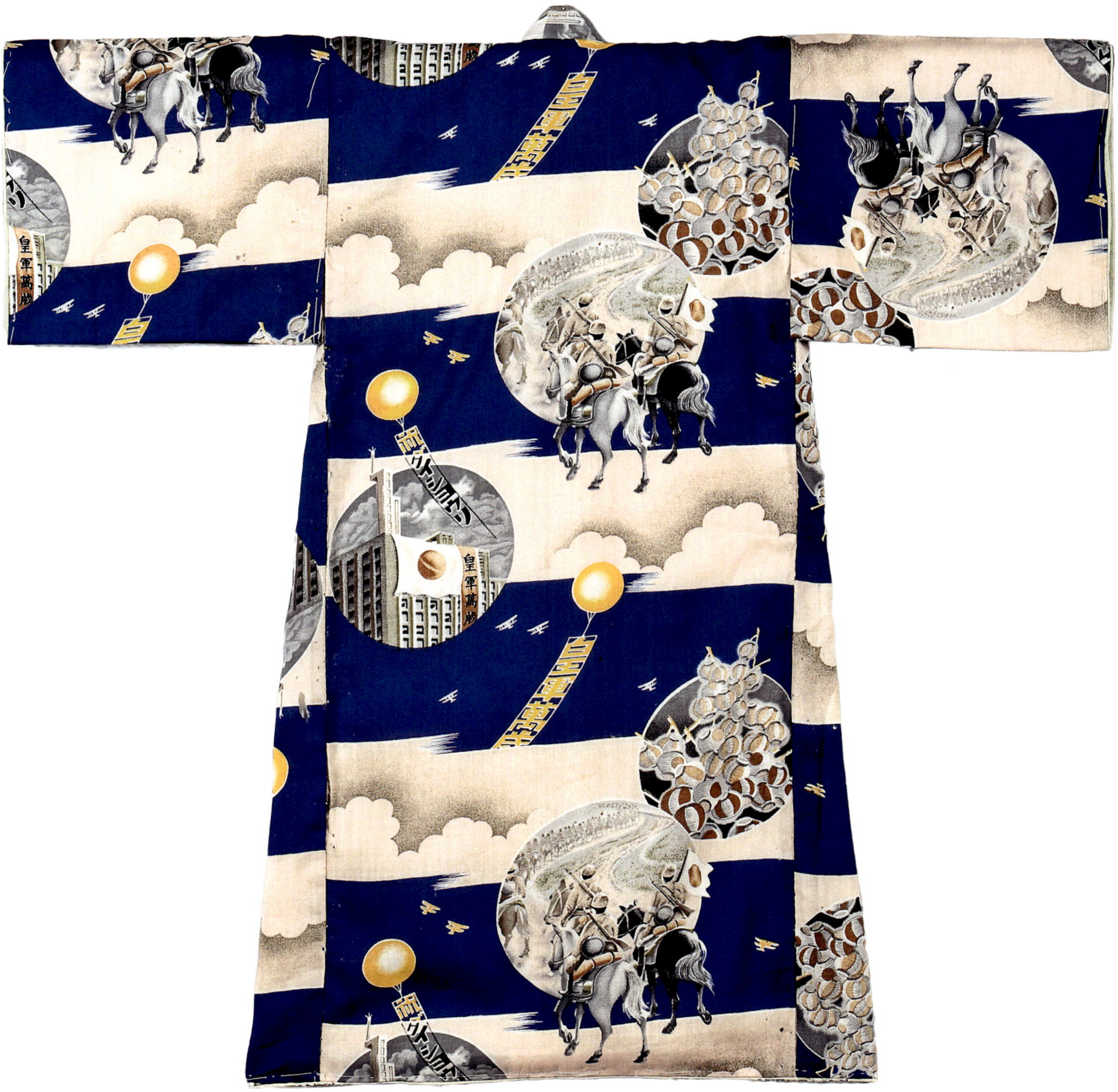

SENSŌGARA

Obi for a woman
An arsenal of war
Shōwa period, 1930s–early 1940s
Rinzu patterned silk overprinted with military designs (front length of obi)
156.0 × 12.0 inches (396 × 30 centimeters)
KM010

This wartime design is an unusual one for a woman. The base fabric is a special silk called *rinzu*, which has a delicate flower design woven directly into the textile that can barely be seen. Where the *rinzu* has been overprinted with the patterns of the multihued military accoutrements, the subtle flowers almost disappear behind the images of the tanks, cannon, and fighter planes. In the bands of solid blue, beige, and creamy yellow, however, the flowers still quietly show themselves in open spaces as a reminder that beauty can still be seen, even in times of war.

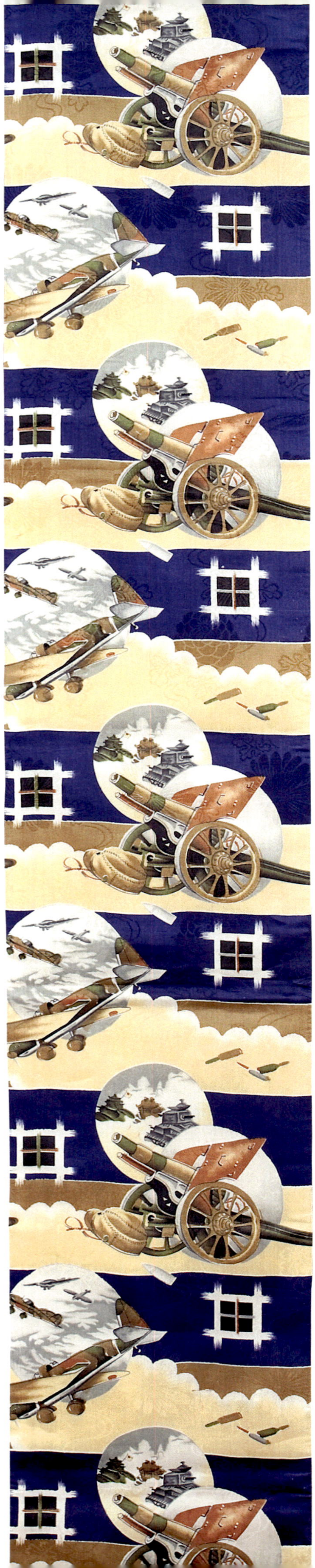

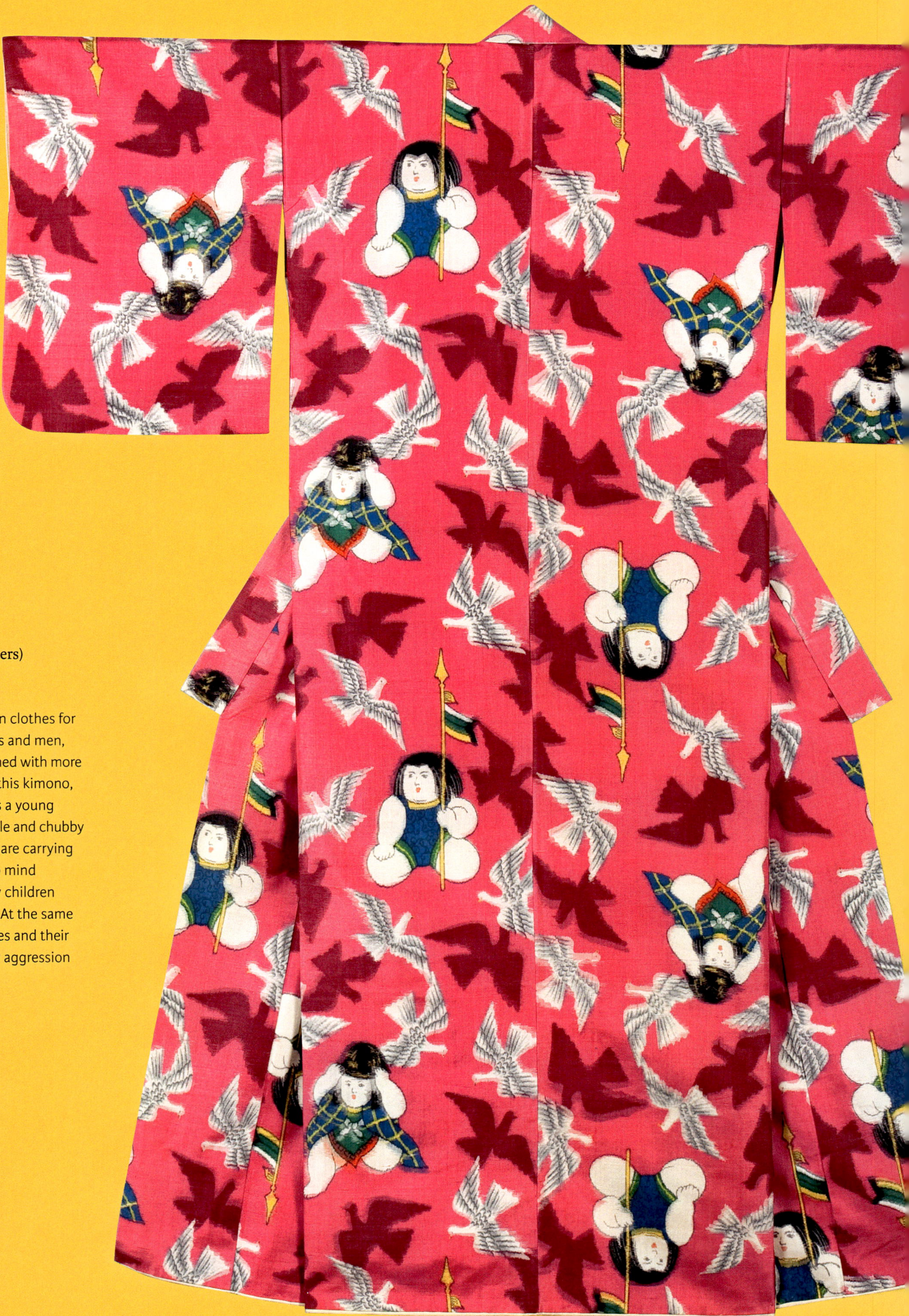

CULTURE

Kimono for a young woman
***Gosho ningyō* (palace doll) at play**
Taishō–Shōwa period, 1930–1940
Silk *meisen*
60.0 × 49.0 inches (152 × 124 centimeters)
KM*011*

War themes appeared less frequently on clothes for women and girls than on those for boys and men, and the female garments were approached with more delicacy and artistry. The deep pink of this kimono, printed in *meisen* technique, marks it as a young woman's robe. The design depicts lovable and chubby *gosho ningyō* ("palace" child dolls) who are carrying spears or wearing helmets and bring to mind Kintarō and Momotarō, both legendary children of superhuman strengths and abilities. At the same time, the background is filled with doves and their shadows, balancing the hint of military aggression with signals that they come in peace.

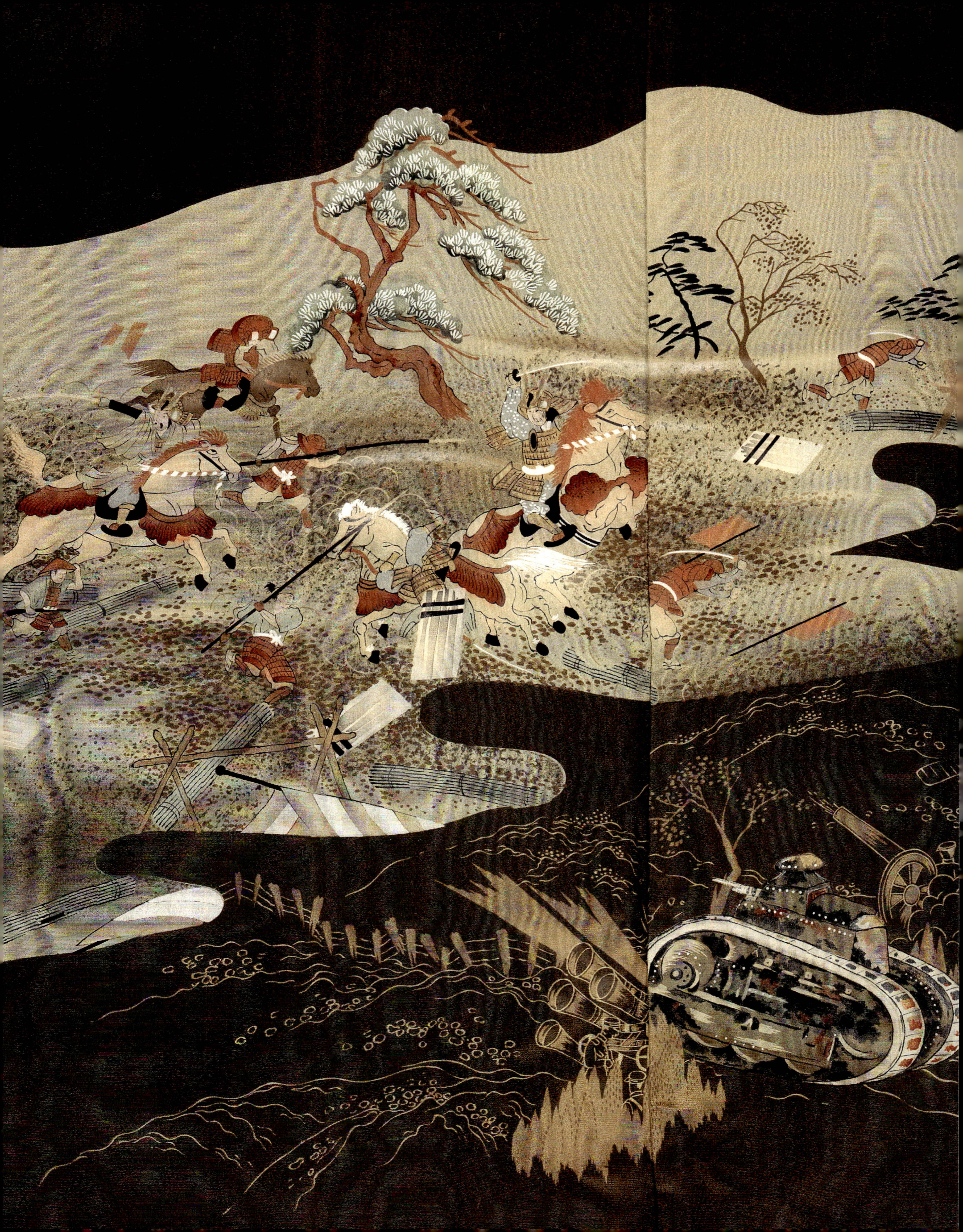

TRADITION AND MODERNITY

Man's *haori* with a decorative lining (*haura*)
Samurai and soldiers, horses and tanks
Taishō–Shōwa period, 1920–1940
Silk plain weave *haori* (outer); printed silk *haura* (lining)
51.0 × 38.0 inches (130 × 97 centimeters)
KM012

The designer of the *haura* of this quietly elegant *haori* brought together a smart blend of traditional and contemporary military imagery so that the design conceptualized the equivalent of the battles of the ancient samurai and the modern army. In their own way, the ancient warriors and the modern soldiers transcended their centuries and are the same: what they both embodied was *yamato damashii*, or the "Japanese spirit." The enemy might possess a material superiority, but the Japanese soldiers claimed a spiritual superiority whose roots were sunk into the not-to-be-forgotten samurai codes of fighting and honor.

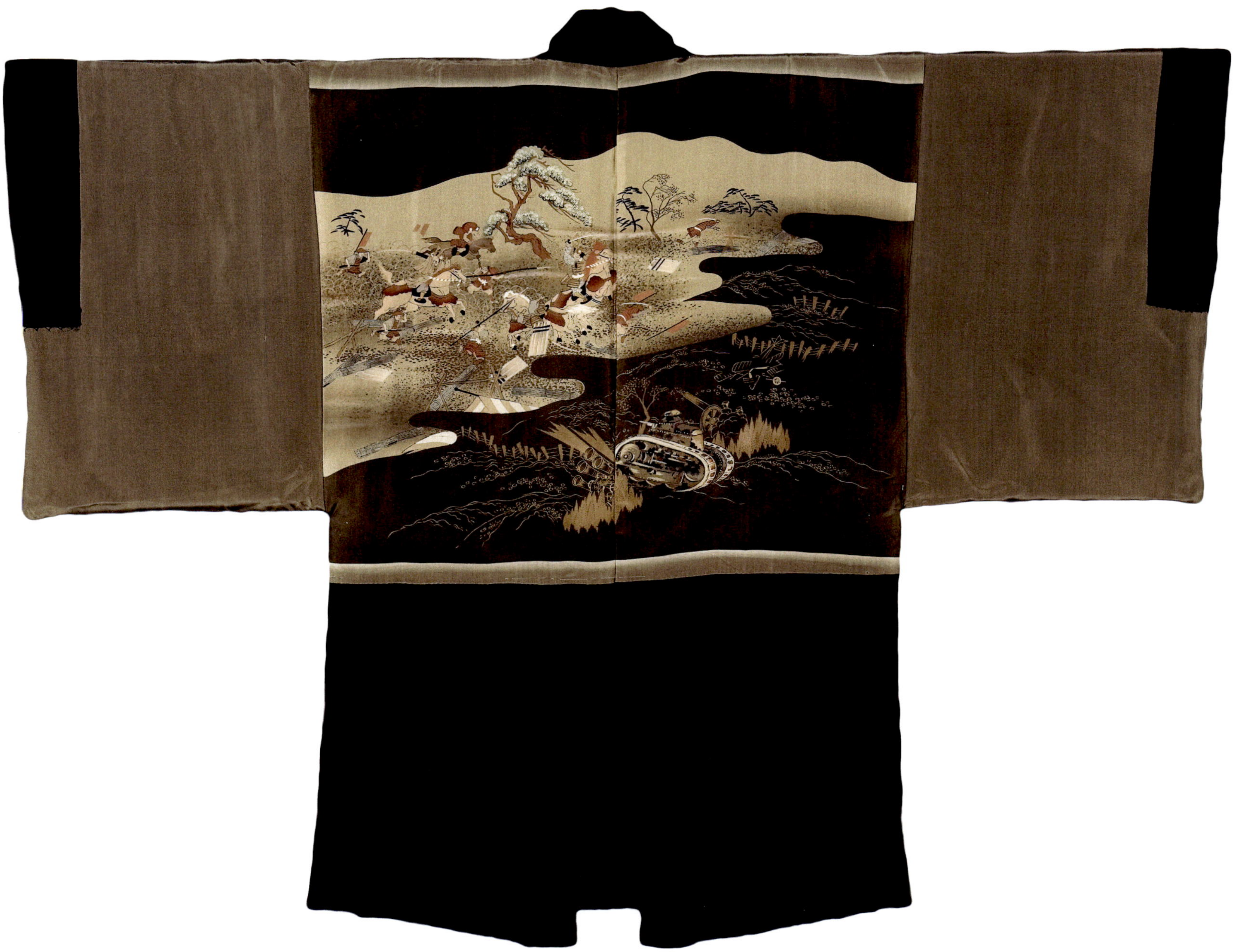

SENSŌGARA/ MACHINE AGE

Man's *haori* with a decorative lining (*haura*)
Design with an acoustic locator and a background of city skyscrapers
Taishō and Shōwa period, late 1920s–early 1930s
Silk plain weave *haori* (outer); *kata-yūzen* discharged printed silk *haura* (lining)
51.5 × 42.0 inches (131 × 107 centimeters)
KM013

The acoustical locator could facilitate passive detection of aircraft from a distance by picking up noise from a plane's engines. It was an unusual instrument of war, although the artist who designed the locator for this *haura* drew it more as an object of technological virtuosity than as a functional wartime tool. This impression was further underscored by the colloquial name of "Japanese war tuba." In spite of their comic appearances, locators played their part in war until they were overridden by radar, which rendered them obsolete. Textile designers, however, found the "war tuba" an ideal novelty design and it became a favorite image for *omoshirogara*.

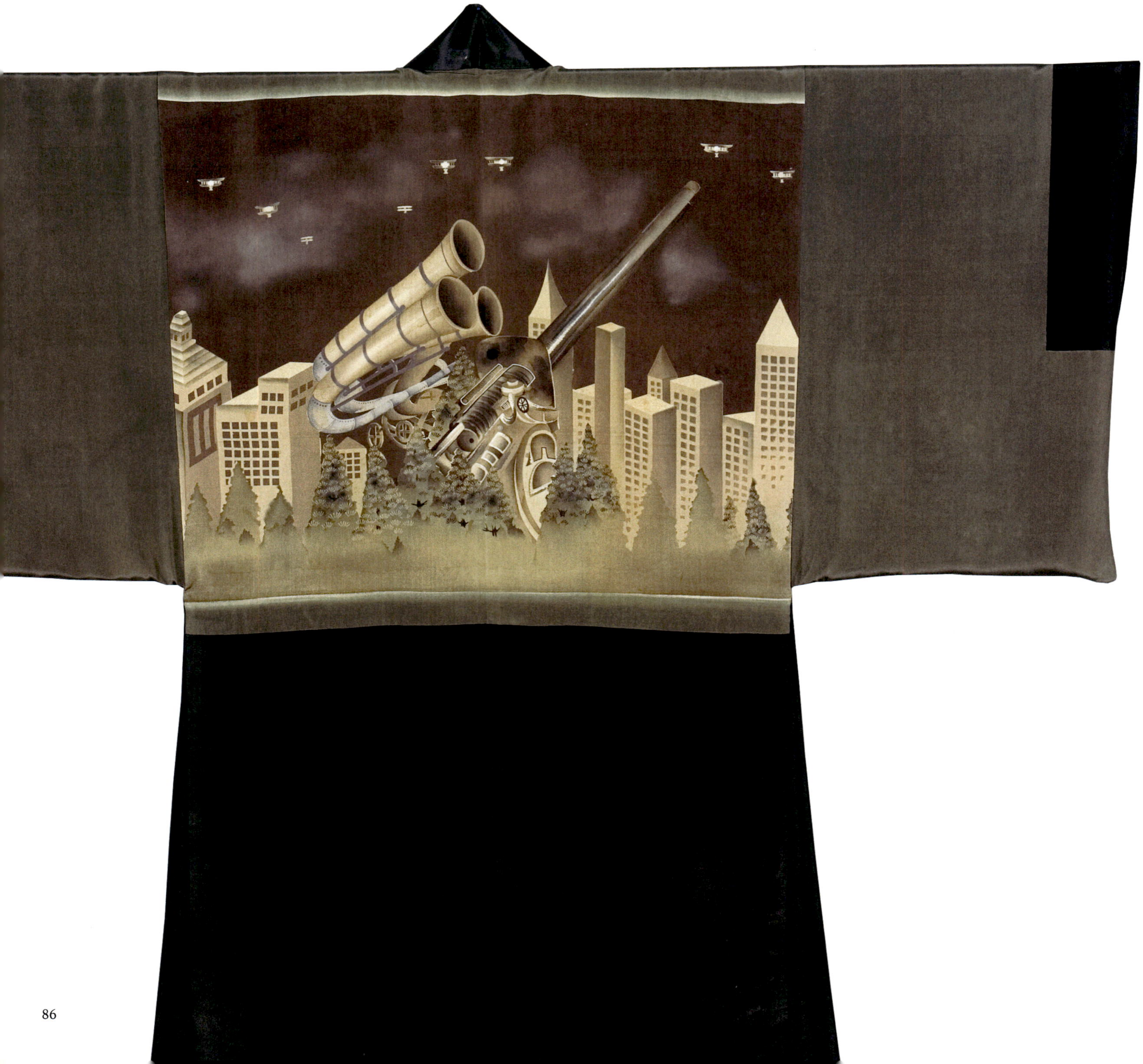

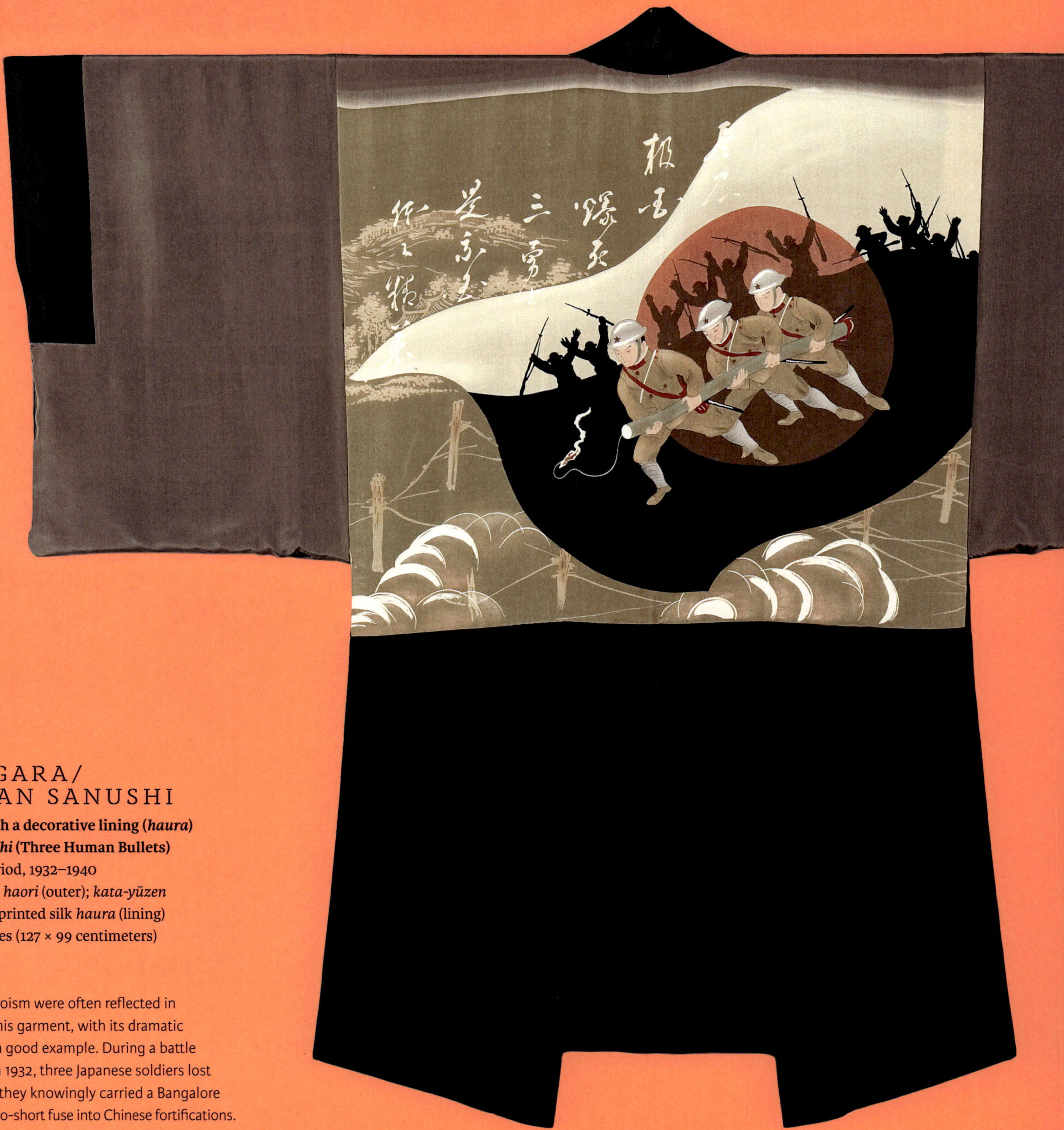

SENSŌGARA/ BAKUDAN SANUSHI

Man's *haori* with a decorative lining (*haura*)
***Bakudan Sanushi* (Three Human Bullets)**
Early Shōwa period, 1932–1940
Silk plain weave *haori* (outer); *kata-yūzen* discharged and printed silk *haura* (lining)
50.0 × 39.0 inches (127 × 99 centimeters)
KM014

Sacrifice and heroism were often reflected in *sensōgara*, and this garment, with its dramatic *haura*, provides a good example. During a battle near Shanghai in 1932, three Japanese soldiers lost their lives when they knowingly carried a Bangalore torpedo with a too-short fuse into Chinese fortifications. The torpedo's explosion killed the three men but gave other soldiers entry to the Chinese territory. The soldiers were named *Bakudan Sanyushi* (Three Human Bullets) and recognized by the Japanese populace as *gunshin* ("military gods") at the Yasukuni Shrine in Tokyo for their selfless act of loyalty and bravery. The text on this *haura* reads in part "three brave soldiers . . . rewarded by death . . . this is our nation's body and soul."

SENSŌGARA

Man's *haori* with a decorative lining (*haura*)
Battleship at war in a raging sea
Late Meiji–Taishō period, 1904–1930
Silk plain weave *haori* (outer); *kata-yūzen* dyed and hand-painted silk *haura* (lining)
52.0 × 39.0 inches (132 × 99 centimeters)
KM015

The *haura* that was made for this *haori* is a complex and starkly stunning composition, due to the fine dyeing and delicate hand painting produced by the textile artist. Only a small part of the warship can be seen in the midst of battle, with the commander and sailors gathered on the decks watching as the naval conflict rages on. The overall pictorial scene, however, even in all its fierce beauty, is rather enigmatic. It is conceivable that the ship depicted here is the *Naniwa*, since it took part in many naval battles and skirmishes in the Sino- and Russo-Japanese Wars, but this is only speculation, as there is no confirmed identification.

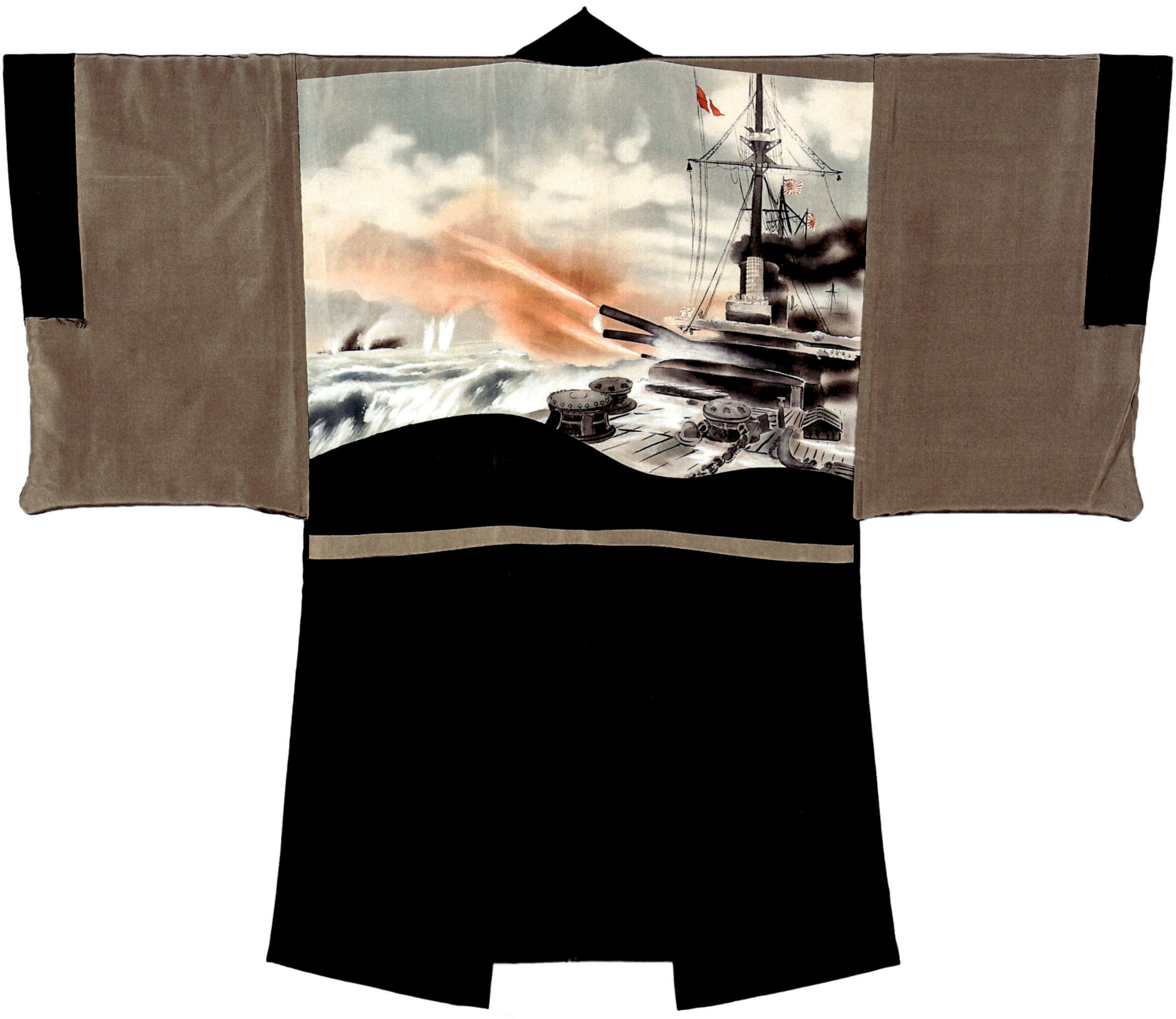

SENSŌGARA

Man's *haori* with a decorative lining (*haura*)
Victorious entry into Mukden
Late Meiji–Taishō period, 1912–1926
Silk plain weave *haori* (outer); *kata-yūzen* discharged and printed silk *haura* (lining)
52.0 × 39.0 inches (132 × 99 centimeters)
KM016

An unknown artist based his design for this *haura* on a famous painting by Kanokogi Takeshirō (1874–1941), *The Mukden Battle in the Russo-Japanese War*.[1] The painting shows the triumphal entry by Commander-in-Chief Oyama Iwao and his troops into the city of Mukden, a victory that helped Japan to win the war. This *haura* was produced in the Taishō era to commemorate Japan's victory in the Russo-Japanese War of 1904–05. The image drawn on the *haura* is quite similar to Kanokogi's painting, although the textile artist chose to depict Oyama on a white horse rather than the russet horse in the original painting, probably to highlight the commander as he entered the city.

1. Kanokogi Takeshirō (1874–1941), *The Mukden Battle in the Russo-Japanese War*, *c.* 1905. Oil on canvas, 9 ft. 8 in. × 6 ft. 9 in. (295 × 206 cm). Collection of The Seitoku Memorial Picture Gallery, Tokyo.

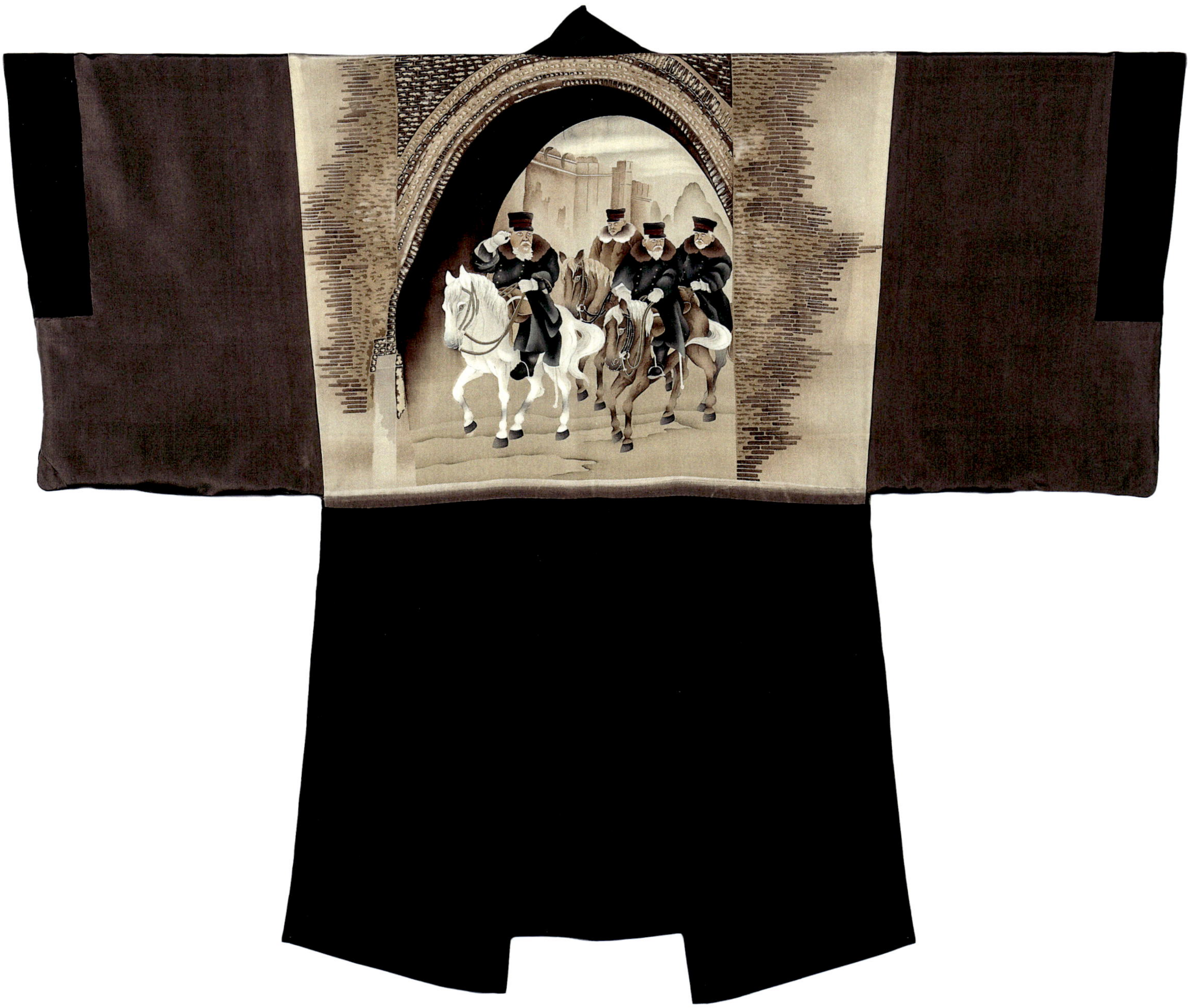

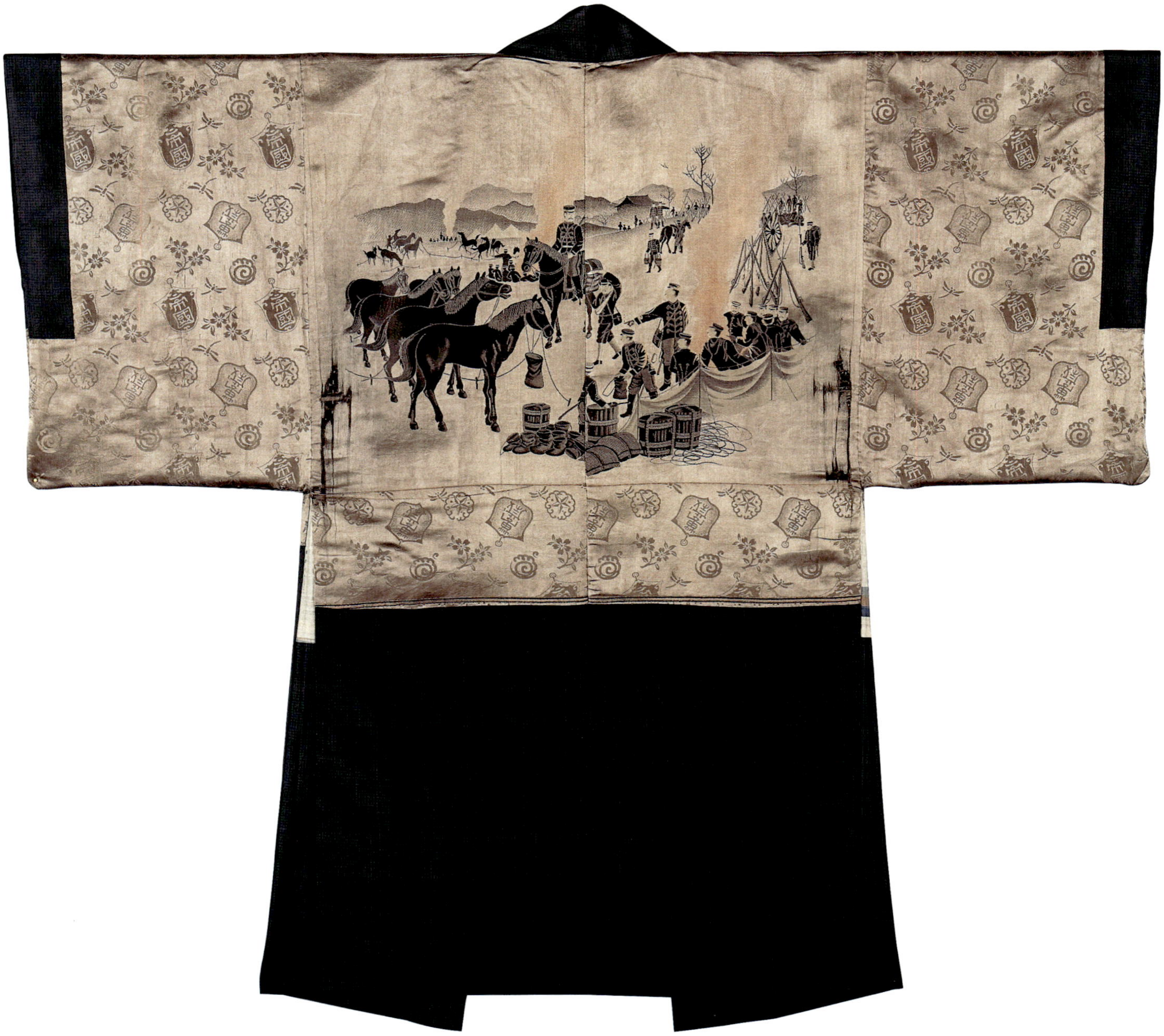

SENSŌGARA

Man's *haori* with a decorative lining (*haura*)
Soldiers and horses gathering at camp
Late Meiji period, 1894–1895
Silk plain weave *haori* (outer); woven silk decorative lining (*haura*), satin silk for inner sleeves
52.0 × 39.0 inches (132 × 99 centimeters)
KM017

This restful camp scene depicts the few quiet moments that the soldiers appreciate as they lounge on the ground or take care that their horses are watered and fed. They know that the Chinese army is not far, and they will soon be required to return to war once more, but the obvious camaraderie between the men solidifies their abilities to work together as they face the next valiant battle. The design for this textile was beautifully developed, and it is possible that it was commissioned from an artist who had participated as a soldier or reporter during the Sino-Japanese War years.

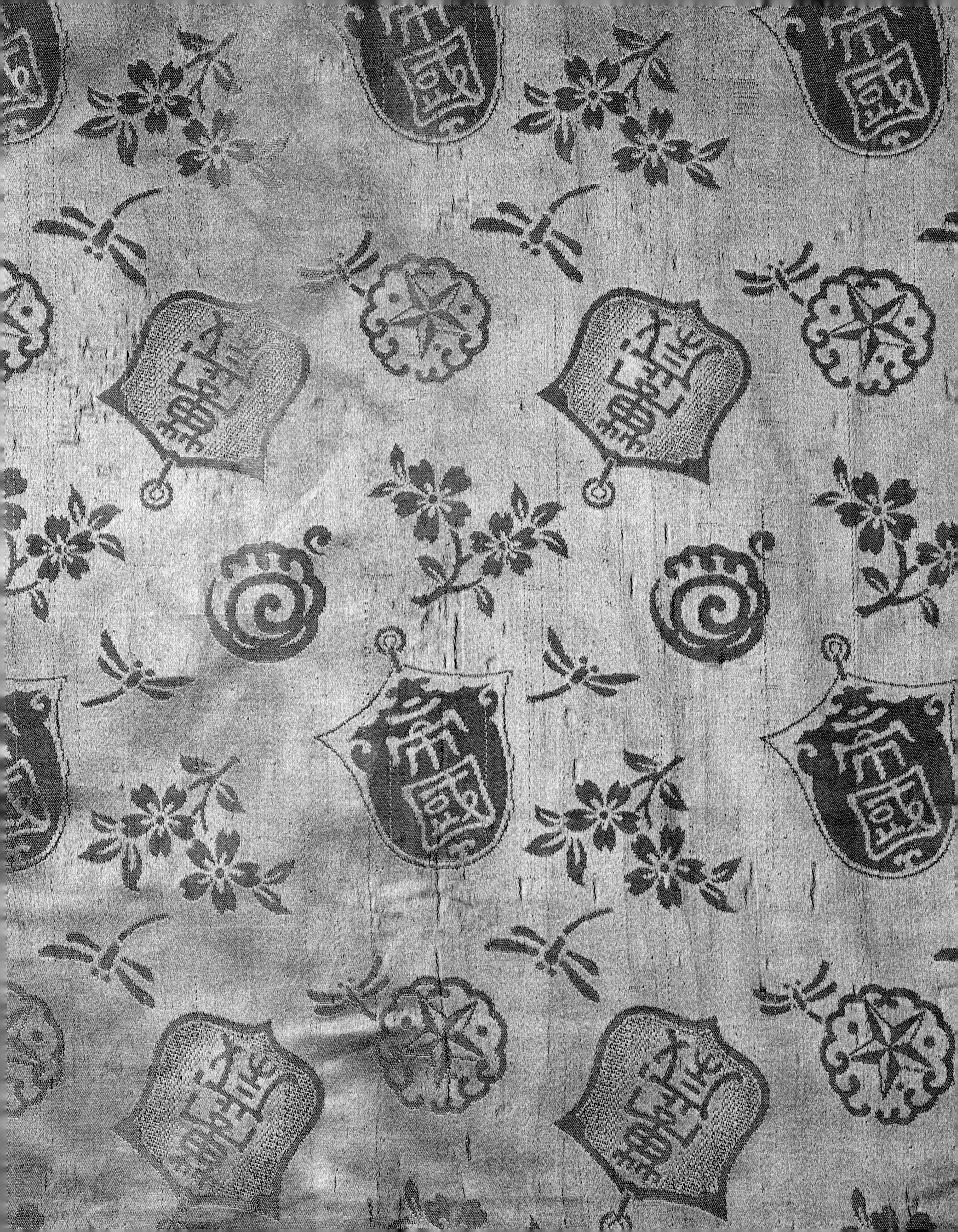

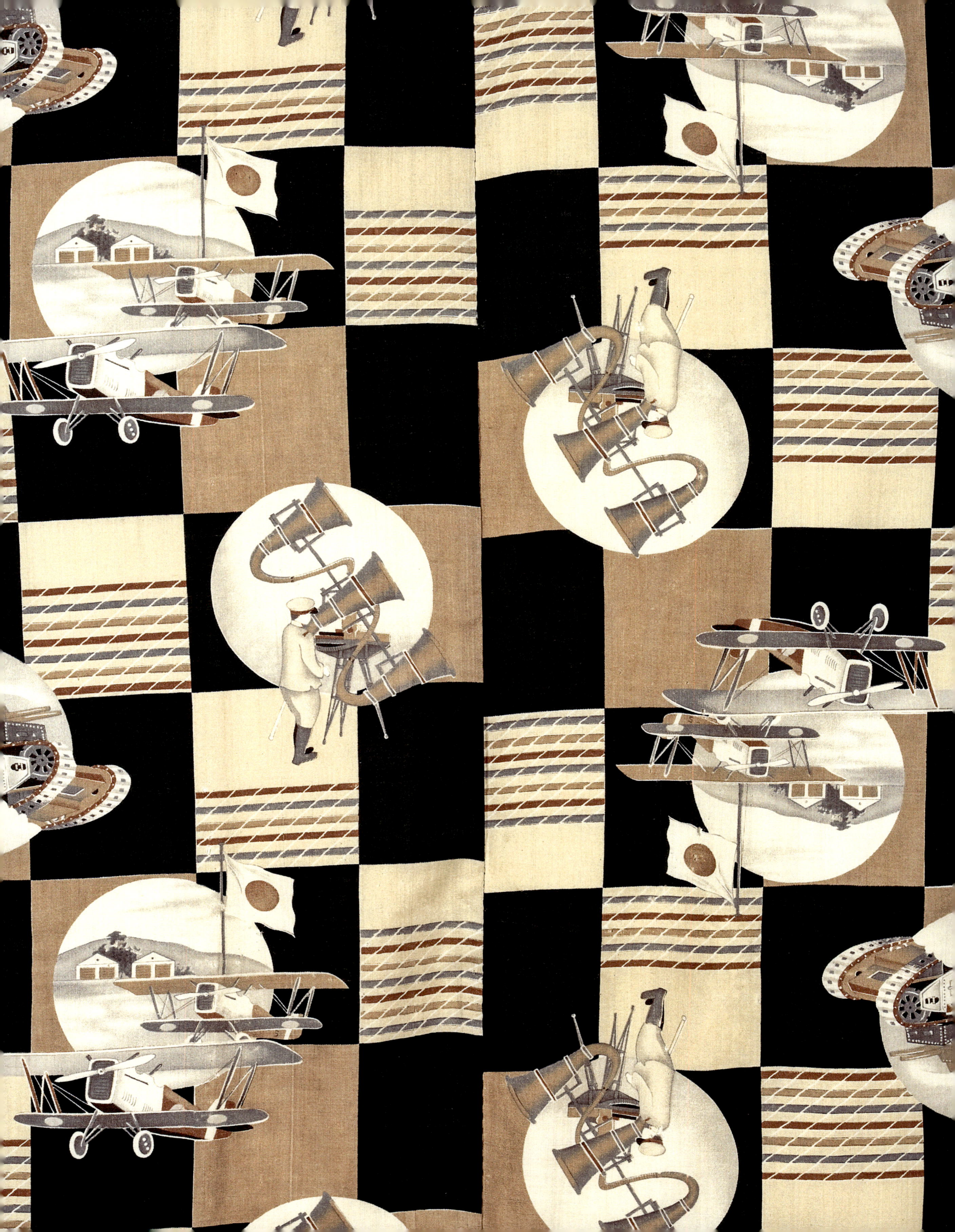

SENSŌGARA/ MACHINE AGE

Man's *juban*
Tubas, tanks, and flight
Late Taishō–early Shōwa period, 1920s–1930s
Printed wool muslin, silk collar
56.0 × 50.0 inches (142 × 127 centimeters)
KM018

The carefully drawn designs for the textile used in this *juban* show three good examples of some of the important modern equipment that was very much wanted by the Japanese military following World War I and into the late Taishō and early Shōwa eras. The aircraft, portable acoustical locators, and military tanks were shown on this textile primarily to draw attention to these technical advances that Japan had been carefully developing, and as an excellent way to encourage the wearer of the *juban* to better appreciate these new elements. The circles and blocks of color serve as a strong background for the planes, locators, and tanks; the overall design produces a vibrant visual impact.

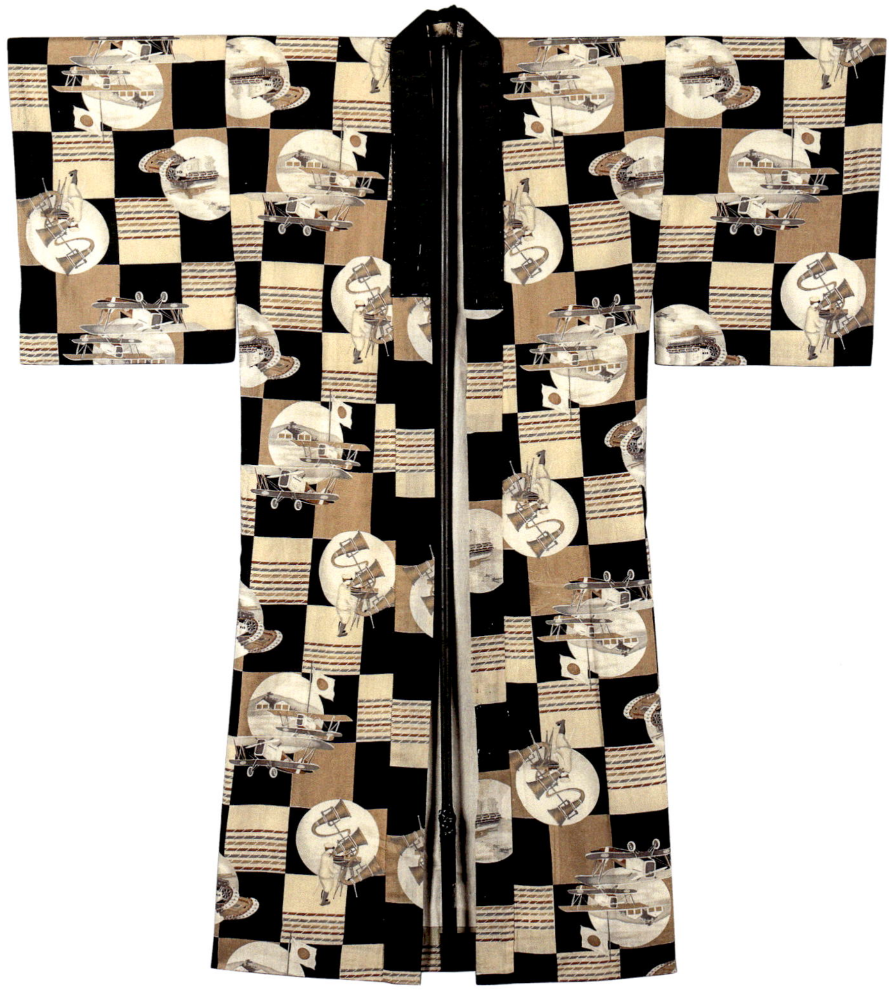

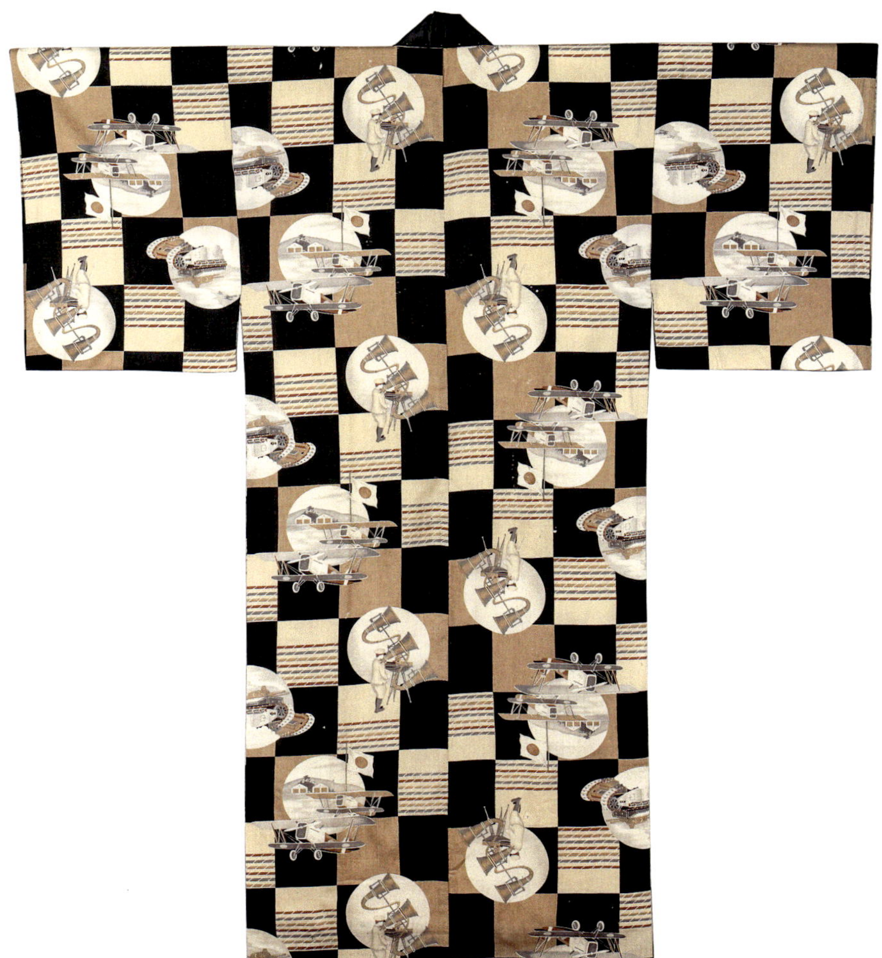

SENSŌGARA/ COSMOPOLITANISM

Woman's *nagajuban*
Anchors and flowers
Late Meiji period, 1904–1906
Silk with board clamp resist (*itajimezome*)
49.0 × 46.0 inches (124 × 117 centimeters)
KM019

This woman's *nagajuban* was dyed using *itajimezome*, a board clamp resist method. In this technique, cloth panels are folded multiple times and tightly clamped between wooden boards that have been carved with a three-dimensional design. Dye is run through the areas of the carved-out clamped boards, and the white area of the design is reserved where the dye cannot penetrate. The carving for this design consists only of one anchor and one spray of cherry blossoms, but thanks to the clever folding and artful carving, each element appears in left and right, up and down positions, which makes the simple design appear much more complex. The pattern is symbolic of the Japanese Navy and serves as a reminder of the naval victories of the Russo-Japanese War (1904–05).

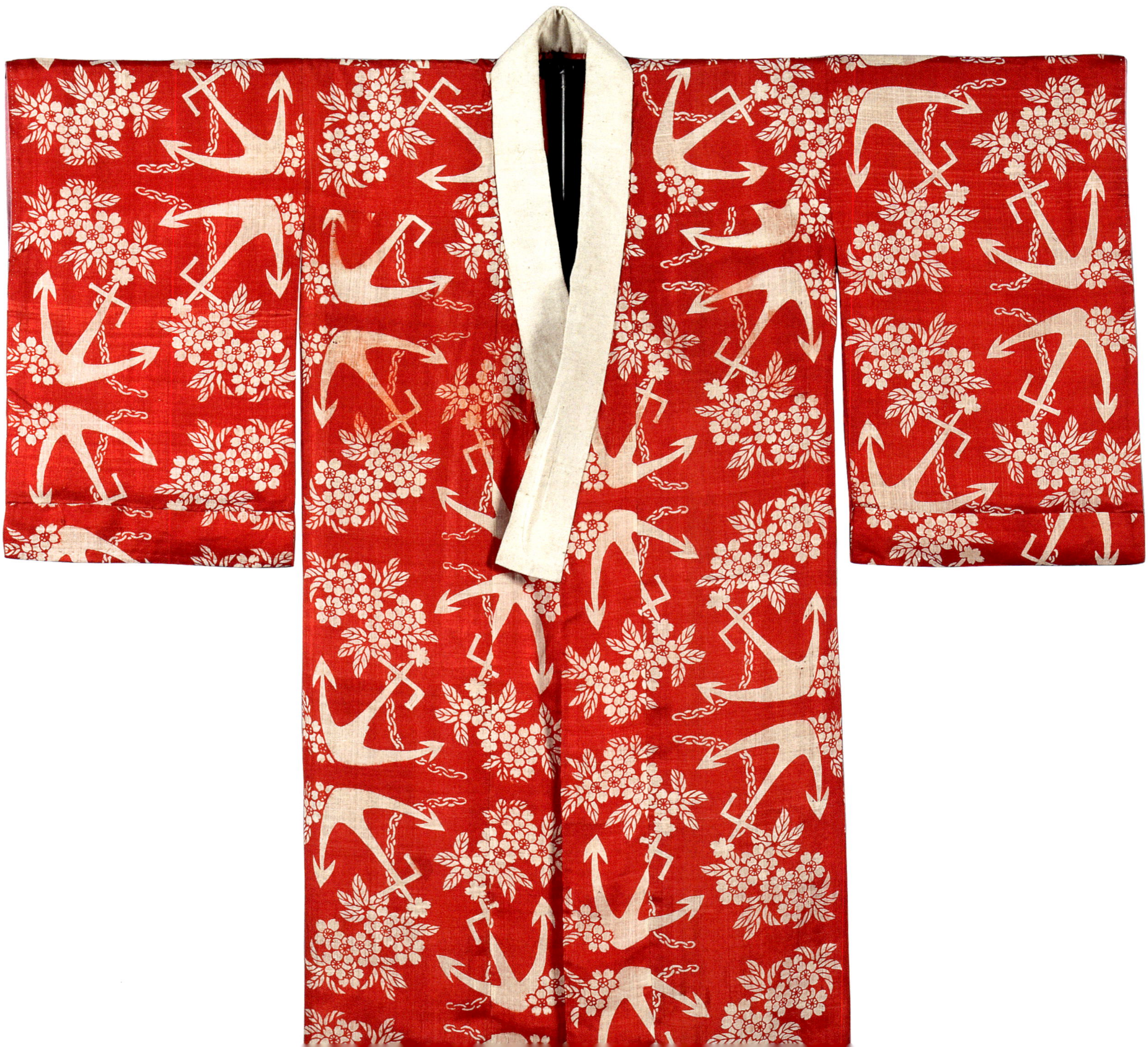

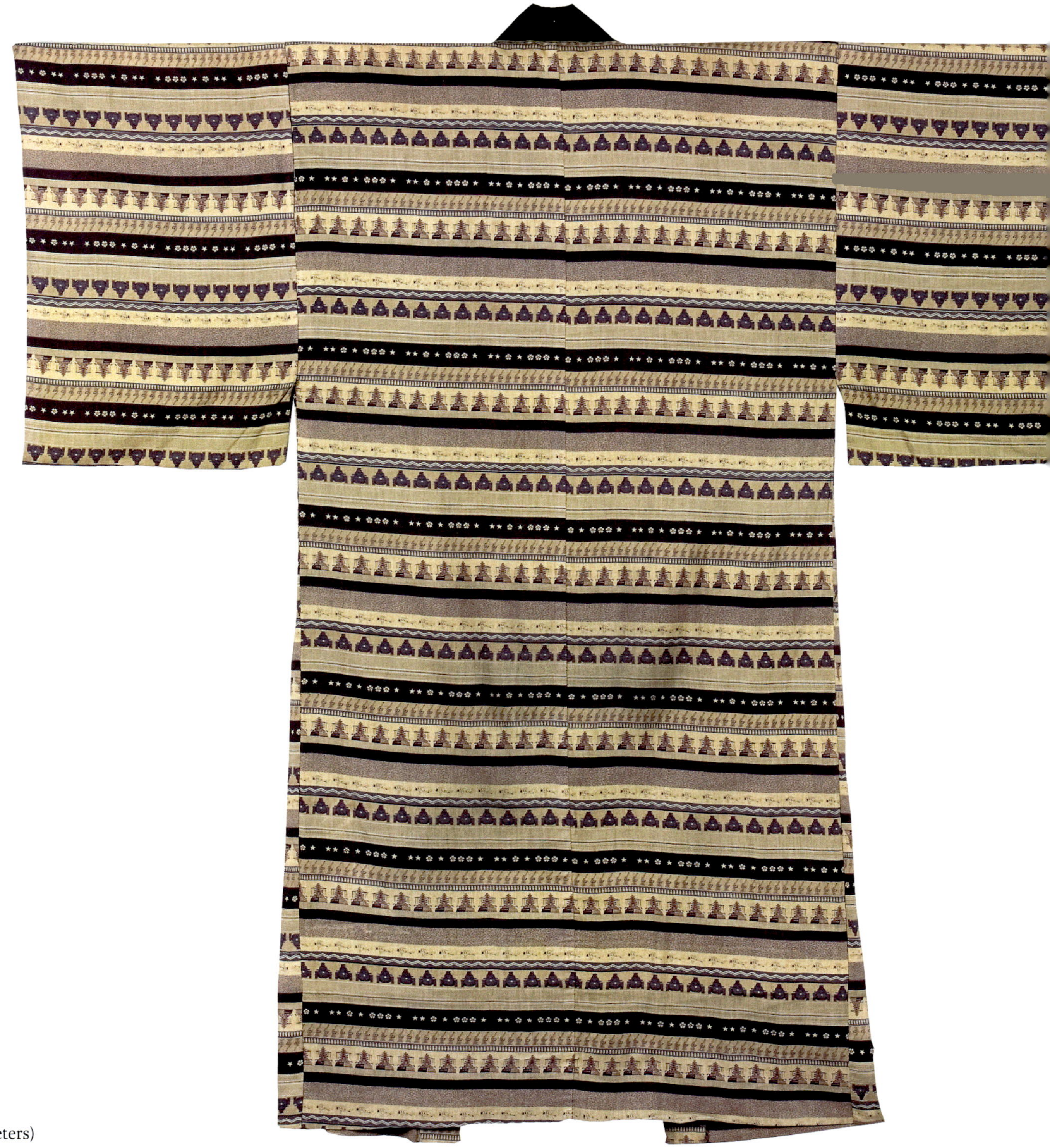

SENSŌGARA

Man's *juban*
Stylized armaments
Early Shōwa period, 1930s–1940s
Printed ramie, silk collar
56.0 × 50.0 inches (142 × 127 centimeters)
KM020

This highly stylized design captures a wide range of military armaments within its repeated horizontal bands. Starting from the top, a row of formidable battleships is followed by a row of airplanes, then by a zigzag design that represents one of the duty flags of the Imperial Japanese Navy. Next is a line of well-armoured tanks, followed by a band of stars and cherry blossoms representing rank badge motifs meant to be worn on uniform collars. Anti-aircraft guns form a lengthy line of protective armaments, close to a band of ammunition ready for fire. This *juban* is made from ramie, a strong open-weave fabric somewhat similar to linen that had been used for centuries. The *sensōgara* design would have been much appreciated by its male wearer.

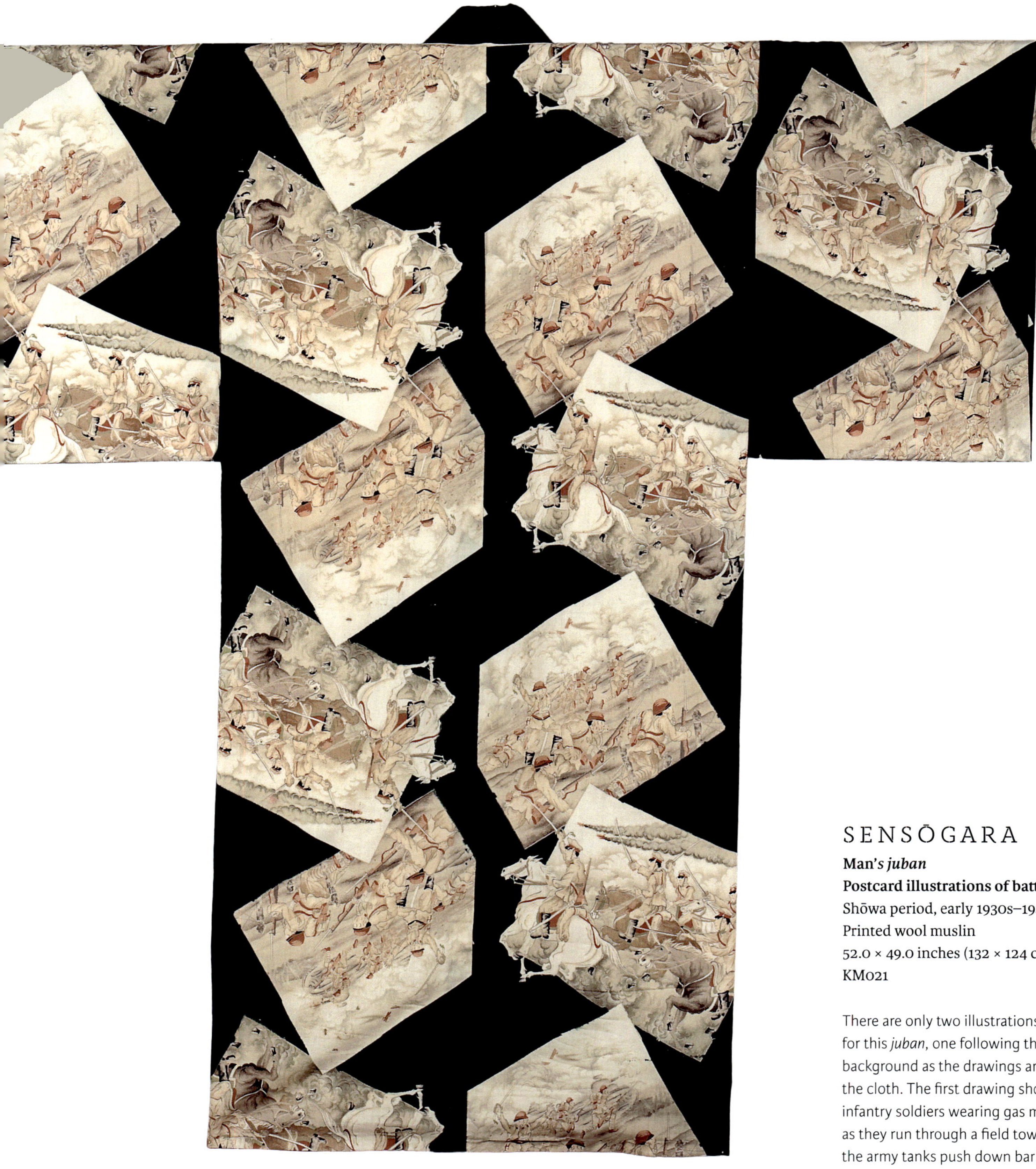

SENSŌGARA

Man's *juban*
Postcard illustrations of battle scenes
Shōwa period, early 1930s–1940s
Printed wool muslin
52.0 × 49.0 inches (132 × 124 centimeters)
KM021

There are only two illustrations used on the textile for this *juban*, one following the other against a black background as the drawings are repetitively placed on the cloth. The first drawing shows a large number of infantry soldiers wearing gas masks and carrying rifles as they run through a field toward the enemy, while the army tanks push down barbed wire fences to allow the soldiers to follow. The second illustration shows the cavalry pushing through clouds of smoke, waving their swords as they rush toward the enemy. Both illustrations show dogfights among the biplanes skirmishing in the air. The images of the raging battle drawn on this textile produce a very powerful impression on anyone who sees this *juban*.

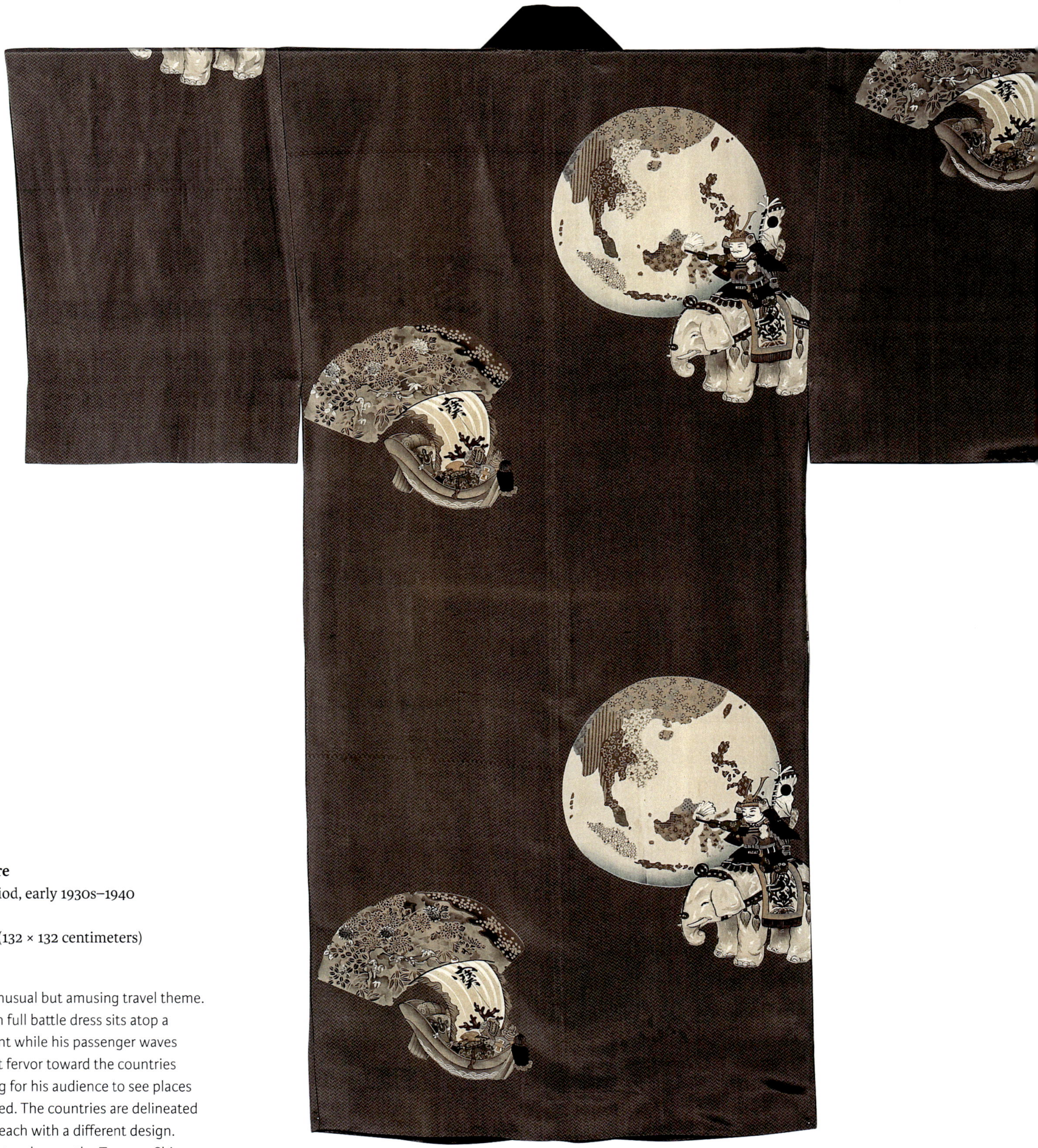

TRAVEL

Man's *juban*
Travel and treasure
Taishō–Shōwa period, early 1930s–1940
Printed silk
52.0 × 52.0 inches (132 × 132 centimeters)
KM022

This *juban* has an unusual but amusing travel theme. A samurai warrior in full battle dress sits atop a complacent elephant while his passenger waves his brush with great fervor toward the countries on the globe, calling for his audience to see places that should be visited. The countries are delineated by textile patterns, each with a different design. A secondary theme touches on the Treasure Ship (*Takarabune*), the ship of the Seven Gods of Good Fortune that is an essential part of New Year celebrations, as legend has it that the ship carrying its treasures sails at this time of year. The sail of the ship carries the character *ju*, meaning longevity.

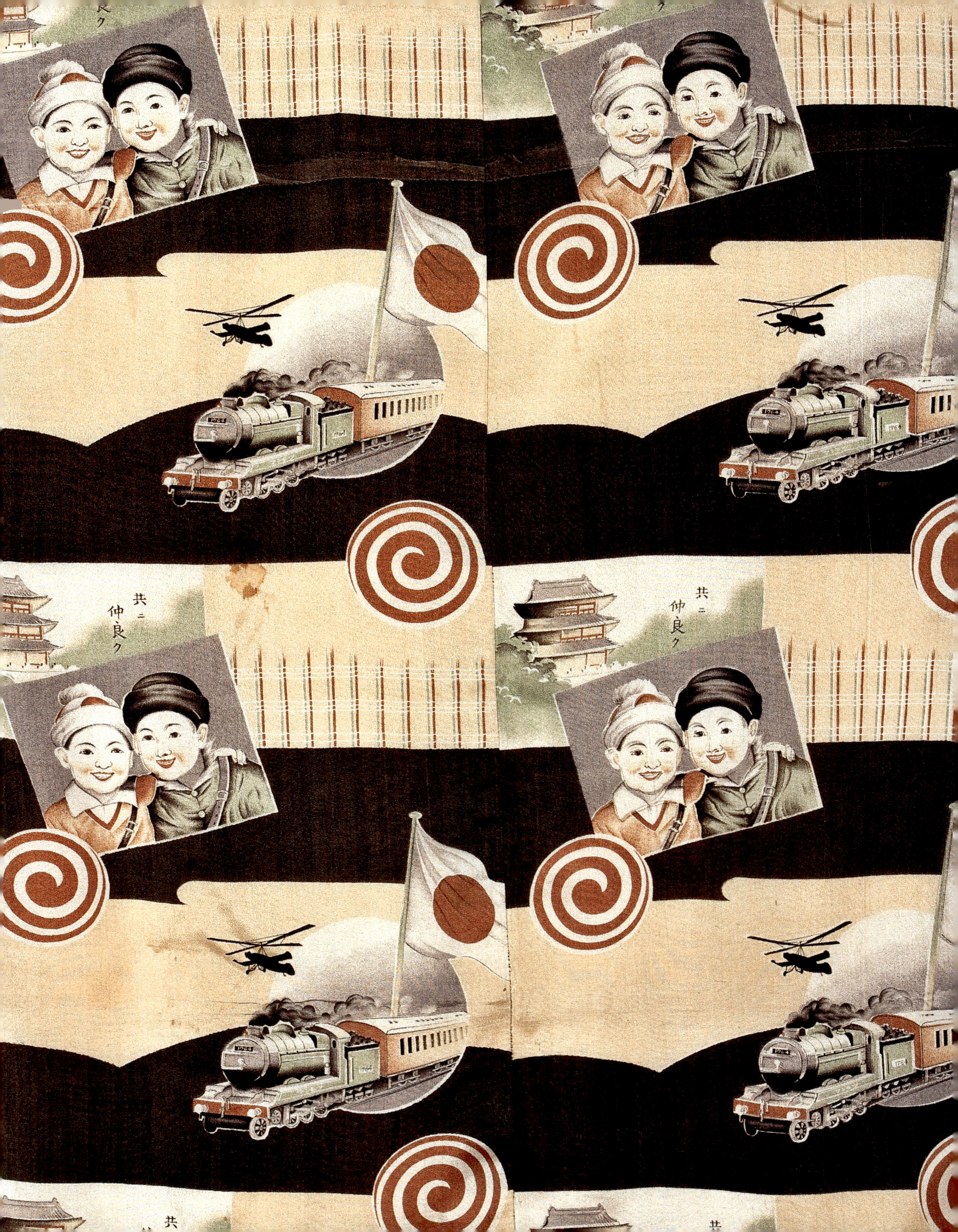
共ニ仲良ク

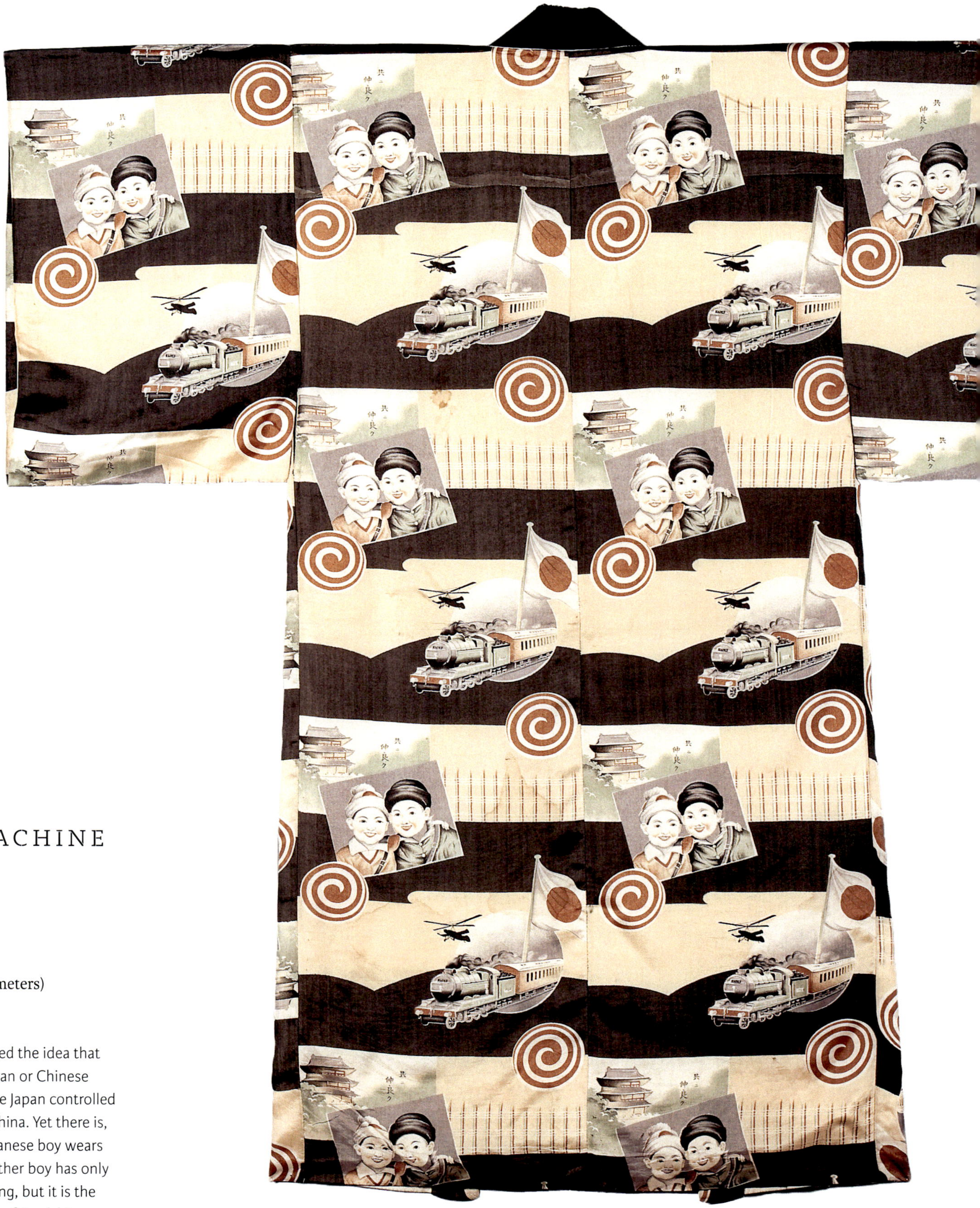

SENSŌGARA/MACHINE AGE

Man's juban
Making friends
Early Shōwa period, 1932–1940s
Printed rayon
50.0 × 45.0 inches (127 × 114 centimeters)
KM023

The design on this textile encouraged the idea that young Japanese boys and Manchurian or Chinese boys could become fast friends once Japan controlled Manchuria and parts of occupied China. Yet there is, perhaps, some dissonance. The Japanese boy wears Western-style clothing, while the other boy has only traditional garments. Both are smiling, but it is the Japanese boy who claims the right to friendship. This design was produced after the Japanese occupation of Manchukuo and parts of China, and the Japanese *hinomaru* flag that flies from a train's engine encourages recognition of Imperial Japan. The autogiro, a predecessor of the modern helicopter, was brought to Japan in the 1930s and was initially developed for use as an observation platform in China.

SENSŌGARA/MEIJI
SHIPS OF WAR

Man's *haori* with a decorative lining (*haura*)
Warships and shrines
Late Meiji period, 1904–1905
Silk plain weave *haori* (outer) with family crests (*mon*); woven silk *haura* (lining), damask patterned silk for inner sleeves
50.0 × 41.0 inches (127 × 104 centimeters)
KM024

The *haura* woven for this *haori* depicts a magnificent display of a flotilla of warships that fills a large harbor. Spaced between the rows of ships are woven pictures of quiet havens that shelter traditional fishing boats and *torii* that lead to shrines hidden in the hills. The juxtaposition of the two elements captures a sense of the old and the new, of the time-honored hills and coves and of the changing face of modernity that leads to a new world. This *mon* (family crest) has a standing arrowhead backed with two blossoms. It was a crest favored by samurai families.

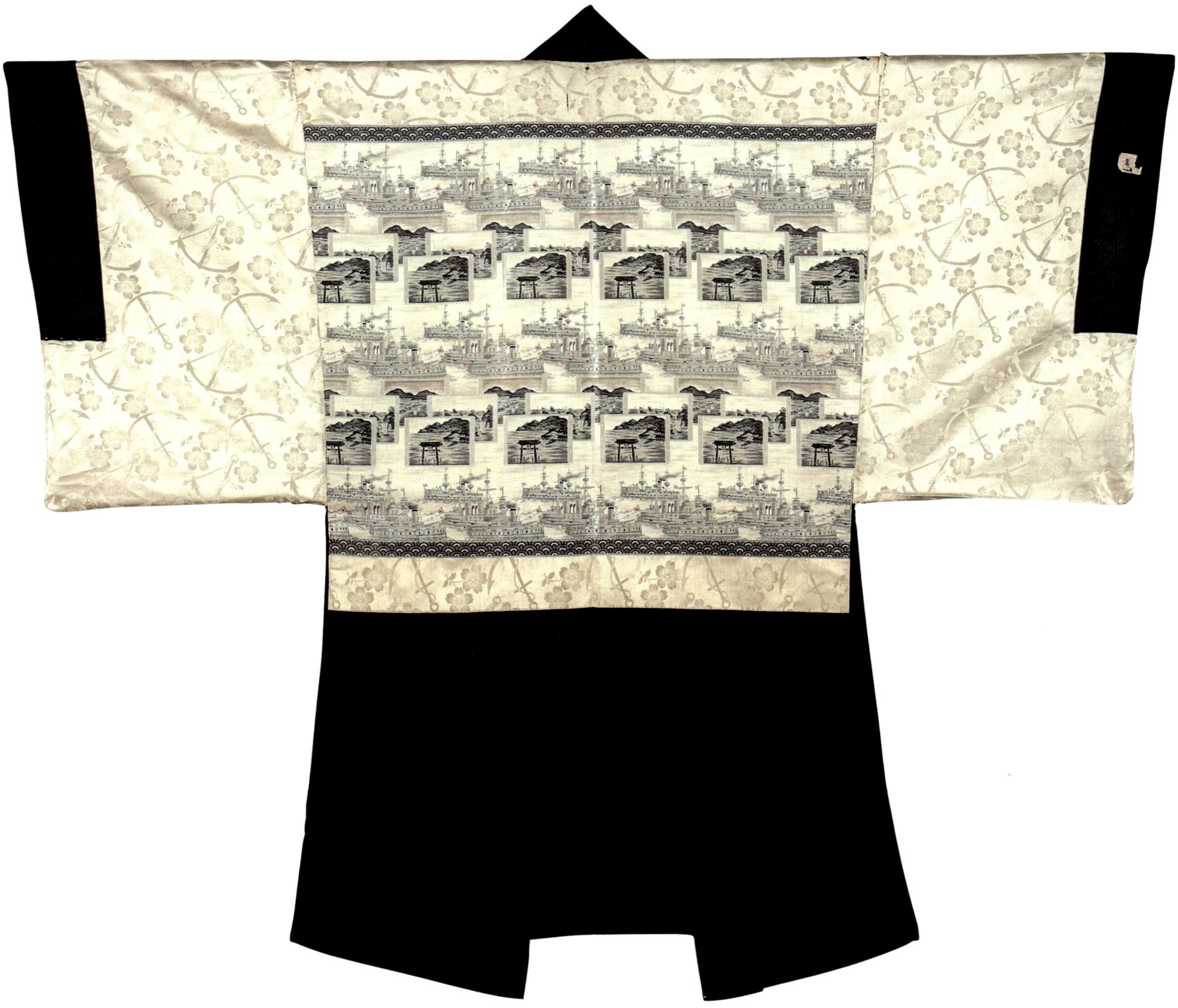

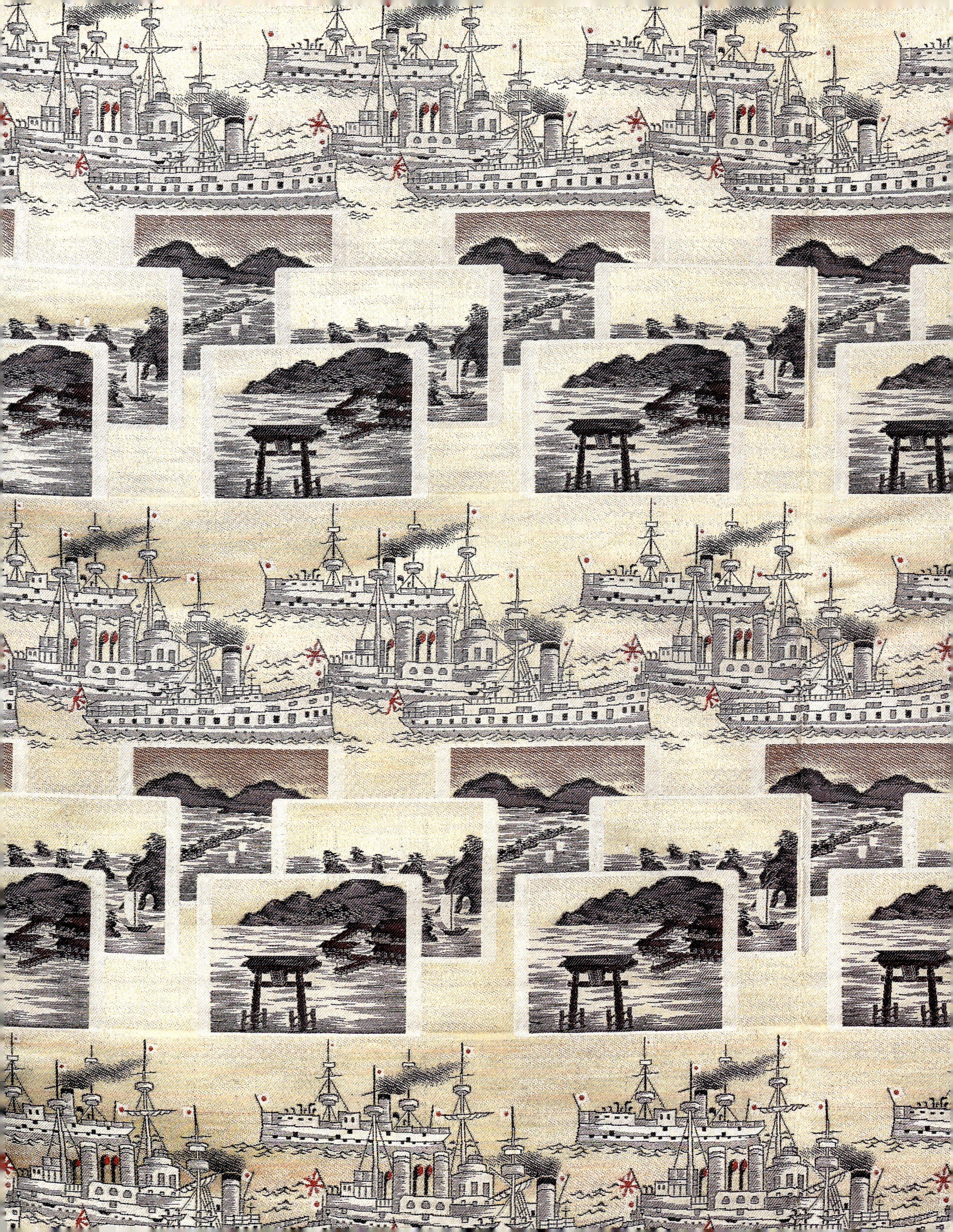

MACHINE AGE

***Tanzen* (cotton jacket for a man)**
The excitement of the New Age
Late Taishō–early Shōwa period, 1920s–1930s
Kasuri exterior; printed cotton interior
51.0 × 35.0 inches (130 × 89 centimeters)
KM025

The magic of airplanes, Zeppelins, armored cars, tanks, and battleships can capture a man's interest in these exciting postcard-like images printed on a deep purple cotton. The small airplanes flit over roads and buildings, perhaps just for fun on a sunny day. The impressive *Graf Zeppelin* was the dirigible that carried the newspaper magnate William Randolph Hearst, his entourage, and members of the Zeppelin Company on an around-the-world publicity tour for the two companies in 1929. The sleek new armored cars, sturdy tanks, and massive battleships also evoke admiration for the formidable armada that Japan could produce.

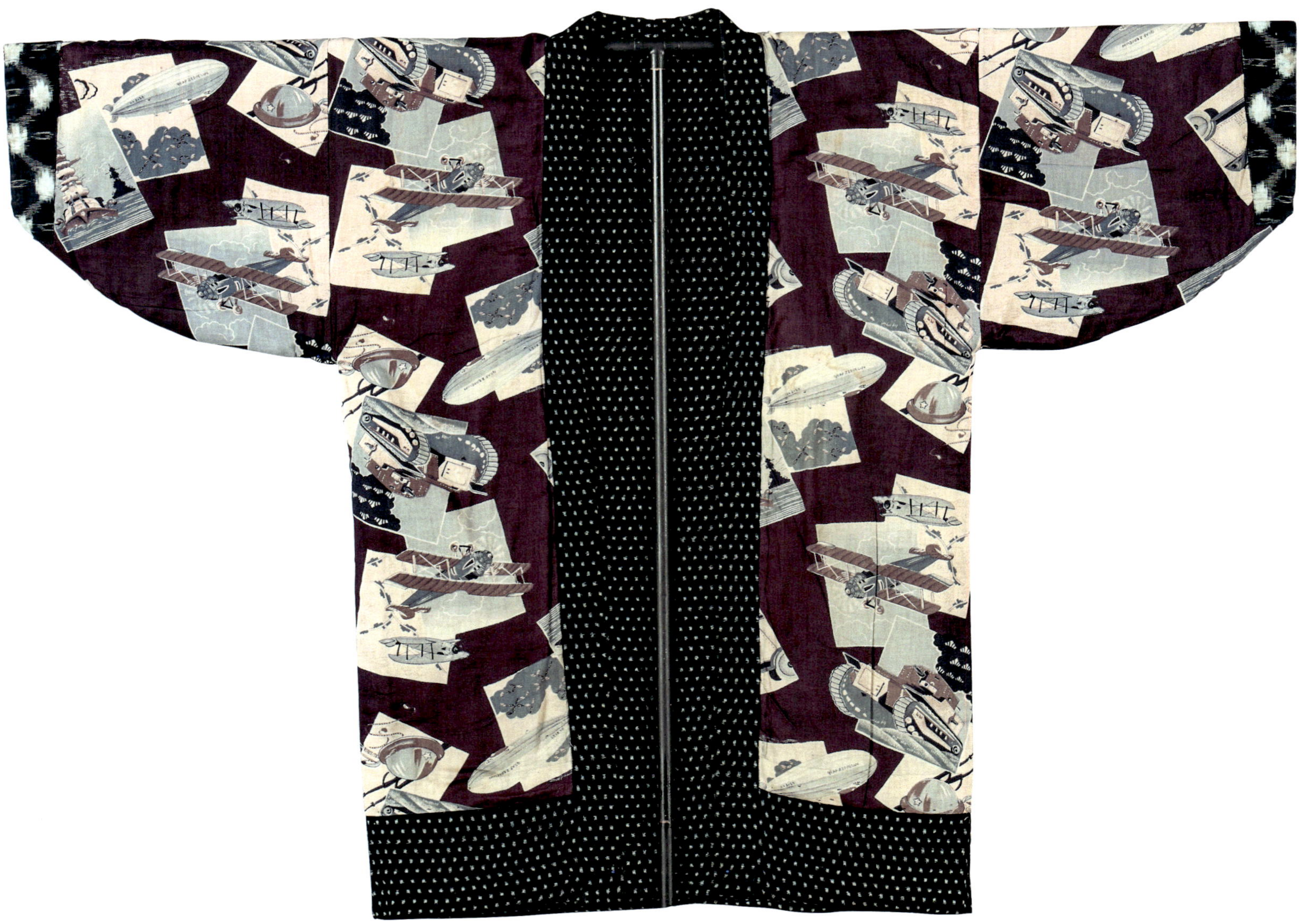

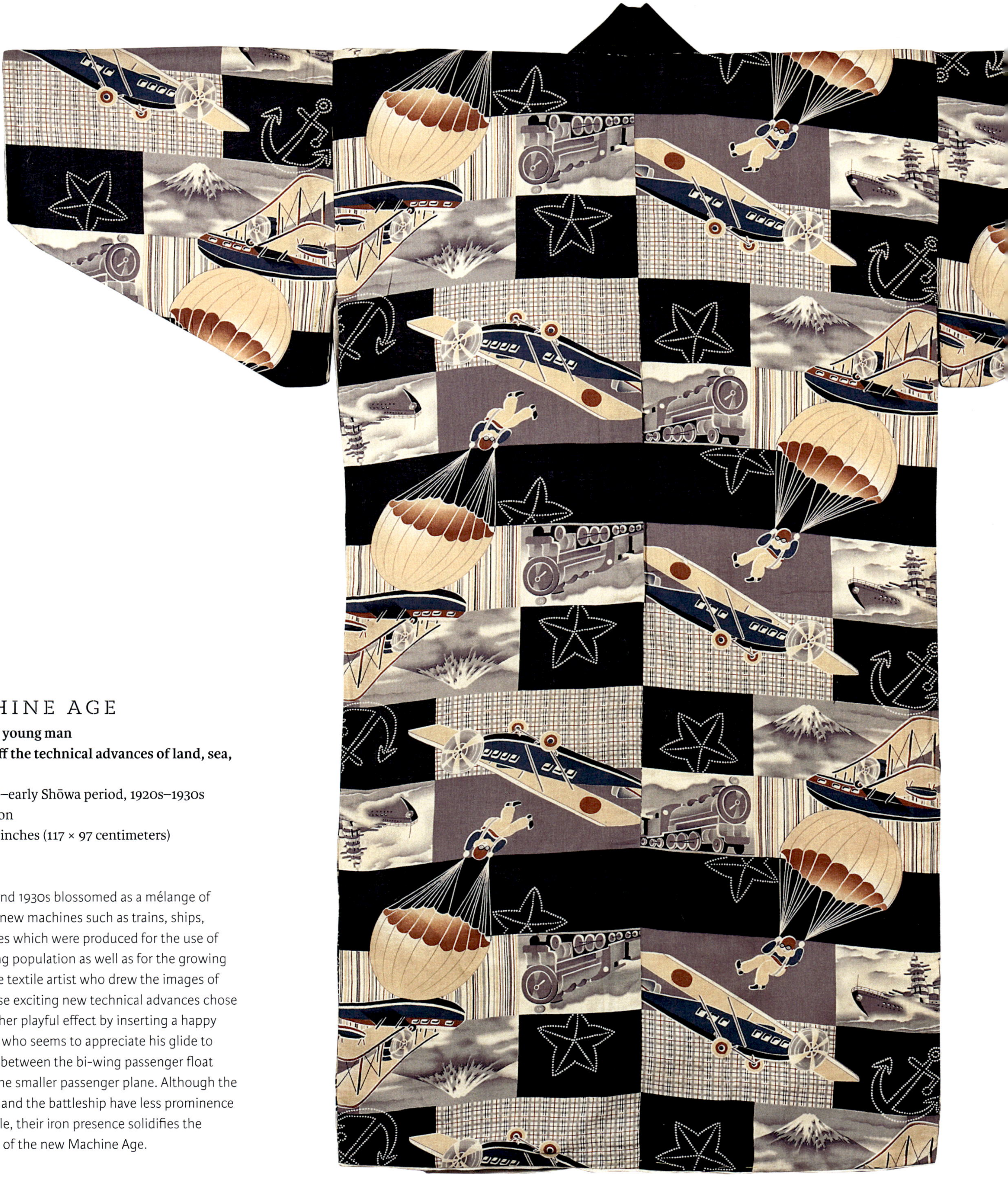

MACHINE AGE

Juban **for a young man**
Showing off the technical advances of land, sea, and sky
Late Taishō–early Shōwa period, 1920s–1930s
Printed rayon
46.0 × 38.0 inches (117 × 97 centimeters)
KM026

The 1920s and 1930s blossomed as a mélange of fascinating new machines such as trains, ships, and airplanes which were produced for the use of an increasing population as well as for the growing military. The textile artist who drew the images of each of these exciting new technical advances chose to add a rather playful effect by inserting a happy parachutist who seems to appreciate his glide to the ground between the bi-wing passenger float plane and the smaller passenger plane. Although the locomotive and the battleship have less prominence on the textile, their iron presence solidifies the importance of the new Machine Age.

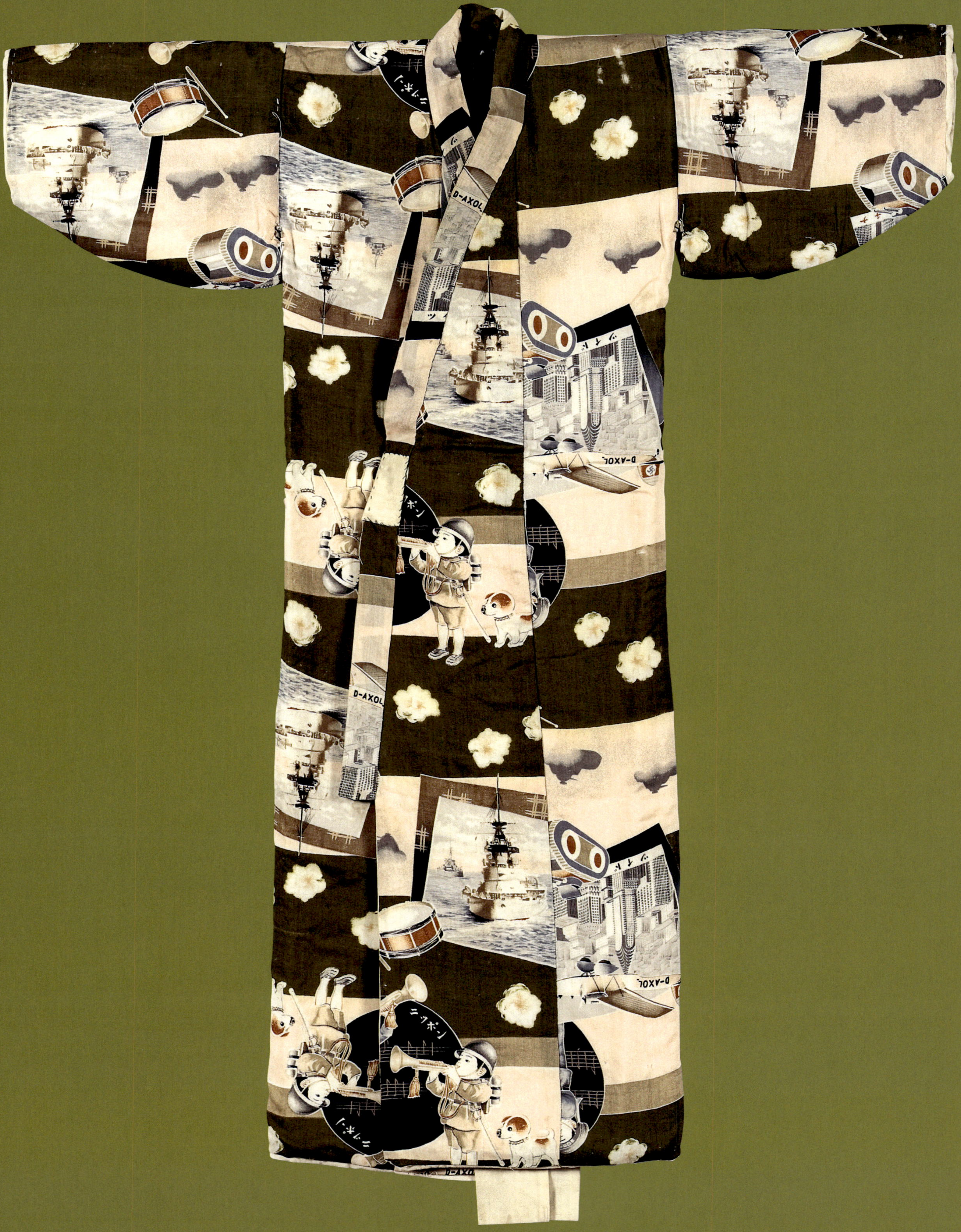

SENSŌGARA

Kimono for a boy child
Boys playing bugles as German airplanes fly about New York
Shōwa period, early 1940s
Printed wool muslin
39.5 × 33.0 inches (100 × 84 centimeters)
KM027

The designs on this little kimono are quite extraordinary. The main motif shows a German Dornier Luftwaffe warplane flying over the famous Chrysler Building in New York City. The plane has a Nazi swastika painted on its tail, and the Japanese characters written below the buildings say *Doitsu* (Germany). The design was probably intended to flaunt would-be victories by the Axis alliance formed by Germany, Italy, and Japan, although the artist's overly optimistic design incites only a patriotic song rather than reality. Another design shows two young buglers who are recognizable as stand-ins for Kiguchi Kohei, a young soldier who blew the battle call on his bugle even though he was mortally wounded during the 1894 Sino-Japanese war. The Japanese text next to the boys reads *Nippon* (Japan).

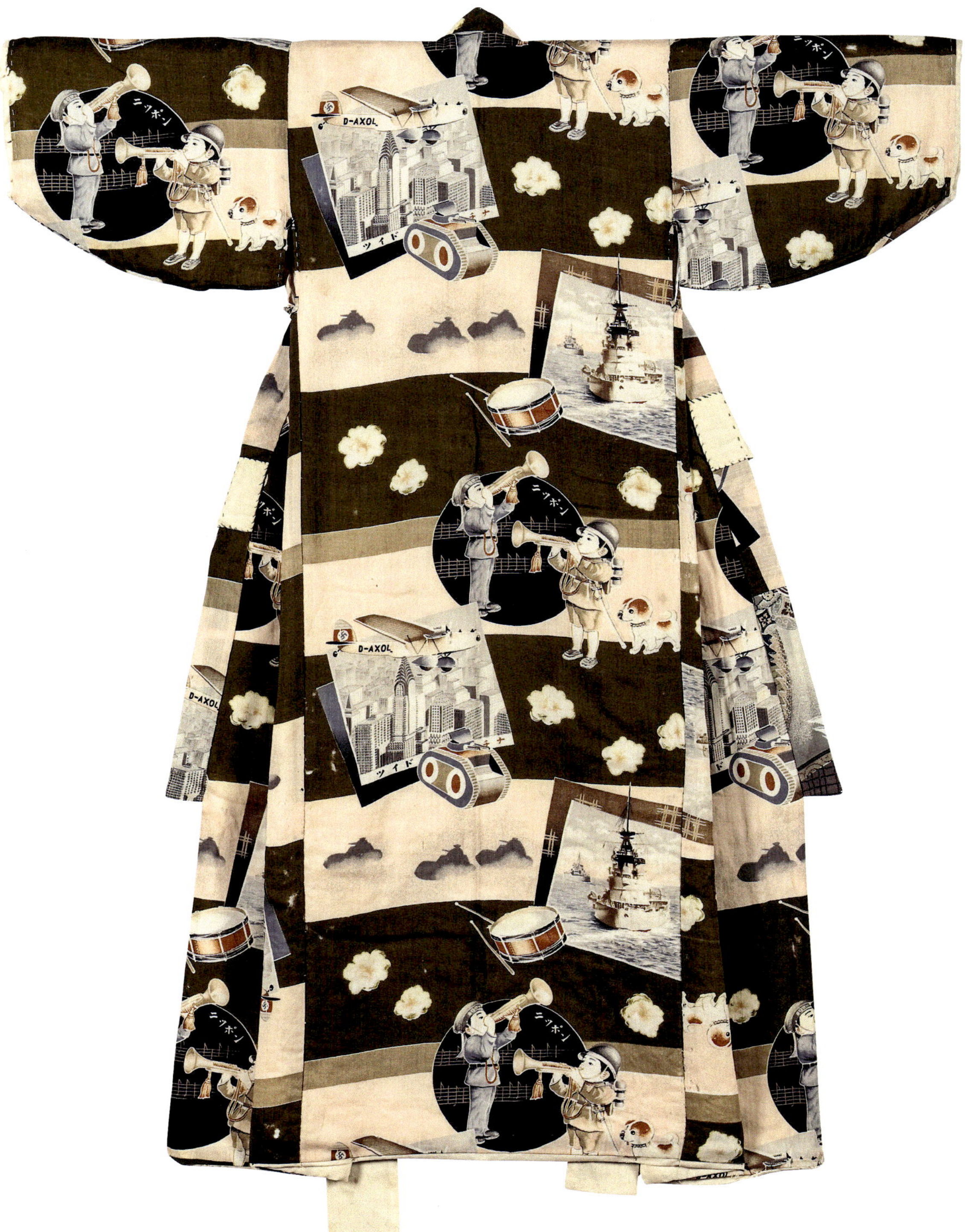

INTERNATIONALISM

Kimono for a boy child
Doves, airplanes, and flags
Early Shōwa period, 1937–1940
Printed silk
32.0 × 26.0 inches (81 × 66 centimeters)
KM028

At first glance, the appealing colors, motifs, and design of this infant's kimono seem to imply peace among nations, but a closer look raises questions. While the flags of Manchukuo and Japan, as well as that of the Kingdom of Italy, a Japanese ally, are all depicted more or less correctly, the American flag flies incorrectly with 56 stars instead of 48, and 14 stripes instead of 13; the French flag is depicted flying backward; and what might be the Dutch flag is depicted upside down. All three of these countries held territories in East Asia that were invaded by Japan in 1942.

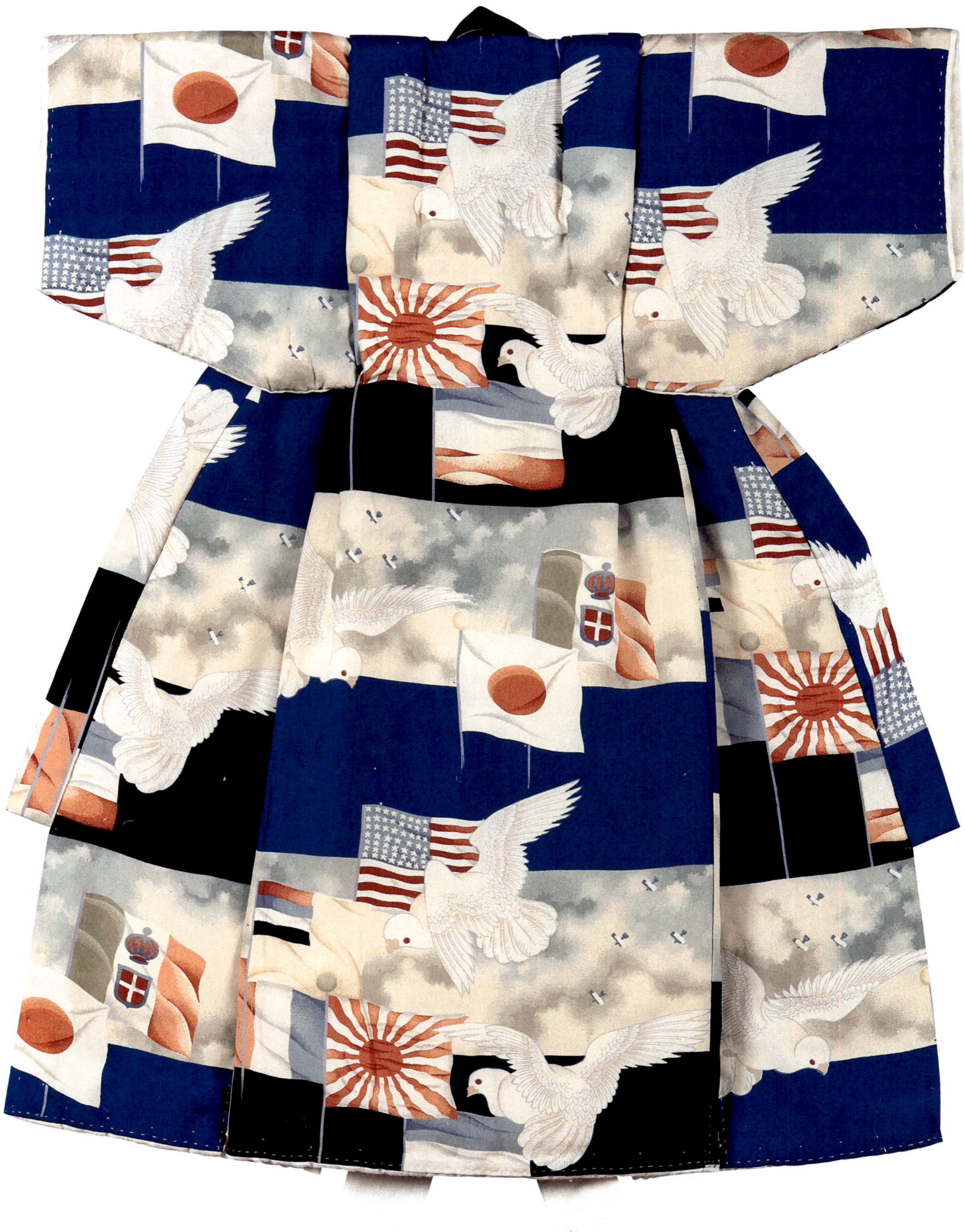

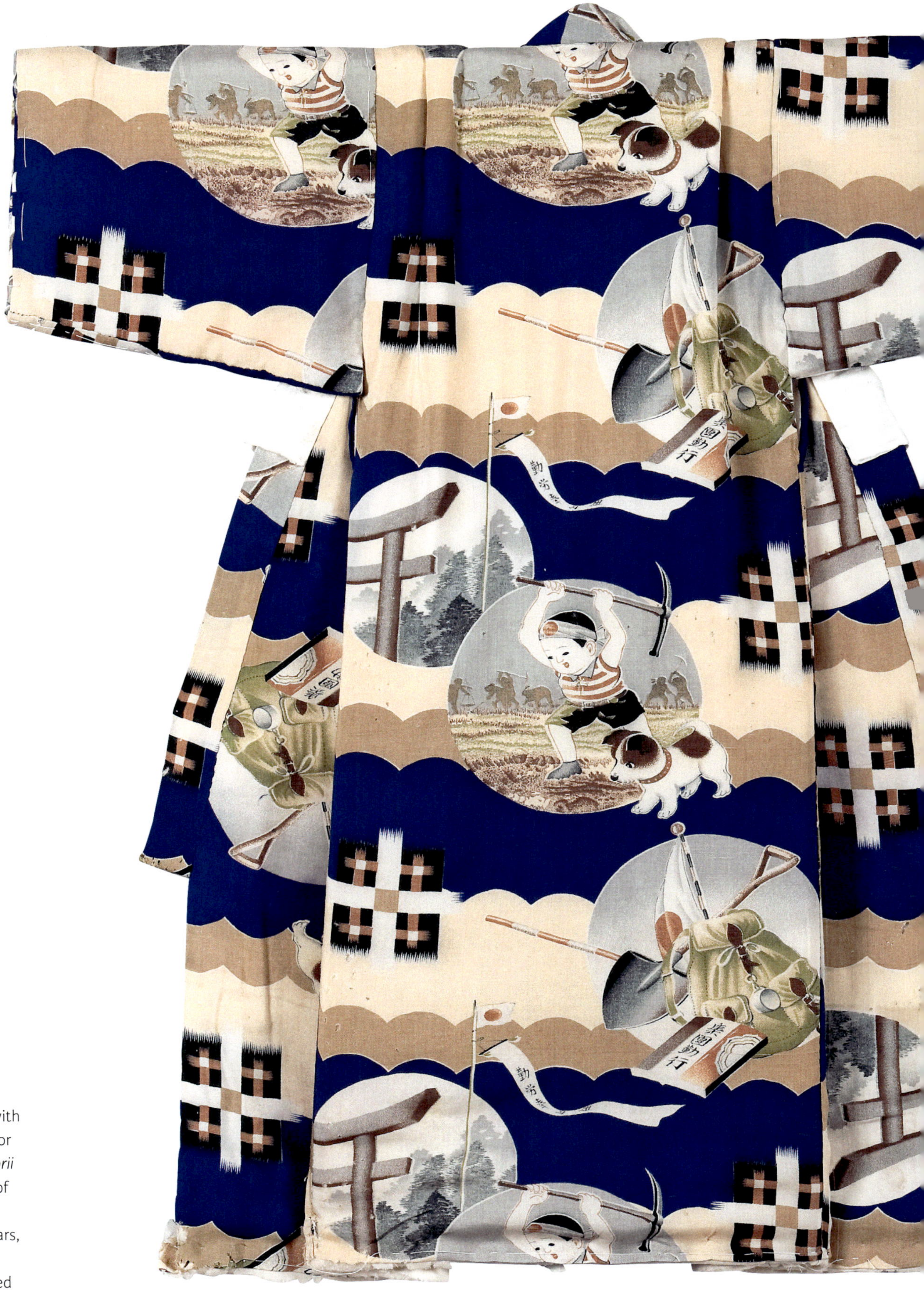

ARCHITECTURE/ ISE SHRINE

Kimono for a small boy
Boy working in a field
Shōwa period, 1930s–1940s
Printed silk
28.0 × 26.0 inches (71 × 66 centimeters)
KM029

This little kimono (*hitotsumi*) is for a small boy, with pleats stitched down at the shoulders to allow for his growth. Partially visible in one roundel is a *torii* gate, possibly that of the Ise Shrine, the center of Shintoism and the state religion of the time. The Ise Shrine is demolished and rebuilt every 20 years, and its completion was scheduled for 1933. This important textile design may have been produced shortly before the completion of the new shrine and used to encourage volunteers to help with the final work. The banner lifted in the breeze acknowledges the donation of labor, and adults are seen breaking ground in the background. The young boy at the forefront of the design is making his own contribution to the shrine by his hard work.

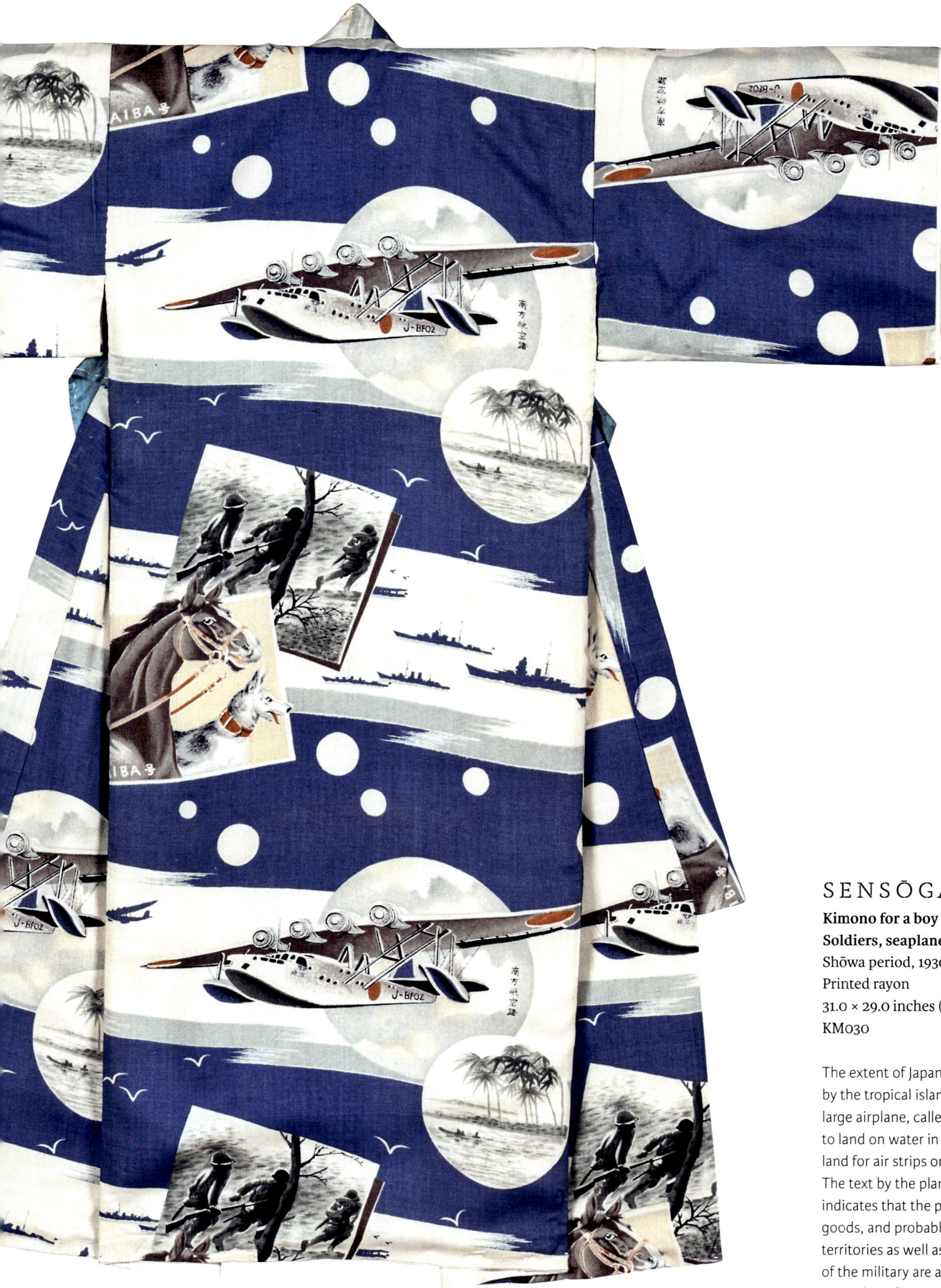

SENSŌGARA/TRAVEL

Kimono for a boy child
Soldiers, seaplanes, horses, and army dogs
Shōwa period, 1930s–1940s
Printed rayon
31.0 × 29.0 inches (79 × 74 centimeters)
KM030

The extent of Japan's territorial conquests is indicated by the tropical island designed for this textile. The large airplane, called a "flying boat," was designed to land on water in response to the lack of adequate land for air strips on the colonized Pacific islands. The text by the plane reads "Southern Air Route" and indicates that the plane carries passengers as well as goods, and probably shuttles between the Japanese territories as well as Japan's major cities. Many aspects of the military are also depicted in this garment: land, air, and sea forces, as well as the canine corps and cavalry. The hard work of the soldiers is also underscored.

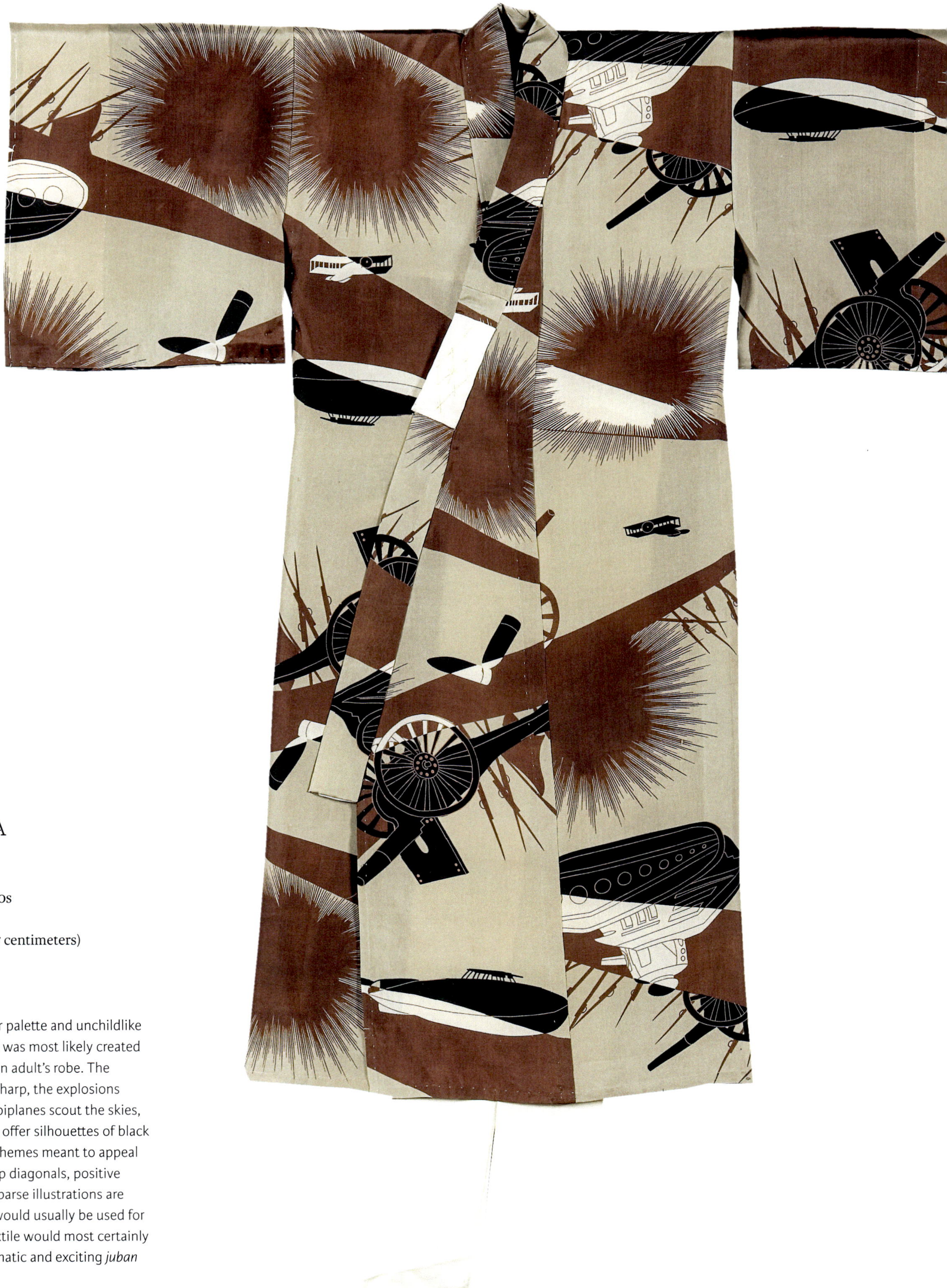

SENSŌGARA

Kimono for a small boy
On the field of battle
Shōwa period, 1930s–1940s
Printed silk
31.0 × 30.5 inches (79 × 77 centimeters)
KM031

Given its very limited color palette and unchildlike design, this little *hitotsumi* was most likely created from leftover fabric from an adult's robe. The silhouetted bayonets are sharp, the explosions enormous, dirigibles and biplanes scout the skies, and the tanks and cannon offer silhouettes of black and brown, not colors or themes meant to appeal to a young child. The sharp diagonals, positive and negative space, and sparse illustrations are more sophisticated than would usually be used for childrenswear, but this textile would most certainly have produced a very dramatic and exciting *juban* for a man.

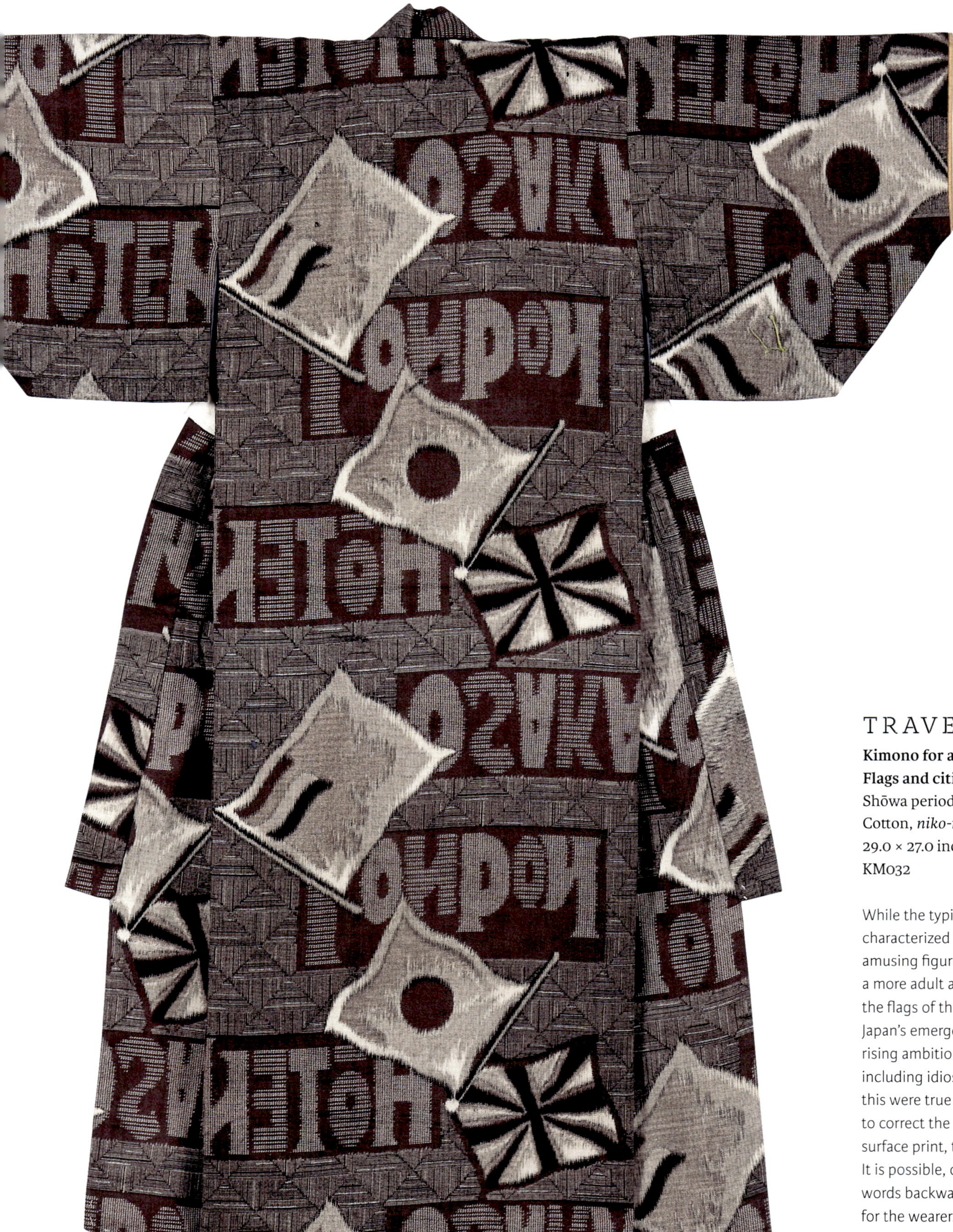

TRAVEL

Kimono for a boy child
Flags and cities (Osaka, London, and Hōten)
Shōwa period, 1930s
Cotton, *niko-niko kasuri*
29.0 × 27.0 inches (74 × 69 centimeters)
KM032

While the typical *niko-niko kasuri* kimono is characterized by medium-sized checks overlaid with amusing figures at regular intervals, this design takes a more adult approach. Three cities are named, with the flags of their respective countries—a reference to Japan's emergence as an international power and its rising ambitions. The design has several anomalies, including idiosyncratic typography and spelling. If this were true *kasuri*, the material could be reversed to correct the writing order, but since *niko-niko* is a surface print, the reverse side of the material is blank. It is possible, of course, that the designer wrote some words backward on purpose, as a playful puzzle for the wearer. There is both novelty and status in commercial use of the Western alphabet in keeping with the drive toward modernization and Westernization, although with occasionally unexpected results.

MACHINE AGE

Kimono for a boy child
Airplanes and helicopters
Shōwa period, 1940s–1950
Cotton, *niko-niko kasuri*
33.0 × 32.0 inches (84 × 81 centimeters)
KM033

Complex traditional Japanese *e-gasuri* ("picture ikat") patterns were once crafted painstakingly by hand, and designs were limited in color and location by the time-consuming process. Once roller printing was introduced, it was possible to mimic the look of *e-gasuri* while speeding up the process and considerably lowering costs. This process was called *niko-niko* ("smile," or "giggle") *kasuri*, and the designs—muted colors, superimposed motifs, and often a checkerboard background—were popular for many years. The printing process allowed for any number of design variations to be brought quickly to market. The near-random placement of airplanes and helicopters on the checkered pattern of this kimono is an important clue that the design was printed and not woven, and offers a pattern that young boys would find very amusing.

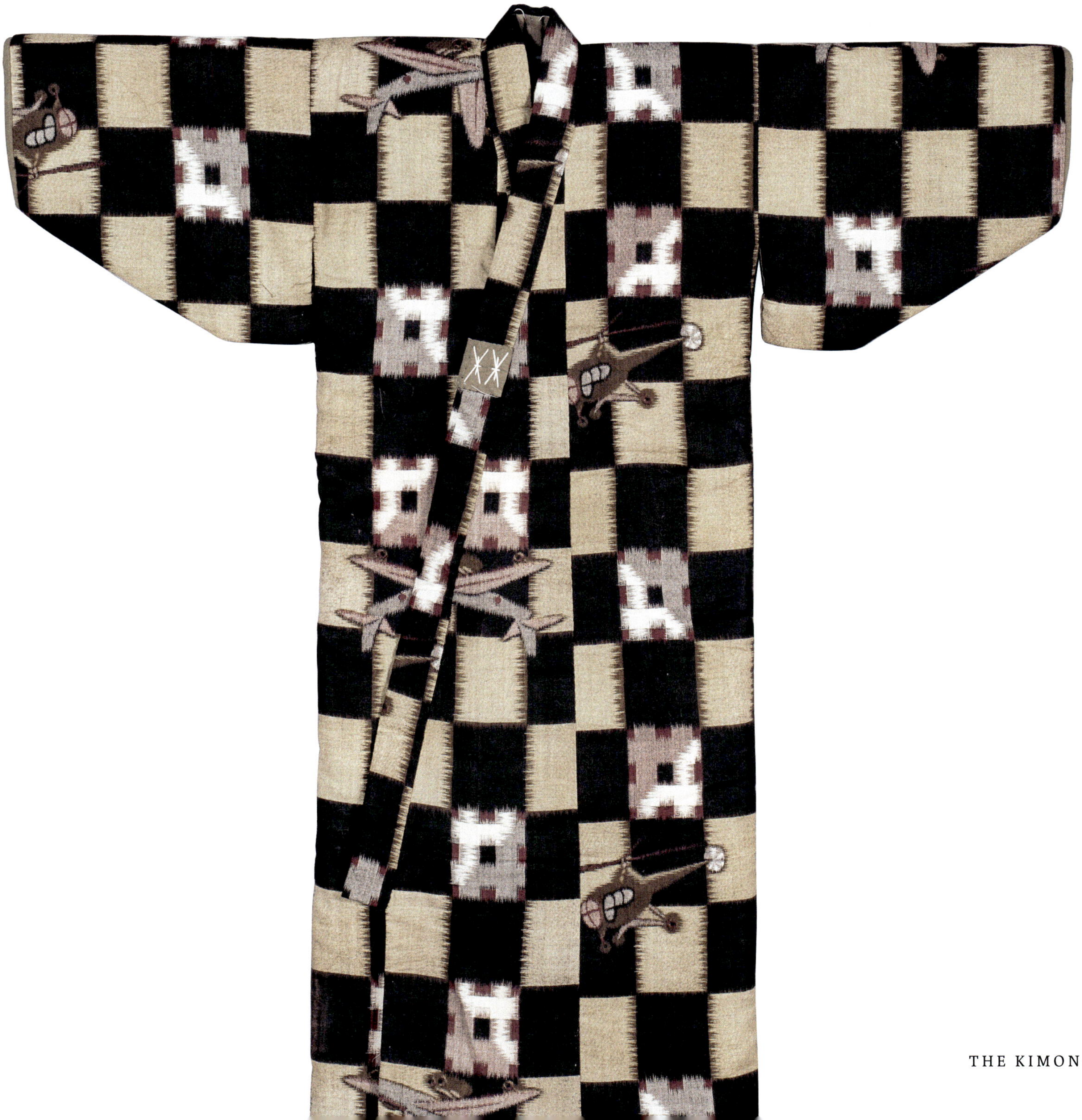

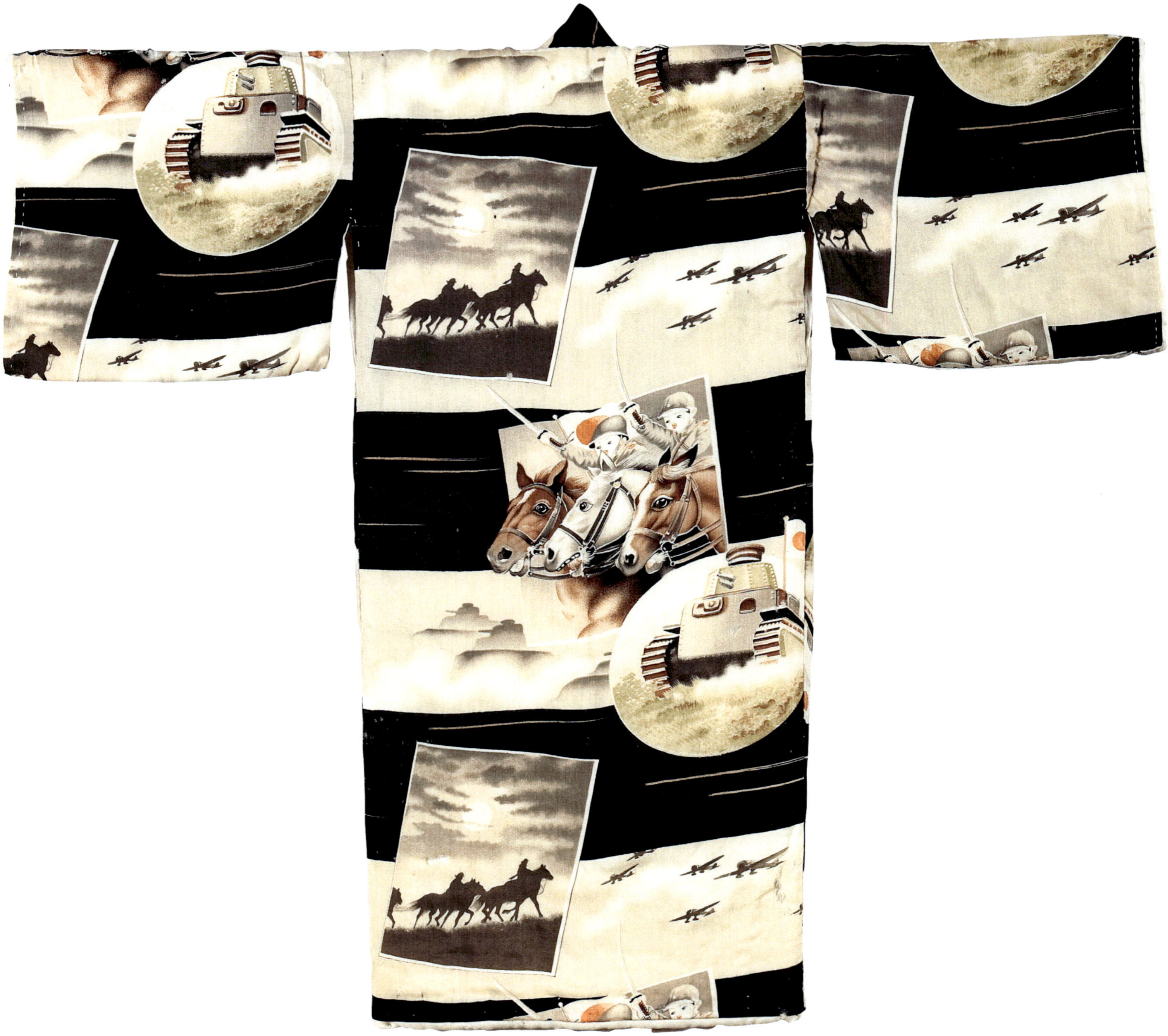

SENSŌGARA

Kimono for a child
Cavalry, tanks, and planes
Shōwa period, 1930s–early 1940s
Printed rayon
28.0 × 24.0 inches (71 × 61 centimeters)
KM034

The designer for this textile employed several artistic techniques to make images of war relatable for children, foremost by placing uniformed children on charging horses in the only illustration squarely in the center of the material. On a kimono of predominantly muted colors, this illustration is the most vibrant, and of all the subjects, is closest to the viewer. After horses were found to be unsuited to military service in China, the cavalry still played a small role in the war, possibly because historic images of samurai on brilliantly outfitted horses contributed to their continued depiction in modern warfare.

SENSŌGARA

***Miyamairi* (boy child's kimono for his first shrine visit)**
Victory celebration
Shōwa period, 1930s–1940s
Hand-painted silk *yūzen*, couched gold
36.0 × 32.0 inches (91 × 81 centimeters)
KM035

Miyamairi often depict images of legendary Japanese heroes at their most shining moments. This *miyamairi*, however, represents a contemporary soldier and his horse—a very dramatic image. The fortress in the background is a Chinese stronghold, the prize of the soldiers, and their arms are uplifted in a gesture of victory as they shout "Banzai" ("Ten thousand years!"). Many *miyamairi* designs are printed, but this one was probably a custom order for a baby boy for his first shrine visit. It is carefully hand-painted, with a wealth of thoughtful details, such as the bright couched metal threads that outline the soldiers' helmets. This garment also sports five *mon* (family crests), two on the front, three on the back. The family used the simple but elegant shape of wood sorrel (*katabami*) for their *mon*.

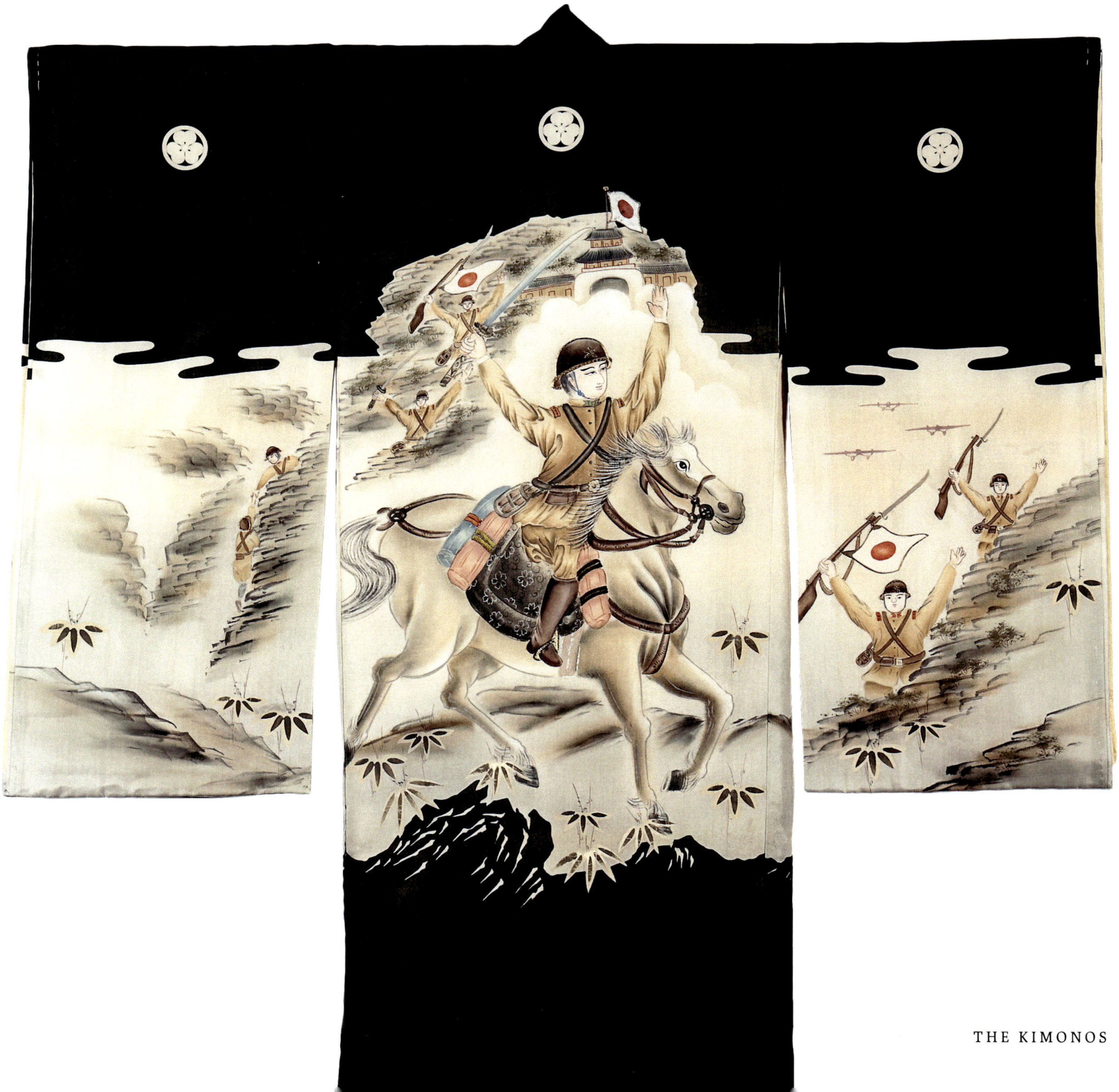

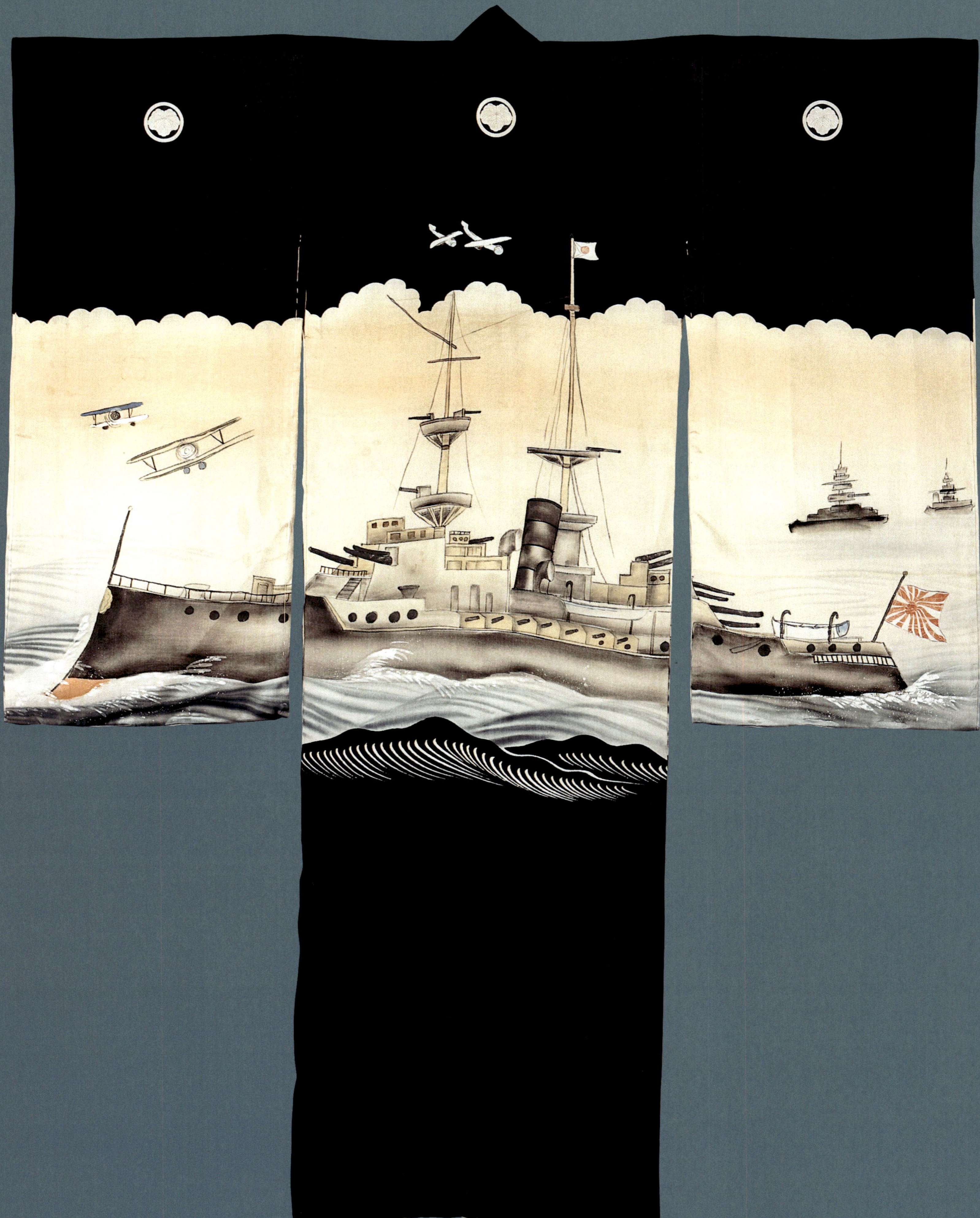

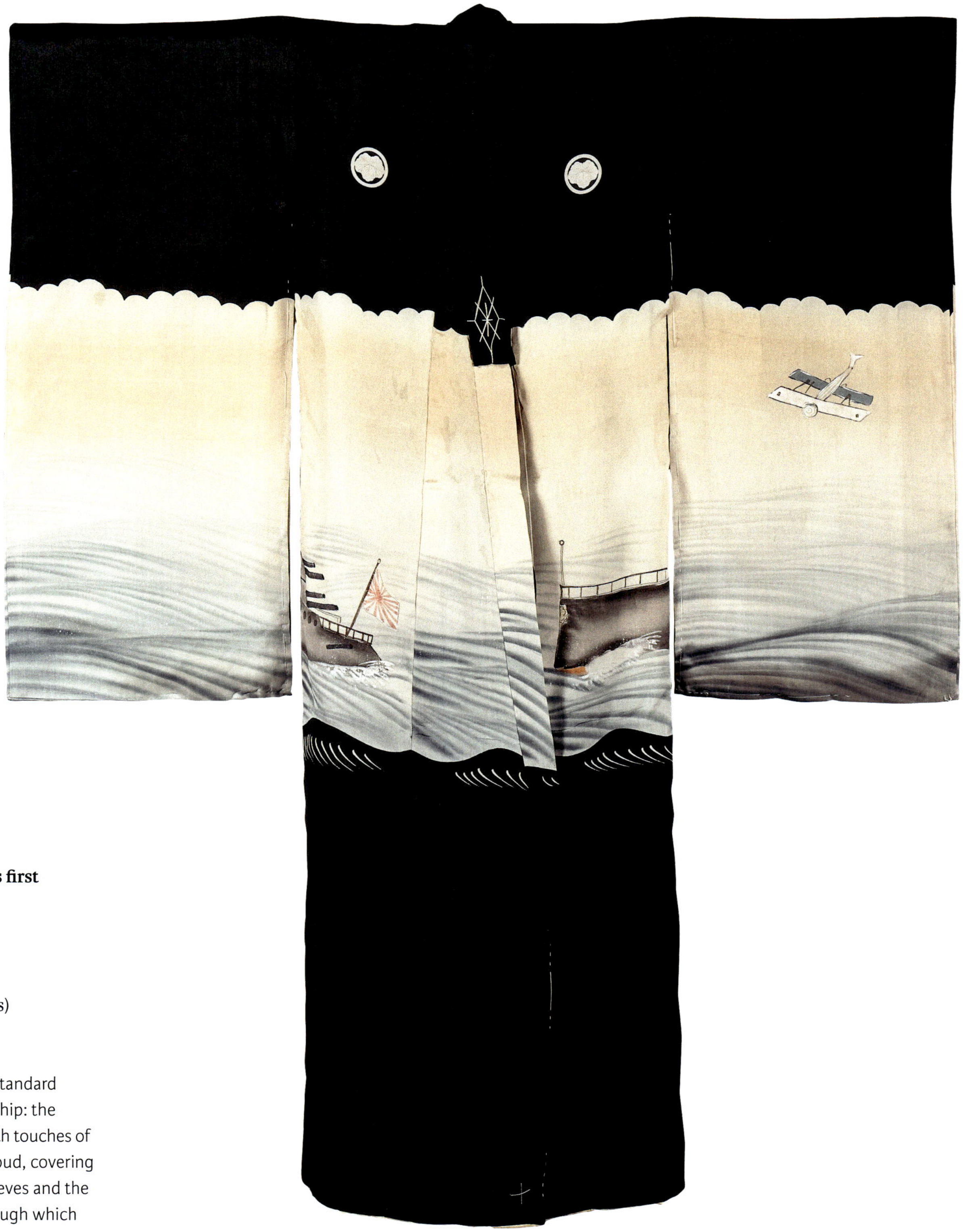

SENSŌGARA

Miyamairi **(boy child's kimono for his first shrine visit)**
Large battleship and airplanes
Taishō–Shōwa period, 1910s–1930s
Hand-painted silk
40.5 × 33.0 inches (103 × 84 centimeters)
KM036

This boy's formal *miyamairi* has several standard features used for a depiction of a battleship: the illusion of clouds, the foaming waters with touches of white paint, and the ship that stands proud, covering the back panel that runs across both sleeves and the center back. This is the main object through which the parents express their wishes for their child: filial piety, moral fortitude, strength, loyalty, and courage. The timing for this *miyamairi* is a bit of a puzzle, however, as the ship is representative of the Russo-Japanese War (1904–05), but the aircraft call for World War I or later. The Japanese flag flies on the highest mast and the military flag at the rear hints at a more peaceful period, so the design may have been chosen simply because the boy was from a naval family.

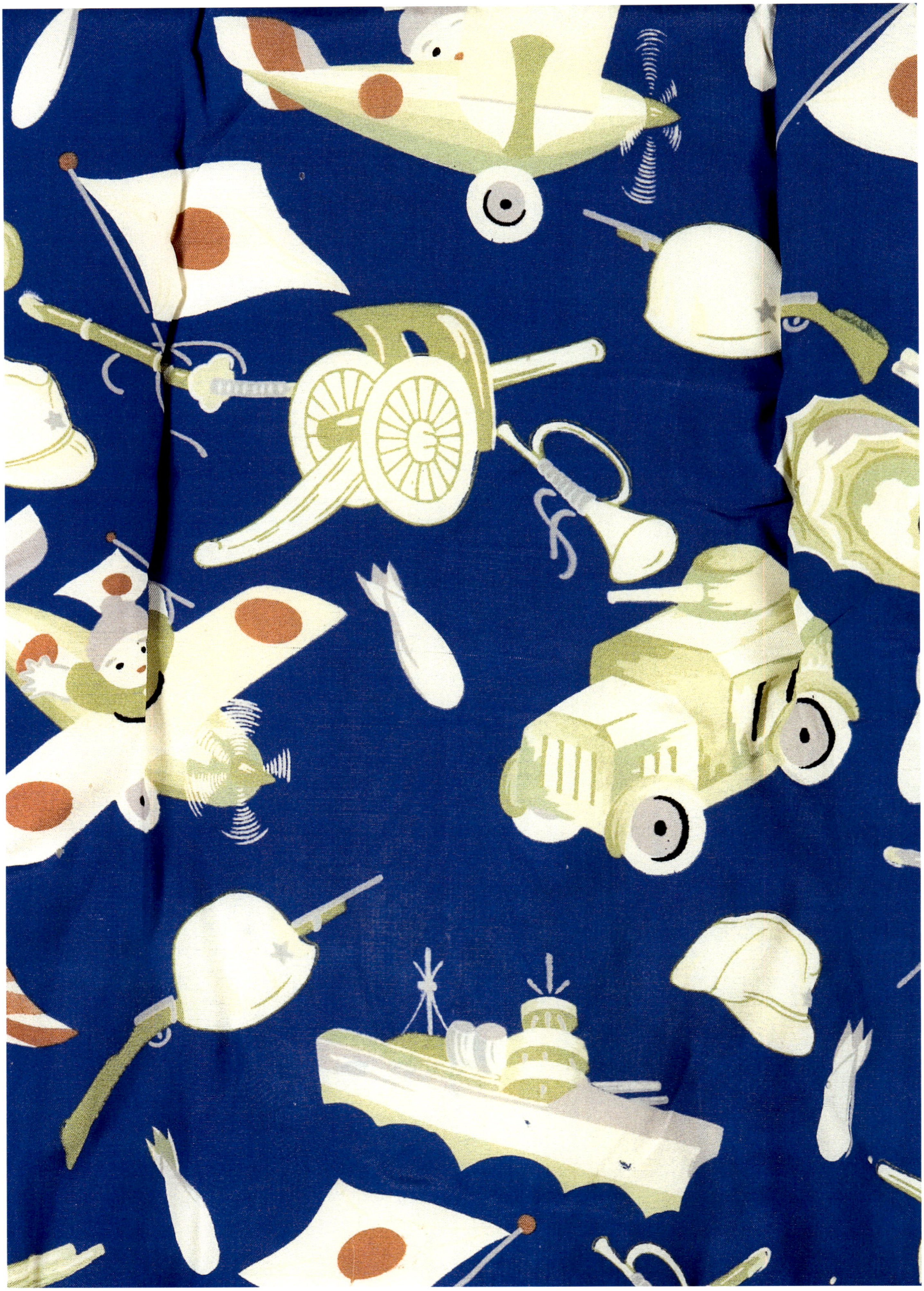

SENSŌGARA

Kimono for a boy child
Playful military toys
Taishō–Shōwa period, 1930s–1940s
Printed silk
27.0 × 25.0 inches (69 × 64 centimeters)
KM037

In Japanese design there is a traditional pattern called *takarazukushi* (a plethora of treasures) that consists of images of the seven Buddhist treasures that signify wealth and good fortune, scattered randomly across the fabric. In this little kimono, the predominant *sensōgara* mood of the time is reflected as the traditional treasures have been replaced by playful military-themed toys (tanks, airplanes, ships, cannon, bugles, and armored cars) that little boys might covet. Note that the kimono has been folded over and stitched down at the back shoulders and the waist; these seams can be let out later so the child can continue to wear it as he grows.

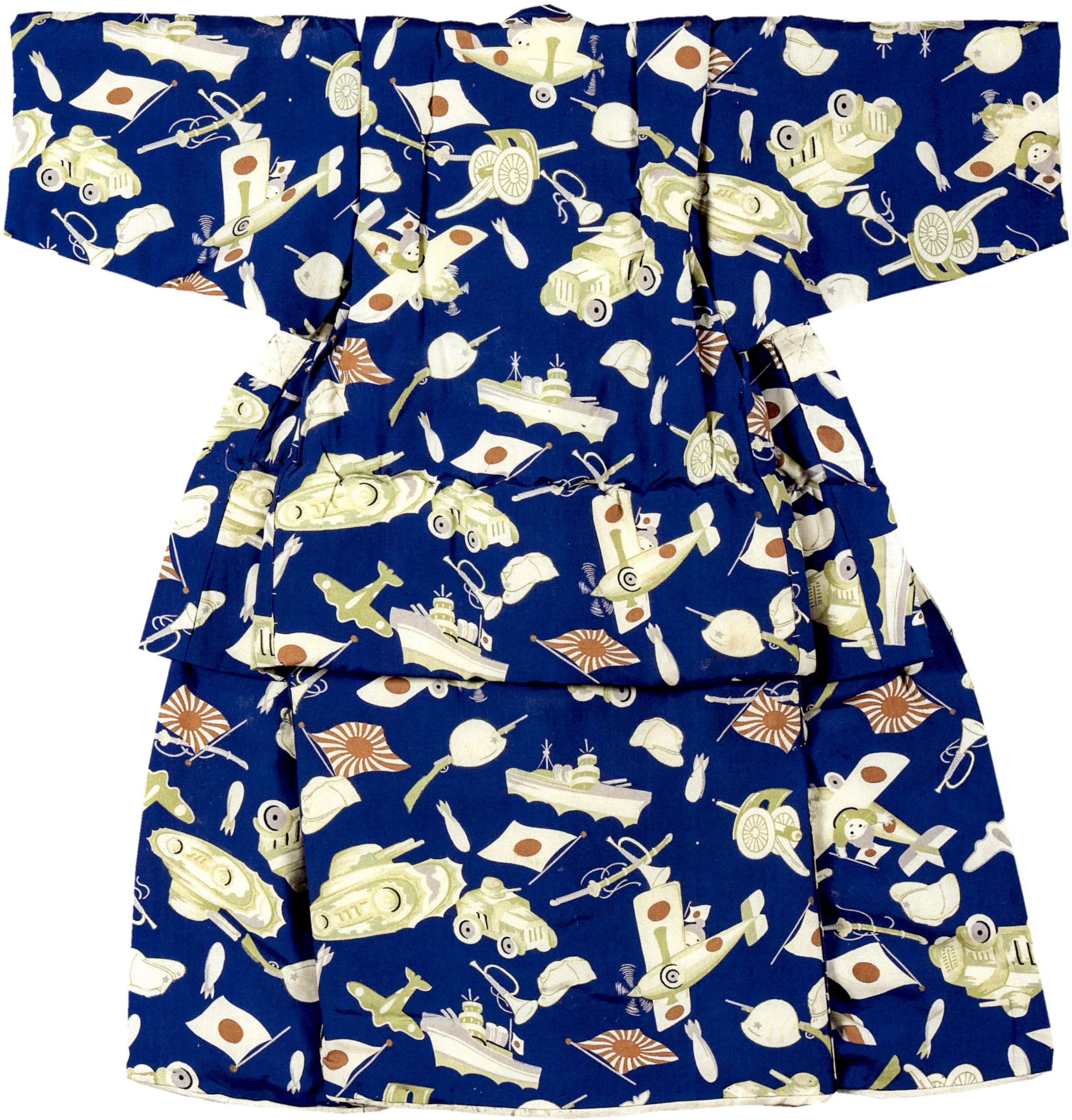

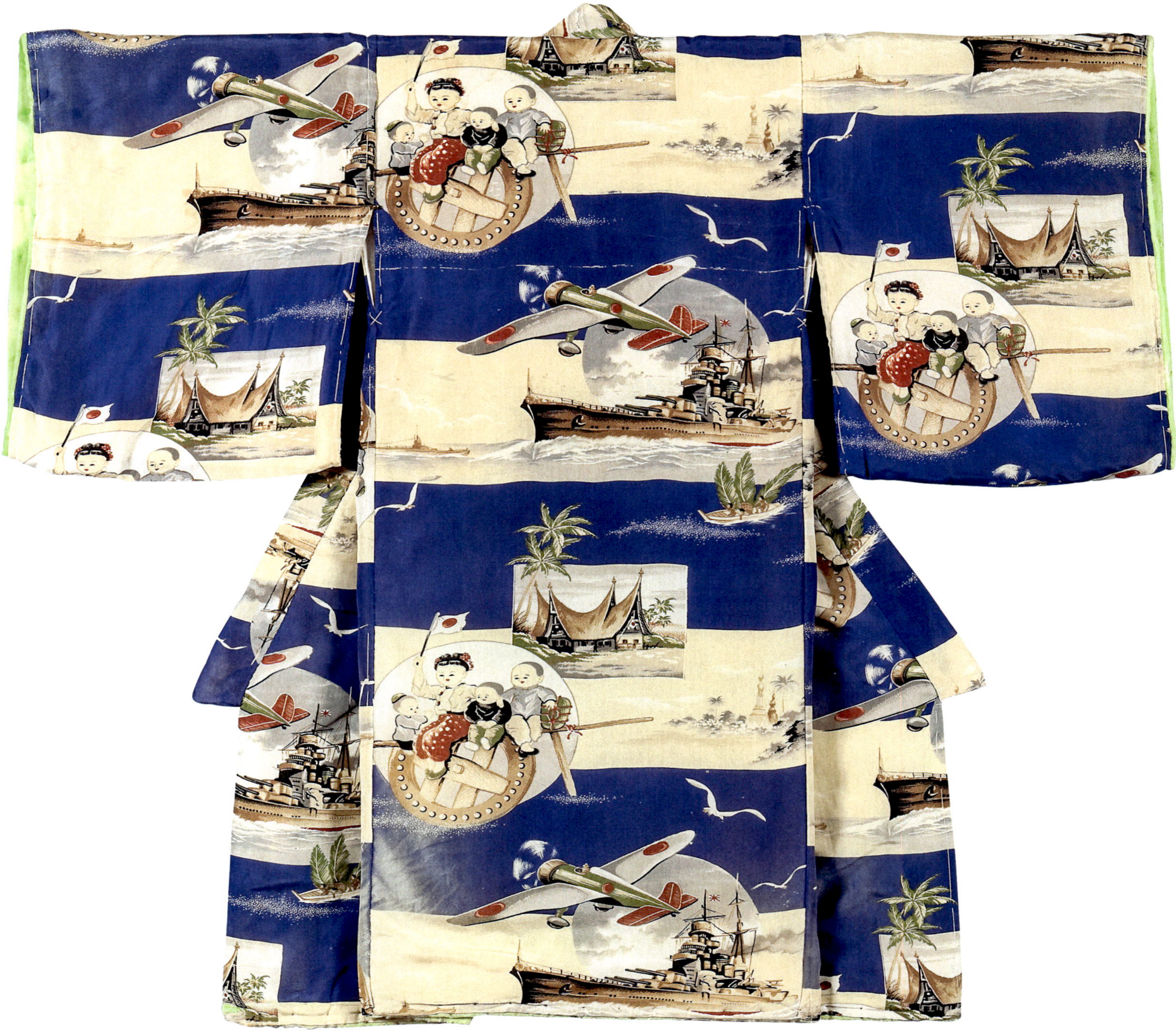

SENSŌGARA

Child's kimono
Children sitting on an ox cart wheel
Shōwa period, early 1940s
Printed silk
32.0 × 31.0 inches (81 × 79 centimeters)
KM038

This kimono reads almost like a pictorial summary of the Japanese occupation of Southeast Asia in 1941 and 1942. The structure with pointed roof tops might indicate Malaya, which the Japanese invaded in 1941. To the right of that are two Buddhist stupas and Japanese army tanks, an image that probably depicts the invasion of Burma, also in 1941. The large roundel on the left shows four indigenous children perched on the wheel of an ox cart; the girl waves a Japanese flag to welcome the Japanese military. These scenes are juxtaposed against modern Japanese ships and planes of the time, implying that the occupied territory will benefit from Japanese leadership.

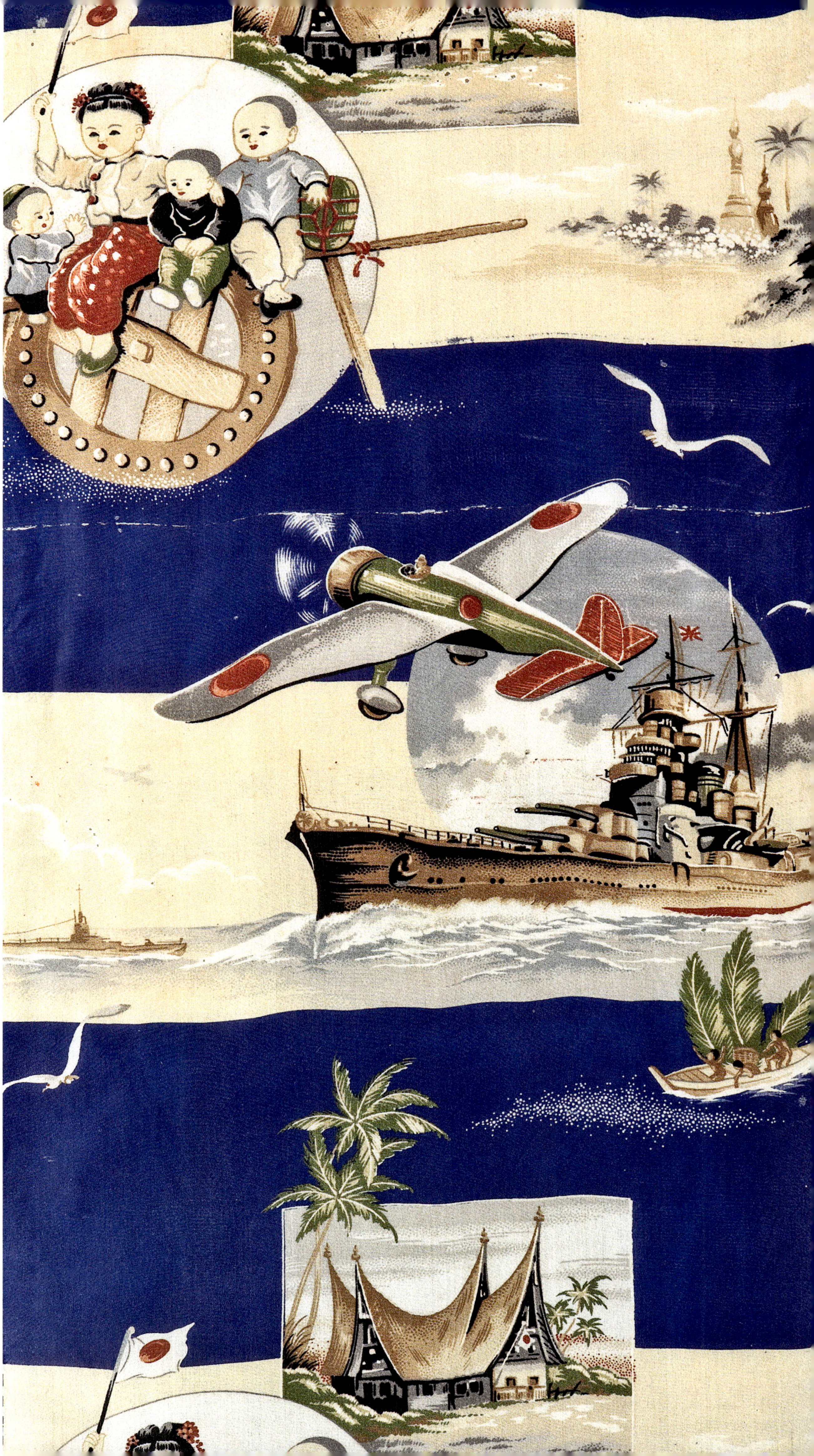

SENSŌGARA

Man's *haori* with a decorative lining (*haura*)
Lonely soldier dreaming of home
Early Shōwa period, 1931–1945
Silk plain-weave *haori* (outer); *haura* (lining) with satin silk and woven silk brocade with decorative gold and silver thread
53.0 × 43.0 inches (135 × 109 centimeters)
KM039

This design captures a single soldier assigned to guard duty on a quiet winter night. The soldier stands guard, but the background of the mountains of China brings poignant memories of the majestic Mount Fuji of his home and family in Japan. A small bush nearby carries early *ume* (plum blossoms) and is another nostalgic memory of home. The heavy satin silk of the *haura* sets the base for the woven twill that gives character and drama to the design as a whole.

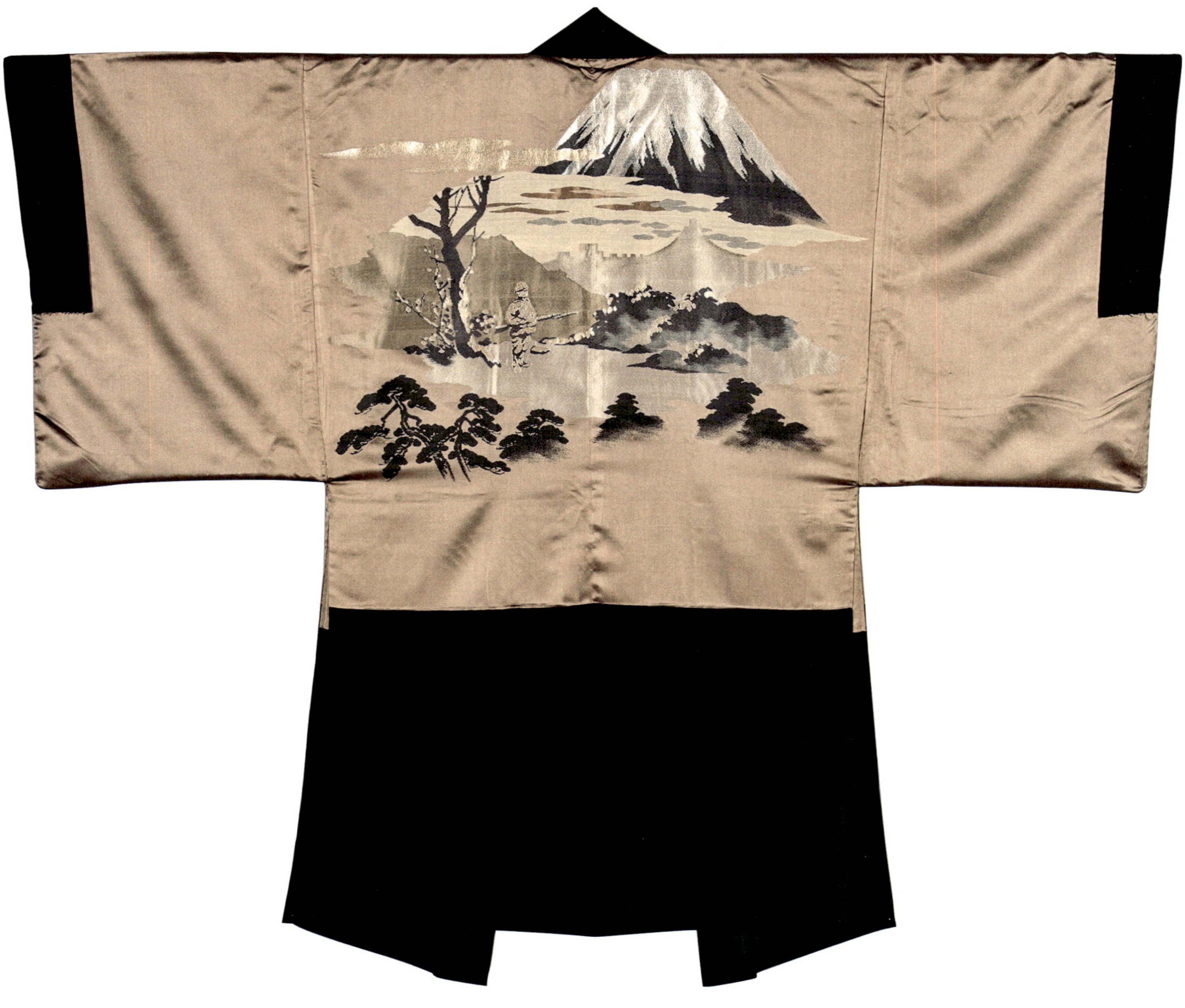

SENSŌGARA

***Juban* for a man**
Soldiers crossing a river at night
Shōwa period, 1930s–1940s
Hand-painted *shibori* silk
52.0 × 50.0 inches (132 × 127 centimeters)
KM040

A delicate mauve silk provides the background for soldiers slipping from their boats to prepare a surprise raid on the Chinese buildings above them. The soldiers, buildings, and brush are hand-painted with great care, as is the light-colored boat at the right. The soldier carefully walks at the boat's bow to guide it to shore. The heavy-looking black and white *shibori* boat is a very unusual design, an anomaly that seems out of context with the other boat, but the designer does not offer more information.

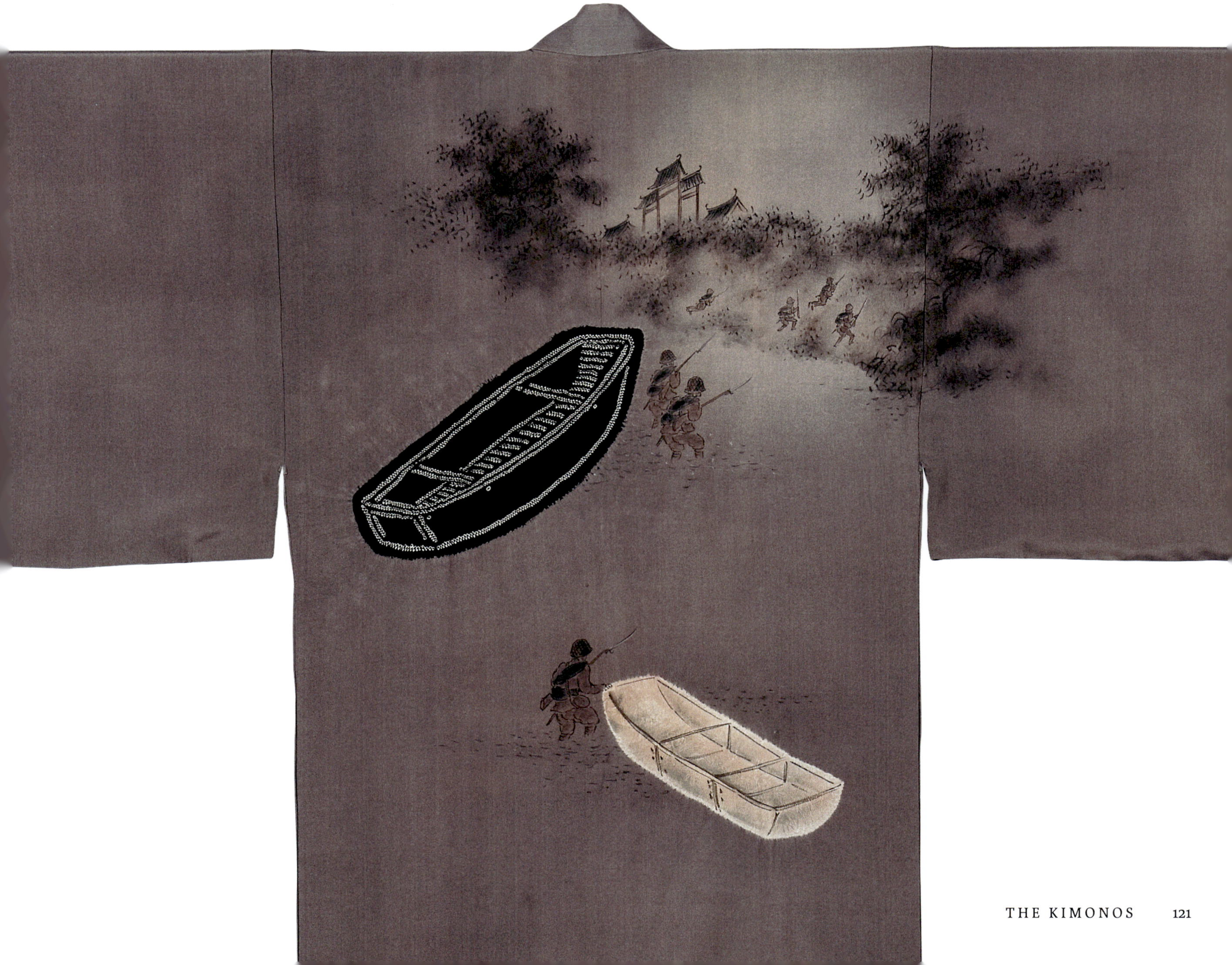

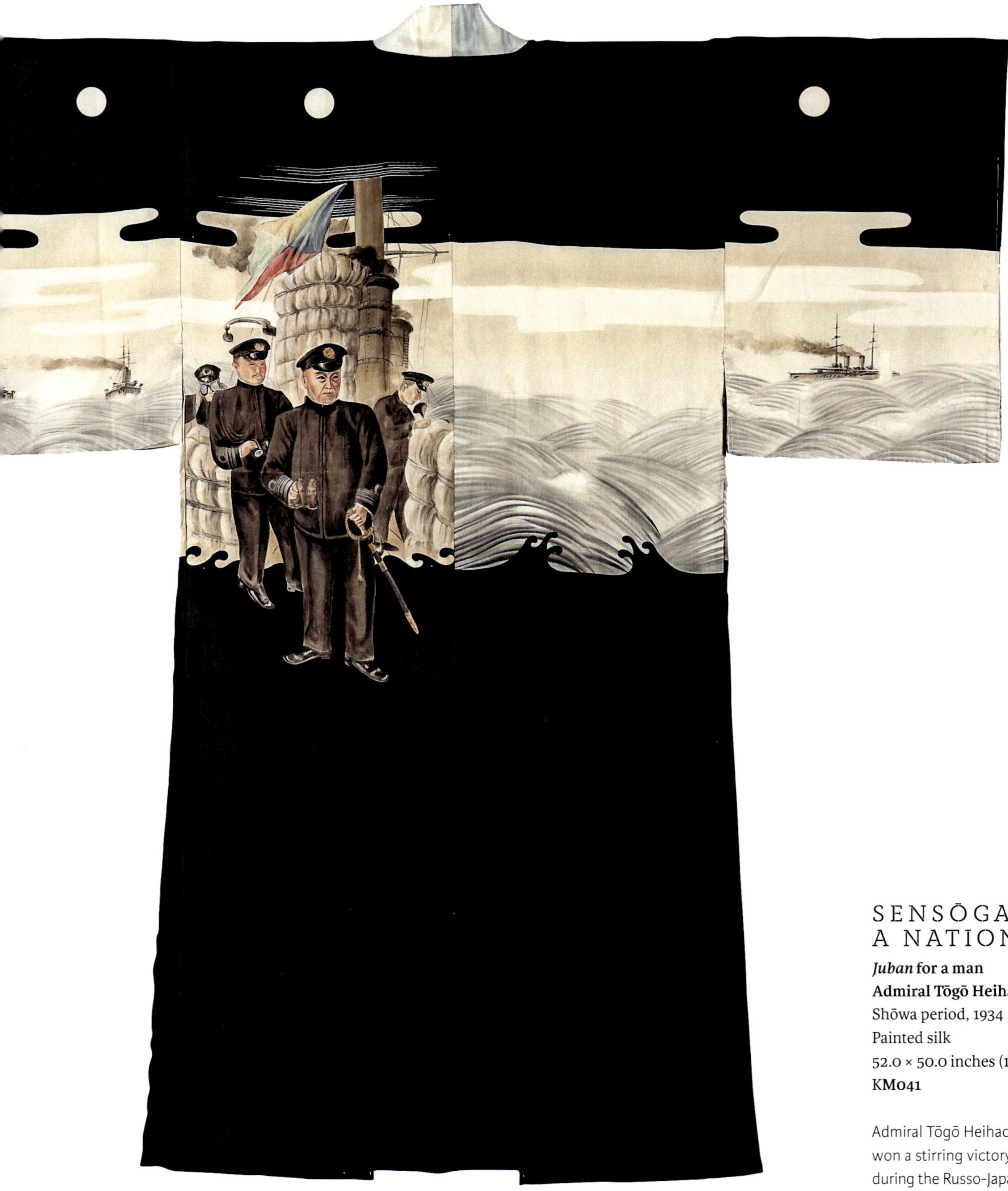

SENSŌGARA/ A NATIONAL HERO

***Juban* for a man**
Admiral Tōgō Heihachirō, a national hero
Shōwa period, 1934
Painted silk
52.0 × 50.0 inches (132 × 127 centimeters)
KM041

Admiral Tōgō Heihachirō was a national hero who won a stirring victory over the Russian Baltic Fleet during the Russo-Japanese War in 1904–05. He was a model of bravery and dedication to his mission, and when he died in 1934 his loss was widely mourned. Many special-order designs were produced in his memory, showing the admiral on the *Mikasa*, his flagship, just before the decisive Battle of Tsushima. The design was based on a painting done in 1906 and reproduced over the years in honor of Admiral Tōgō, and this *juban* was undoubtedly produced for just such a design. It may never have been purchased, however, as the white circles would have been painted with the family crest after the *juban* was bought.

SENSŌGARA

Boy's *haregi* (kimono used for special events)
Samurai and soldiers
Early Shōwa period, 1930s–1940s
Printed silk
33.0 × 33.0 inches (84 × 84 centimeters)
KM042

The message on this young boy's *haregi* is wonderfully conceived and dramatically delivered. This formal kimono carefully blends traditional and contemporary military imagery to express continuity between ancient samurai and the modern soldier. The weapons and strategies have changed, but the valor of the 20th-century soldier is as formidable as the bravery of any historical samurai; both groups are infused with *yamato damashii*, or Japanese spirit. The two groups are positioned above and below, facing in opposite directions, and each following a commander, a design that provides excellent thematic and visual balance.

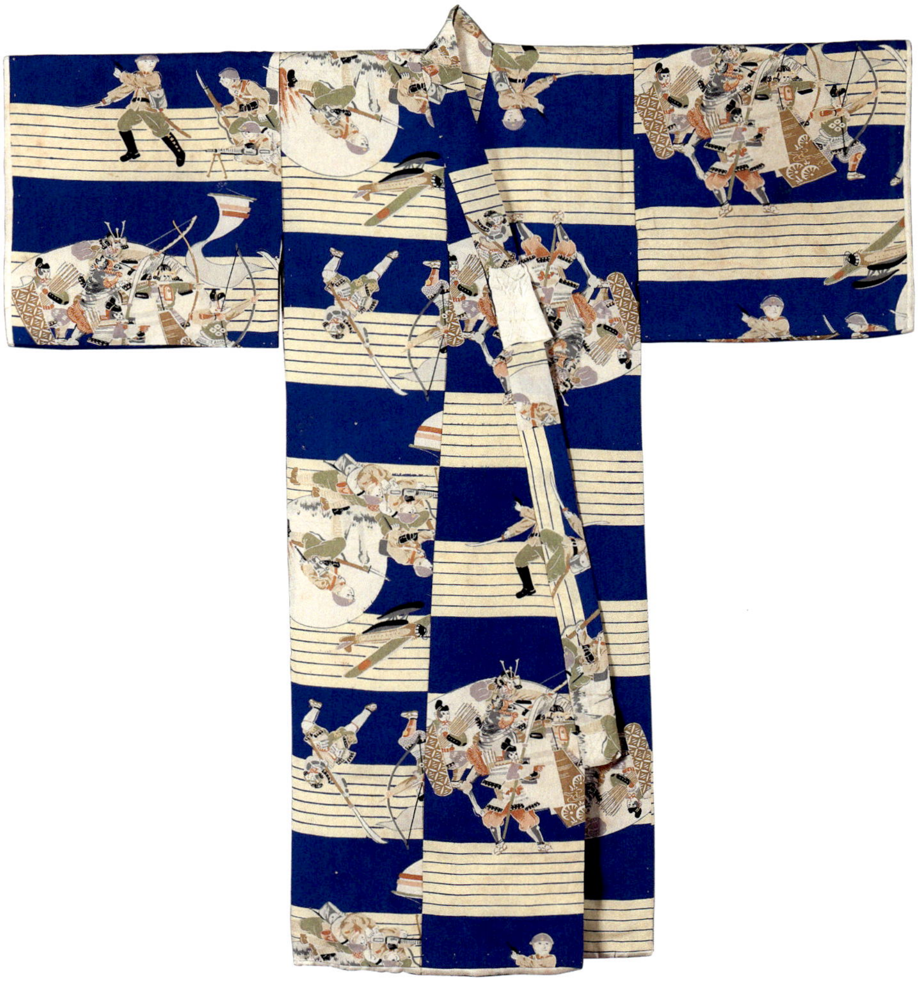

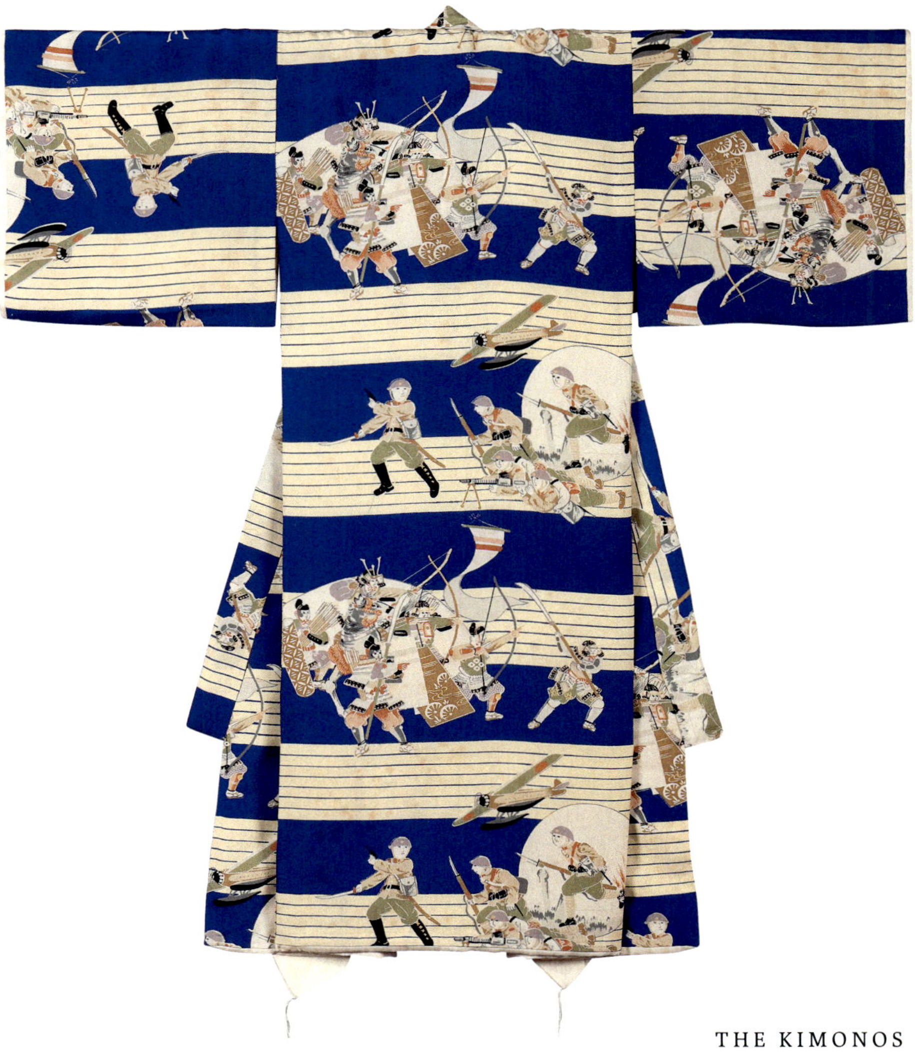

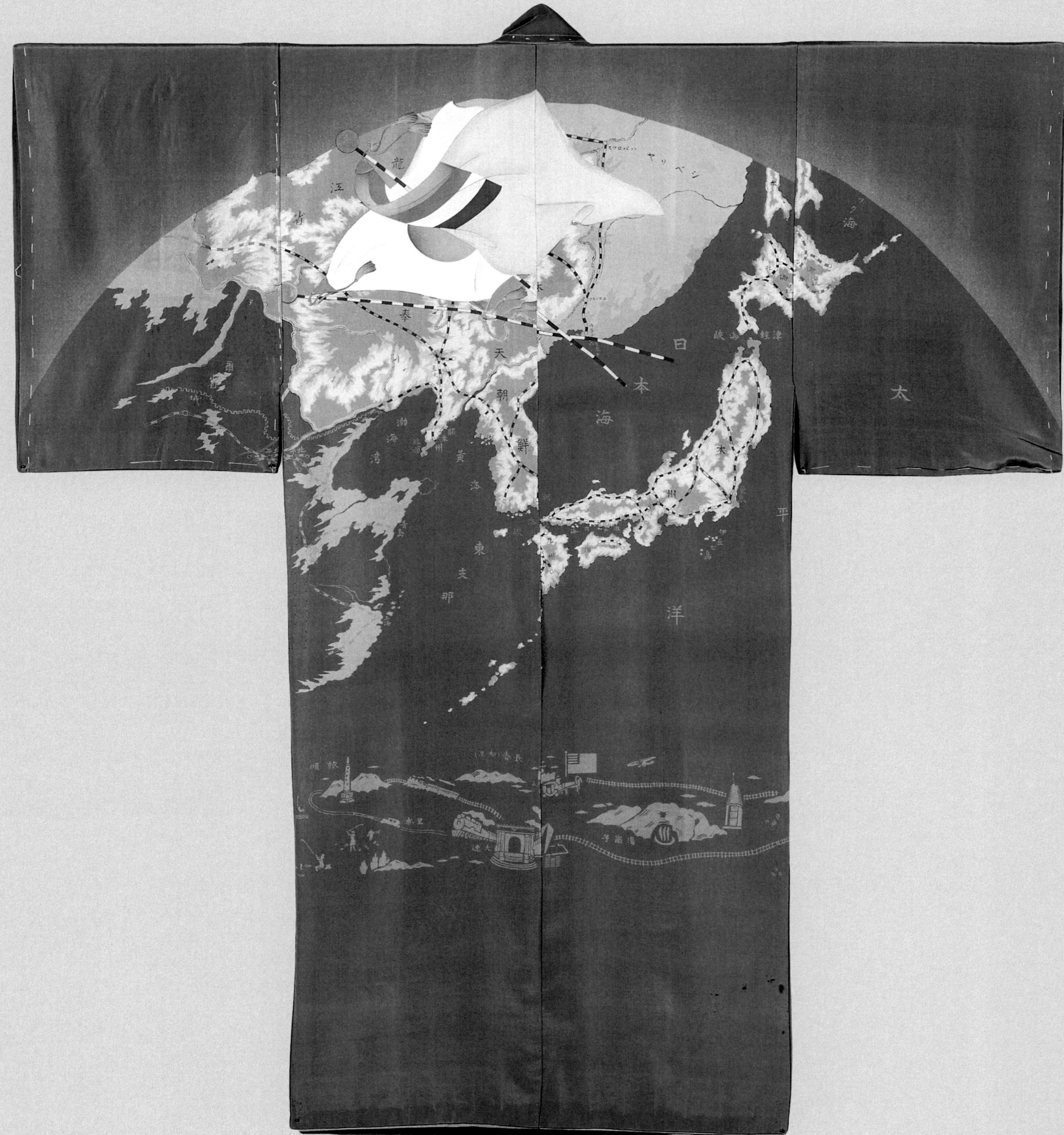
日本海
太平洋
朝鮮
奉天
黄海
東支那
渤海湾
津軽海峡

TRAVEL/MODERNITY

Man's *juban*
Manchukuo and tourists
Shōwa period, mid-1930s
Yūzen-dyed and printed silk
52.0 × 50.0 in (132 × 127 centimeters)
KM043

The flags of Japan and Manchukuo flying together over a map of Manchuria and Japan are the principal images chosen for this dramatic *juban*. The map highlights the railway tracks that ran through Japan, Korea, and Manchuria, further emphasizing the extent of the Japanese empire in the 1930s. Manchukuo especially resonated with the Japanese public as a utopian ideal, and it soon became a popular destination for Japanese tourists. A subsidiary design on the lower part of the *juban* offered an array of images that had great appeal for visitors, from leisure activities such as golf, fishing, and bathing in hot springs to historic sites such as the Chūreitō, a tall, slim tower erected in 1907 to honor the Japanese soldiers killed at the Siege of Port Arthur during the Russo-Japanese War in 1904–05.

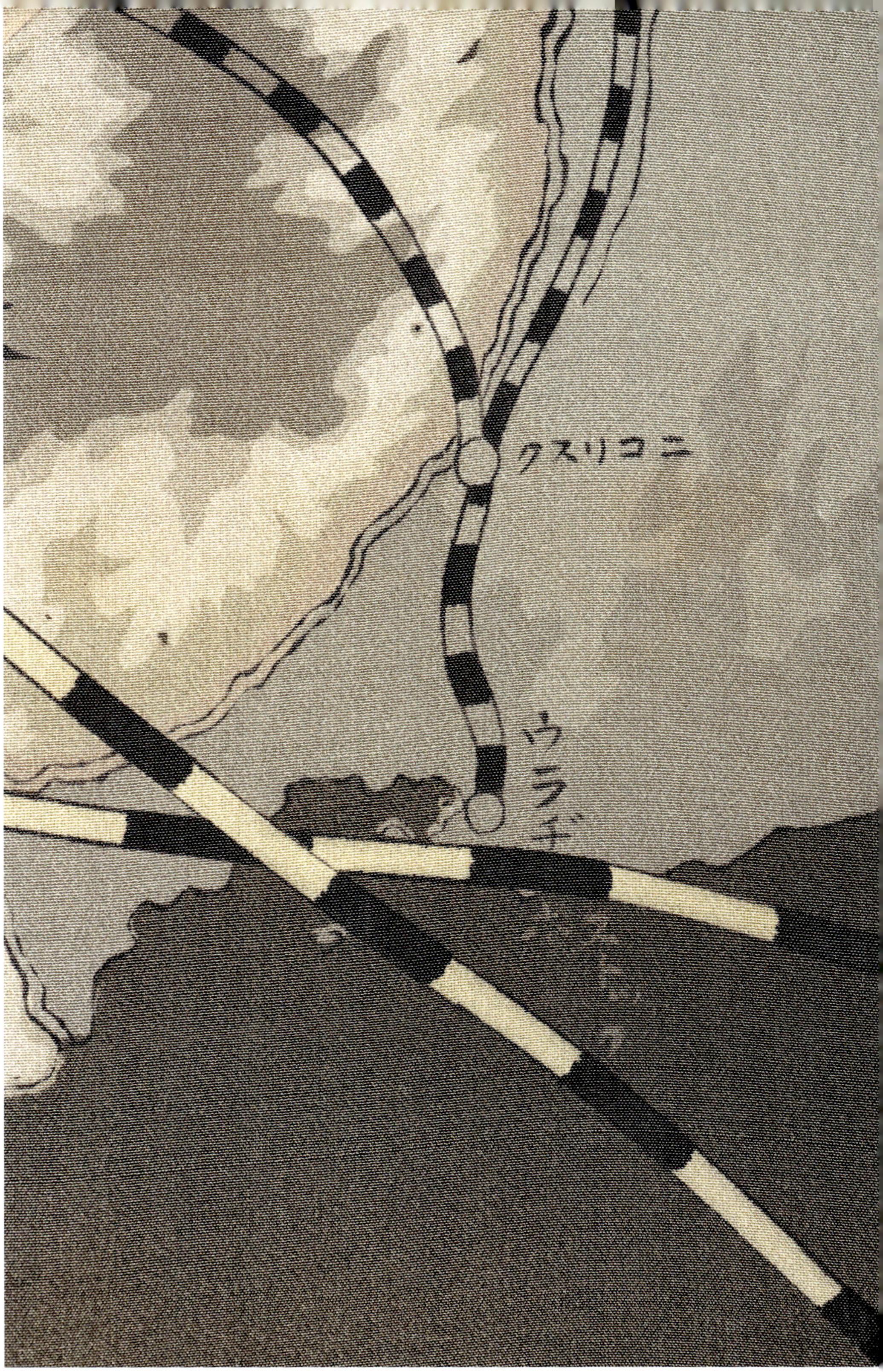

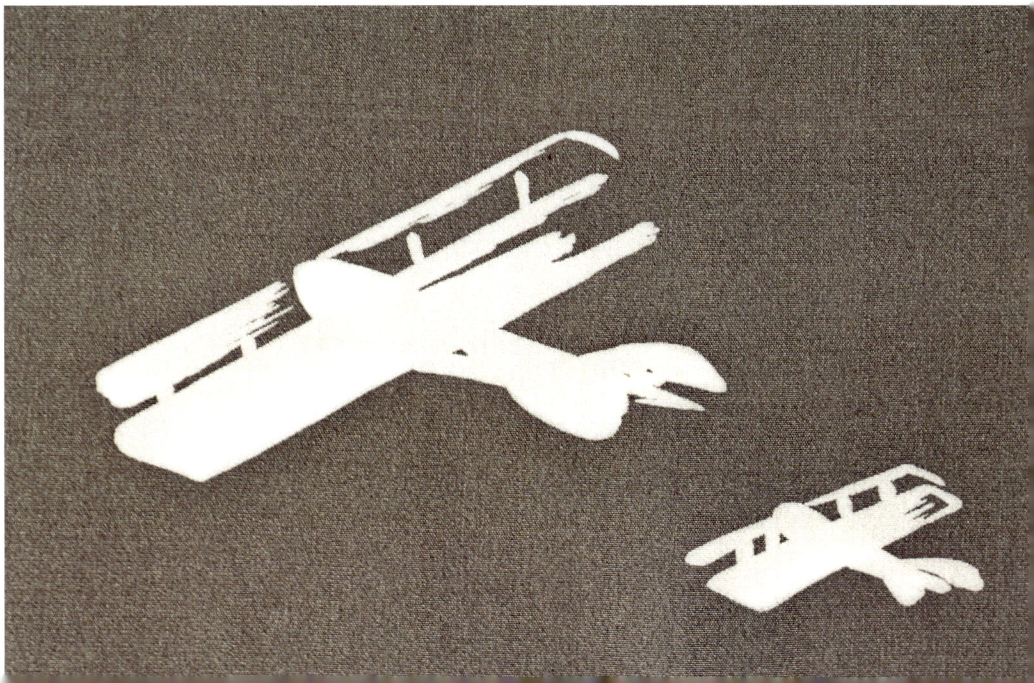

COSMOPOLITANISM/ PALACE DOLL

***Juban* for a woman**
***Gosho ningyō* and koi**
Taishō–Shōwa period, 1930s–1940s
Printed wool muslin
50.0 × 47.0 inches (127 × 119 centimeters)
KM044

The *gosho ningyō* (palace doll) and carp (koi) are two traditional symbols of the national holiday known as Boys' Day. The *ningyō* wears a bib that carries a family crest, and he is invested with characteristics such as vitality, bravery, and loyalty that are deeply desired in sons. He has also taken on the persona of a modern-day warrior who wears a modern helmet and carries a military flag, but still he wears a traditional *jinbaori*—a vest that warrior leaders wore over their armor—and a classic samurai sword hangs at his side. The carp represents strength and perseverance and is a common motif on boys' garments.

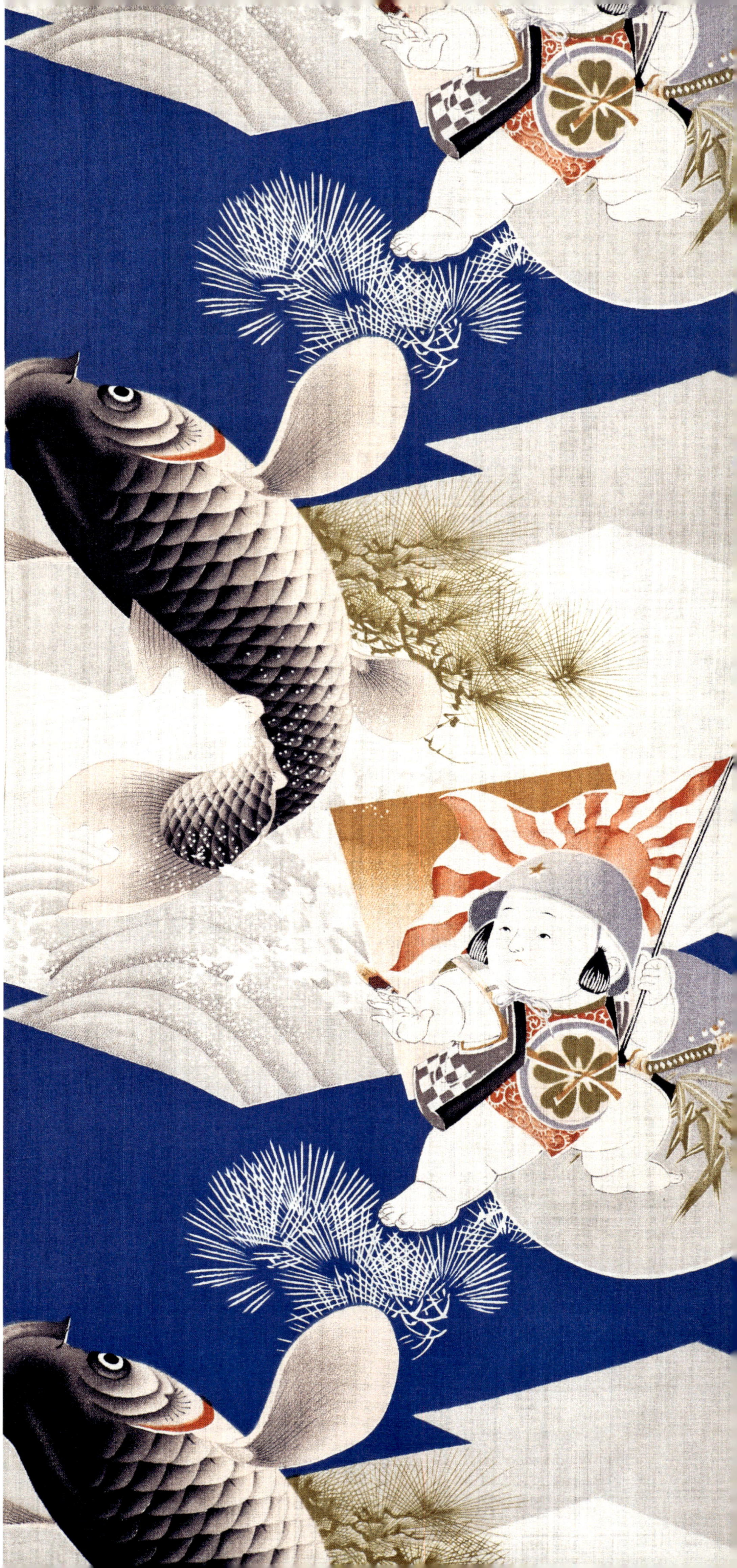

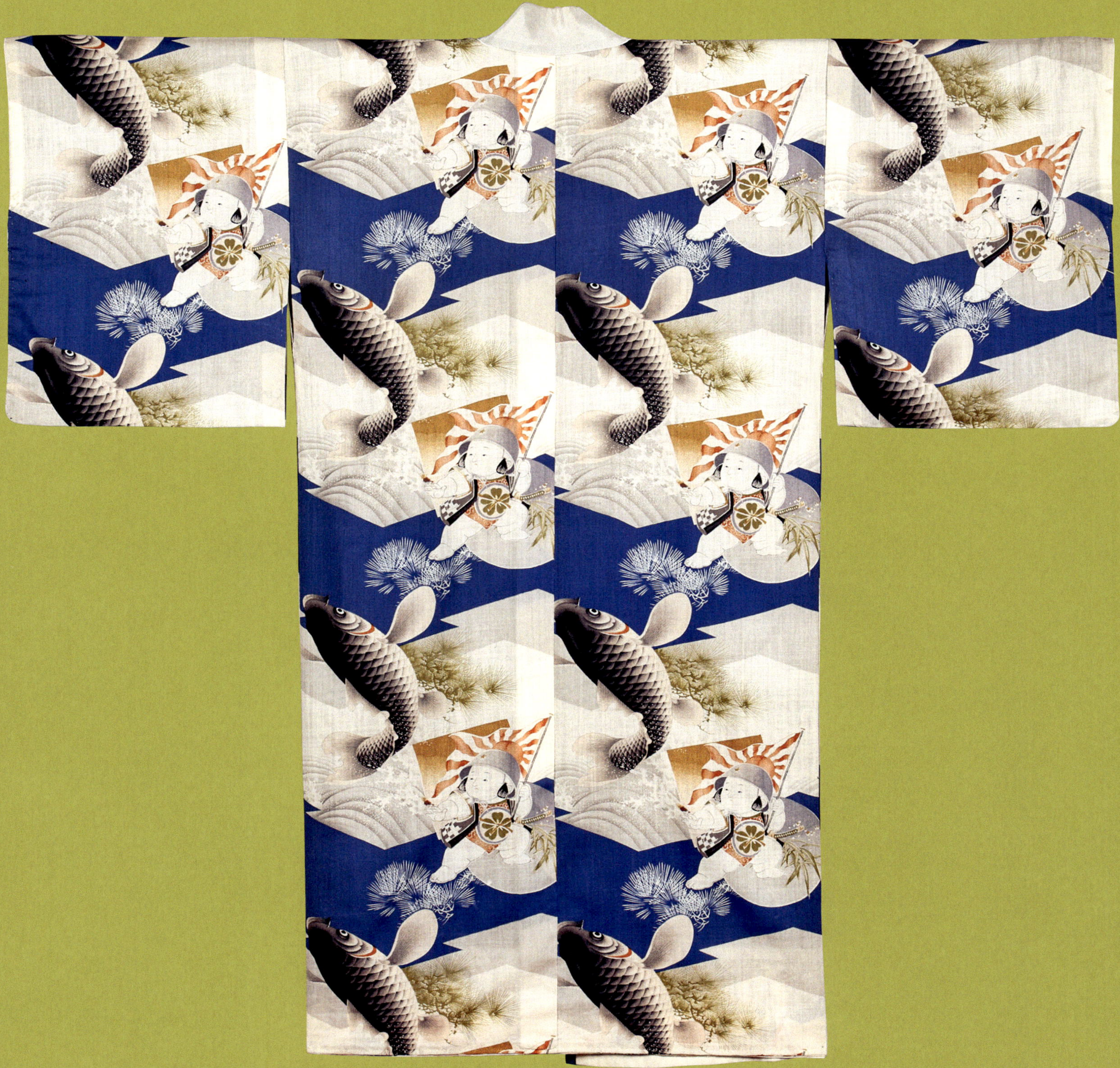

MEMORIAL/ A NATIONAL HERO

***Haori* for a man**
A tribute to Admiral Tōgō Heihachirō
Shōwa period, 1934–1935
Silk plain-weave *haori* (outer); satin silk and woven silk brocade with decorative gold and silver thread (*haura* lining)
51.0 × 41.0 inches (130 × 104 centimeters)
KM045

This dramatic and stunningly beautiful *haura* was woven to capture the announcement of Admiral Tōgō Heihachirō to his fleet as they prepared to engage Russian ships at the Battle of Tsushima. Tōgō's words—"The fate of the empire depends upon this event. Let every man do his utmost"—were similar to Admiral Horatio Nelson's charge to his ships ("England expects that every man will do his duty") as he prepared for action at the Battle of Trafalgar in 1805. This *haura* was undoubtedly prepared as a special memorial for Tōgō in the year of his death (1934). It is a compelling reminder of Tōgō's valor and loyalty to the emperor and served as a source of inspiration and determination as Japan edged closer to another war.

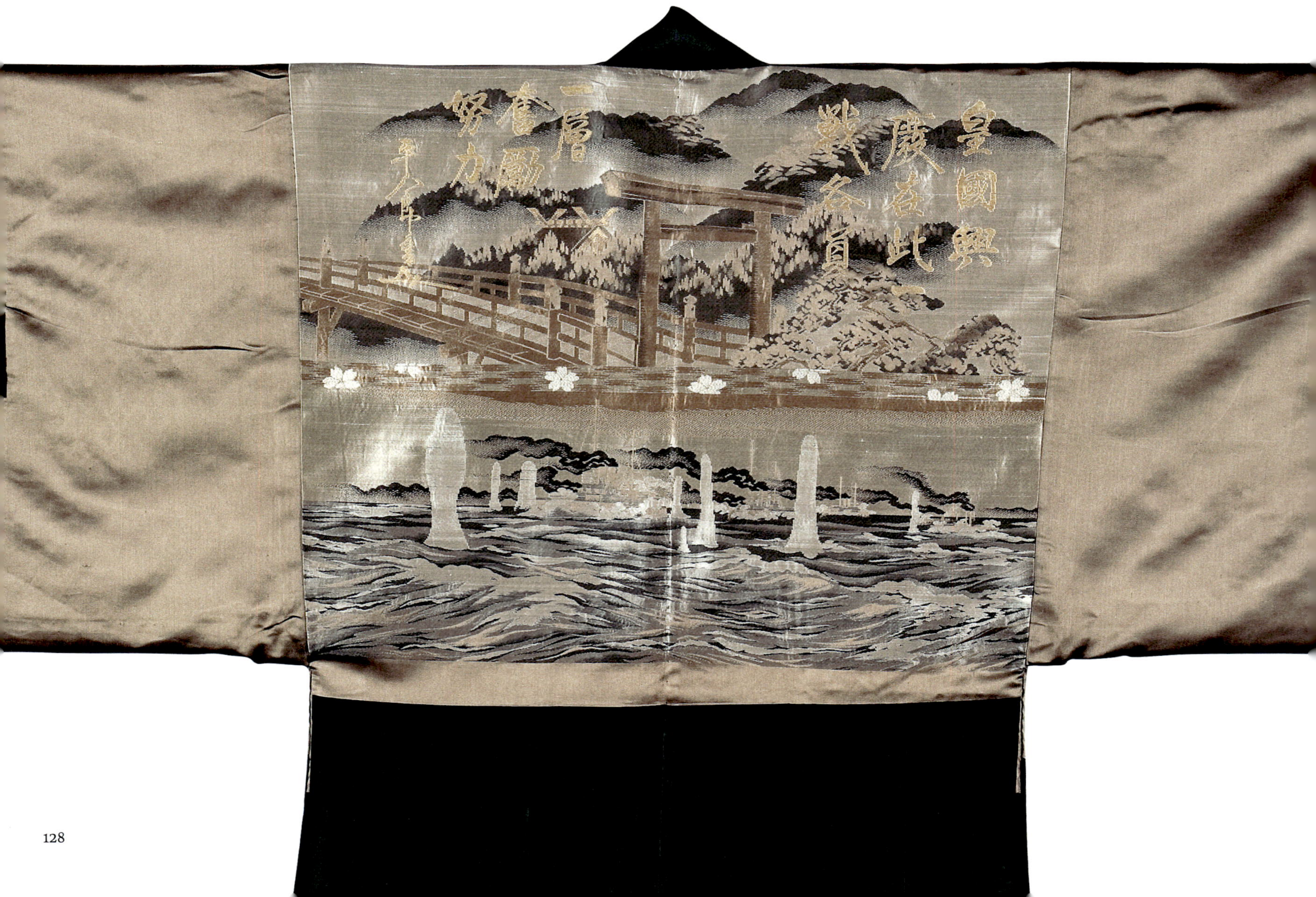

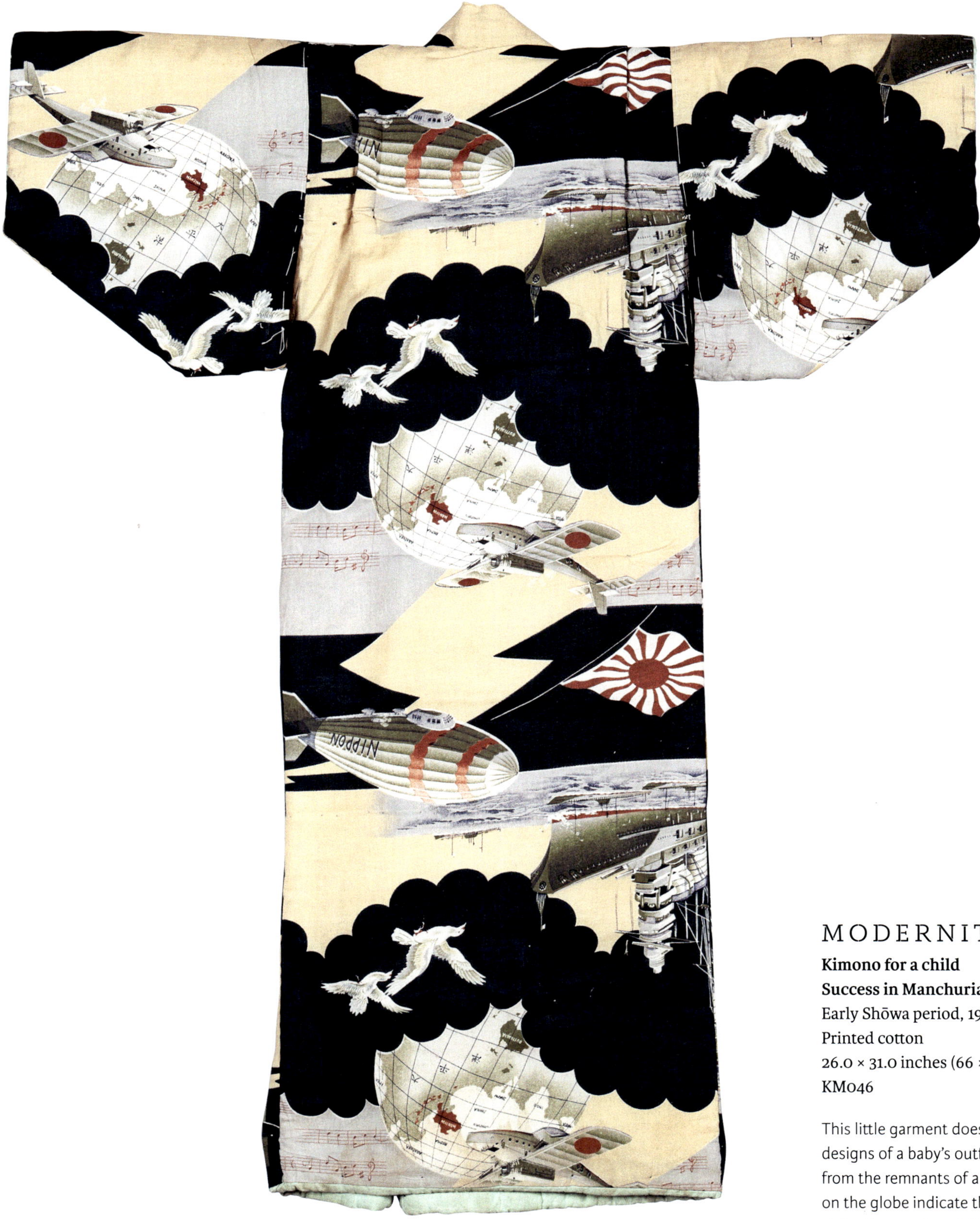

MODERNITY

Kimono for a child
Success in Manchuria
Early Shōwa period, 1930s
Printed cotton
26.0 × 31.0 inches (66 × 79 centimeters)
KM046

This little garment does not have the brightly colored designs of a baby's outfit, so it was probably made from the remnants of a larger robe. The red territories on the globe indicate the reach of Japan's influence at the time and mark its growing place in the world. The addition of so-called *romaji* (Roman letters) was fashionable at the time, and few would have noticed the misspellings. The plane shown here was adapted to sea landings and assisted in the delivery of supplies and personnel to locations under Japan's domination. Doves indicate peaceful intentions. Japan's army and navy both invested in dirigibles, but eventually they were phased out in the early 1930s, helping to date this kimono.

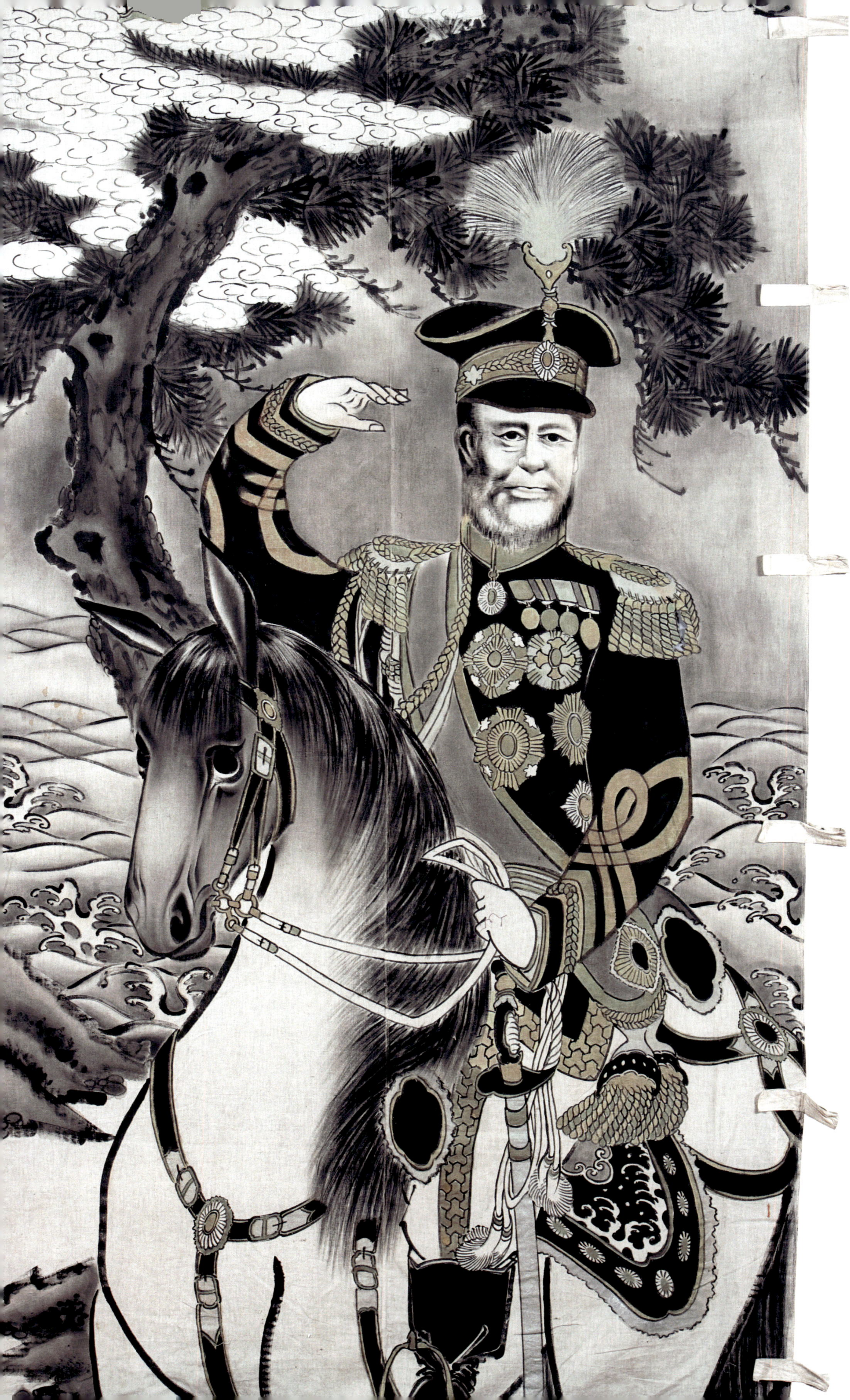

OPPOSITE

MODERNITY

***Nobori* (banner)**
Tokugawa Yoshinobu
Meiji period, 1900–1912
Painted cotton
316.0 × 57.0 inches (803 × 145 centimeters)
KM047

This *nobori* (a banner for a festival) has been carefully painted to show a well-outfitted military man adorned with medals of bravery and riding his horse with elegance. There is no definitive identification for the man, but the *nobori* artist copied a newspaper photo for his face, and it is possible that this man was Tokugawa Yoshinobu, the last shogun of Japan, who ultimately surrendered his position under the new Imperial Court and emperor in 1868. Although he was nominally confined as an Enemy of the Court, he was allowed to retire in Mito. Later, in 1902, he was pardoned by the Meiji Emperor (whose face is also on the *nobori*) and was granted the rank of *kōshaku* (prince). The family crest on this *nobori* carries the encircled mandarin orange known as a *tachibana*.

RIGHT

MACHINE AGE

Woman's obi
The beauty of flight
Taishō–Shōwa period, late 1920s–early 1930s
Printed and painted silk, embroidery, metallic threads, gold and silver leaf
6.0–12.0 × 130.0 inches (15–30 × 330 centimeters)
KM048

This lovely obi matches elements of contemporary graphic design with the modernity of the aircraft. The colors appear to shimmer against the brilliant blue of the clouds and sky as the aircraft cut diagonal flight paths across the fabric. Each of the three different types of aircraft provides a heady sense of speed and motion, helped by the embroidered metallic threads tied to the bodies and wings of the planes. Drifts of gold and silver leaf further enhance the beauty of flight. This obi would provide a dazzling statement when worn.

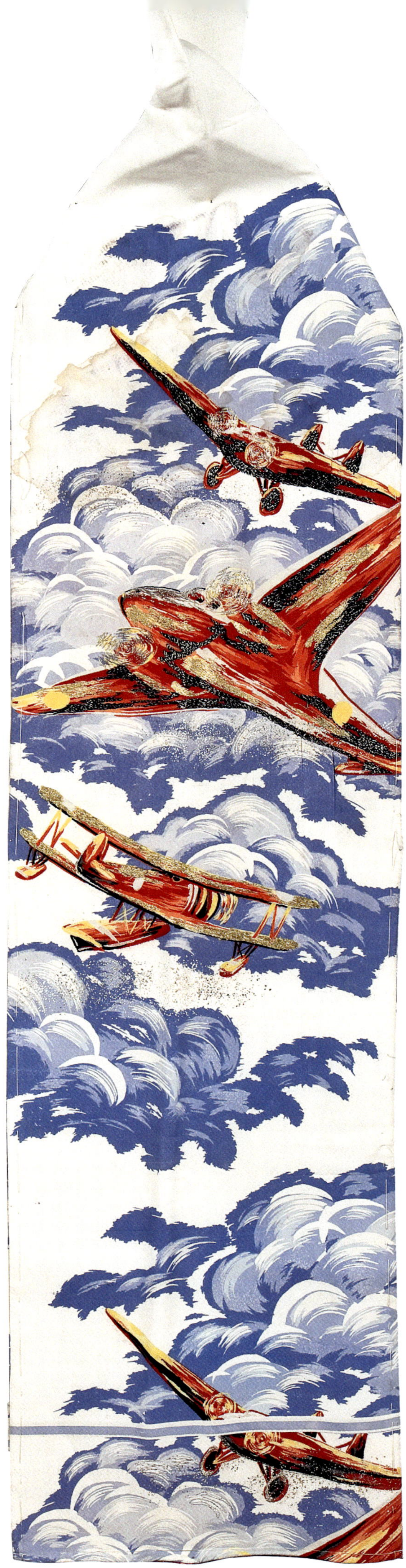

SENSŌGARA/SAMPLES

***Niko-niko* sample book**
Illustrated cover
Shōwa period, 1937–1945
Printed cotton
KM049

Textile sample books were often advertised for purchase or browsing in department stores for those who wished to see potential new goods. This sample book contains a group of *niko-niko* pieces that, as shown on a dramatic *sensōgara* cover, would soon be available for purchase. This group of samples would most likely be greatly appreciated by young boys, as the *niko-niko* designs give a taste of exciting wartime elements, from aircraft to battleships, artillery, and more. *Niko-niko* has some resemblance to the much more elegant *kasuri*, but it is a sturdy cotton textile that can offer exciting images for boys as well as being long-lasting—something that a mother would appreciate.

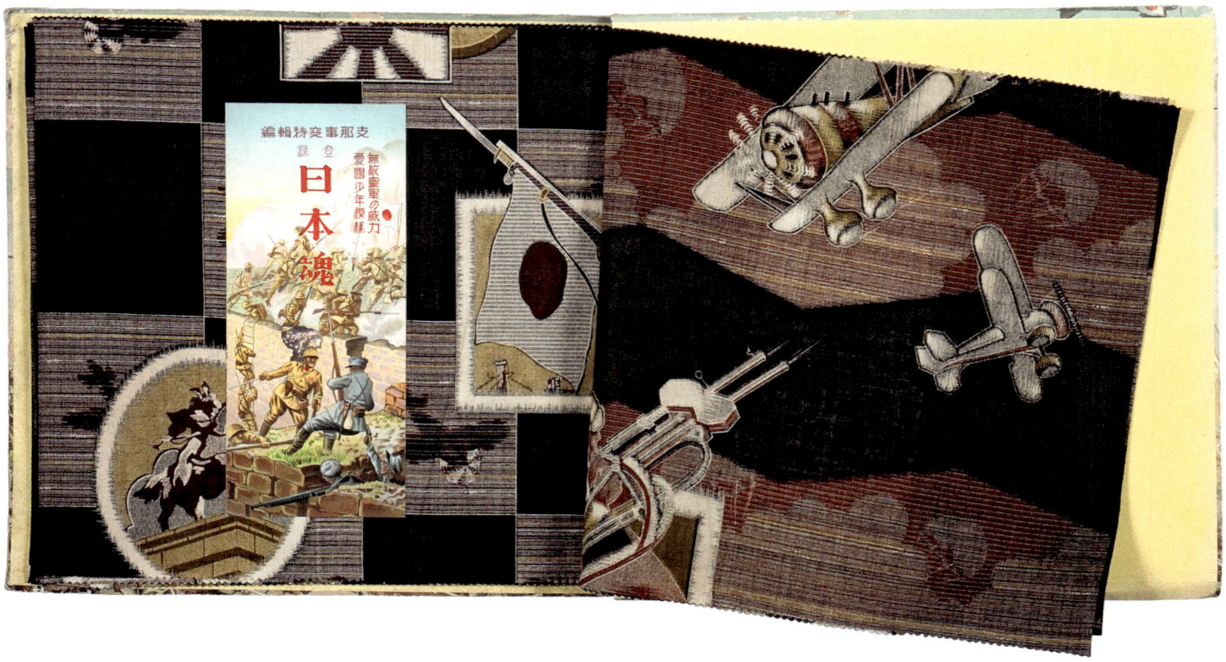

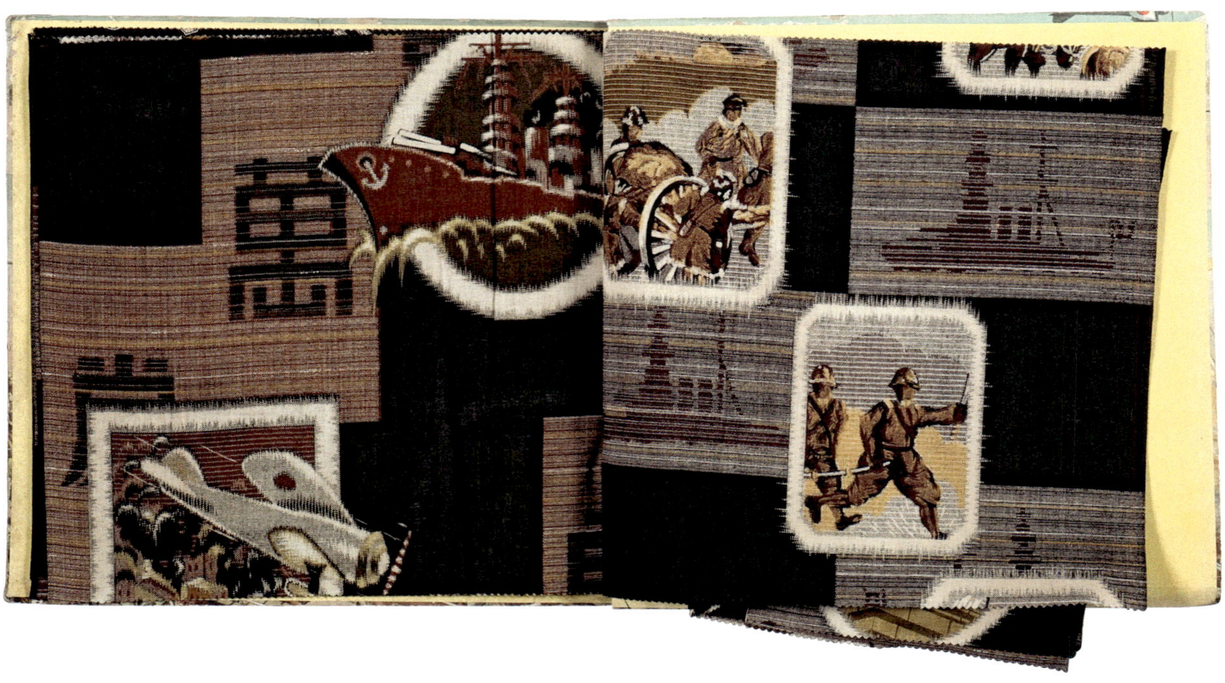

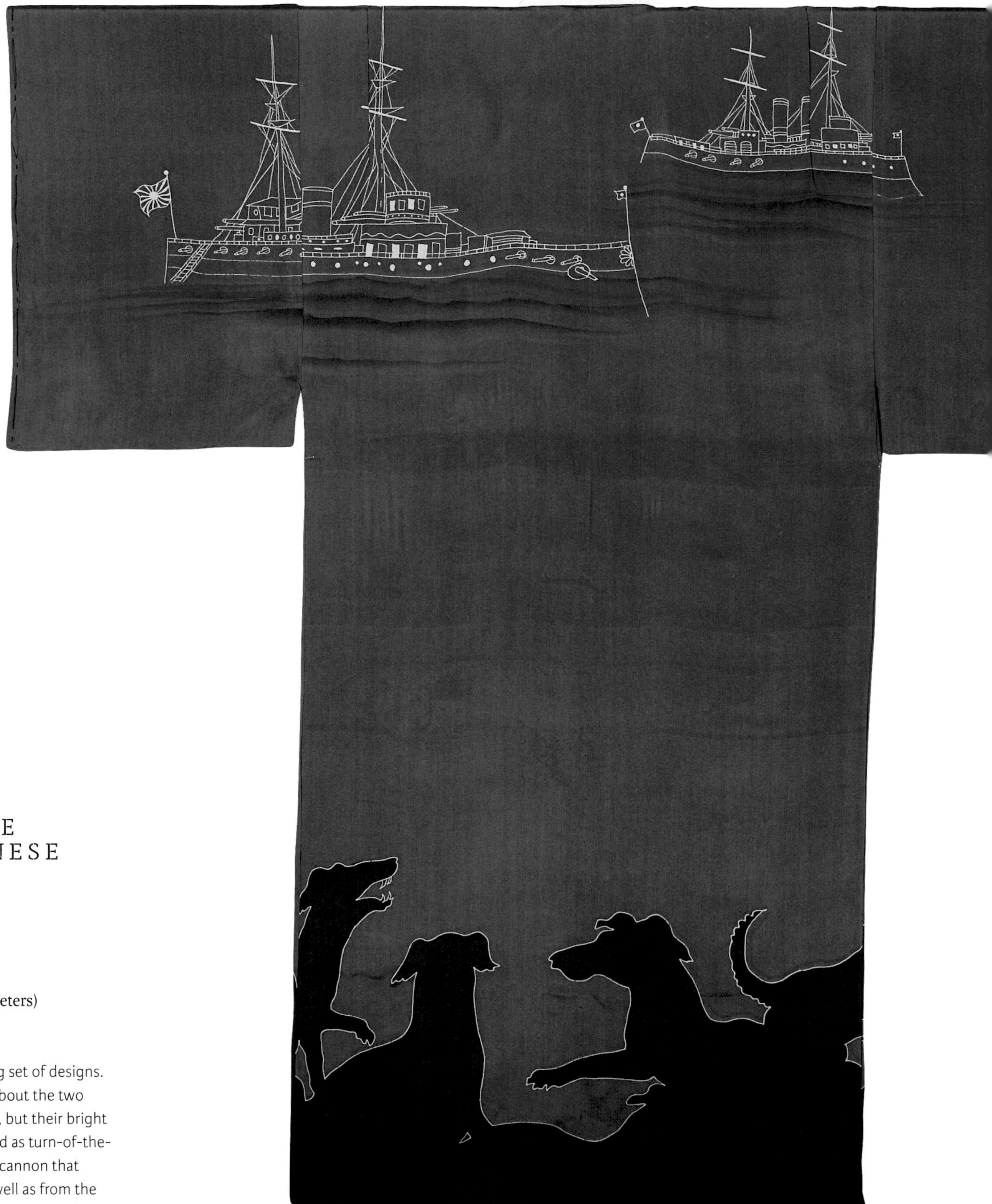

SENSŌGARA/THE IMPERIAL JAPANESE NAVY

***Juban* for a man**
Dreadnoughts and dogs
Meiji–Taishō period, 1890s–1930s
Yuzen-dyed silk
54.0 × 50.0 inches (137 × 127 centimeters)
KM050

This *juban* has a simple but intriguing set of designs. There is little information available about the two ships on the upper back of the *juban*, but their bright white outlines can be easily identified as turn-of-the-century warships by the numbers of cannon that reach out from the ships' turrets as well as from the lower-deck openings. The chrysanthemum on the prow of the larger ship (the imperial motif of the Meiji Emperor) and the military flag of the Imperial Japanese Navy also indicate the importance of these ships as they steam toward their goals. The rowdy dogs shown on this garment are somewhat difficult to decipher, but it might simply be that the dogs did not appreciate the noise of the ships.

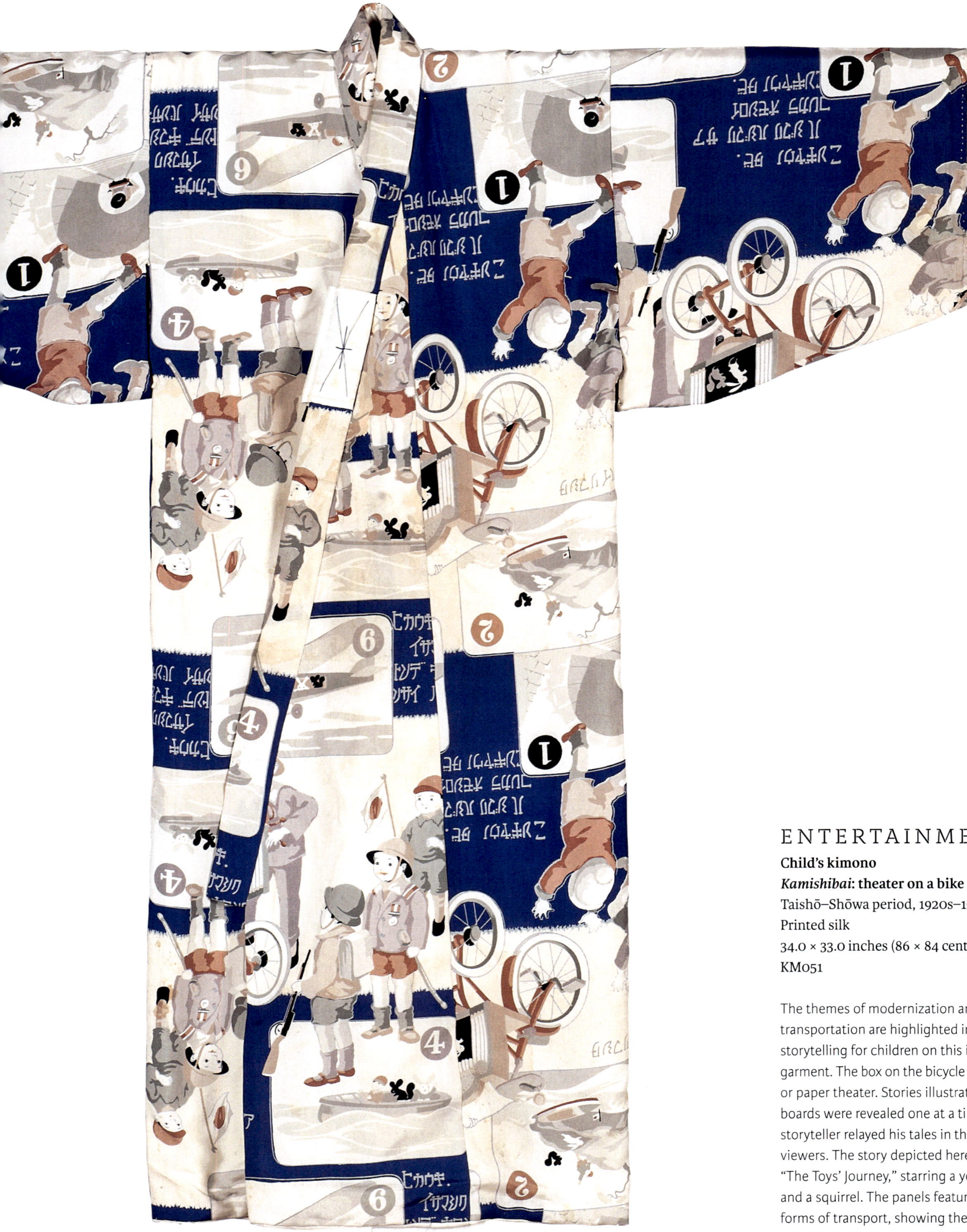

ENTERTAINMENT

Child's kimono
***Kamishibai*: theater on a bike**
Taishō–Shōwa period, 1920s–1930s
Printed silk
34.0 × 33.0 inches (86 × 84 centimeters)
KM051

The themes of modernization and high-speed transportation are highlighted in the form of storytelling for children on this infant's charming garment. The box on the bicycle was called *kamishibai*, or paper theater. Stories illustrated on numbered boards were revealed one at a time as the itinerant storyteller relayed his tales in the streets for local viewers. The story depicted here seems to be "The Toys' Journey," starring a young boy, a rabbit, and a squirrel. The panels featured new and exciting forms of transport, showing the stages of their trip. Modernization was closely intertwined with militarism, as can be discerned from the children's clothing, weapons, and flags.

SENSŌGARA

Man's *haori* with a decorative lining (*haura*)
Warships in rolling waves
Late Meiji period, 1904–1910
Silk plain-weave *haori* (outer); woven silk brocade with metal threads for *haura* (lining)
50.0 × 42.0 inches (127 × x 107 centimeters)
KM052

The dramatic images of warships and Mount Fuji were carefully prepared for this *haura*, as its silk brocade had metal threads woven into the designs of the foremost ships to give extra sheen to their outside armament. These two warships were most likely built in London for the Japanese government before 1900, as large-scale wartime production in Japan had not as yet been fully developed. The outside of this kimono carried a family crest (*mon*) on the back and front of the garment. The *mon* design for this family—the arrowhead plant, also known as the "victory plant" (*shōgunsō*)—had a martial connotation that was greatly favored by many samurai families by the end of the Edo period.

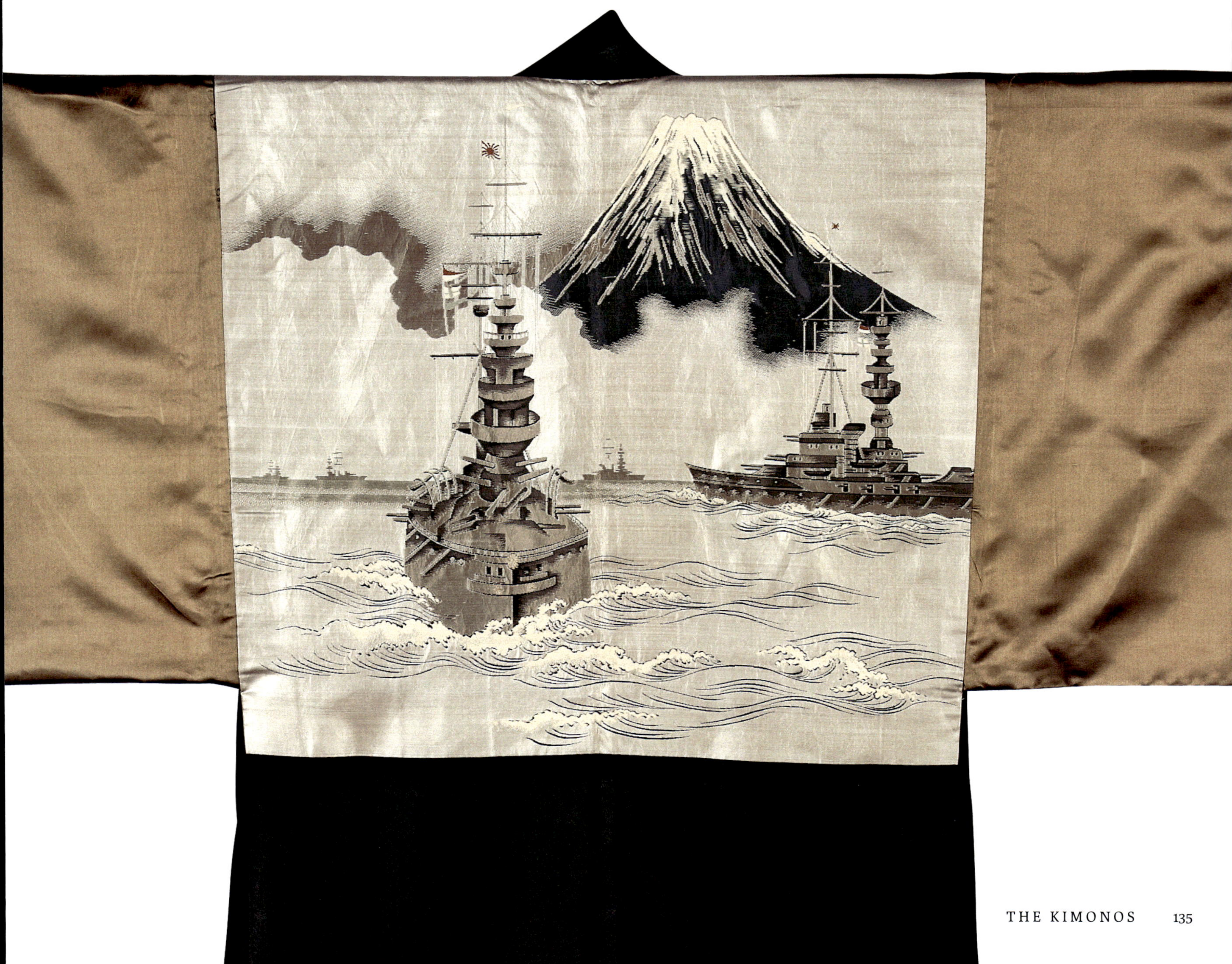

SENSŌGARA

Man's *haori* with a decorative lining (*haura*)
At war in the fields
Shōwa period, 1930s–1940
Silk pongee *haori* (outer); *kata-yūzen* dyed silk *haura* (lining); plain silk sleeves (interior)
52.0 × 41.5 inches (132 × 105 centimeters)
KM053

The artist for this kimono has produced a superb *haura* that shows a very early foggy and misty morning as soldiers prepare to quietly position the caissons, cannon, and other equipment that will soon be used for battle. The man who walks behind the soldiers encourages the men as he issues information on the proper positions of the artillery. It seems to be a serene and quiet, almost tranquil, moment as the men carry out their work, but the thunder of guns will begin all too soon. The *haura* has been dyed and painted with a steady hand that honors the soldiers' work.

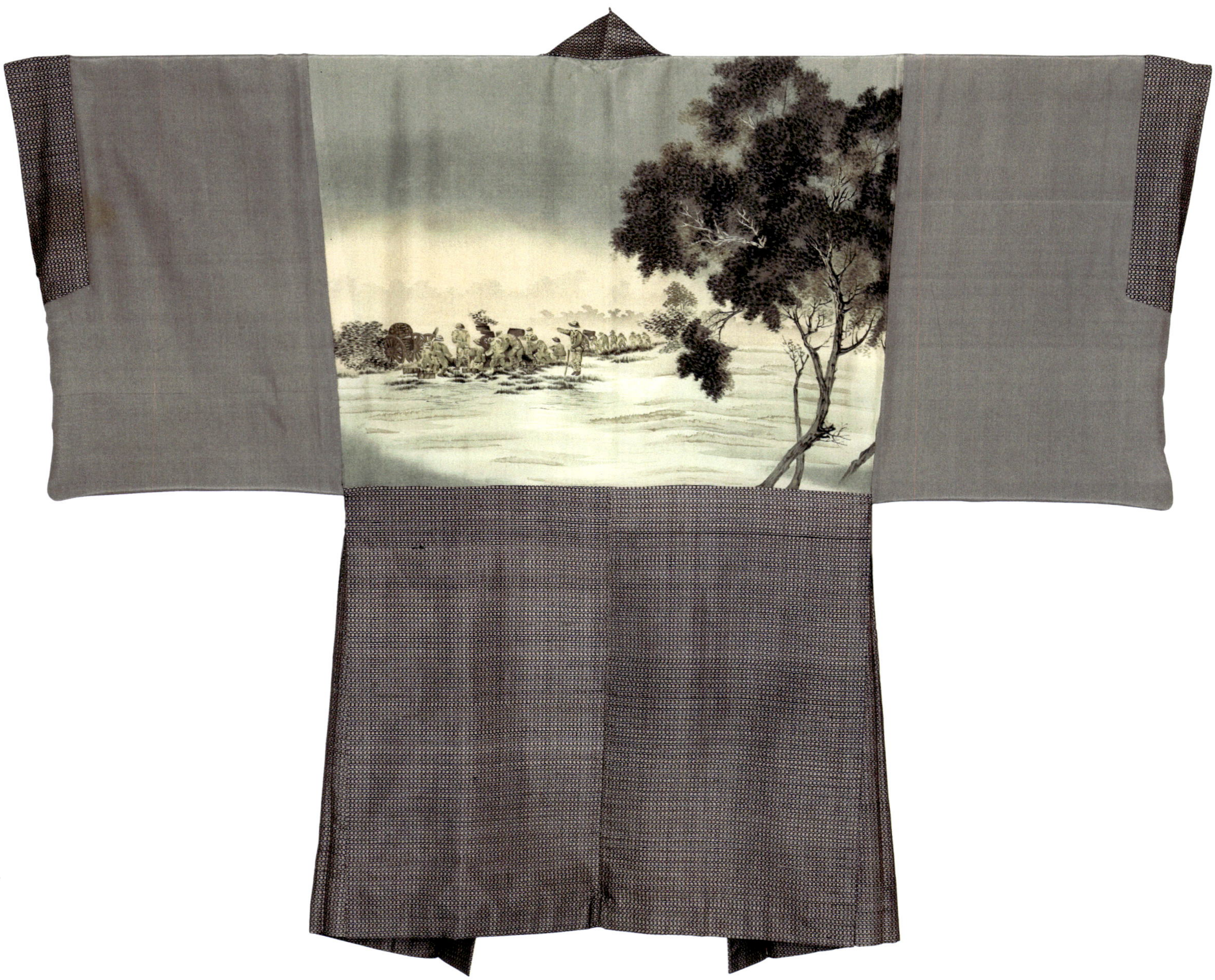

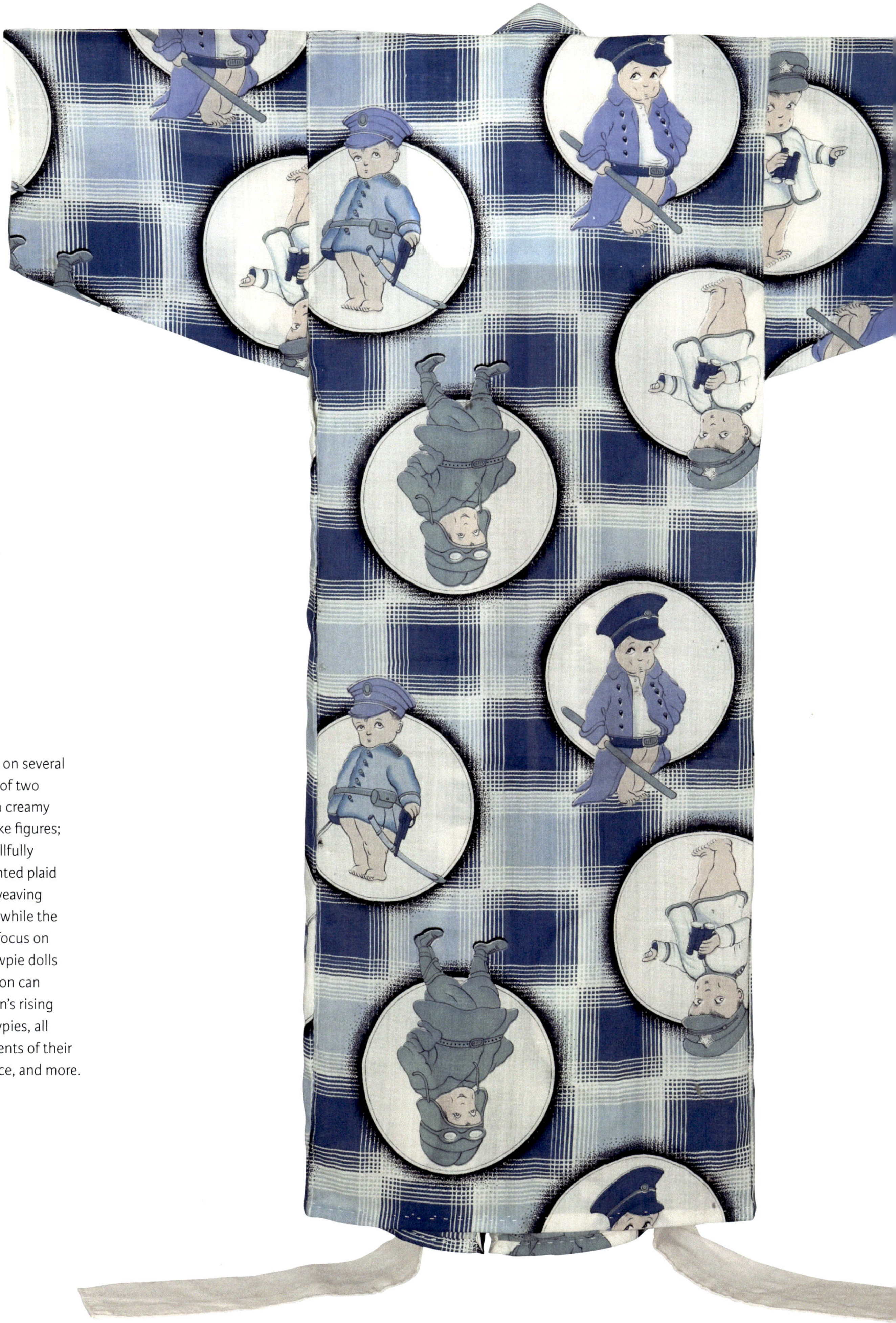

ENTERTAINMENT/ KEWPIES

Kimono for a child
Kewpies in uniform
Taishō period, 1914–1918
Printed wool muslin
33.0 × 29.0 inches (84 × 74 centimeters)
KM054

The design of this garment is compelling on several levels. The design is composed primarily of two colors, blue and white; the third color is a creamy pink, applied to the skin of the Kewpie-like figures; the darker and lighter blue shades are skillfully used to stand in for other colors. The printed plaid background imitates the traditional interweaving of blue and white warp and weft threads while the roundels in the foreground, by contrast, focus on modernization. Japan fell in love with Kewpie dolls in the early 20th century, and that affection can be seen in these Kewpie-like babies. Japan's rising militarization can also be seen in the Kewpies, all of whom are male and wearing the garments of their military trades, such as army, navy, air force, and more.

SENSŌGARA

Woman's *juban*
Lantern parades and cherry blossoms
Shōwa period, early 1930s–early 1940s
Yūzen dyed silk
50.0 × 47.0 inches (127 × 119 centimeters)
KM055

Flags, lanterns, and flowers made for an ideal textile for a young woman, who could wear this colorful *juban* under her kimono so she could join the cheering populace when the victory parades were in full force. Although she would not wish to show her *juban* in public, on her return home she could slip off her kimono and continue to enjoy wearing the *juban* for relaxing in the evening. The designs used for this silk *juban* include lanterns printed or painted with parade slogans, cherry blossoms to honor the *gunshin* ("military gods"), and national and military flags.

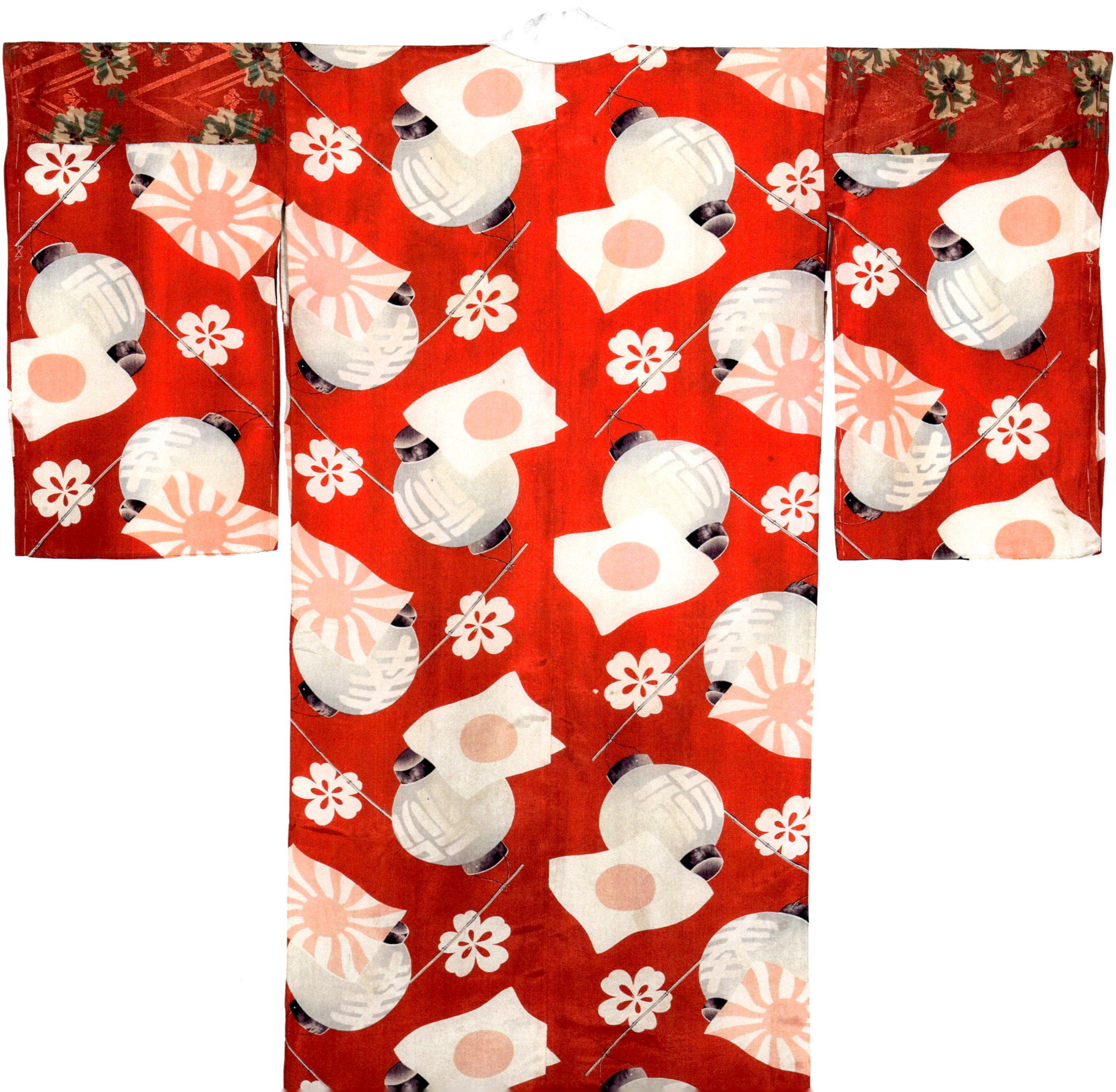

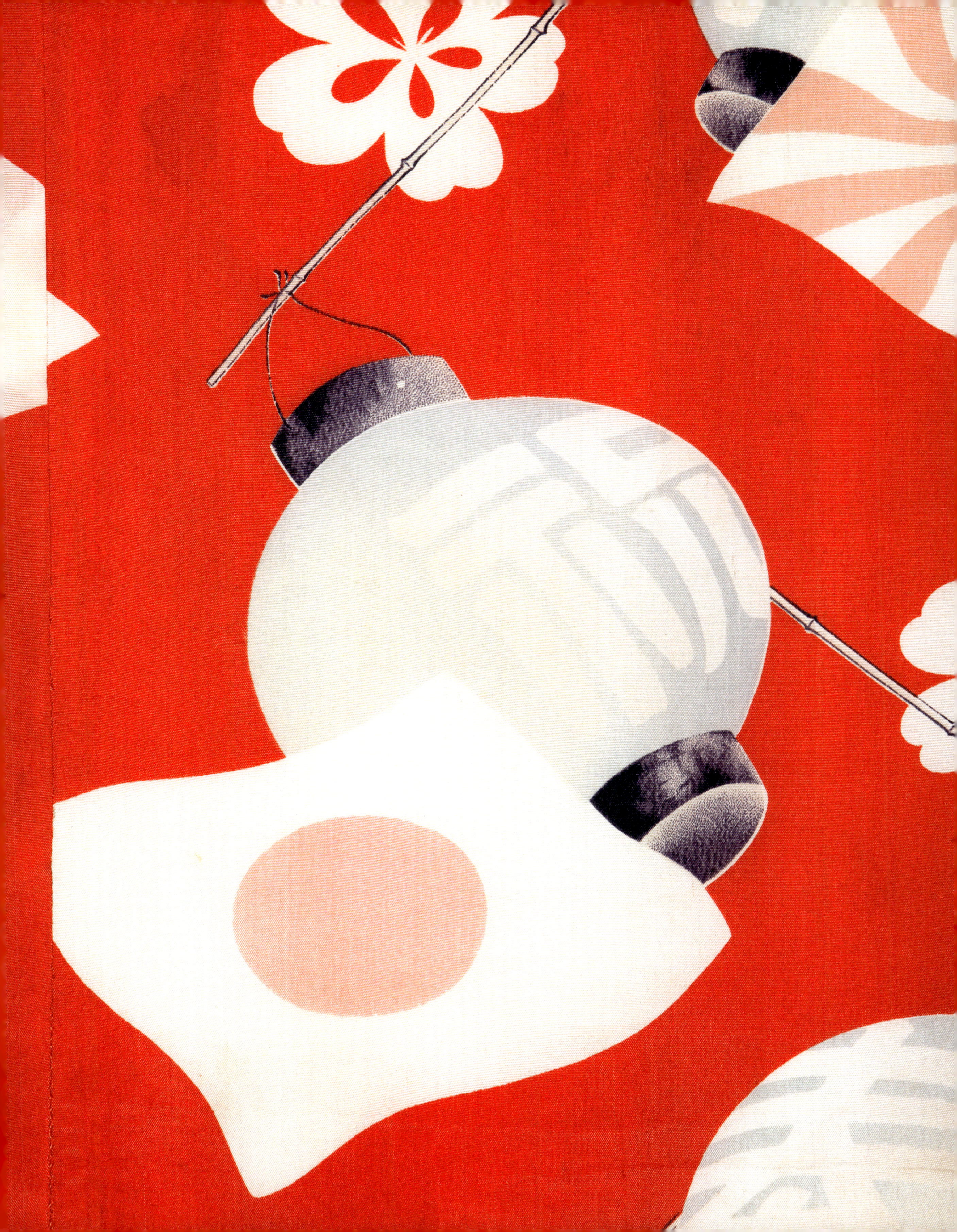

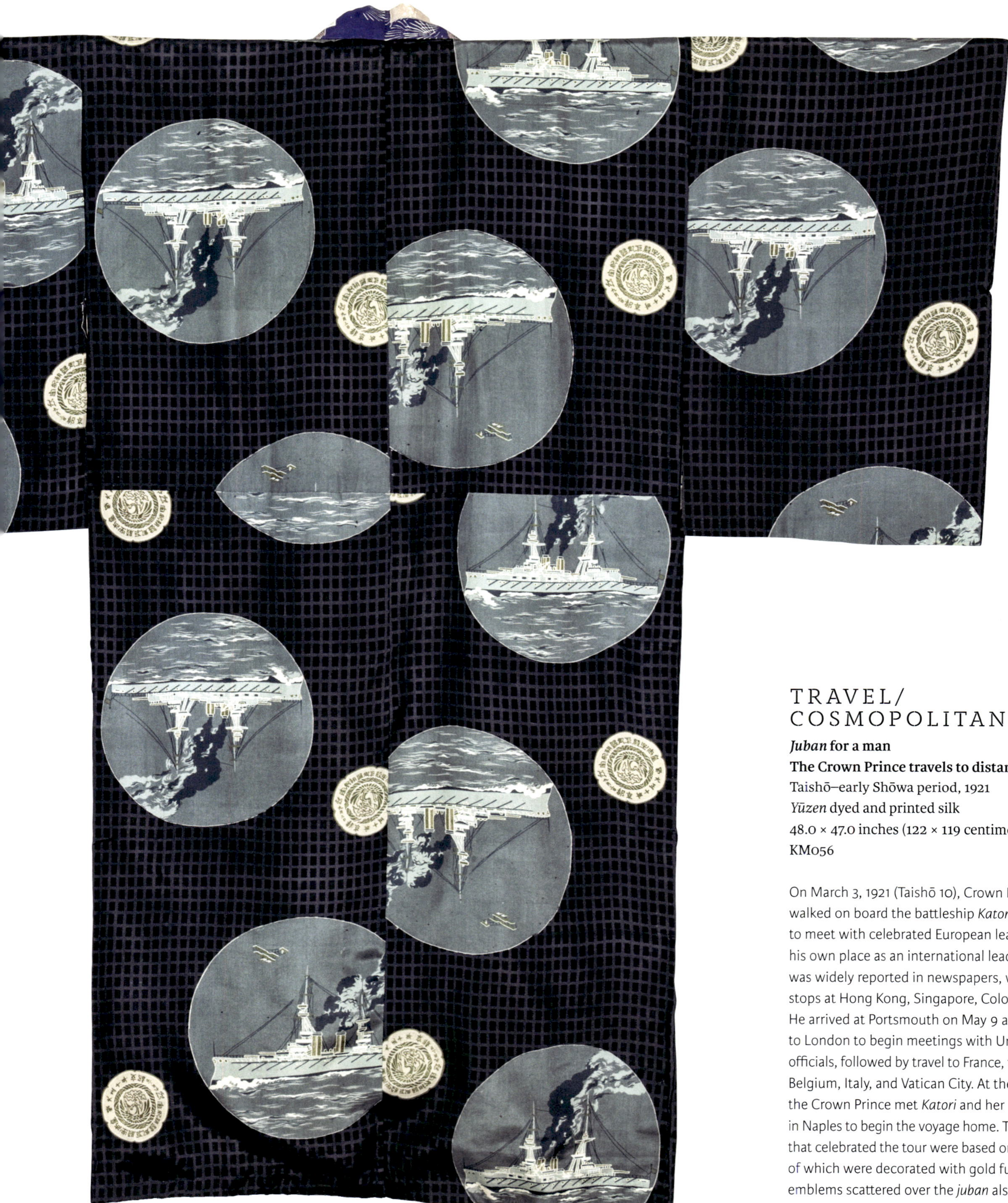

TRAVEL/ COSMOPOLITANISM

***Juban* for a man**
The Crown Prince travels to distant lands
Taishō–early Shōwa period, 1921
Yūzen dyed and printed silk
48.0 × 47.0 inches (122 × 119 centimeters)
KM056

On March 3, 1921 (Taishō 10), Crown Prince Hirohito walked on board the battleship *Katori* to travel abroad to meet with celebrated European leaders and take his own place as an international leader. His journey was widely reported in newspapers, which noted his stops at Hong Kong, Singapore, Colombo, and Suez. He arrived at Portsmouth on May 9 and went directly to London to begin meetings with United Kingdom officials, followed by travel to France, the Netherlands, Belgium, Italy, and Vatican City. At the end of the tour, the Crown Prince met *Katori* and her escort, *Kashima*, in Naples to begin the voyage home. The textile designs that celebrated the tour were based on the ships, both of which were decorated with gold funnels. Circular emblems scattered over the *juban* also showed the importance of the date Hirohito left Japan.

MACHINE AGE

***Miyamairi* (boy child's kimono for his first shrine visit)**
Maritime machines
Late Taishō–early Shōwa period, 1920s–1940
Kata-yūzen dyed and printed silk
40.0 × 31.0 inches (102 × 79 centimeters)
KM057

As an island nation, with no citizen more than 100 miles from the coastline, much of Japan's military success depended on its maritime prowess, showcased here on this infant boy's *miyamairi* in the form of toy-like floatplanes, battleships, and yachts. The talisman stitched to the *miyamairi* back, as seen here, is meant to protect the boy who wears this garment. The main background colors for this kimono are soft brown and deep blue and were printed with chemical dyes. Ironically, these colors corresponded well to two traditional and popular natural colors: *bengara*, a brown pigment derived from iron oxide, and indigo, derived from the widely cultivated indigo plant.

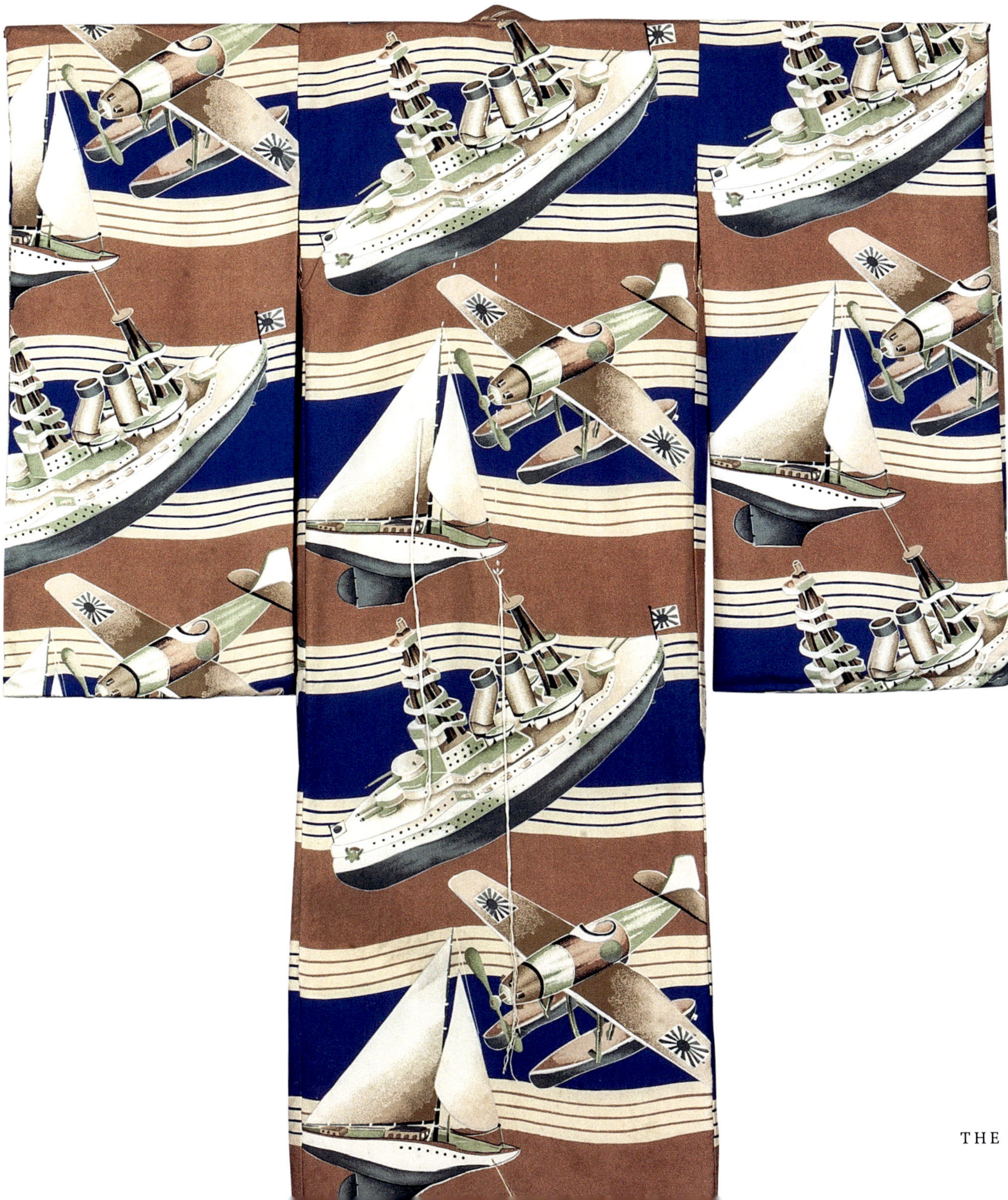

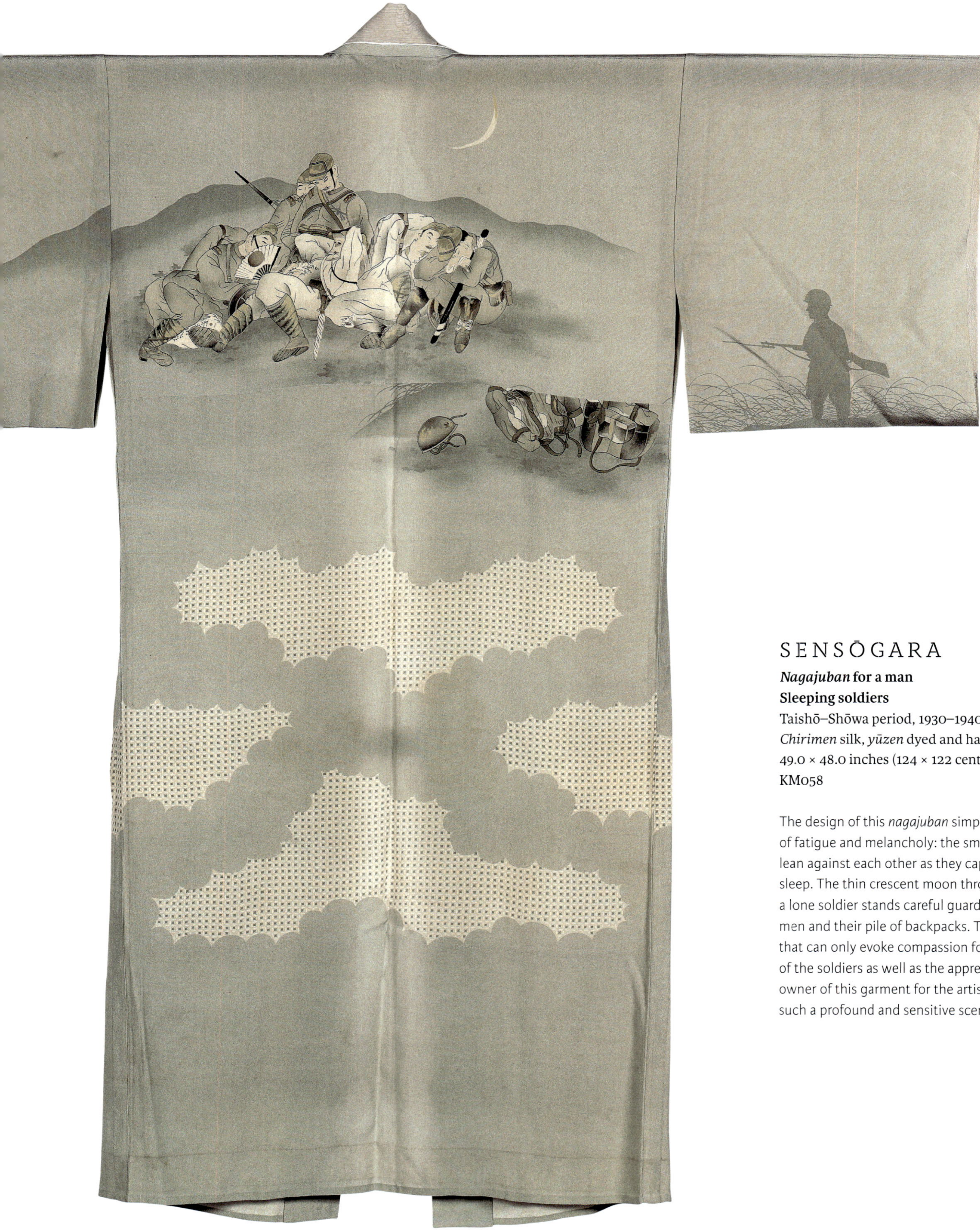

SENSŌGARA

***Nagajuban* for a man**
Sleeping soldiers
Taishō–Shōwa period, 1930–1940s
Chirimen silk, *yūzen* dyed and hand-painted
49.0 × 48.0 inches (124 × 122 centimeters)
KM058

The design of this *nagajuban* simply radiates a time of fatigue and melancholy: the small group of soldiers lean against each other as they capture a few hours of sleep. The thin crescent moon throws a faint light as a lone soldier stands careful guard over the exhausted men and their pile of backpacks. The design is one that can only evoke compassion for the exhaustion of the soldiers as well as the appreciation by the owner of this garment for the artist who produced such a profound and sensitive scene of men and war.

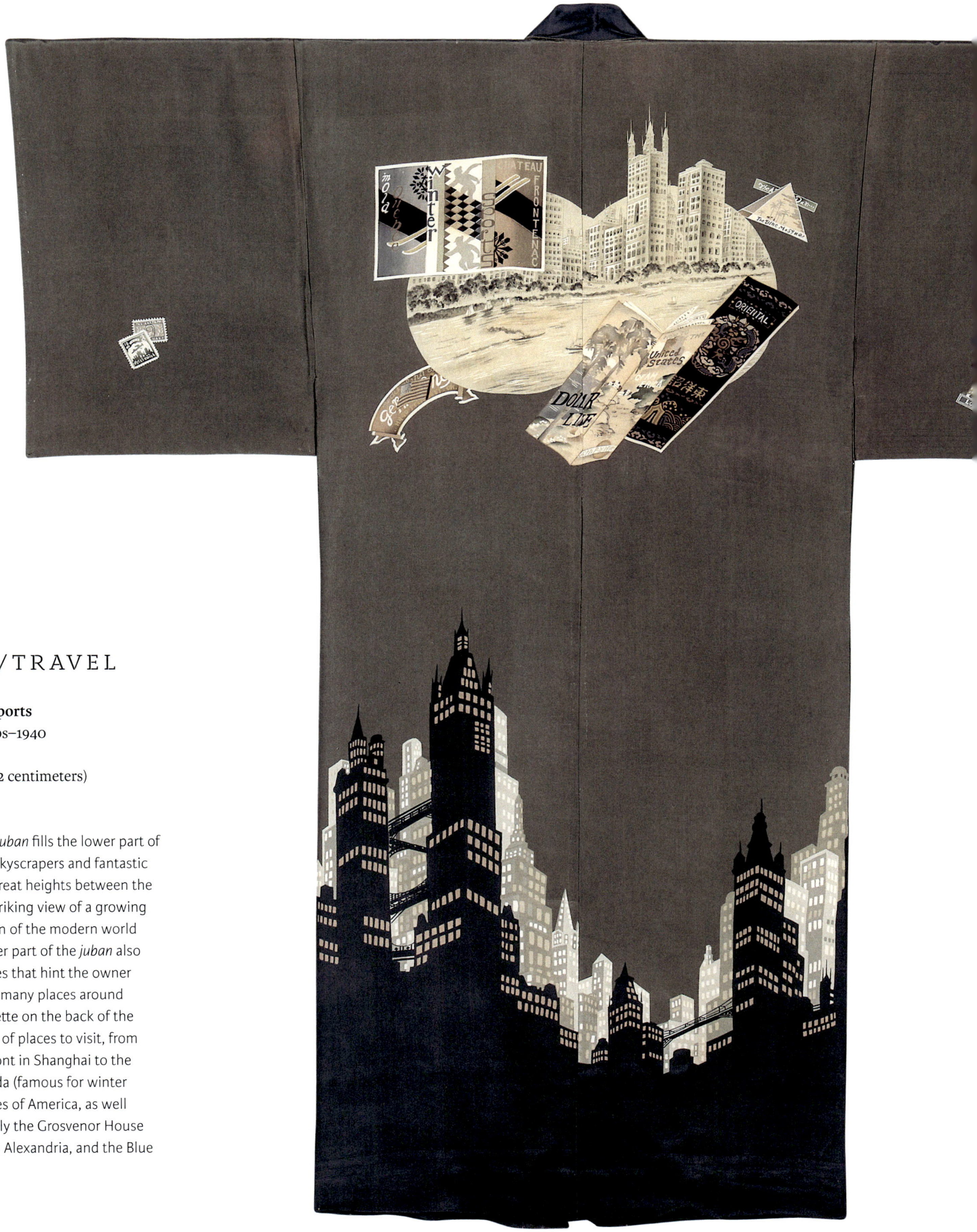

MODERNITY/TRAVEL

***Juban* for a man**
Skyscrapers, travel, and sports
Taishō–Shōwa period, 1920s–1940
Kata-yūzen dyed silk
53.0 × 52.0 inches (135 × 132 centimeters)
KM059

The primary design on this *juban* fills the lower part of the garment with majestic skyscrapers and fantastic walking bridges that span great heights between the towering buildings. It is a striking view of a growing city that is a bold declaration of the modern world as well as the new. The upper part of the *juban* also features interesting vignettes that hint the owner might be an avid traveler to many places around the world. The central vignette on the back of the garment shows a collection of places to visit, from the Bund along the waterfront in Shanghai to the Château Frontenac in Canada (famous for winter sports) and the United States of America, as well as a "London Hotel" (possibly the Grosvenor House Hotel), the Oriental Hotel in Alexandria, and the Blue Mosque in Turkey.

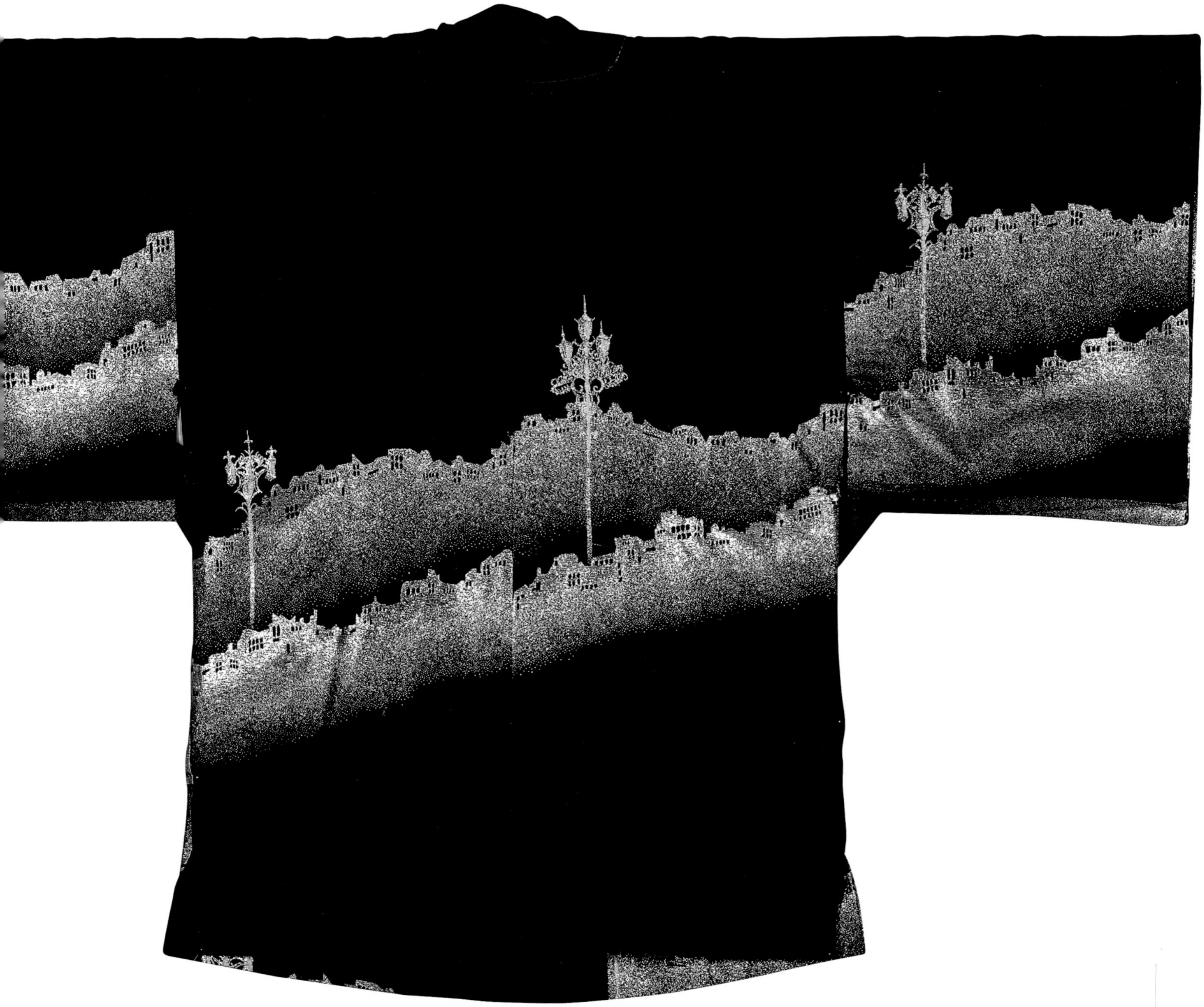

CITY LIFE

Woman's *haori*
Night-time cityscape with lit lamp posts
Taishō–Shōwa period, 1920s–1940
Silk with woven *urushi* threads design
51.0 × 38.0 inches (130 × 97 centimeters)
KM060

The design of this simple but very elegant *haori* demonstrates the special skill of the designer. A dark sky without stars provides a dramatic background for a midnight walk along the paths of a city's central park, but the tall lantern-like lamps posted along the way give enough bright light to help the verdant shrubs shine in the dark. The smooth black silk has been stitched with great care for the metallic density of the bushes, which helps to make the walkway feel as though it has turned into an iridescent fairyland for an exciting evening.

MODERNITY/CITY LIFE

Man's *haori* with a decorative lining (*haura*)
City interiors
Taishō–Shōwa period, 1920s–1940
Silk plain weave *haori* (outer); *kata-yūzen* dyed and printed silk *haura* (lining)
52.0 × 42.0 inches (132 × 107 centimeters)
KM061

Men's *haori* were at the height of their popularity from the Taishō era into the early Shōwa era of the 1940s. While many men followed the *haori* trends of abstract, geometric, and Cubist-inspired designs of the 1920s and early 1930s, some chose designs that offered a new sense of living space. This *haori*'s *haura* shows an image of a flat furnished in Western style that overlooks the city. The room contains books, plants, a unique lamp, wallpaper, pictures, decorative objects, and a very interesting credenza with modern designs on it. It could very well be a comfortable place in which to live.

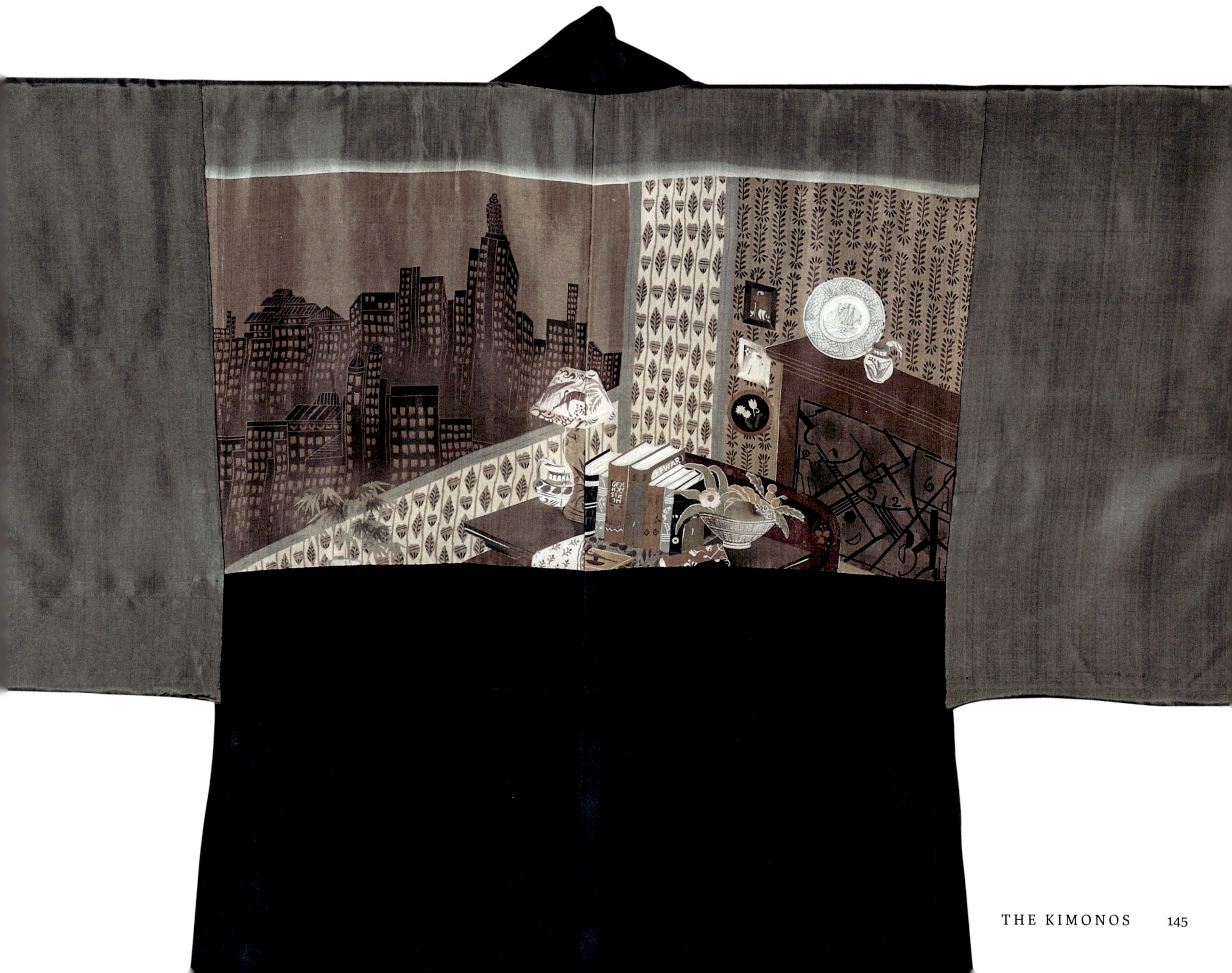

MODERNITY

Man's *haori* with a decorative lining (*haura*)
A changing world
Traditional and modern bridges
Taishō–Shōwa period, 1920s–1940
Silk plain weave *haori* (outer); *kata-yūzen* dyed and printed silk *haura* (lining)
53.0 × 44.0 inches (135 × 112 centimeters)
KM062

These two contrasting scenes show a traditional bridge and a very modern bridge, and those who viewed these images must have immediately seen the clash between the two worlds. One scene captures the past of Japan: a wooden bridge that leads travelers, workers, and neighbors to the clusters of small houses, tea shops, and stores that are the livelihood of this little town. The second scene opens on a much larger world, one that expands so far that the earlier town has all but disappeared. The new metropolis not only features a large railroad bridge spanning the river, but shows off multi-story houses, churches, viaducts, and more. It is indeed a new world.

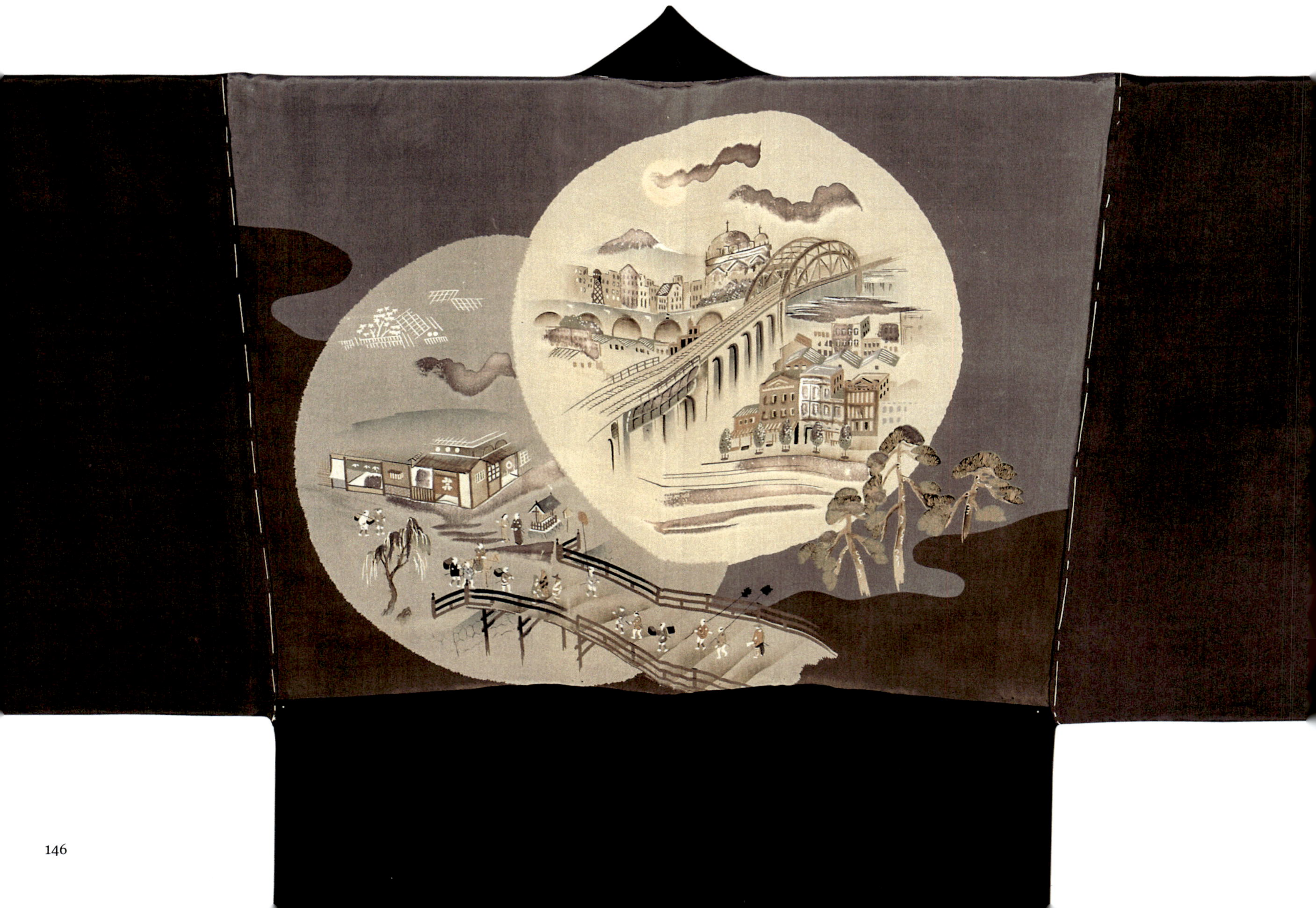

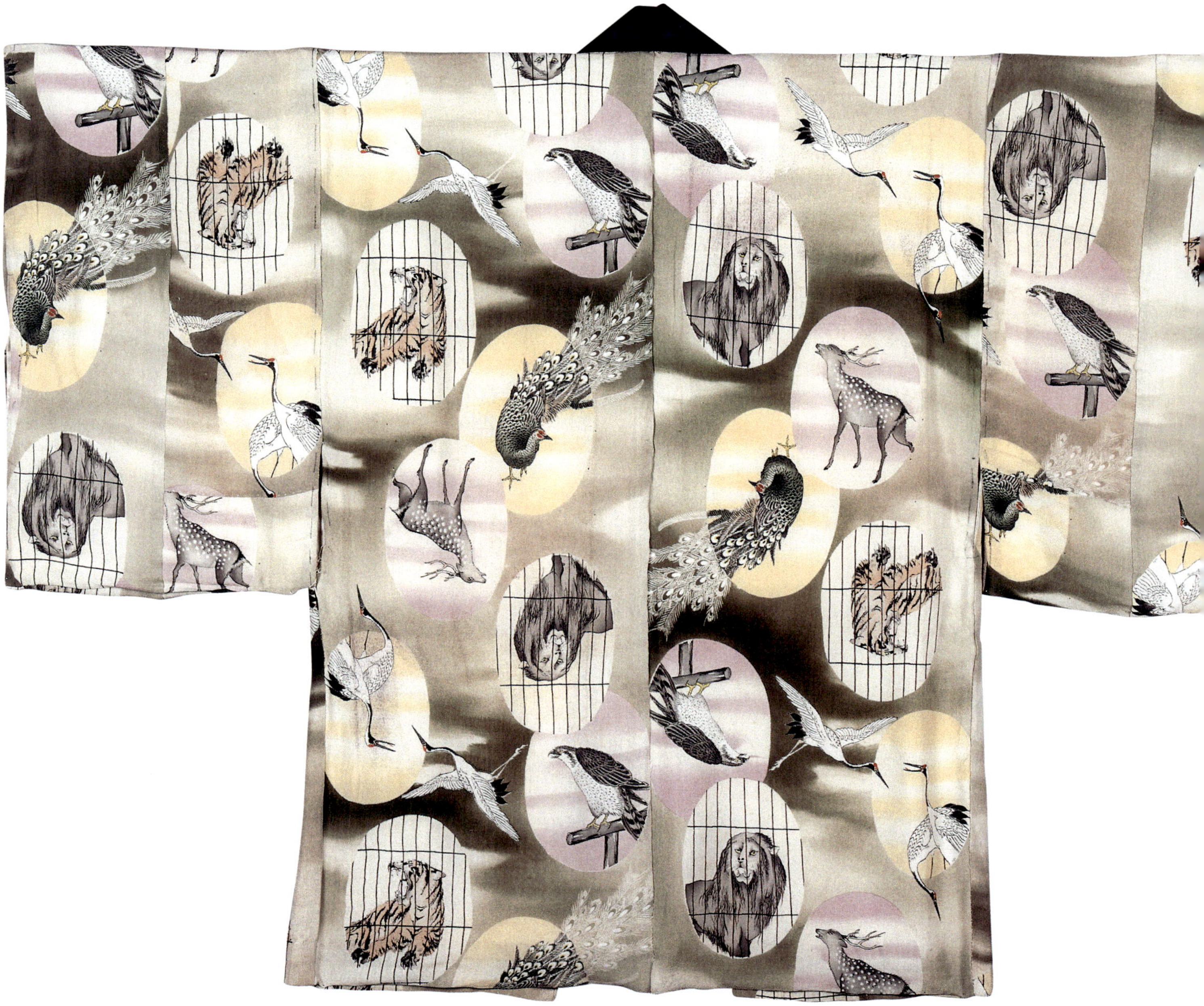

LEISURE ACTIVITIES/ ZOO

Woman's *hanjuban*
A visit to the zoo
Taishō–Shōwa period, 1920s–1940
Hand-painted *chirimen* (silk crepe)
48.0 × 37.0 inches (122 × 94 centimeters)
KM063

The Ueno Zoological Gardens started life as a menagerie attached to the National Museum of Natural History in Tokyo. The menagerie was converted into a public zoo in 1882, to the delight of the citizens of Tokyo. The grounds were originally part of the estate of the imperial family, but they were granted to the municipal government on the occasion of the Crown Prince Hirohito's wedding in 1924. This is Japan's oldest zoo, and it is now home to more than 3,000 animals. This lovely rendering of several of the most popular animals in the zoo was done during the Taishō or early Shōwa period. Undoubtedly the regal lion and snarling Sumatran tiger would have been special favorites of visitors at that time.

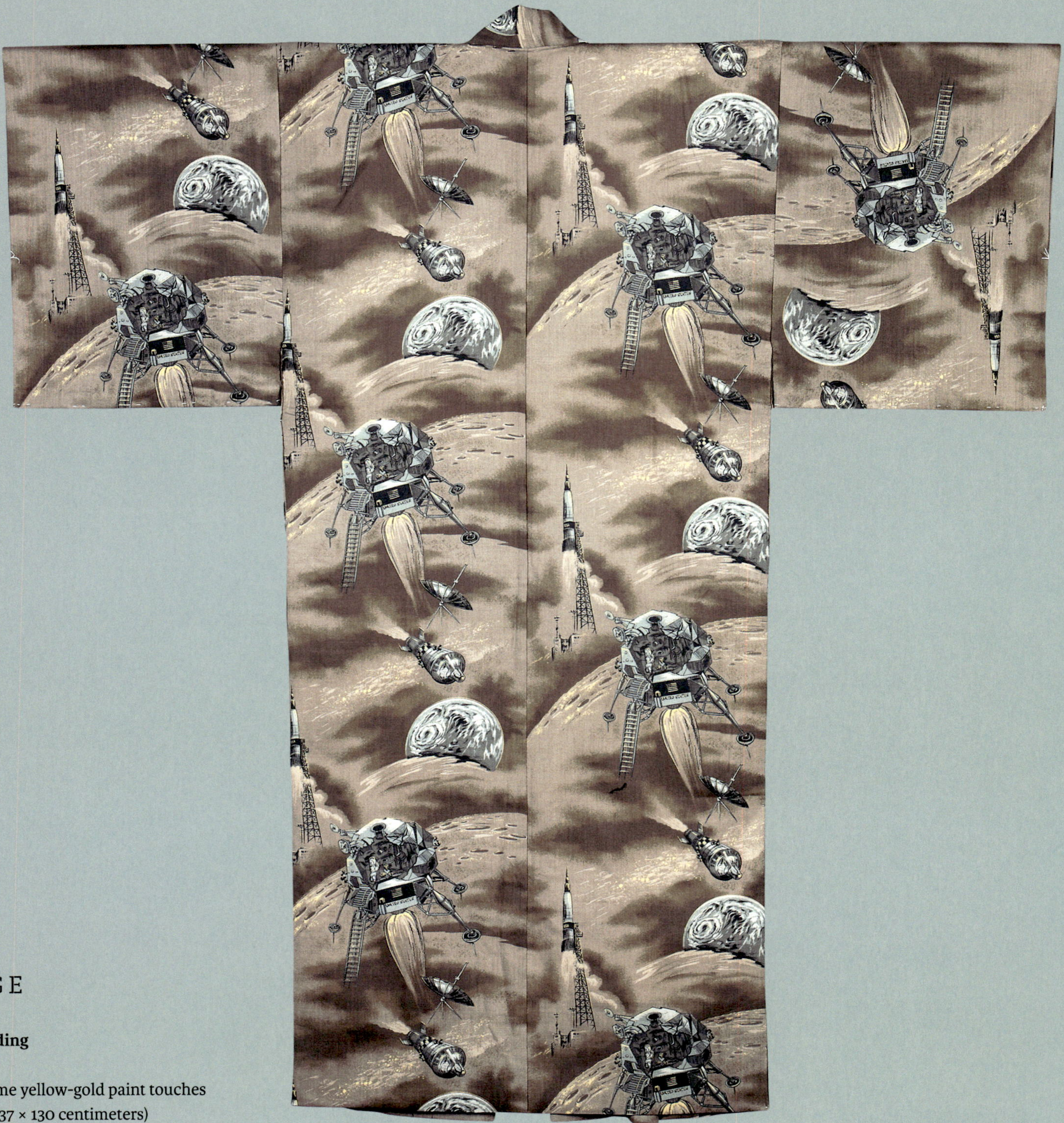

SPACE AGE

***Juban* for a man**
The first moon landing
Shōwa period, 1969
Printed silk with some yellow-gold paint touches
54.0 × 51.0 inches (137 × 130 centimeters)
KM064

This *juban* was a commemoration of the Apollo Lunar Module Eagle, in which humans first landed on the moon. The first step of Commander Neil Armstrong onto the lunar surface was broadcast on live TV to a worldwide audience. About two-thirds of the audience were from the United States, the rest from 55 other countries (including Japan). Millions more around the world listened to radio broadcasts, and 20 percent of the world's population watched humans walk on the moon for the first time. It was, without question, a not-to-be-missed event for those who waited with bated breath for Armstrong's famous words as he stepped onto the moon: "One small step for man, one giant leap for mankind."

CITY LIFE

Man's *haori* with a decorative lining (*haura*)
Early modern Japan vs. "The New Modern"
Taishō–Shōwa period, 1912–1940
Silk plain weave *haori* (outer); *kata-yūzen* dyed and printed silk *haura* (lining)
52.0 × 42.0 inches (132 × 107 centimeters)
KM065

The *haura* sewn onto this *haori* carries a mélange of the old and the new Tokyo. The circle encompasses a traditional street scene lined with shops, where women wear old-style kimono and coats as they buy food and take time to chat with neighbors in the chilly morning. However, a man wearing a Western-style jacket and hat and a telephone pole that rises between the shops indicate that this street is well on its way to modernity. The "New Modern" of Tokyo has taken over, with a large clock that shows day and night, nightclubs, new apartment buildings, Western card games, and a suspension bridge above it all.

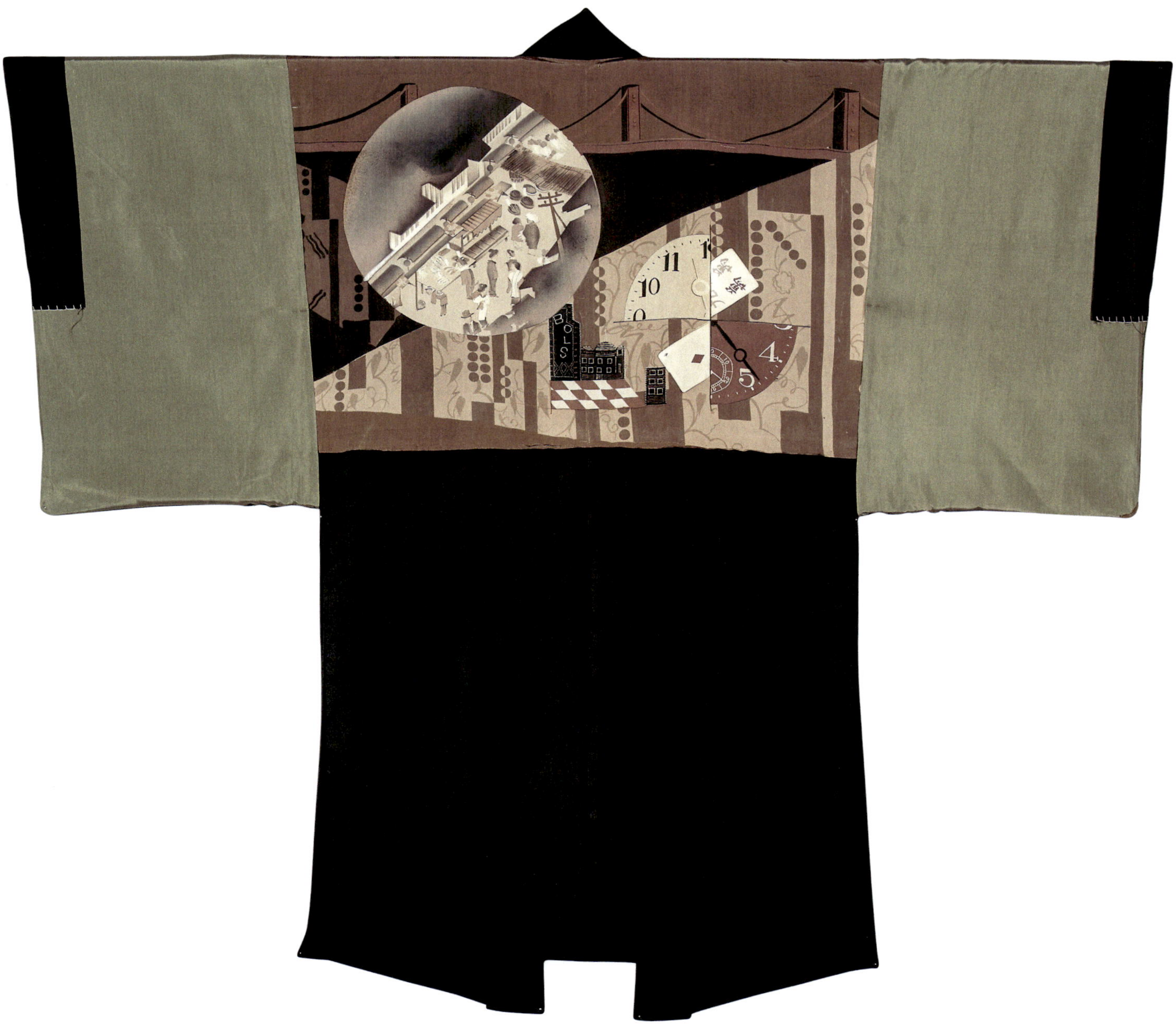

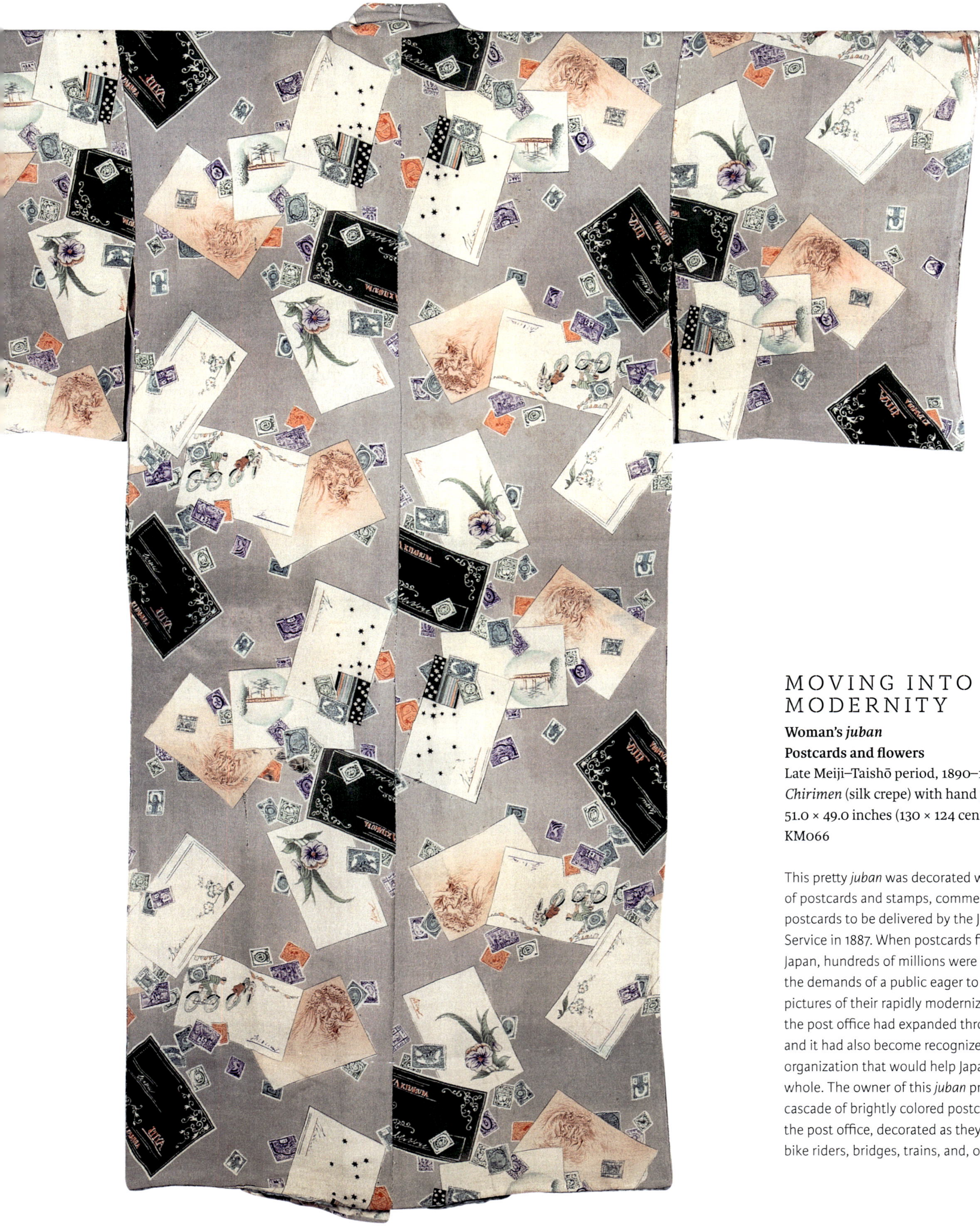

MOVING INTO MODERNITY

Woman's *juban*
Postcards and flowers
Late Meiji–Taishō period, 1890–1920s
Chirimen (silk crepe) with hand painting
51.0 × 49.0 inches (130 × 124 centimeters)
KM066

This pretty *juban* was decorated with a flowery deluge of postcards and stamps, commemorating the first postcards to be delivered by the Japanese Postal Service in 1887. When postcards first appeared in Japan, hundreds of millions were produced to meet the demands of a public eager to acquire words and pictures of their rapidly modernizing nation. By 1900, the post office had expanded throughout the country, and it had also become recognized as a profitable organization that would help Japan's economy as a whole. The owner of this *juban* probably enjoyed this cascade of brightly colored postcards produced by the post office, decorated as they were with racing bike riders, bridges, trains, and, of course, flowers.

MODERNITY

Man's *haori* with a decorative lining (*haura*)
A street scene and cigarettes
Taishō–Shōwa period, 1920s–1930s
Silk plain weave *haori* (outer); *yūzen* dyed and printed silk *haura* (lining)
51.0 × 44.0 inches (130 × 112 centimeters)
KM067

The *haura* of this man's *haori* is an excellent example of the changing cityscape. The energy of everyday life becomes apparent as the street fills with hurrying people. Some are rushing for buses and tramcars; others, below ground, await subway trains as they go to work. An abundance of bicyclists cruise through the streets as a policeman stands on his box, carefully watching to ensure the busy traffic makes no mistakes. Telephone poles and lines are ubiquitous, as are the electric lines overhead that power the trams. The street scene is framed with a bevy of cigarette boxes, each with amusing covers that serve well as advertisements.

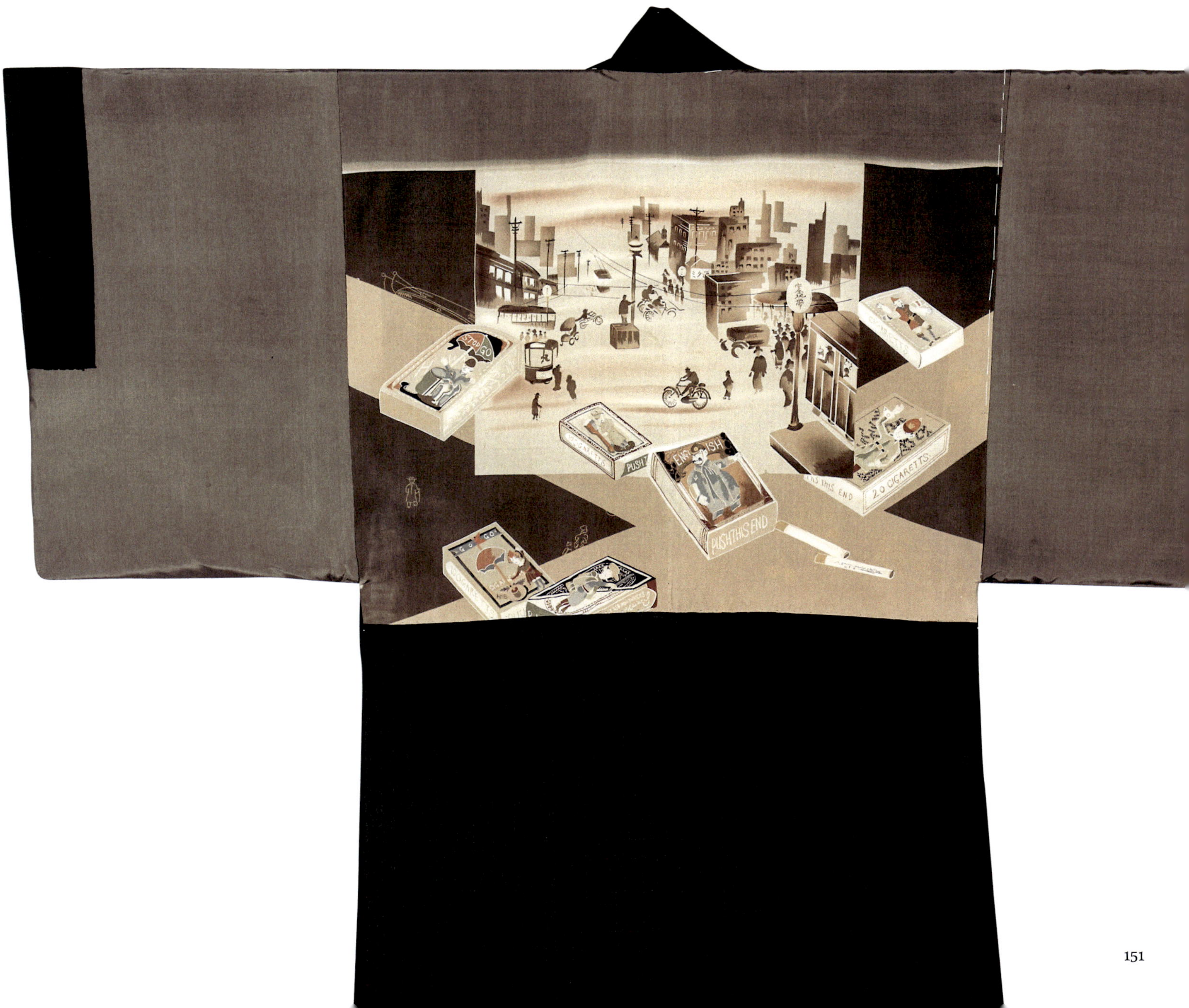

MODERNITY

Man's *haori* with a decorative lining
Books, calendars, and cigarettes
Shōwa period, 1930s
Silk plain weave *haori* (outer); *kata-yūzen* dyed and printed silk lining (includes sleeves)
52.0 × 37.0 inches (132 × 94 centimeters)
KM068

This is a rather odd presentation for this *haori*. The background has neatly placed marching rows of cigarettes and matches, and the foreground shows cigarette cases and matchboxes, a calendar for Tuesday, November 3, 1932 (a leap year), an inkwell with a feather pen, an unopened envelope, and two books. The *Annual of American Design 1932* may be a fabrication; the *Annual of American Design* was published in 1931. The other book is written by Joseph Wood Krutch (1893–1970), an American writer, critic, and naturalist: it is his *Experience and Art: Some Aspects of the Esthetics of Literature* (1932), although the entire book title is not given here.

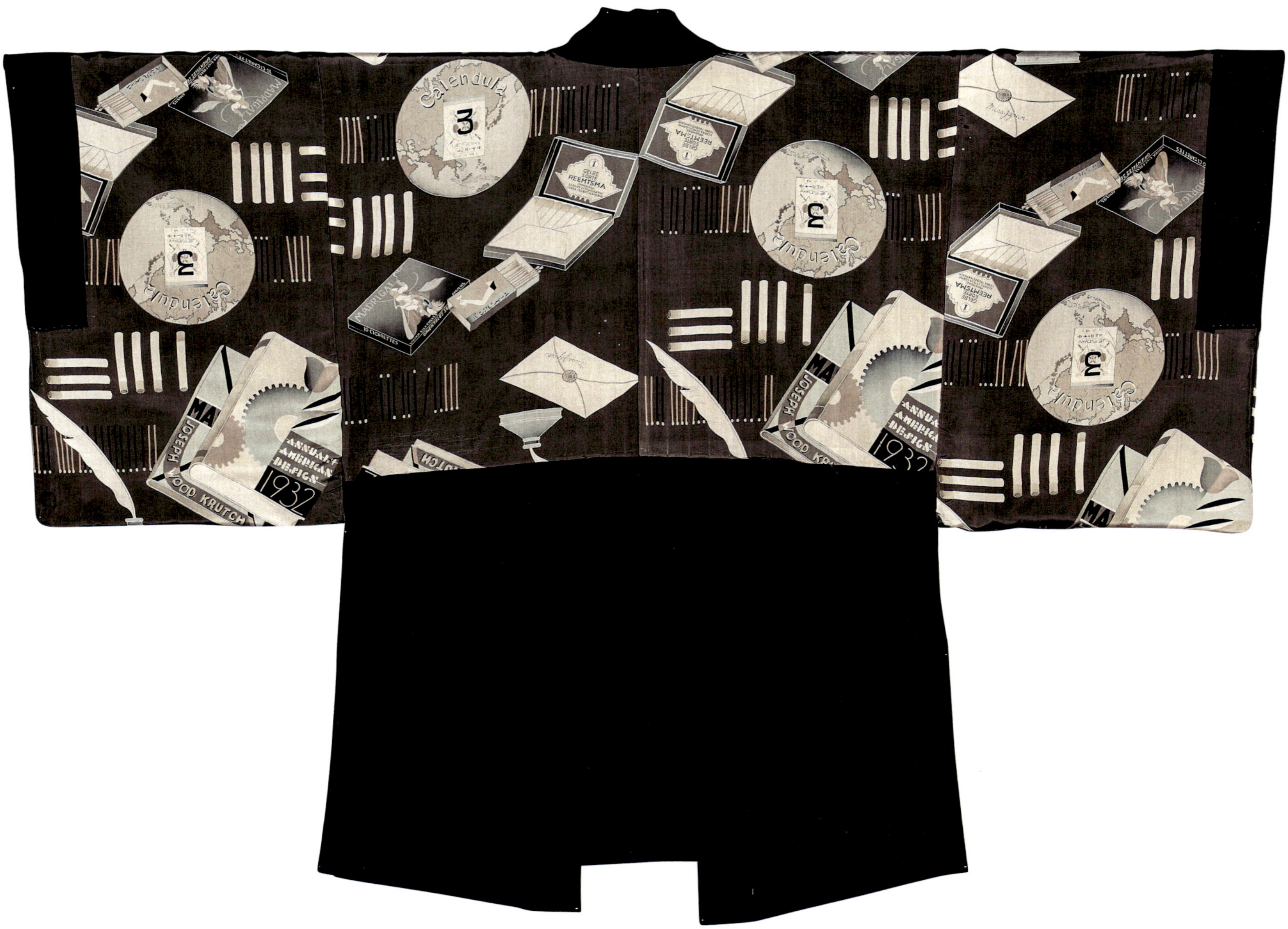

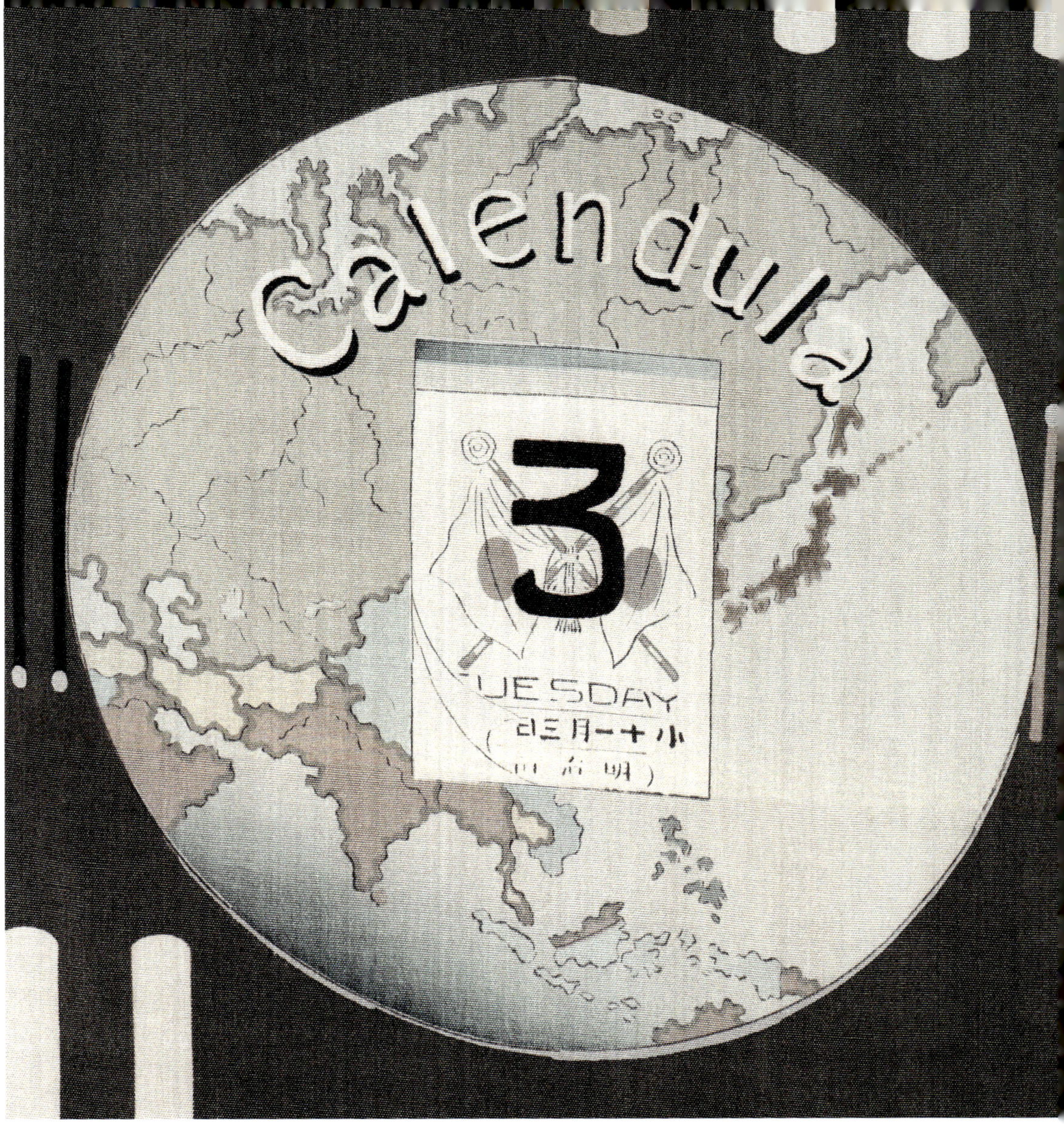
Calendula
3
UESDAY

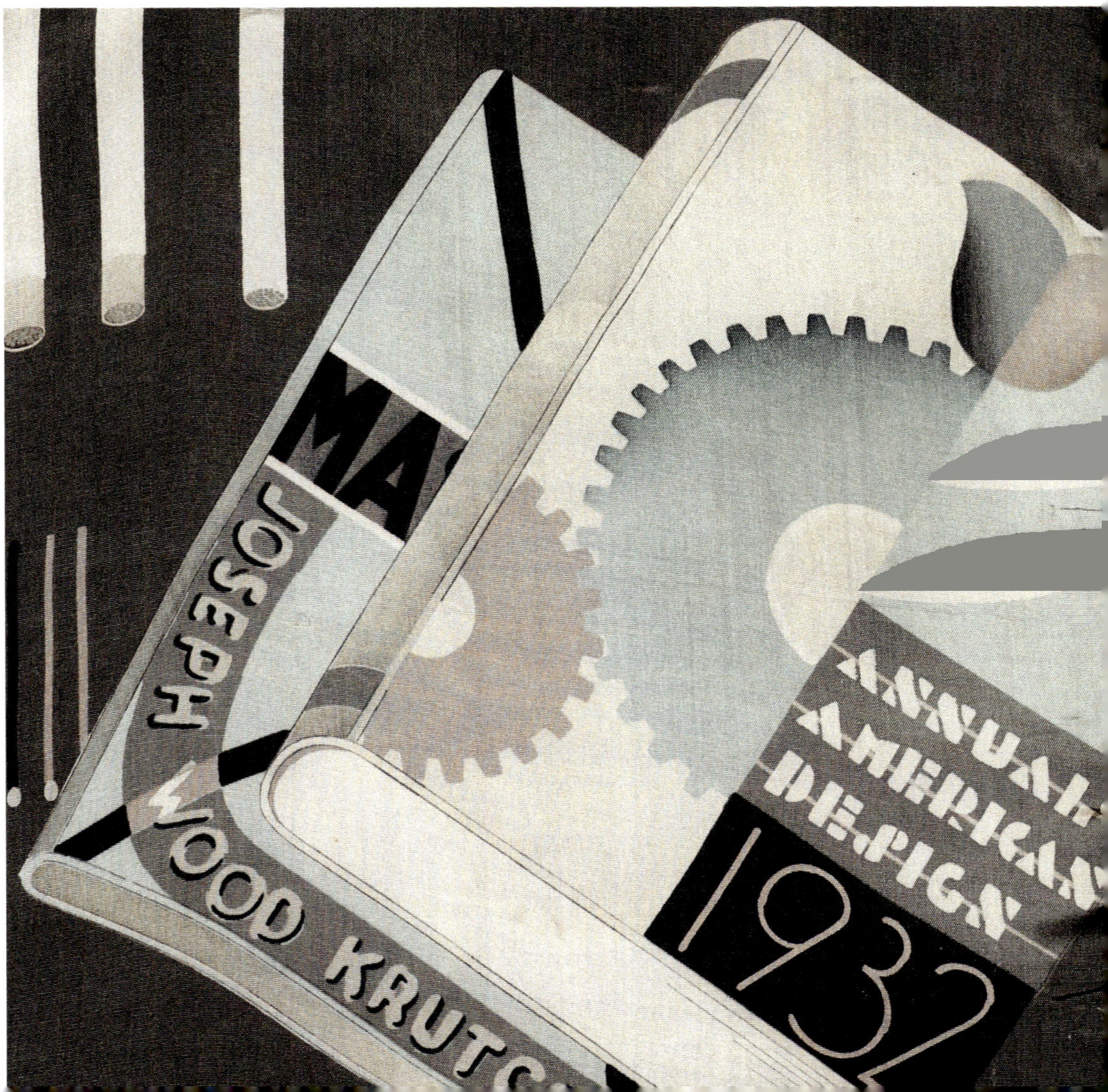
MA
JOSEPH
WOOD KRUTC
ANNUAL
AMERICAN
DESIGN
1932

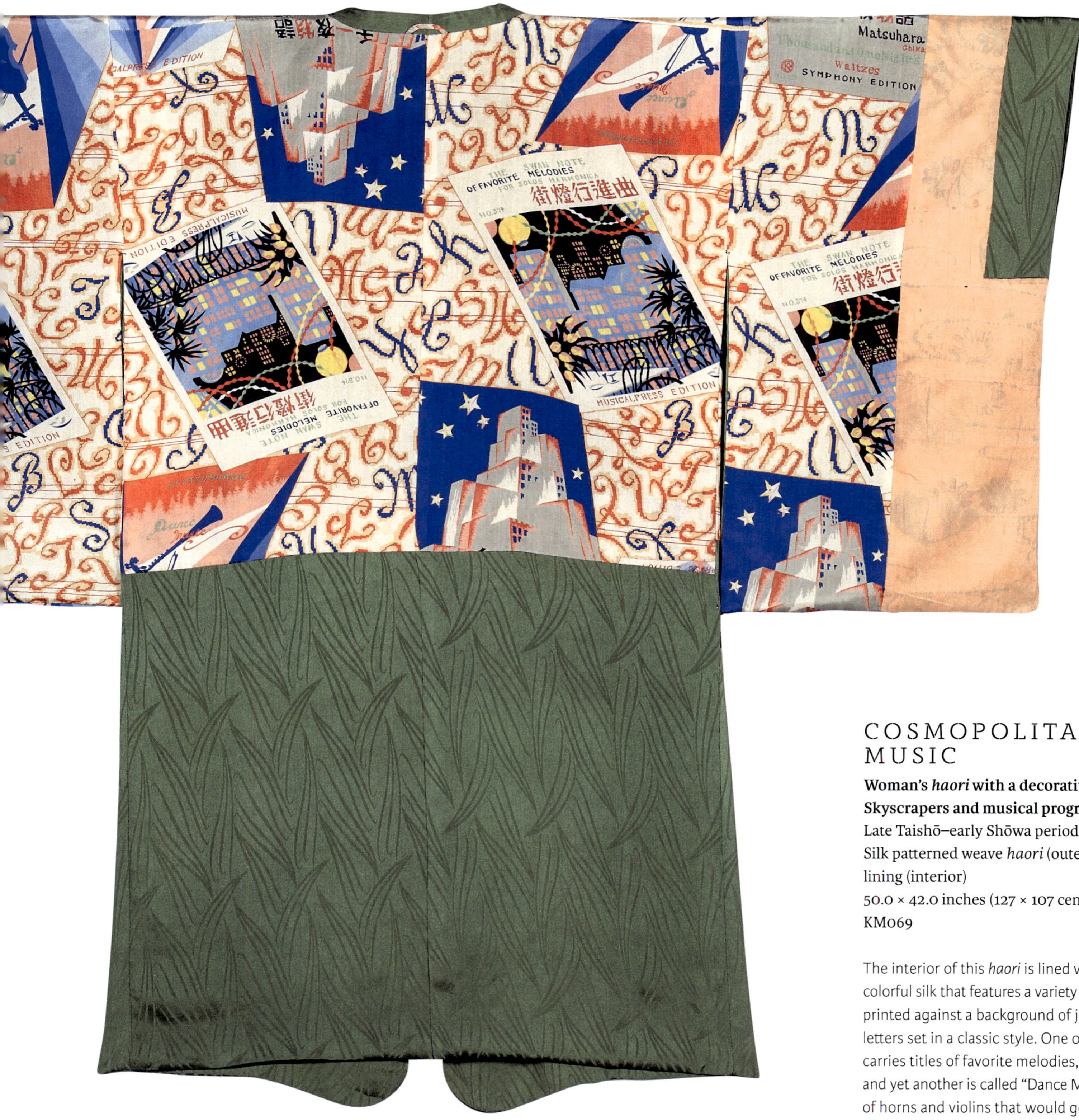

COSMOPOLITANISM/ MUSIC

Woman's *haori* with a decorative lining
Skyscrapers and musical programs
Late Taishō–early Shōwa period, 1920s–1940
Silk patterned weave *haori* (outer); printed silk lining (interior)
50.0 × 42.0 inches (127 × 107 centimeters)
KM069

The interior of this *haori* is lined with bright and colorful silk that features a variety of musical programs printed against a background of jumbled alphabet letters set in a classic style. One of the programs carries titles of favorite melodies, another of waltzes, and yet another is called "Dance Music," with drawings of horns and violins that would go with the music. The outer textile used for this *haori* is a very pretty green patterned silk, and when the *haori* is taken off, the colorful interior lining can be seen and appreciated.

MODERNITY/CITY LIFE

Man's *haori* with a decorative lining (*haura*)
Bars, billiards, music, and tea
Taishō–Shōwa period, 1920–1940
Silk plain weave *haori* (outer); *kata-yūzen* dyed and printed silk *haura* (lining)
51.0 × 42.0 inches (130 × 107 centimeters)
KM070

The design for this *haori* called for a large, roofed space, tall, elegant columns, and Matisse-like frescoes that float high behind the columns. It may depict a music hall or symphony space, as indicated by the musical posters on the walls, and other cozy, intimate spaces where wine bars and tea salons put forth food and drink, or billiards and booze. All in all, this is a heady mix of the possibilities that can be found in the new and modern metropolises of Japan.

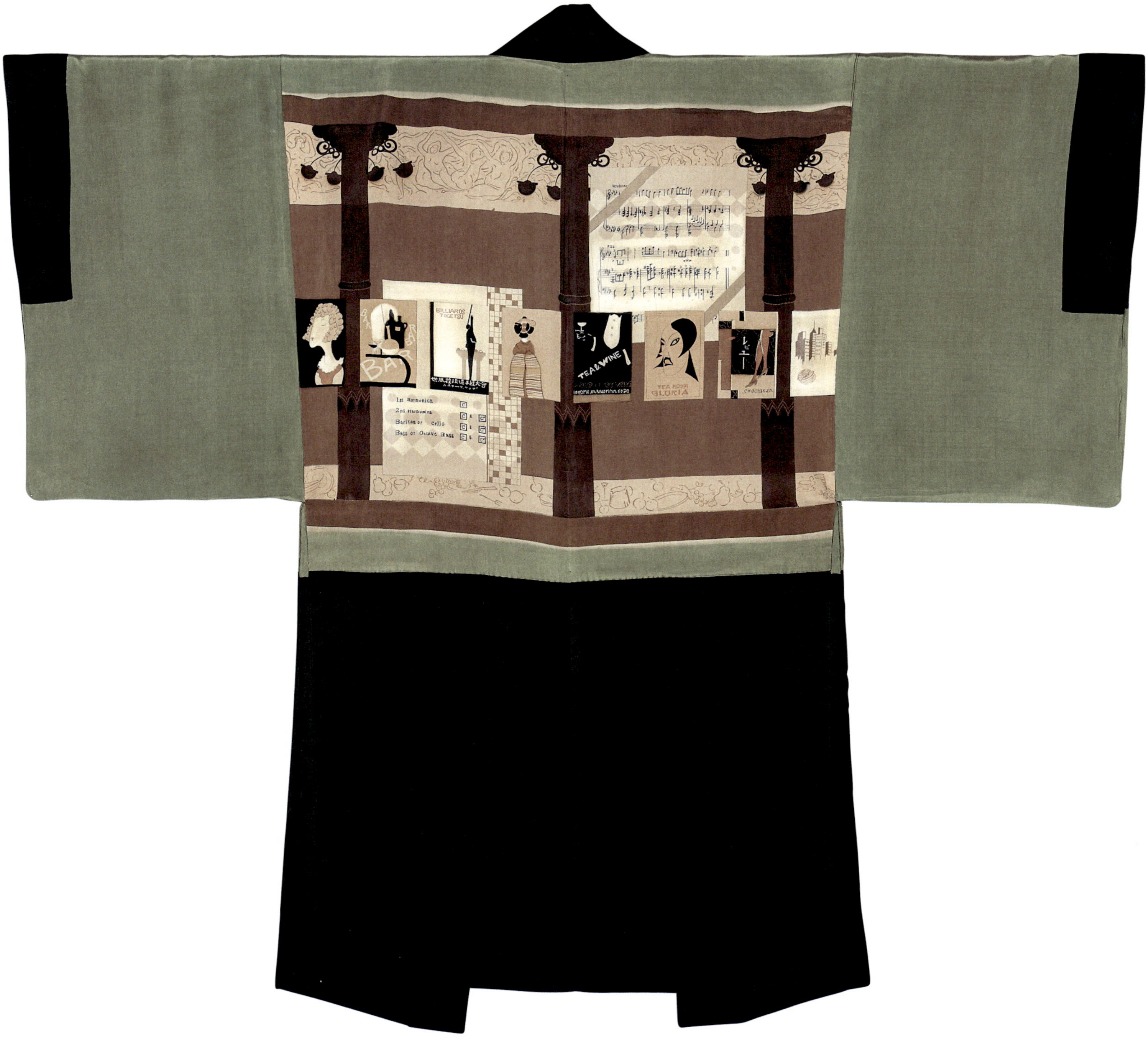

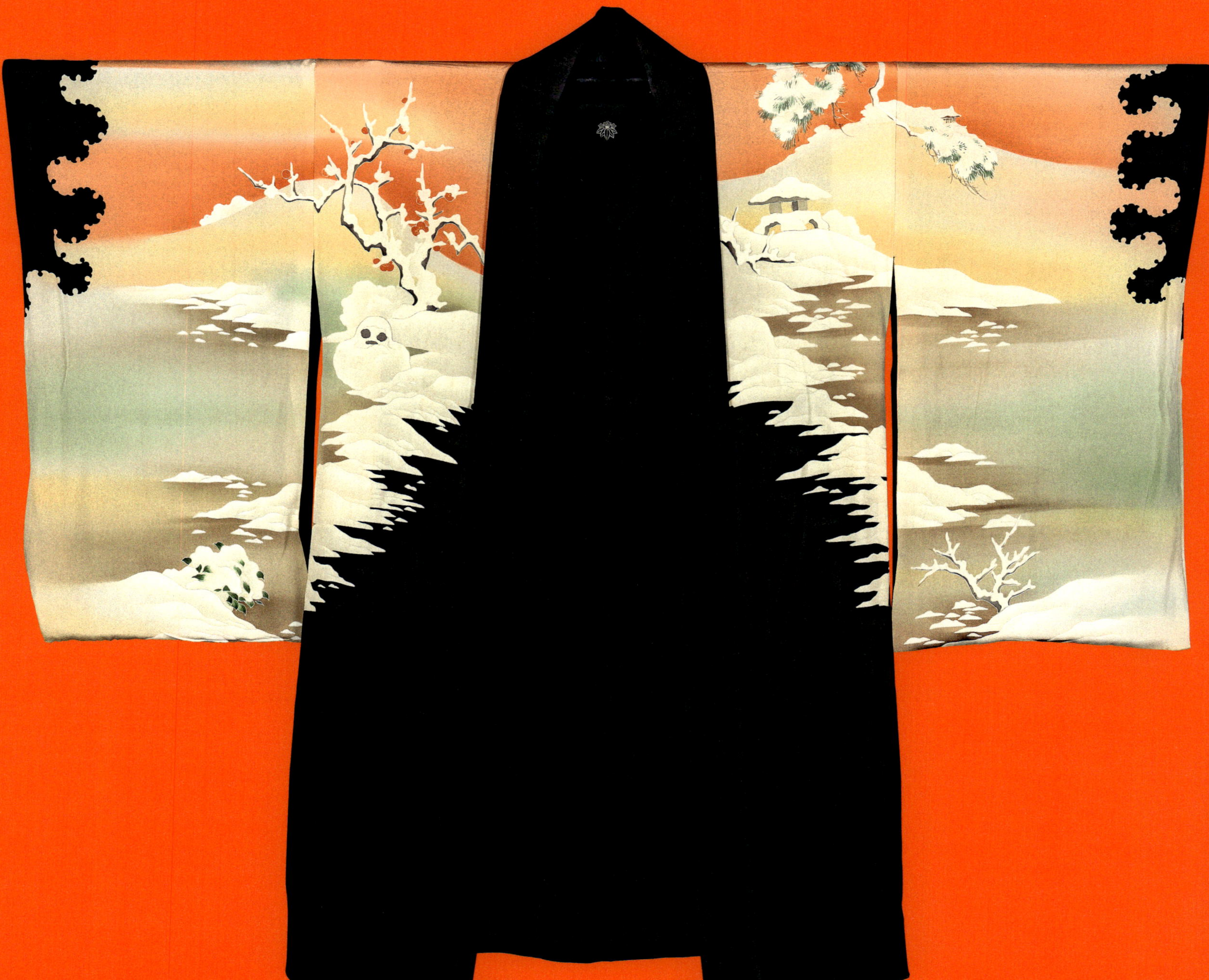

THE BEAUTY OF ART

***Muso haori* with a decorative interior**
Children building a snowman
Taishō–Shōwa period, 1912–1930s
Yūzen dyed and painted silk
49.0 × 42.0 inches (124 × 107 centimeters)
KM071

A *muso haori* is quite different from other *haori*, as there is no cutting of the fabric between the inside and the outside of the garment. The interior silk textile for this *haori* has been carefully dyed and painted to show white, wintry motifs as well as a spectacular orange sky. Two children are shown carefully building a snowman under a pine tree laden with snow while other children watch their friends at work. The garment's front interior textile panels show another snowman under a pomegranate tree on one side and a snow-laden small stone garden temple on the other. Occasionally these interior designs might seep to the outer side of the cloth, as intended by the textile artist. The formal family crest here uses gentian flowers and bamboo leaves; the crest was used mostly by court nobles.

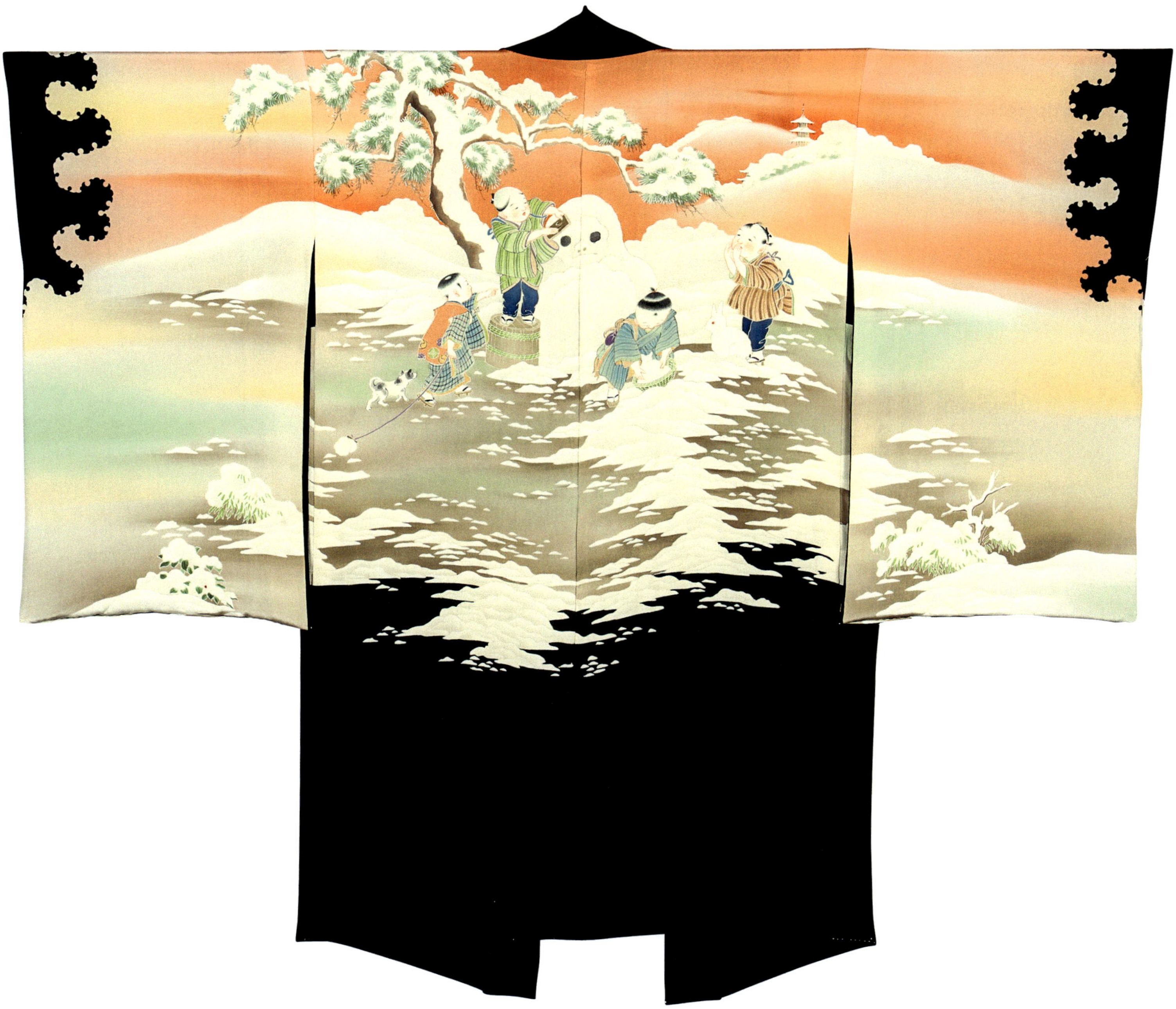

CARTOONS

Kimono for a child
Rambunctious children and dogs
Shōwa period, late 1940s–1950s
Kata-yūzen dyed silk
25.0 × 24.0 inches (64 × 61 centimeters)
KM072

Japanese textile artists were tireless in their search for new designs to catch the buyer's eye. Here, the source of inspiration was the popular cartoon "Blondie." In this child's kimono, Blondie and her husband Dagwood Bumstead don't appear; the focus is instead on the two children (Alexander and Cookie), the family dog Daisy, and her thundering herd of puppies. Collections of the "Blondie" cartoon strips were published as books during the 1940s, and a Japanese artist probably copied the designs on this kimono directly from one of those books. The figures almost leap off the kimono and look exactly as they do in the books.

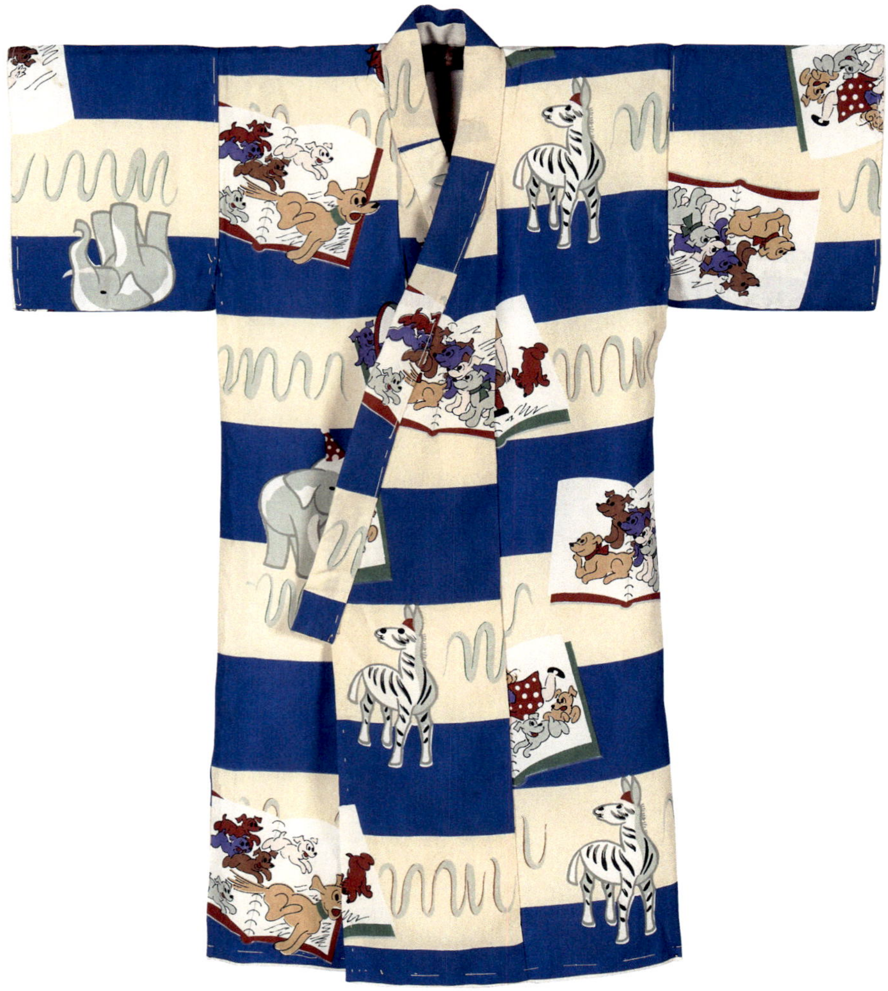

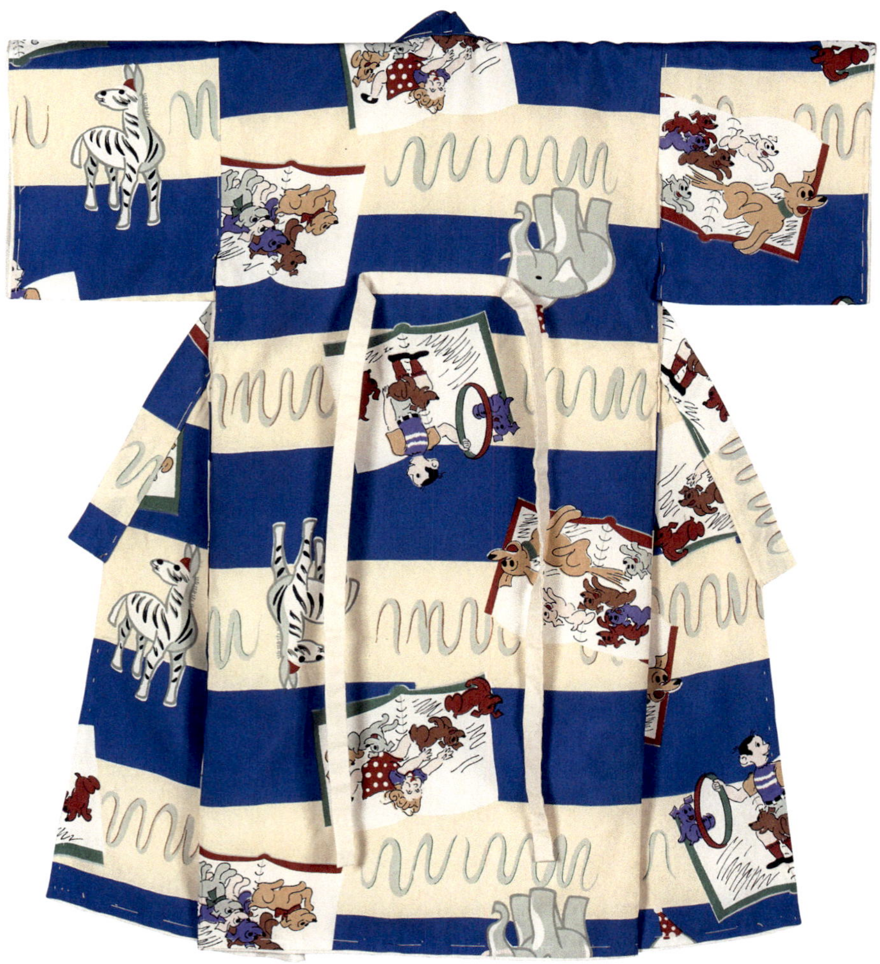

CARTOONS

Kimono for a child
Dumbo and other circus friends
Shōwa period, *c.* 1950s
Kata-yūzen dyed cotton with silver highlighting
33.0 × 32.0 inches (84 × 81 centimeters)
KM073

Cartoons and movies were a rich source of inspiration for Japan's modern textile designers, and Walt Disney's movies were particularly loved by the Japanese. One of Disney's most popular films was *Dumbo*, based on an enchanting children's story created by Helen Aberson-Mayer. Disney quickly bought the rights to her book, and *Dumbo* was released in 1941. Because of the war, *Dumbo* was not released in Japan until the 1950s, but the designer who drew Dumbo and his friends on this child's kimono certainly created a festive atmosphere, with giraffes, seals, elephants, birds, camels, horses with carriages—and Dumbo, the star of the show, of course—that would be much enjoyed by those who saw the movie.

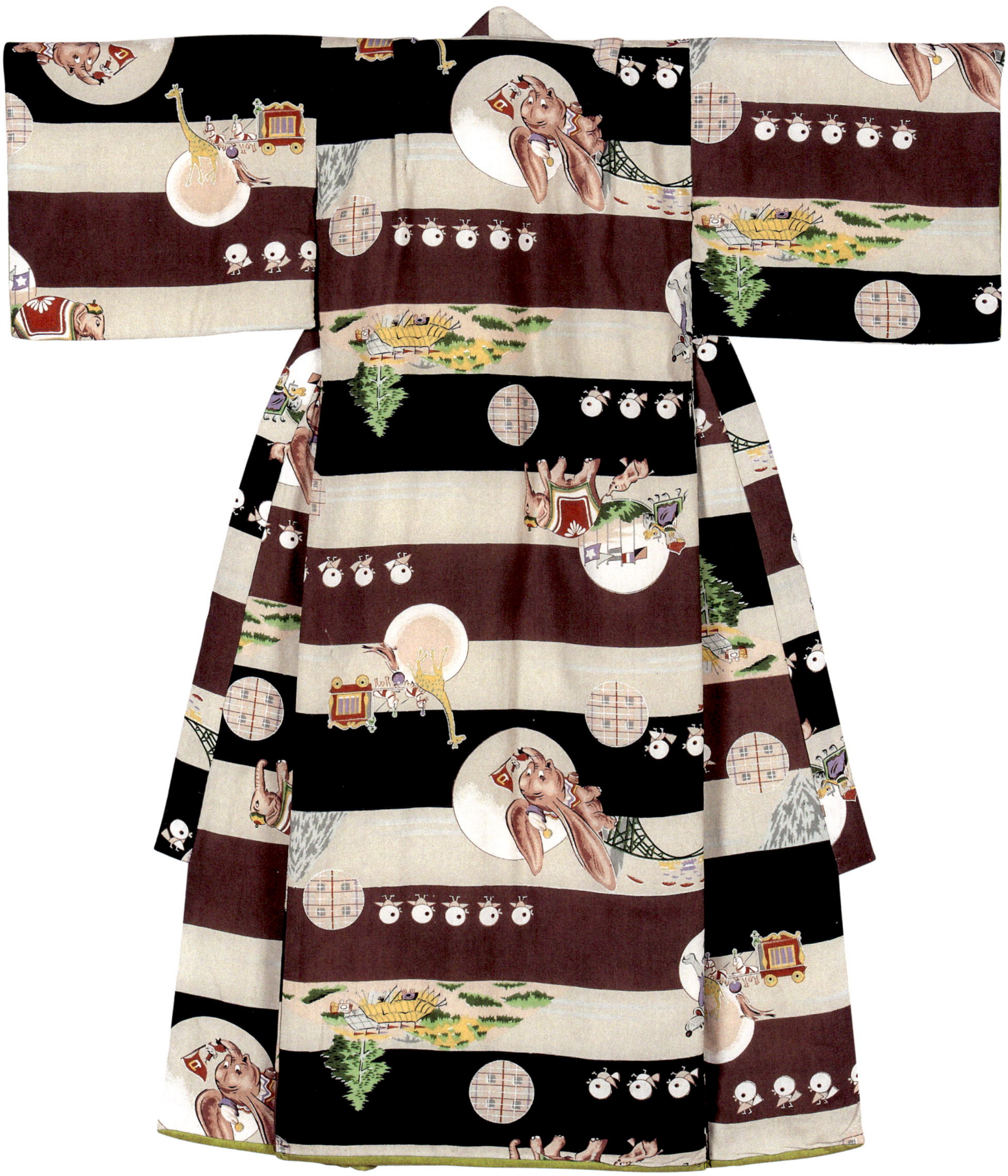

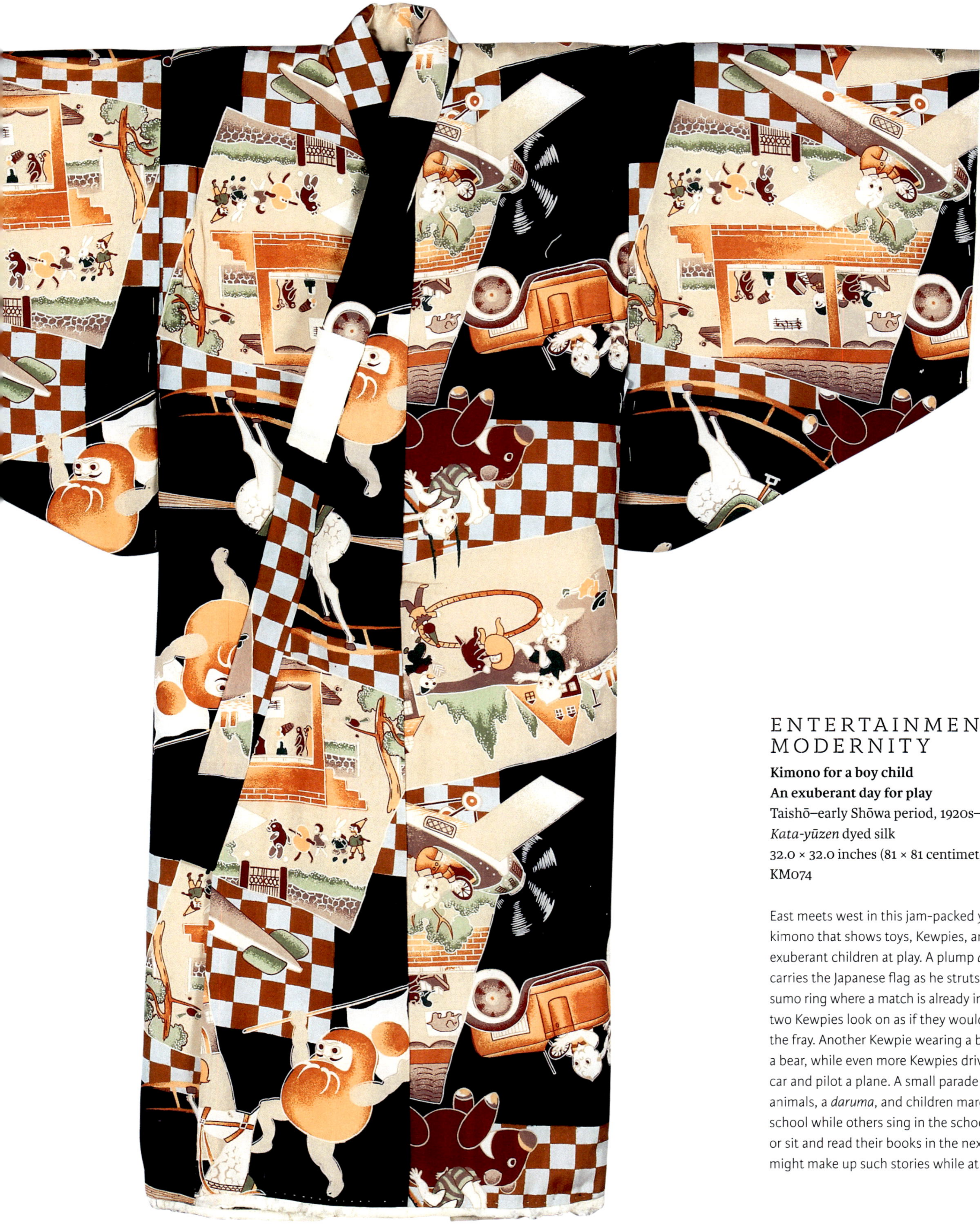

ENTERTAINMENT/ MODERNITY

Kimono for a boy child
An exuberant day for play
Taishō–early Shōwa period, 1920s–1930s
Kata-yūzen dyed silk
32.0 × 32.0 inches (81 × 81 centimeters)
KM074

East meets west in this jam-packed young boy's kimono that shows toys, Kewpies, animals, and exuberant children at play. A plump *daruma* with legs carries the Japanese flag as he struts toward a small sumo ring where a match is already in progress, and two Kewpies look on as if they would like to join the fray. Another Kewpie wearing a bathing suit rides a bear, while even more Kewpies drive a "modern" car and pilot a plane. A small parade consisting of animals, a *daruma*, and children march outside the school while others sing in the school's music room or sit and read their books in the next room. A child might make up such stories while at play.

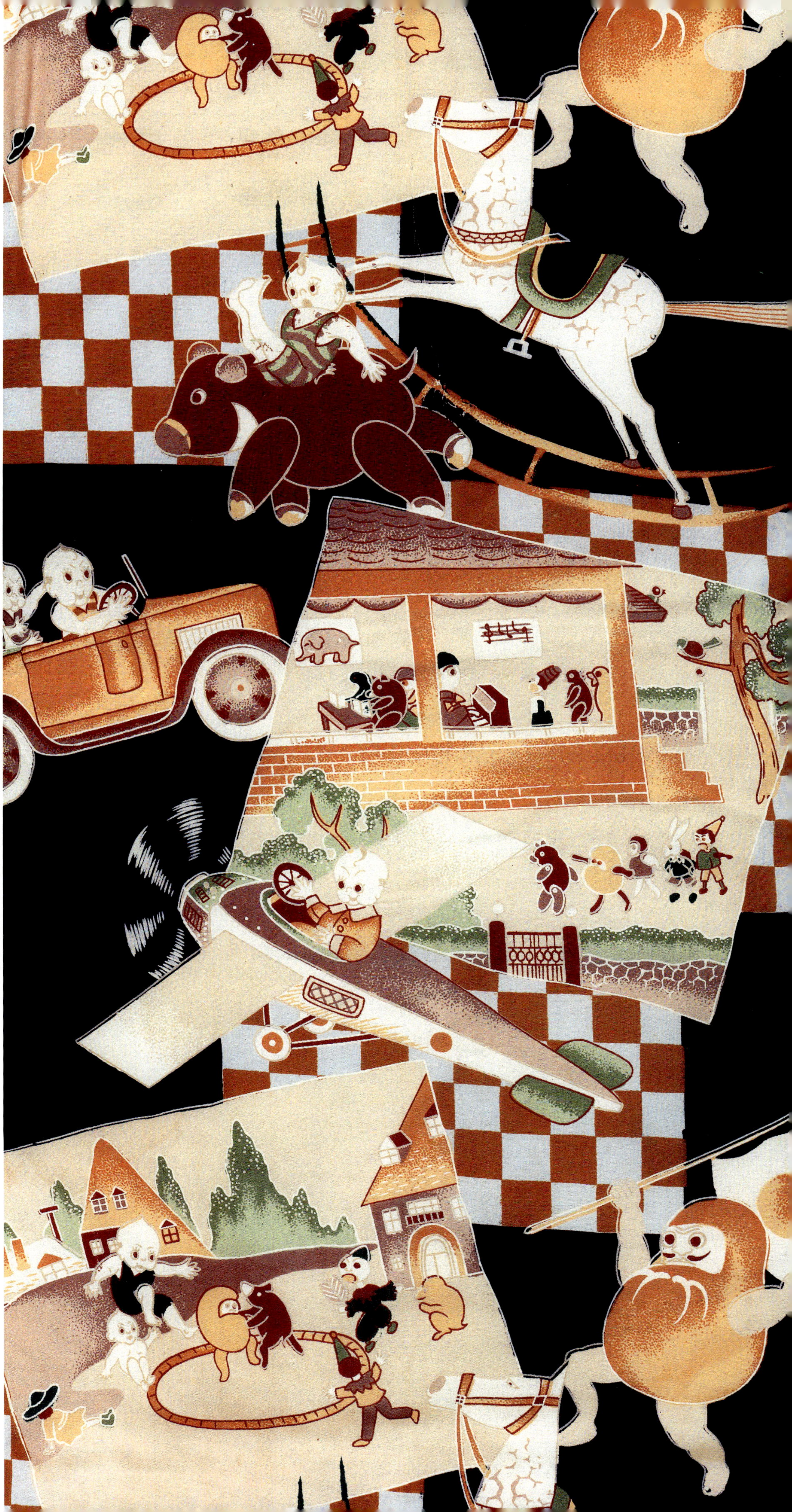

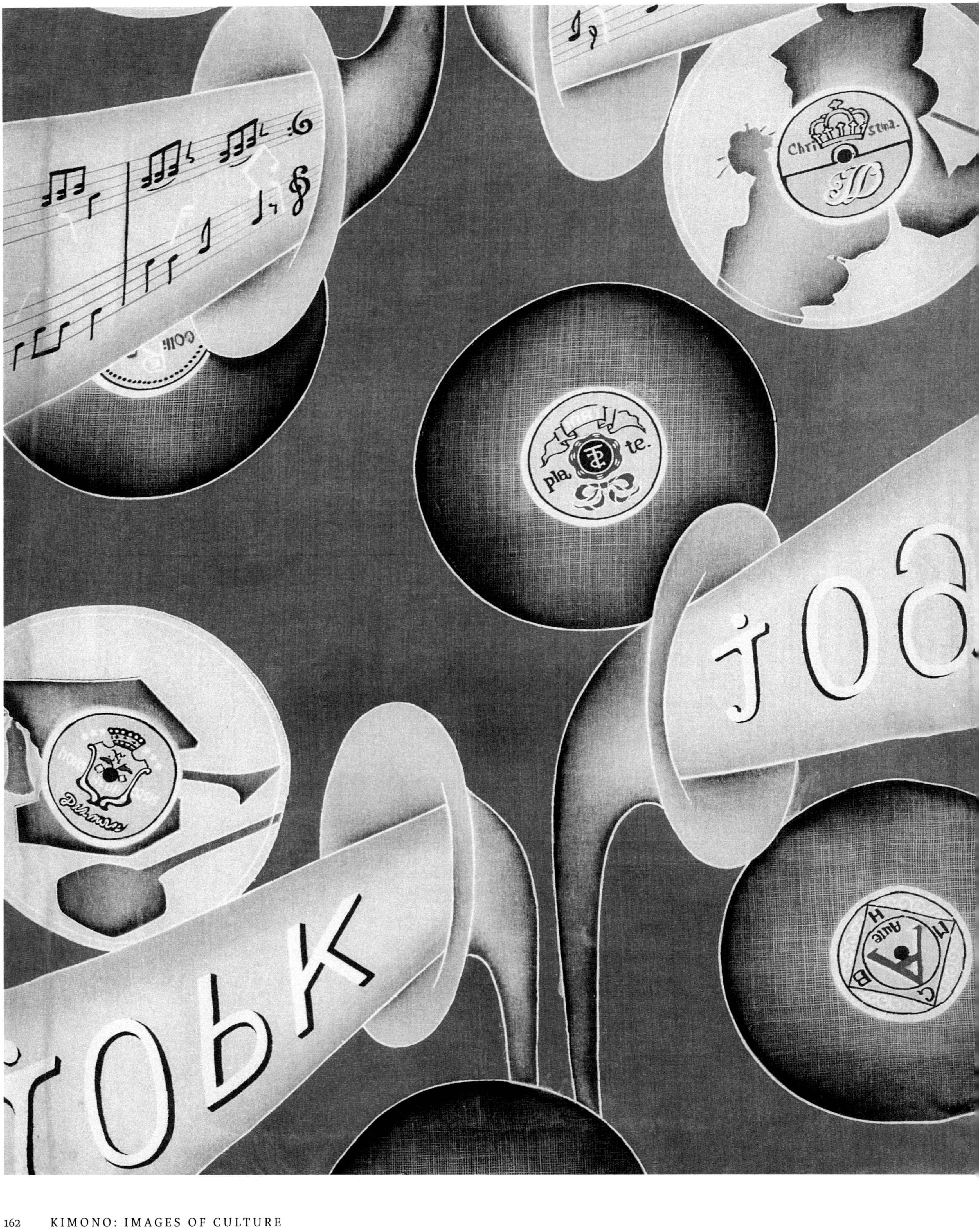
Chri stina.
pla. te.

MUSIC

***Juban* for a man**
Making music
Taishō–early Shōwa period, 1920s–1930s
Kata-yūzen dyed silk
50.0 × 50.0 inches (127 × 127 centimeters)
KM075

The textile designs used for this *juban* would have made for a wonderful complementary garment to wear while listening to music. The textile is covered with images of the records that were broadcast from the Tokyo Broadcasting Station via its call letters JOAK and JOKB (sometimes written backwards here). The design of this *juban* shows the station's call letters as well as music from the records flying out of strange-looking horns; these helped to create better acoustics when connected to radios. The designs on the faces of the records indicate what instruments might be played, or perhaps what conductor or ballet might be heard.

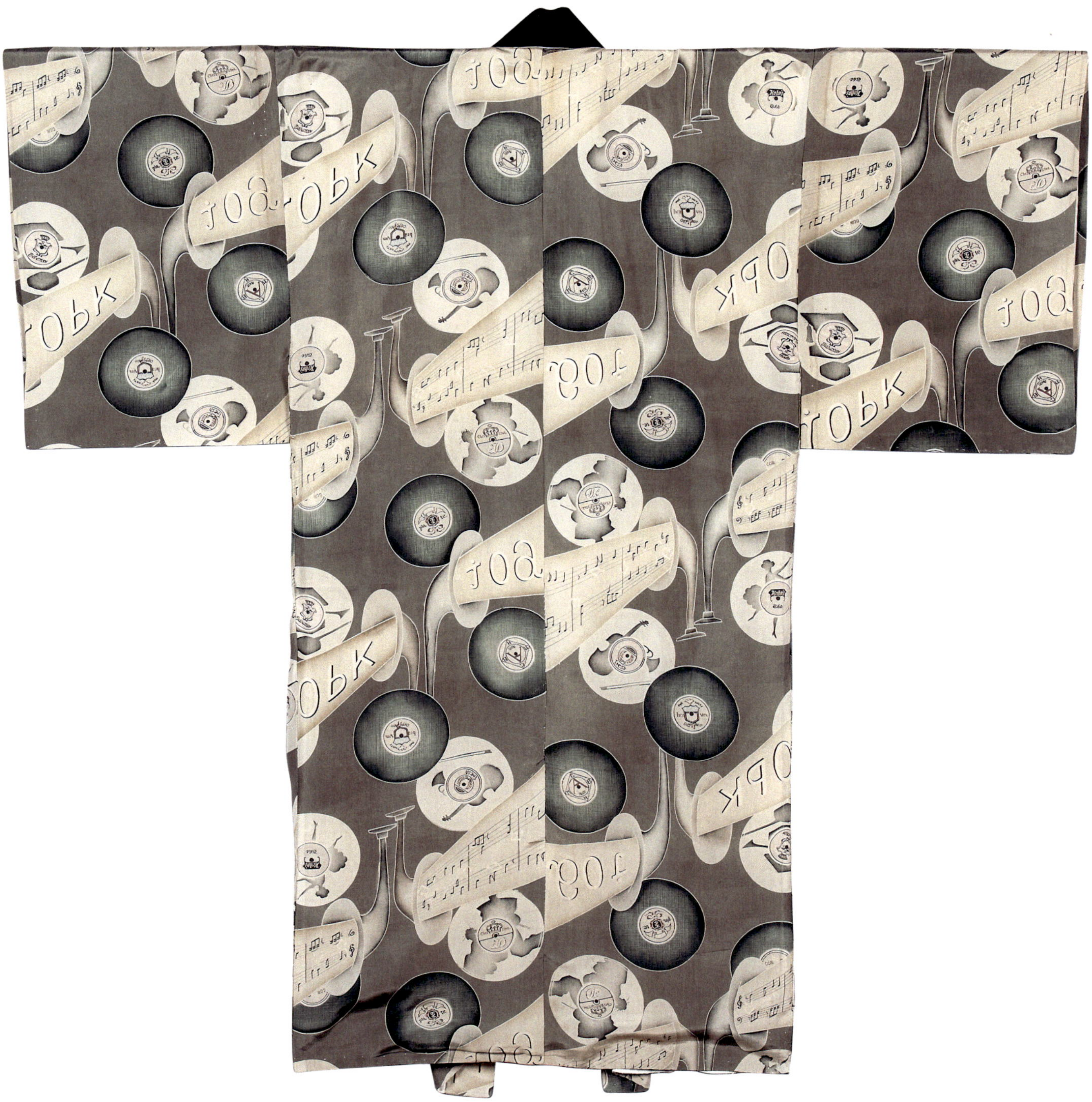

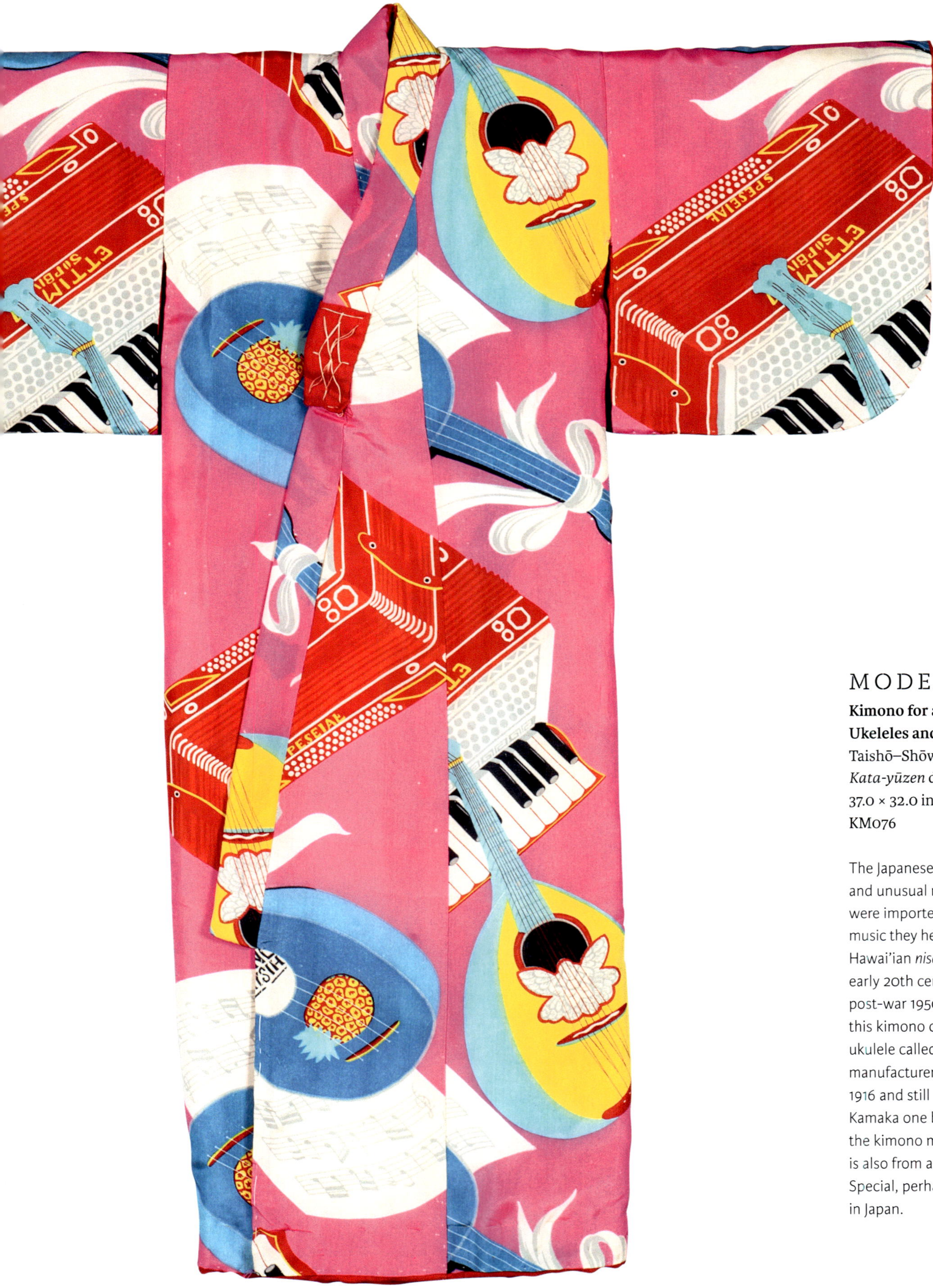

MODERNITY

Kimono for a girl child
Ukeleles and accordions
Taishō–Shōwa period, 1930s–1950s
Kata-yūzen dyed and printed silk
37.0 × 32.0 inches (94 × 81 centimeters)
KM076

The Japanese had a keen interest in Western music, and unusual musical instruments such as ukuleles were imported so musicians could reproduce the music they heard on records and in movies. Although Hawai'ian *nisei* brought ukuleles to Japan in the early 20th century, the ukulele's heyday was in the post-war 1950s. The artist who crafted patterns for this kimono chose to make a delightful copy of a ukulele called the "Pineapple," made by the Hawai'ian manufacturer Kamaka Hawai'i, Inc. (established in 1916 and still in business). The interior label is not a Kamaka one but more likely to be a coy reference to the kimono maker. The accordion drawn on the textile is also from a real-life model, the Settimio Soprani Special, perhaps made by the owner of the store in Japan.

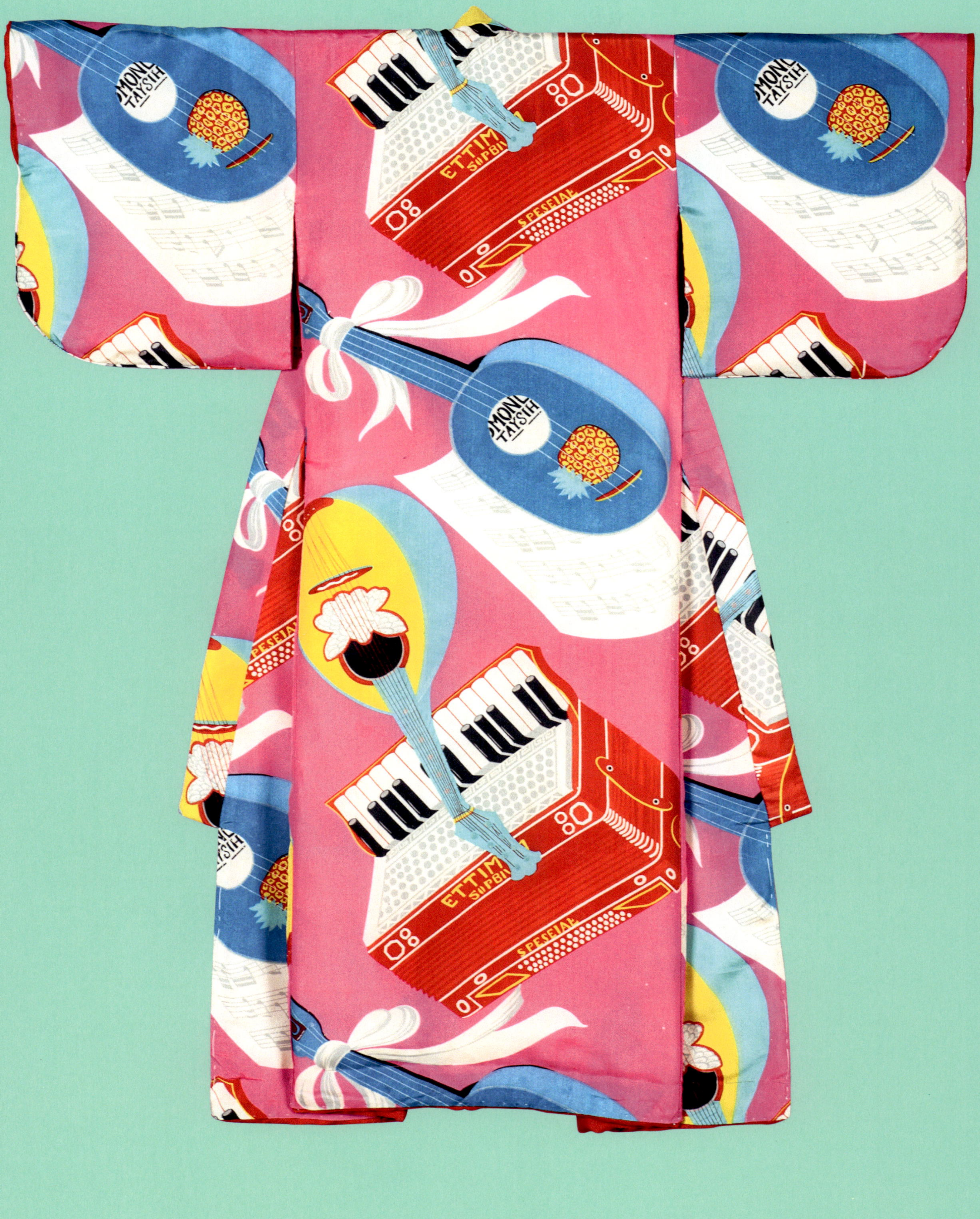

COSMOPOLITANISM/ CITY LIFE

Woman's *haori* with a decorative lining
Living the city life
Taishō–early Shōwa period, 1920s–1930s
Printed feather design on silk (outer); *kata-yūzen* dyed and printed silk lining
49.0 × 35.0 inches (124 × 89 centimeters)
KM077

The artist developed an exceptionally vibrant design for this textile, one that brings with it an imaginative covey of people, music, and busy city life. Music is a primary element: a woman plays records, a pianist and an elaborately dressed soloist sing a melody, and a male band play instruments and prance with gusto as their nightclub rocks with tunes. There are hints of modern city life, too: tables with books, lamps and lanterns; bars with glasses, wine, and whiskey; a lady relaxing with a book in a modern chair, sitting on an ottoman while talking on a phone, and making an entrance in a petal dress; and a *moga* ("modern girl") looking bored on a small bench.

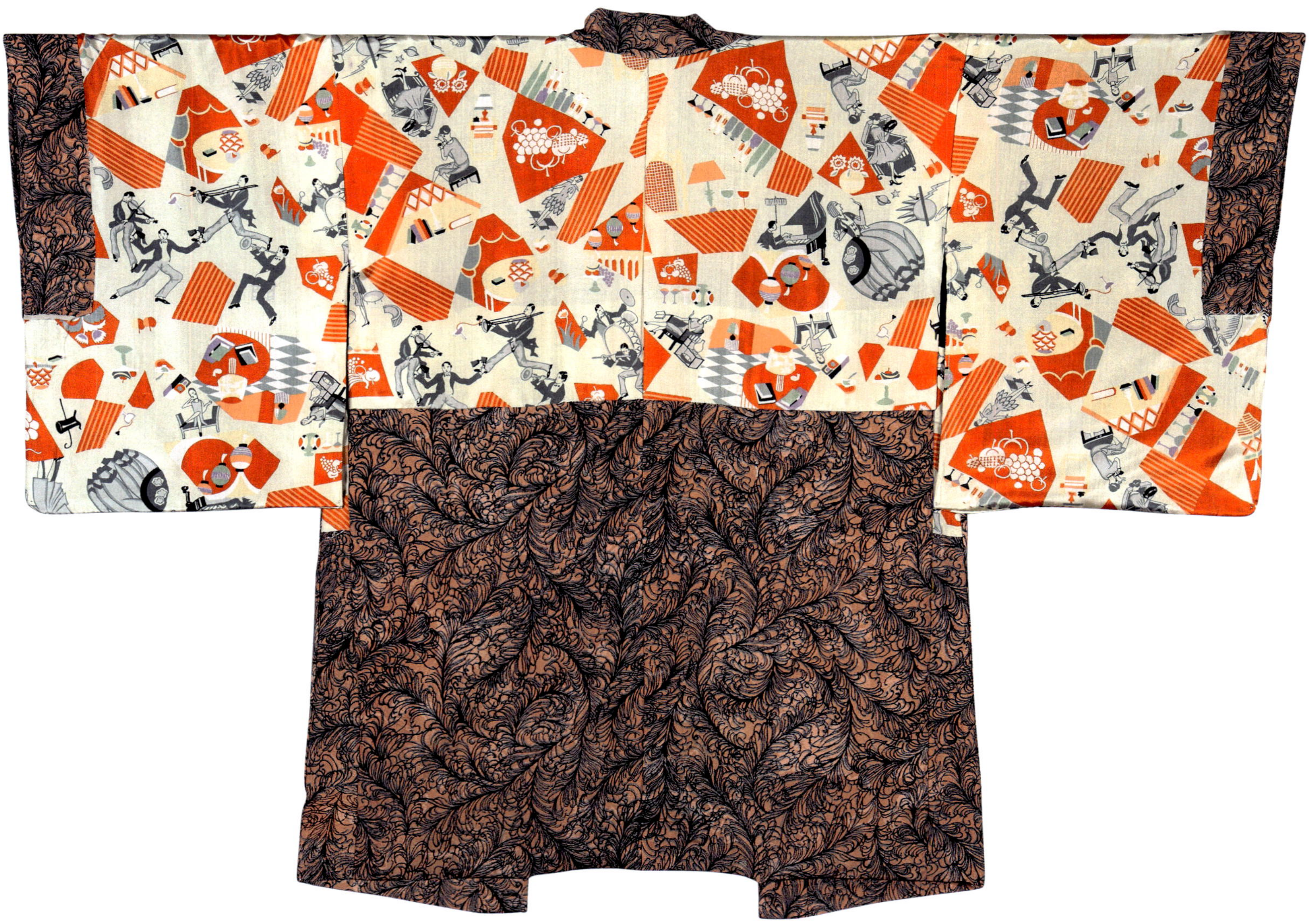

SPORTS/HIKING/ CLIMBING

Man's *haori* with a decorative lining (*haura*)
Hiking and climbing
Taishō–Shōwa period, 1920s–1940
Silk plain weave (outer); printed and hand-painted silk *haura* (lining)
41.0 × 41.0 inches (104 × 104 centimeters)
KM078

This stunning mountain range has been beautifully crafted for the *haura* used for this *haori*. This particular group of mountains (possibly the Valais or Pennine Alps) may not be placed in their exact true positions, but the famous Matterhorn certainly might play a major role in this work. The equipment placed in the foreground—backpack, binoculars, mountain ice axe, compass, rolled small blanket, and even an emergency can of food—show the gear that a hiker (or climber) would be sure to need for his planned adventure in the mountains.

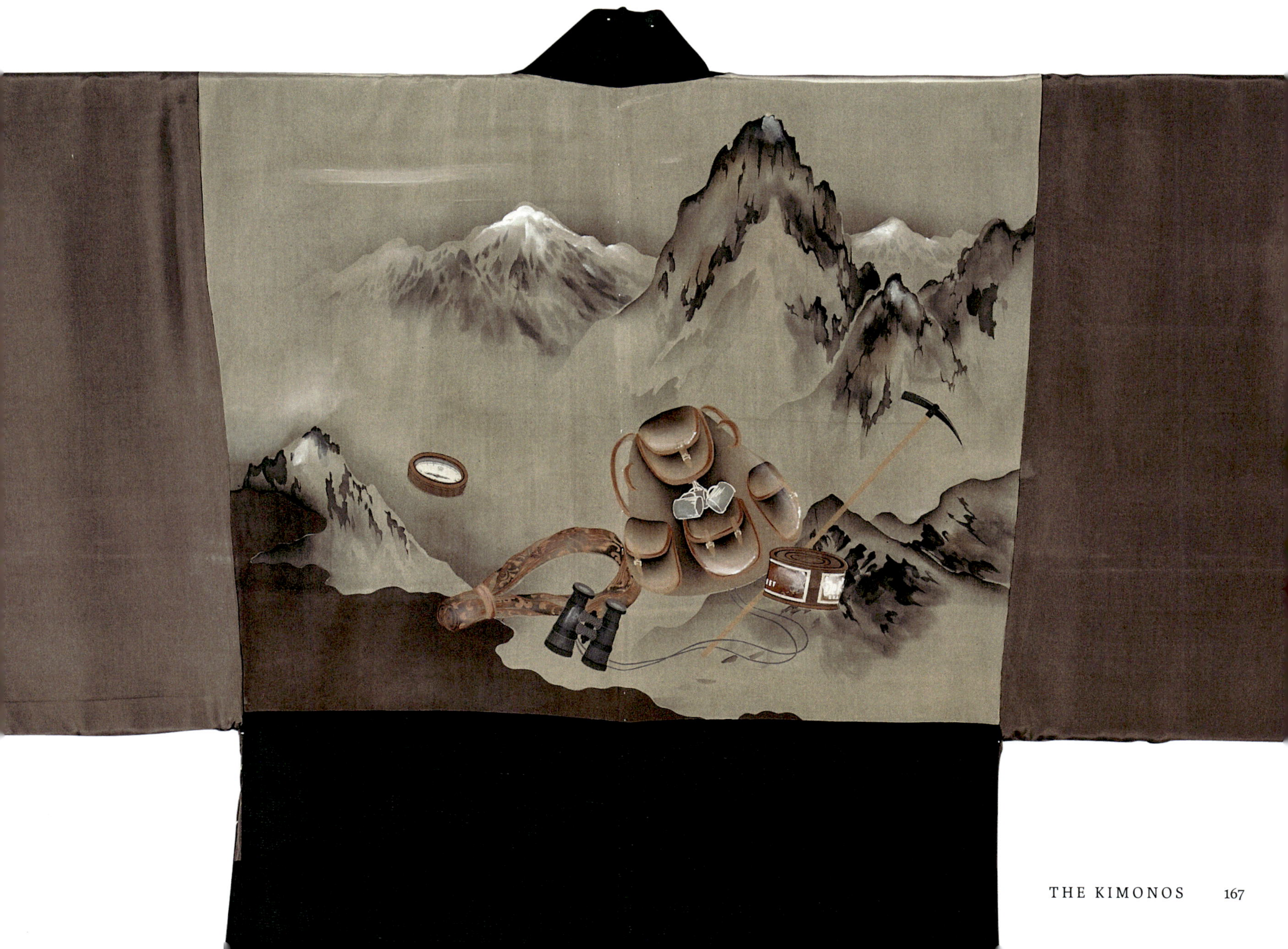

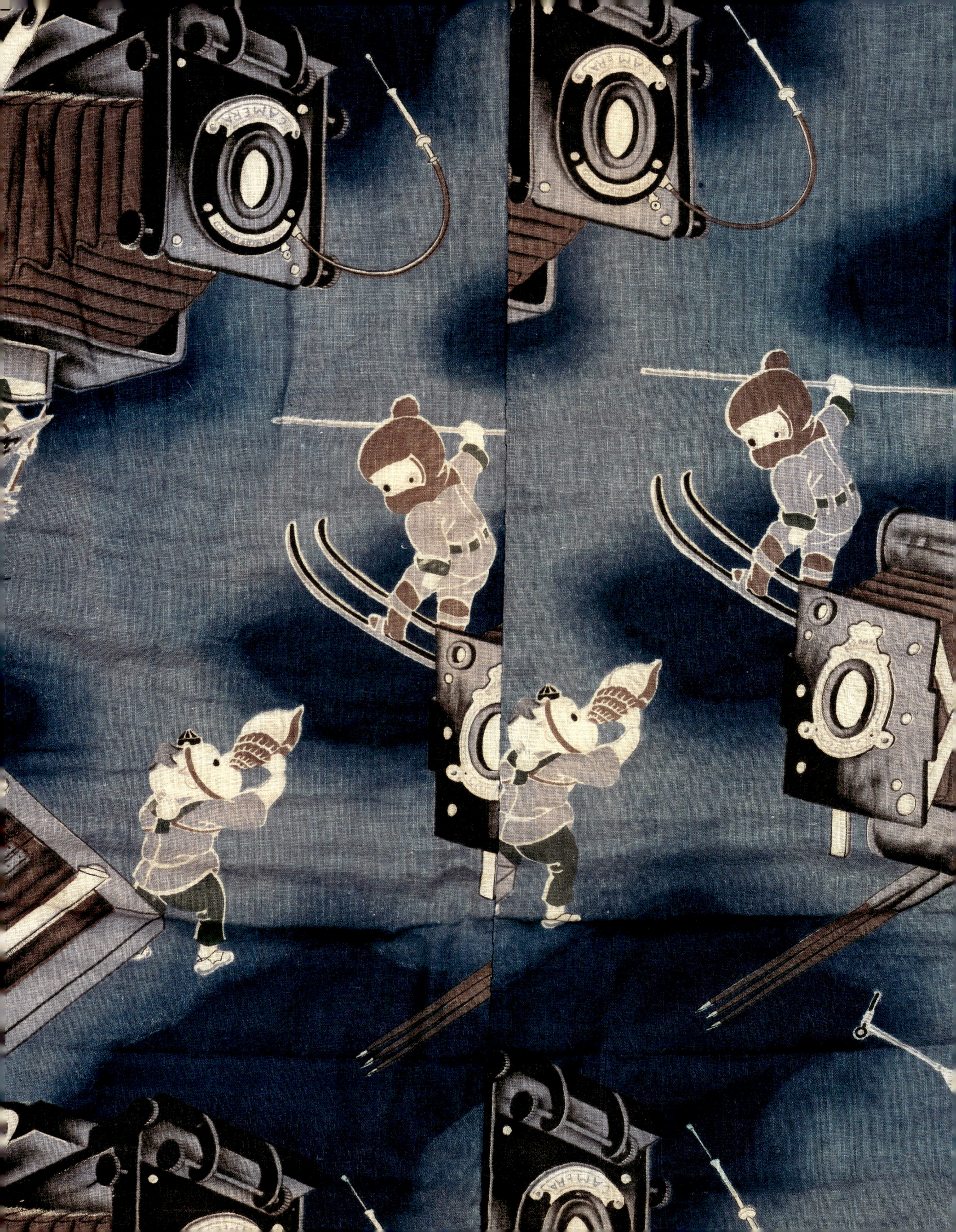
CAMERA

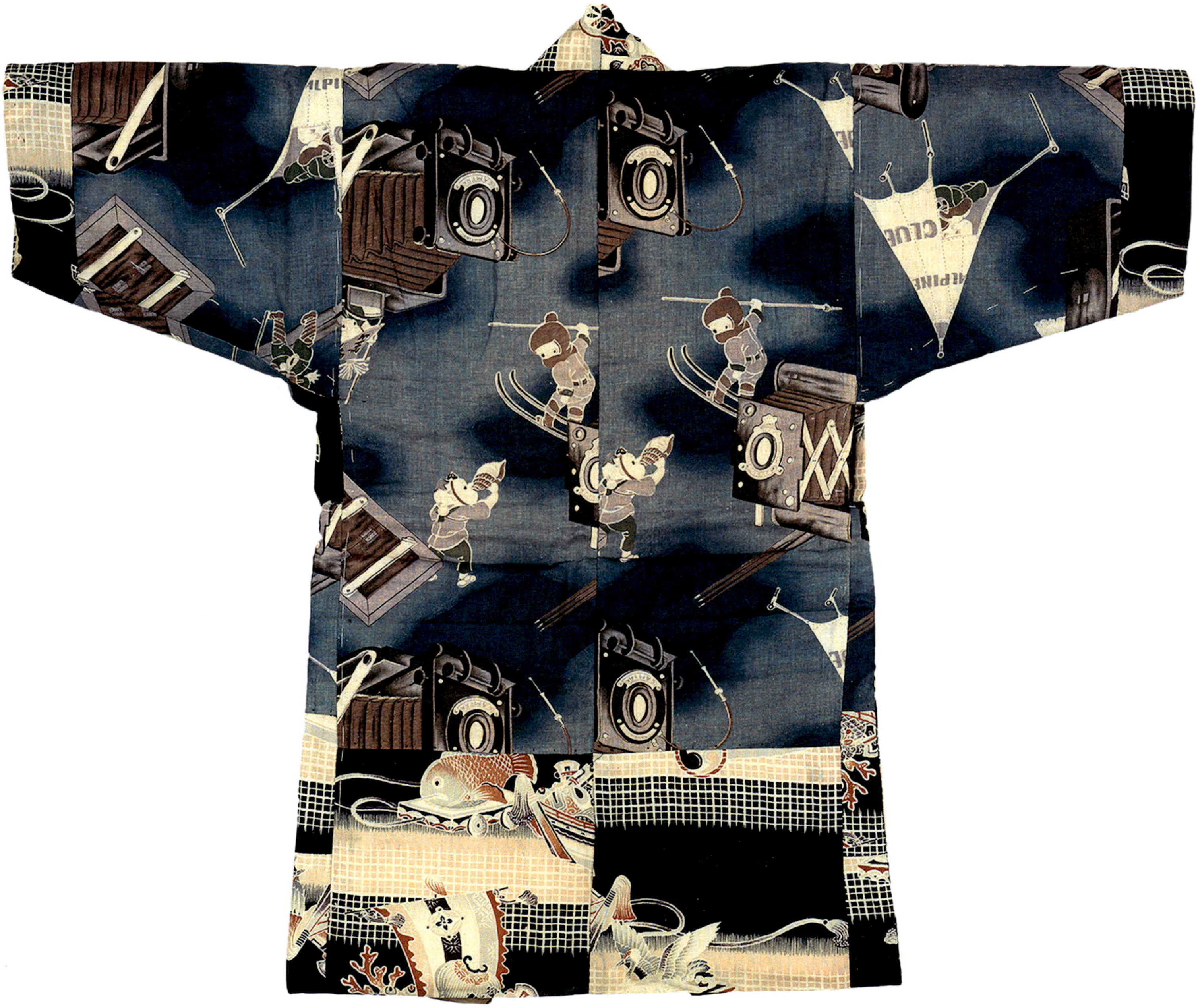

ENTERTAINMENT/ KEWPIES

Kimono jacket for a young boy
Skiing, cameras, and Kewpies
Taishō–Shōwa period, 1920–1940
Kata-yūzen dyed cotton
34.5 × 30.0 inches (88 × 76 centimeters)
KM079

This little patchwork kimono demonstrates the Japanese custom of using and reusing cloth when necessary. The outside of the young boy's jacket is decorated with a make-believe treasure ship, a toy sea bream on wheels, and a crane, all symbols of the coming New Year. Turned inside out, we can see that cloth with a different design was added as a lining as there was not enough of the outer cloth. Luckily, the mother found remnants enough to complete the inner lining for her child from a former garment. That cloth has several very playful objects pictured on it—cameras, Kewpie skiers, and a tent for the Alpine Club—and the child would surely have enjoyed wearing the jacket both for exterior and interior.

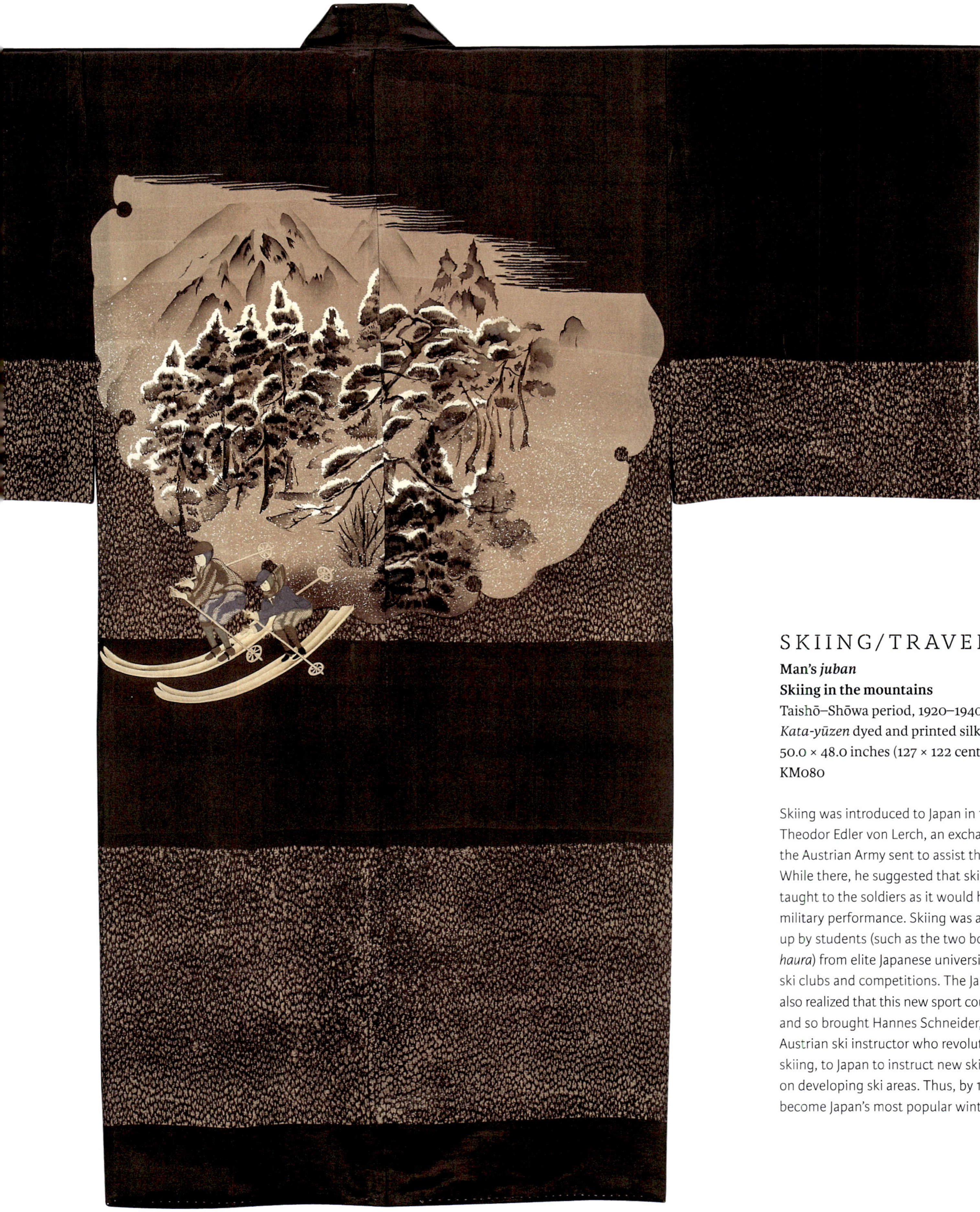

SKIING/TRAVEL

Man's *juban*
Skiing in the mountains
Taishō–Shōwa period, 1920–1940
Kata-yūzen dyed and printed silk
50.0 × 48.0 inches (127 × 122 centimeters)
KM080

Skiing was introduced to Japan in 1910 by Major Theodor Edler von Lerch, an exchange officer from the Austrian Army sent to assist the Japanese army. While there, he suggested that skiing should be taught to the soldiers as it would help to boost military performance. Skiing was also quickly taken up by students (such as the two boys drawn on this *haura*) from elite Japanese universities who formed ski clubs and competitions. The Japanese government also realized that this new sport could promote tourism and so brought Hannes Schneider, a well-known Austrian ski instructor who revolutionized downhill skiing, to Japan to instruct new skiers and consult on developing ski areas. Thus, by 1930, skiing had become Japan's most popular winter sport.

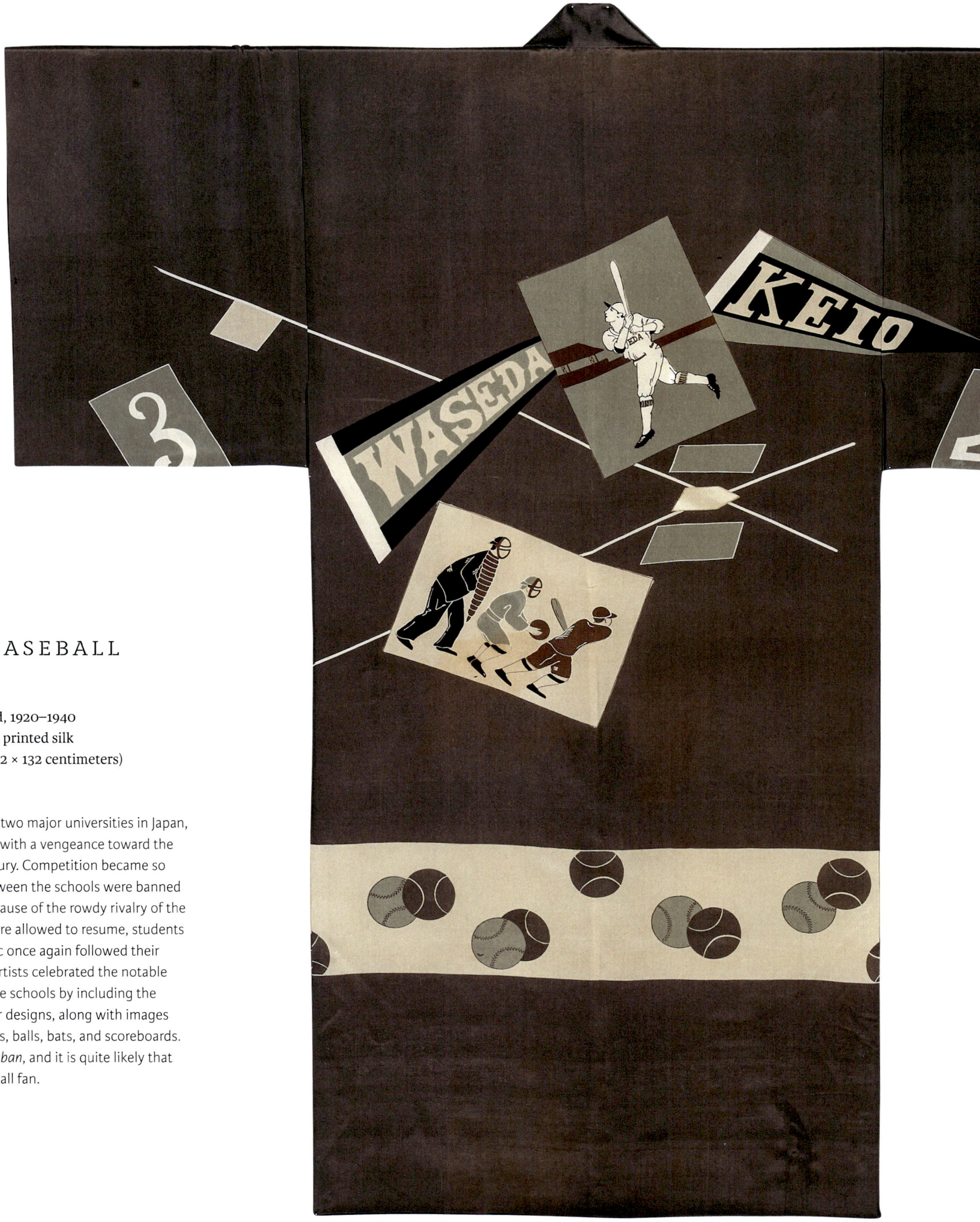

SPORTS/BASEBALL

Man's *juban*
Keio vs. Waseda
Taishō–Shōwa period, 1920–1940
Kata-yūzen dyed and printed silk
52.0 × 52.0 inches (132 × 132 centimeters)
KM081

Keio and Waseda, the two major universities in Japan, had taken to baseball with a vengeance toward the close of the 19th century. Competition became so fierce that games between the schools were banned from 1905 to 1925 because of the rowdy rivalry of the fans. When games were allowed to resume, students and the general public once again followed their teams avidly. Textile artists celebrated the notable competitiveness of the schools by including the names of both in their designs, along with images of the players, umpires, balls, bats, and scoreboards. This is a really great *juban*, and it is quite likely that its owner was a baseball fan.

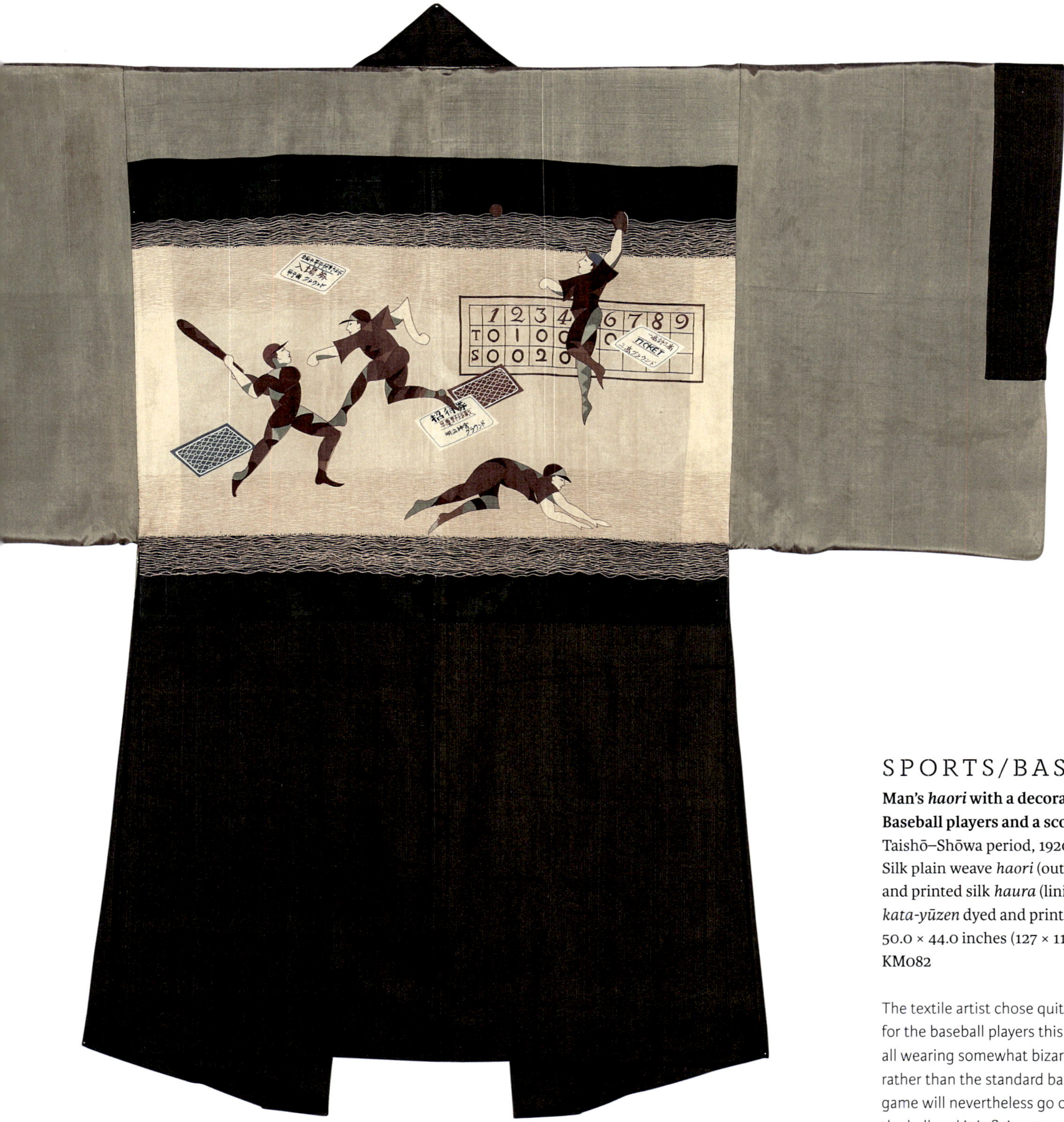

SPORTS/BASEBALL

Man's *haori* with a decorative lining (*haura*)
Baseball players and a scoreboard
Taishō–Shōwa period, 1920–1940
Silk plain weave *haori* (outer); *kata-yūzen* dyed and printed silk *haura* (lining)
kata-yūzen dyed and printed silk
50.0 × 44.0 inches (127 × 112 centimeters)
KM082

The textile artist chose quite a different uniform for the baseball players this time. The players are all wearing somewhat bizarre harlequin-like outfits rather than the standard baseball uniforms, but the game will nevertheless go on. The batter has just hit the ball and it is flying toward the outfielder, who has jumped high off the ground to try to catch it. The other two players seem to be trying to steal bases. The score board shows that the game is at the top of the sixth inning, but the game will not end until the ninth inning.

SPORTS/TENNIS

Man's *haori* with a decorative lining (*haura*)
Anyone for tennis?
Taishō period, 1920s
Oshima silk *haori* (outer); printed silk *haura* (lining)
50.0 × 45.0 inches (127 × 114 centimeters)
KM083

This *haori* offers an interesting view of a man and woman who appear to be seriously engaged in playing a game of tennis. Although the man and the woman are left nameless on this textile, their faces show that they are probably not simply anonymous figures, but people known for their tennis and other abilities. The man might possibly be Ichiya Kumagae, a famous tennis player best known for winning two silver medals at the 1920 Antwerp Olympics, the first Olympic medals won by any Japanese athlete. He was also tennis instructor to Princess Nagako, who became the wife of the Emperor Hirohito in 1924. She was a most enthusiastic tennis player, and especially good at a forehand stroke. The woman on this *haori* has some likeness to Nagako, and she and Kumagae could have played tennis together when he was an instructor.

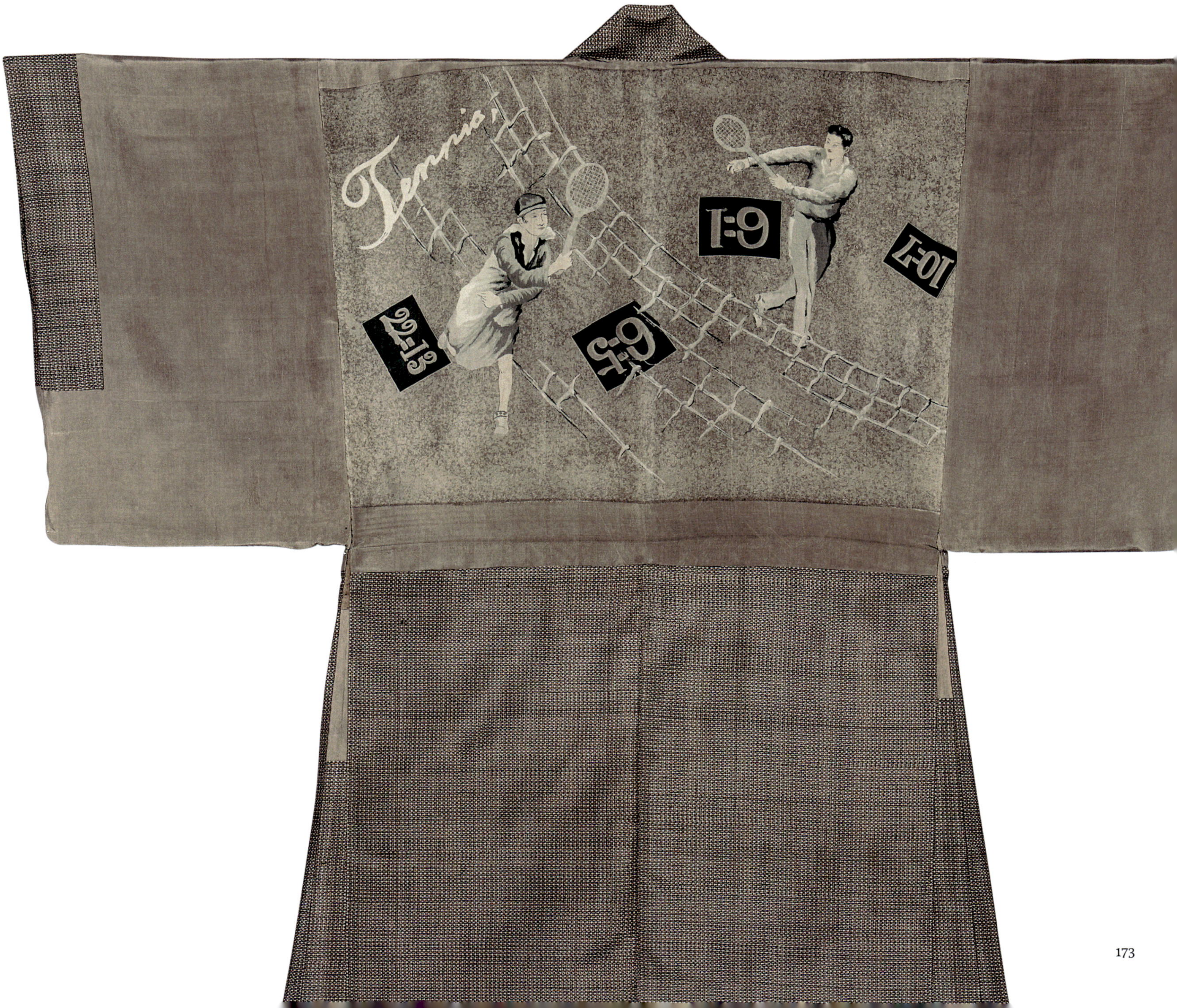

SPORTS/HORSE RACES

Man's *juban*
On the racetrack
Taishō–Shōwa period, 1920–1940
Kata-yūzen dyed silk
57.0 × 52.0 inches (145 × 132 centimeters)
KM084

This is an excellent design for this *juban*, and the artist has done a superb job of drawing and coloring the horses and jockeys. He has also captured the exciting sense of the traditional oval racetrack as horses and jockeys, who are well into their race, draw the attention of the roaring crowd in the pavilion as they come to their feet. The jockey for Number 5 has a tight lead, and Number 4 is working hard to bring his charge to the front, but Number 3 may try to pass the other riders to gain the outside as first position. The tickets floating above indicate that this race is being held in the fall.

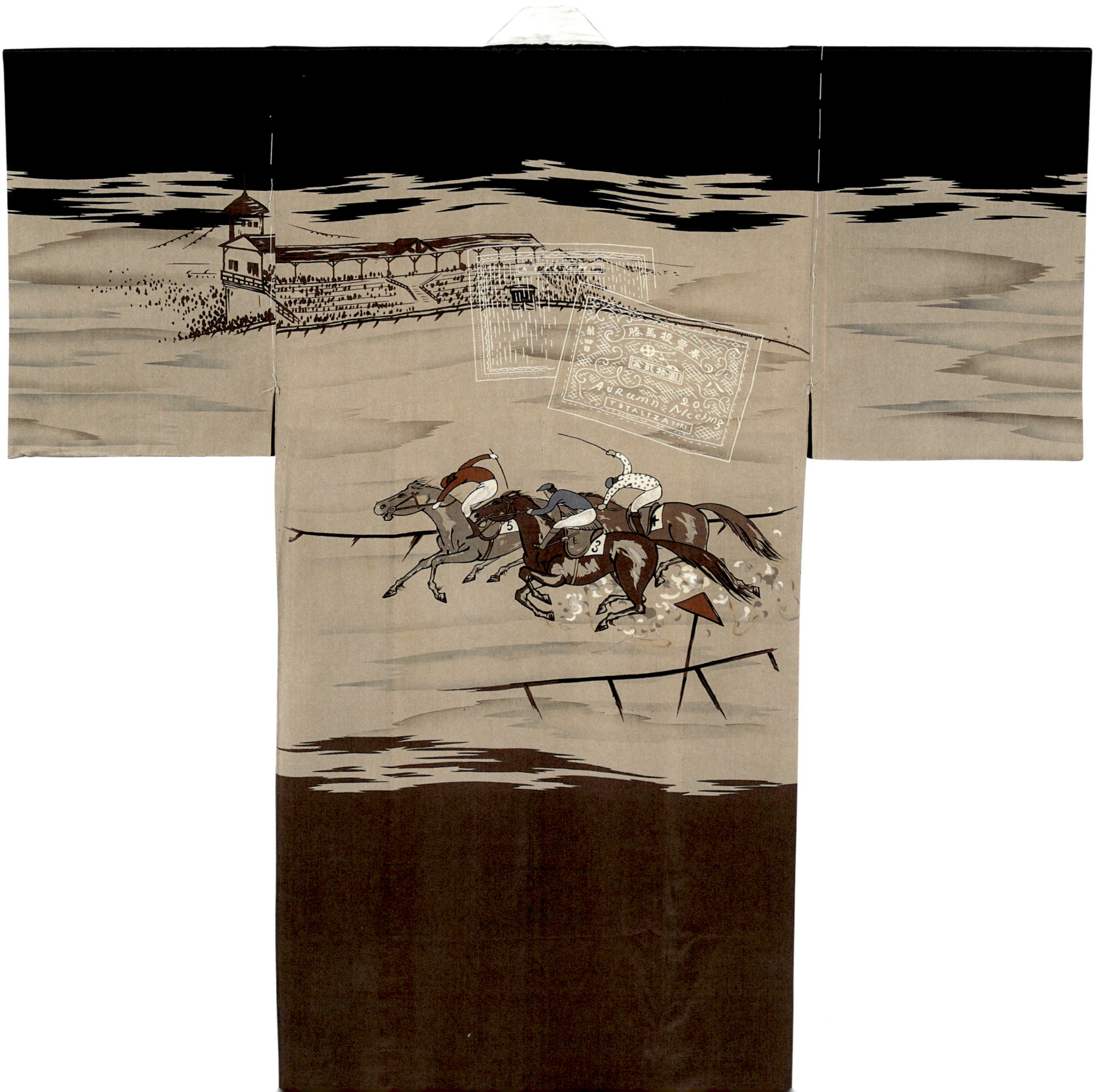

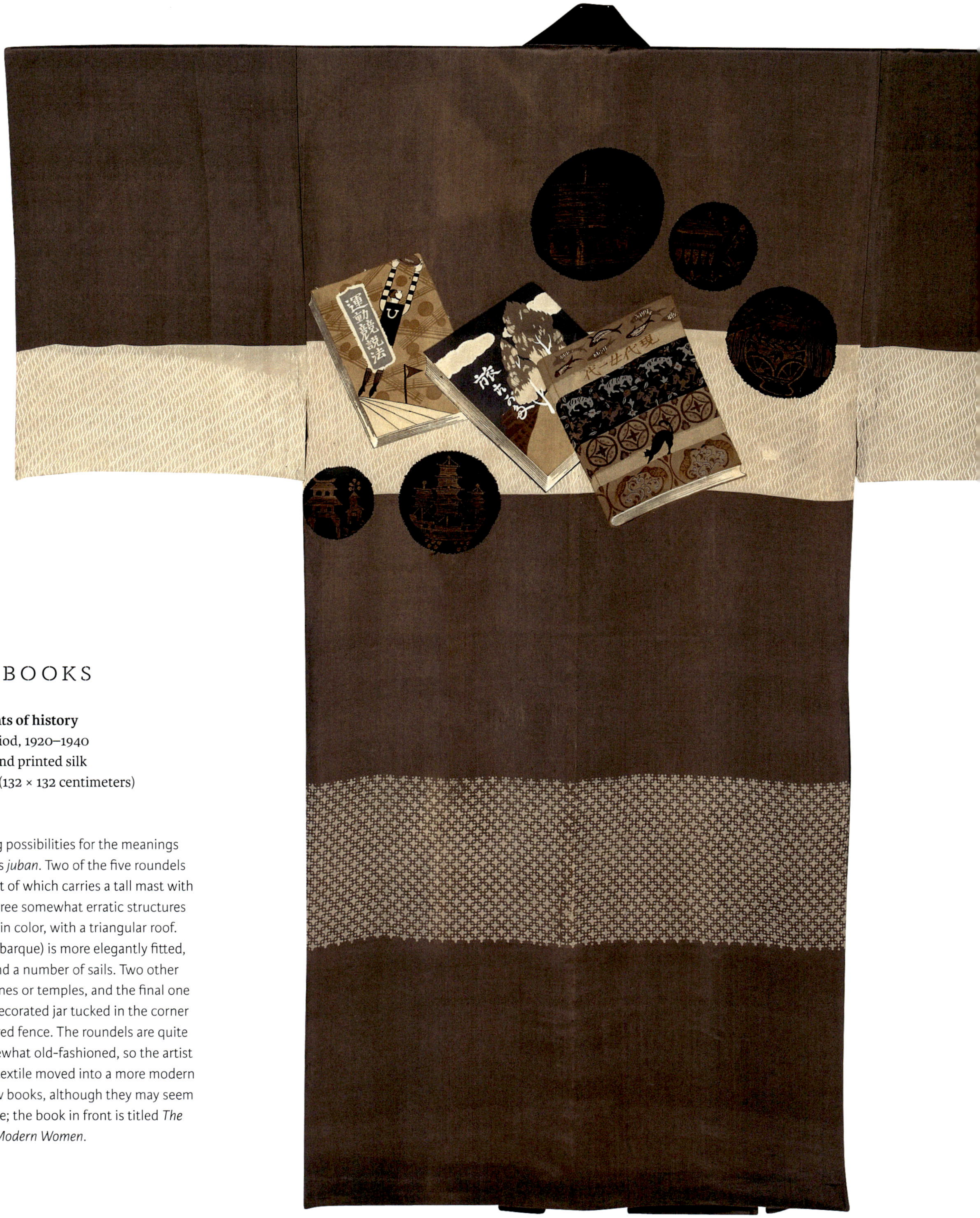

TRAVEL/BOOKS

Man's *juban*
Books and thoughts of history
Taishō–Shōwa period, 1920–1940
Kata-yūzen dyed and printed silk
52.0 × 52.0 inches (132 × 132 centimeters)
KM085

There are intriguing possibilities for the meanings of the design of this *juban*. Two of the five roundels show ships, the first of which carries a tall mast with a sizable sail and three somewhat erratic structures on deck, one black in color, with a triangular roof. The second ship (a barque) is more elegantly fitted, with three masts and a number of sails. Two other roundels show shrines or temples, and the final one is an overly-large decorated jar tucked in the corner of a simple structured fence. The roundels are quite charming but somewhat old-fashioned, so the artist who designed the textile moved into a more modern age by adding a few books, although they may seem to be a little obscure; the book in front is titled *The First Generation of Modern Women*.

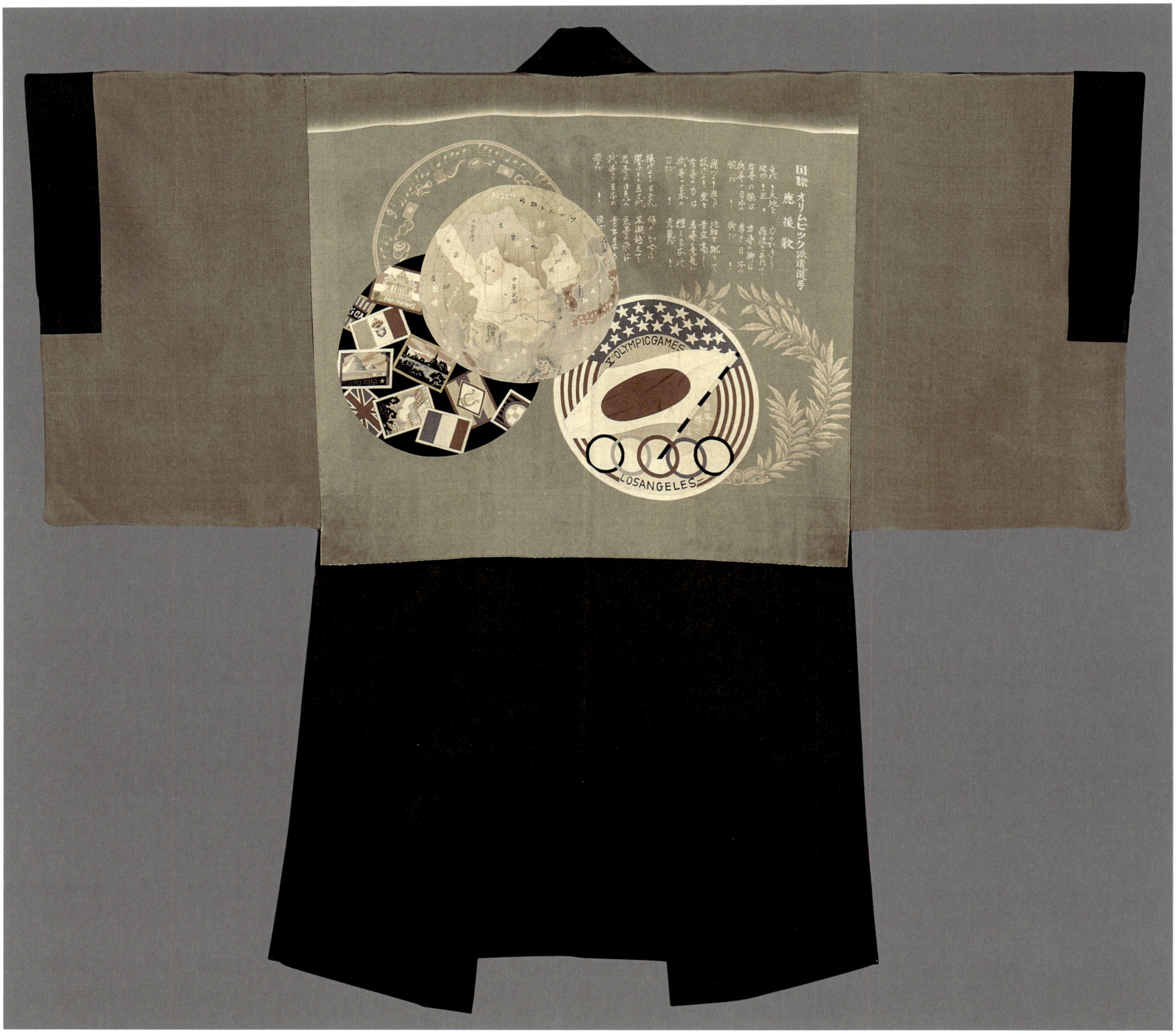

THE OLYMPICS

Man's *haori* with a decorative lining (*haura*)
1932 Olympics
Shōwa period, 1932
Silk plain weave *haori* (outer); *kata-yūzen* dyed and printed silk *haura* (lining)
51.0 × 41.0 inches (130 × 104 centimeters)
KM086

The 1932 Summer Olympics, officially known as the Games of the X Olympiad, were held in Los Angeles, California, during the worldwide Great Depression. Only 37 nations competed, as some were unable to pay for the trip to Los Angeles. The Japanese took all titles except one in the men's swimming events, and Baron Takeichi Nishi was the gold medalist (with his horse Uranus) in the equestrian show-jumping event. The design used for this *haura*, with maps, text, music, and pictures of flags and countries, is very informative. The five interlocked Olympiad rings and the flag design for the host country are very nicely conceived, as is the Japanese flag.

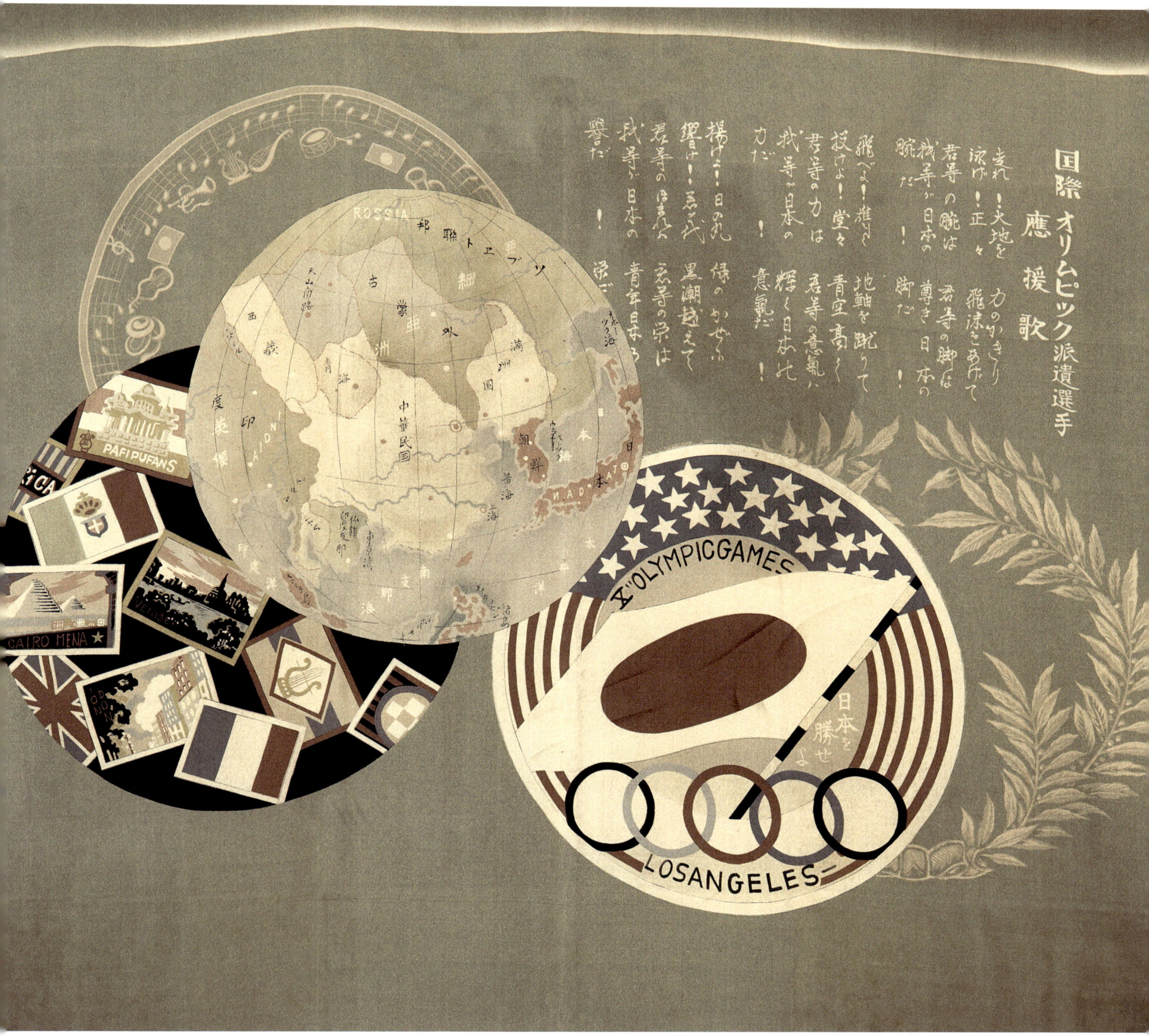
国際オリムピック派遣選手
應援歌
走れ！天地を　力のかぎり
泳げ！正々　飛沫をあげて
君等の腕は　君等の脚は
我等が日本の　尊き日本の
腕だ！　脚だ！
飛べよ！雄々しく　地軸を蹴りて
投げよ！堂々　青空高く
君等の力は　君等の意氣は
我等が日本の　輝く日本の
力だ！　意氣だ！
揚げよ！日の丸　緑のかぜふく
響け！君が代　黒潮越えて
君等のほまれ　君等の栄は
我等が日本の　青年日本の
譽だ！
ROSSIA
中華民国
満洲国
朝鮮
黄海
上海
CAIRO MENA
OLYMPICGAMES
LOSANGELES
日本を勝せよ

THE OLYMPICS/SPORTS

Child's *yukata*
The Olympiad
Shōwa period, 1936–1940
Kata-yūzen dyed and printed cotton
33.0 × 29.0 inches (84 × 74 centimeters)
KM087

Five interlocked rings always refer to the Olympics, and thus help date textiles printed with that motif. In 1936, amid much controversy, Japan was awarded its first Olympiad, scheduled to be held in Tokyo in 1940. In keeping with Japan's efforts to be recognized as a world power, this signal honor was commemorated in a myriad of ways, including children's garments, as seen here. The designer chose to highlight swimming, triple jumping, and pole vaulting, all sports in which Japan had won gold medals in the 1936 Berlin Olympics. The horse and rider most likely refer to Colonel Baron Takeichi Nishi, who won the gold medal for show jumping in the 1932 Olympics in Los Angeles.

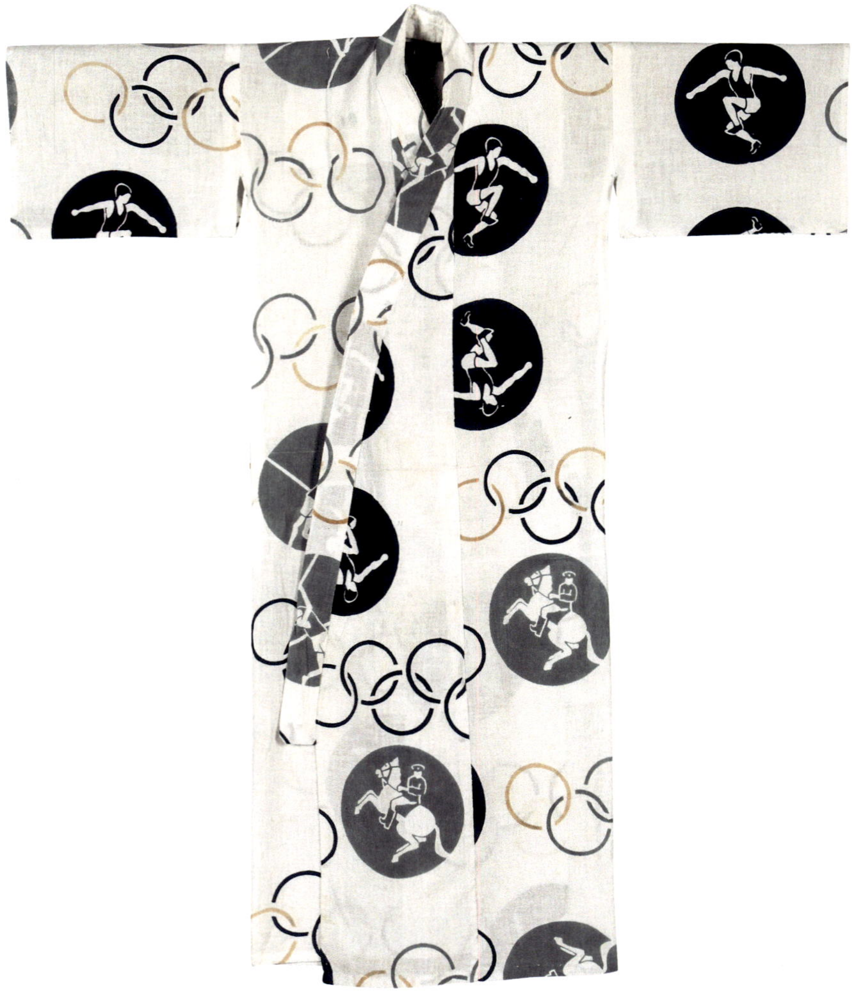

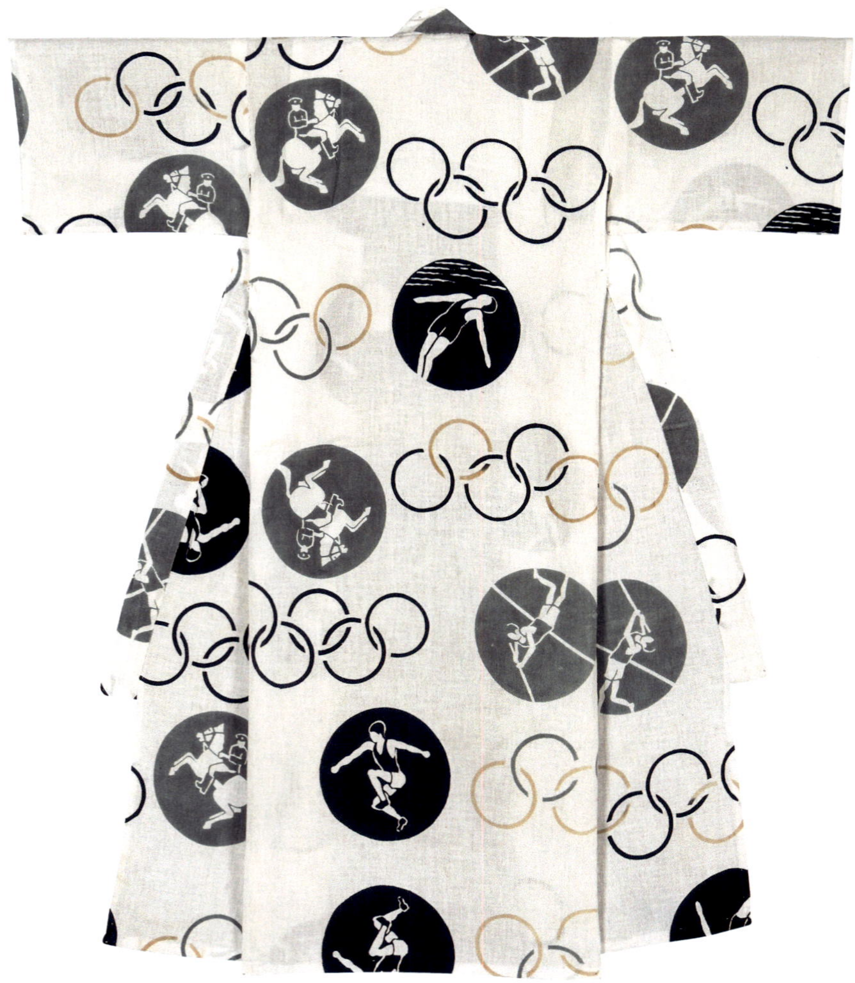

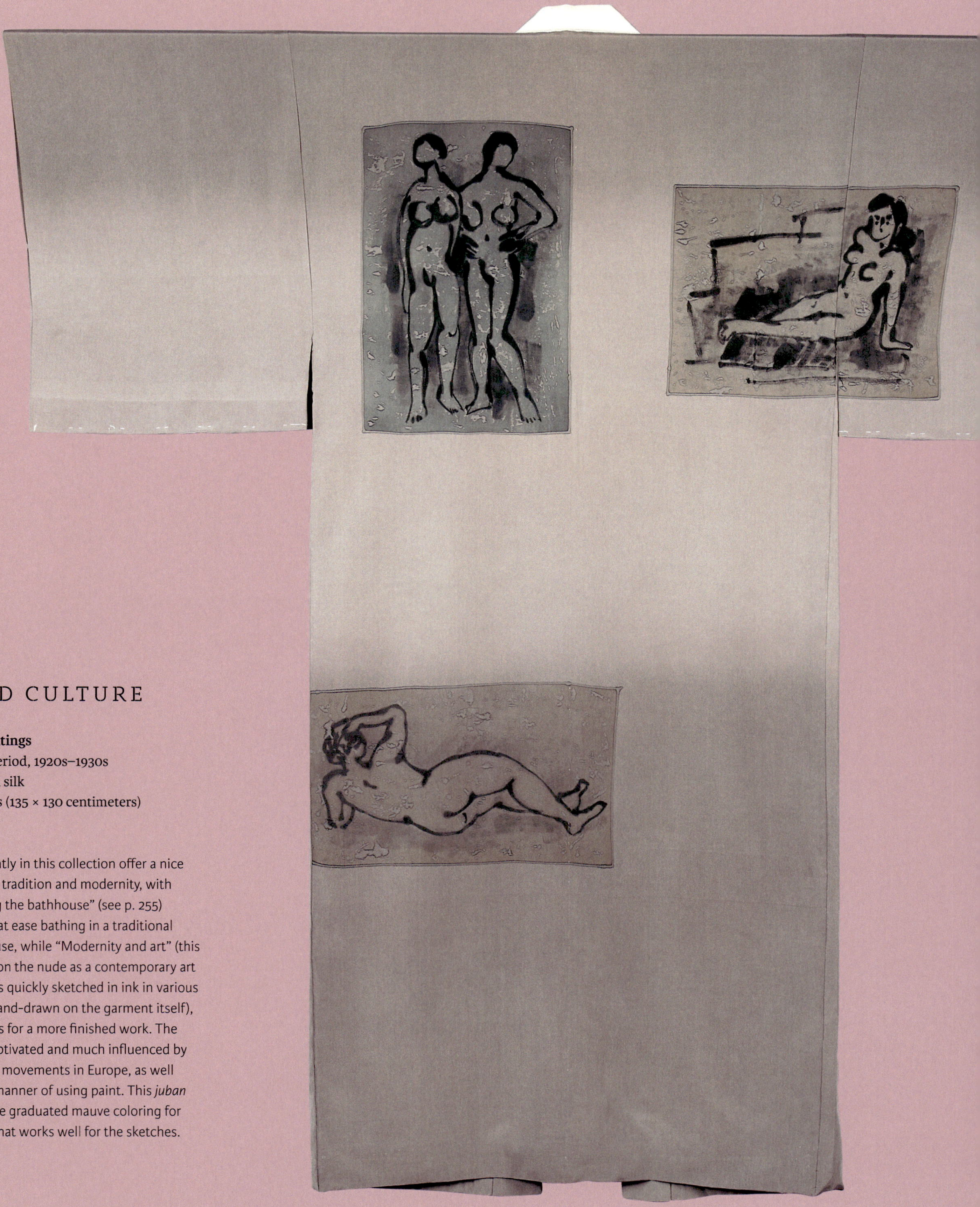

ART AND CULTURE

Man's *juban*
Three nude paintings
Taishō–Shōwa period, 1920s–1930s
Kata-yūzen-dyed silk
53.0 × 51.0 inches (135 × 130 centimeters)
KM088

Two works presently in this collection offer a nice contrast between tradition and modernity, with "Women enjoying the bathhouse" (see p. 255) showing women at ease bathing in a traditional Japanese bathhouse, while "Modernity and art" (this kimono) focuses on the nude as a contemporary art form, with models quickly sketched in ink in various poses (possibly hand-drawn on the garment itself), perhaps as studies for a more finished work. The Japanese were captivated and much influenced by contemporary art movements in Europe, as well as the European manner of using paint. This *juban* also offers a subtle graduated mauve coloring for the background that works well for the sketches.

MACHINE AGE/ MODERNITY

Man's *haori* with a decorative lining (*haura*)
A pilot all alone
Early Shōwa period, 1930s
Silk plain weave *haori* (outer); *kata-yūzen* dyed and printed silk.
54.0 × 33.0 inches (137 × 84 centimeters)
KM089

The decorative lining of this *haori* is quite charmingly playful, especially this pint-sized single-engine "sports" floatplane built in 1931 by Junkers, a major aircraft manufacturer in Germany. The owner of a Japanese newspaper (*Hochi Shimbun*) in Tokyo had become infatuated with this "Junkers Junior" aircraft, bought it, and planned to have it flown nonstop from Tokyo to Los Angeles. The inside design of the *haori* shows a dramatic range of mountains that the plane would fly near, and a map that spells out the route from Tokyo to Los Angeles. The floatplane design has a slightly comic look, as does the pilot, who wears an aviation jacket, helmet, and goggles as well as a formal white shirt and tie. Unfortunately, a first attempt to cross the north Atlantic Ocean from Tokyo to Los Angeles failed when the aircraft crashed into the sea some 40 miles off the Kurile Islands. Plane and pilot were rescued, and the pilot attempted a second nonstop flight to Los Angeles. This time, the aircraft crashed into Nemuro Bay in Hokkaido. The pilot was rescued, but the plane sank and was lost.

Note: The family crest with intersecting arrow feathers (*yabane*) on the outside of the *haori* is one of the more recognizable martial motifs in Japanese heraldry.

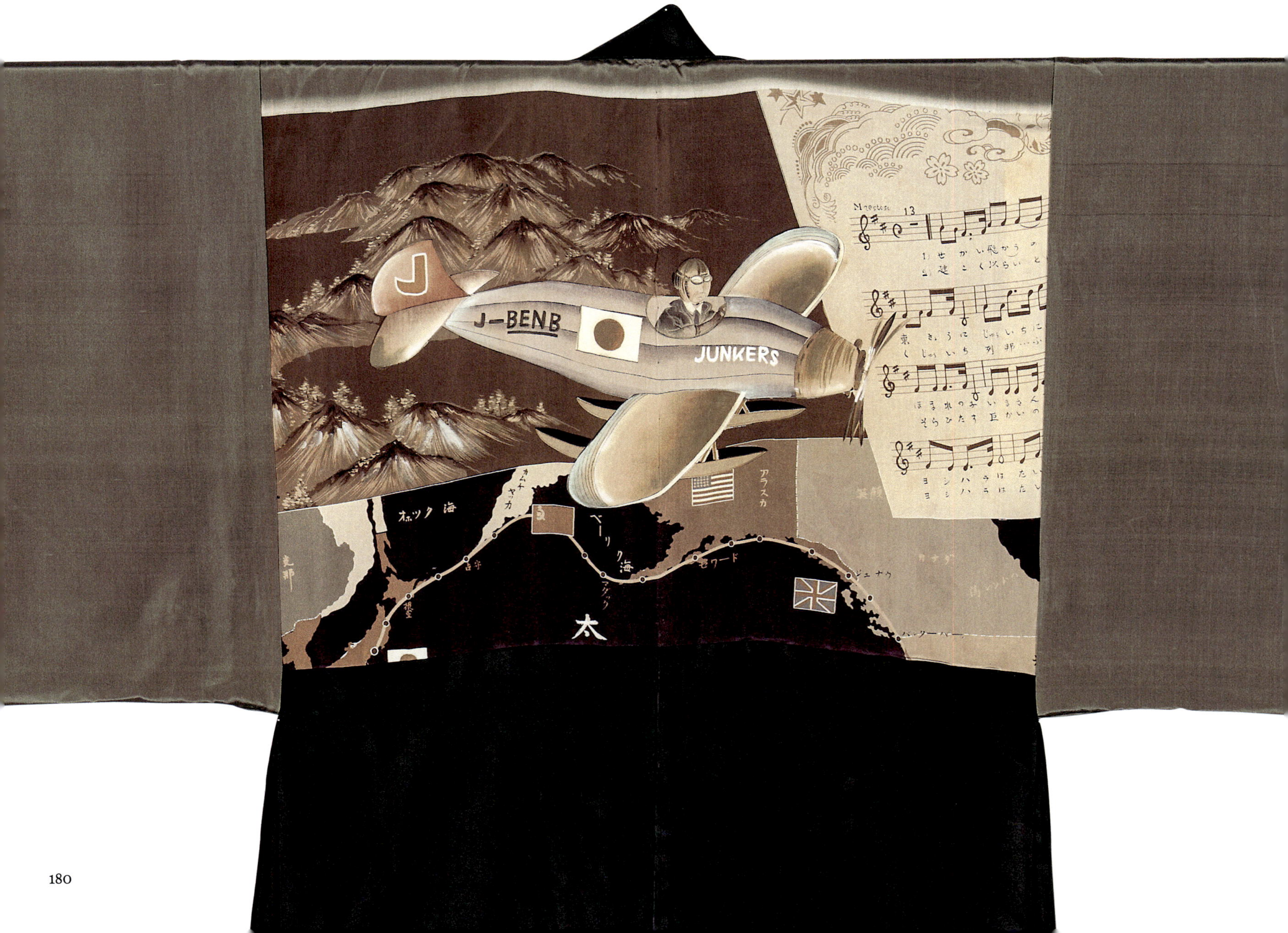

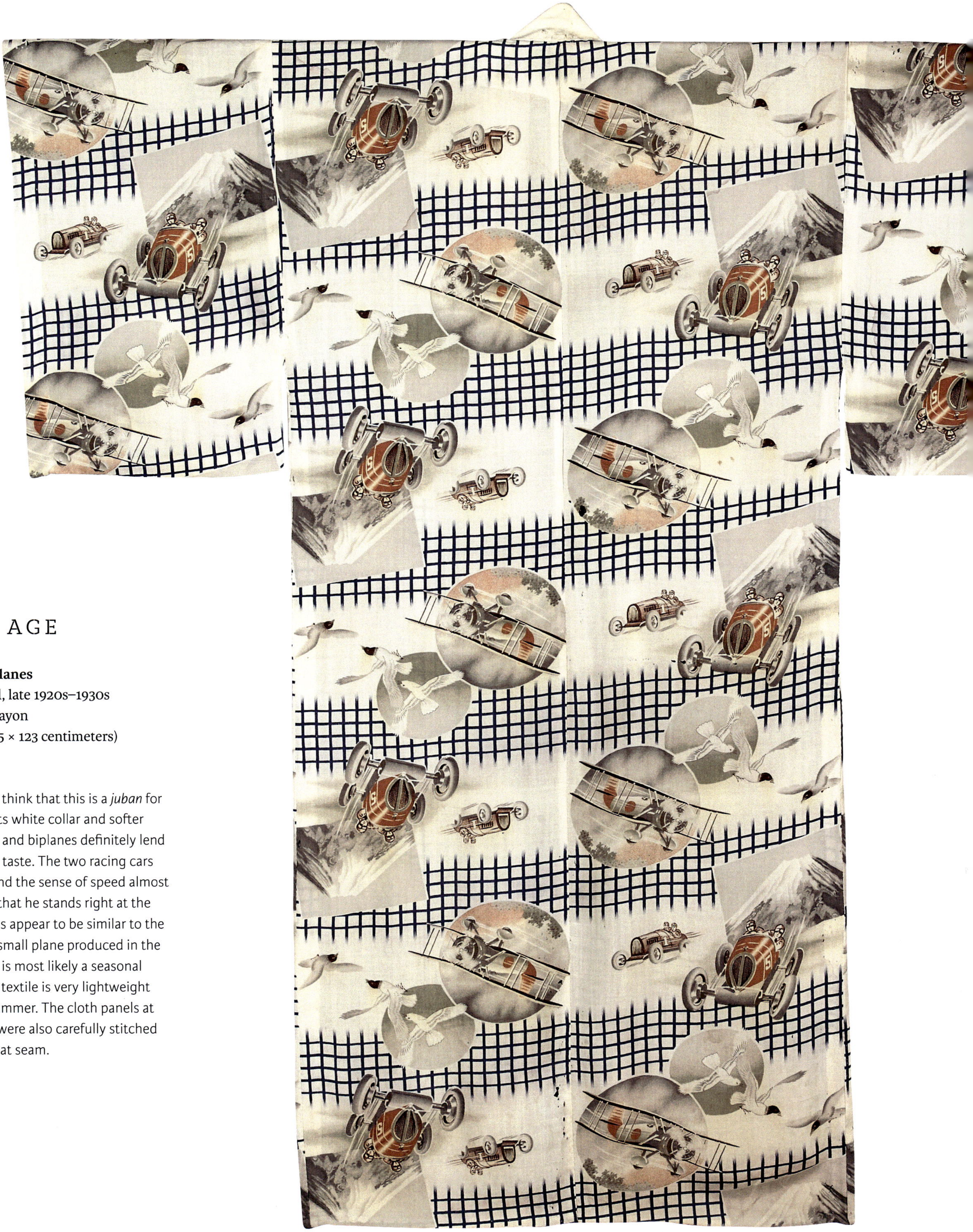

MACHINE AGE

Man's *juban*
Racing cars and airplanes
Taishō–Shōwa period, late 1920s–1930s
Lightweight printed rayon
53.0 × 48.5 inches (135 × 123 centimeters)
KM090

Although some might think that this is a *juban* for a woman because of its white collar and softer colors, the racing cars and biplanes definitely lend themselves to a man's taste. The two racing cars are very well drawn, and the sense of speed almost convinces the viewer that he stands right at the racetrack. The biplanes appear to be similar to the Aichi D1A, a compact small plane produced in the early 1930s. The *juban* is most likely a seasonal garment, as the rayon textile is very lightweight and appropriate for summer. The cloth panels at the back of the *juban* were also carefully stitched together to make a neat seam.

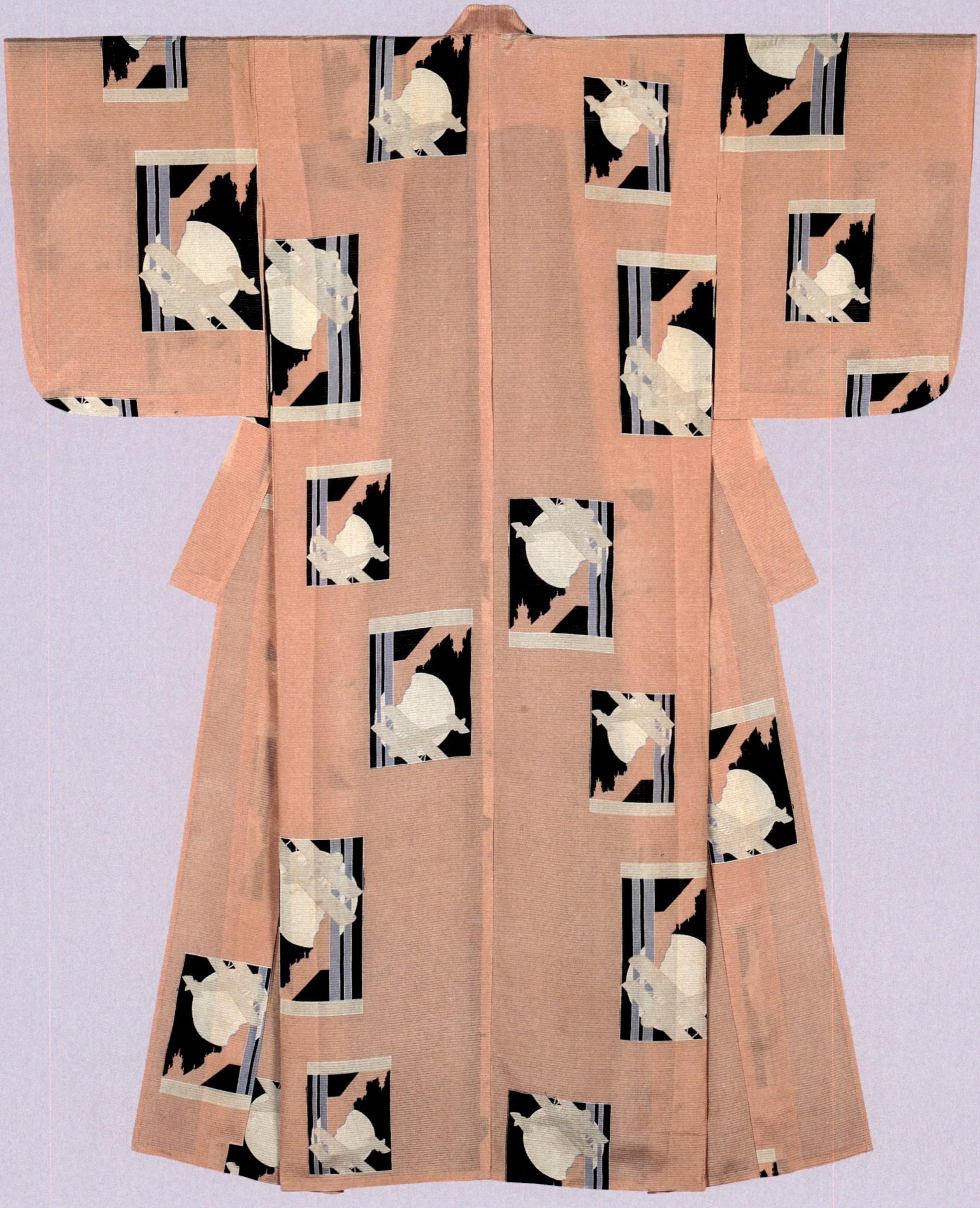

SUMMER MOONLIGHT

Woman's kimono
The airplane, the moon, and the city
Taishō–Shōwa period, 1920s–early 1930s
Kata-yuzen dyed and printed *rō* (a summer silk)
58.0 × 48.0 inches (147 × 122 centimeters)
KM091

This airy, gauze-like leno-weave silk fabric was chosen for this summer kimono, and it is exceptionally attractive. The textile pattern is quite unusual and gives great character to the ghost-like airplane, the moon, and the silhouetted cityscape captured within the rectangles that outline the design. The soft colors are offset by the black background, which helps to delineate the fine peach-colored line that meanders around the planes and the delicate violet blue that creeps toward the moon. The delicate *rō* lines of the cloth give a sense of elegance to the kimono.

MACHINE AGE

Man's *juban*
Searchlight in the night
Taishō–Shōwa period, 1920s–1930s
Kata-yuzen dyed and stenciled silk
52.0 × 50.0 inches (132 × 127 centimeters)
KM092

This well-designed *omoshirogara* robe is quite intriguing. The airplane was built by Junkers, a German manufacturer, and was bought in 1928 by the Japanese Imperial Maritime Defence Volunteer Association, a patriotic organization, and registered with the letters J-BALG. In 1934, the plane was taken over by Nippon Kaiji Kentei Kyokai (NKKK) and used for airmail cargo service for the Japanese Imperial Navy. Unfortunately, J-BALG crashed in March 1934 in unknown circumstances somewhere in Japan, and the crew's fate also remains unknown. This plane had served Japan well over some six years, and it is highly likely that the design for this *juban* included the large searchlight to imply the hope that J-BALG could be found. The two smaller planes were also included as part of the search party.

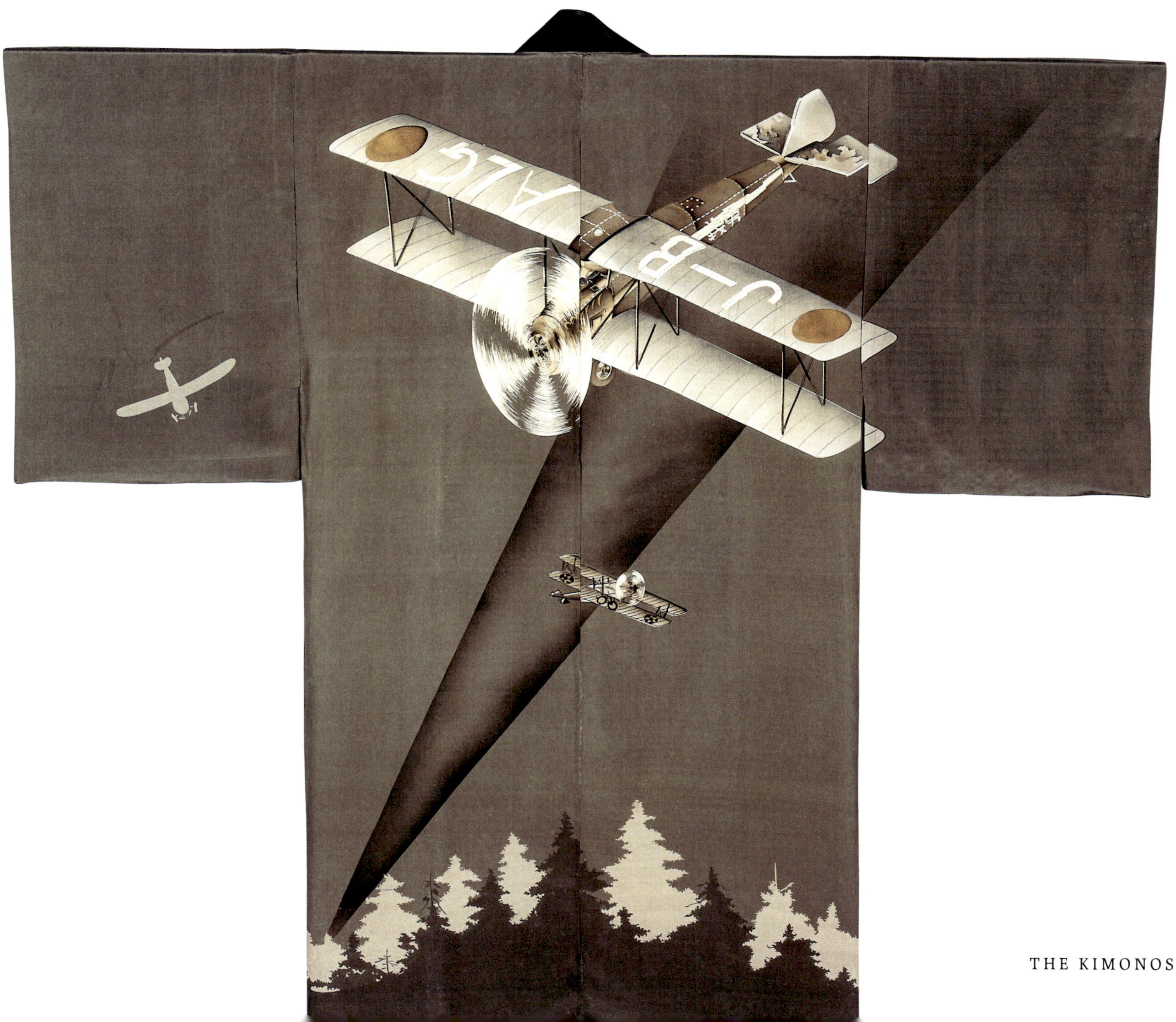

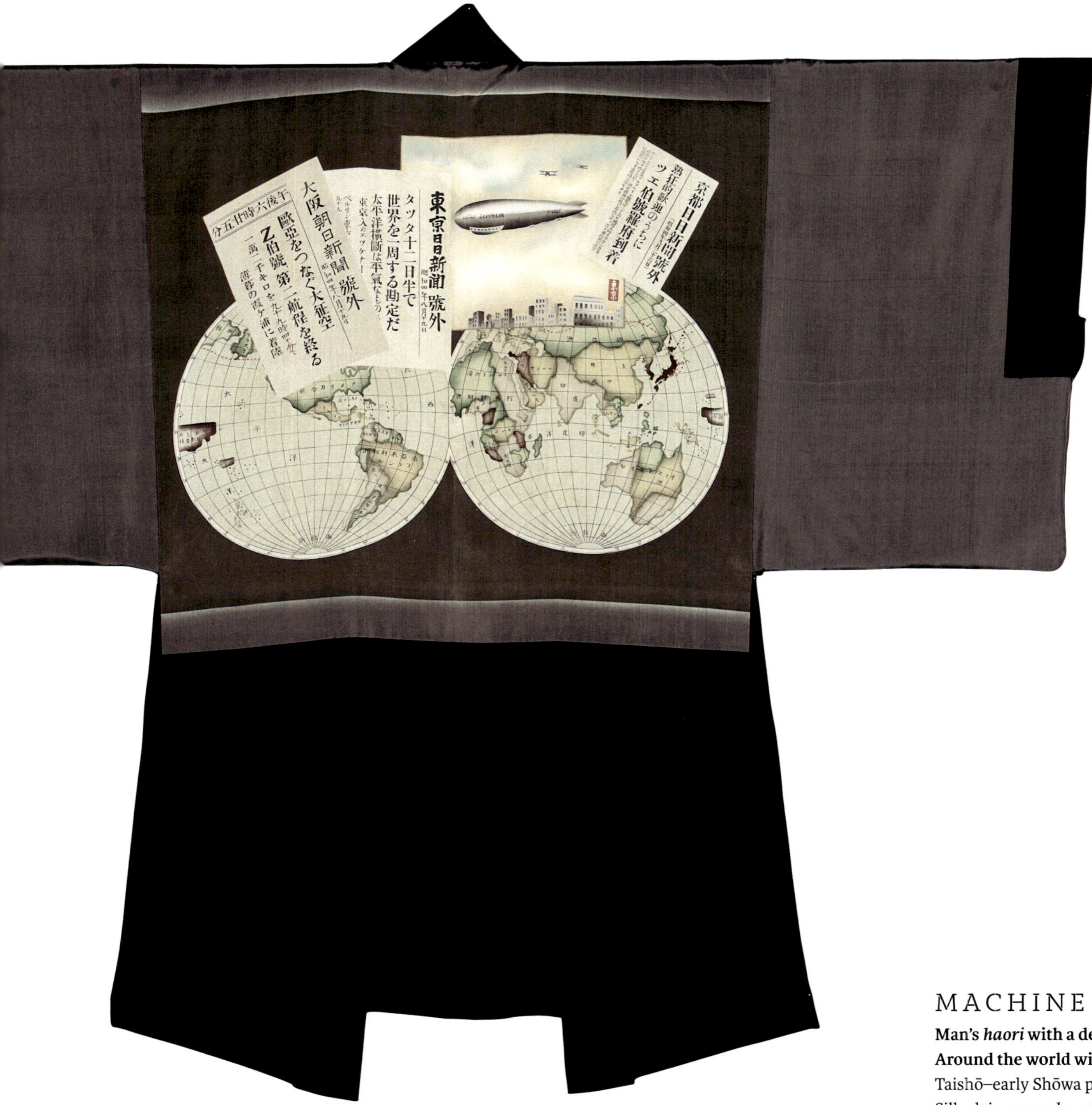

MACHINE AGE

Man's *haori* with a decorative lining (*haura*)
Around the world with the *Graf Zeppelin*
Taishō–early Shōwa period, 1920s–1930s
Silk plain weave *haori* (outer); *kata-yūzen* stencil-printed silk *haura* (lining)
51.0 × 44.0 inches (130 × 112 centimeters)
KM093

The interior *haura* design of this *haori* was prepared by a textile artist who produced outstanding designs that, one might say, covered the world, given the east and west faces of the globe. The first image prepared for the *haura* shows the *Graf Zeppelin* afloat in the skies, displaying its modernistic silvery sleekness as two biplanes fly nearby to serve as consorts. A second image shows poster-like pages that indicate the times when the populace of Osaka, Tokyo, and Kyoto should look upward as the *Graf Zeppelin* makes its stately way to the Kasumigaura Naval Air Station in Tokyo. The east and west faces of the globe show the third design, a carefully placed trail of red arrows followed by the airship as it flies around the world.

MACHINE AGE

Child's kimono
Trams, trains, and puppies
Taishō–Shōwa period, 1920s–1940
Kata-yuzen dyed and printed silk
32.0 × 30.0 inches (81 × 76 centimeters)
KM094

On this tiny kimono, a train chugs through the green countryside, bringing with it the benefits of modernization. A brand-new tram is additionally shown, and it is proudly noted as a "gasolin car." Overall, there is a sense of calmness and tranquility, as a little girl happily feeds crumbs to the local pigeons. In Japanese, the same word, *hato*, describes both pigeons and doves. A small talisman for protection is embroidered on the fold of the front collar of the child's kimono. Talismans were once so standard on childrenswear that embroidered samples were compiled in small books, enabling mothers and grandmothers to easily recreate designs of their choice.

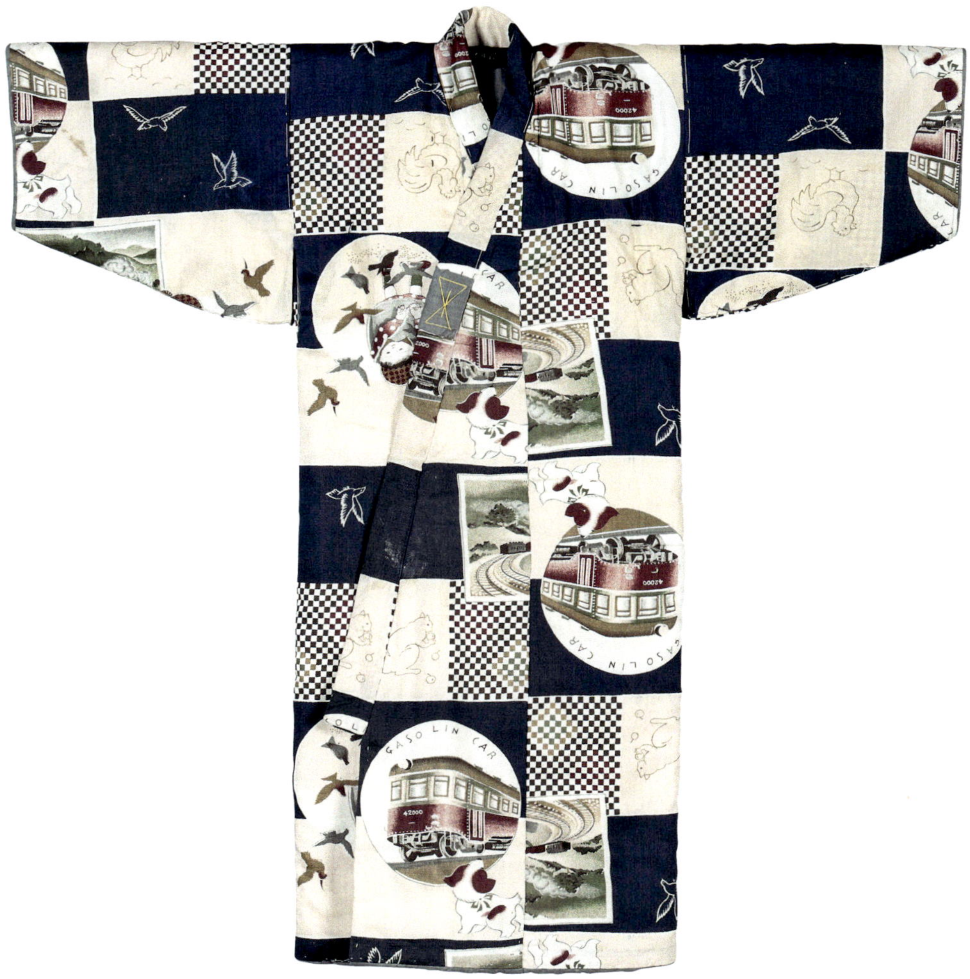

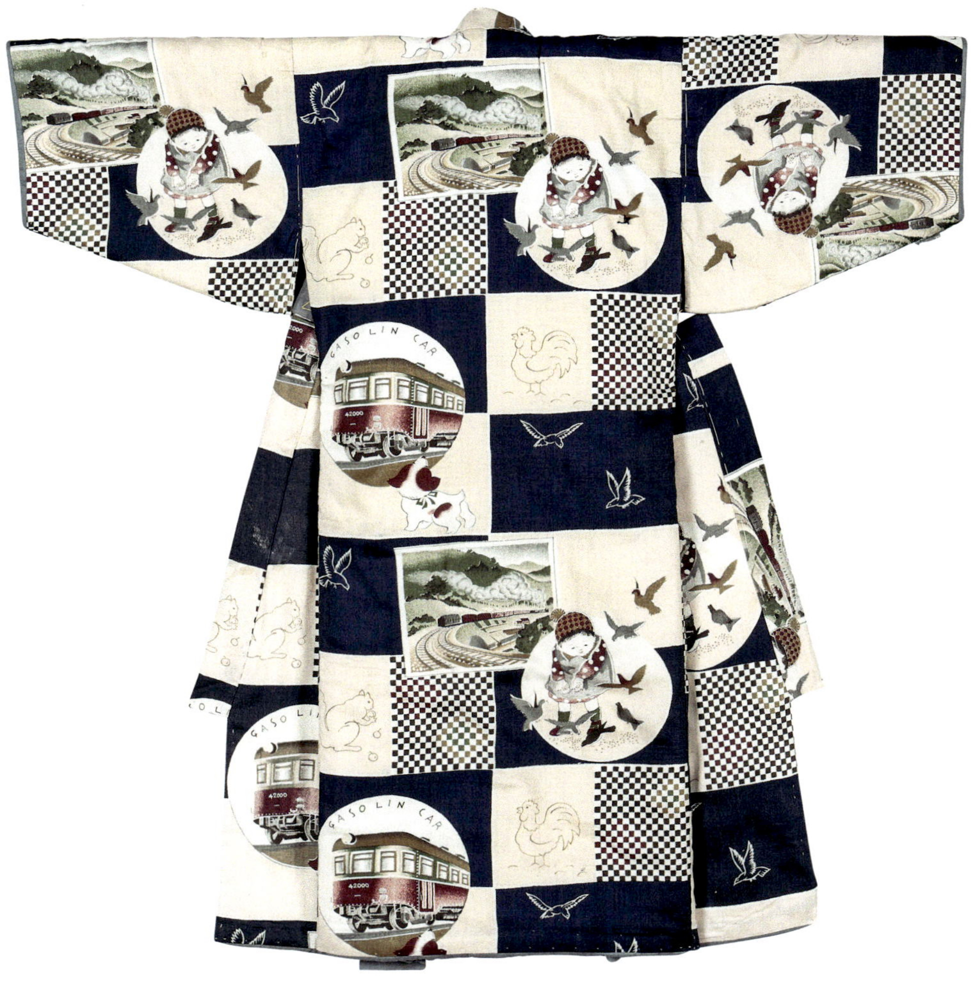

MODERNITY

Man's *haori* with a decorative lining (*haura*)
The flight of the *Kamikaze*
Shōwa period, 1930s
Silk plain weave (*haori* exterior); *kata-yūzen* dyed and printed silk *haura* (lining)
50.0 × 38.0 inches (127 × 97 centimeters)
KM095

This design celebrates the flight of the *Kamikaze* (Divine Wind) from Tokyo to London in honor of the coronation of King George VI of the UK in April 1937. The *Kamikaze* was sponsored by the *Asahi Shimbun* (a Japanese newspaper), and its sleek shape and high-tech styling made it an artistic favorite, as well as a benchmark of modernity for Japan. *Kamikaze* was the first Japanese plane to set an aviation record (a flight completed in just over 54 hours), and its route and refueling stops are shown in the inset map. The sheet music denotes a popular symphony by Tchaikovsky, who is depicted below the music, and Lenin's image joins him there.

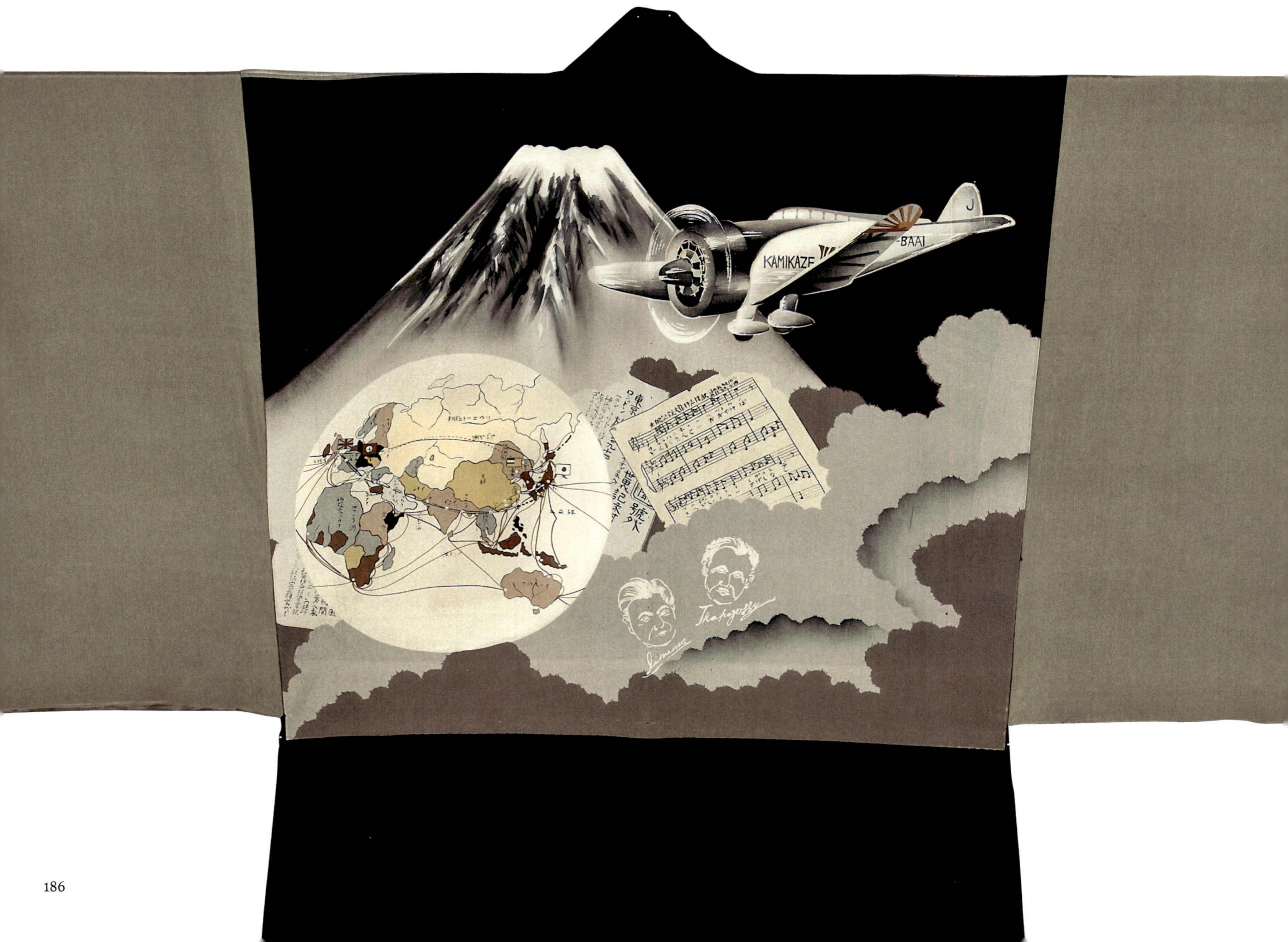

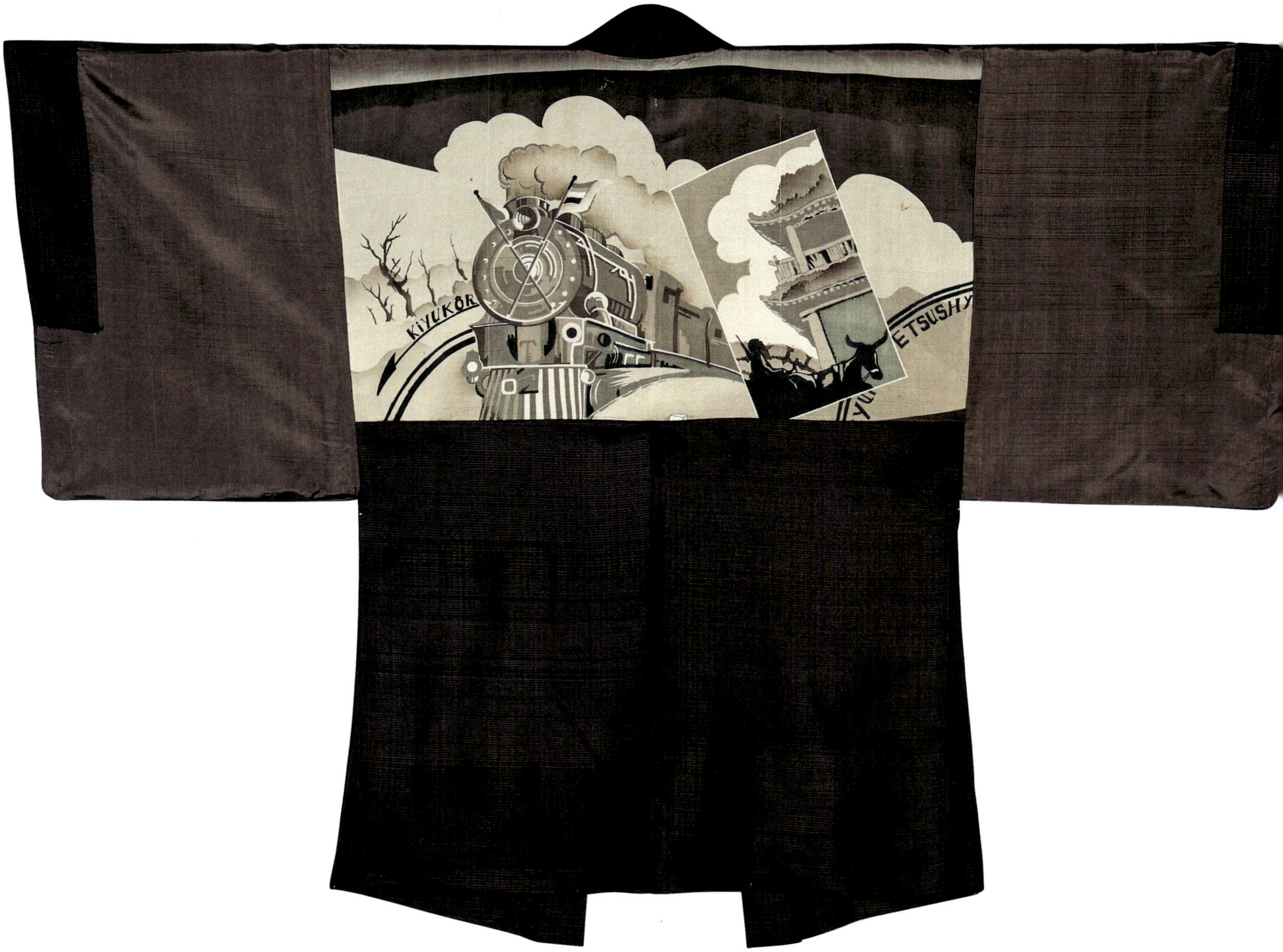

MACHINE AGE/TRAVEL

Man's *haori* with a decorative lining (*haura*)
The Mantetsu Express
Taishō–Shōwa period, 1930–1940s
Silk plain-weave (*haori* exterior); *kata-yuzen* dyed and printed silk (interior lining)
50.0 × 35.0 inches (127 × 89 centimeters)
KM096

This textile rendering of a roaring locomotive was based on posters advertising the South Manchurian Railway, which lay at the heart of Japan's neocolonial presence north of the Great Wall of China. Such images elicited pride in Japan's technological prowess, as well as excitement about the pioneering challenge of developing the new puppet state of Manchukuo (Manchuria). The engine here is shown carrying both the Japanese Hinomaru flag and the Manchukuo flag, and the poster showing the silhouette of a man driving a donkey cart hints at Manchukuo as a tourist paradise.

COSMOPOLITANISM

Woman's *juban*
Following the European style
Taishō–Shōwa period, 1920s–1940
Chirimen silk, and *kata-yuzen* dyed and hand-painted
51.0 × 49.0 inches (130 × 124 centimeters)
KM097

The designs on this *juban* offer two different tableaux that showcase open-air terraces, each furnished with a different ornate European-style table and chair. Each table is supplied with a very decorative vase with prolific masses of flowers as well as wine glasses or a small teapot, a hint that full service will soon be provided. The open terrace settings offer fascinating vistas of rivers, bridges, and elegant classic buildings of European architecture to delight new visitors. The owner of this *juban* would most certainly have enjoyed contemplating these carefully drawn and painted designs of the European style.

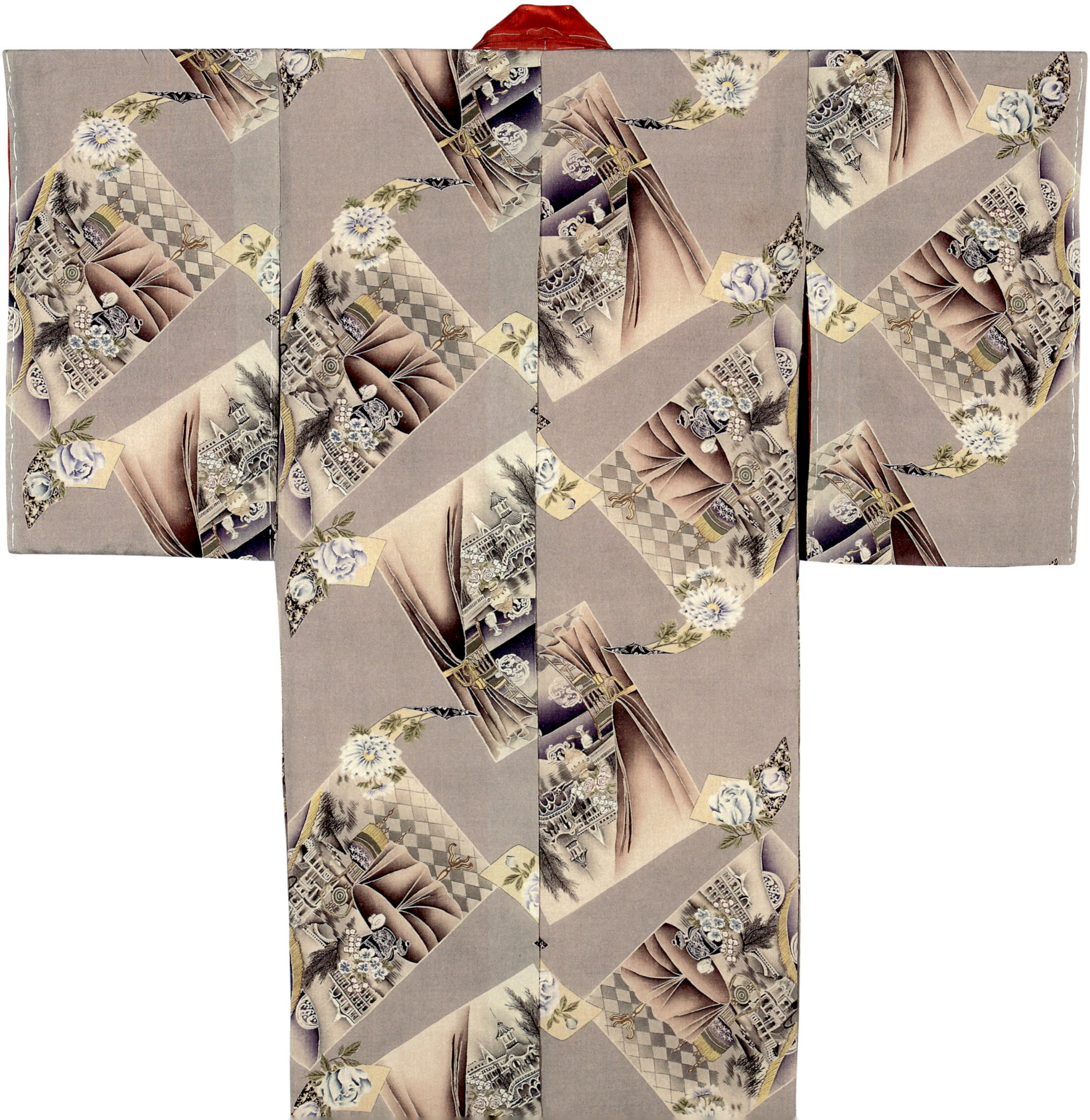

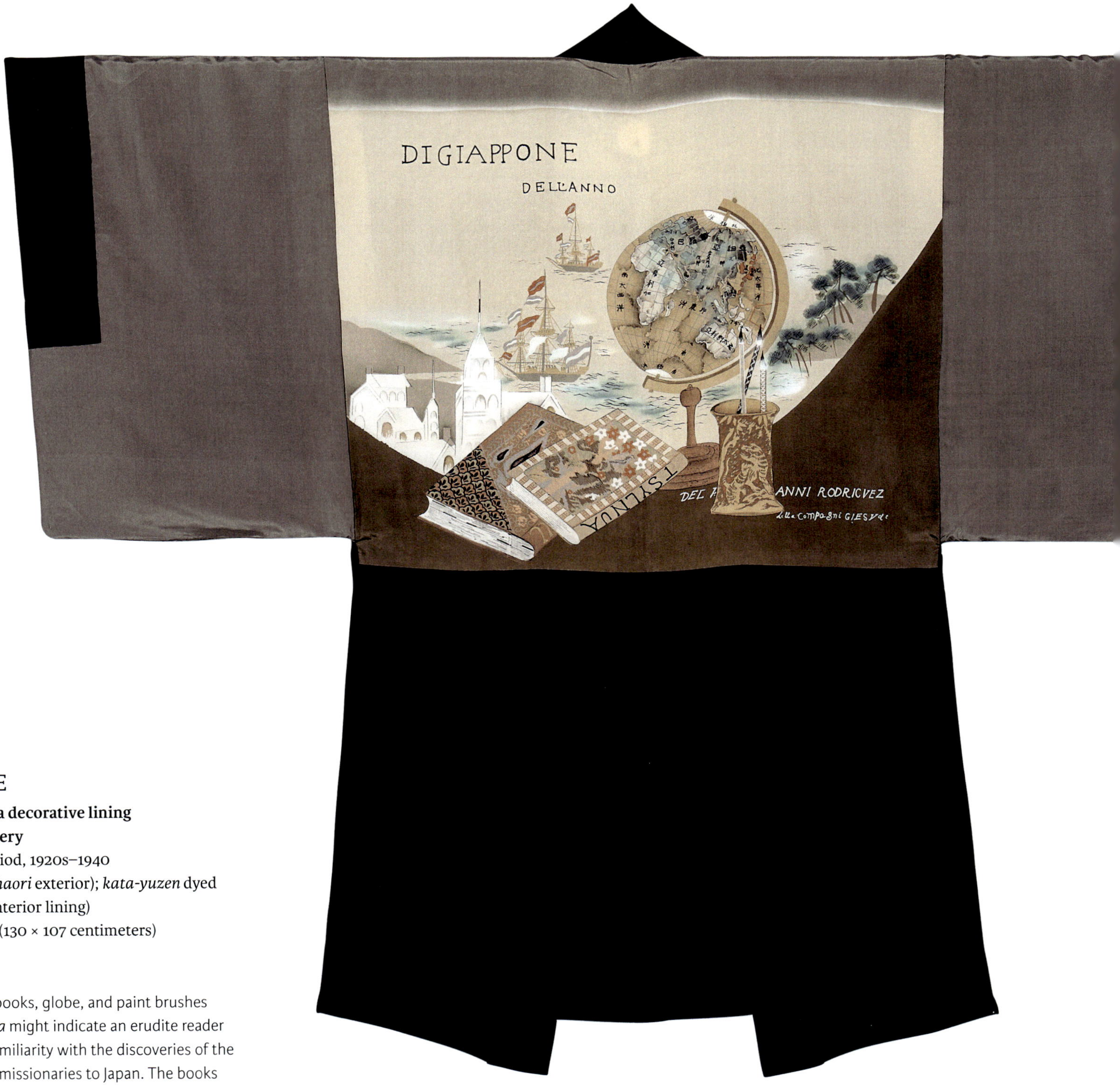

CULTURE

Man's *haori* with a decorative lining
Voyages of discovery
Taishō–Shōwa period, 1920s–1940
Silk plain-weave (*haori* exterior); *kata-yuzen* dyed and printed silk (interior lining)
51.0 × 42.0 inches (130 × 107 centimeters)
KM098

The design of the books, globe, and paint brushes drawn on this *haura* might indicate an erudite reader who has a broad familiarity with the discoveries of the early travelers and missionaries to Japan. The books probably represent volumes that carried copies of the annual correspondence sent from Japan to Rome by members of the Jesuit order who had gone to Japan as missionaries. The few lines of text shown on this *haura* come from one of the letters sent to Rome by Fra Giovanni Rodriguez, a Jesuit missionary who resided in Japan from 1606 to 1610. The background shows European ships apparently leaving Japan to return to their home base with various accounts of life in Japan.

TRAVEL

Man's *juban*
Luggage, liners, and adventure
Taishō–Shōwa period, 1920s–1940
Kata-yūzen dyed and printed silk
51.0 × 49.0 inches (130 × 124 centimeters)
KM099

The lively labels printed on this silk *juban* offered a wide range of places to visit for adventurous travelers. Top of the list is the NYK (Nippon Yusen Kaisha) Line, which covered a large shipping territory throughout the world, and whose passenger ships sailed to many places. Not all travelers used the NKY lines, but, as the *juban* images show, many other travel possibilities could appeal to them. The many pieces of luggage, destination tags, and travel passes demonstrate that voyagers would want very much to visit exciting or elegant places, be it Davos in Switzerland, The Hague, the Netherlands, the Hotel Terminus in Utrecht (Netherlands), or a stateroom on the Dollar Steamship Line in the Orient.

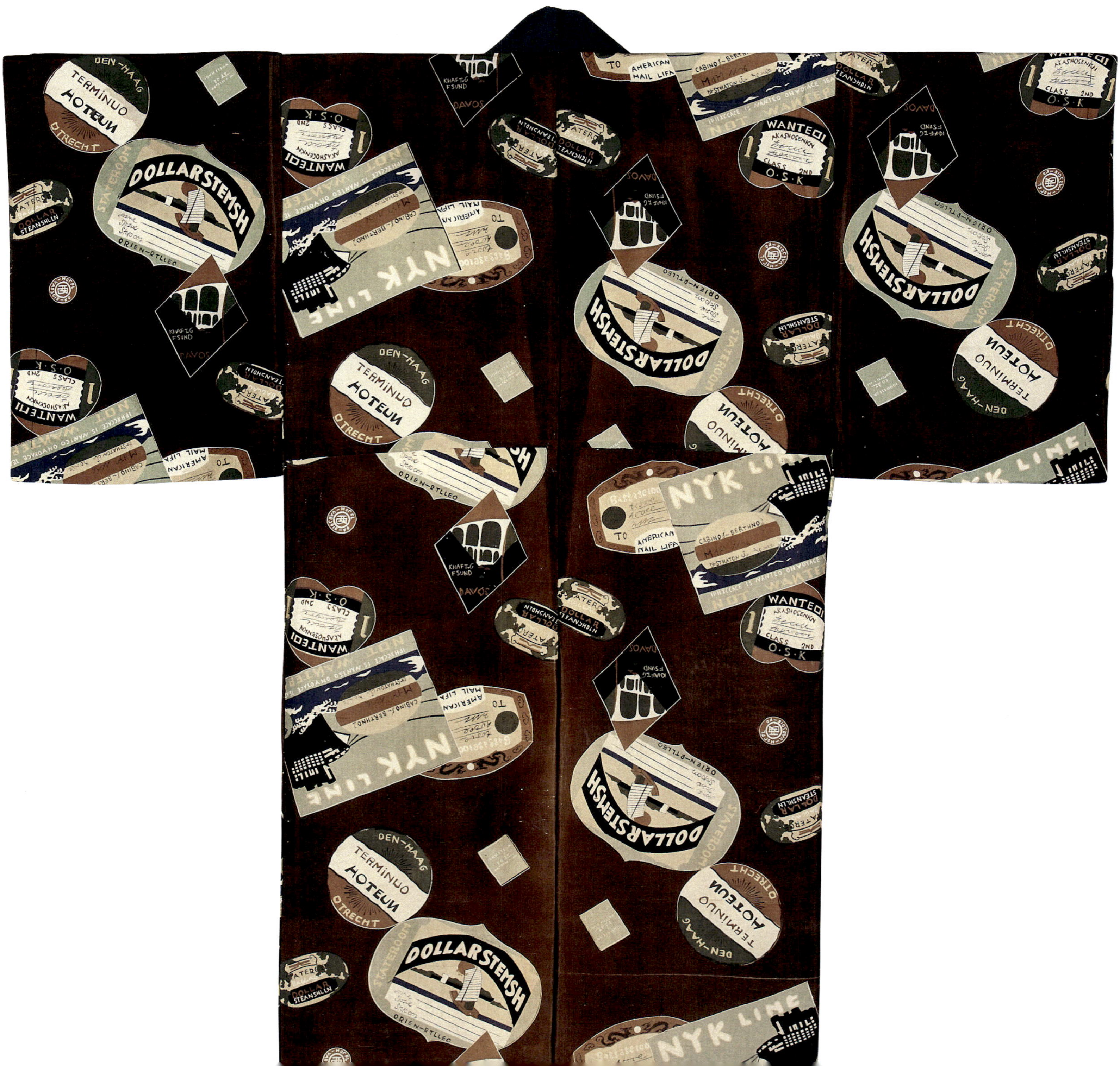

COSMOPOLITANISM/ WORLD EXHIBITIONS

Man's *juban*
Architecture from around the world
Shōwa period, 1940s–1950s
Printed silk
50.0 × 50.0 inches (127 × 127 centimeters)
KM100

The designs drawn on many of the buildings placed on this *juban* are quite spectacular. They were built to commemorate the World Expo held in Osaka, Japan, in 1970. Some of the dramatically marvelous architectural structures produced for the Expo carried their national names, such as American Park, Australia, Belgium (misspelled in the text), Canada, Colombia, United Kingdom, and USSR. Others were special pavilions, such as the Textiles Pavilion and Santau Pavilion. Several other structures carried titles (such as the dramatic Paingal Tower), but they did not relate to formal national names. This remarkable garment is of the most recent vintage of this collection, and it is well worth contemplating the architectural patterns of its time.

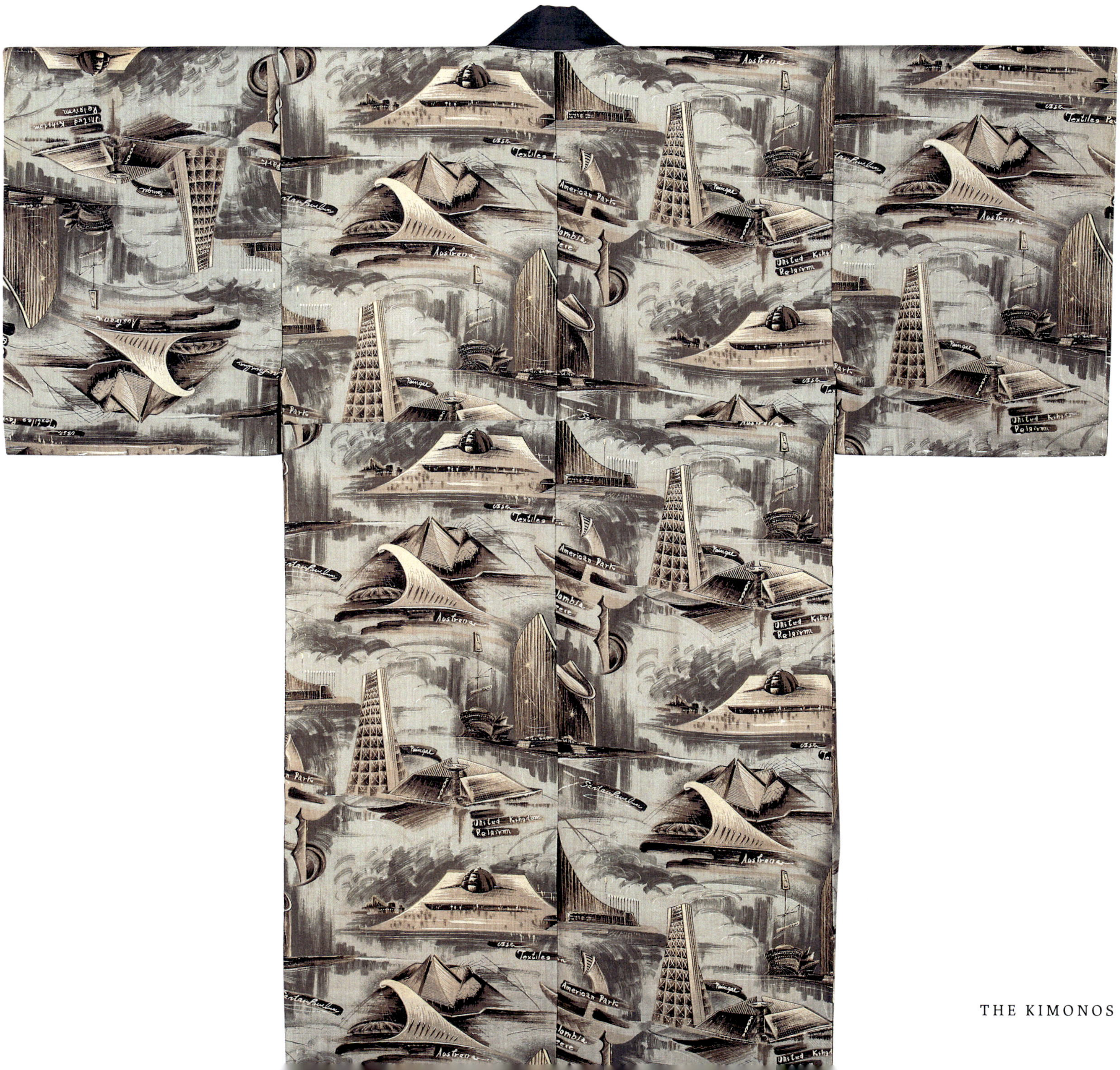

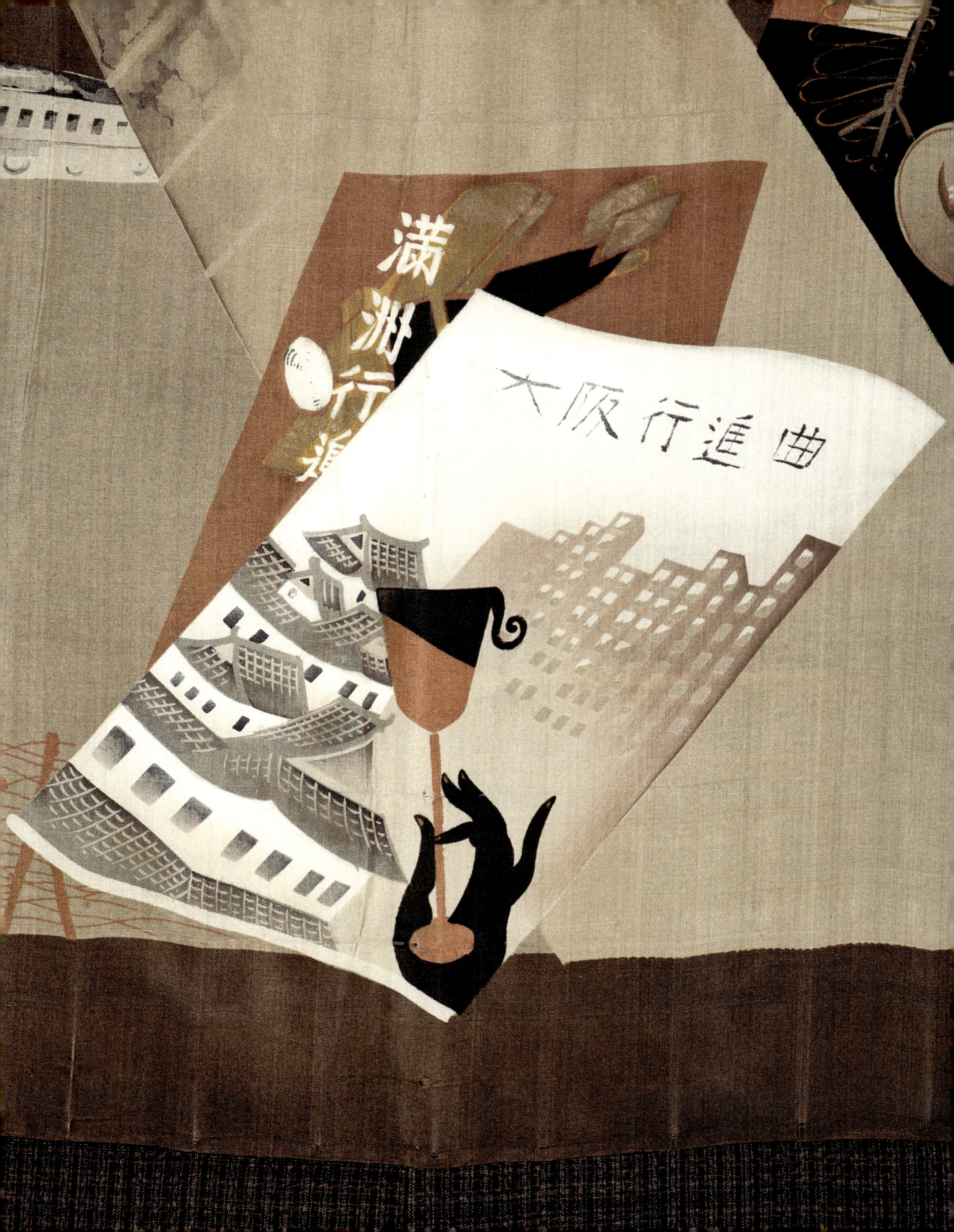
満洲行進
大阪行進曲

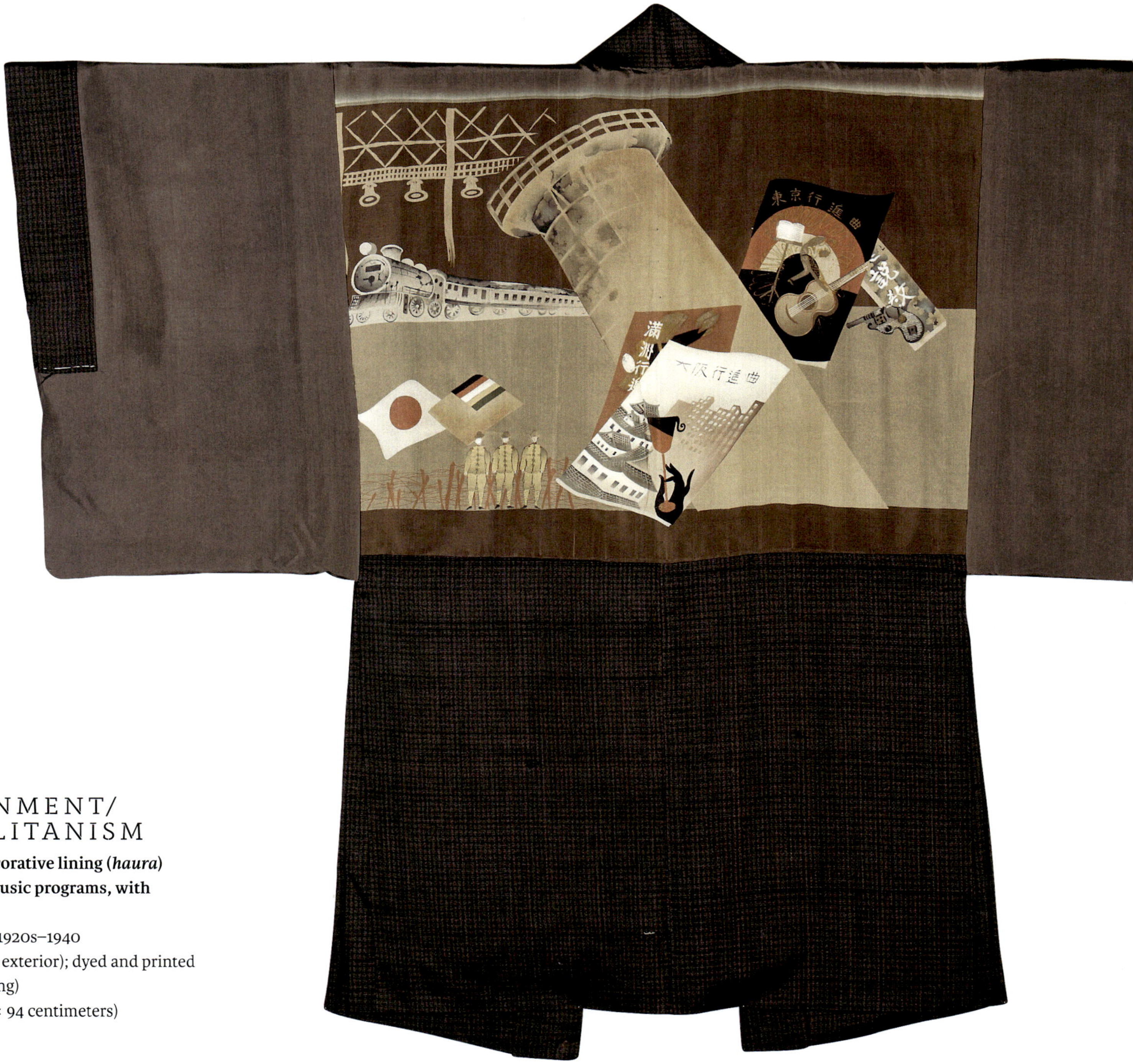

ENTERTAINMENT/ COSMOPOLITANISM

Man's *haori* with a decorative lining (*haura*)
Trains, theatre, and music programs, with soldiers and flags
Taishō–Shōwa period, 1920s–1940
Silk plain-weave (*haori* exterior); dyed and printed silk *haura* (interior lining)
51.0 × 37.0 inches (130 × 94 centimeters)
KM101

Empire was a major concept underlying many of the designs of the wartime textiles in the 1930s, and they were often presented in a complex way. The lining of this *haori*, for example, shows the Japanese and Manchuria flags together to indicate their national ties. The three soldiers standing in a battlefield are without guns, which perhaps hints at a camaraderie of sorts. Above the flags, the engine pulls a long line of military cars, possibly bringing more soldiers to the front, or perhaps even sending soldiers home. The three posters are labeled *Tokyo Marching Music*, *Osaka Marching Music*, and *Manshu Marching Music*, and they also show lively nightclub activities: dance, drink, and music. Neither the revolver nor the massive leaning column can be easily explained.

TRAVEL

Man's *haori* with a decorative lining (*haura*)
Manchukuo as a vacation playland
Shōwa period, 1930s–1940s
Silk *kasuri* (*haori* exterior); printed rayon (*haura*)
50.0 × 42.0 inches (127 × 107 centimeters)
KM102

The lining for this *haori* serves as a promotional tool for adventurous tourists who seek the wonders of Manchukuo (Manchuria). The broad white bands are filled with the many attractions of Manchukuo: the great passenger terminal at Dairen Harbor (with a docked ocean liner), the imposing walled city of Changchun, golfing resorts, hot springs, Buddhist stupa, and the Chūreitō, a famous historical monument (for the Japanese) in Manchuria. The design captures these major sights, although the designer carefully referenced the idea of empire through the Manchukuo flag that floats gracefully with flags of Britain, Italy, Brazil, and Japan, implying interest in internationalism as well as imperialism. Overall, the design offers the complex meanings Manchukuo held for Japan, from the expansion of empire to the opportunities offered for both work and play.

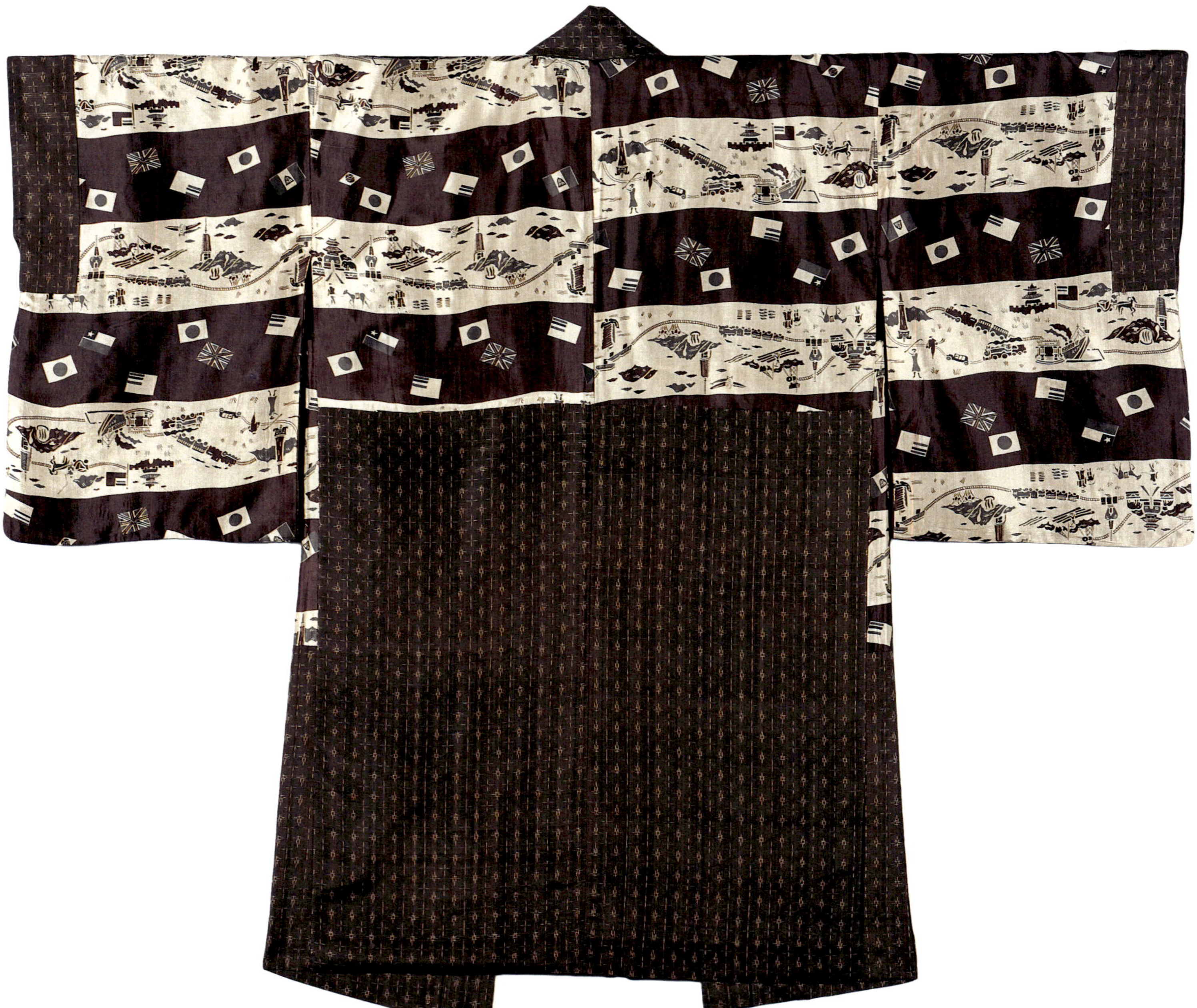

TRAVEL

***Juban* for a man**
Trains, ships, and a bicycle
Late Meiji–Taishō period, 1900–1914
Chirimen (silk crepe), hand-printed and
kata-yūzen dyed
51.0 × 51.0 inches (130 × 130 centimeters)
KM103

This length of *chirimen* was produced in the early years of the twentieth century and gives an interesting perspective on the changes that were occurring during the late Meiji period. Japan had reached an era of great change since the Meiji Restoration, when trains and ships began to supply new modes of travel throughout Japan's islands. The notes that float over the textile are tickets, envelopes, and perhaps even some paper money that would be needed for these new worlds of travel. Note the bicycle that peeks from behind the ticket.

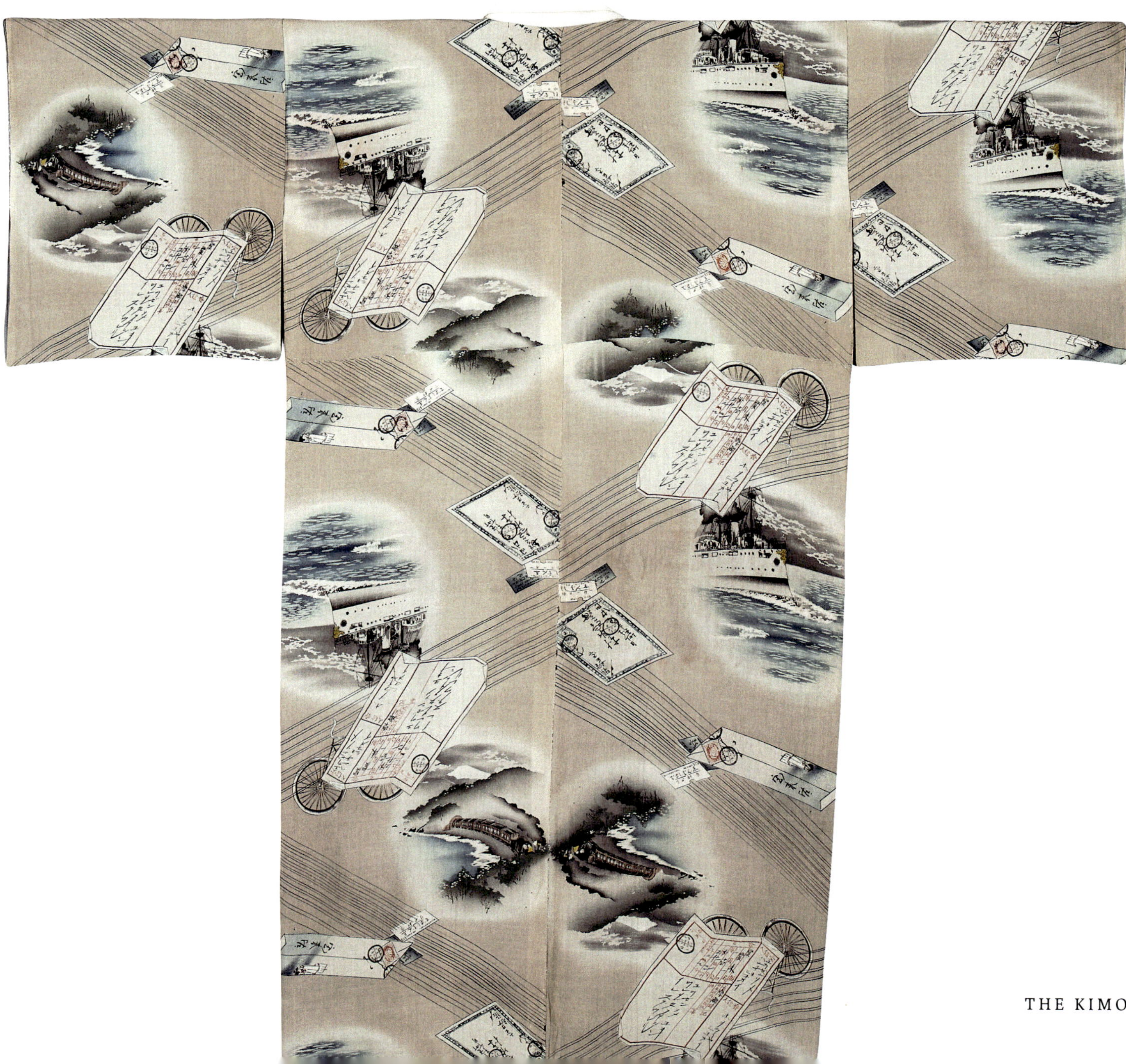

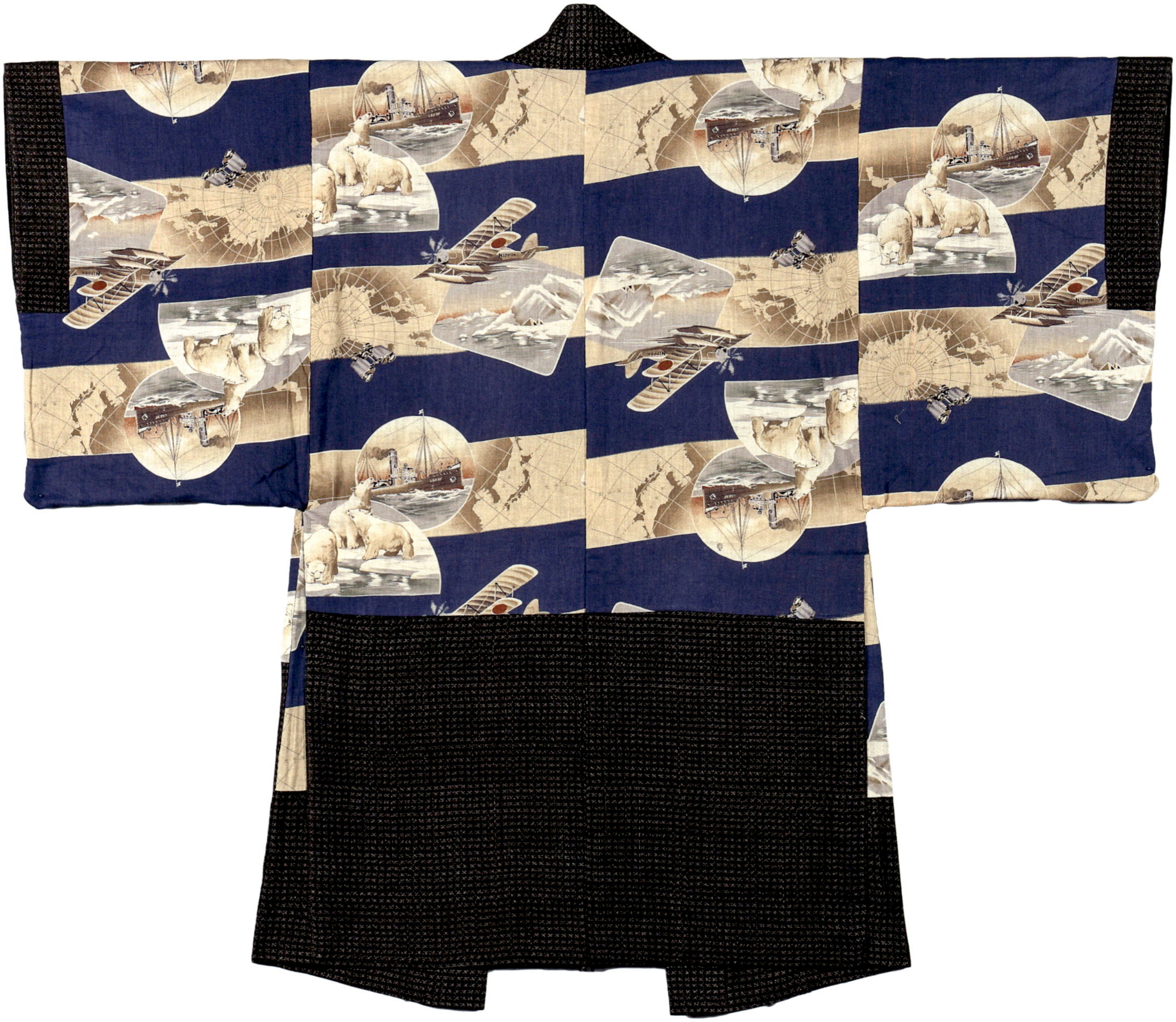

MODERNITY

Man's *haori* with a decorative lining (*haura*) Celebration of the Second International Polar Year

Taishō–Shōwa period, 1928–1930s
Kasuri silk (exterior); printed cotton interior
49.0 × 38.5 inches (124 × 98 centimeters)
KM104

The designs on this *haori* played a part in the Second International Polar Year (IPY) that was celebrated in 1932–33. Members of the International Meteorological Organization helped to bring together 44 nations to participate in this Arctic research program for advances in the fields of meteorology, magnetism, atmospheric science, and the mapping of ionospheric phenomena that helped to move radio science further ahead. Twenty-seven observation stations were established in the Arctic during 1932–33, and a vast amount of data was also collected during the program. Japan provided float planes as well as ships during the polar explorations. The artist included images of these planes and ships on the *haori*, capturing the fascination of the work of the IPY for those who wore these garments. The image of the polar bears also offered a light touch, as the bears seem to be in awe of the work taking place around them.

SENSŌGARA/ MIYAMAIRI

***Miyamairi* (boy child's kimono for a first shrine visit)**
A special garment
Taishō–Shōwa period, 1920s–1940s
Kata-yūzen dyed and painted silk
37.0 × 34.0 inches (94 × 86 centimeters)
KM105

The warship on this *miyamairi* is painted with loving detail, and the warplanes above look almost playful in flight. The shoulders and skirt are dyed the olive green of military uniforms, enfolding the tiny wearer in the spirit of the times. This formal robe has three crests at the back and two at the front, showing five identical small planes rather than familial crests. Some *miyamairi* have images of the Seven Treasures on the shoulders and hem, indicating that the child would want for nothing, but here the Treasures are replaced with tanks, helmets, and bugles. The bugles symbolize the poignant story of Kiguchi Kohei, a bugler who, although mortally wounded during the Sino-Japanese war, continued to sound his horn. This child's parents hoped their son would grow up to be selfless and courageous.

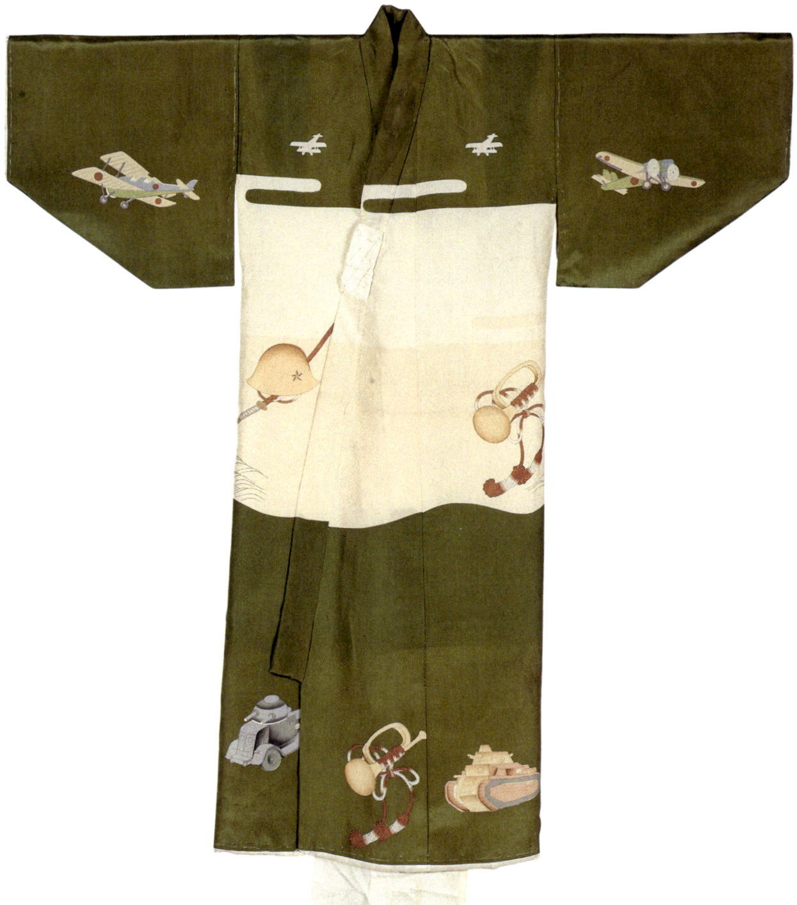

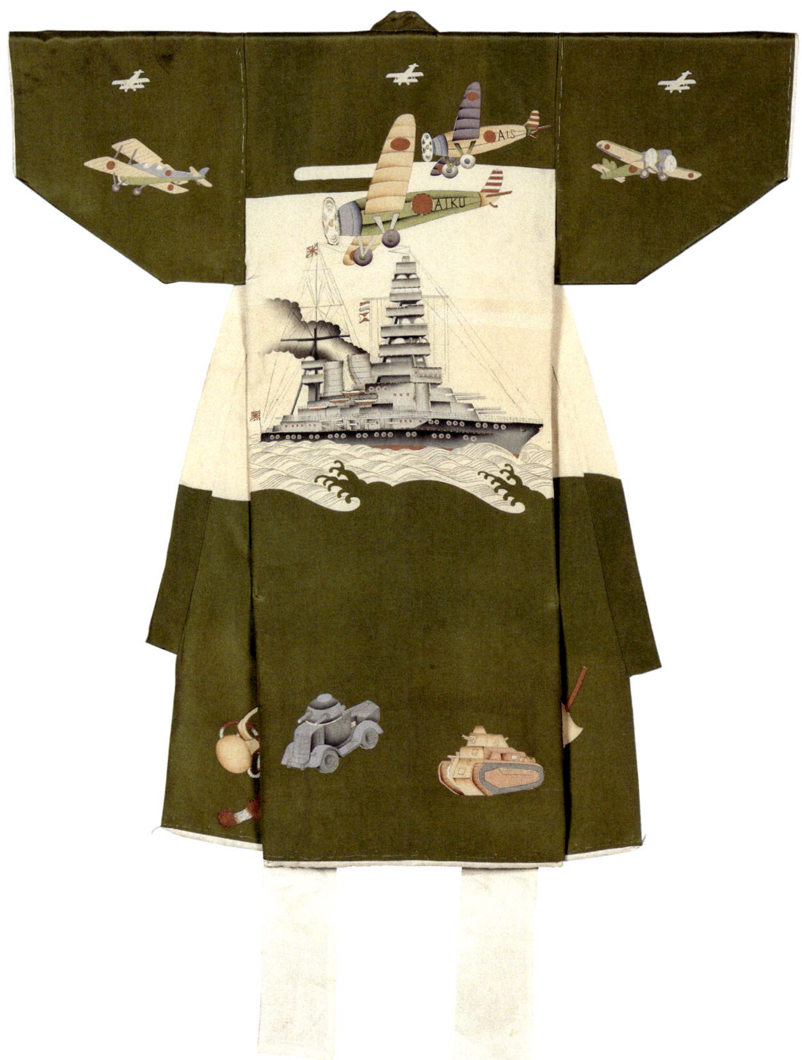

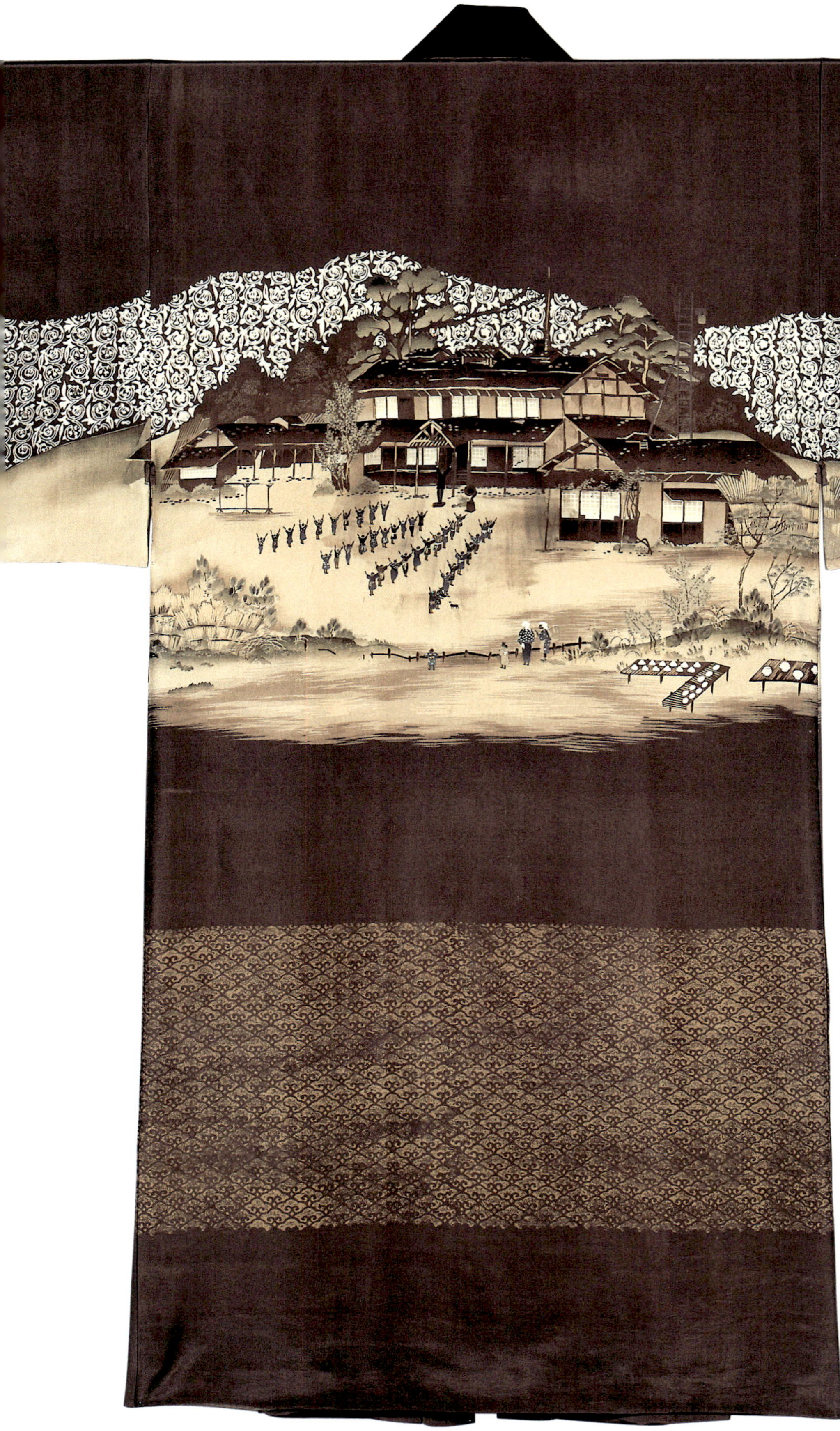

MODERNITY

Man's *juban*
Morning exercises at school
Taishō–Shōwa period, 1920s–1940s
Kata-yūzen dyed and painted silk
54.0 × 51.0 inches (137 × 130 centimeters)
KM106

The artist who produced this elegant *juban* chose a thoughtful subject. The building is an academy in a rural area and the teacher is seen opening a morning class with exercises for the 40 students—all boys—who vigorously follow their teacher's motions. There is a music box with a horn attached so all the students can hear and follow the music as they exercise. The serving women have set up a table with food that awaits the boys, who are very likely to be hungry after exercises. The design of structures, people, and foliage for the dyed and painted *juban* were carefully planned, and the subtle browns and beiges touched here and there with blue, white, and green capture the eye for further appreciation of the scene.

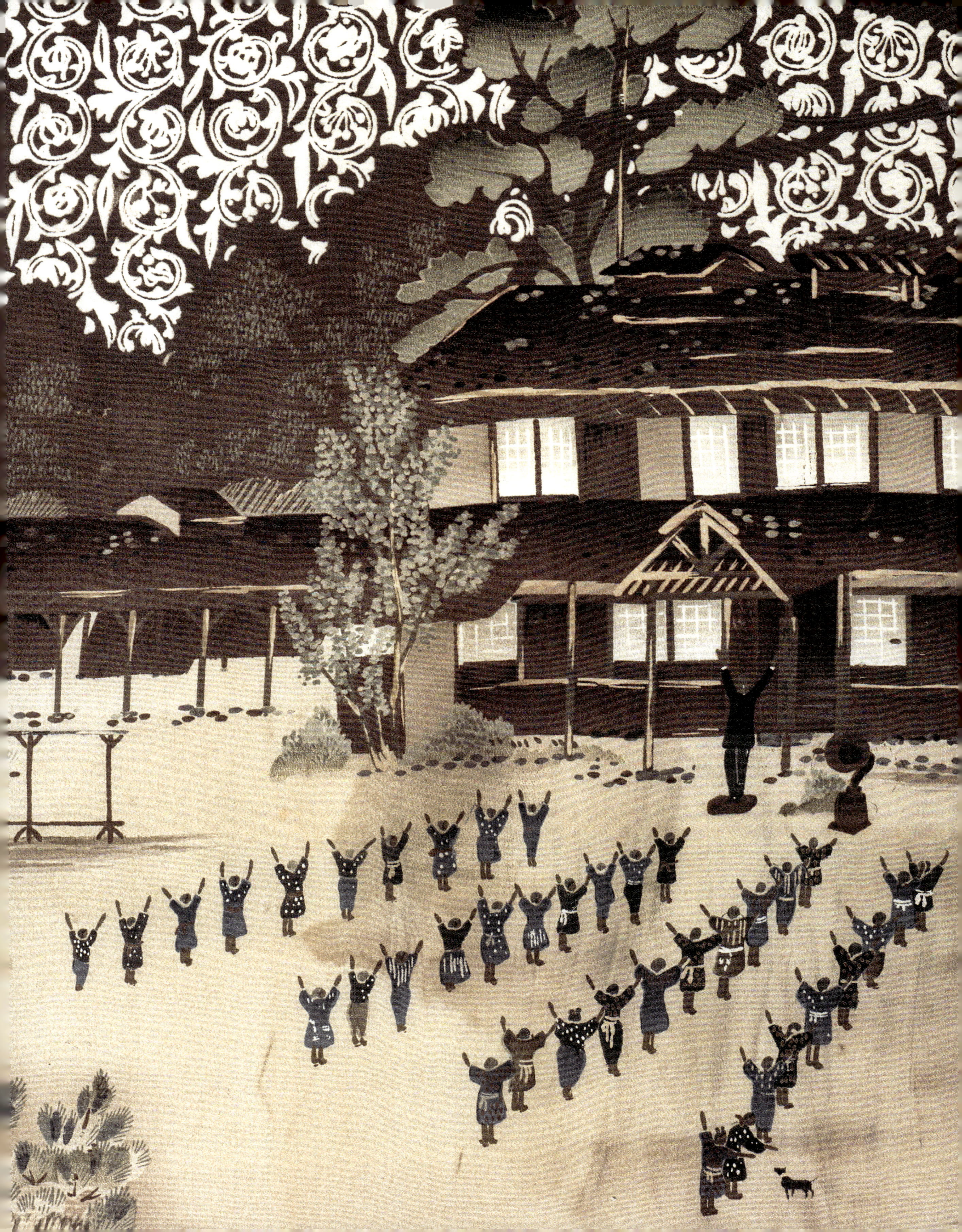

TRAVEL

Man's *haori* with a decorative lining (*haura*)
From Bangkok to New York City
Taishō–Shōwa period, 1920s–1930s
Silk plain-weave *haori* (outer); woven twill and heavy silk with metal threads for *haura* (lining)
50.0 × 38.0 inches (127 × 97 centimeters)
KM107

Two stunning images are depicted on this man's *haori*. The *haura* is a *tour de force* of the craftsmanship required for the brocade and twill techniques on the silk cloth. The depictions of the two famous cities—New York's famous skyscrapers and the Brooklyn Bridge in America, and Bangkok's majestically constructed temples in Siam (known as Thailand since 1949)—create a spectacular tour of two sides of the world. The iconic Mount Fuji also plays a part, showing its clouded snow-drenched shoulders just below its peak. At the lower left, a misty fog slightly hides a traditional Japanese boat as it leaves the bay. The owner of this garment has undoubtedly purchased a textile treasure.

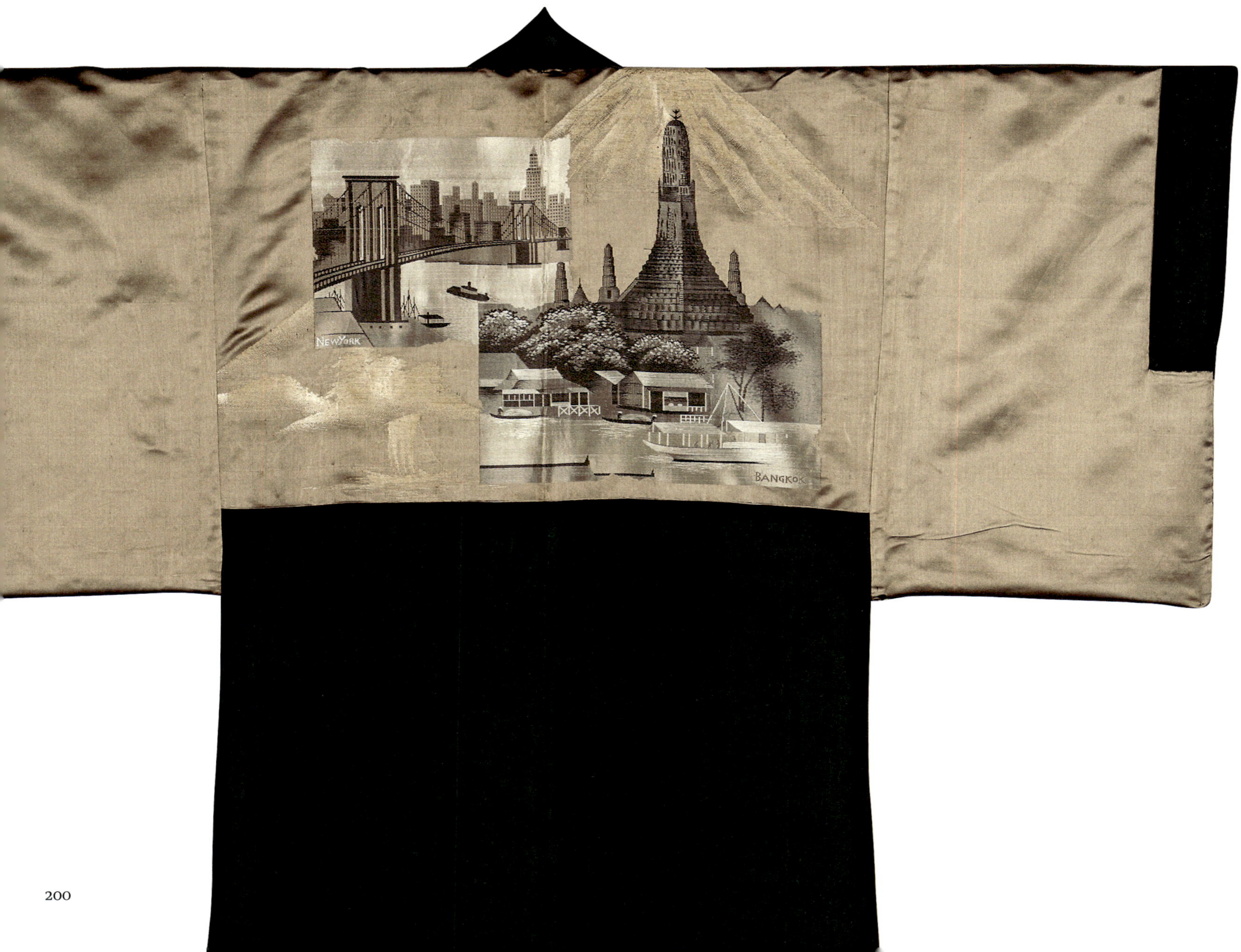

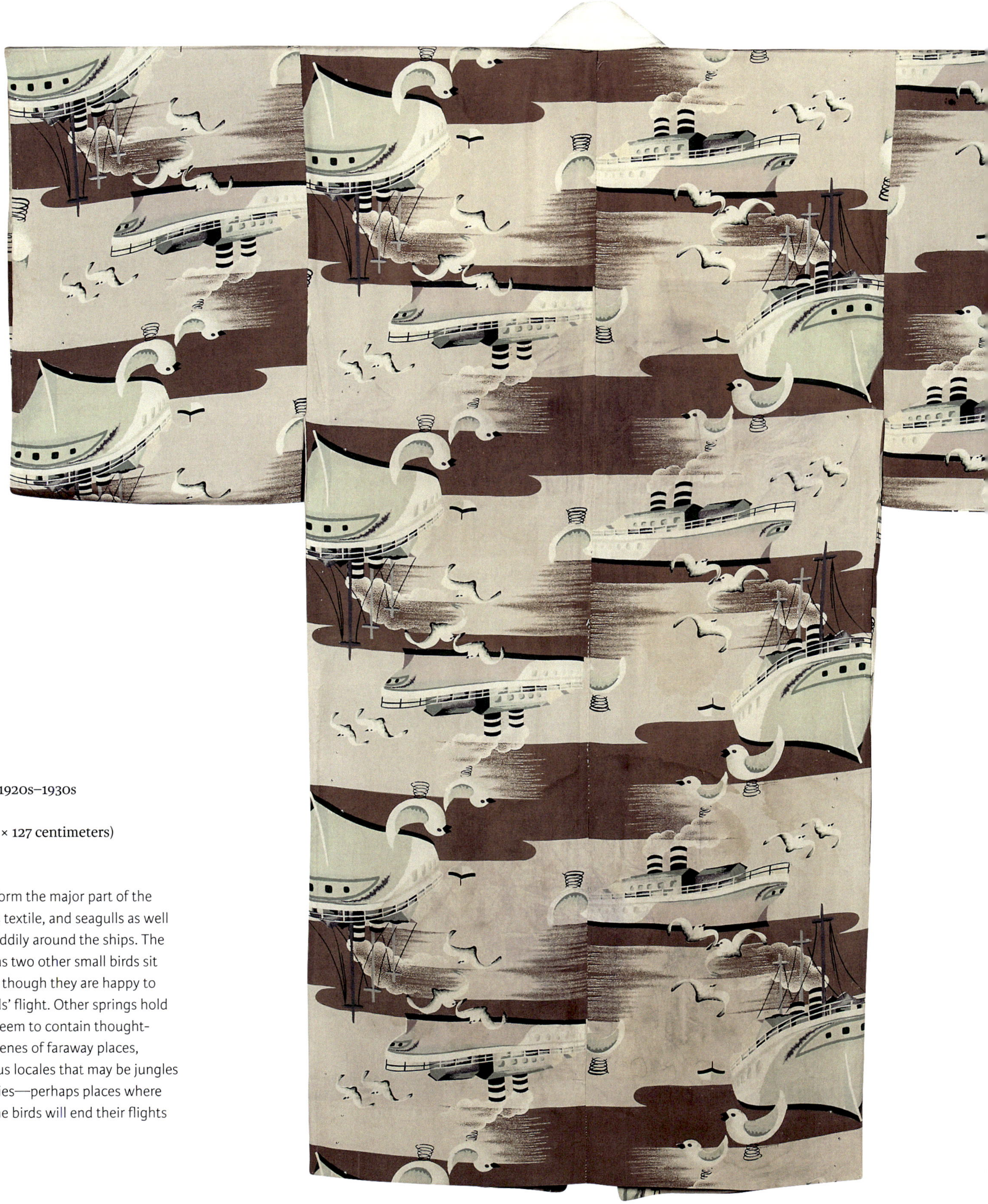

TRAVEL

***Juban* for a man**
Mysterious meanings
Taishō–Shōwa period, 1920s–1930s
Printed silk
50.0 × 50.0 inches (127 × 127 centimeters)
KM108

Two large ocean liners form the major part of the design intended for this textile, and seagulls as well as *chidori* (plovers) fly giddily around the ships. The design is quite playful, as two other small birds sit on springs, cheeping as though they are happy to be part of the other birds' flight. Other springs hold up arc-like pieces that seem to contain thought-provoking shadowed scenes of faraway places, unknown and mysterious locales that may be jungles or possibly towns or cities—perhaps places where the ships will dock or the birds will end their flights in comfort.

LEISURE ACTIVITIES

Kimono for a child
Children at home
Taishō–Shōwa period, late 1920s–1930s
Printed silk
38.0 × 32.0 inches (97 × 81 centimeters)
KM109

As with many children's kimono in the period leading up to the war, hints of the military are evident without being the focal point of the design. In this kimono, which depicts a spacious, well-appointed home with a number of Western features, there are two scenes of a boy at play. In one, he appears to be quietly engrossed in fixing a radio, surrounded by stuffed toys. In the other, he has a toy machine gun, and the stuffed toys have been replaced by toy planes and tanks. The implicit message seems to be that a child must be raised to understand his role in society, both in peacetime and in wartime.

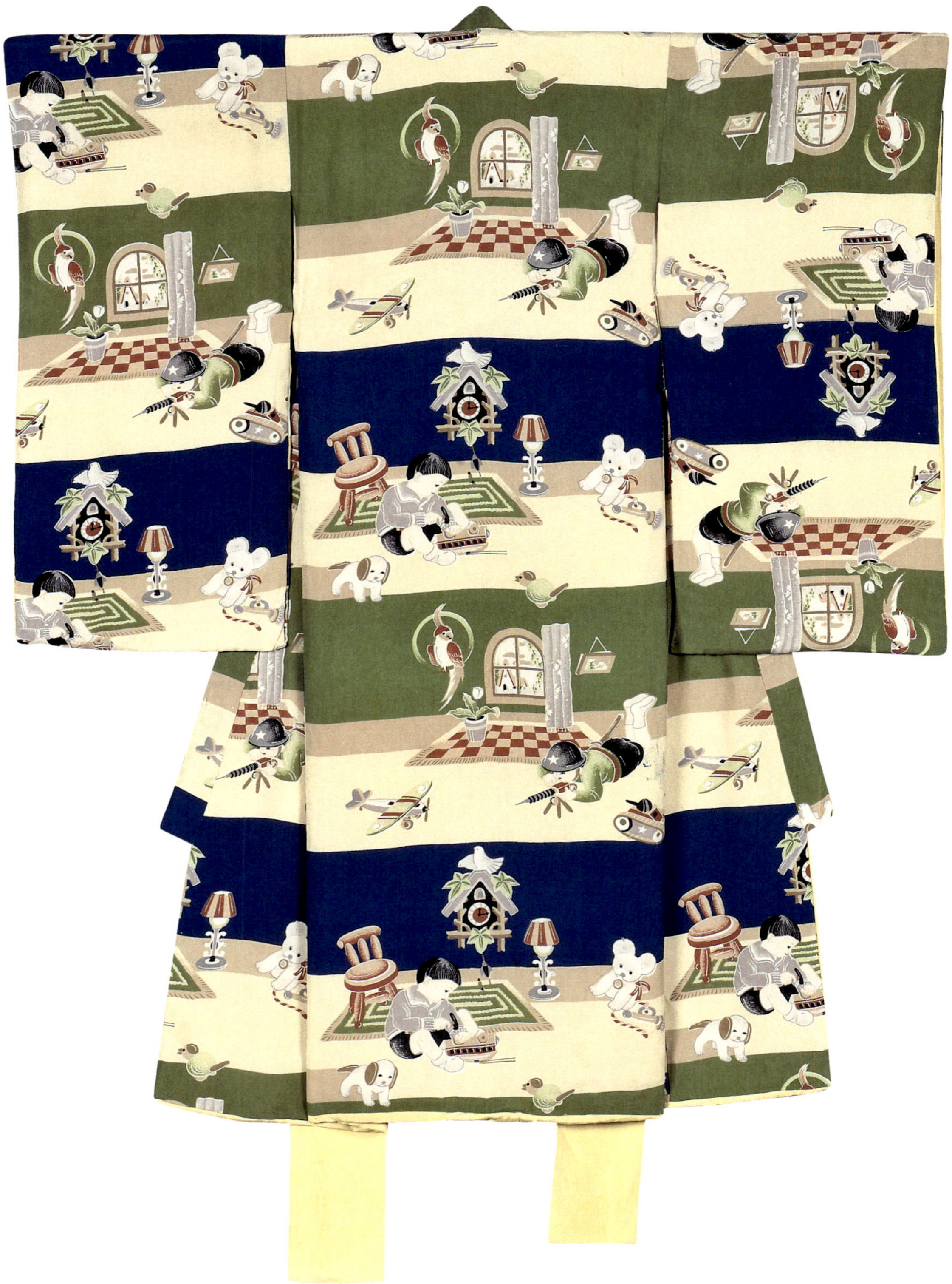

ENTERTAINMENT

Kimono for a woman
Animals and soldiers
Early Shōwa period, 1930s–1940
Kata-yūzen dyed silk
54.0 × 54.0 inches (137 × 137 centimeters)
KM110

A child's favorite toys take flight in this fanciful *juban* that showcases bauble-like balloons that fly through the air with passengers in baskets or attached to harnesses. The design is playful, with well-known friends such as Mickey and Minnie Mouse making guest appearances, along with the rabbit in the moon. The adorable teddy bears, a dressed-up elephant, and even the toy soldier, the sole hint of the political climate of the times, are all perfectly at ease as they float through the deep blue sky. The amusing textile for this garment would be delightful attire for women or men.

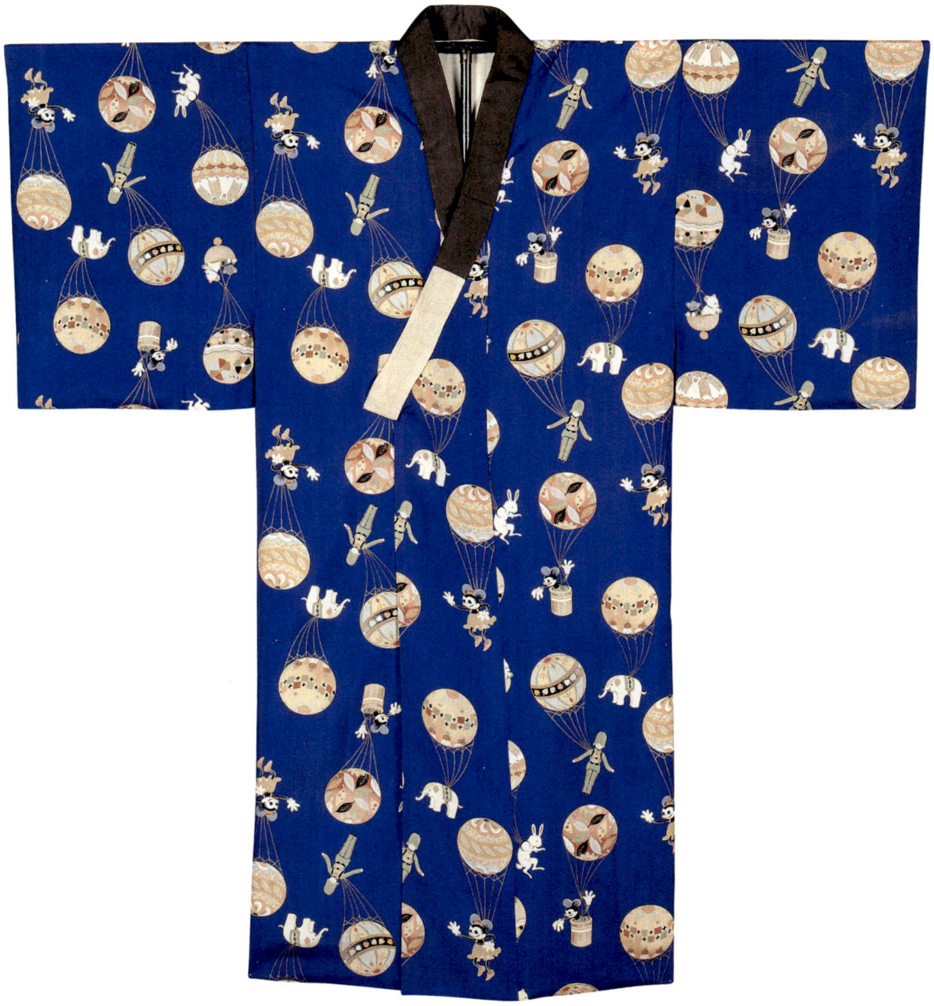

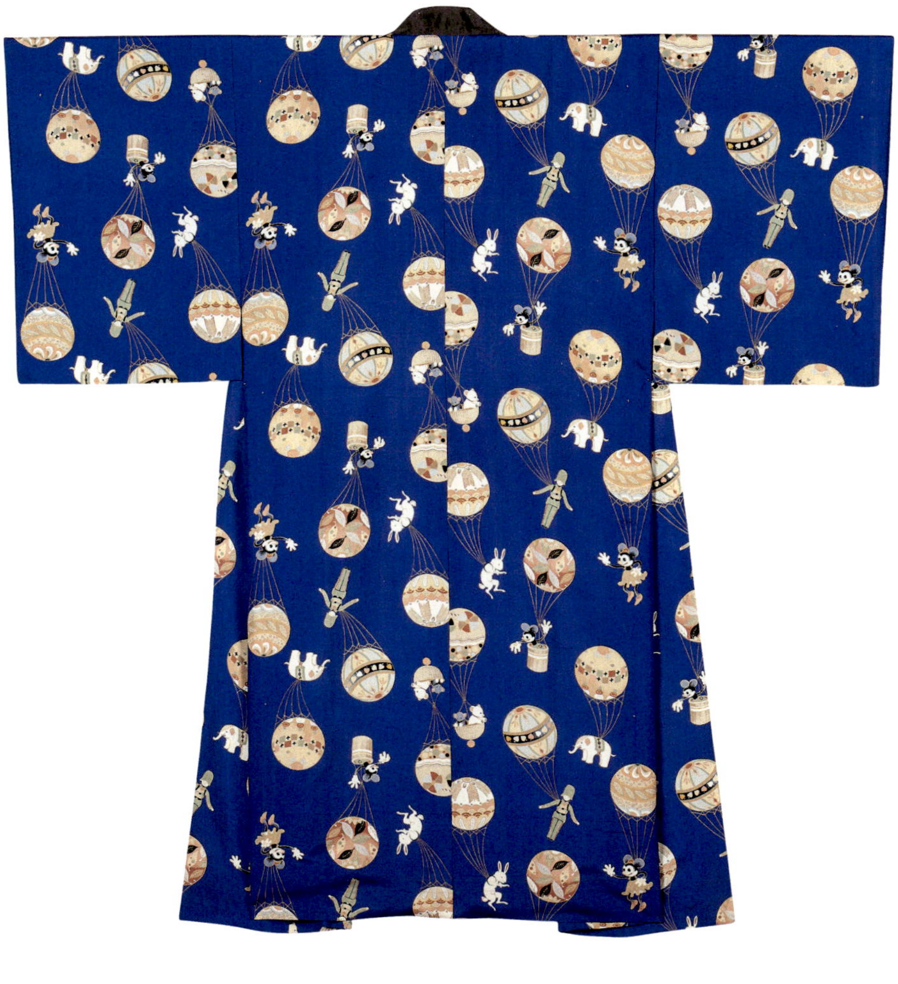

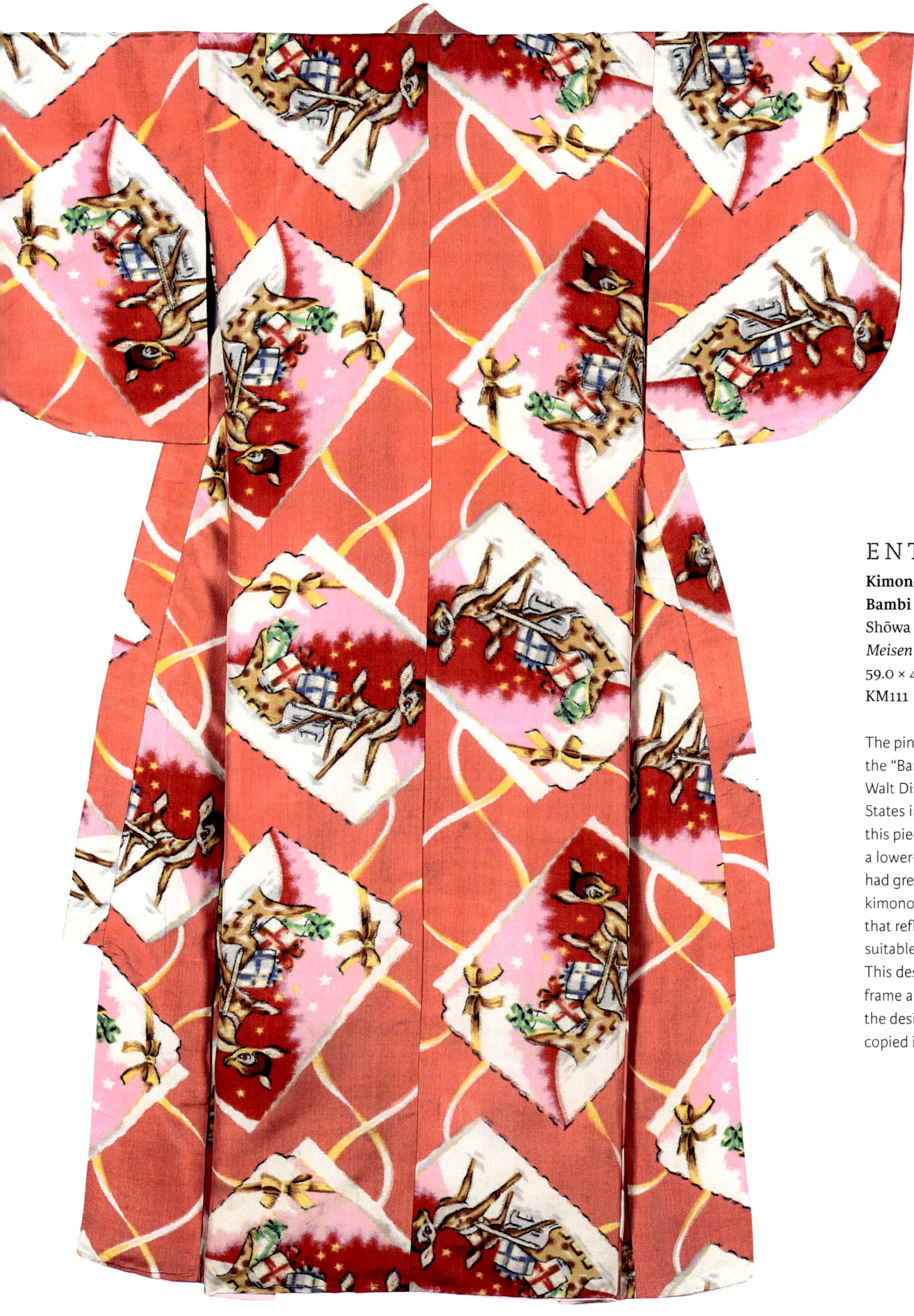

ENTERTAINMENT

Kimono for a girl child
Bambi with a sled of presents
Shōwa period, 1940s–1950s
Meisen silk
59.0 × 43.0 inches (150 × 109 centimeters)
KM111

The pink and red colors of this kimono, along with the "Bambi" motif, clearly mark it as a girl's robe. Walt Disney's *Bambi* was released in the United States in 1942, and in Japan in 1951, helping to date this piece. Because *meisen* kimono were made of a lower-quality silk, they were less expensive and had great commercial success. Lower prices allowed kimono manufacturers to print novelty patterns that reflected short-lived trends and fads and were suitable for casual wear rather than formal occasions. This design, with its long rectangular deckled-edge frame and golden bow, looks very much as though the designer found a Western Christmas card and copied it, along with its envelope.

ENTERTAINMENT

***Juban* for a man**
Come to the cabaret
Taishō–early Shōwa period, 1920s–early 1930s
Stenciled and dyed *kata-yūzen* silk
51.0 × 51.0 inches (130 × 130 centimeters)
KM112

The decorative designs on this man's *nagajuban* capture a new type of contemporary popular entertainment—the musical revue—for the Taishō and early Shōwa periods. The stenciled figures of the dancing girls are possibly based on an actual vaudeville performance known in one of the burlesque houses in Japan. The lounging lady adds an element of mystery and provocative sexuality as she relaxes, perhaps on a would-be sand dune, while the shadow of a giant wave that appears to be poised to wash over her gives a slightly ominous cast to an otherwise playful and frivolous design. Overall, the design encapsulates the erotic grotesque nonsense of the 1930s.

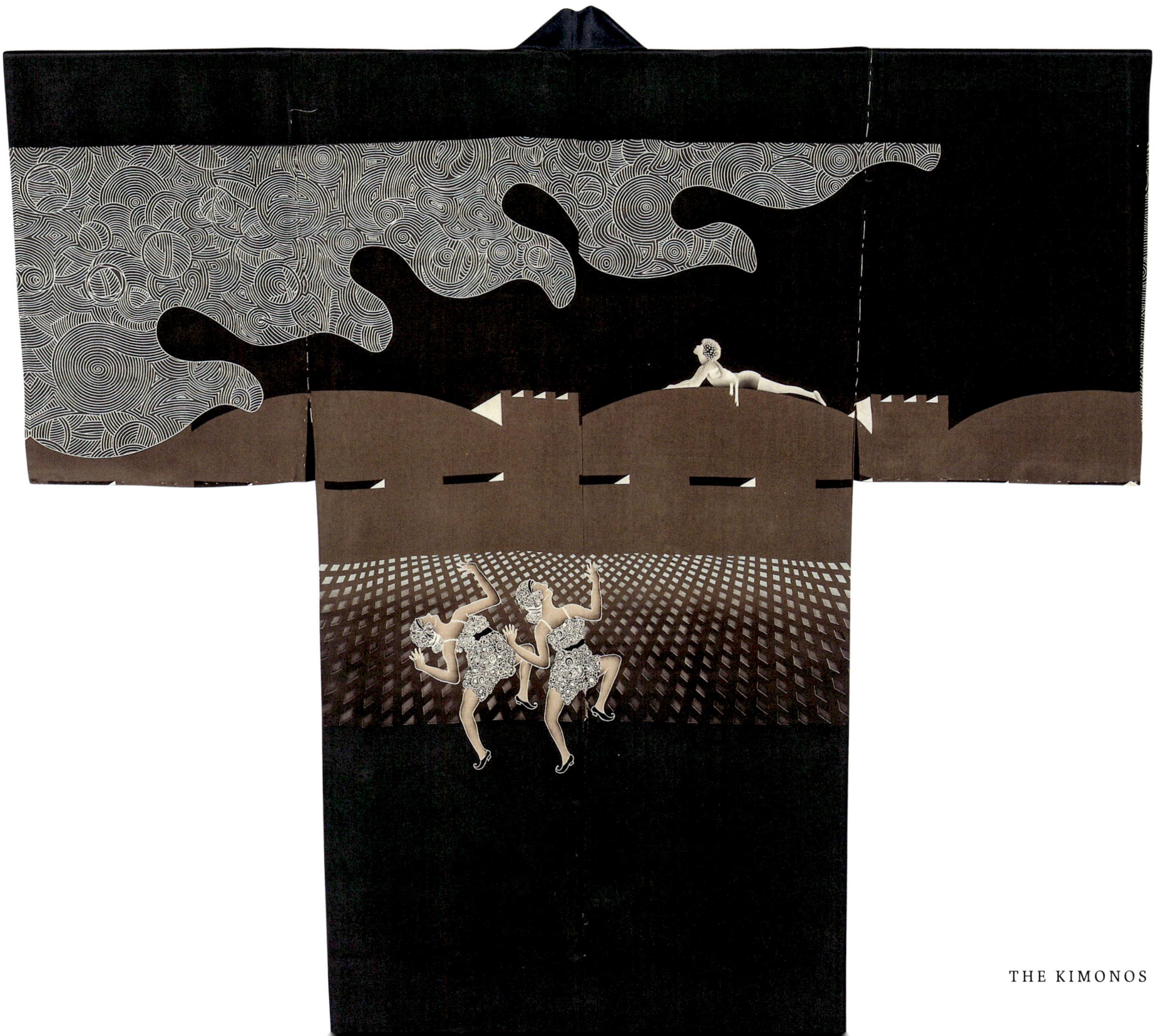

MACHINE AGE

***Yukata* for a child**
Airplanes in formation
Late Taishō–early Shōwa period, late 1920s–early 1930s
Printed cotton
35.0 × 32.0 inches (89 × 81 centimeters)
KM113

Airplanes were a popular motif in the textiles that young boys liked to wear. This *yukata*, though visually simple, is actually very sophisticated in its design. Blue and white stripes are an old traditional design in a country steeped in reverence for tradition. The placement of the planes simultaneously in both color fields results in a striking juxtaposition of positive and negative space. These striking graphics are particularly ingenious in highlighting the *hinomaru* (the rising sun motif) on the wings of the plane, subtly referencing patriotism and nationalism. Further, the rhythmic 1-2-1-2 pattern of the planes suggests the precision of military formation.

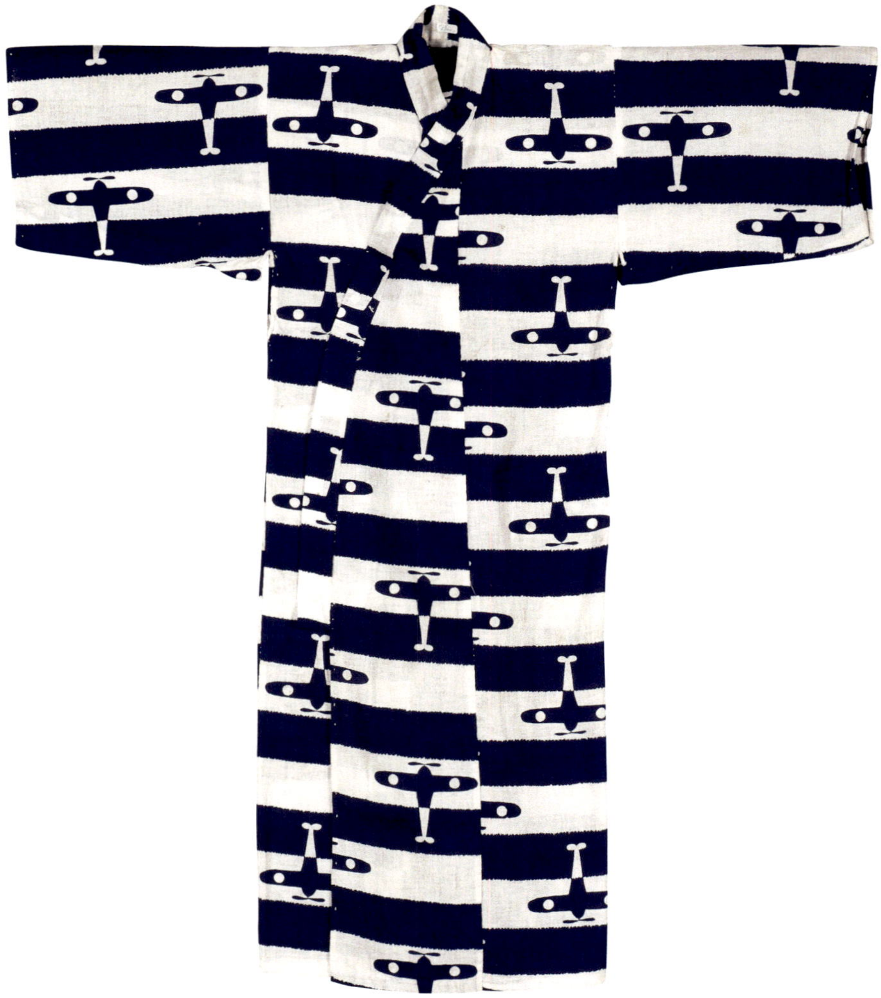

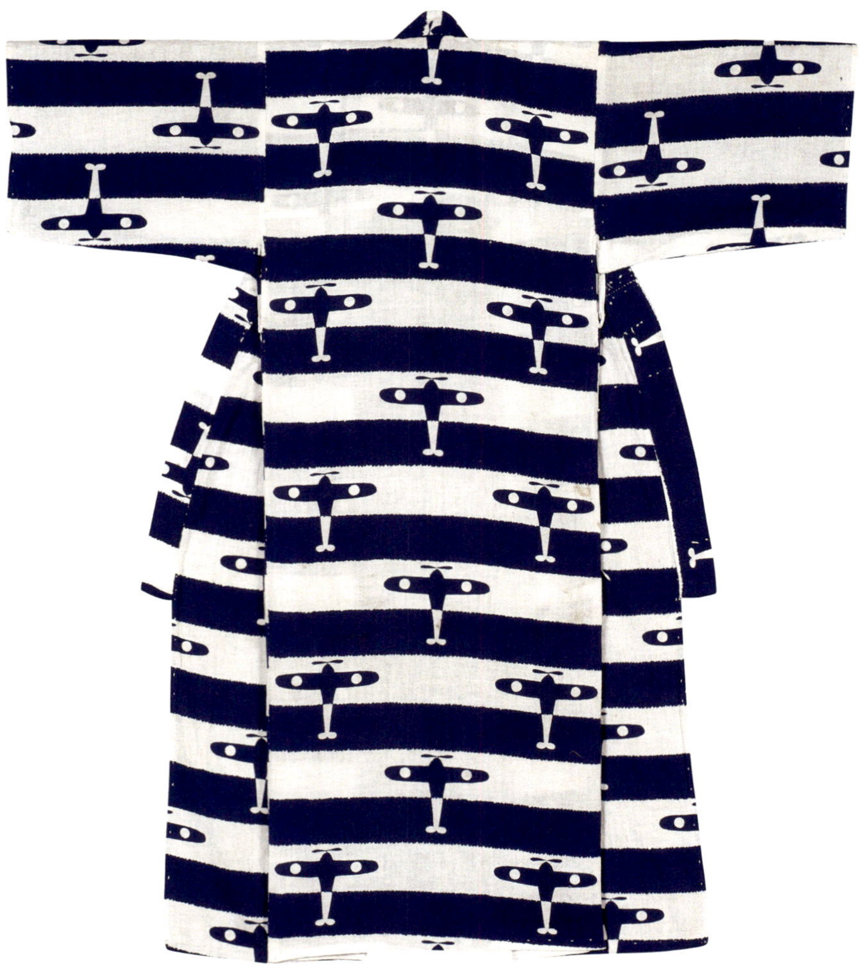

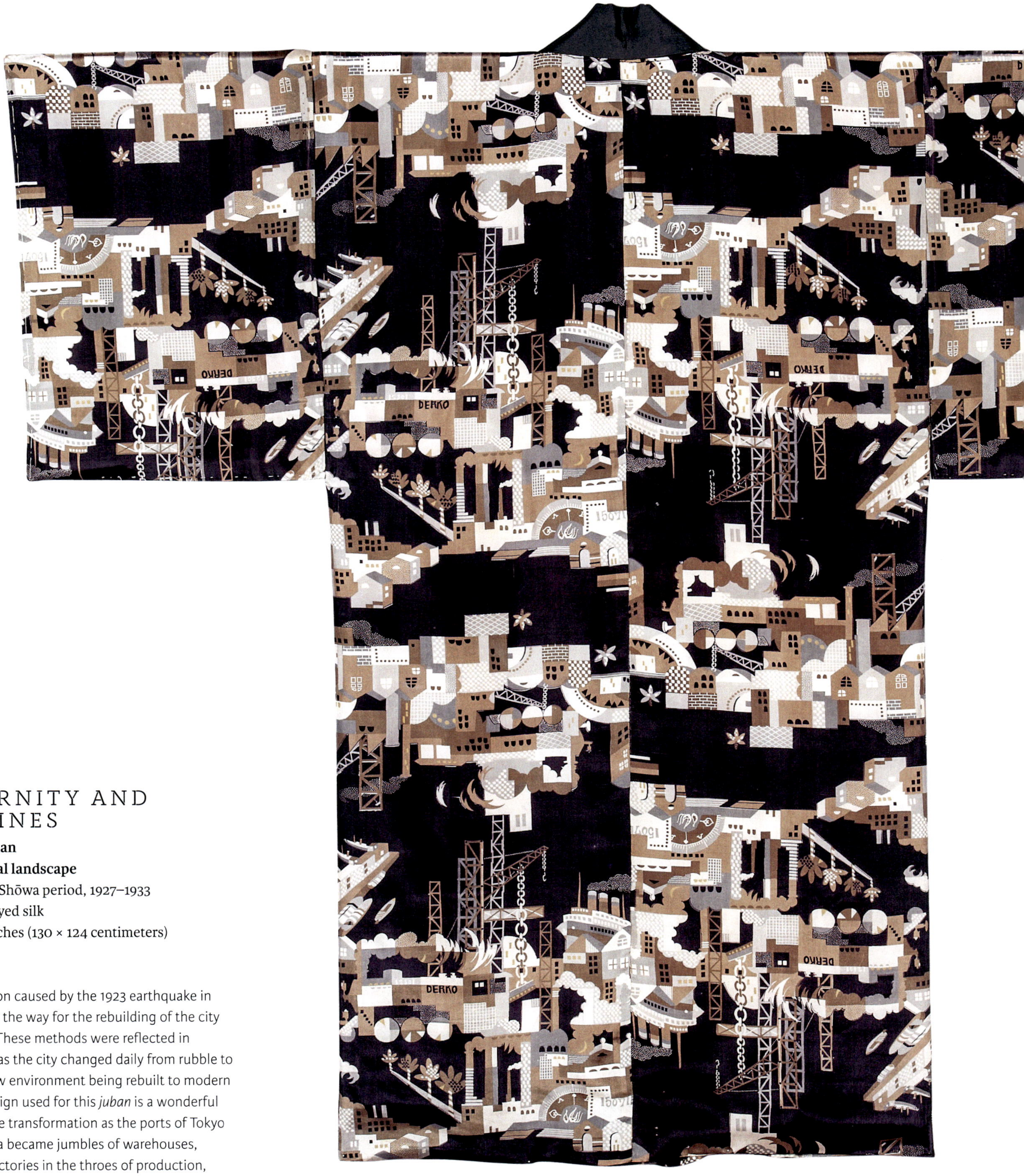

MODERNITY AND MACHINES

***Juban* for a man**
The industrial landscape
Taishō–early Shōwa period, 1927–1933
Kata-yūzen dyed silk
51.0 × 49.0 inches (130 × 124 centimeters)
KM114

The destruction caused by the 1923 earthquake in Tokyo opened the way for the rebuilding of the city in new ways. These methods were reflected in *omoshirogara* as the city changed daily from rubble to a dynamic new environment being rebuilt to modern scale. The design used for this *juban* is a wonderful example of the transformation as the ports of Tokyo and Yokohama became jumbles of warehouses, new docks, factories in the throes of production, and buildings glowing with electric light. As seen in the *juban* design, construction cranes were constant features along the skyline. A counterpart in a contemporary work of art by Yamagata Komatarō (*Cranes*, 1928; Miyagi Museum of Art, Sendai) may have been what inspired this striking *juban*.

CINEMA/ ENTERTAINMENT

***Juban* for a man**
Film strips showing *samurai* in battle
Taishō–early Shōwa period, late 1920s–early 1930s
Kata-yūzen dyed and printed silk
49.0 × 49.0 inches (124 × 124 centimeters)
KM115

The cinema was loved by the Japanese public, and people rushed to see their preferred movies, which ranged from comedies and cartoons to serious dramas as well as light and colorful musicals. The owner of this *juban* perhaps had a preference for films that depicted dark and dramatic narratives drawn from the samurai stories of the past. The filmstrip images on this textile show swordplay, recognizable actors who played moody or evil parts, and even a brief comedy segment where several unhappy men (and, perhaps, a large, partially hidden fish) fall over as a protagonist easily challenges their intent.

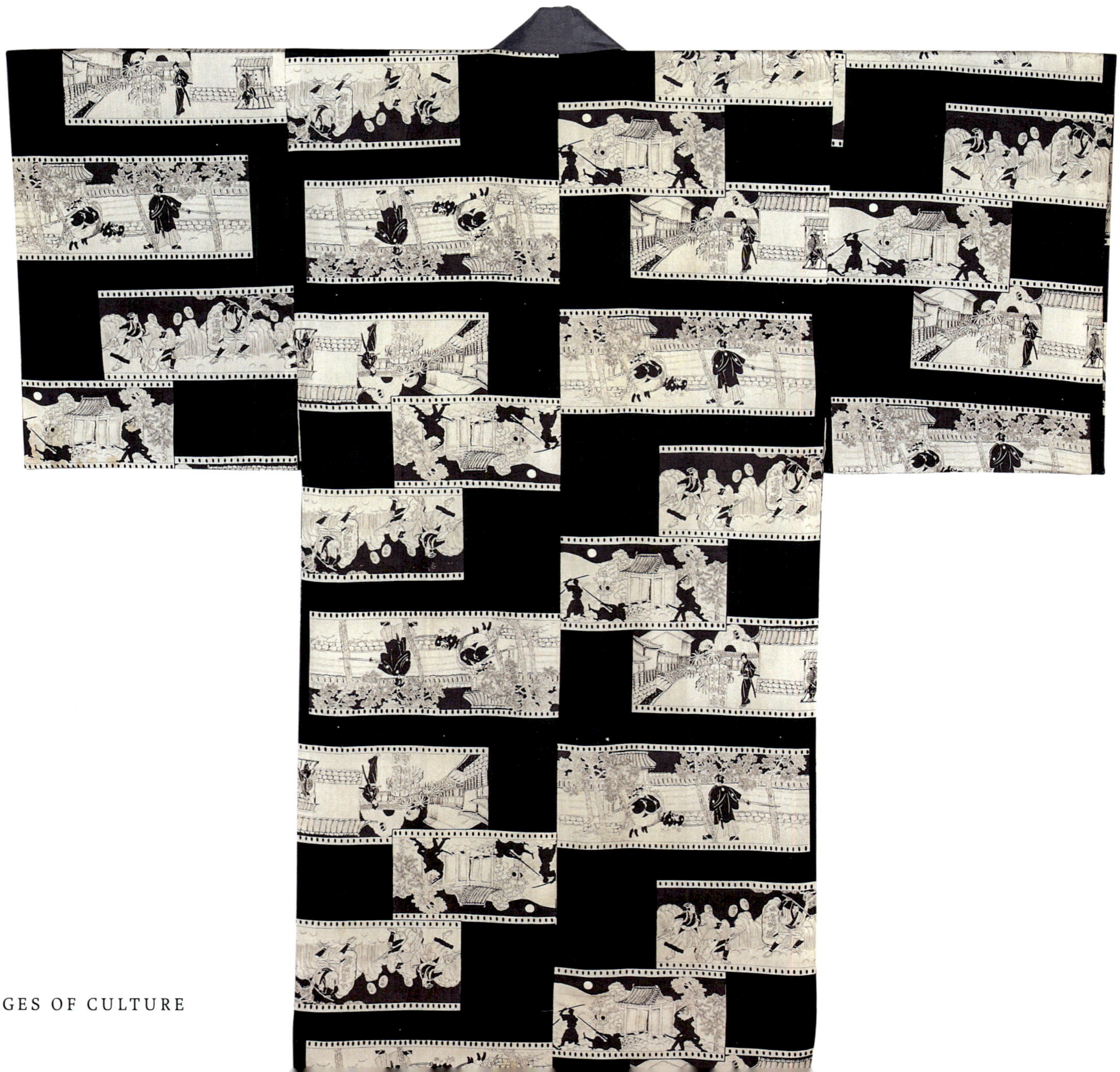

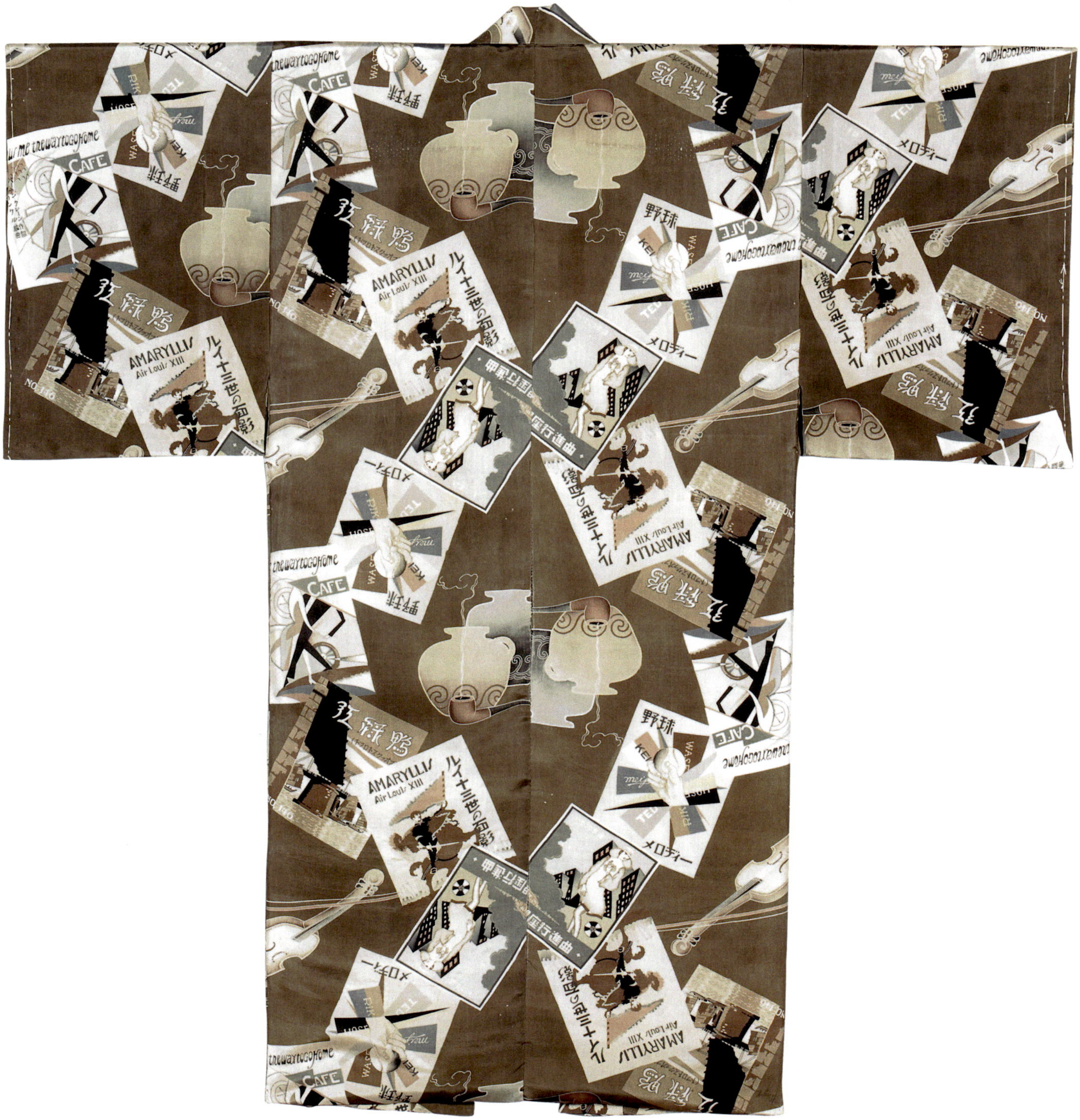

MODERN LIFE/ ENTERTAINMENT

Man's *juban*
Posters, pipes, and music
Taishō–early Shōwa period, 1920s–1930s
Kata-yūzen dyed and printed silk
53.0 × 51.0 inches (135 × 130 centimeters)
KM116

There is a wild mix of posters, vases, pipes, and violins on this *juban*. The posters themselves offer a great variety of choices for entertainment. One poster shows a café named "The Way to Go Home"; it was based on the British song "Show Me the Way to Go Home," which has been an enduring hit from 1925 until today. Another poster advertises *Amaryllis*, a musical performance composed by King Louis XIII of France (1601–1643). The excitement of baseball is brought to the fore on a poster showing pennants from the six main Japanese universities that held the highest baseball rankings. Areas of the *juban* are also nicely shaded, adding a special flavor to the designs.

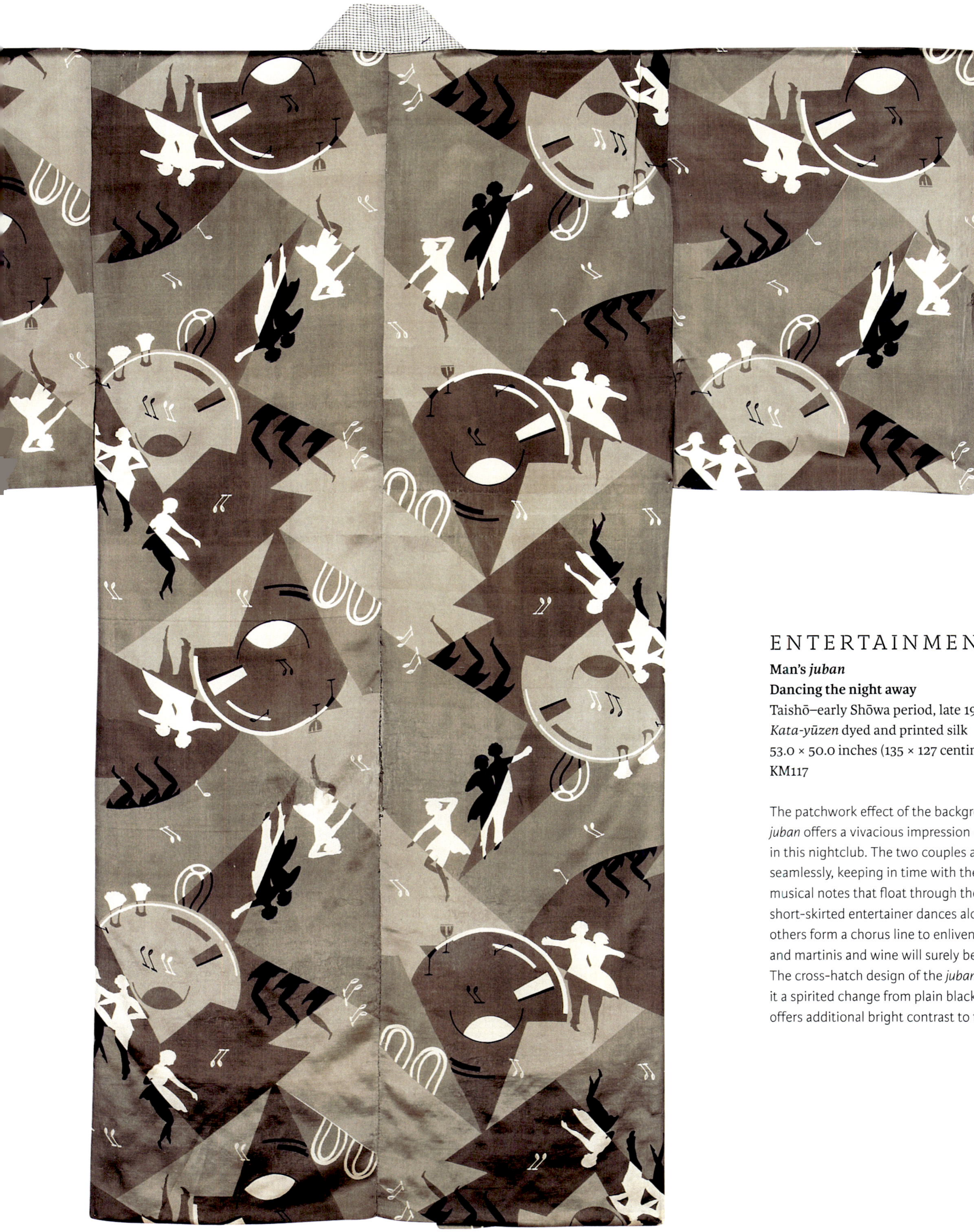

ENTERTAINMENT

Man's *juban*
Dancing the night away
Taishō–early Shōwa period, late 1920s–early 1930s
Kata-yūzen dyed and printed silk
53.0 × 50.0 inches (135 × 127 centimeters)
KM117

The patchwork effect of the background of this *juban* offers a vivacious impression of the dancers in this nightclub. The two couples appear to waltz seamlessly, keeping in time with the records and musical notes that float through the air. One short-skirted entertainer dances alone, while several others form a chorus line to enliven the evening, and martinis and wine will surely be appreciated. The cross-hatch design of the *juban*'s collar gives it a spirited change from plain black or white and offers additional bright contrast to the main textile.

MODERNITY

Man's *haori* with a decorative lining (*haura*)
City of the future
Taishō–early Shōwa period, late 1920s–early 1930s
Silk plain-weave *haori* (outer), *yūzen*-dyed and hand-painted silk *haura* (lining)
50.0 × 41.0 inches (127 × 104 centimeters)
KM118

The artist of this *haura* created an idealized modern city that contains skyscrapers galore, along with a sleek dirigible and two airplanes. The buildings show elevated roadways that seem to pass through several of the buildings without cars or people, creating a subtle sense of mystery to this design. The artist's delicate touch of paint in the lightning in the darkened clouds also underscores the details in this design. The wearer's audience would have found much interest in this sartorial display once the garment was removed and carefully shown by the owner.

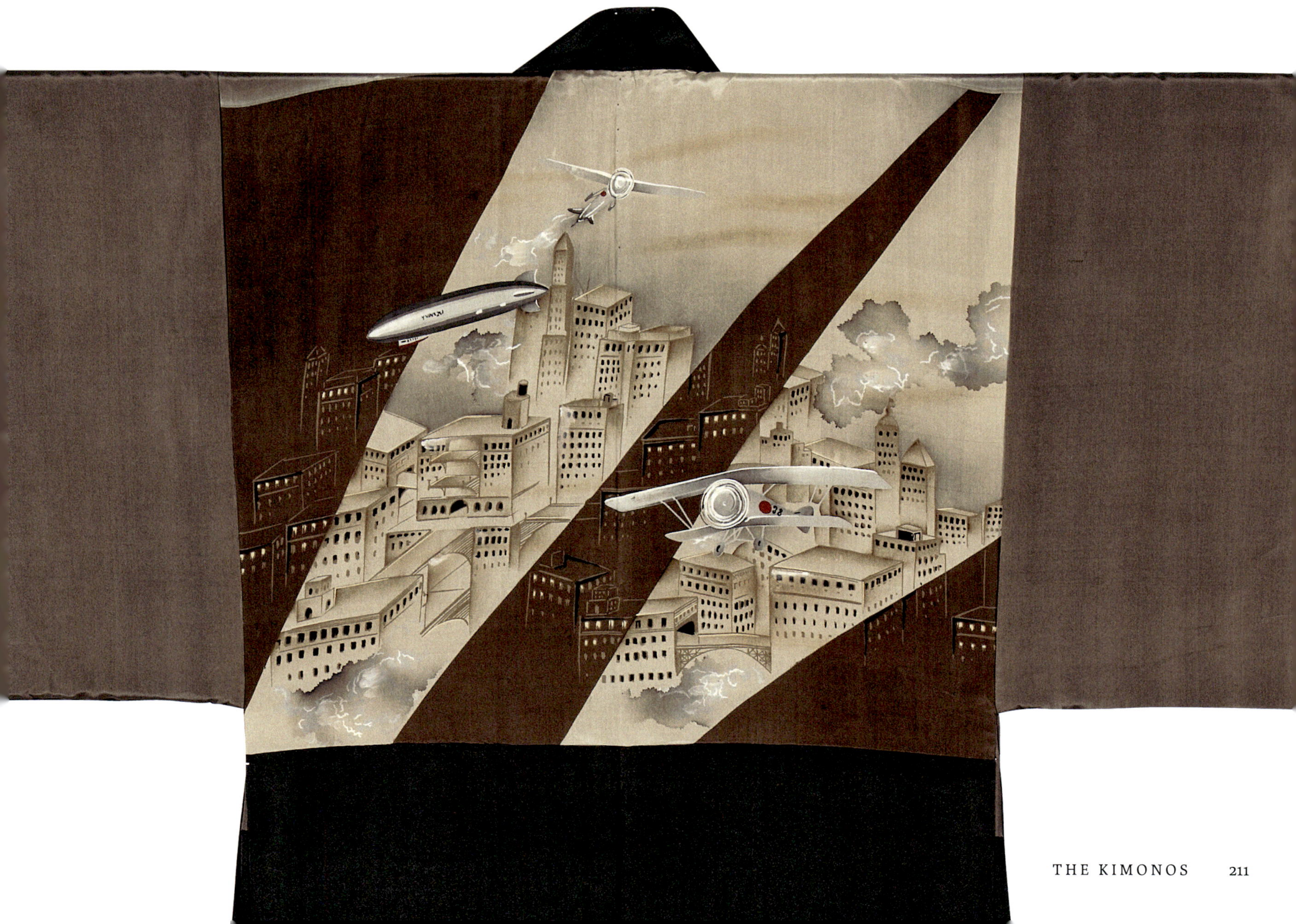

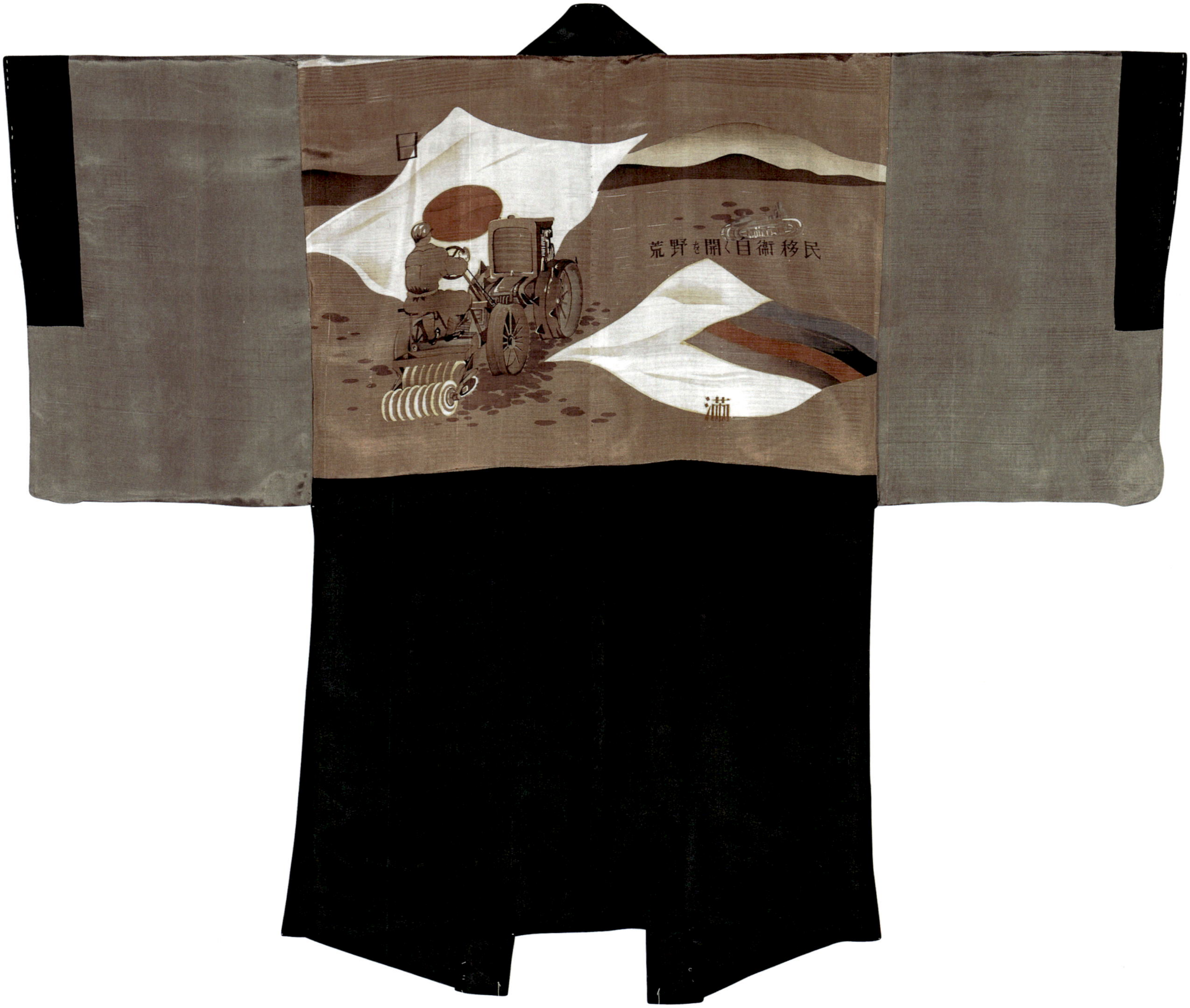

TRAVEL

Man's *haori* with a decorative lining (*haura*)
'Emigrate to Manchuria'
Shōwa period, 1937/1938
Silk plain-weave *haori* (outer), *yūzen*-dyed and hand-painted silk *haura* (lining)
51.0 × 39.0 inches (130 × 99 centimeters)
KM119

Manchuria offered many of the natural resources that Japan lacked, including land for space-starved Japanese people to farm. The Japanese government hoped to send one million immigrants to Manchuria, and, between 1937 and 1941, some 80,000 people actually emigrated. The design of this *haura* shows a farmer driving a tractor to prepare his fields for planting, precisely the image the government wished to portray. The artist also designed text for the *haura* that extolled the opening of the "wilderness" to provide a better life for the Japanese immigrants. The text, with the inclusion of the flags of both countries, helped to symbolize the connection between Japan and Manchukuo.

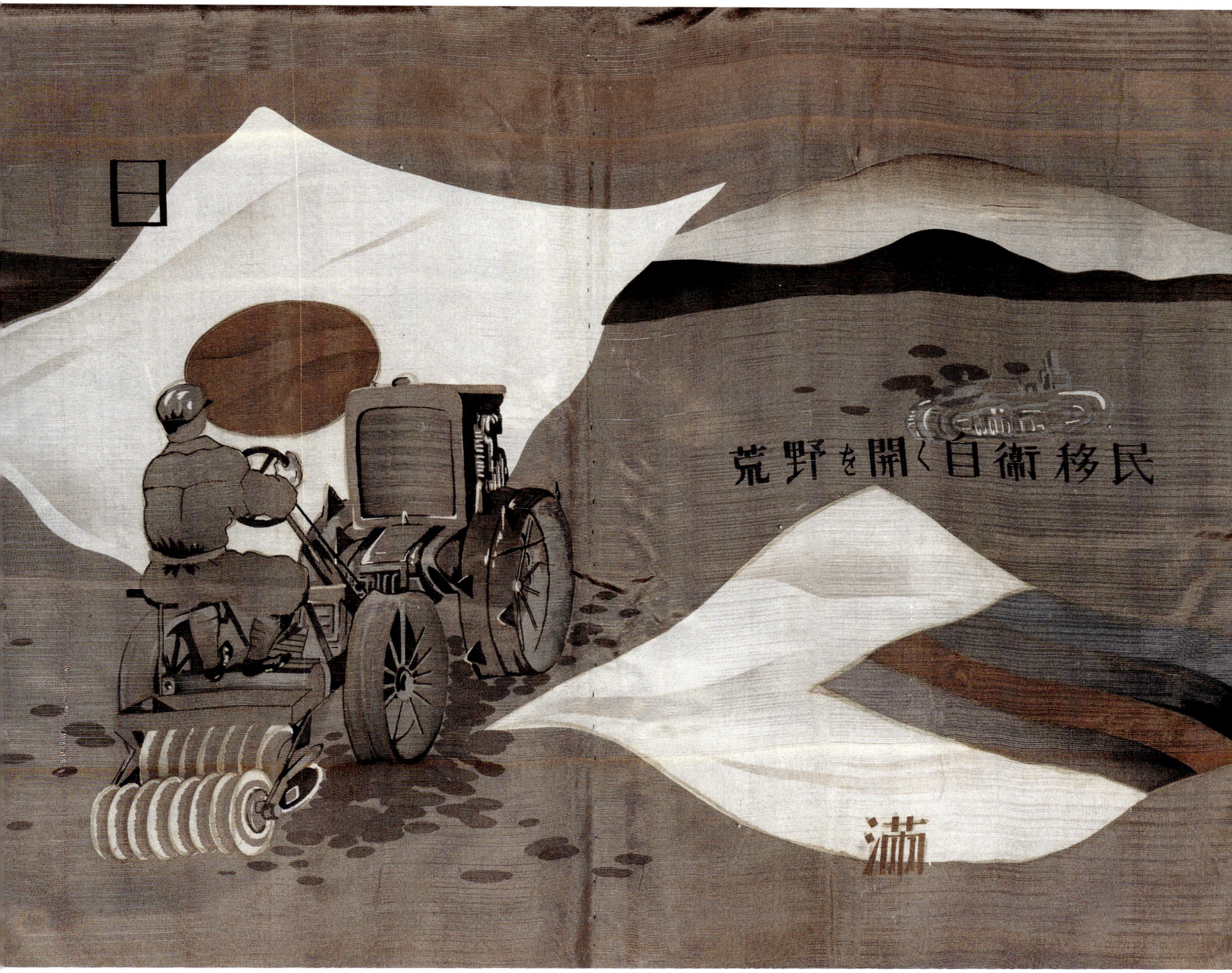
日
荒野を開く自衛移民
満

TRAVEL

Man's *juban*
From Fuji to Cairo
Taishō–early Shōwa period, late 1920s–early 1930s
Kata-yuzen dyed silk
52.0 × 50.0 inches (132 × 127 centimeters)
KM120

This *juban* is a travelogue *par excellence*. It covers a goodly portion of the world, beginning at home (Mount Fuji, of course), then a vignette follows with an exotic safari in India, led by an elephant topped with a swaying box from where the traveler can perhaps find shooting sport with aid from two servants. The last vignette shows skyscrapers of modern cities, quite possibly New York. Additional cards carry names from many countries: Hotel Venise (Venice); the Municipal Hotel in Agra; the Tower of Pisa in Italy; Mena House in Cairo, close to the pyramids; Terminus Hotel in The Hague, Utrecht (Netherlands); and the Astor Hotel in Shanghai. In all, an imaginative adventure for the *juban* wearer.

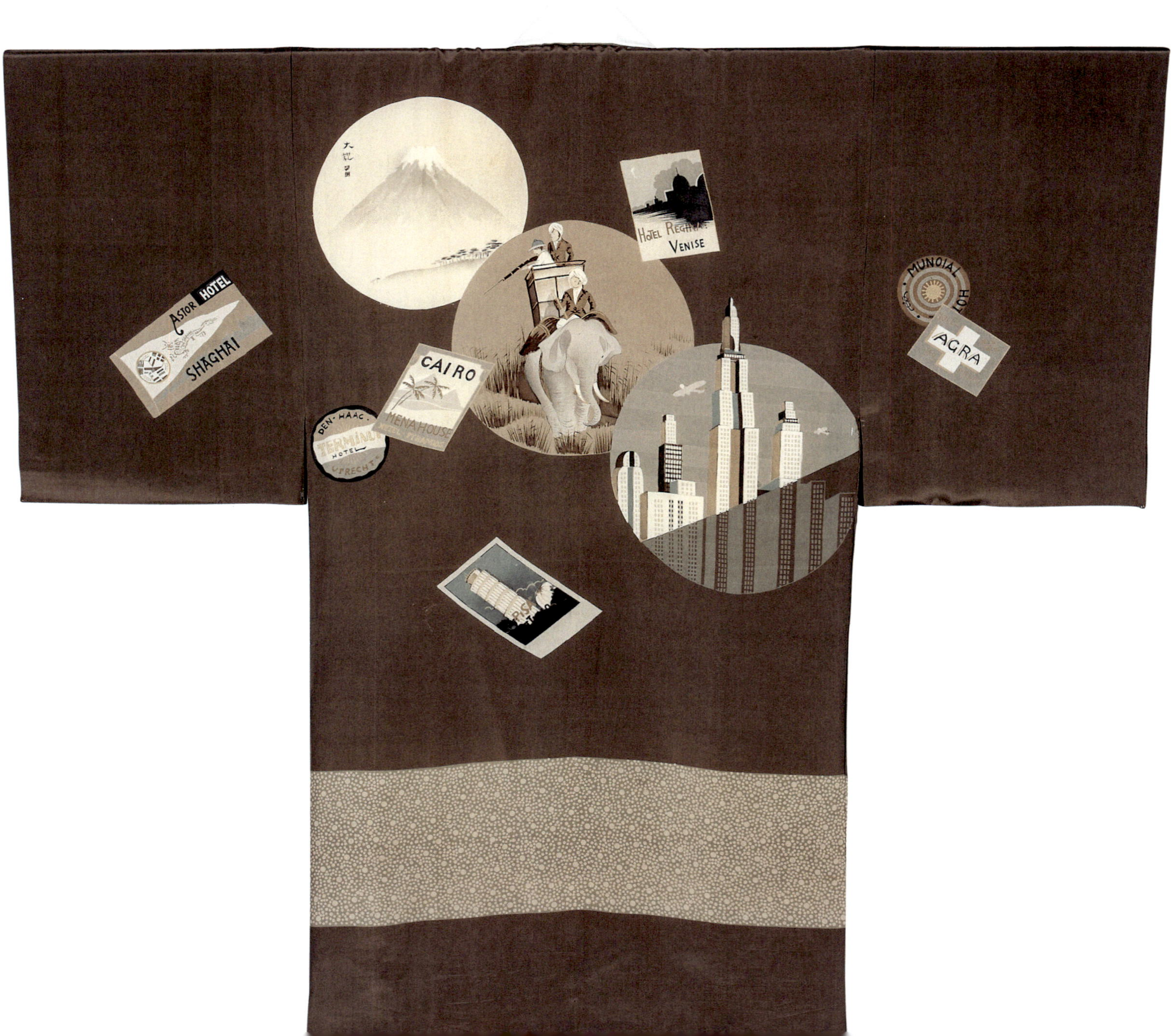

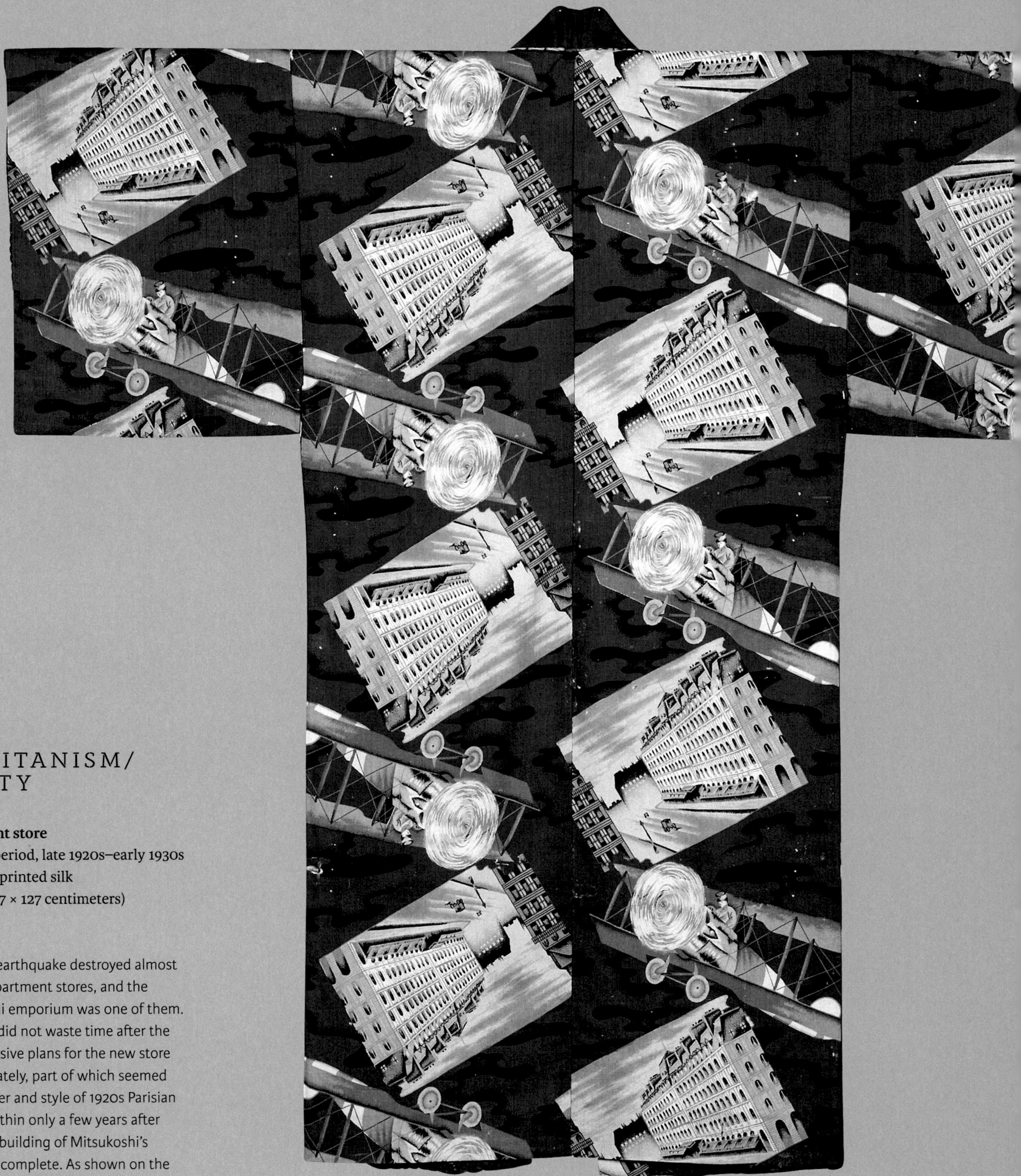

COMOPOLITANISM/ MODERNITY

Man's *juban*
A modern department store
Taishō–early Shōwa period, late 1920s–early 1930s
Kata-yūzen dyed and printed silk
50.0 × 50.0 inches (127 × 127 centimeters)
KM121

The 1923 Great Kanto earthquake destroyed almost all of Tokyo's great department stores, and the high-status Mitsukoshi emporium was one of them. Mitsukoshi, however, did not waste time after the earthquake, and extensive plans for the new store began almost immediately, part of which seemed to capture the character and style of 1920s Parisian department stores. Within only a few years after the earthquake, the rebuilding of Mitsukoshi's department store was complete. As shown on the *juban* here, the building was not only expanded in size but included features that would easily draw its customer base, which included rooftop gardens and a panoramic view of the New Tokyo. A biplane also flits through the *juban*'s textile, presumably to acknowledge the beauty and elegance of the new Mitsukoshi flagship.

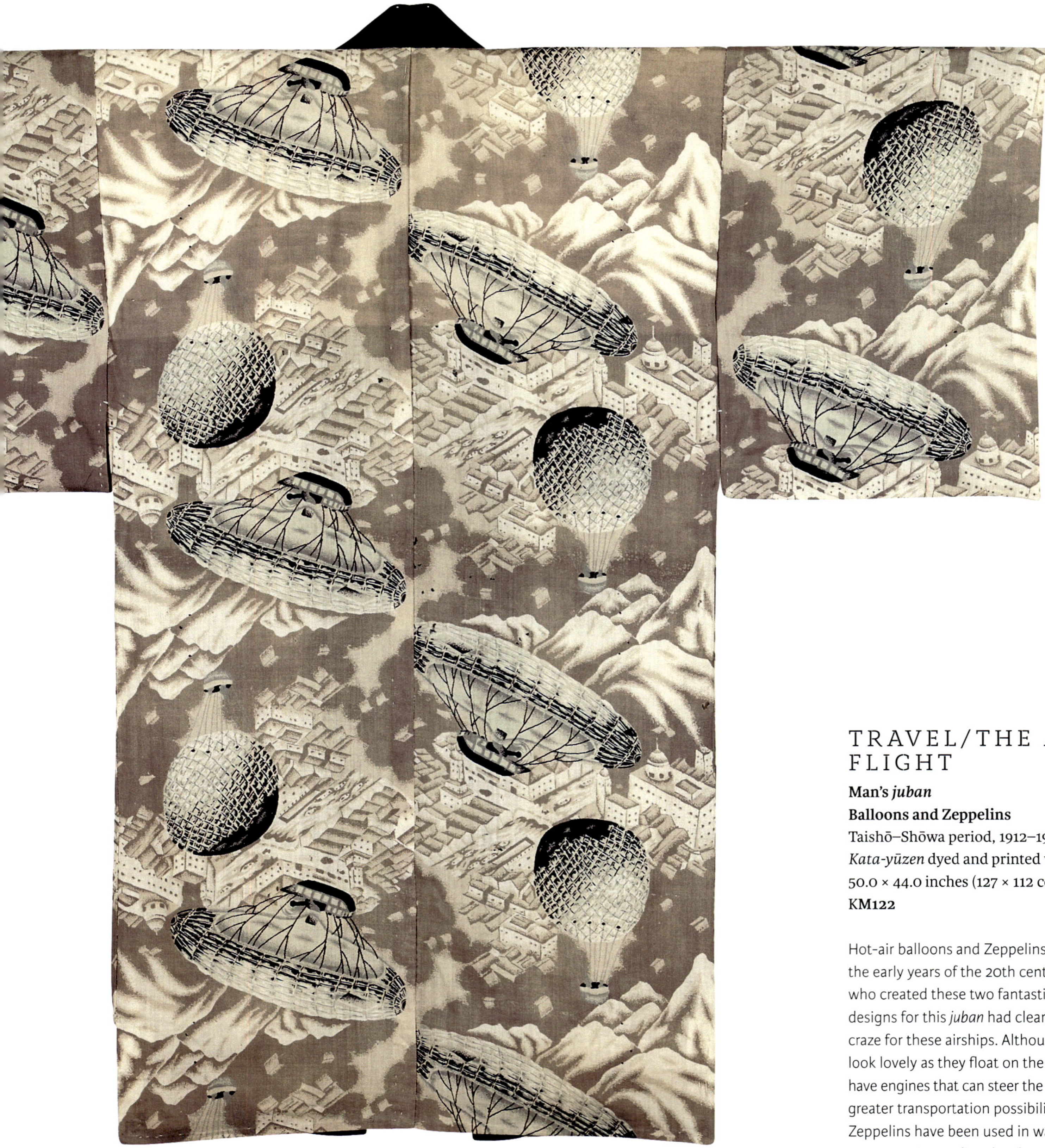

TRAVEL/THE AGE OF FLIGHT

Man's *juban*
Balloons and Zeppelins
Taishō–Shōwa period, 1912–1940
Kata-yūzen dyed and printed wool muslin
50.0 × 44.0 inches (127 × 112 centimeters)
KM122

Hot-air balloons and Zeppelins were all the rage in the early years of the 20th century, and the designer who created these two fantastically imaginative designs for this *juban* had clearly taken to heart the craze for these airships. Although the hot-air balloons look lovely as they float on the wind, the Zeppelins have engines that can steer the airships, which gives greater transportation possibilities to travelers. Zeppelins have been used in wartime to observe enemy positions, but they have also been used for advertisements. Here, both airships ride over the cities below, seemingly on pleasure cruises as the occupants get the special treat of seeing the imposing mountain ranges in the background.

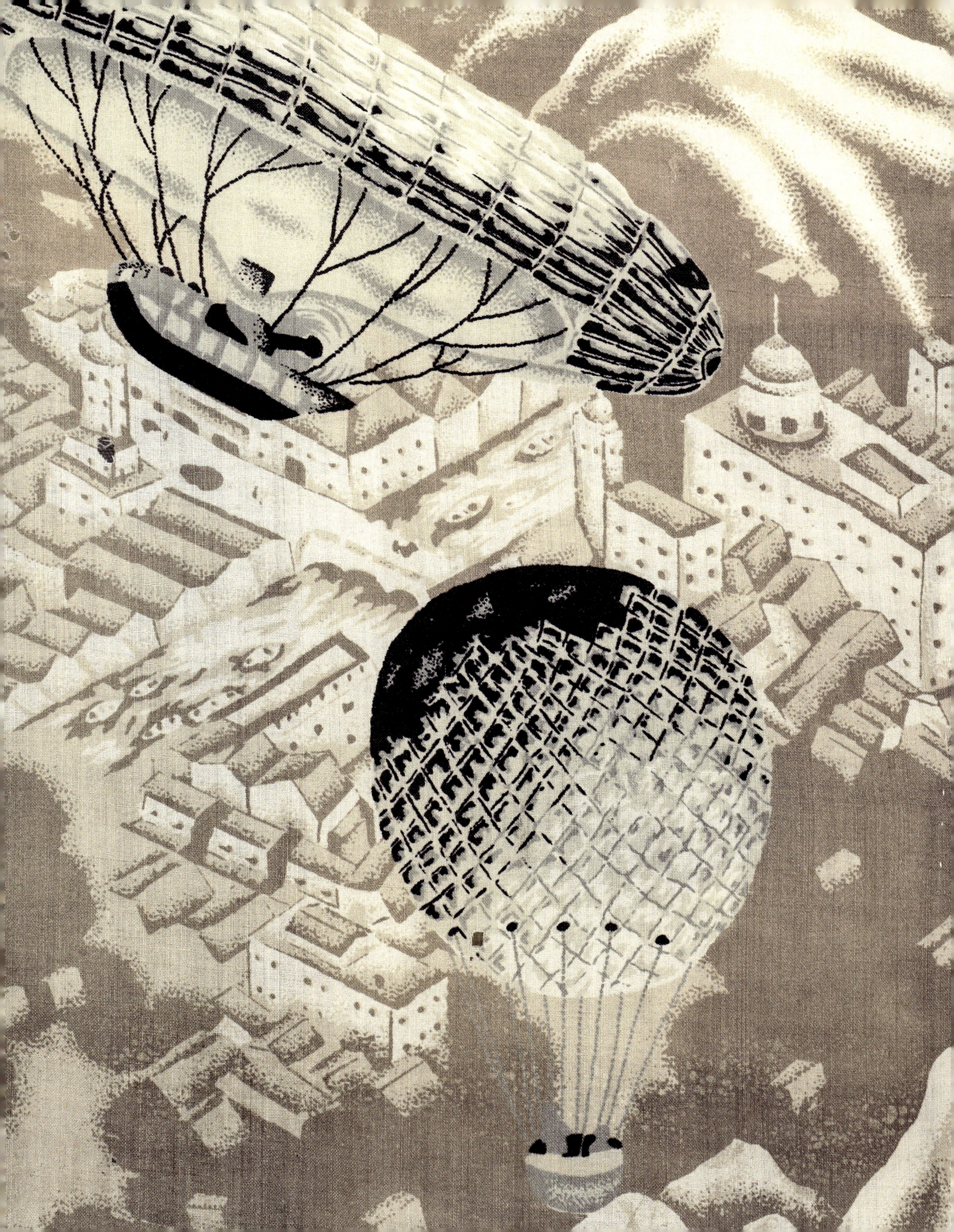

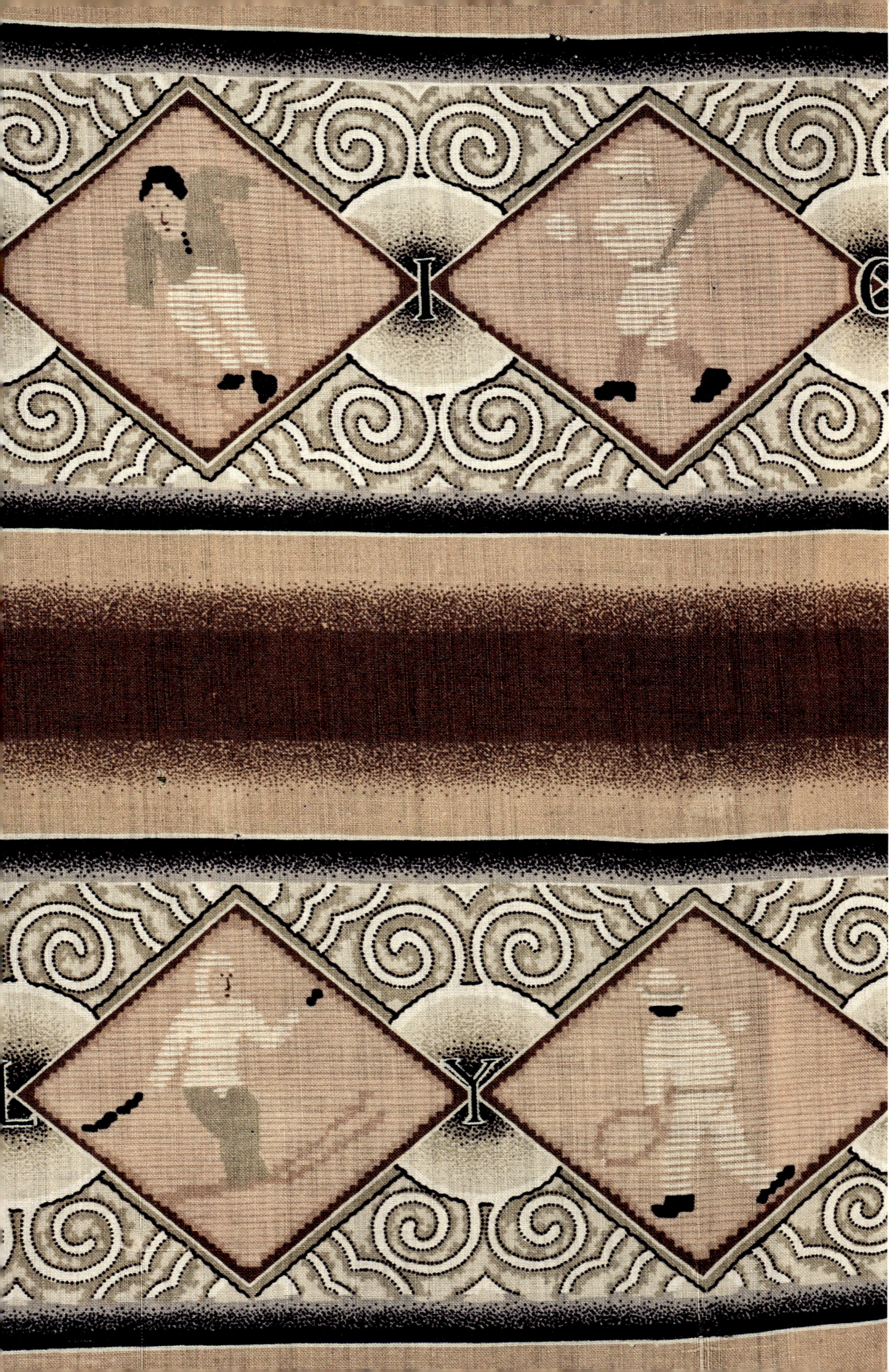
I
Y

SPORTS/OLYMPICS

Man's *juban*
Olympic sports
Taishō–Shōwa period, 1920s–1930s
Printed wool muslin
51.0 × 50.0 inches (130 × 127 centimeters)
KM123

The designer chose a very interesting pattern for this *juban* as he laid out the decorative panels, which give the appearance of friezes. Rhomboids were set against the decorative curlicue background, and each shows a sports figure—baseball batter, bowler, sprinter, baseball catcher, skier, and tennis player. Circles sit between the rhomboid sections, and, at the center of each circle, a symbolic letter is placed. When all seven essential letters are placed, they carefully spell out O-L-Y-M-P-I-C. This design was planned to help highlight the upcoming International Olympic Games, which were intended to be held in Japan in 1940, but the expanding pressure of war prevented this.

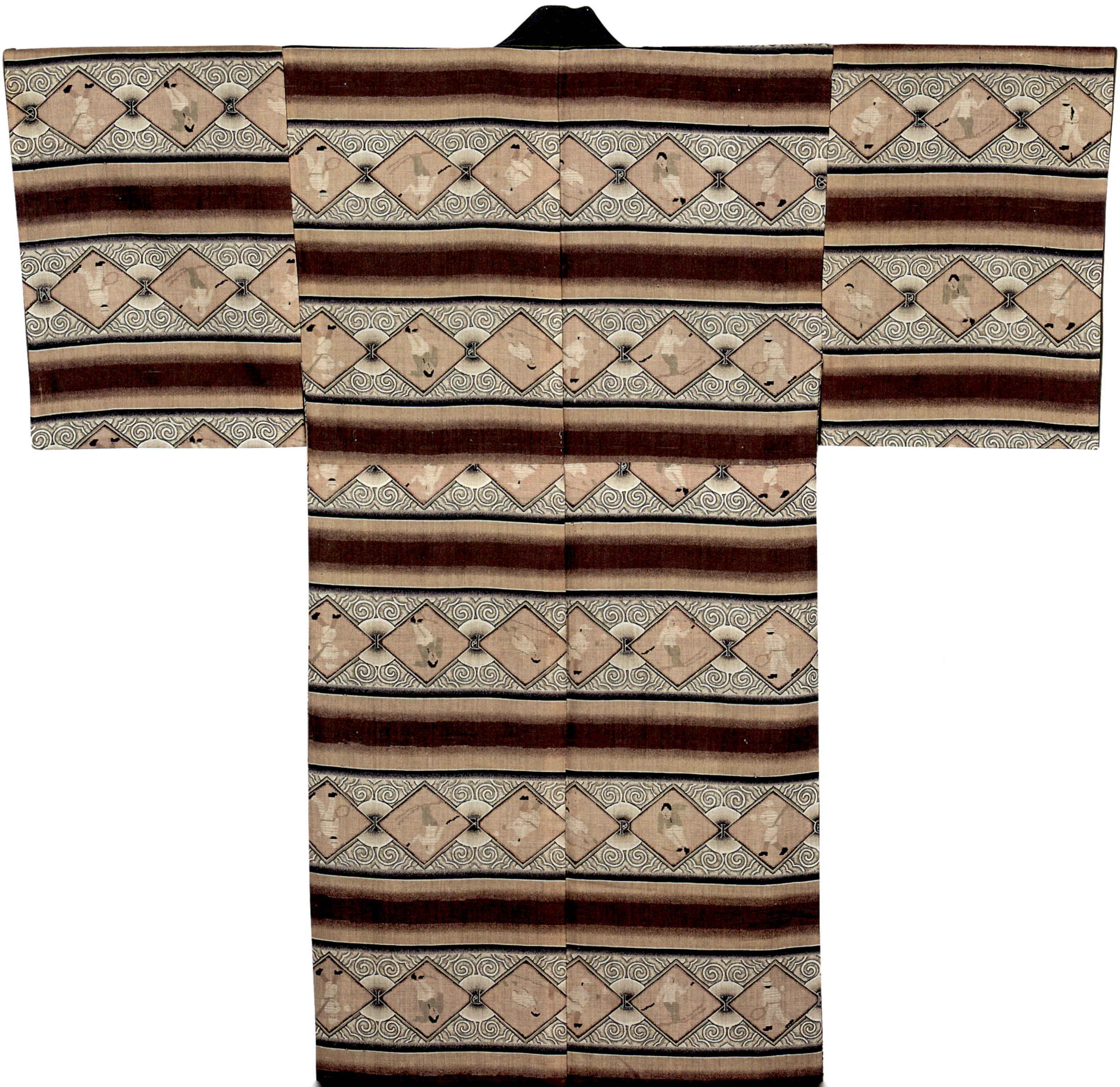

MACHINE AGE

Fireman's *hanten*
A hot-air balloon
Taishō–Shōwa period, 1920s–early 1930s
Sashiko, resist-dyed cotton
47.0 × 38.0 inches (119 × 97 centimeters)
KM124

This simple but well-designed hot-air balloon has been placed in the exact center of the *hanten*. The boy (or man) who manages the balloon appears to sit in comfort in the basket, and he has positioned a flag on each side to offer extra decoration. This design is the interior of the *hanten*, but it can be worn inside-out for parades and other events. The outside also looks good, as it sports a static but intriguing design. The Japanese character in the middle of the back of the *hanten* is the symbol used to let the public know the name of this fireman's brigade.

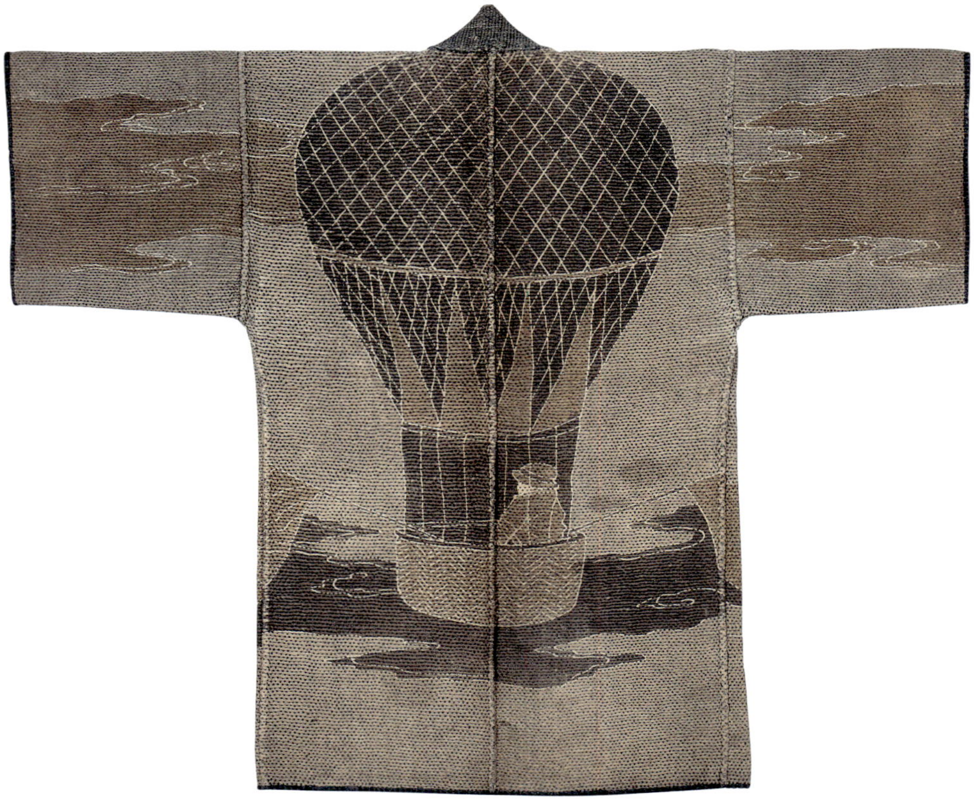

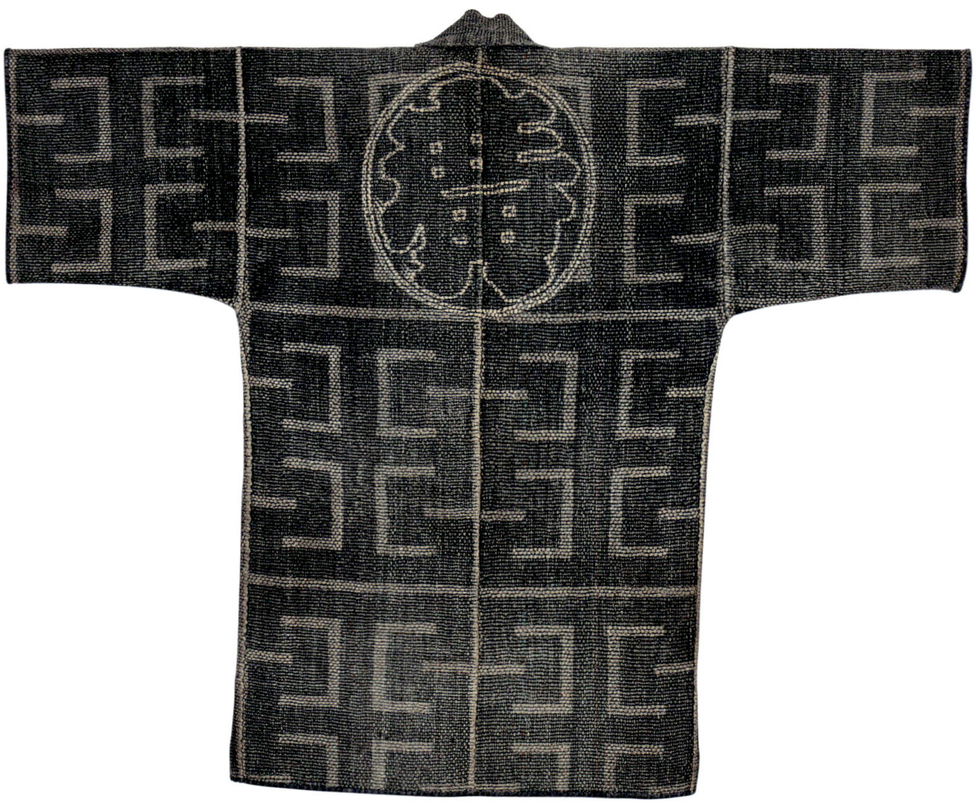

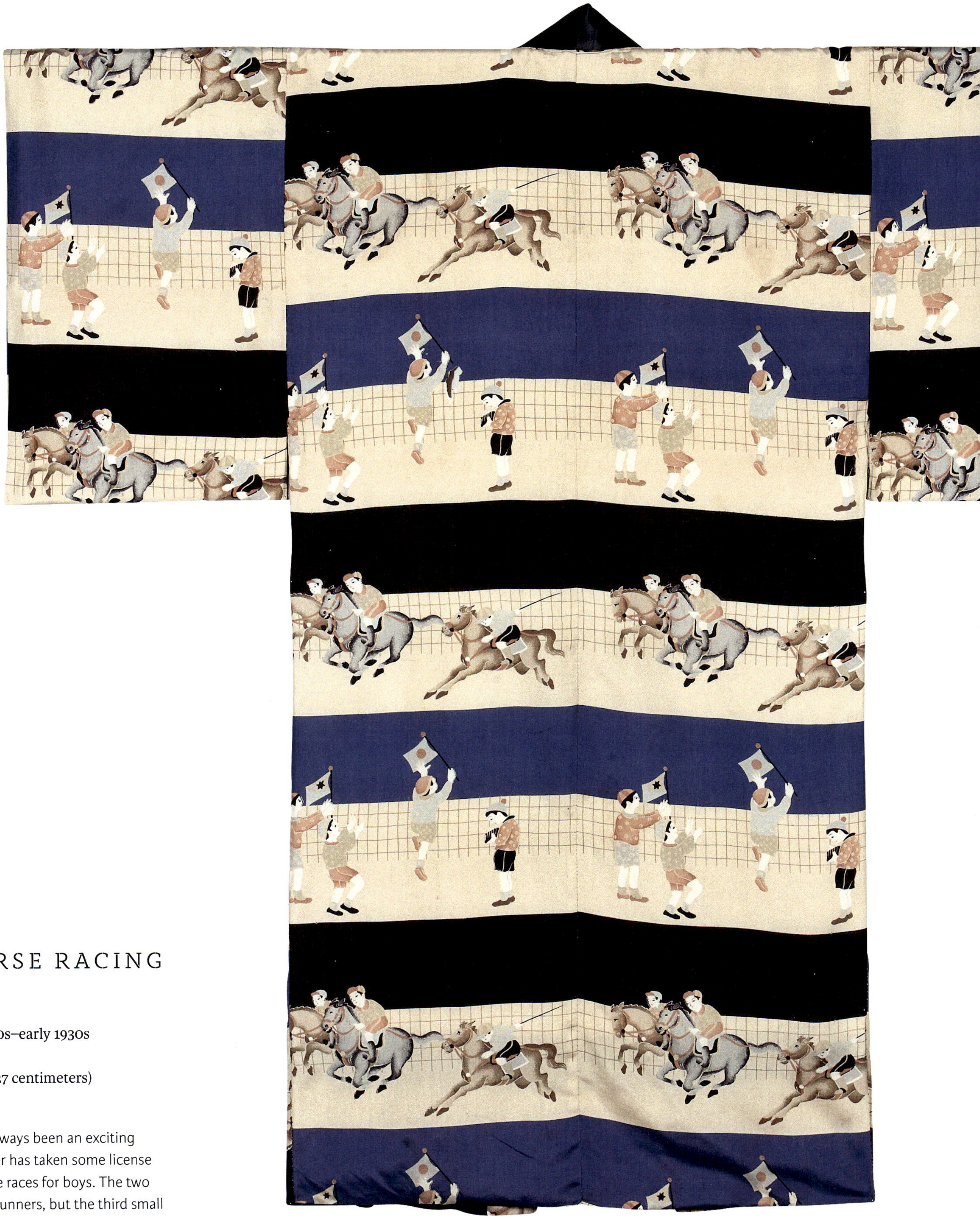

SPORTS/HORSE RACING

Man's *juban*
Who will win?
Taishō–Shōwa period, 1920s–early 1930s
Printed silk
52.0 × 50.0 inches (132 × 127 centimeters)
KM125

Horse racing in Japan has always been an exciting event, and here the designer has taken some license (just for fun) to depict horse races for boys. The two young men are close front runners, but the third small boy on a horse is trying hard to get ahead. Three of the boys behind the fences are excitedly jumping up and down and cheering while watching the race; the fourth boy looks quite serious as he carefully handles his camera to take photos of his friends and the young jockeys on the racetrack. The designer has also dressed the boys in rather fanciful shirts and pants, which gives extra color and style to their outfits.

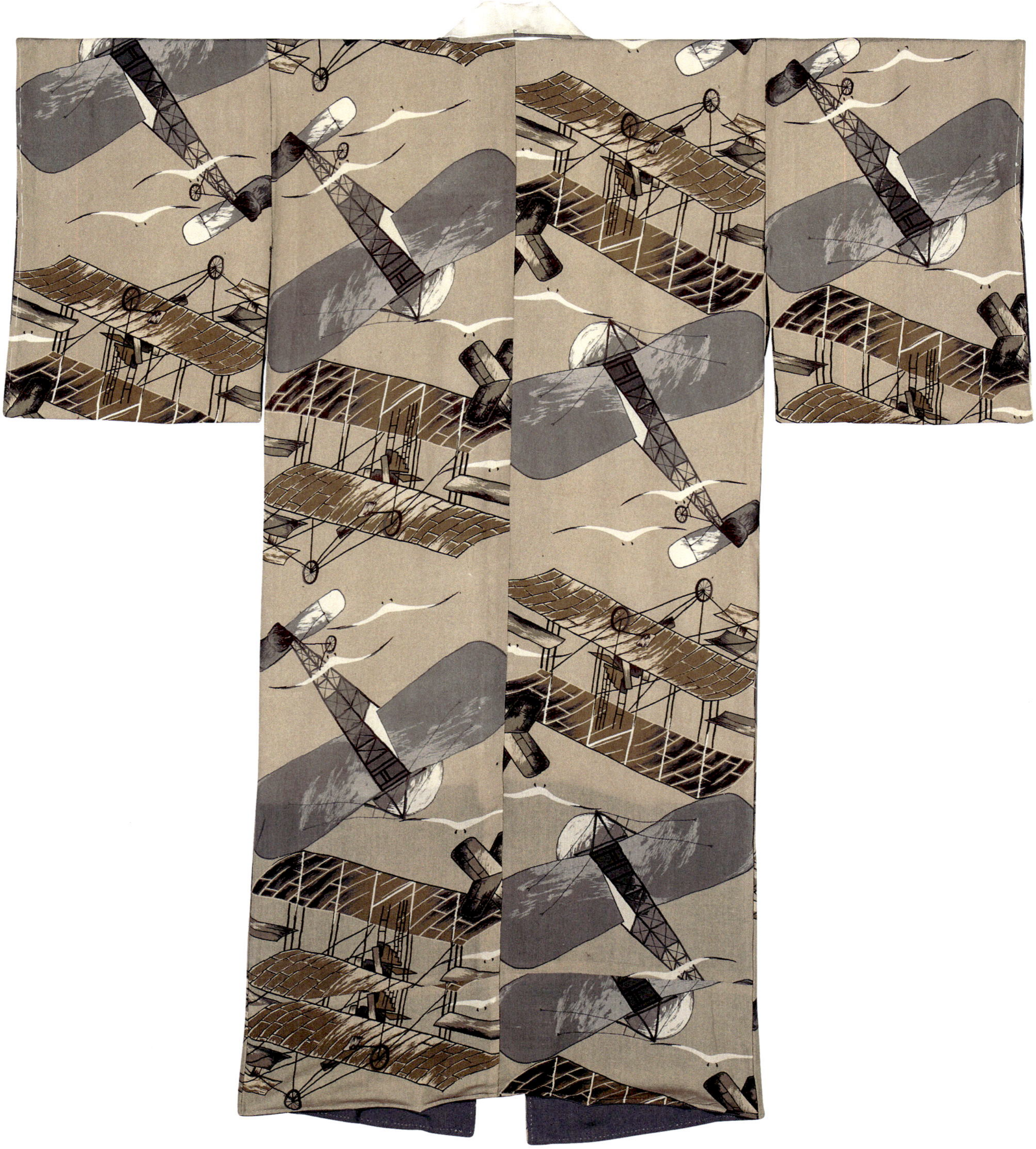

AIRPLANES/MACHINE AGE

Man's *juban*
The art of flight
Taishō–Shōwa period, 1912–1930
Kata-yūzen dyed *chirimen* silk
51.0 × 49.0 inches (130 × 124 centimeters)
KM126

The person who purchased this *juban* was indeed a lover of flight. The textile artist chose to feature only two flying machines, both, perhaps, unreal, yet they capture the eyes and the mind. The first drawing is of a glider/biplane, and brings to mind a somewhat similar aircraft built by Wilbur and Orville Wright, two brothers who made the first controlled and sustained powered flight by a biplane/glider in 1903 at Kitty Hawk in the United States. The second drawing is probably based on the monoplane flown by Louis Blériot, a French aviator who became world-famous in 1908 when he made the first flight in an aircraft across the English Channel and won a prize of £1,000.

MACHINE AGE

***Juban* for a young man**
New transport for the world
Taishō–Shōwa period, 1920s–1930s
Kata-yūzen dyed silk
51.0 × 50.0 inches (130 × 127 centimeters)
KM127

Themes of modernity, international transport, and masculinity are all visible in this young man's *juban*. The ocean liners, airplanes, cars, and Zeppelins are drawn in a simple, newspaper-like fashion. The puppies might seem more appropriate for a child's kimono, but in general this design can be considered appropriate for a young man who is, perhaps, ready to leave home as he prepares to enter university. The latticework in the broad horizontal strips hints at the traditional samurai *noshime kosode*, which usually has a wide hip band with a warp and weft *kasuri* pattern woven for an additional touch of interest.

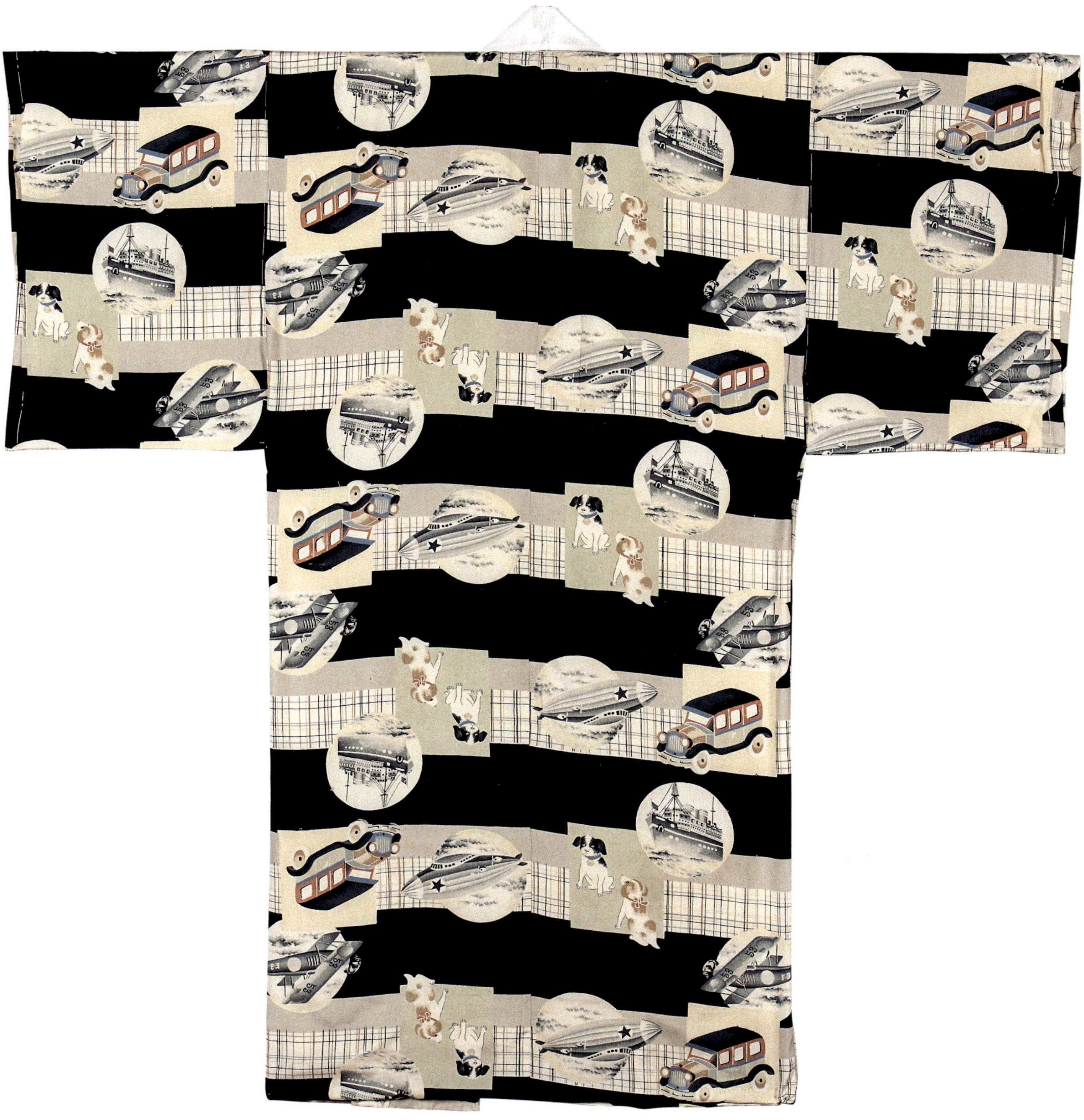

SPORTS/BASEBALL

Man's *haori* with a decorative lining (*haura*)
Two baseball players in the field
Taishō–Shōwa period, late 1920s–1930s
Silk pongee (*haori* exterior); *kata-yūzen* dyed and painted silk *haura* (lining)
51.0 × 45.0 inches (130 × 114 centimeters)
KM128

A large image such as this is quite extraordinary, and provides a dramatic scene of a tense clash on the ballfield. Minimal color has been used by the textile artist, but the shadowing of the creases of the painted outfits show clearly that this is a sunny day, one well chosen for a significant baseball game. It is difficult to tell which player is winning, as they may clash together just as the ball touches home base. Baseball games played by Tokyo universities were wildly popular as well as highly competitive, and a game such as this would have meant much to the winning team.

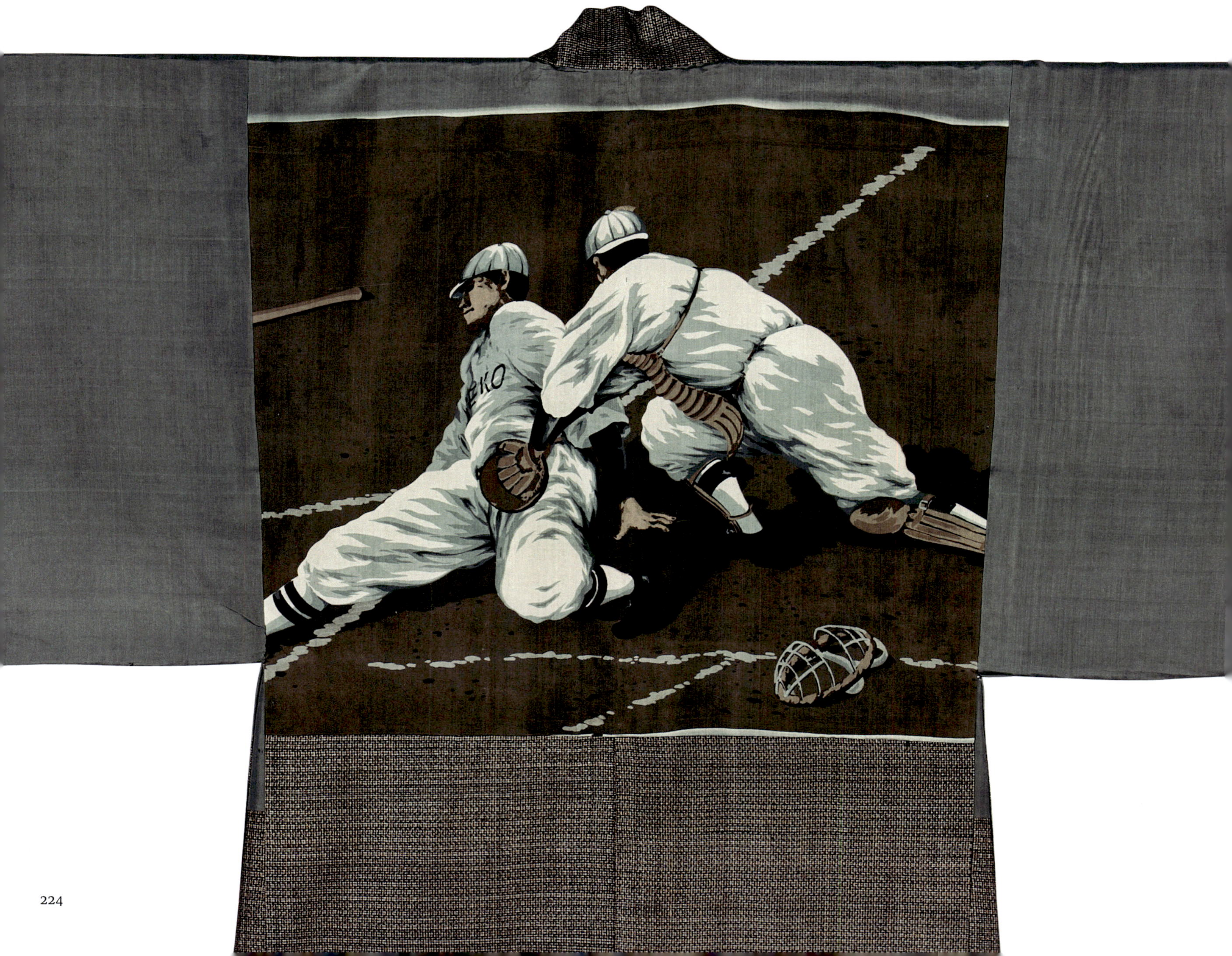

SPORTS/TENNIS

Man's *haori* with a decorative lining (*haura*)
Tennis balls in play
Taishō–Shōwa period, late 1920s–1940
Silk plain weave (*haori* exterior), *kata-yuzen* dyed and stencil-printed silk *haura* (lining)
50.0 × 37.0 inches (127 × 94 centimeters)
KM129

This *haori*'s lining has an unusual design. A tennis court serves as a background, and two different pictures—one showing a net with two tennis players, and the other a country scene with a church or school nearby—are positioned above the court. The tennis players are playing a doubles game, as is noted on the garment, but the competition is not seen. The players are also wearing somewhat bizarre harlequin-like outfits rather than standard tennis outfits. The second picture is somewhat obscure, as there is no hint of how the building relates to the game.

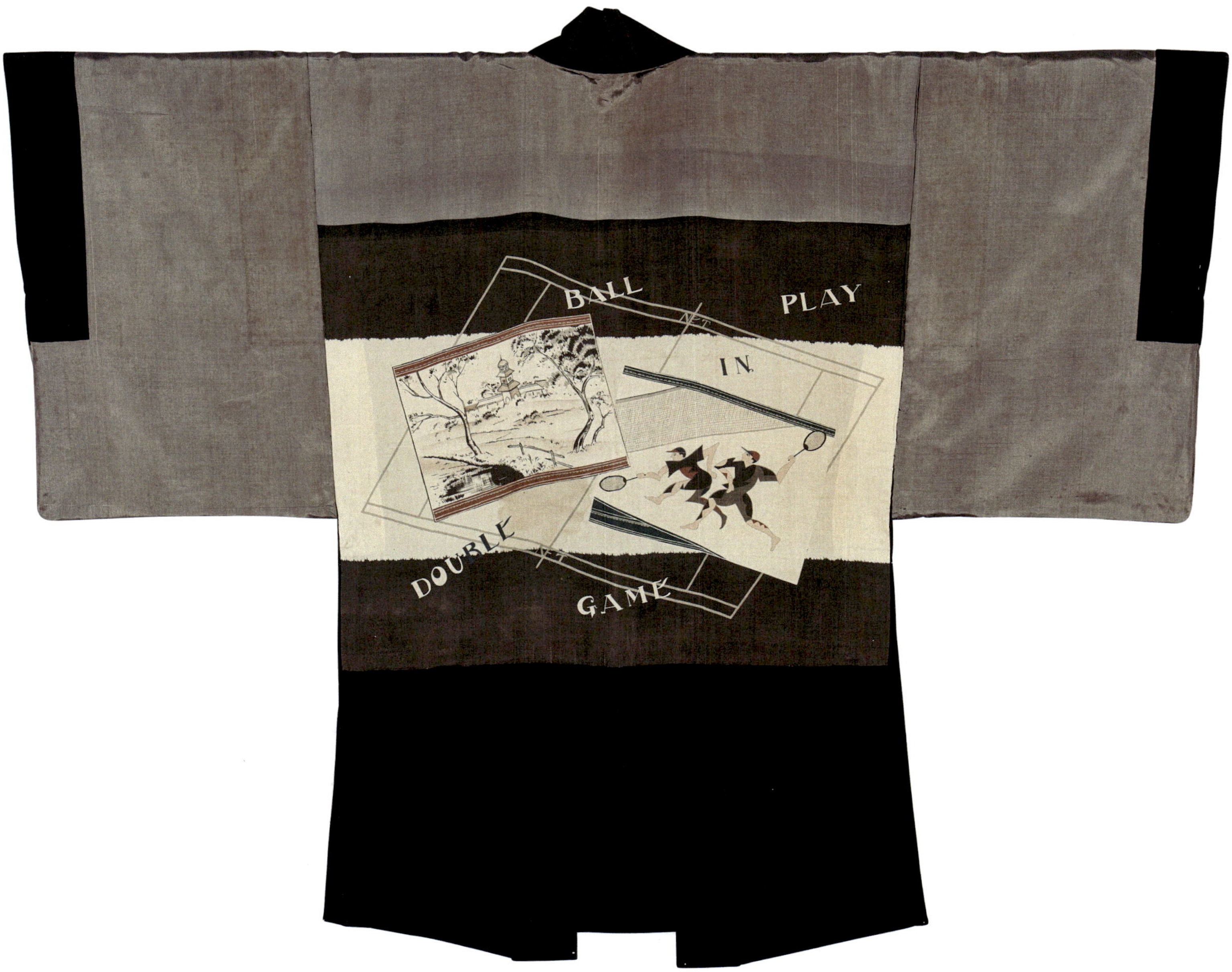

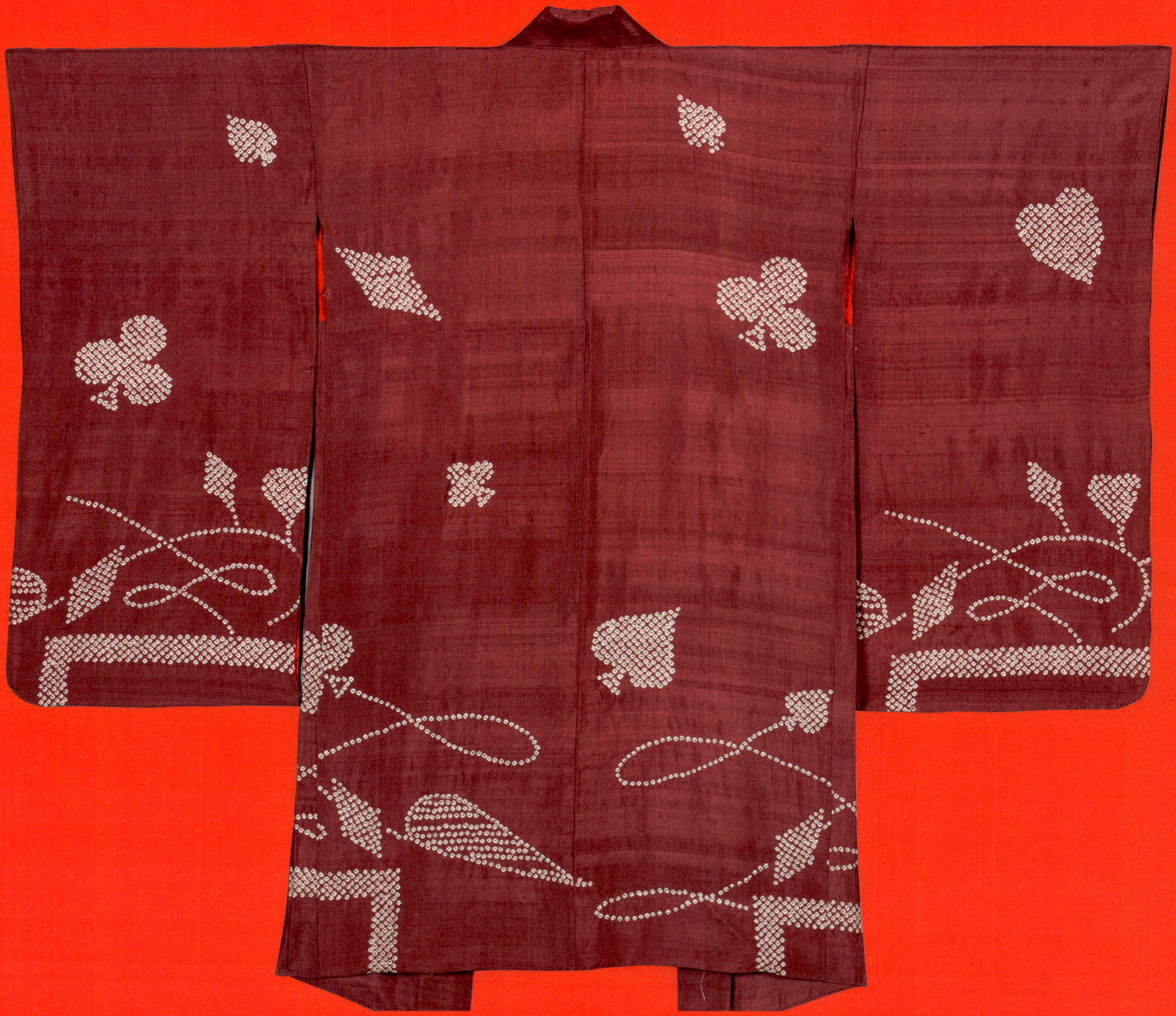

GAMES/ ENTERTAINMENT

***Haori* for a woman**
Playing cards
Taishō–Shōwa period, late 1920s–1940
Silk *shibori* (outer jacket), *rinzu* (patterned silk) lining
49.0 × 44.0 inches (124 × 112 centimeters)
KM130

This stunning *haori* is patterned with a Western-style playing cards motif. It is a very simple jacket that would be worn by a young woman (because of the length of the sleeves), and the design, color, and technique are beautiful. The playing cards—hearts, spades, diamonds, and clubs—are done with *shibori*, as are the patterned bands at the edges of the sleeves and the hem of the *haori*. The playing cards look almost as though they are growing off the *shibori* bands. Thin, swirling stems hold the cards as though they are to be played. The inner lining is a gorgeous red *rinzu* patterned silk, with the silk patterning representing chrysanthemums.

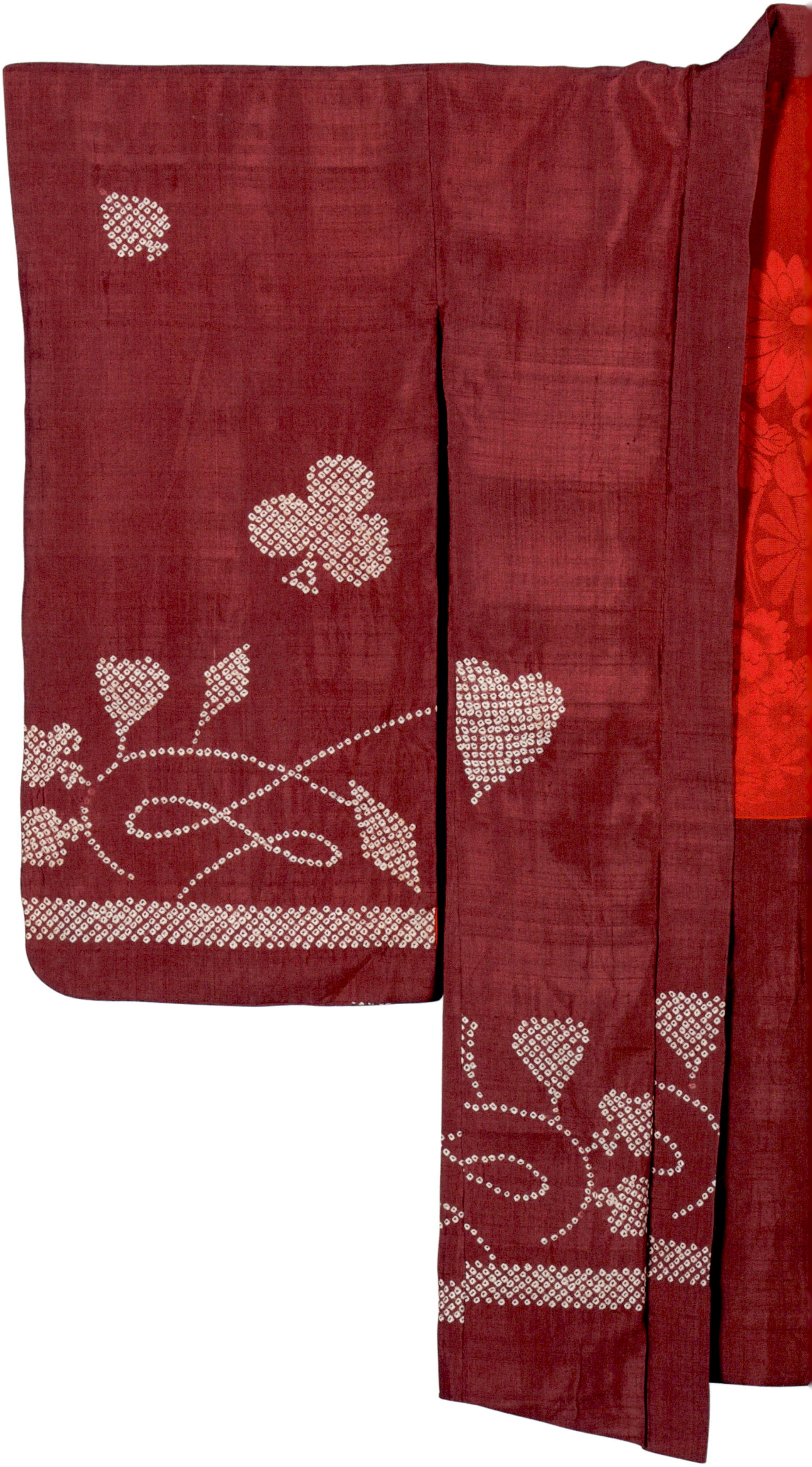

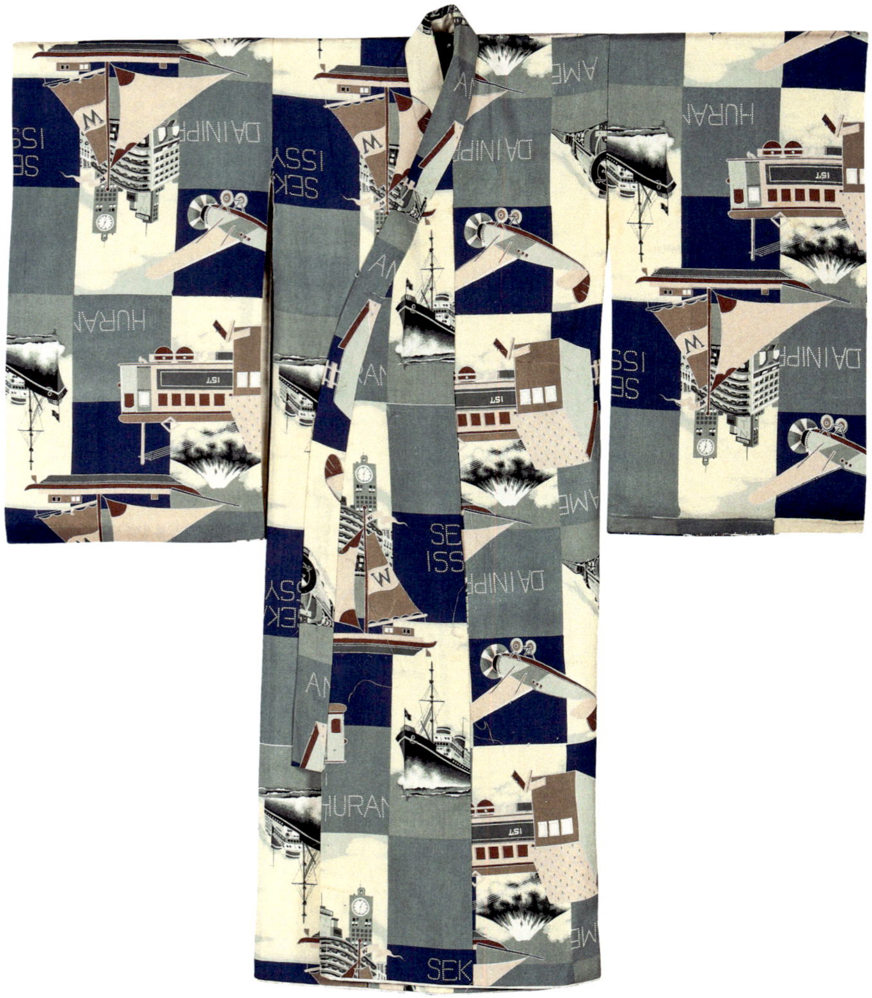

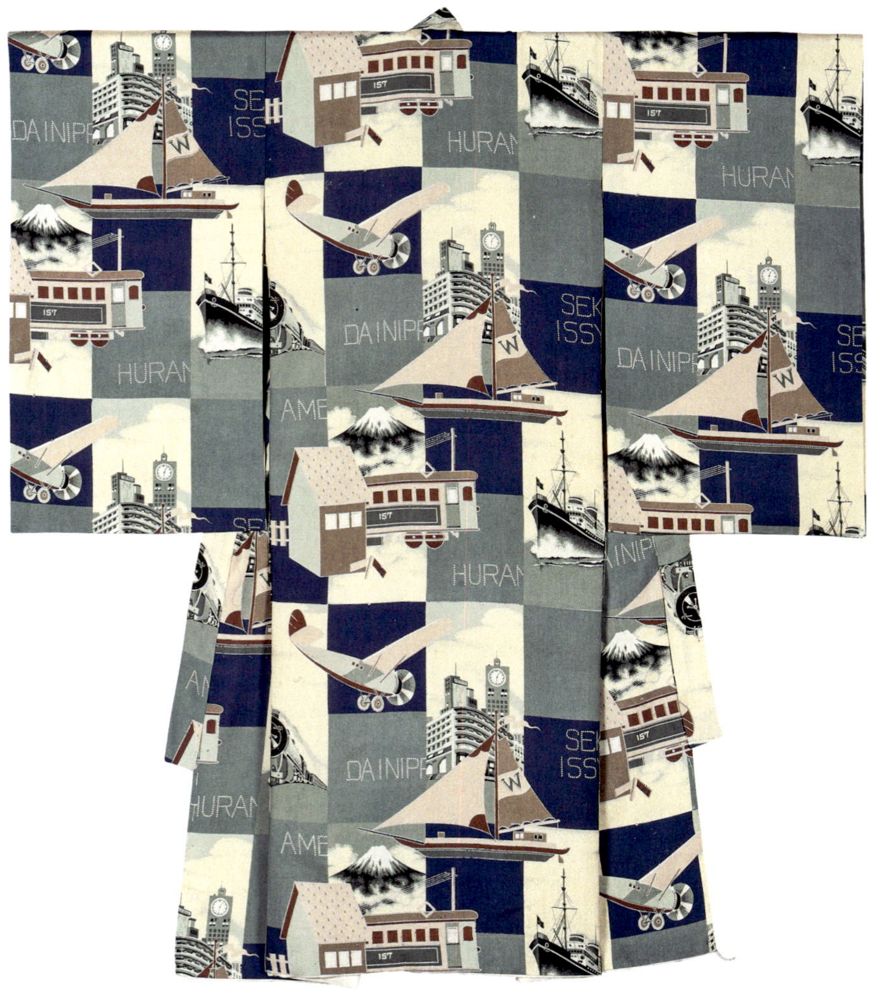

MODERNITY/ MACHINE AGE

Miyamairi **(child's kimono for first shrine visit)**
Modern industrialized Japan
Taishō–Shōwa period, late 1920s–1940
Kata-yuzen dyed and printed silk
37.0 × 33.0 inches (94 × 84 centimeters)
KM131

Modernity, transportation, and internationality were popular themes in 1930s Japan, as reflected in this textile for a *miyamairi*. The tall clock tower is instantly recognizable as the Hattori Building (now the Wako Building), which, when constructed on the Ginza in 1932, was among the first of a new wave of modern buildings in Tokyo following the Great Kanto Earthquake of 1923. The Western alphabet was used in an attempt to underscore the international themes on the textile. *Dai Nippon* and *America* are immediately recognizable; *Huran* is the beginning of a Japanese phonetic transcription of France. *Sek Issy* is most likely *Sekai Isshu* (Around the World), suggesting that a nation that formerly looked inward was now enthusiastically embracing the world outside itself.

MODERNITY/TRAVEL

Man's *haori* with a decorative lining (*haura*)
Ocean and sky
Taishō–early Shōwa period, 1929–1930s
Silk plain weave *haori* (outer); *kata-yūzen* printed silk fabric for *haura* (lining)
50.0 × 40.0 inches (127 × 102 centimeters)
KM132

In this *haori*, the elegance of a magnificent ocean liner is juxtaposed with the equally elegant Chrysler Building of New York City. These two images stood as symbolizing progress, innovation, and modernity. The Art Deco Chrysler Building, with its high, needle-like spire reaching for the sky, was spectacular, and would awe any visitor. The ocean liner here is without a name, but it fits well with images of the *Asama Maru*, a ship designed and built in Japan for the NYK (Nippon Yusen Kaisha) Line in 1929. The ship had both maritime ingenuity and opulence, offering a highly sophisticated world to its passengers. *Asama Maru* regularly visited principal ports-of-call, including Hong Kong, Shanghai, Kobe, Yokohama, Honolulu, Los Angeles, and San Francisco.

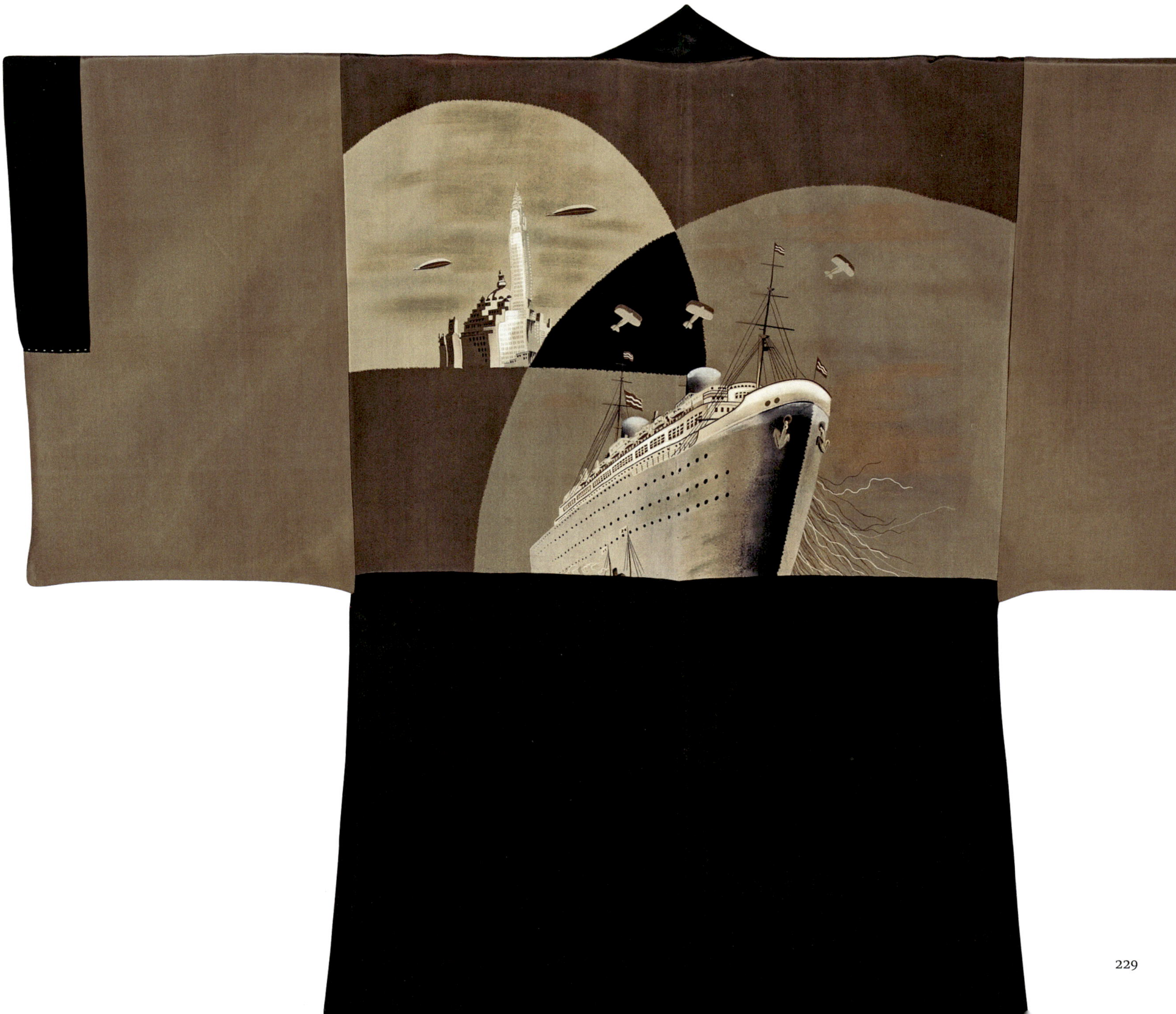

ENTERTAINMENT/ BILLIKEN

Man's *haori* with a decorative lining (*haura*)
The Billiken: Things as they ought to be
Taishō–early Shōwa period, 1920–1930
Silk plain weave *haori* (outer); *kata-yūzen* printed silk *haura* (lining)
50.0 × 38.0 inches (127 × 97 centimeters)
KM133

The Billiken, with his smirking sneer and squinting eyes, was always able to frighten demons away with his role as "the god of things as they ought to be." Unlike the fleeing demons, Billiken's many visitors enjoyed dropping coins in his donation box and were not at all afraid of him—they were always happy to rub the soles of his feet to make their wishes come true. The textile flowing behind Billiken served as a good-luck charm, with images of a bag of fortune, scrolls of wisdom, a magic mallet, a hat of invisibility, and more. This *haori* carries a family crest (*mon*) on its front and back. It shows nine bamboo leaves enclosed within a circle, a design commonly used as subtle mimicry in Japanese heraldry.

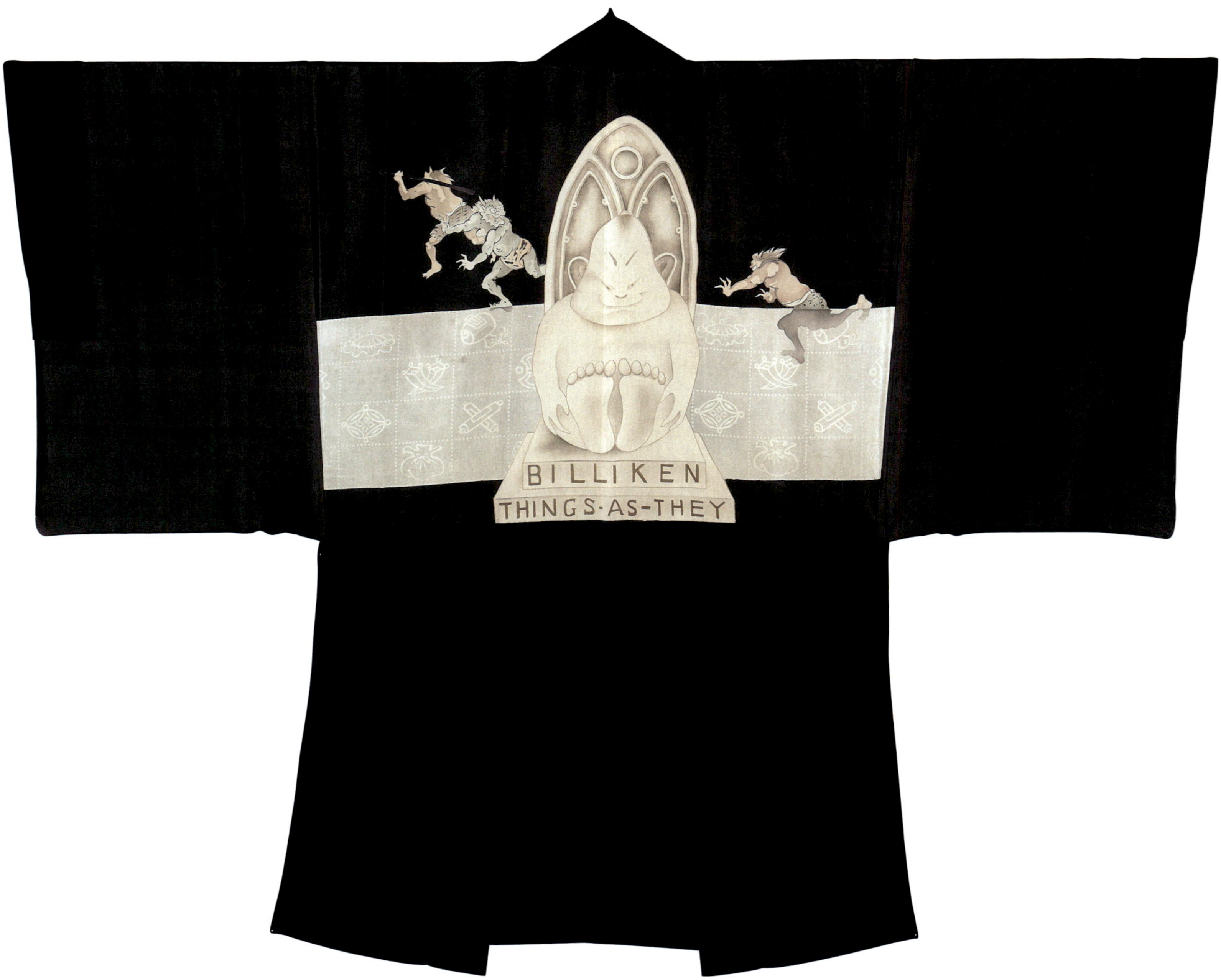

CITYSCAPE/ MODERNITY

Man's *juban*
Modern Tokyo
Taishō–early Shōwa period, 1920s–1930s
Stenciled and hand-painted printed silk
49.0 × 47.0 inches (124 × 119 centimeters)
KM134

This *juban* is a delight, with its modern cityscape of buildings big and small, cars and trams driving on city streets or across bridges, telephone lines and power lines for trams, and lights, lights, lights: bright lights in the buildings, street lamps, the lights of theaters and advertising signs, lights for traffic, and so much more. The gentle cloud-like effect of the city, with all its bustle and hype, still retains a magical feeling for all those who live there, work there, and visit. The text on the lower part of the *juban*—"Modan Tokiyo Warera no Miyako"—translates as "Modern Tokyo, Our Metropolis."

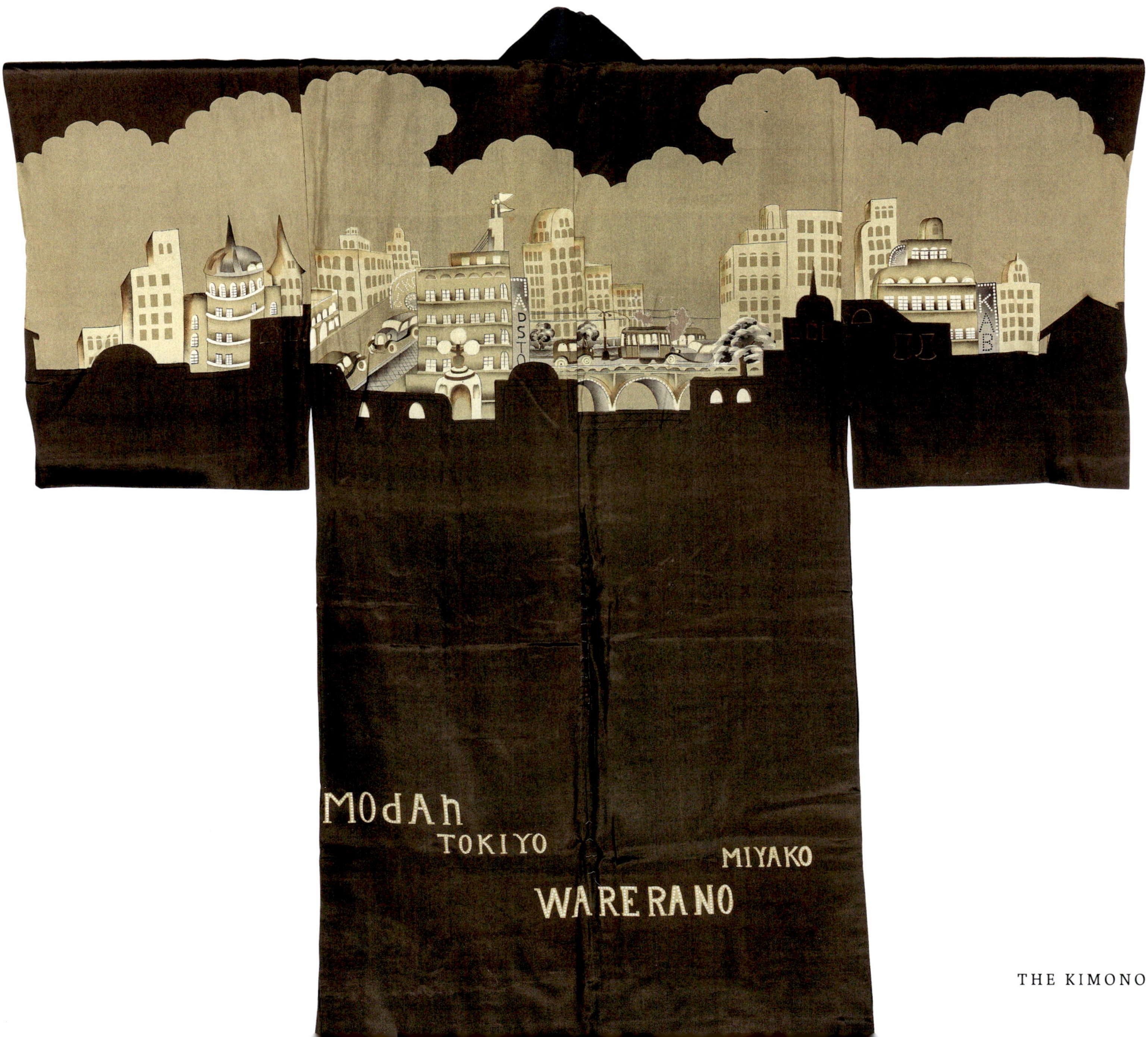

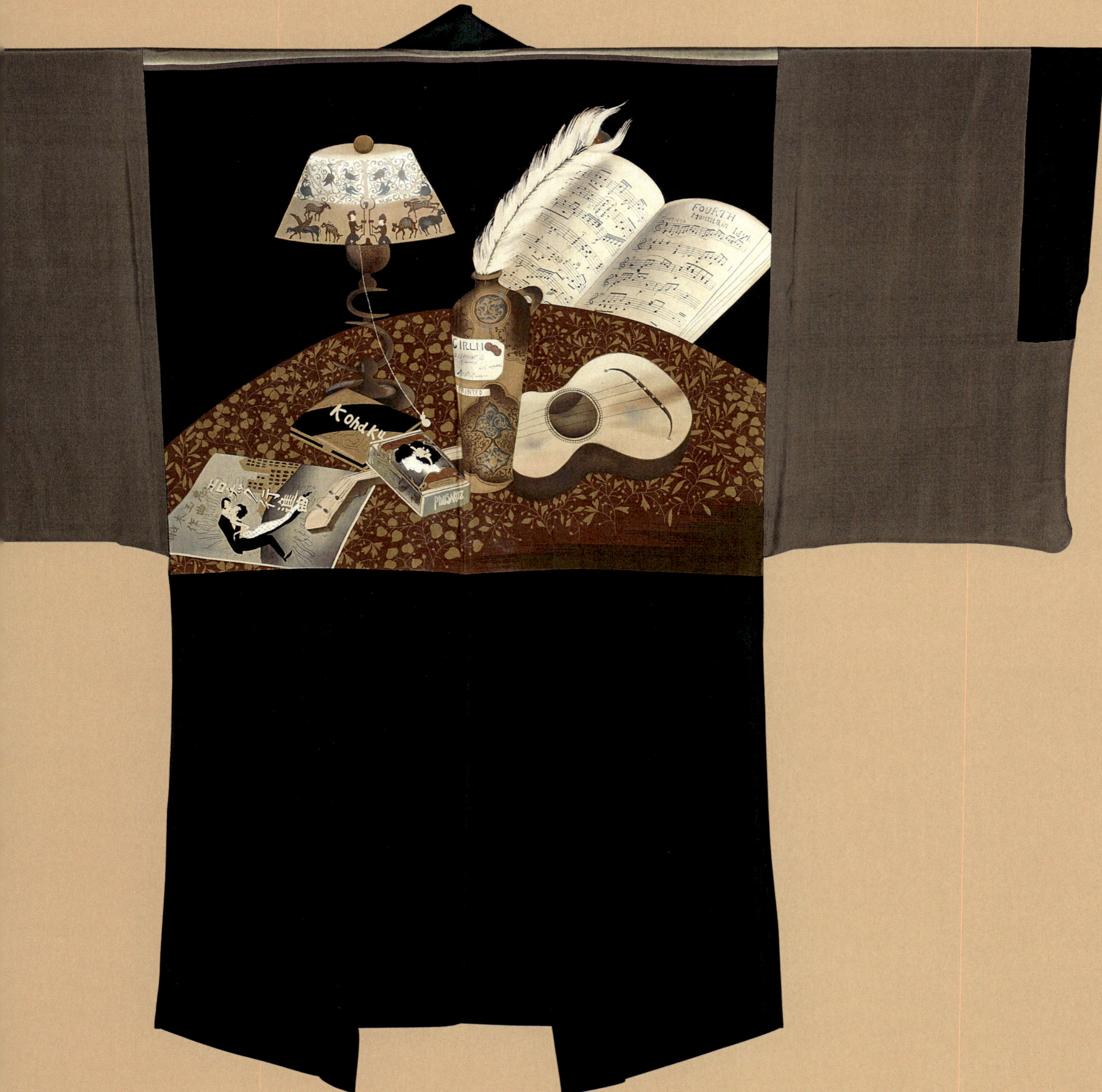

COSMOPOLITANISM/ INTERIORS

Man's *haori* with a decorative lining (*haura*)
A table of objects
Taishō–early Shōwa period, 1920s–1930s
Silk plain weave *haori* (outer); *kata-yūzen* dyed and printed silk *haura* (lining)
51.0 × 43.0 inches (130 × 109 centimeters)
KM135

On first glance, the design for this *haura* may seem quite unassuming, but a closer look can easily offer items of interest. Music seems to be an important element, starting with a musical composition opened to the "Fourth Mountain Idyll," possibly a favorite melody, and one occasionally played by the guitar on the table. Another interesting musical work rests on the front of the table; its title is "Erotica: A Musical Piece." A stylized lamp and a one-time wine bottle that now holds a feather are quirky choices, but perhaps objects of special meaning for the owner. A packet of cigarettes as well as a cigarette case could also be favored objects.

SPORTS/BASEBALL

Man's *haori* with a decorative lining (*haura*)
Baseball on a pitch
Taishō–early Shōwa period, 1912–1930
Silk plain weave *haori* (outer); *kata-yūzen* dyed and printed silk *haura* (lining)
51.0 × 42.0 inches (130 × 107 centimeters)
KM136

In the late 19th century, baseball became very popular in elite boys' schools in Japan. Although schools initially looked on it as an amateur school sport that would build character and team loyalty, in 1896 the Tokyo Itchikō High School team won a string of victories over the Yokohama baseball teams of mostly American foreign residents. Newspapers lauded the young Japanese team as national heroes, which further advanced baseball as a major school sport. By 1915, the newspaper *Osaka Asahi Shimbun* organized the First National Secondary School Baseball Championship to celebrate the winning school teams of the year. Many schools were in attendance, and their teams helped to form the shape and stitching of a baseball "on a pitch" in the field; it was a great display. The prize trophy, laurel garland, and crossed bats are iconic reminders of the games.

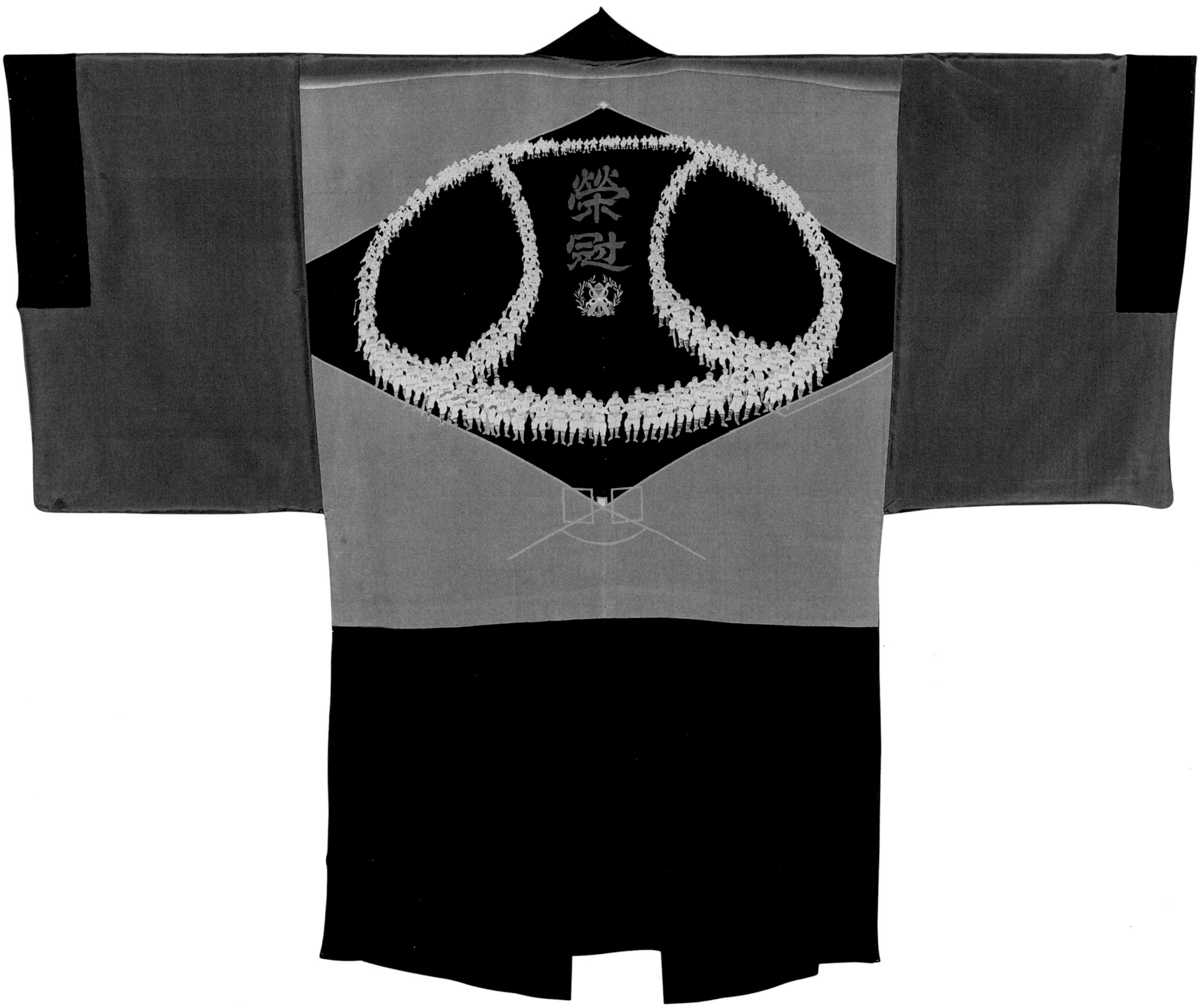

ENTERTAINMENT

Man's *haori* with a decorative lining (*haura*)
Ballroom dancing
Taishō–Shōwa period, 1920–1940
Silk plain weave *haori* (outer); *kata-yūzen* dyed and printed silk *haura* (lining)
50.0 × 43.0 inches (127 × 109 centimeters)
KM137

The images used for the *haura* of this *haori* show the interior of the Shochiku-za Theatre, the first one of its kind, which opened in Osaka in 1923. The theatre became very successful in showing films, plays, and music, all of which can be seen in different rooms. This became a highly popular modern concept of entertainment, and it was so profitable that five other Shochiku-za theatres were soon opened in other Japanese cities. The brown ticket below the room for the musicians is for the Shochiku-za, and the price can be seen on its face: "A" seats are 1.50 yen; "B" seats are less expensive at 1 yen.

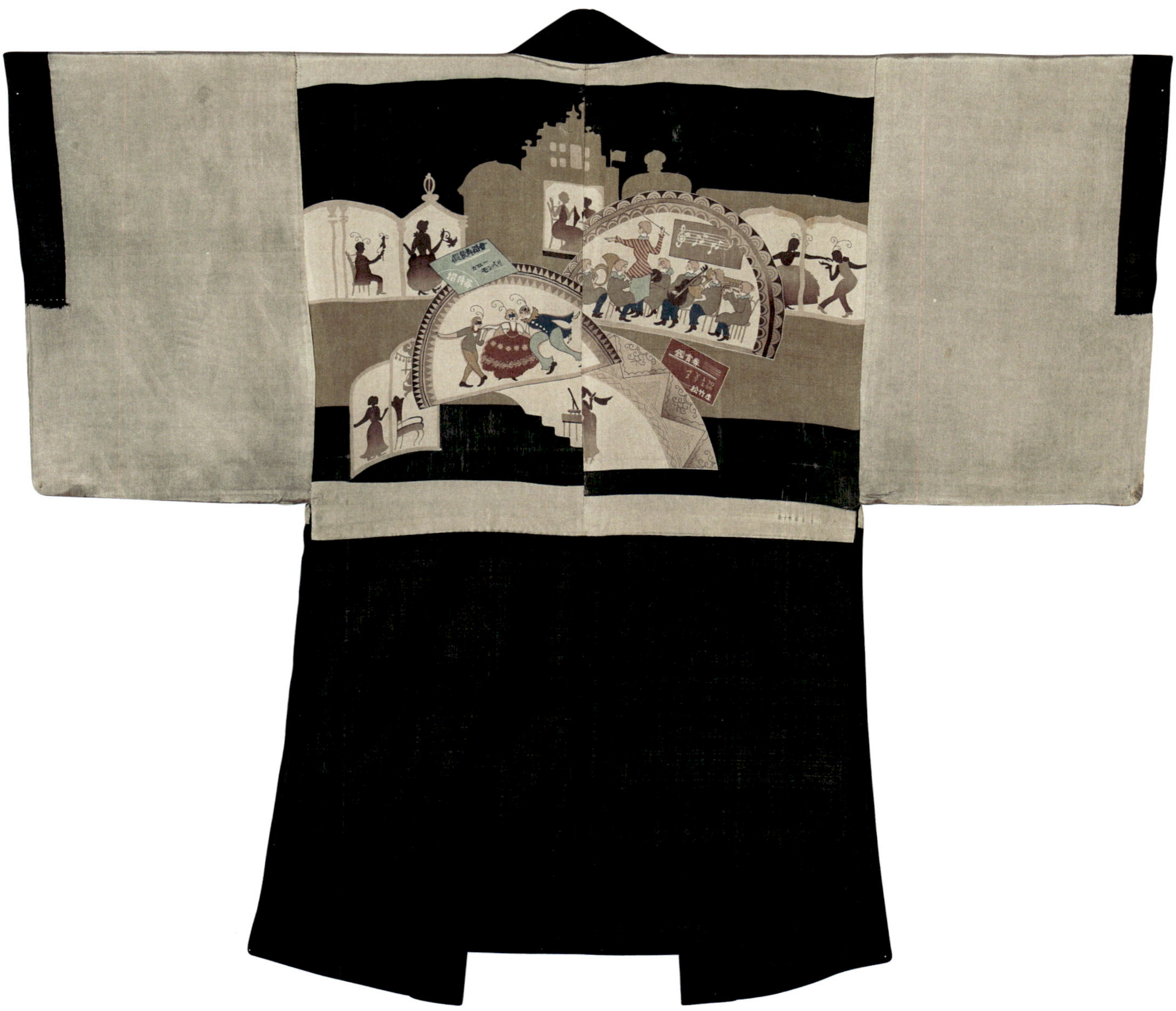

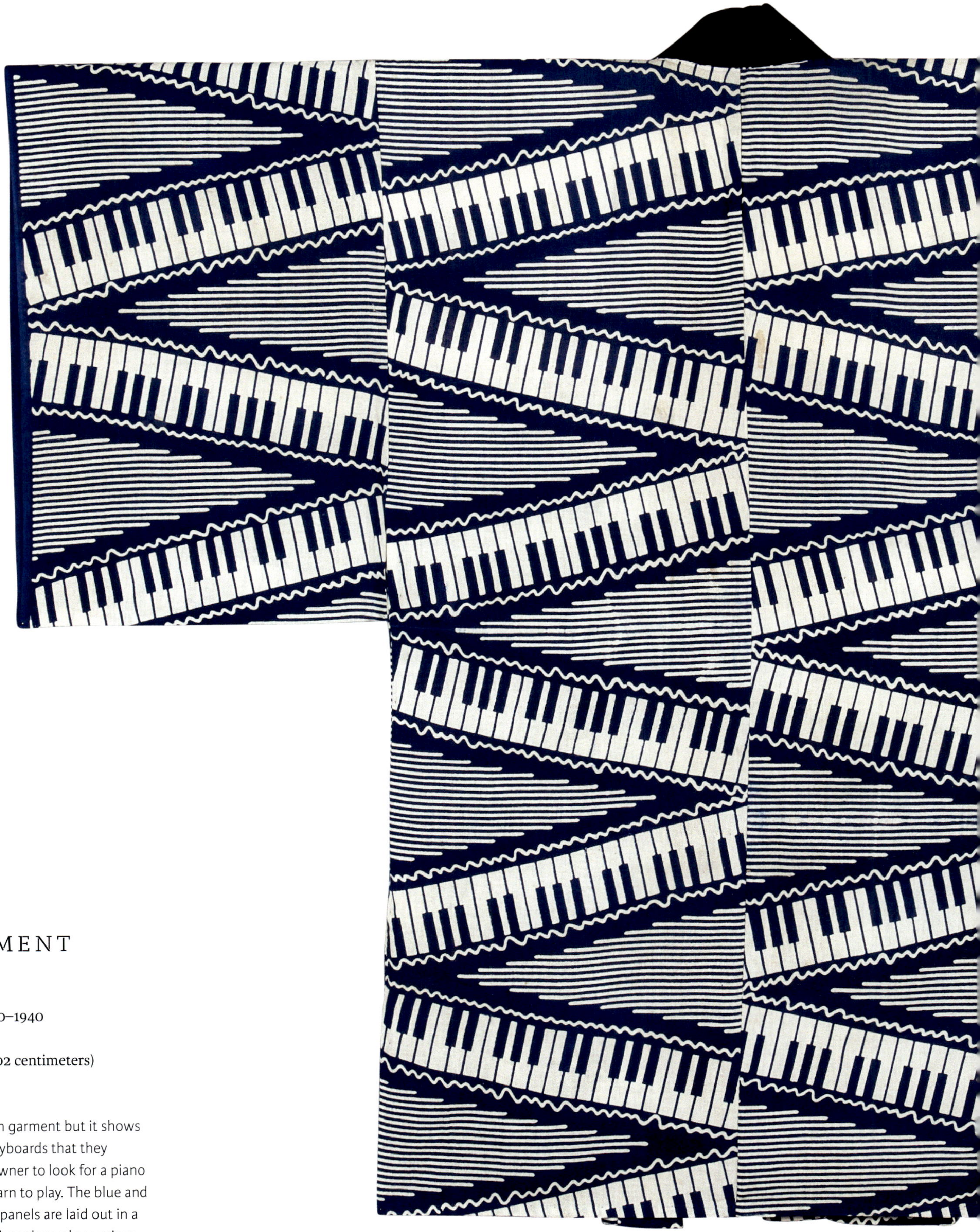

ENTERTAINMENT

Man's *juban*
Playing the keyboards
Taishō–Shōwa period, 1920–1940
Stenciled cotton
51.0 × 40.0 inches (130 × 102 centimeters)
KM138

This *juban* is a simple cotton garment but it shows such a lively grouping of keyboards that they probably encouraged the owner to look for a piano immediately so he could learn to play. The blue and white zigzags of the textile panels are laid out in a manner that allows the keyboards to play against each other at the center back seam of the *juban*, and the sleeves are also set to match the panels appropriately. This light cotton *juban*, with its bright blue and white theme, would be a comfortable garment to wear in the house, or when taking a walk in the cool of a summer evening.

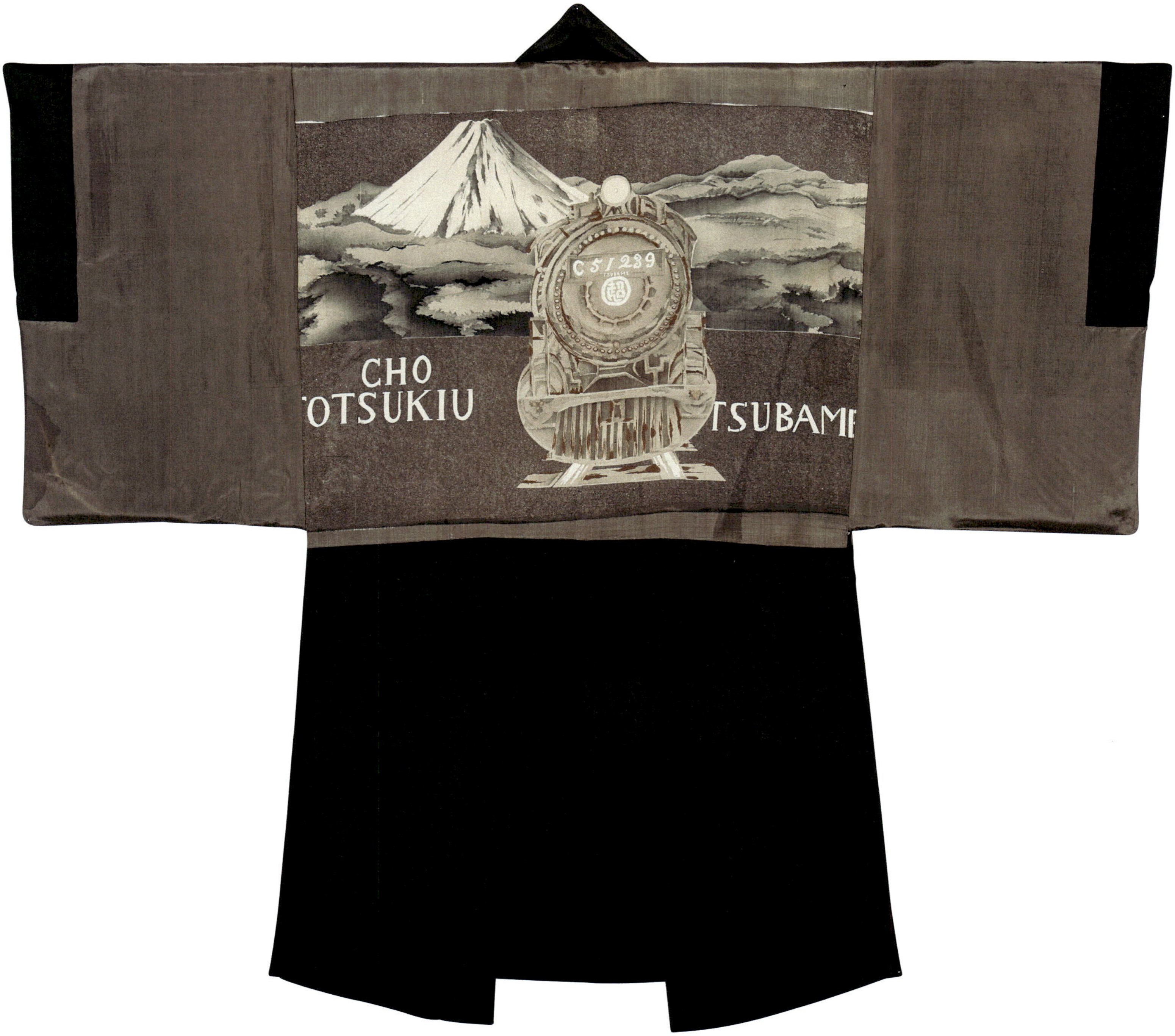

MACHINE AGE/"THE SPEED ERA"

Man's *haori* with a decorative lining (*haura*)
The *Swallow* Super Express
Taishō–early Shōwa period, 1920s–1940s
Silk plain weave (*haori* exterior); *kata-yuzen* dyed silk lining (*haura*)
50.5 × 40.5 inches (128 × 103 centimeters)
KM139

The Super Express *Tsubame* ("Swallow") was the first super express train in Japan, and the locomotive (C51-239) built to power the train was known as the "miraculous revival engine." The *Tsubame* had early test runs in 1929, and its final trial run, from Tokyo to Kobe, was held on July 3, 1930. The station was jammed that day with passengers as well as photographers and news reporters, who called *Tsubame* "the forerunner of the Speed Era." The train was a huge success, as the 375 miles (600 kilometers) between Tokyo and Kobe took only 8 hours and 55 minutes each way. This *haori* was probably made as a celebratory textile for the new Super Express, and the *haura*'s powerful designs of both locomotive and Mount Fuji would appeal to men eager to wear such a prize.

SPORTS/ SAILING

Man's *haori* with a decorative lining (*haura*)
Full speed
Taishō–Shōwa period, 1920s–1940s
Silk plain weave (*haori* exterior); silk lining with hand painting for the *haura*
51.0 × 39.0 inches (130 × 99 centimeters)
KM140

This image shows a stunningly beautiful racing schooner that was built in the United States and launched in 1925. The textile artist who drew this image probably had a photograph of the schooner under sail, and he copied it to perfection. The textile used was a high-quality silk, and the artist handled both dyeing and painting superbly to give real character to this vessel. The grayish-brown background on which this schooner image has been painted is *makinori* ("sprinkled rice paste"), a special dyeing technique that produces a pointillist effect. The *haori* family crest (*mon*) uses a design of three *chidori* (plovers) within a circle; two are on the front, three on the back.

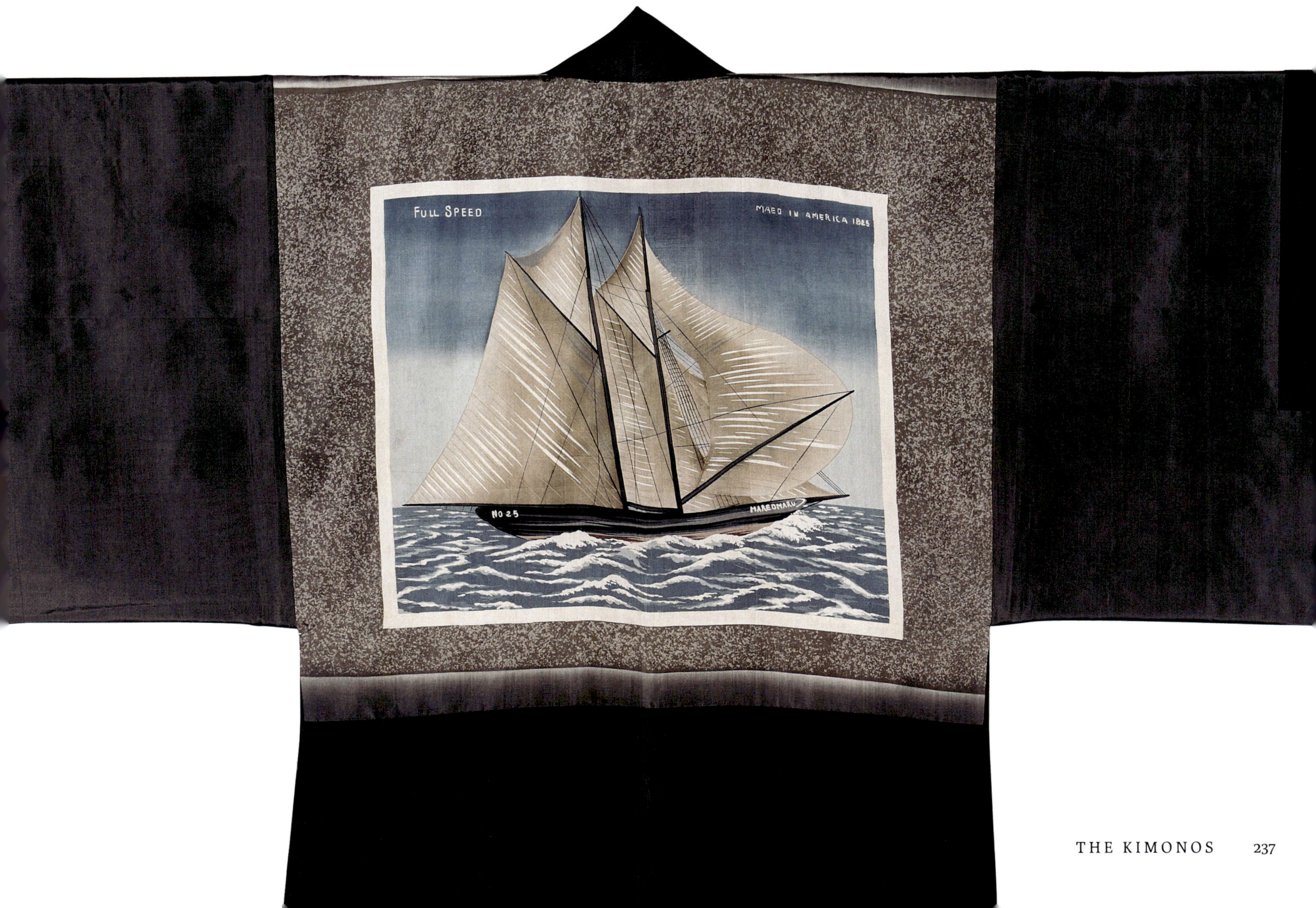

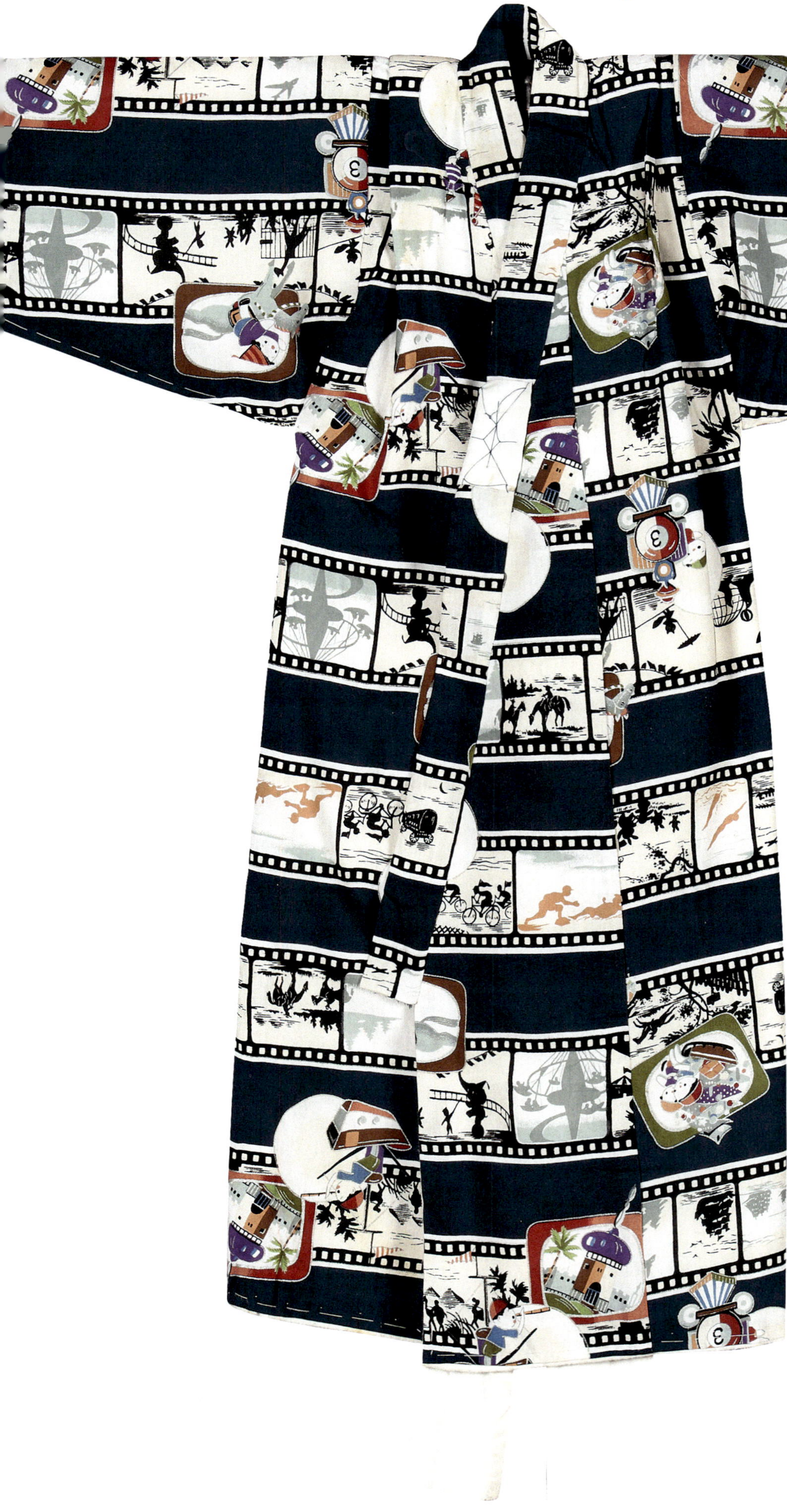

A NEW AGE/ ENTERTAINMENT

Kimono for a very young boy
Color television at last!
Shōwa period, 1960s
Printed silk or printed rayon
32.0 × 28.0 inches (81 × 71 centimeters)
KM141

As noted earlier, television broadcasts were banned during World War II. The broadcasts could not be started again until 1953, but by 1960, NHK (Nippon Hōsō Kyōkai, called Japan Broadcasting Corporation) and other stations were developing color broadcasts in Tokyo and Osaka. Initially, color broadcasts showed for only an hour a day, with programs squeezed into very little time. One short cartoon became a wild success with the public, and the colorful designs on this little boy's kimono may have captured both the sense of this lively cartoon and its amusing characters. The kimono also shows black and white film images used for broadcasts. These include cowboys and horses, zoos and circuses, travelogues with ships, airplanes, pyramids, and camels—all the excitement of television as viewers began to comprehend the demands of a new age.

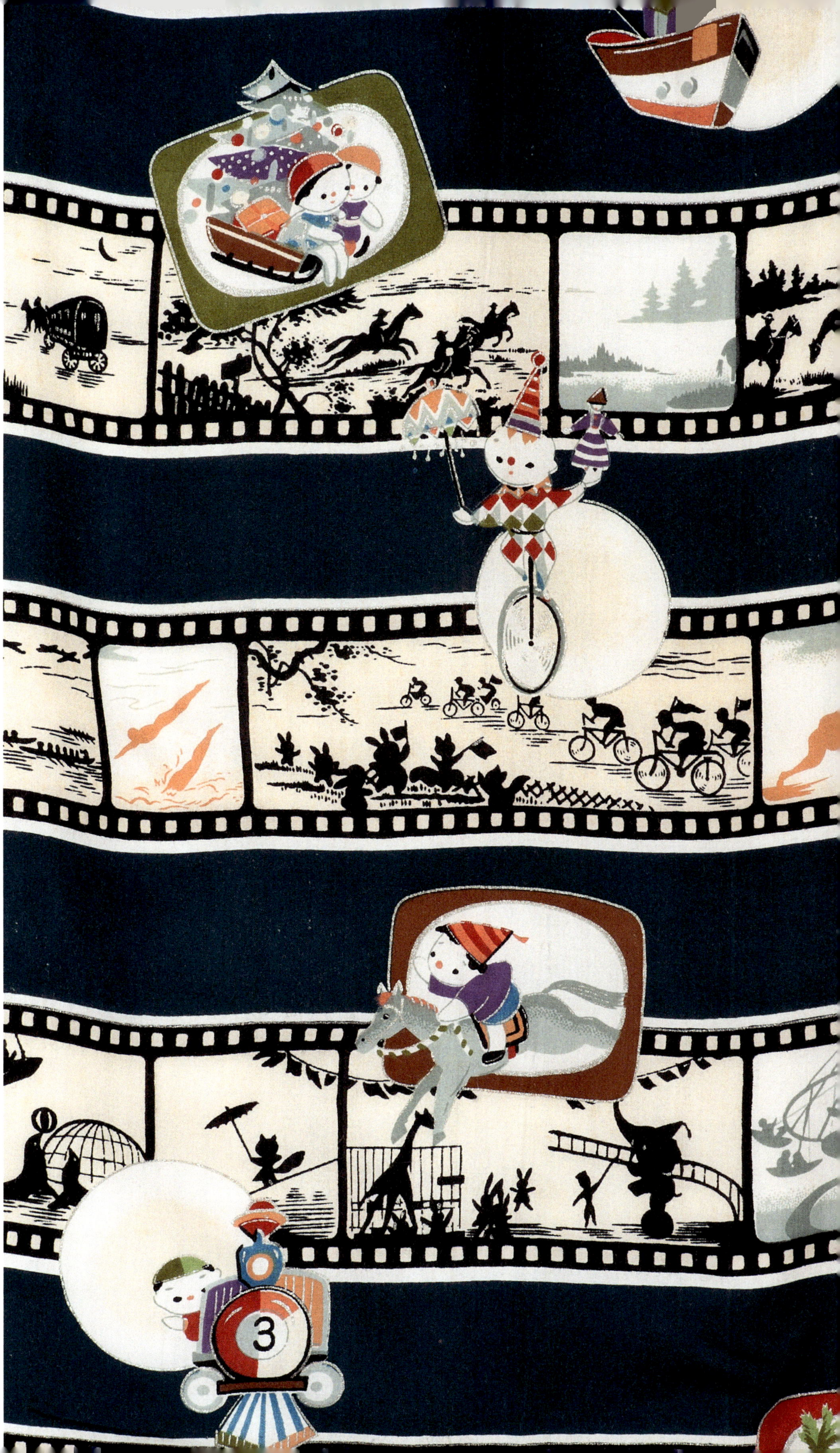

CINEMA/ ENTERTAINMENT

Woman's *juban*
Mickey Mouse and friends
Shōwa period, late 1930s–1940
Stenciled rayon
50.0 × 48.0 inches (127 × 122 centimeters)
KM142

The artist for this colorful *juban* brought together a lively medley of cartoon characters: Mickey Mouse, Minnie Mouse, Donald Duck, Bugs Bunny, Pluto, and Porky Pig—some of the most famous names in Hollywood. These wide-eyed characters were drawn with great accuracy on this textile, although with a few idiosyncratic touches. Mickey sports an olive fatigue cap that carries a single central star, usually associated with Japanese military wear, and Practical Pig wears a simple cap and overalls, as opposed to his ostentatious brothers. As Japan's war mobilization gathered steam in 1940, citizens were urged to conserve resources, so rayon, an inexpensive substitute for cotton and silk, was used for this *juban*. Rayon was generally accepted by the public because of its soft texture and affinity for dyes.

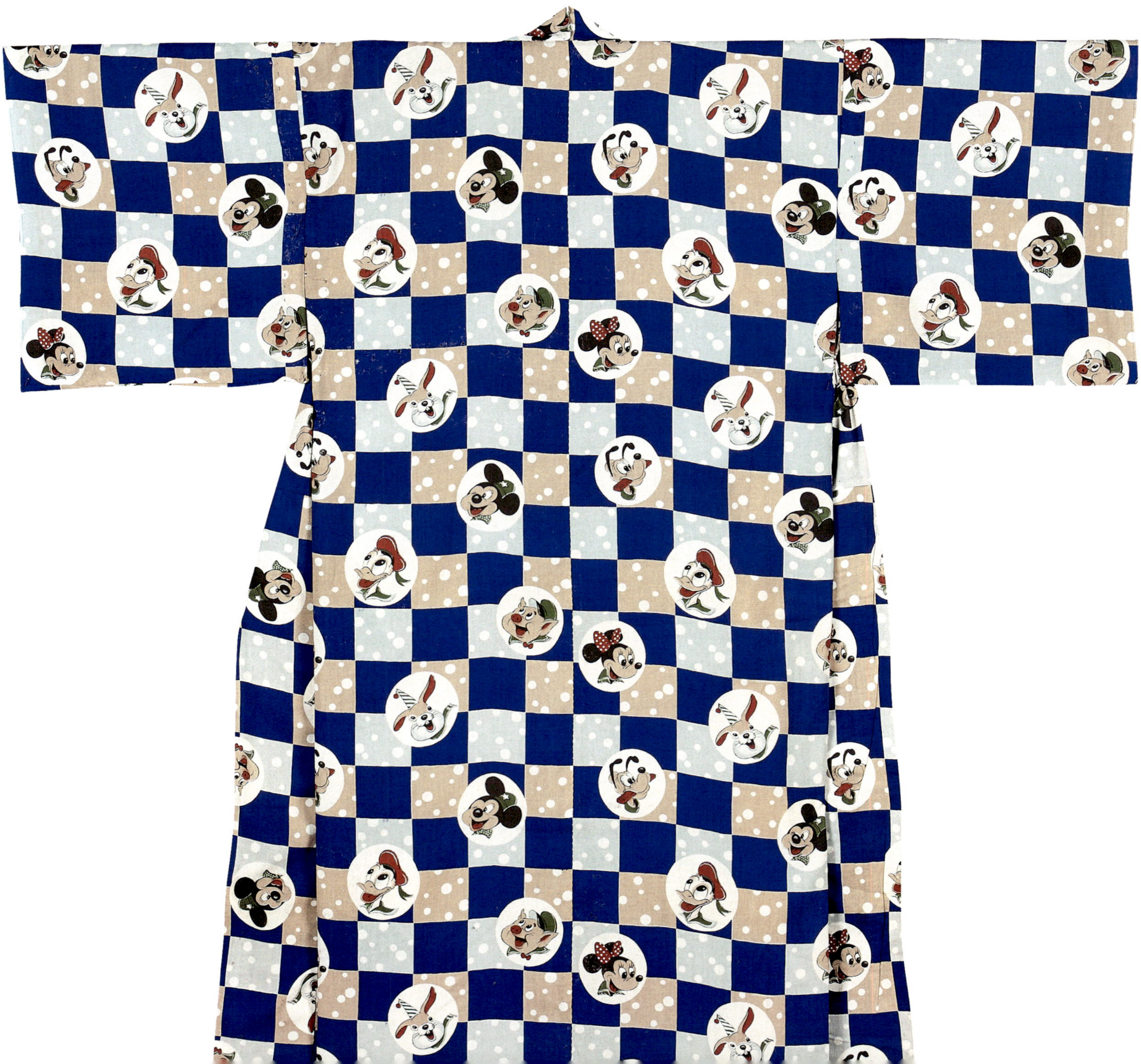

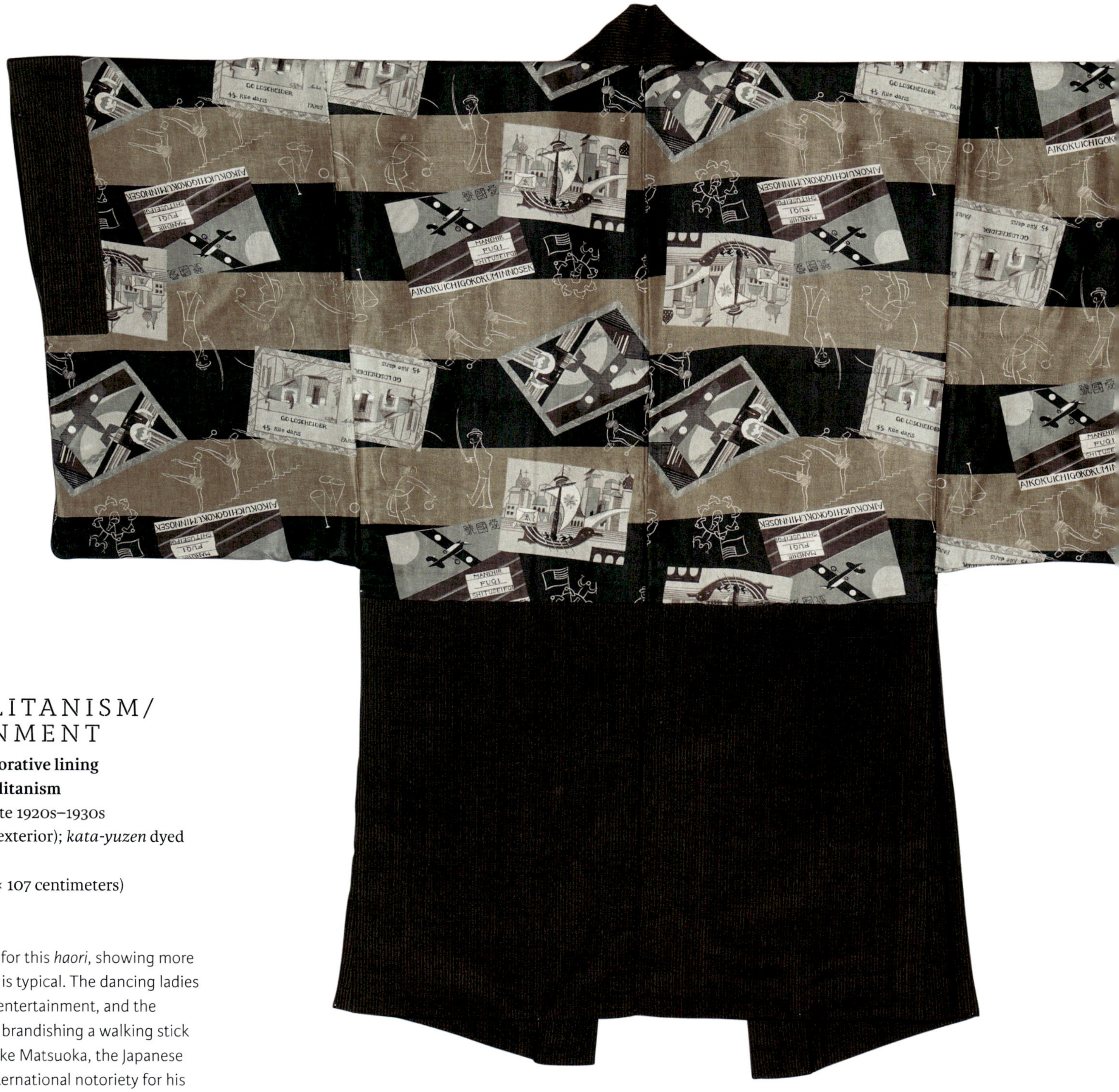

COSMOPOLITANISM/ ENTERTAINMENT

Man's *haori* with a decorative lining
The allure of cosmopolitanism
Taihō–Shōwa period, late 1920s–1930s
Silk plain weave (*haori* exterior); *kata-yuzen* dyed and printed silk lining
51.0 × 42.0 inches (130 × 107 centimeters)
KM143

This is an unusual lining for this *haori*, showing more white-lined figures than is typical. The dancing ladies and tennis players offer entertainment, and the dapper, mustached man brandishing a walking stick possibly represents Yōsuke Matsuoka, the Japanese diplomat who gained international notoriety for his 1933 speech condemning the League of Nations in Geneva. Matsuoka then announced Japan's withdrawal and led the Japanese delegation out of the League's assembly hall, thus ending Japan's further diplomatic participation. The figure raising his arms at the table with the Manchukuo flag also represents Matsuoka. The "*Aikoku/Ichigo/Kokumin/Nosek[i]*" text card calls for "Love of Nation/United Harmony/One People/ National Character." Another text carrying the name "Goldscheider" has a Parisian address, probably representing Arthur Goldscheider, a Jewish art dealer who owned one of the best-known galleries in Paris. In the 1930s, Matsuoka was supporting the Japanese government's plan to resettle Jews from Nazi-occupied Europe to Japanese territories in the East, and if he had met Goldscheider, this might have galvanized his support even further.

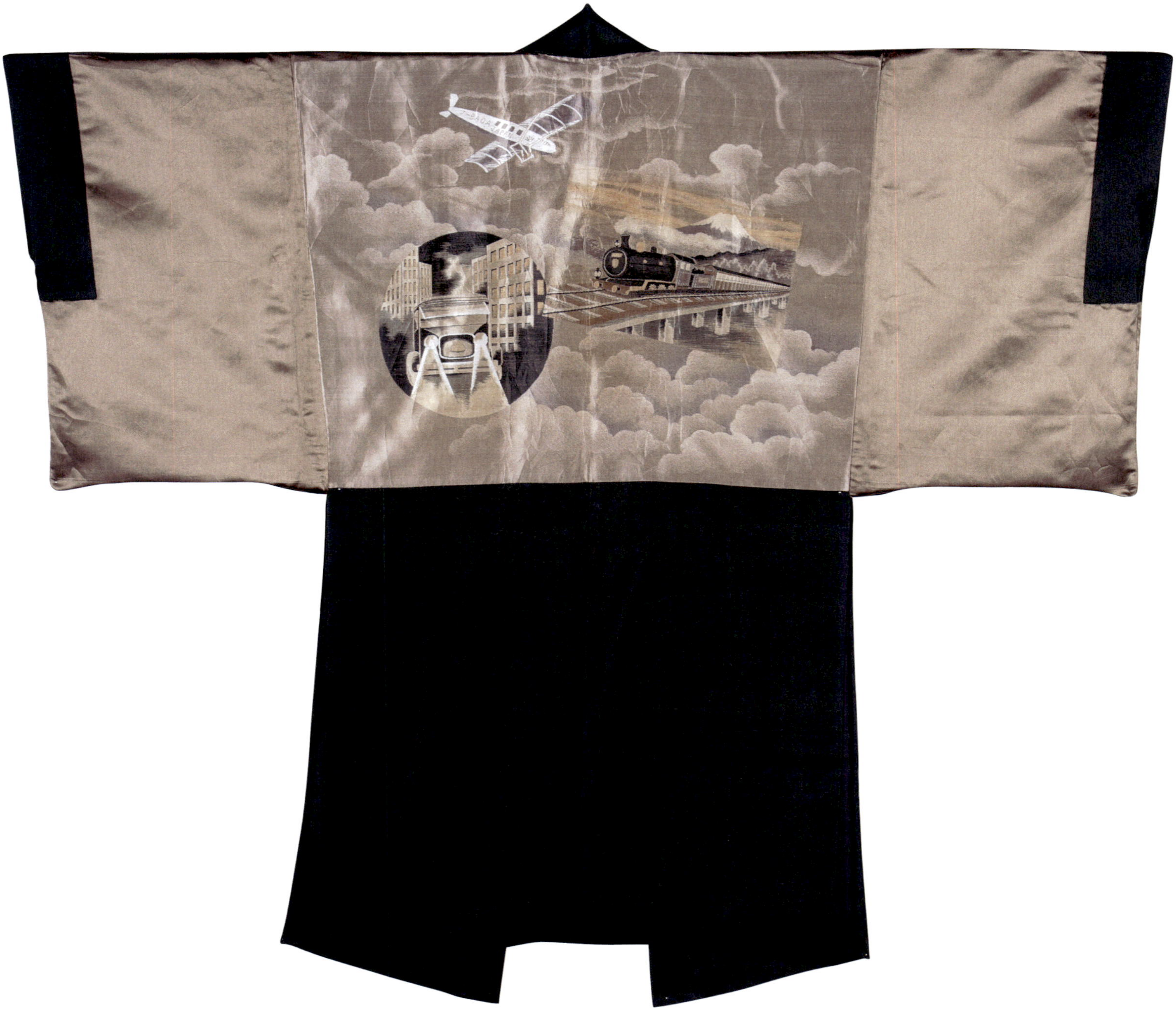

MACHINE AGE

Man's *haori* with a decorative lining (*haura*)
Machines on the ground and in the clouds
Taishō–Shōwa period, 1920s–1930s
Silk plain weave (*haori* exterior); brocaded silk *haura* (lining) with metal threads
53.0 × 45.0 inches (135 × 114 centimeters)
KM144

The *haura* of this garment is beautifully crafted with silk and metal threads. The design is carefully woven, with segments letting each of the major elements—the plane, the locomotive, and the trolleybus—stand out in the dramatic positions the artist provided. The use of the yellow-gold in the sky above the locomotive and the golden reflections in the windows of the buildings above the trolleybus add extra background emphasis. The airplane shown here (strange though it may look) was based on air transportation pioneered by the Japan Air Transport Company; it provided air services to Korea, Manchuria, and Japan until the late 1930s. Mount Fuji is always an important icon to be noted during travels.

ENTERTAINMENT/ KEWPIES

***Miyamairi* (child's kimono for first shrine visit)**
Cheering Kewpies and music
Taishō–early Shōwa, early 1920s–early 1930s
Kata-yuzen dyed silk
40.5 × 32.5 inches (103 × 83 centimeters)
KM145

Mass production in the early 20th century gave rise to textiles in Japan that could be manufactured relatively inexpensively. One result of this was *omoshirogara* prints—novelty designs that reflected new trends. This design reveals several elements of contemporary popular culture and hints at the vibrant and decadent culture of Weimar Germany. The Kewpie dolls that took the world by storm in 1914 were originally manufactured in Germany, and by the mid-1920s, they were being made in many forms in Japan. These odd little dolls were widely known for their cherubic smiles and warm coloring, but the staring Kewpies printed on this textile seem almost menacing. The background sheet music is *Karatachi no Hana* (Wild Orange Blossoms), written in 1928 by Kosaku Yamada, a celebrated Japanese composer.

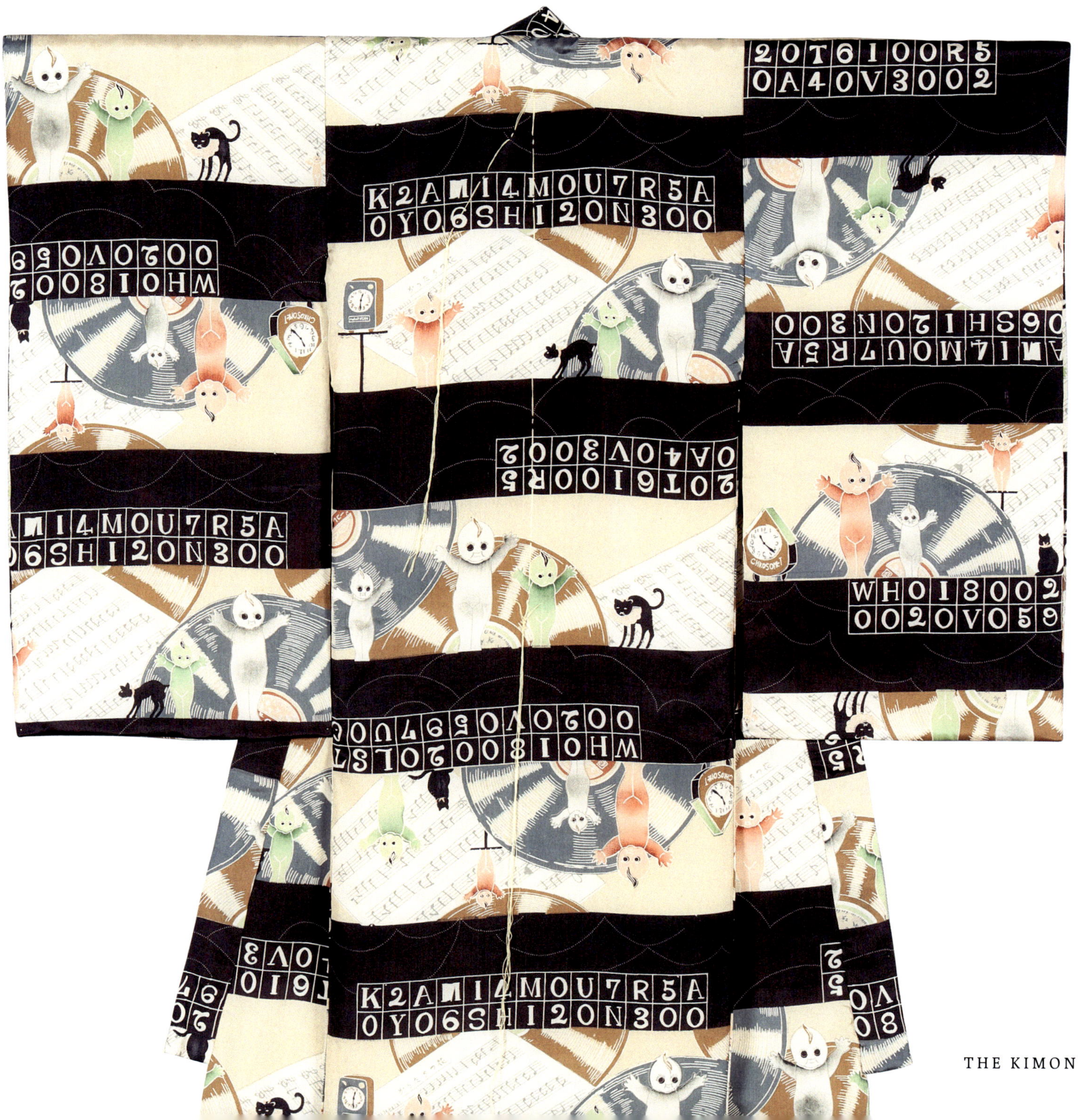

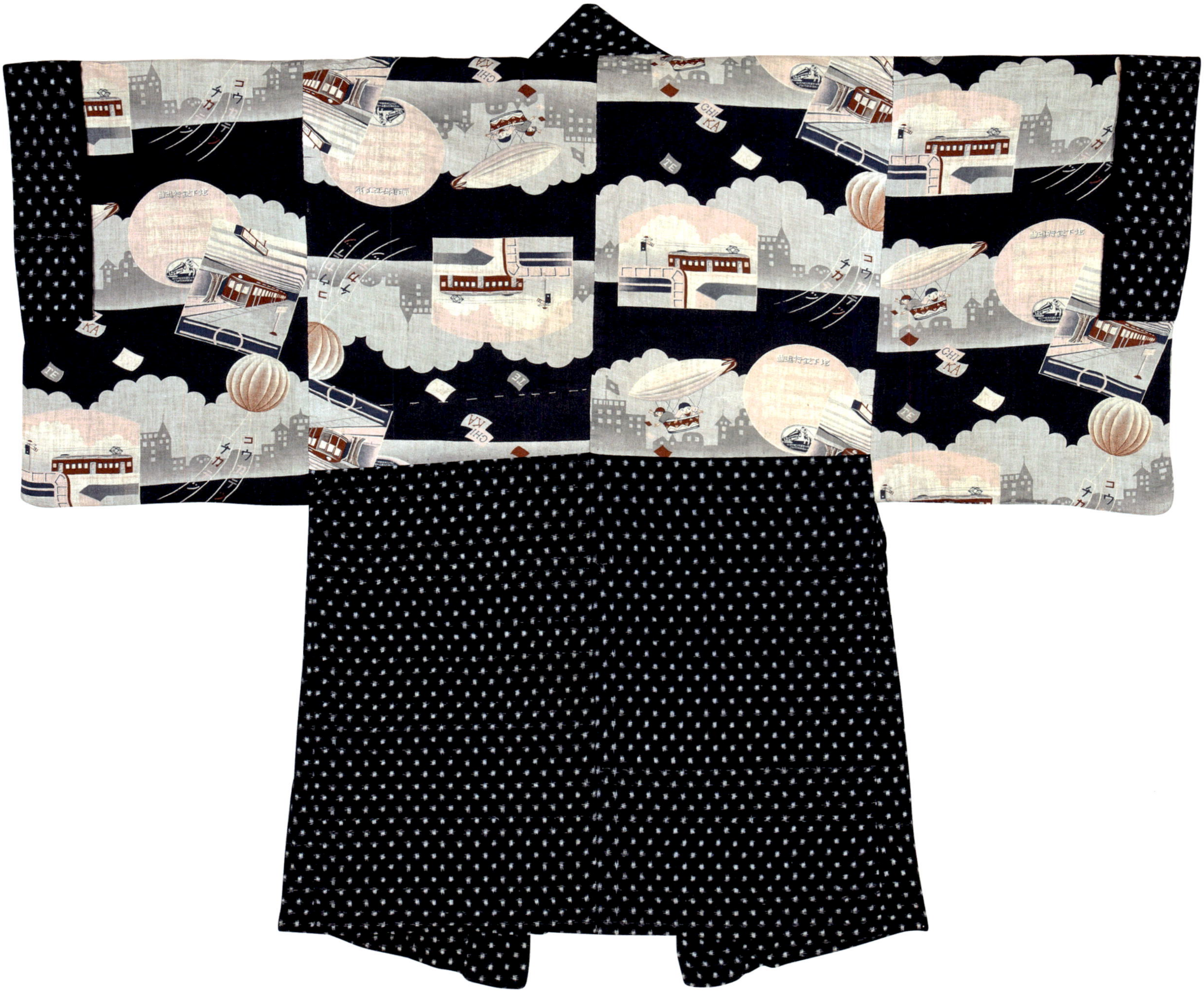

THE MODERN AGE

Man's informal *haori* with a decorative lining
Trains, dirigibles, and "His Master's Voice" (HMV)
Shōwa period, 1933
Woven *kasuri* (exterior); printed cotton lining
50.0 × 36.0 inches (127 × 91 centimeters)
KM146

The printed cotton lining of this *haori* has lively designs set against a cityscape background. The city is Osaka, and the 1933 opening of the new Osaka *chikatetsu* (an underground train) is about to be commemorated. Two grinning boys drop *chikatetsu* flyers from their dirigible basket while an orange balloon floats with two banners, one spelling *Chikatetsu* and the other *Kokutetsu* (underground and overground railway respectively). The final design is the music set within the round disk. "His Master's Voice" (the logo of the record company) refers to a song specially written for the occasion, but unfortunately the cloth is now too faded to read. The outside of this *haori* is *kasuri*. It is a spot-dyed double weave, with both warp and weft yarns tied and resist-dyed before being woven into a single textile.

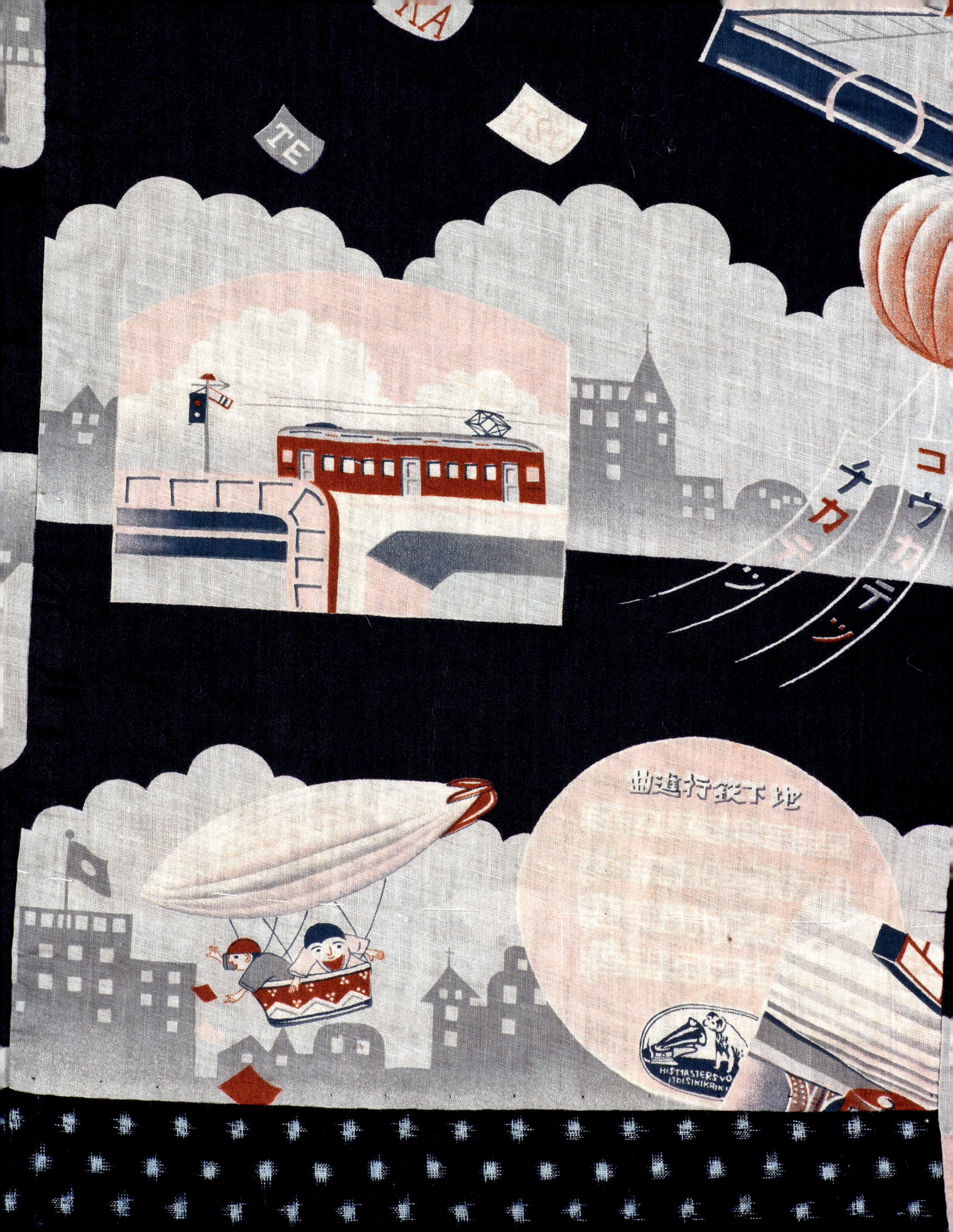

KA
TE
コウカデン
地下鉄行進曲

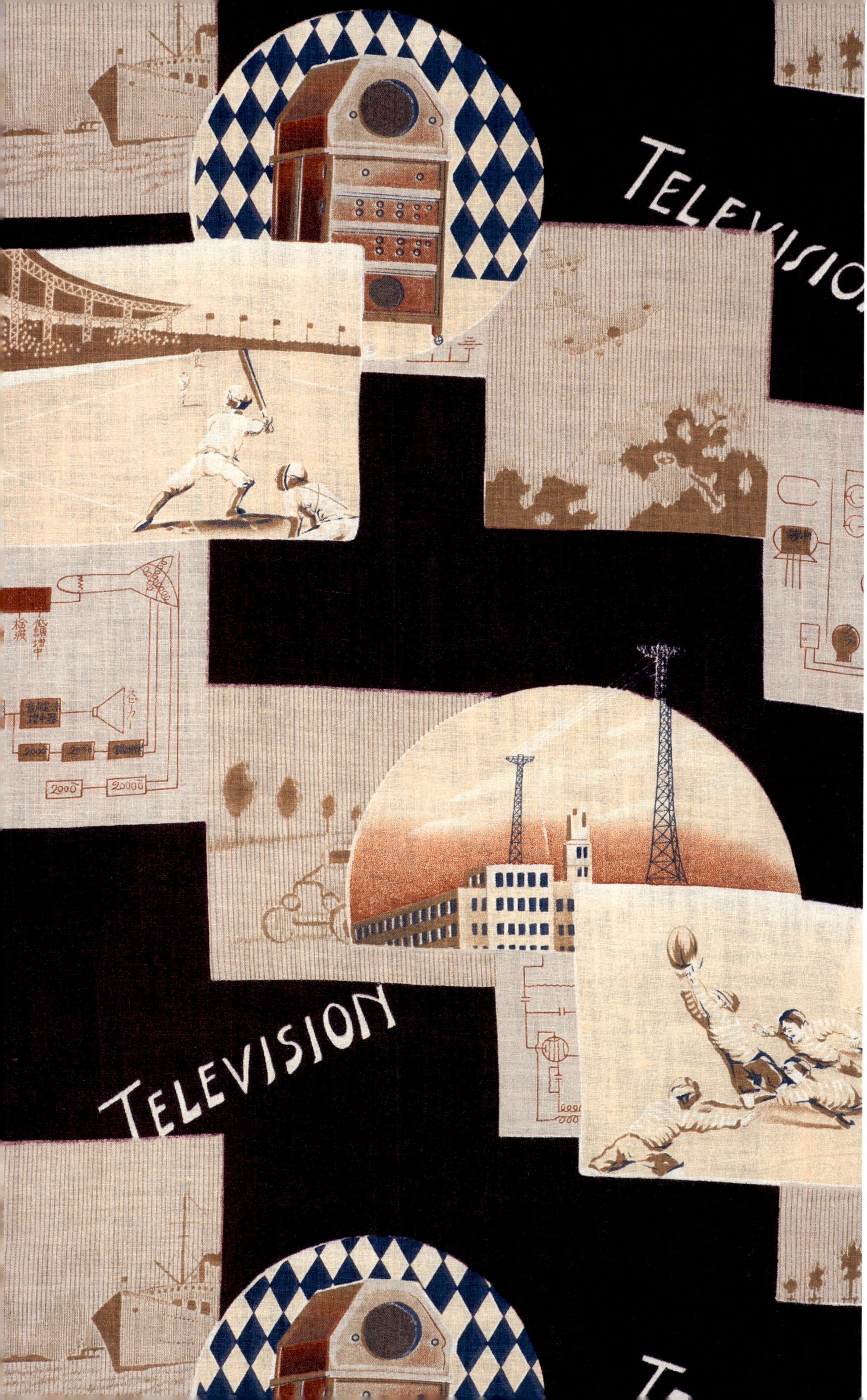
TELEVISION

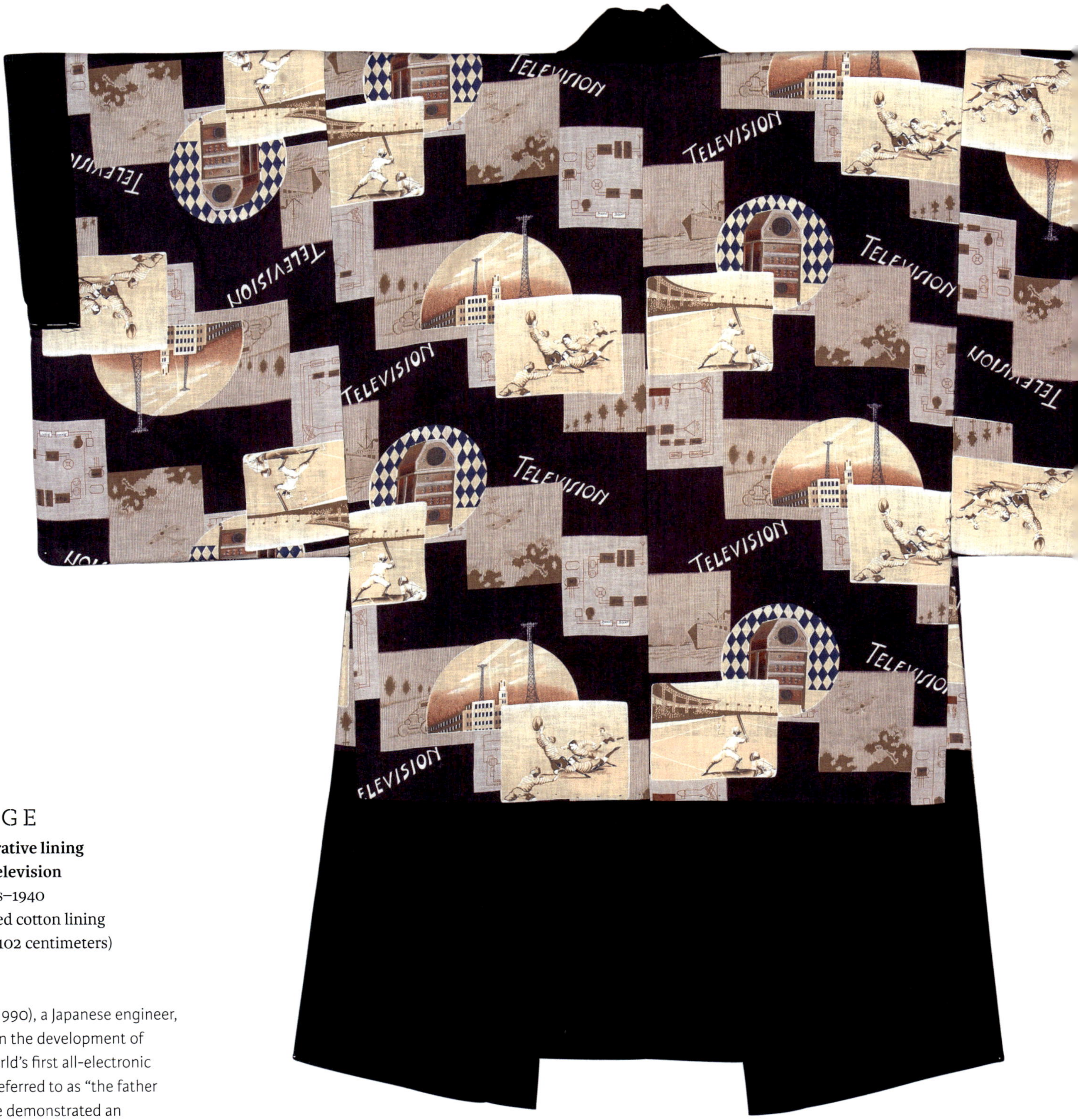

MACHINE AGE

Man's *haori* with a decorative lining
The father of Japanese television
Shōwa period, early 1930s–1940
Heavy silk exterior; printed cotton lining
50.0 × 40.0 inches (127 × 102 centimeters)
KM147

Kenjiro Takayanagi (1899–1990), a Japanese engineer, was a significant pioneer in the development of television. He built the world's first all-electronic television receiver and is referred to as "the father of Japanese television." He demonstrated an all-electronic television system in 1935, and his success brought television broadcasting to the Japanese public in the late 1930s. Further television broadcasting in Japan, however, was halted by World War II, and broadcasting did not begin again until 1953. This *haori* was produced not only to celebrate the return of television broadcasting in Japan in 1953 but also to offer a tribute to Takayanagi's work through the designs in the lining of the *haori*.

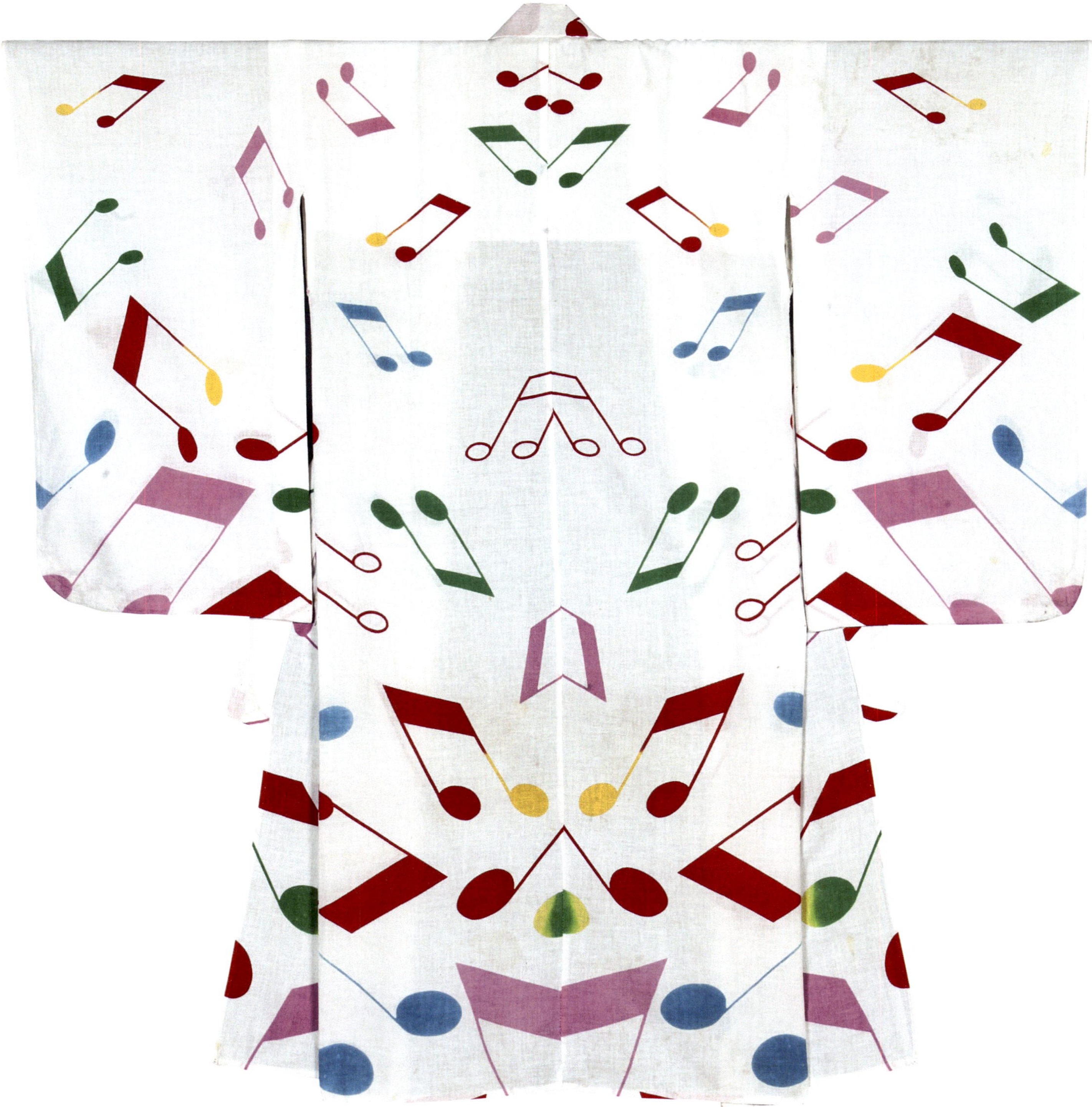

MUSIC

Kimono for a young girl
Musical notes
Taishō–early Shōwa period, 1929–1930s
Stenciled cotton
45.0 × 39.0 inches (114 × 99 centimeters)
KM148

The airy, almost sheer cotton used for this beautiful kimono was intended for summer wear. It was probably worn over a white cotton or silk *juban* that would help to offset summer heat and present a light sense of coolness. The kimono carries what first appears to be a simple stenciled design of musical notes starting from the kimono hem to the collar, but, as the notes gradually ascend, it becomes obvious that they have been carefully printed to become just slightly smaller as each note climbs higher. The fabric has been exactly duplicated from one side to the other.

TRAVEL

Woman's *haori*
Windmills and a red haze
Taishō–early Shōwa period, 1929–1930s
Hand-painted silk and embroidered gold thread
48.0 × 41.0 inches (122 × 104 centimeters)
KM149

This is both a mystical and a magical scene for this *haori*; it is one that would rarely be seen. The windmill looks like a tower suitable for the golden-haired Rapunzel of the celebrated fairy tale. The rough stonework of the tower has been painted almost as a medieval icon would be, and the long, thin, oversized blades of the windmill look dangerous enough to let only the bravest people pass. The blood-dark blades can be imagined gaining speed as winds rush wildly through the sky, while an enigmatic red haze wraps itself around the tower. Hand-painted colors and embroidered gold thread give great presence to this work.

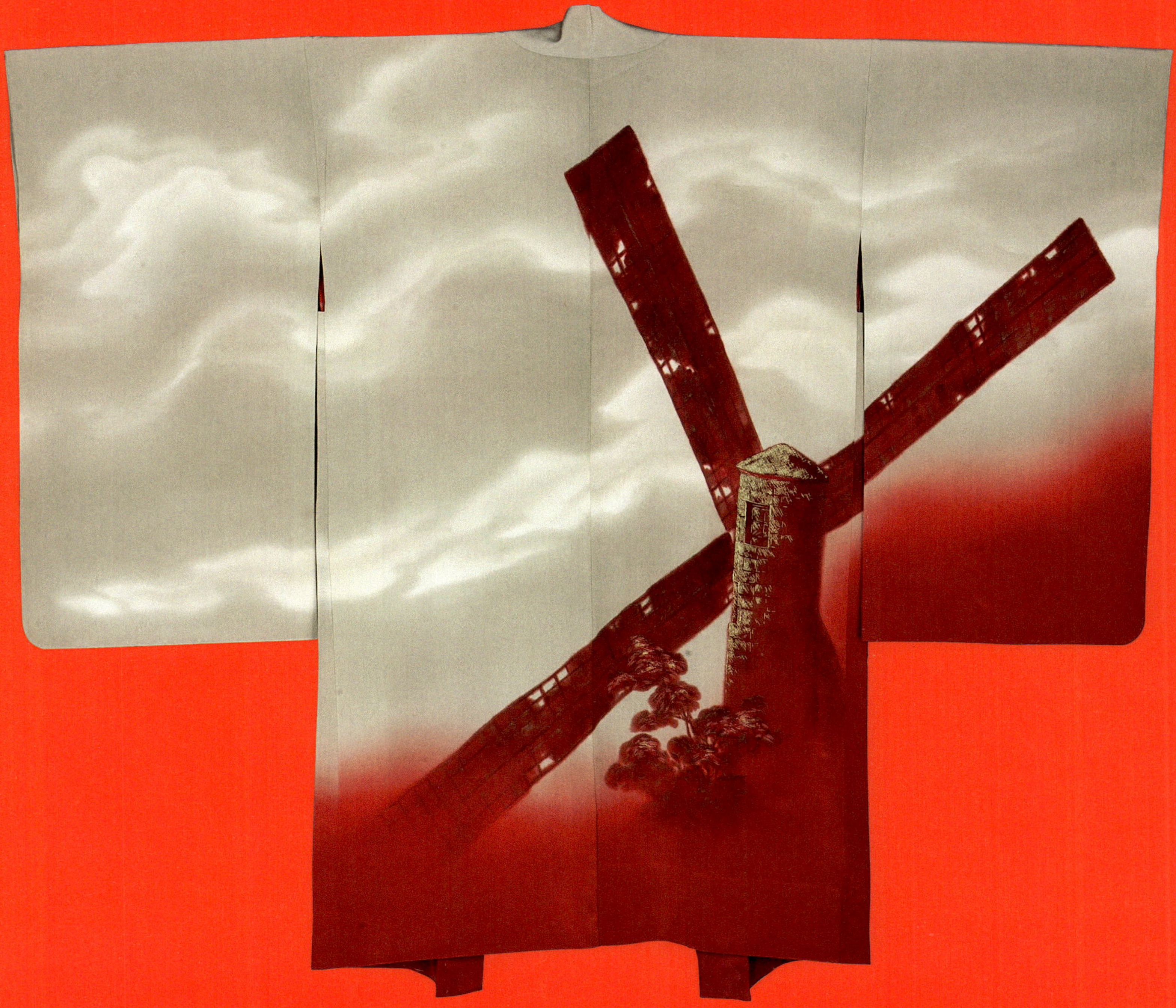

CULTURE/ART

Man's *haori* with a decorative lining (*haura*)
Paintings, sculpture, and trees
Taishō–Shōwa period, 1920–1940
Silk plain weave *haori* (outer); *kata-yūzen* dyed silk *haura* (lining)
48.0 × 33.0 inches (122 × 84 centimeters)
KM150

The choice for the *haura* in this *haori* offers an interesting design. It is probably meant to be seen as part of an art museum or gallery that has both traditional Japanese and modern art. The largest painting captures Mount Fuji at the top, a traditional castle in the background, a wooden bridge, a cherry tree in full bloom, a woman watching deer, and a man approaching a shrine across the river. The middle picture shows a hunter and his dog walking through the trees as snow falls gently, and the final image features two boatmen fighting the rapids. The nude woman reaching to tie her hair and the man posed to throw an iron ball are both intended to be sculptures for the modern age.

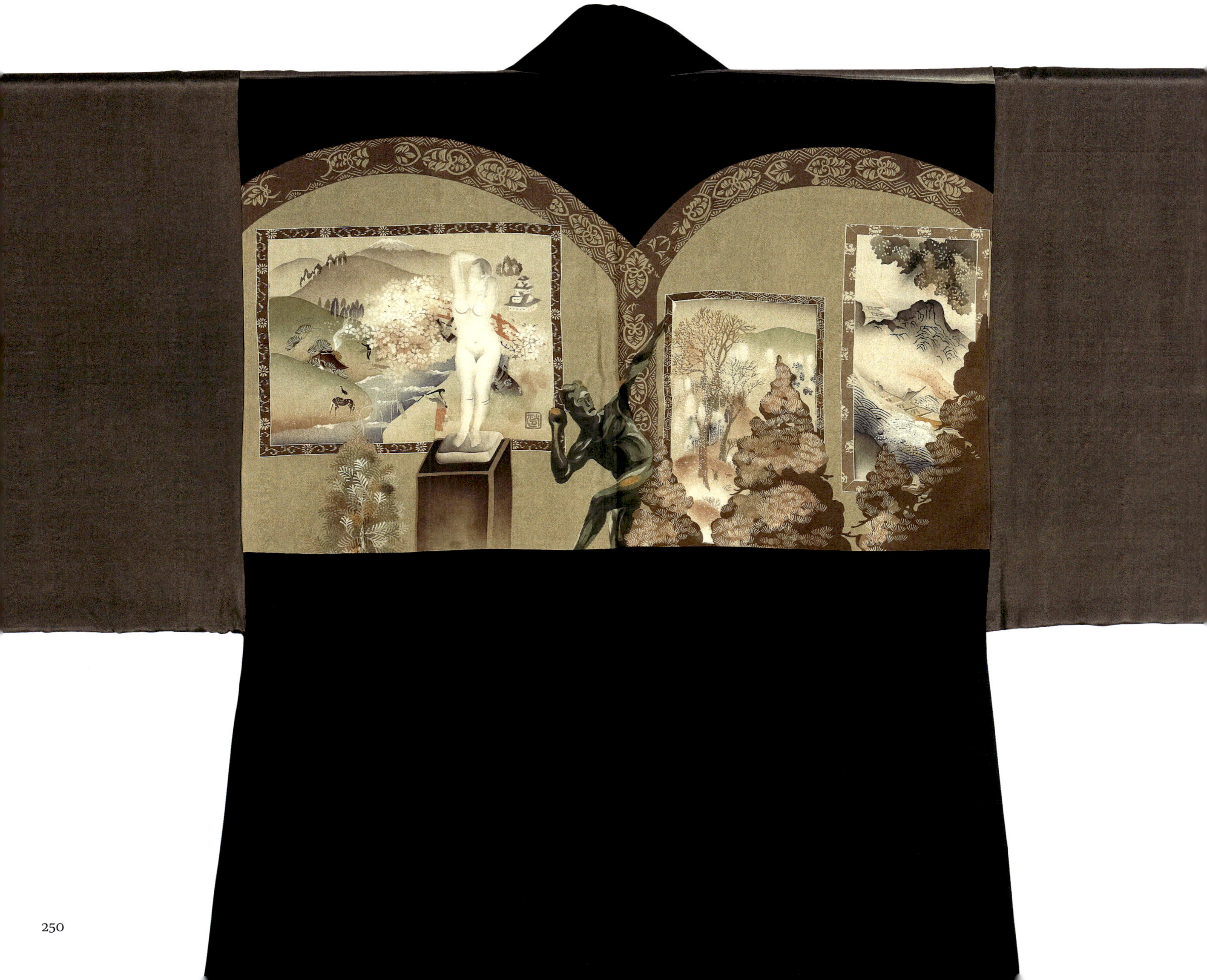

MACHINE AGE

Man's *haori* with a decorative lining (*haura*)
First launch
Taishō–Shōwa period, 1910s–1920s
Silk plain weave *haori* (outer) with pre-dyed scoured threads to create a very dark, almost invisible stripe; heavy woven silk *haura* (lining), damask patterned silk for inner sleeves.
55.0 × 43.0 inches (140 × 109 centimeters)
KM151

This huge ship has just been prepared for its first launch, and the many spectators attending this event are madly cheering as the leviathan slowly slides into the ocean waters. It is likely that this is one of the first warships that Japan produced; it was built for the Imperial Japanese Navy, as indicated by the emblem on the prow. The *haura* is superbly woven; the graceful lines of the ship create an impact of its own as it hits the water. The weaving also carefully captures the figures and garments of the spectators. The figures are woven into three repetitive sections; the tall man who faces the ship and waves his hat high in the air is easily identified in each section.

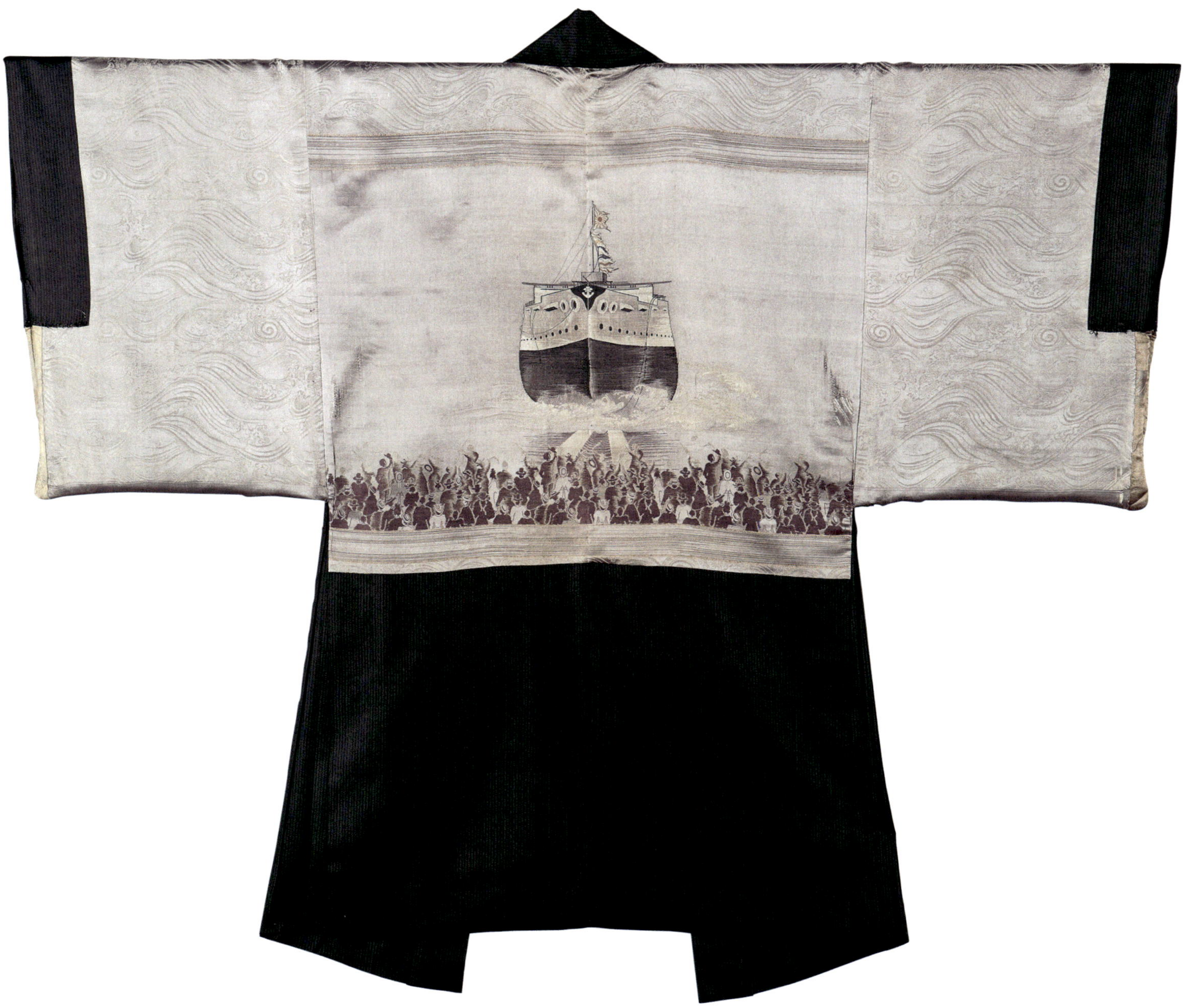

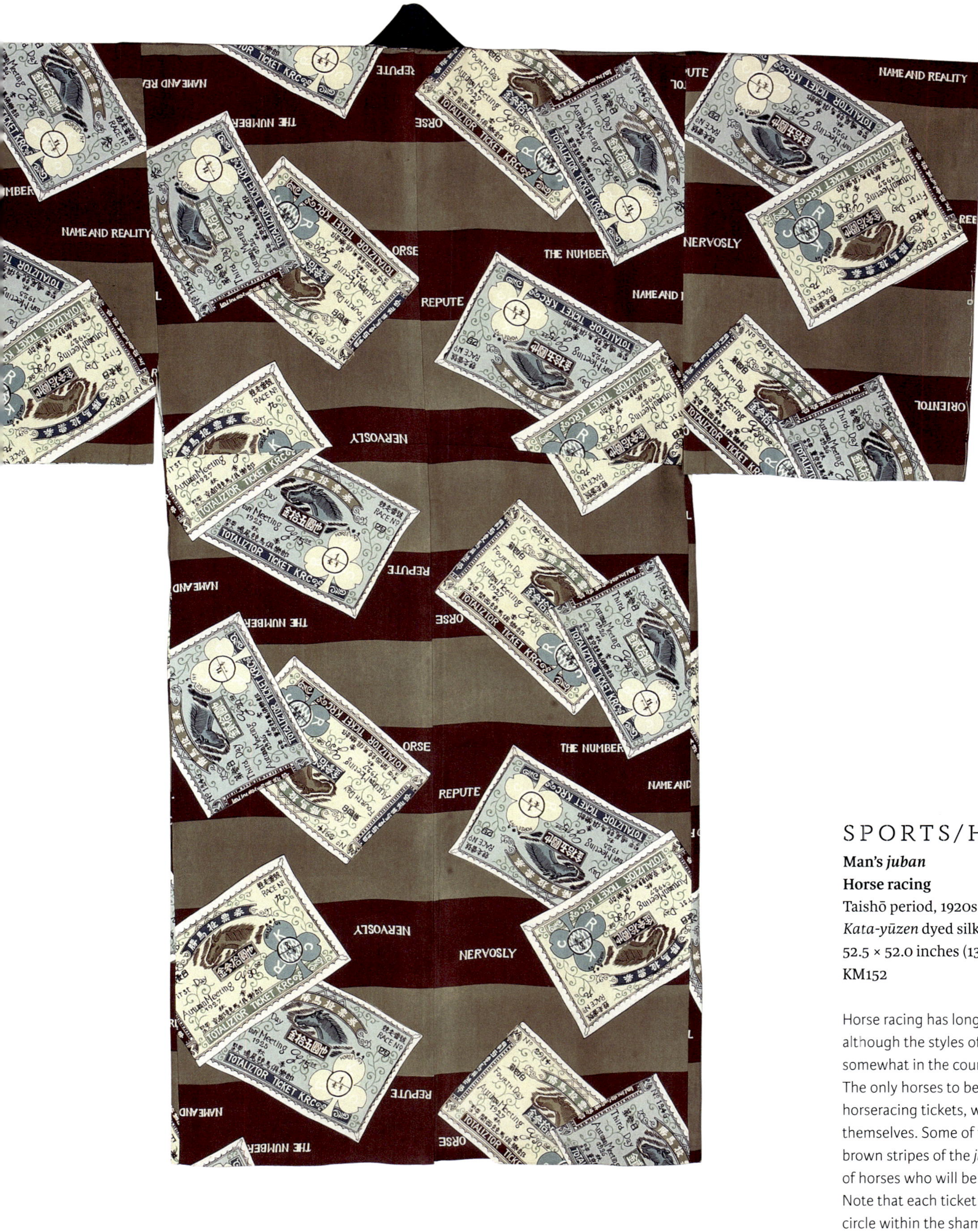

SPORTS/HORSE RACING

Man's *juban*
Horse racing
Taishō period, 1920s
Kata-yūzen dyed silk
52.5 × 52.0 inches (133 × 132 centimeters)
KM152

Horse racing has long been an exciting sport in Japan, although the styles of riding and racing have changed somewhat in the country from the 1500s to the 1920s. The only horses to be seen on this *juban* are on the horseracing tickets, which provide access to the races themselves. Some of the words scattered on the brown stripes of the *juban* are most likely the names of horses who will be racing at the fall meetings. Note that each ticket carries a shamrock, and the circle within the shamrock gives a number for one horse; that number indicates the race in which the horse will run—and possibly win.

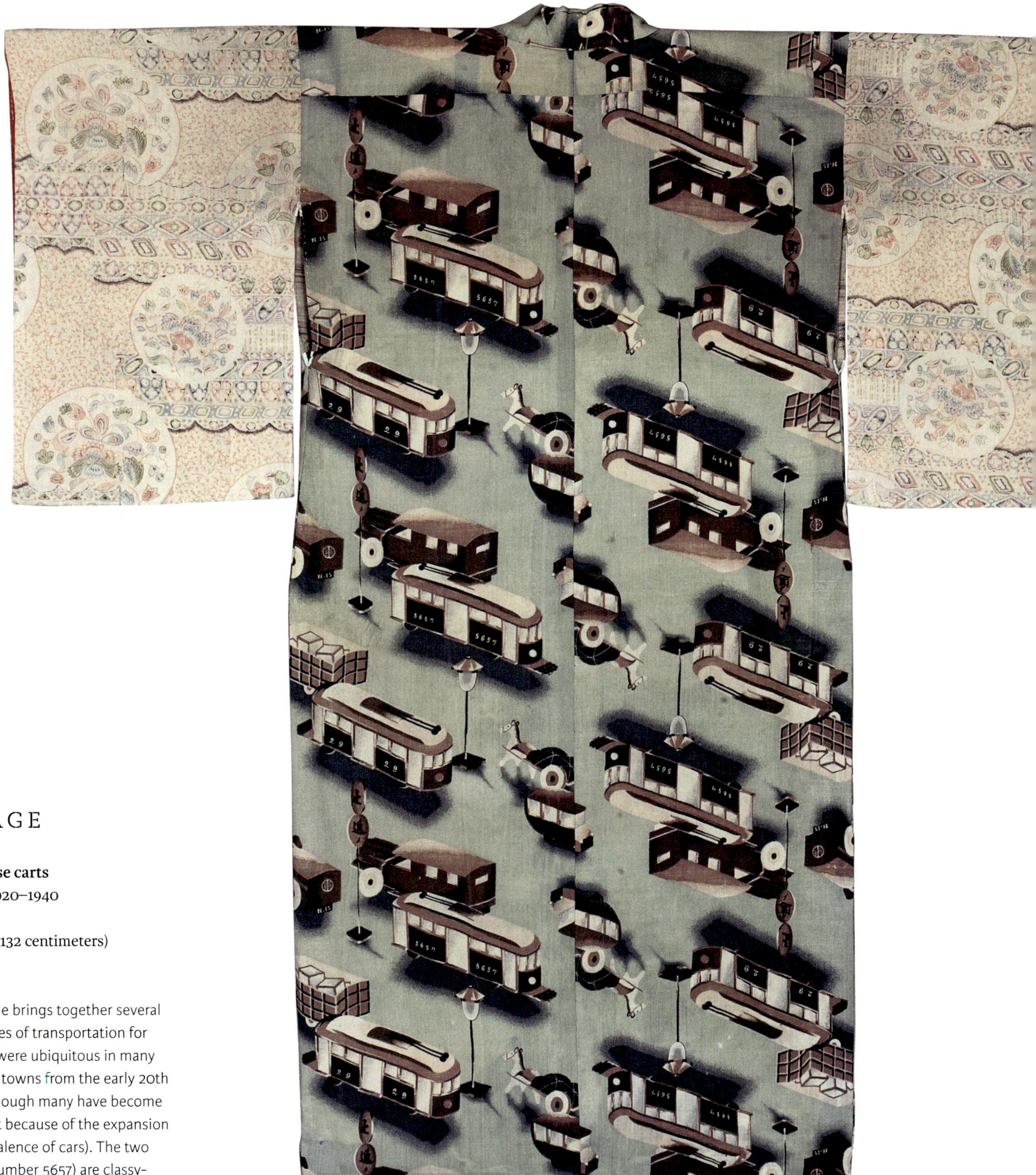

MACHINE AGE

Woman's *juban*
Trams, trucks, and horse carts
Taishō–Shōwa period, 1920–1940
Printed wool muslin
53.0 × 52.0 inches (135 × 132 centimeters)
KM153

This prettily colored textile brings together several new and interesting modes of transportation for Japan. Trams (streetcars) were ubiquitous in many of Japan's large cities and towns from the early 20th century to the 1960s, although many have become almost a thing of the past because of the expansion of subways (and the prevalence of cars). The two trams (Number 29 and Number 5657) are classy-looking and worthy of their time. In addition to trams, the streets pictured on this textile show many closed and open trucks, vans, and (perhaps for amusement) a small horse that proudly prances in the street as he pulls a two-wheeled cart loaded with goods.

MODERNITY

Man's *juban*
Factories on strike
Taishō–Shōwa period, 1920–1940
Kata-yūzen dyed silk
51.0 × 48.0 inches (130 × 122 centimeters)
KM154

This is a most interesting *juban*. It is a wonderful example of an *omoshirogara* (novelty) textile, both in terms of its unusual "patchwork" design and in the many elements that make up the overall composite image. There are hints of modernity, from the gears, belts, and smokestacks indicating industrialization and mass production, to the clusters of factories flanked by cranes that indicate future expansion is already poised to happen. Most of the text imagery in the design is advertisements for British manufacturers and suppliers of machinery or materials related to the textile industry. Overall, however, the entire design carries a sense of narrative and unrest, underscored by workers on strike who carry flags representative of the Communist Party.

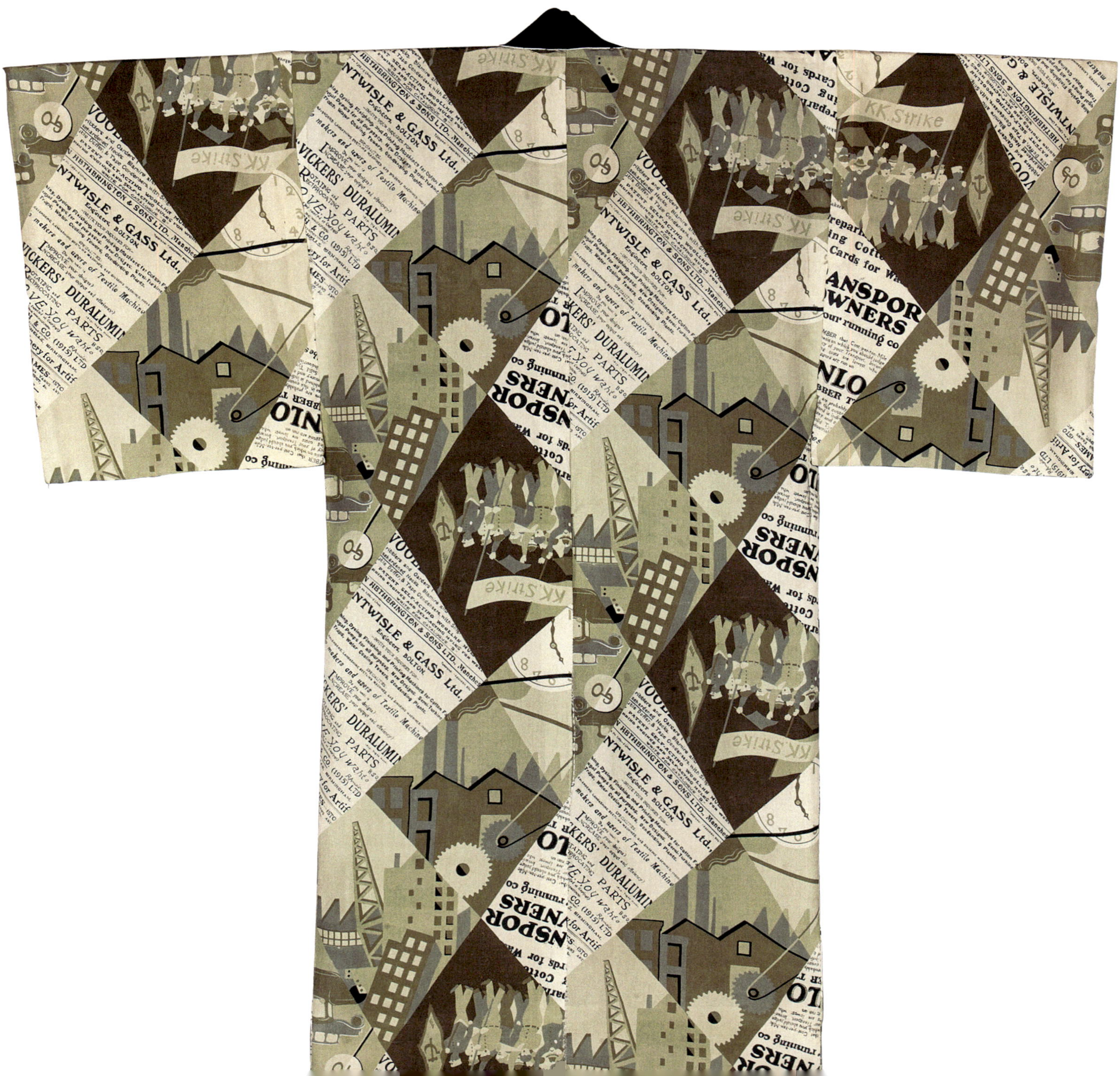

LEISURE TIME

Man's *haori* with a decorative lining
Women enjoying the bathhouse
Taishō–early Shōwa period, 1912–1930s
Silk plain weave *haori* (outer); *kata-yūzen*-dyed silk lining (interior)
48.0 × 40.0 inches (122 × 102 centimeters)
KM155

There is a sense of double entendre in regarding the images of the women in the communal bathhouse on the interior of this *haori*. The women bathing could be seen as enticing entertainment, but the printed sheet of paper is a program for a sumo contest—although one between men and women. The women are listed on the left side of the flyer, and the men are on the right, followed by their rankings, each of which, quite oddly, contains abstract descriptions of the genitalia of both the women and the men. This erotic fantasy is something that men may enjoy, but the ladies bathing might not be so happy should they see the interior of this *haori*.

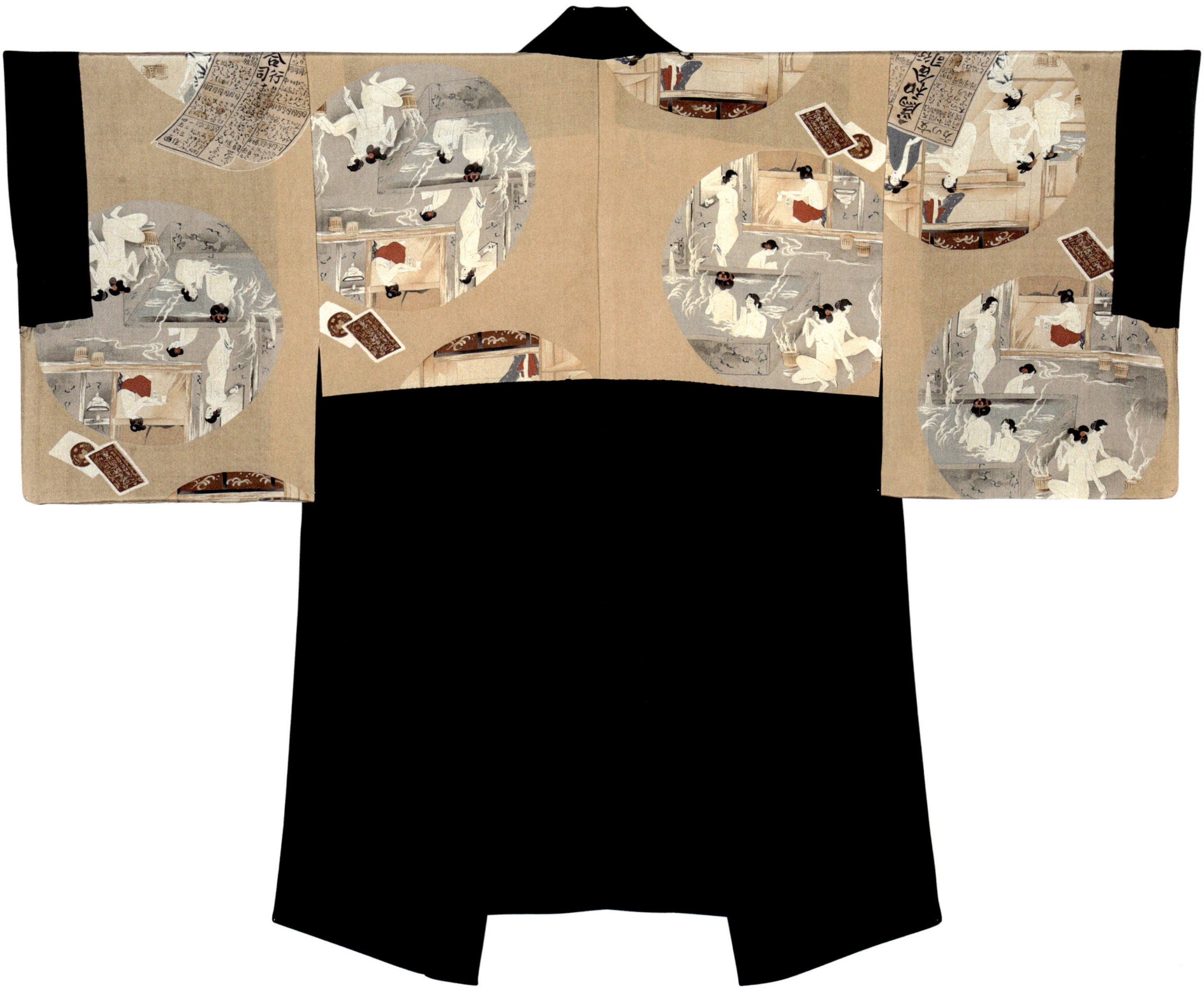

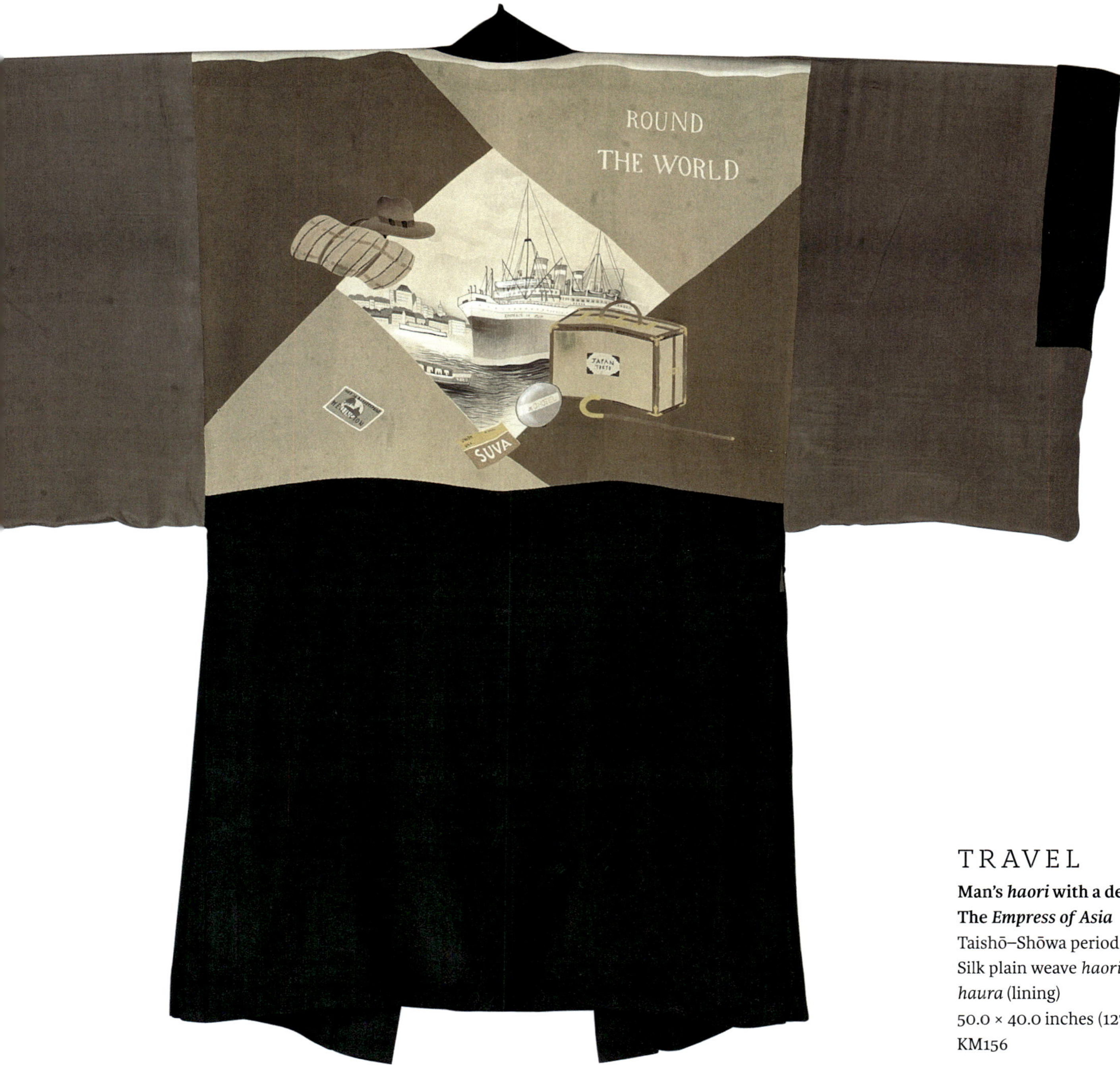

TRAVEL

Man's *haori* with a decorative lining (*haura*)
The *Empress of Asia*
Taishō–Shōwa period, 1920–1940
Silk plain weave *haori* (outer); *kata-yūzen*-dyed silk *haura* (lining)
50.0 × 40.0 inches (127 × 102 centimeters)
KM156

Travel had become almost an obsession for the Japanese in the 1920s and 1930s, and the design in this *haori* shows some of the intriguing places ripe for exploration. The *Empress of Asia*, an ocean liner owned by the Canadian Pacific Steamships Company, would be an ideal base for traveling the world. Choices for an exciting trip might be Wellington, New Zealand; Suva, Fiji; and a visit to the E&O Hotel, one of the most popular hotels in Malaysia. The traveler would probably be from Tokyo, as his luggage, hat, and blanket are already primed for travel. As well as being a passenger liner in peacetime, the *Empress of Asia* also served as an armed merchant cruiser and a troopship in wartime.

MACHINE AGE

Woman's *haori*
Stylized airplanes
Taishō–Shōwa period, 1920–1940
Yūzen-dyed silk with woven *urushi* metallic thread for the airplanes
48.0 × 39.5 inches (122 × 100 centimeters)
KM157

The stylized airplanes of this *haori* are drawn from playful patterns that flit over hazy white clouds backed by a black silk background. The patterns are woven of silver, copper, and gold metallic threads that shimmer as the silk of the *haori* moves with the woman who wears it. The *haori* also carries three crests on the back of the robe and two on the front; the design of the crest (or *mon*) is taken from *myōga*, a variant of the ginger family. Sometimes *myōga* is read as an audacious pun as, written with different ideographs, it also means "divine protection."

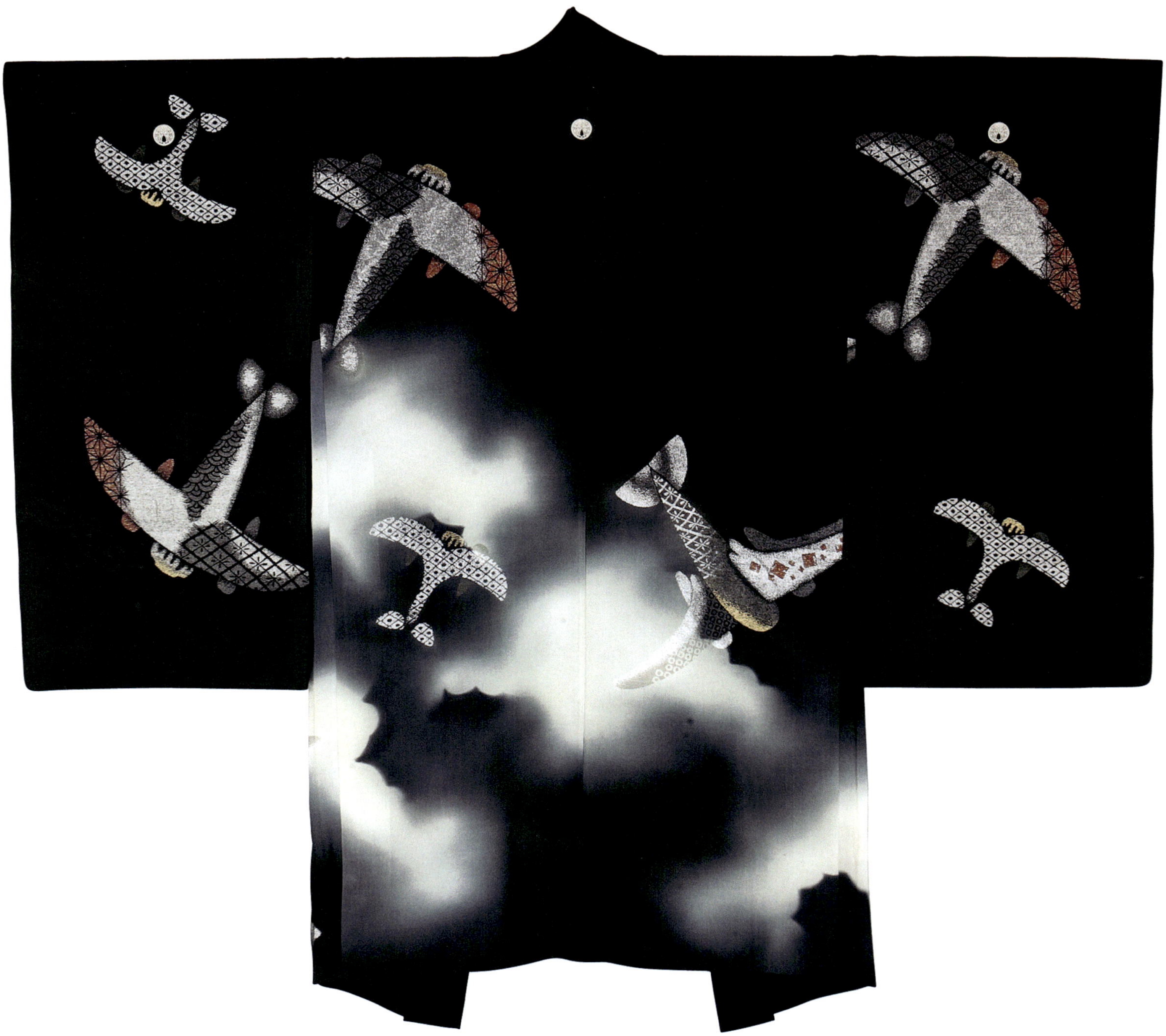

MODERNITY

Man's *haori* with a decorative lining (*haura*)
The old and the new
Taishō–early Shōwa period, 1920s–1930s
Silk plain weave *haori* (outer); *yūzen*-dyed and some hand-painted silk *haura* (lining)
54.0 × 44.1 inches (137 × 112 centimeters)
KM158

The artist who developed this scenic interior *haura* blends views of bridges and buildings, some old, some very new, as Japan moves from the Meiji past to the new Taishō future. The solid new bridge that spans the front of the *haura* carries iron posts with glowing lamps that light the city throughout the night; the older wooden bridge can be seen behind. The multi-storied building sits in the center of town, with traditional buildings behind, while Mount Fuji offers its ever-present dominance. The artist produced some very delicate shading for the hills at the back of the buildings and for the snow on the willows; the touches of silver on the other trees are also well done.

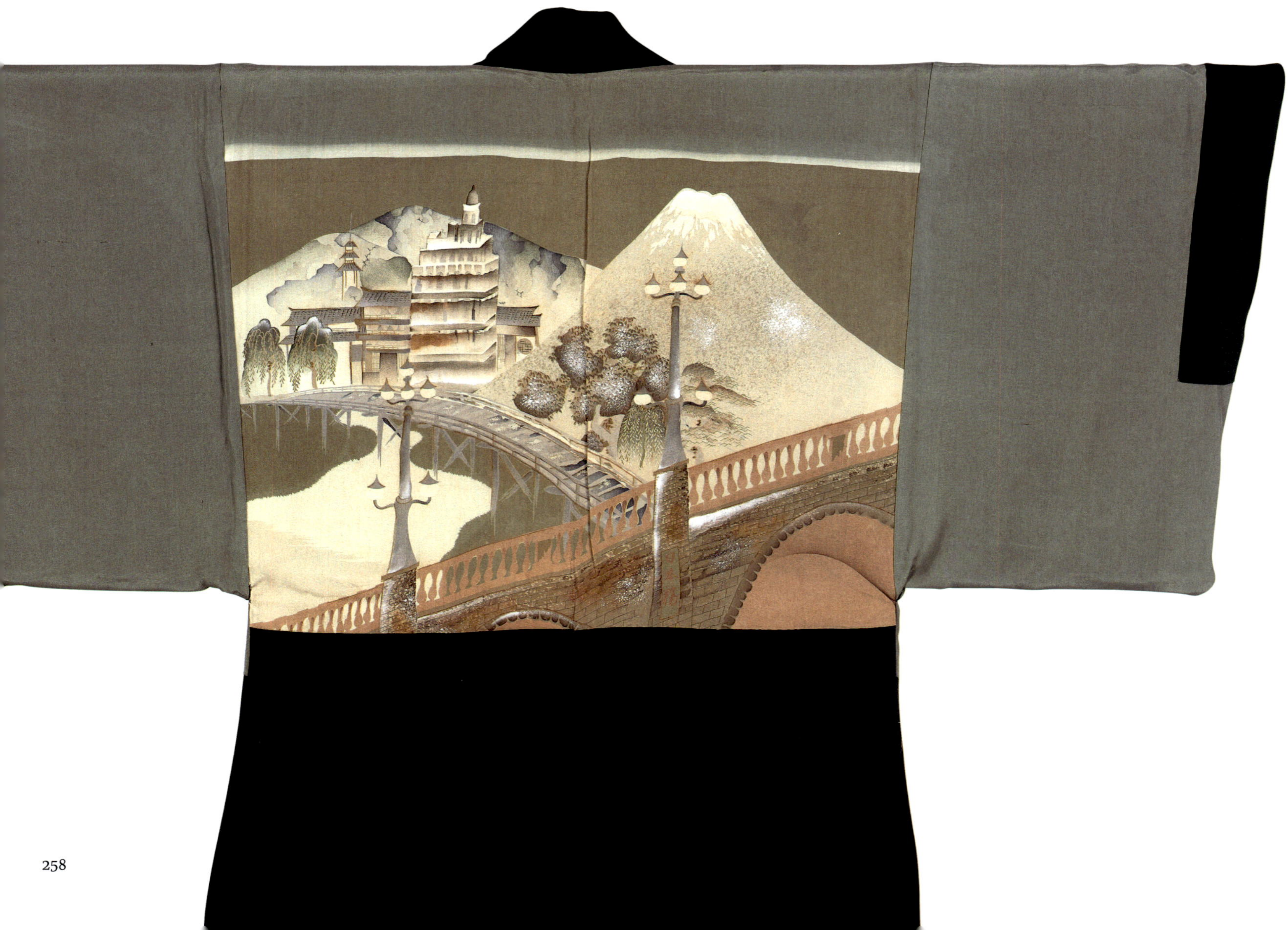

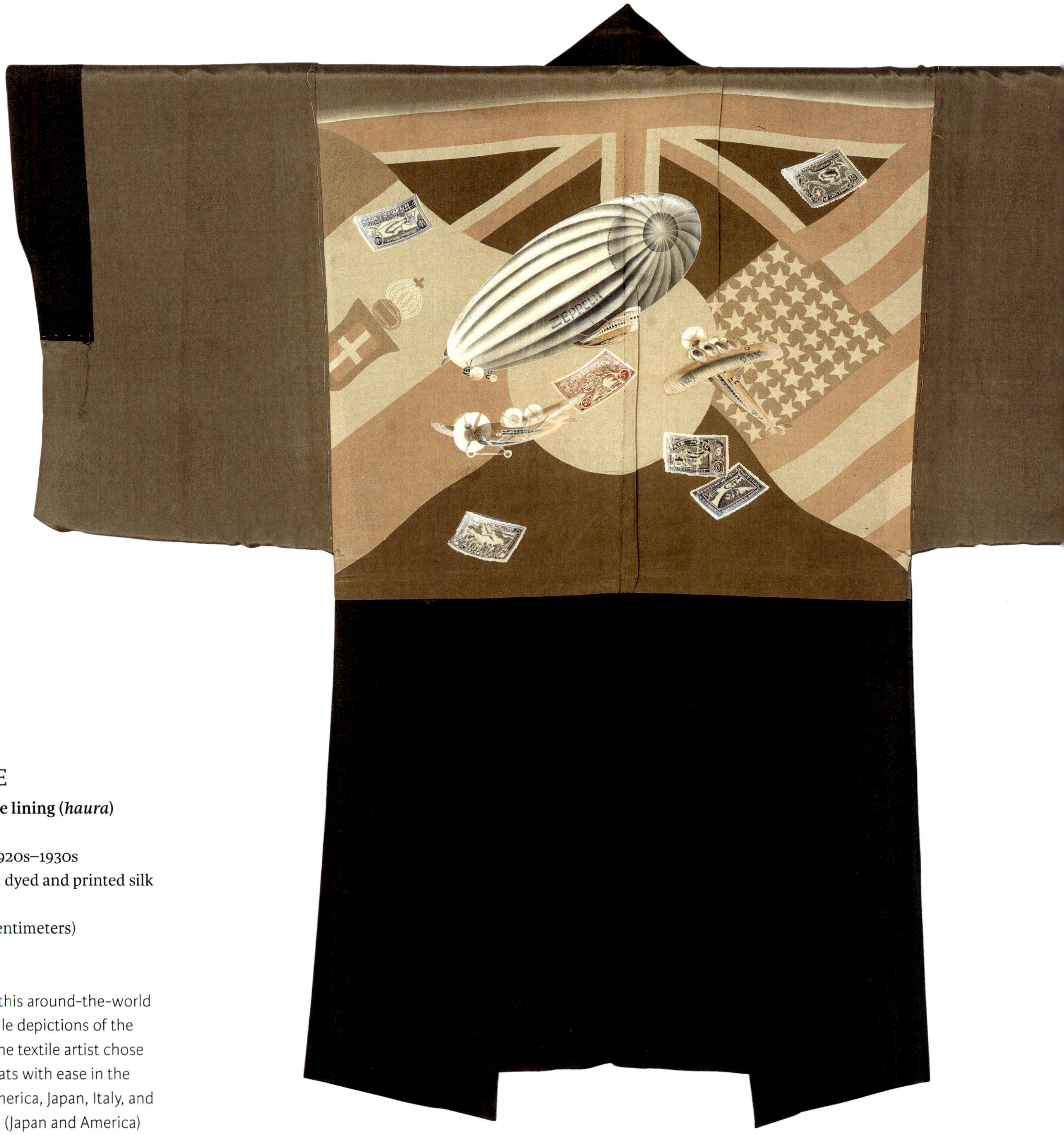

MACHINE AGE

Man's *haori* with a decorative lining (*haura*)
The *Graf Zeppelin* on tour
Taishō–early Shōwa period, 1920s–1930s
Silk plain weave *haori* (outer); dyed and printed silk *haura* (lining)
54.0 × 44.1 inches (137 × 112 centimeters)
KM159

The Japanese commemorated this around-the-world odyssey with many varied textile depictions of the beautiful *Graf Zeppelin*. Here, the textile artist chose to illustrate the airship as it floats with ease in the midst of four national flags: America, Japan, Italy, and the UK. Two of these countries (Japan and America) were visited by the *Graf Zeppelin* as part of the joint global publicity tour for William Randolph Hearst's newspaper empire and the Zeppelin Company.
The airship opened the tour on August 8, 1929, at Lakehurst, New Jersey, crossed the Atlantic Ocean, refueled at Friedrichshafen, Germany, then flew across Eastern Europe and Russia to Tokyo on a non-stop 102-hour leg covering 7,297 miles. There was no question that Tokyo had wildly excited throngs of people when the *Graf Zeppelin* came to visit their city for five days.

MODERNITY

Man's *haori* with a decorative lining (*haura*)
The Empire State Building in New York City
Taishō–Shōwa period, late 1920s–1930s
Silk plain weave *haori* (outer); *yūzen*-dyed and hand-painted silk *haura* (lining)
54.0 × 44.0 inches (137 × 112 centimeters)
KM160

This glorious Art Deco skyscraper is none other than the towering Empire State Building in New York City. The 102-story building is an American cultural icon, and when work was completed in 1931, it had reached a height of 1,454 feet. The mast on top was originally a mooring for dirigibles, which were considered to be the future of air travel in the 1930s. The textile artist who produced the rendering of this dramatic skyscraper for the *haori* also captured images of the many buildings that make up the city of New York. The artist added an unexpected feature for the *haura*: he sketched in the bevy of biplanes to cheer the opening of the Empire State Building.

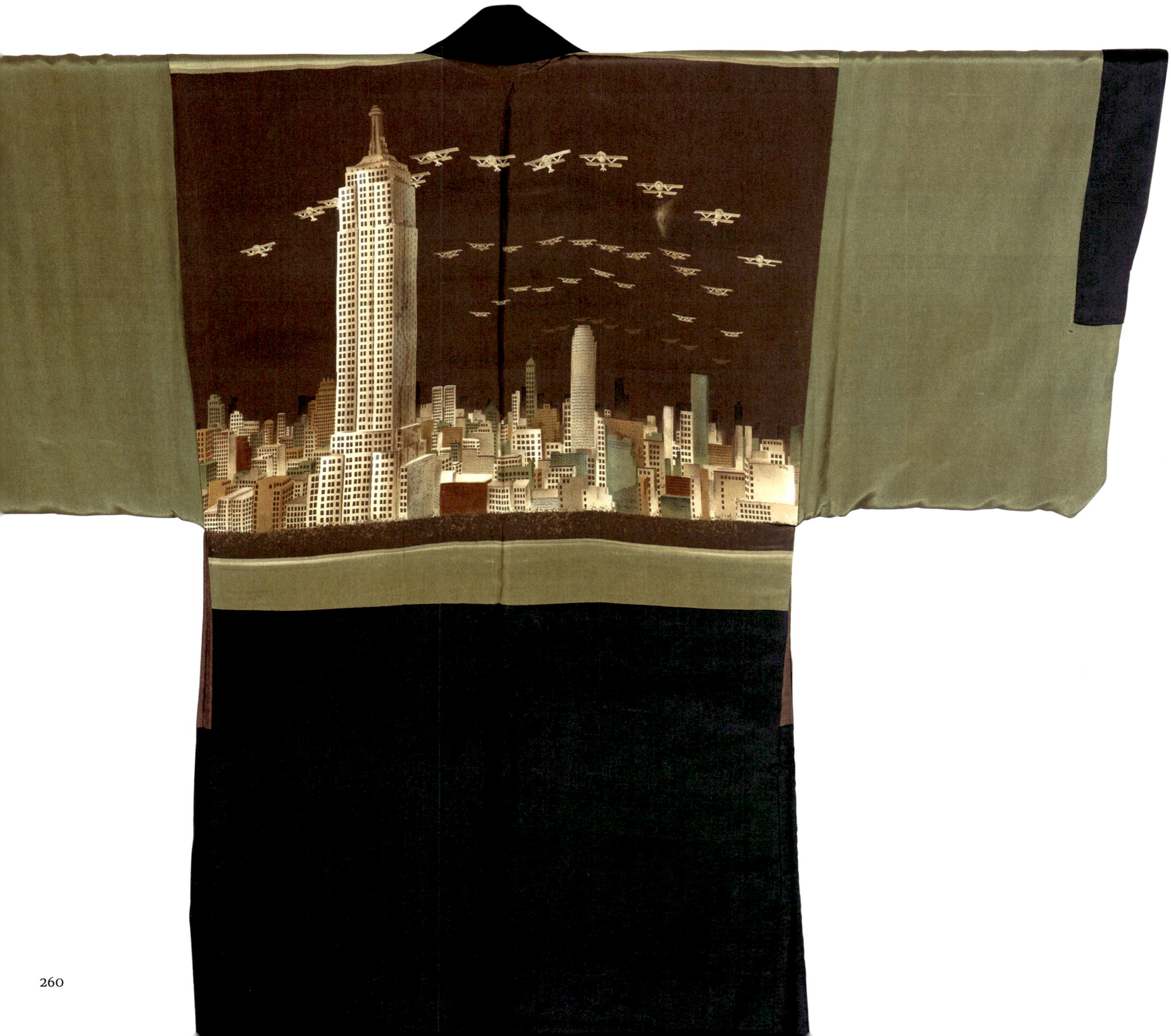

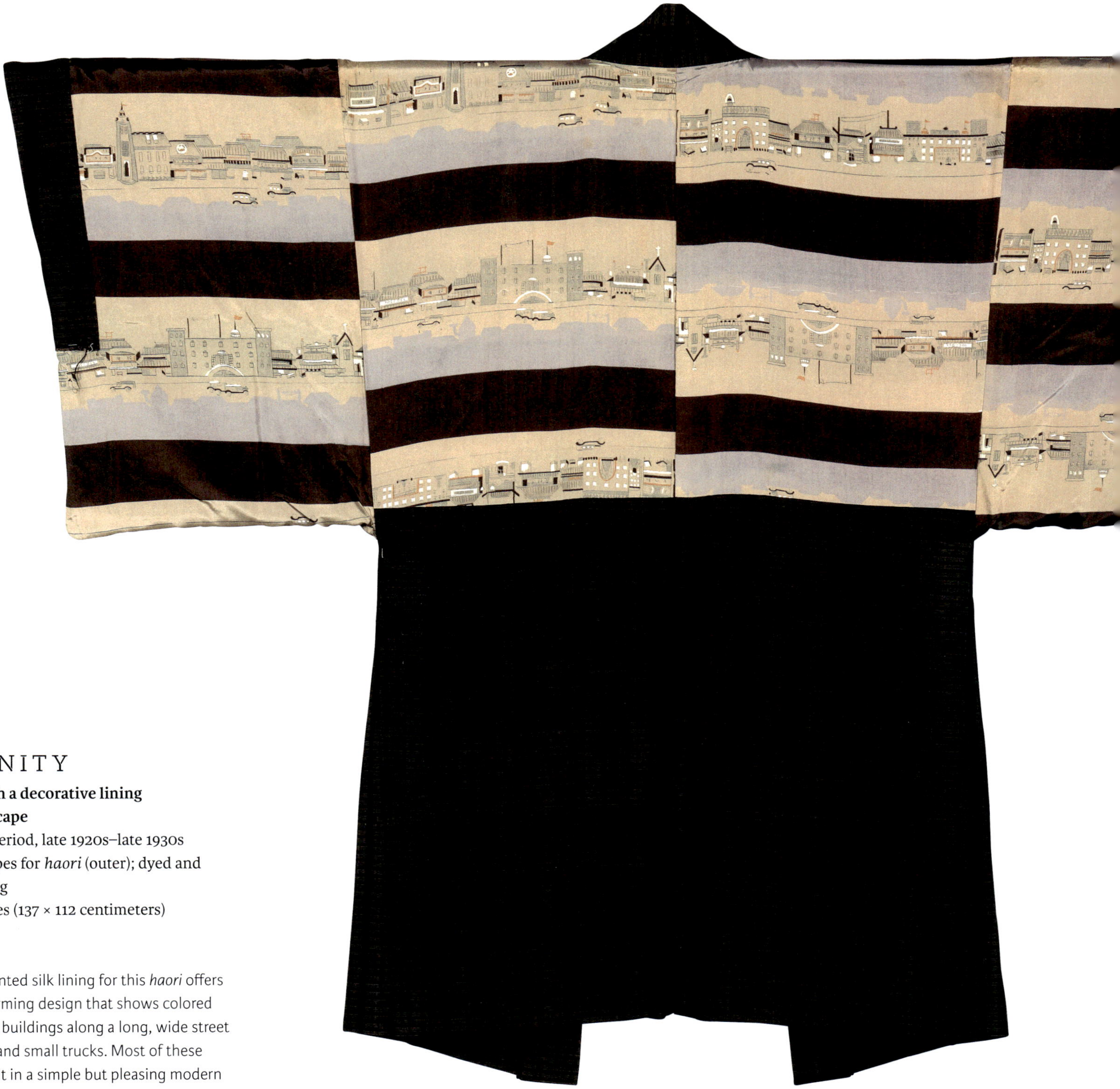

MODERNITY

Man's *haori* with a decorative lining
A modern cityscape
Taishō–Shōwa period, late 1920s–late 1930s
Dark woven stripes for *haori* (outer); dyed and printed silk lining
54.0 × 44.0 inches (137 × 112 centimeters)
KM161

The dyed and printed silk lining for this *haori* offers a simple but charming design that shows colored bands of modest buildings along a long, wide street that carries cars and small trucks. Most of these buildings are built in a simple but pleasing modern style. Many were clearly designed to be comfortable residential apartments, although here and there are some small office buildings and a church as well as traditional-style Japanese restaurants. The buildings sport telephone lines as well as electric lines, indicating that this area of the city has modern conveniences installed for the comfort of the neighborhood.

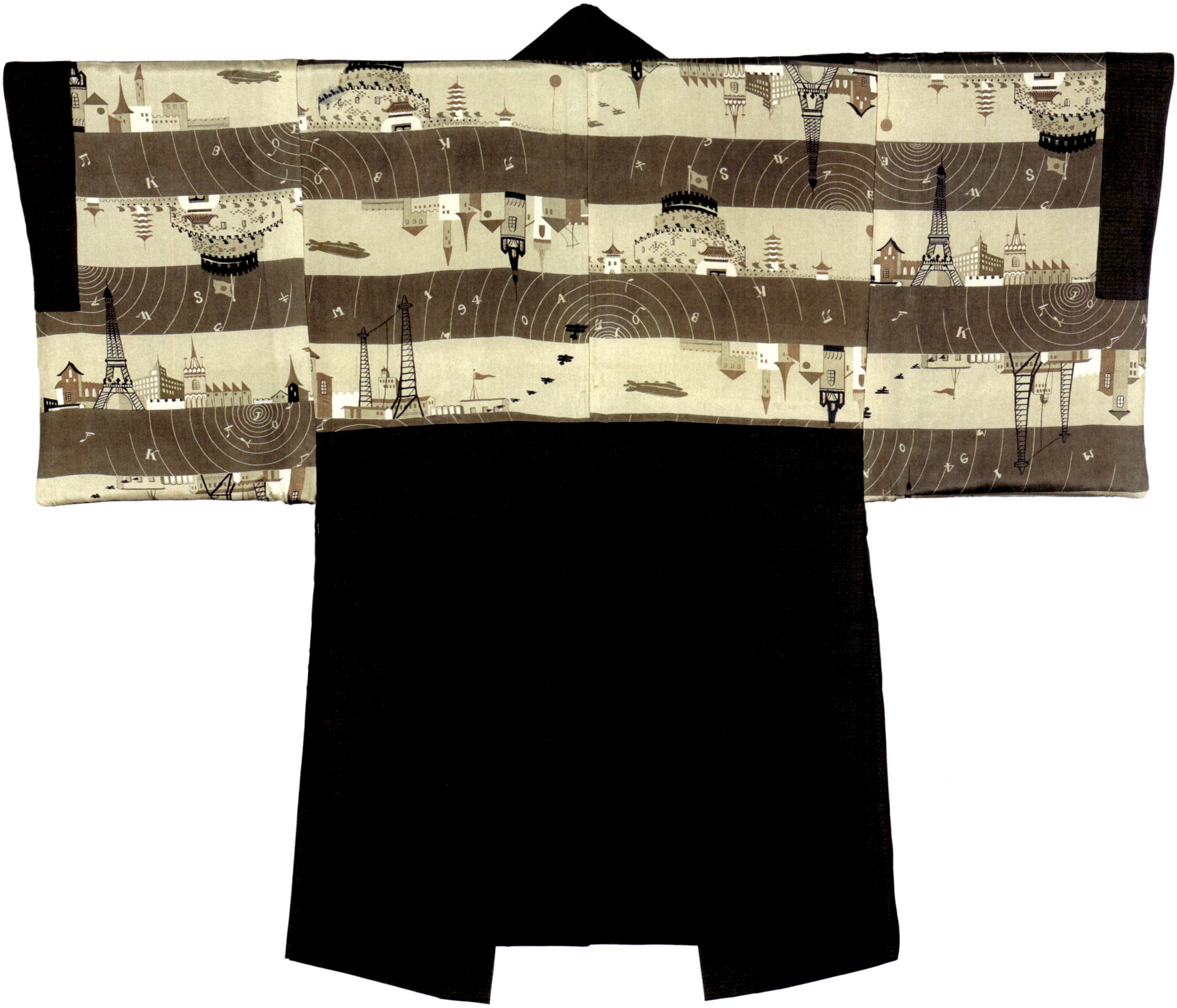

MACHINE AGE

Man's *haori* with a decorative lining
"JOAK! JOAK! JOKB! This is Tokyo Broadcasting."
Late Taishō–early Shōwa period, 1925
Heavy silk (outer); printed silk (inner lining)
50.0 × 44.0 inches (127 × 112 centimeters)
KM162

The design of the fabric used as a lining in this *haori* honors the first public radio address broadcast ever made in Japan. That broadcast was produced by the Tokyo Broadcasting Station on March 22, 1925, at 9:30 a.m. and used the station's call letters (JOAK and JOKB) to reach their audiences. The broadcasting station was intended to reach many faraway places, such as the Eiffel Tower in Paris and the lofty towers of Manchuria and China. The design of this *haori* lining captured the station's call letters flying through the air to create a fascinating picture of the voice of Tokyo throughout the world—a thrill for Japan in 1925.

ARCHITECTURE

Woman's *haori* with a decorative lining
Cityscape with houses, water towers, and telephone and electrical poles
Taishō–early Shōwa period, 1920s–1930s
Printed rayon (outer); *kata-yūzen* stencil-printed silk (interior)
50.0 × 36.0 inches (127 × 91 centimeters)
KM163

For many years, the *haori* was an exclusively male garment, but some women (primarily geisha) began to adopt this jacket style in the late Meiji period. By the early 1920s, however, women of all classes began to wear *haori* over their kimono as a matter of course, and this brightly colored jacket would no doubt have been coordinated with the wearer's kimono. The interior lining for this *haori* depicts a cityscape, indicating the growing modern amenities (electricity, telephones, Western-style houses) of the 1920s and 1930s that hinted at a more comfortable life for the Japanese.

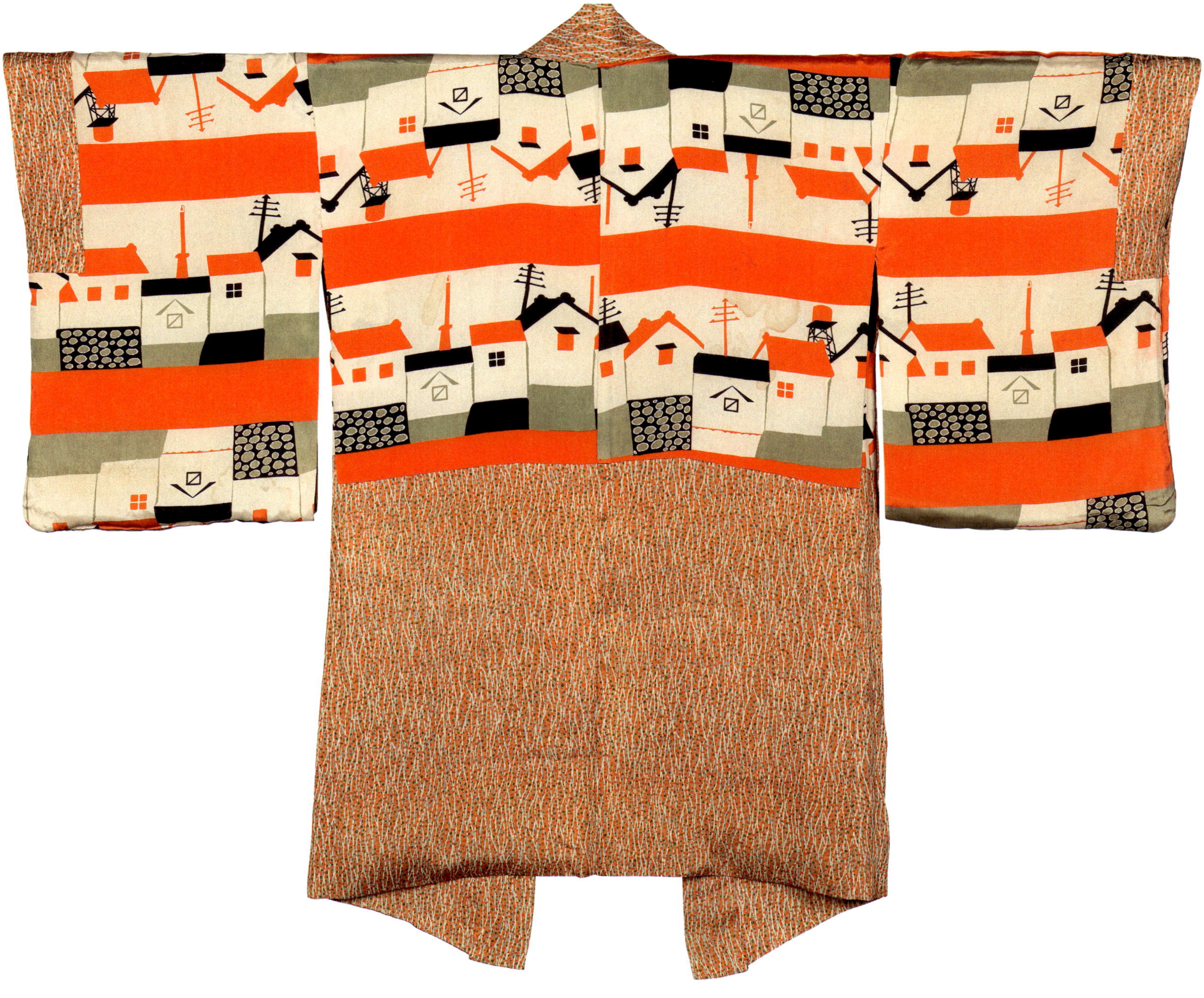

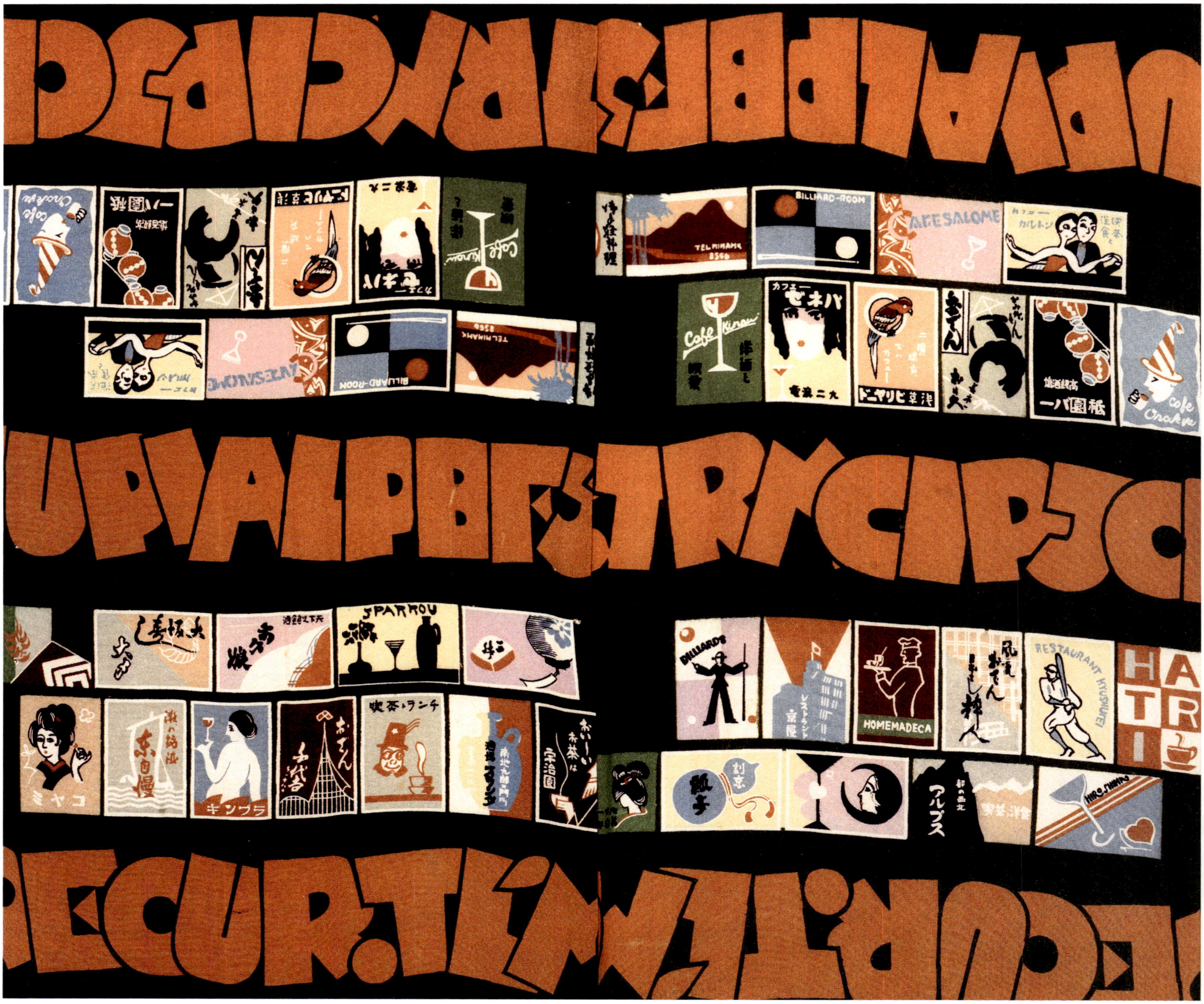

MODERNITY

Man's *juban*

Matchboxes with labels advertising a variety of activities

Taishō period, 1920s

Kata-yūzen stencil-printed silk fabric

57.0 × 49.0 inches (145 × 124 centimeters)

KM164

Men often chose designs for their *juban* that were entertaining, sometimes comical, and sometimes witty. The artist responsible for the design of this garment took a broad look at the many aspects of lively modern life in the early 20th century by copying matchbox covers that carry the names of bars, billiard rooms, restaurants, cafes, and coffee shops—places where drinking, dancing, and games can offer a wide range of diversions in the evenings. The play with letters taken from the Western alphabet show that the artist also had an uninhibited and playful sense of humor.

MODERNITY

Woman's obi

Cigarettes, cigars, pipe, and matchboxes

Late Taishō–early Shōwa period, 1920s–1930s

Kata-yūzen stencil-printed silk fabric

138.0 × 12.0 inches (351 × 30 centimeters)

KM165

In the early 20th century, foreign cigarettes, cigars, and pipes took an exciting hold among the *moga* ("modern girls") and *mobo* ("modern boys"), as well as some of the bolder members of the Japanese upper crust. Many similar products were also produced in Japan, but the more elegant of these foreign offerings, especially with those packed in stylish or well-designed boxes, gave distinction to those who could show them off. A woman with this obi might find it a charming and playful *omoshirogara* textile to pair with an equally stylish kimono.

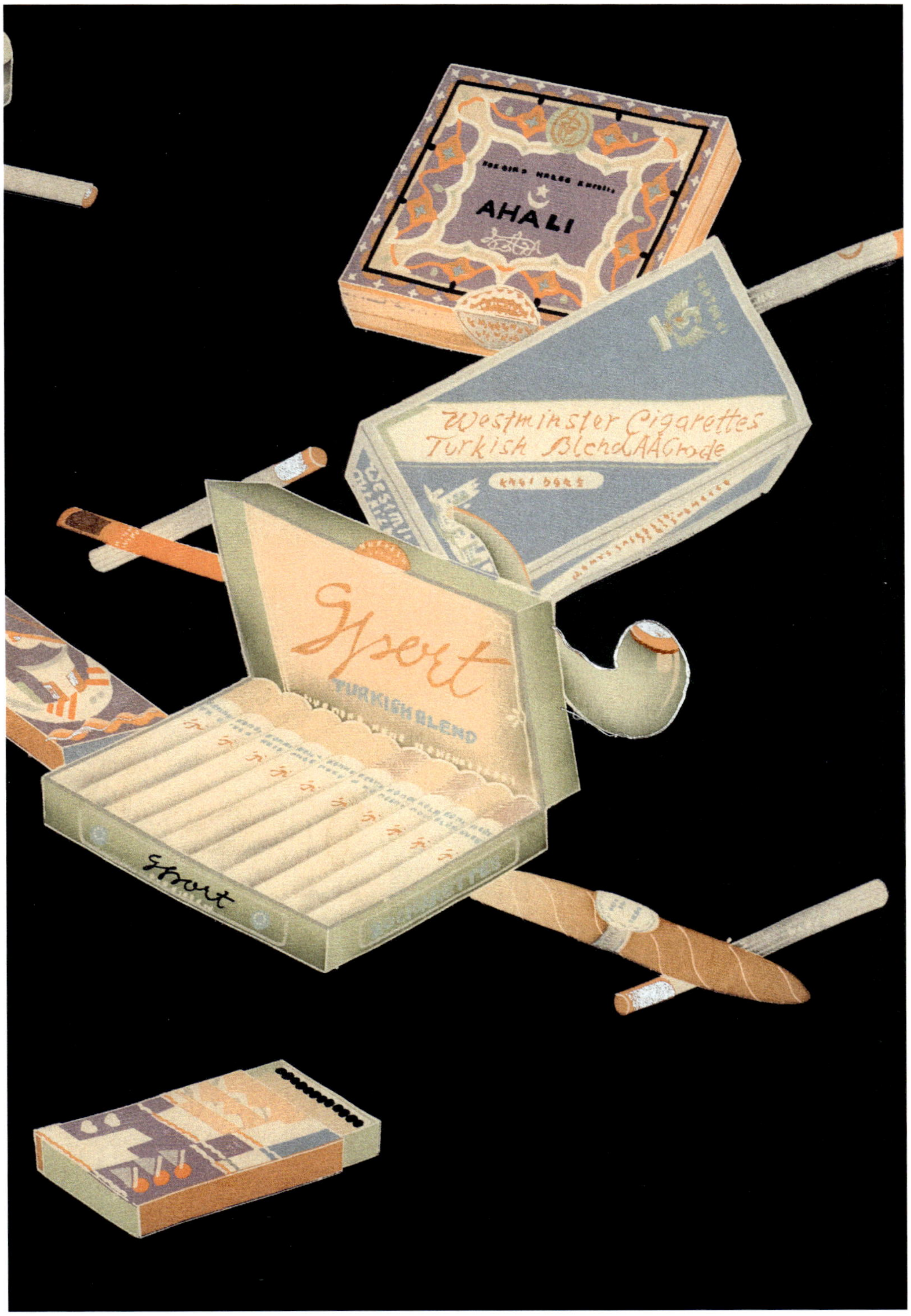

ENTERTAINMENT

Man's *haori* with a decorative lining (*haura*)
Dancers in a Ballroom
Taishō–early Shōwa period, 1924–1930
Silk *haori; yūzen*-dyed and hand-painted silk *haura* (lining)
50.0 × 45.0 inches (127 × 114 centimeters)
KM166

This garment is an excellent example of *omoshirogara*, as the many facets of modernity reflect Japan's growing cosmopolitanism through new and sophisticated urban pleasures. The artist apparently chose to base his *haura* design on a ballroom scene that appears in *Naomi*, a well-known novel by Junichiro Tanazaki.[1] The scene depicted is very similar to the book, with several women sitting on comfortable couches as they watch the dancers circling the room, and the men, who outnumber the women, wait on the sidelines for their opportunity to dance. The men are shown in Western formal evening attire. Several of the women show off pretty Western dresses that float with the dance and others wear elegant kimono with ornate designs. The city skyline of tall buildings in the background offers an additional element of modernity to the scene.

1. Tanizaki Junichiro, *Naomi*, Trans. Anthony H. Chambers (New York: Vintage, 2001; original Japanese publication serialized in *Osaka Asahi* (newspaper) and *Josei* (women's magazine), 1924–25.

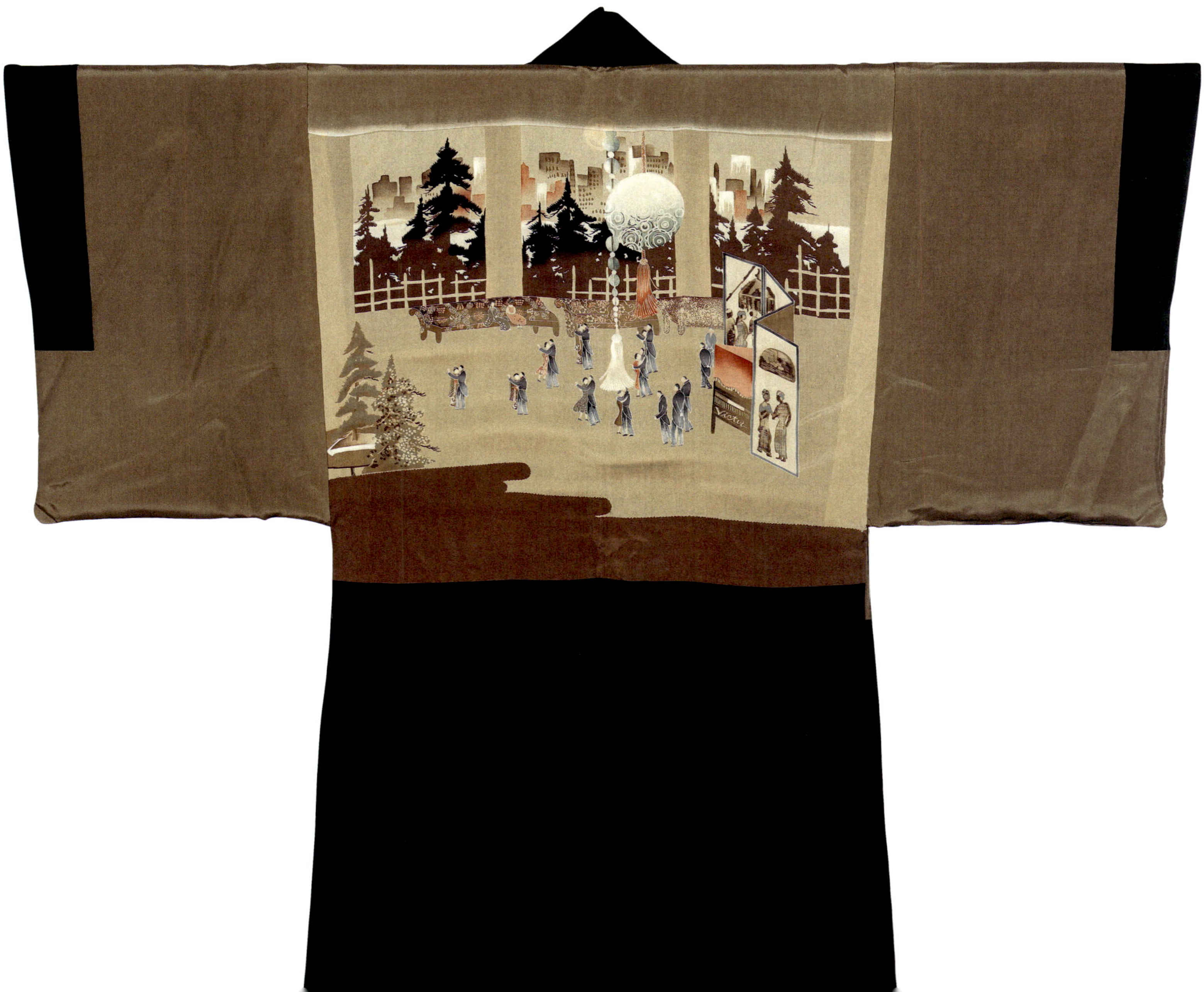

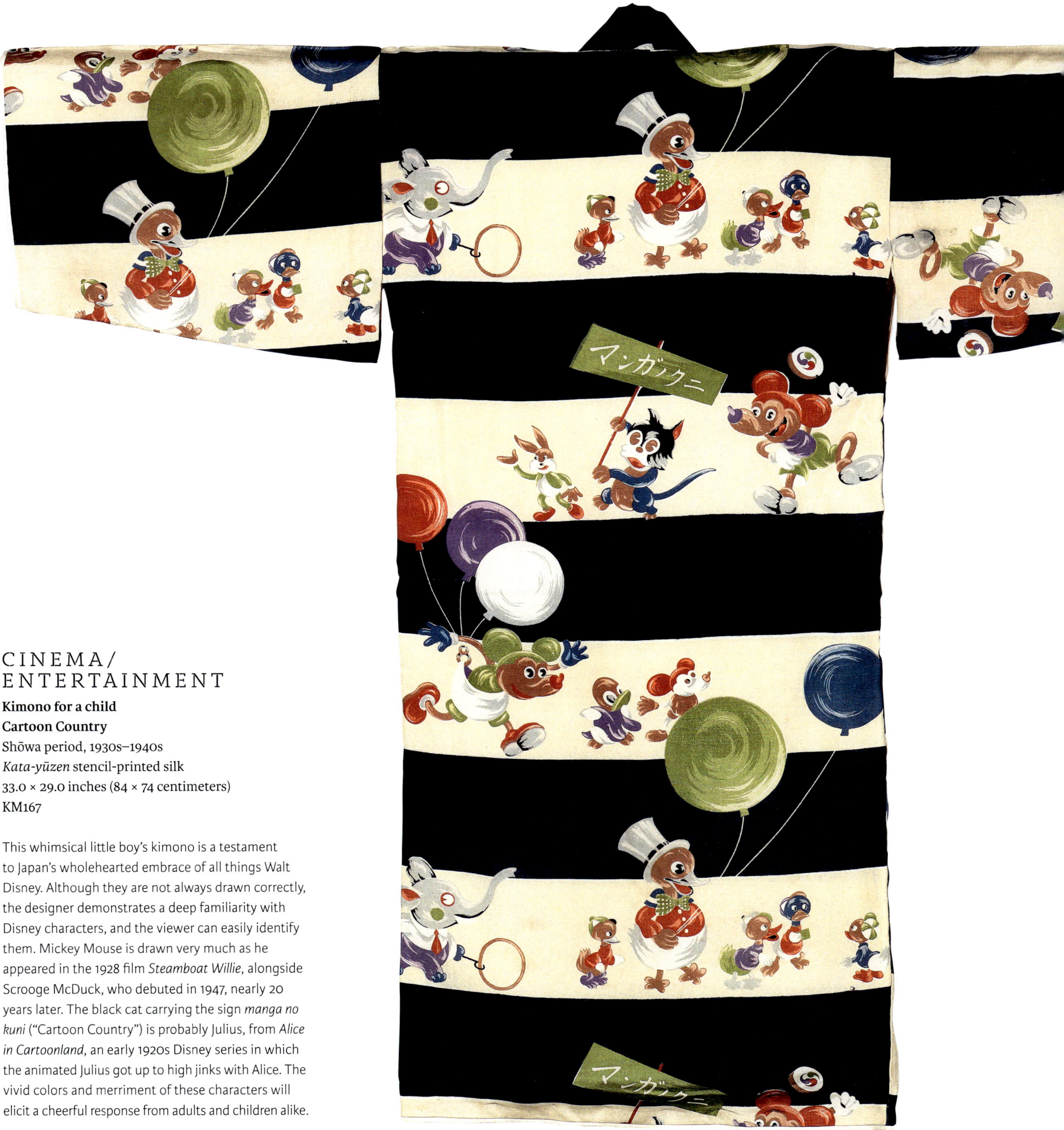

CINEMA/ ENTERTAINMENT

Kimono for a child
Cartoon Country
Shōwa period, 1930s–1940s
Kata-yūzen stencil-printed silk
33.0 × 29.0 inches (84 × 74 centimeters)
KM167

This whimsical little boy's kimono is a testament to Japan's wholehearted embrace of all things Walt Disney. Although they are not always drawn correctly, the designer demonstrates a deep familiarity with Disney characters, and the viewer can easily identify them. Mickey Mouse is drawn very much as he appeared in the 1928 film *Steamboat Willie*, alongside Scrooge McDuck, who debuted in 1947, nearly 20 years later. The black cat carrying the sign *manga no kuni* ("Cartoon Country") is probably Julius, from *Alice in Cartoonland*, an early 1920s Disney series in which the animated Julius got up to high jinks with Alice. The vivid colors and merriment of these characters will elicit a cheerful response from adults and children alike.

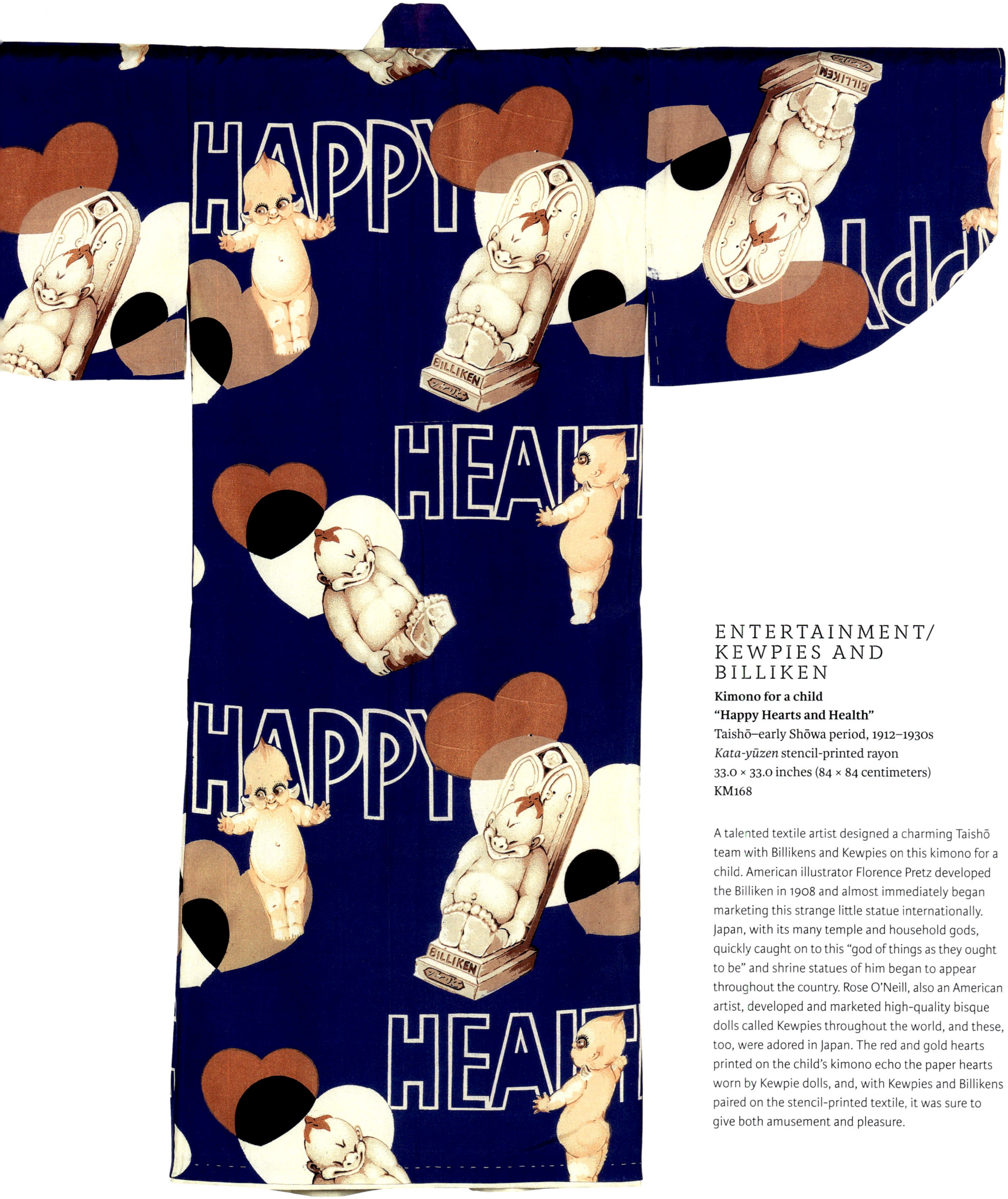

ENTERTAINMENT/ KEWPIES AND BILLIKEN

Kimono for a child
"Happy Hearts and Health"
Taishō–early Shōwa period, 1912–1930s
Kata-yūzen stencil-printed rayon
33.0 × 33.0 inches (84 × 84 centimeters)
KM168

A talented textile artist designed a charming Taishō team with Billikens and Kewpies on this kimono for a child. American illustrator Florence Pretz developed the Billiken in 1908 and almost immediately began marketing this strange little statue internationally. Japan, with its many temple and household gods, quickly caught on to this "god of things as they ought to be" and shrine statues of him began to appear throughout the country. Rose O'Neill, also an American artist, developed and marketed high-quality bisque dolls called Kewpies throughout the world, and these, too, were adored in Japan. The red and gold hearts printed on the child's kimono echo the paper hearts worn by Kewpie dolls, and, with Kewpies and Billikens paired on the stencil-printed textile, it was sure to give both amusement and pleasure.

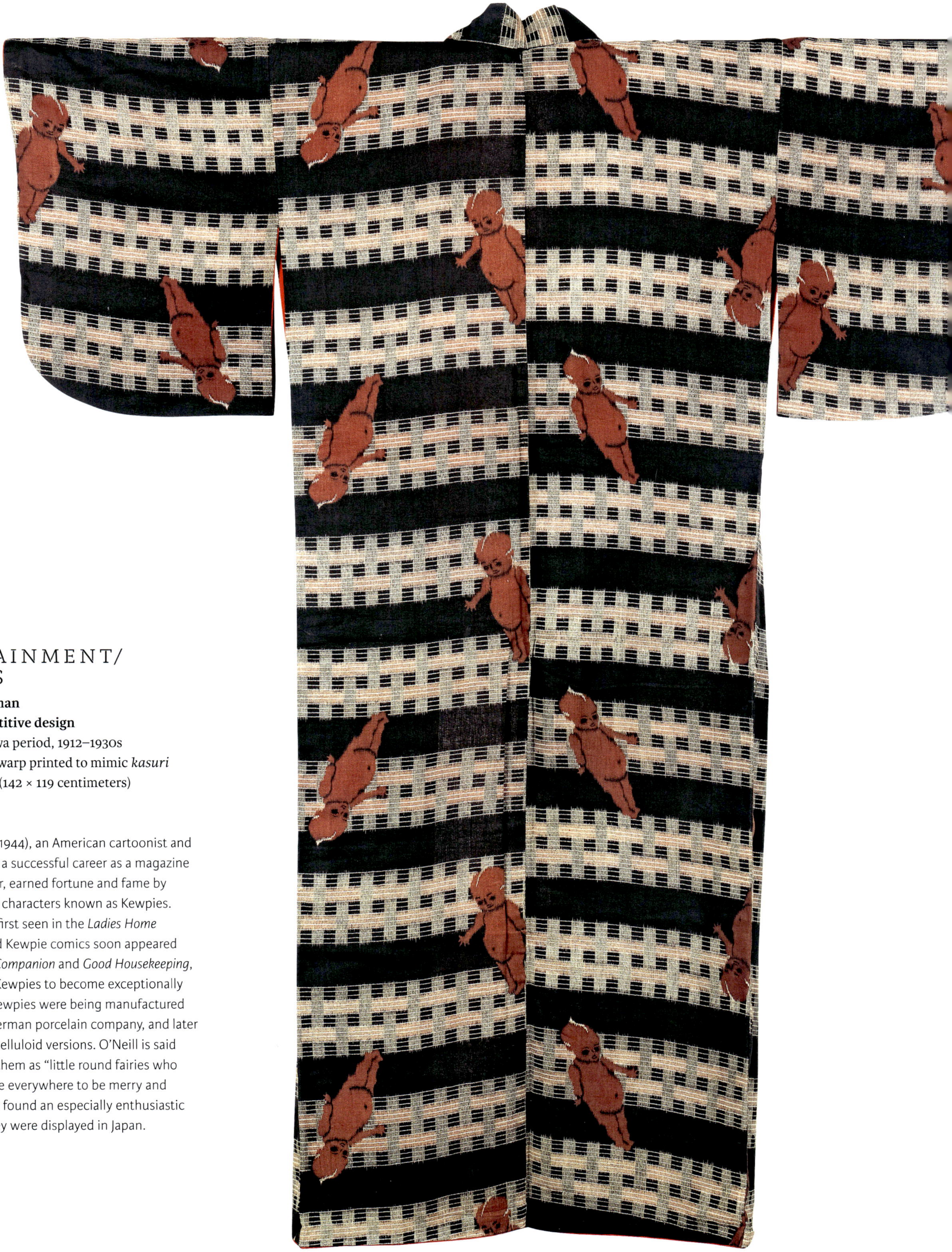

ENTERTAINMENT/ KEWPIES

Kimono for a woman
Kewpies in a repetitive design
Taishō–early Shōwa period, 1912–1930s
Cotton, *niko-niko* warp printed to mimic *kasuri*
56.0 × 47.0 inches (142 × 119 centimeters)
KM169

Rose O'Neill (1874–1944), an American cartoonist and designer who built a successful career as a magazine and book illustrator, earned fortune and fame by creating whimsical characters known as Kewpies. Her Kewpies were first seen in the *Ladies Home Journal* in 1909, and Kewpie comics soon appeared in *Woman's Home Companion* and *Good Housekeeping*, which helped the Kewpies to become exceptionally popular. By 1912, Kewpies were being manufactured as figurines by a German porcelain company, and later were produced in celluloid versions. O'Neill is said to have described them as "little round fairies who would teach people everywhere to be merry and kind." Her Kewpies found an especially enthusiastic audience when they were displayed in Japan.

ENTERTAINMENT/ KEWPIES

***Juban* for a woman**
Happy Kewpies in Japanese dress
Taishō–early Shōwa period, 1912–1930s
Kata-yūzen stencil-printed silk
51.0 × 50.0 inches (130 × 127 centimeters)
KM170

Kewpie dolls, as noted earlier, were a highly successful 1908 product by Rose O'Neill, an American artist. O'Neill engineered her first introduction of Kewpies made of unglazed porcelain in German factories, and they were an immediate international hit. By 1913, the Kewpie craze had swept across the globe, but when World War I began, O'Neill realized that it was impractical to import dolls from Germany, and so moved production to factories in England, France, the United States, and Japan. Her Kewpies were favorites among the Japanese, and, as can be seen in this lively textile design for a *juban*, dressing the sweetly smiling Kewpies in festival garments made them even more appreciated by the Japanese audience.

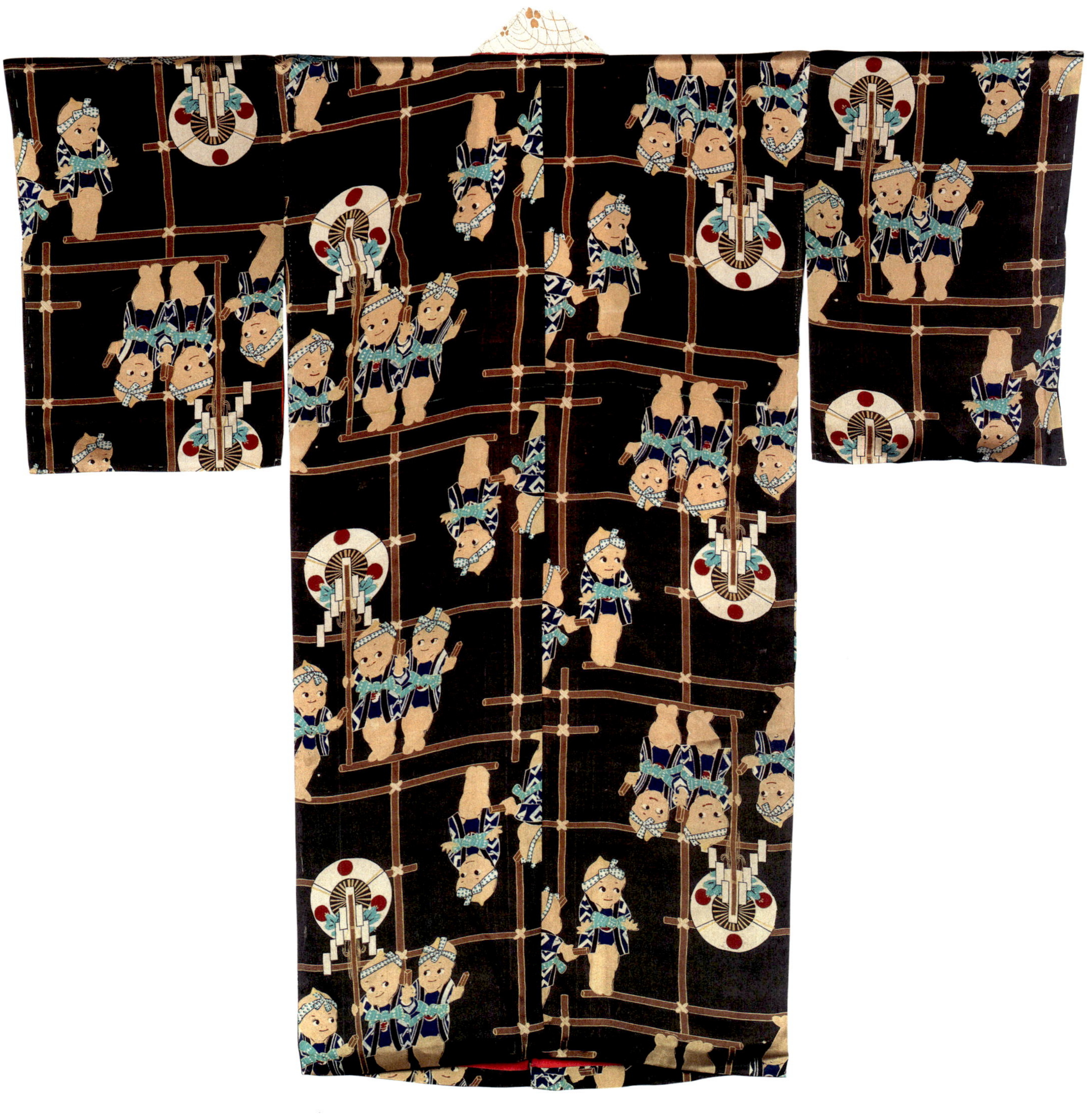

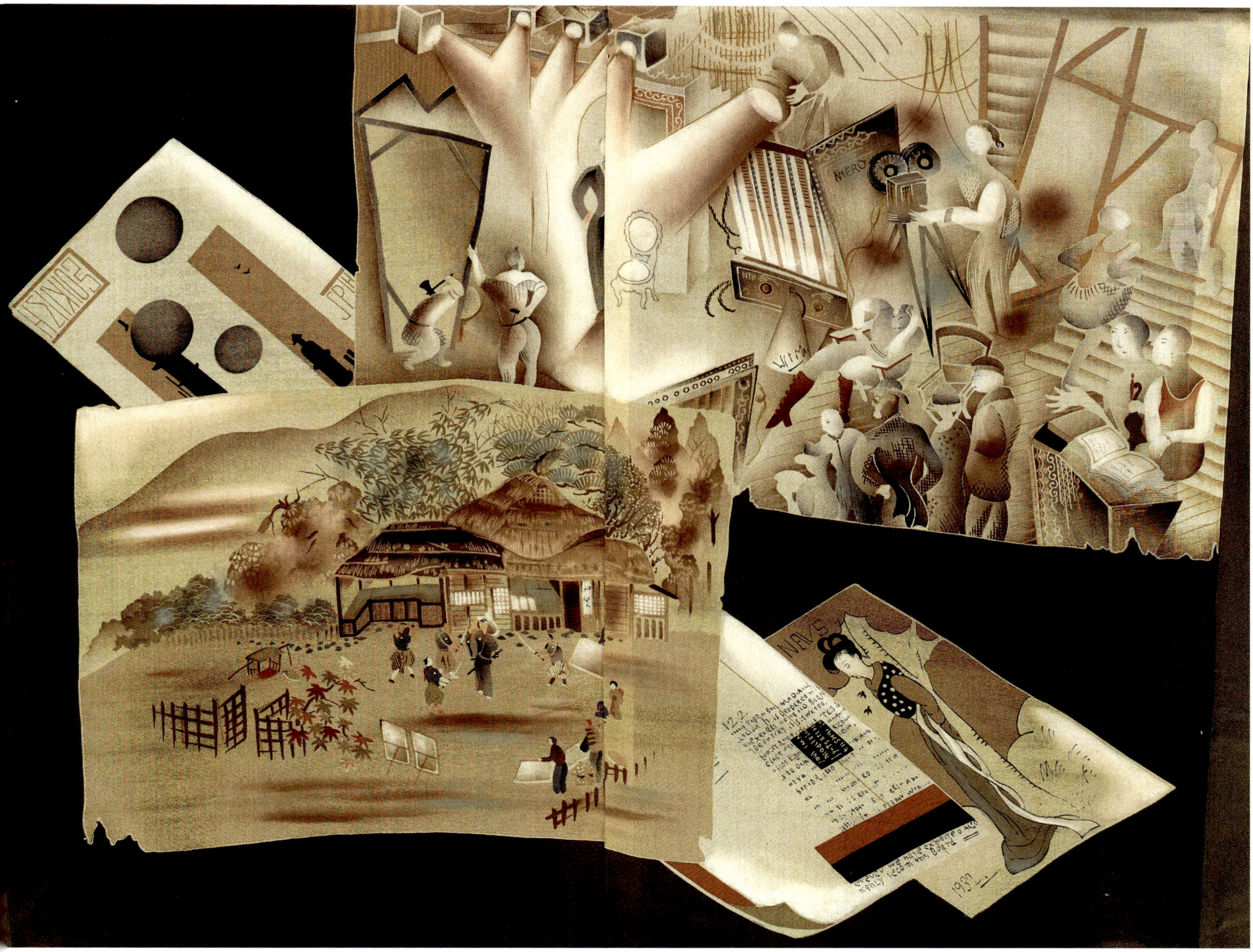

MODERNITY AND TRADITION/ THE CINEMA

Man's *haori* with a decorative lining (*haura*)
Filming for the cinema: modernity and tradition
Taishō–early Shōwa period, late 1920s–early 1930s
Silk *haori* (outer); *kata-yūzen* dyed and stencil-printed silk *haura* (lining)
51.0 × 43.0 inches (130 × 109 centimeters)
KM171

Motion pictures were a benchmark of modernity for the Japanese population in the 1930s. In this *haori*, the *haura* features two vignettes that show glimpses behind the scenes of movie-making. One shows a stylized rendition of the controlled chaos of filming a musical extravaganza on a soundstage, replete with actors, dancers, cameramen, and more; the other presents an outdoor setting for the filming of an historical samurai drama, complete with thatched-roof huts and sword-wielding actors in traditional clothing. The sharp contrast of the modern and the traditional was elegantly captured by the artist who created these scenes.

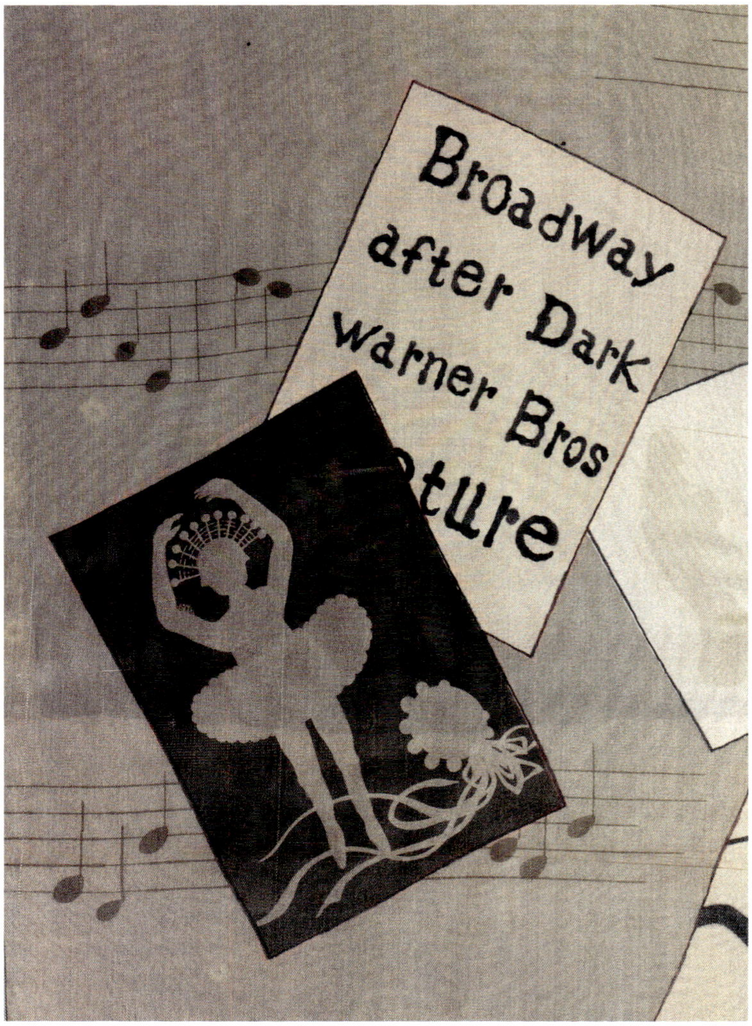

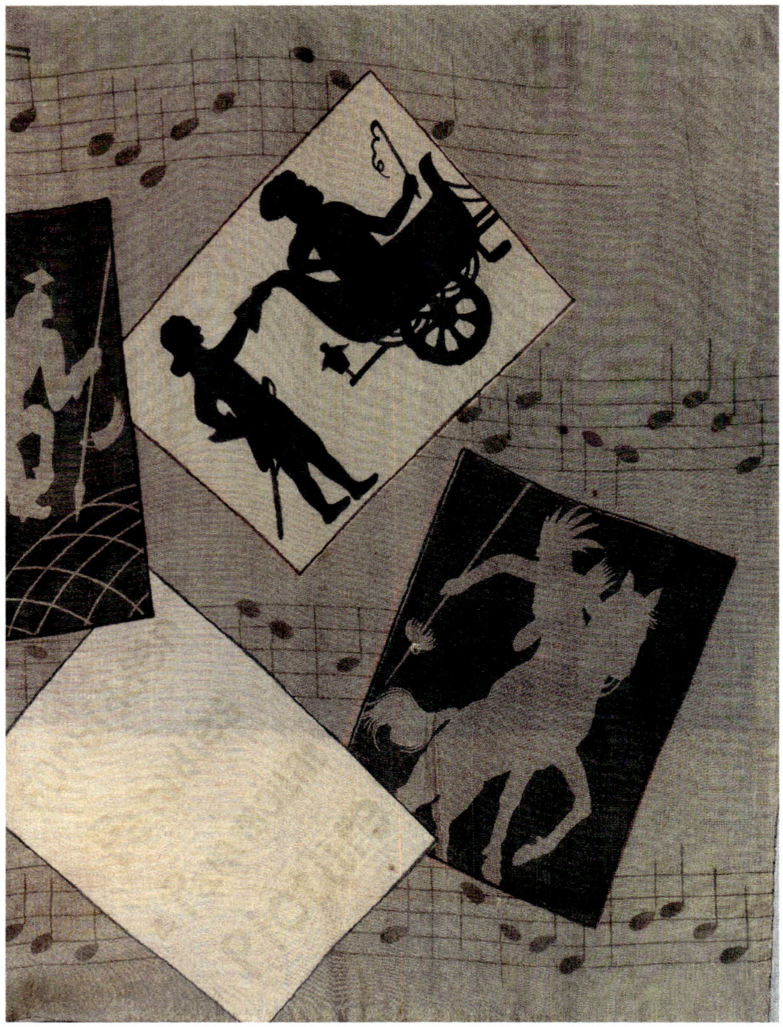

THE CINEMA/ ENTERTAINMENT

Man's *haori* with a decorative lining (*haura*)
Broadway After Dark
Taishō–early Shōwa period, 1920s–1930s
Oshima silk (outer); *kata-yūzen* stencil-printed silk *haura* (lining)
51.0 × 50.0 inches (130 × 127 centimeters)
KM172

The artist who produced the lively motifs on the lining of this *haori* chose advertising posters and silhouette cards made to promote two Hollywood movies: *Broadway After Dark*, from Warner Bros. Studios, and *Forbidden Paradise*, from Paramount Pictures. Both were produced in the 1920s, and the musical background probably relates to the melodies in the films. This *haori*, like several other *haori* in this book, is considered an informal garment. The outer textile is not a solid black silk, but silk pongee, a fabric tied, dyed, and woven to create very small geometric designs typical of Oshima silk. These tiny designs came into favor in the Edo era for the samurai class, and they continue to be popular today in male dress.

MODERNITY/ ENTERTAINMENT

Woman's *haori* with decorative lining
Japanese movie stars
Late Taishō–early Shōwa period, 1920s–1930s
Printed silk (outer); photo transfer rayon lining
48.0 × 35.0 inches (122 × 89 centimeters)
KM173

As Japan modernized, photographs of popular actresses and actors quickly took the place of the woodblock prints of favorite kabuki actors of earlier years. The textile interior of this *haori* shows photos of a lovely young actress who may have only recently started in the film industry. The smiling older woman who stands close to the young actress is quite possibly her mother, as she wears a kimono. The actress wears a jaunty little cloche on her head and pearls around her neck, appropriately modern dress for an actress. The bright orange textile carries images of numerous cards and notes, probably related to films in which the actress appeared.

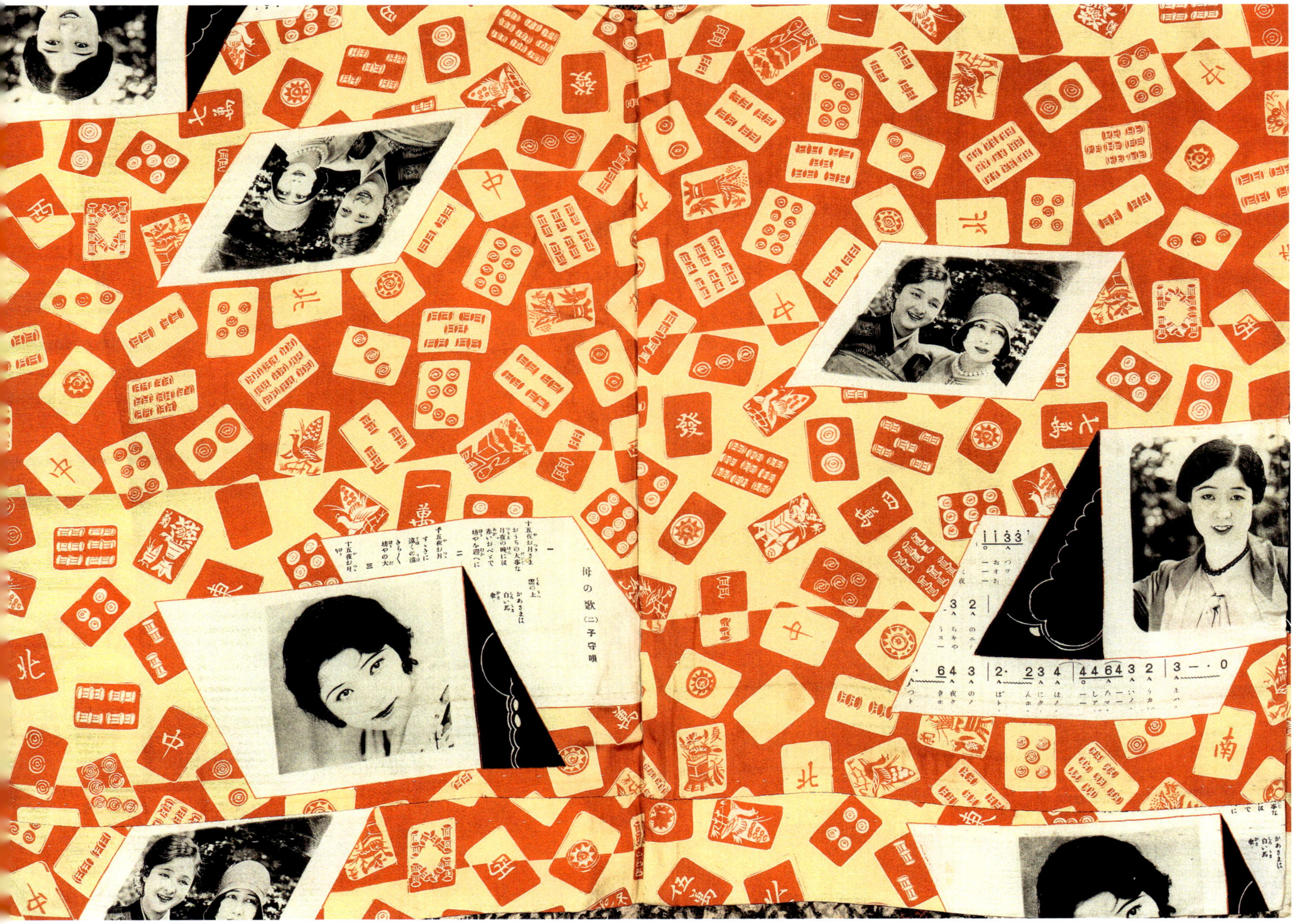

SPORTS

***Juban* for a man**
Baseball on the radio
Taishō–Shōwa period, 1920s–1940
Kata-yūzen stencil-printed silk; thin threaded metallic strips
52.5 × 49.5 inches (133 × 126 centimeters)
KM174

The man who wears this elegant *juban* is probably a great fan of baseball. If he could not attend games in person, he could listen to them on the radio. The design on this *juban* shows what a radio might have looked like in 1925. The "horn" strengthens the sound so listeners can clearly hear the announcer as he narrates what is happening on the baseball field. Additional designs show other baseball players, the umpire, and the scoreboard, all part of the excitement of the game. On the lower part of the *juban*, a band woven in thin metallic strips gives an exciting sheen to that part of the garment.

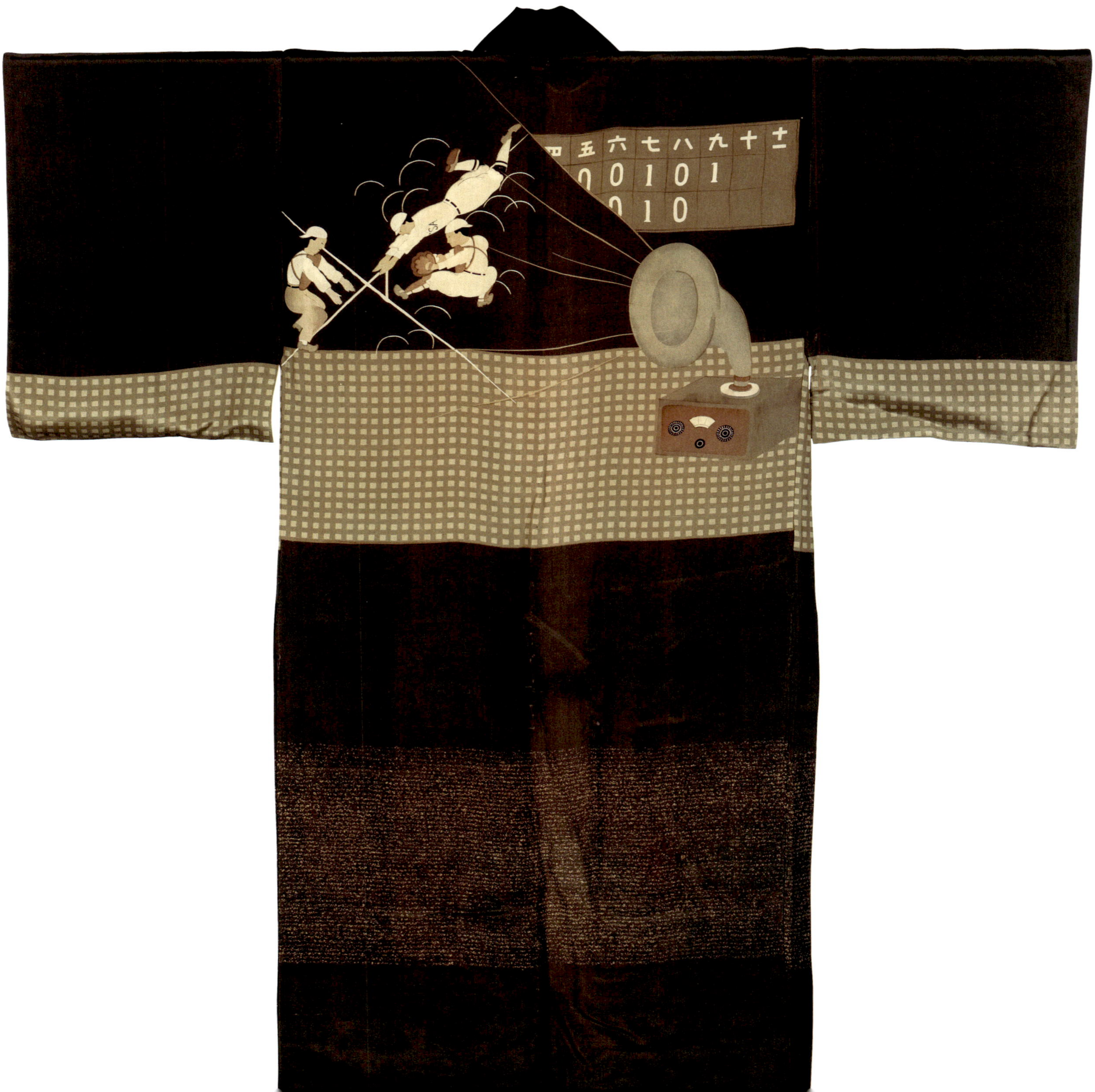

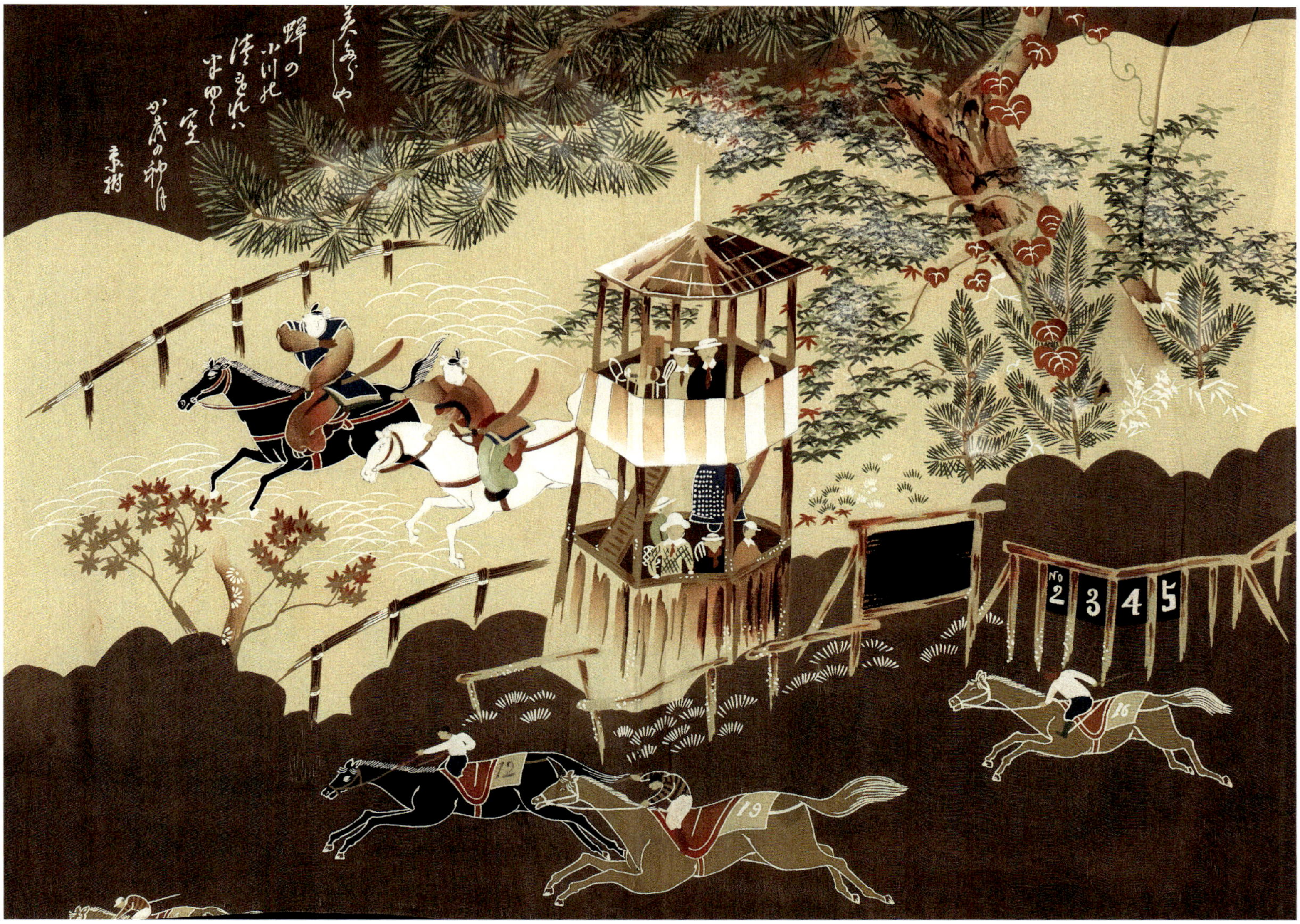

SPORTS/HORSE RACING

Man's *haori* with a decorative lining (*haura*)
Horse racing past and present
Taishō–Shōwa period, 1920s–1940
Silk plain weave (outer); *kata-yūzen* stencil-printed silk *haura* (lining)
52.0 × 41.0 inches (132 × 104 centimeters)
KM175

Horse racing has been a favorite sport in Japan for many hundreds of years. Although it was initially promoted as a religious ceremony, horseracing rapidly became a welcome pastime that flourished throughout the country. Races were held at shrines, temples, and events that allowed commoners to participate, even with the aristocracy that was part of the feudal system. The traditional artistic sense of competition set here in clever contrast to modern racing is graphically very eye-catching and an interesting juxtaposition of old and new.

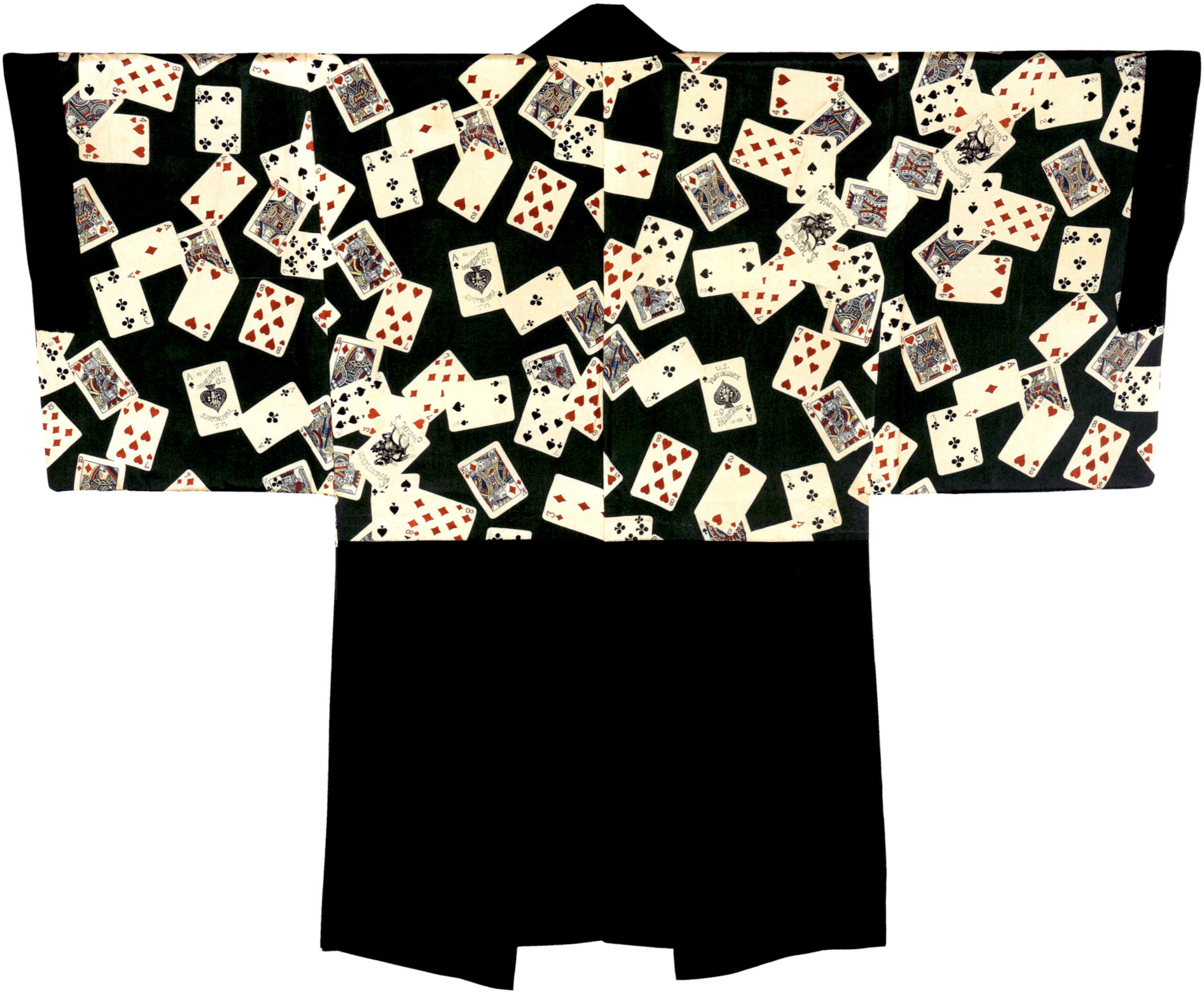

LEISURE

Man's *haori* with a decorative lining European and American playing cards
Taishō–Shōwa period, 1920s–1940
Silk plain weave (outer); printed silk lining
52.0 × 40.0 inches (132 × 102 centimeters)
KM176

Although there were a number of popular Japanese card games, playing European or American card games was soon embraced by metropolitan Japanese people. They found that the images of the Western playing cards were quite different from the Japanese playing cards, and the jokers of the Western cards seemed to capture the most interest. In general, both European and American playing cards were soon adopted by the Japanese as signifiers of modernity, concepts that could lead to a closer understanding of how to live the modern European or American life.

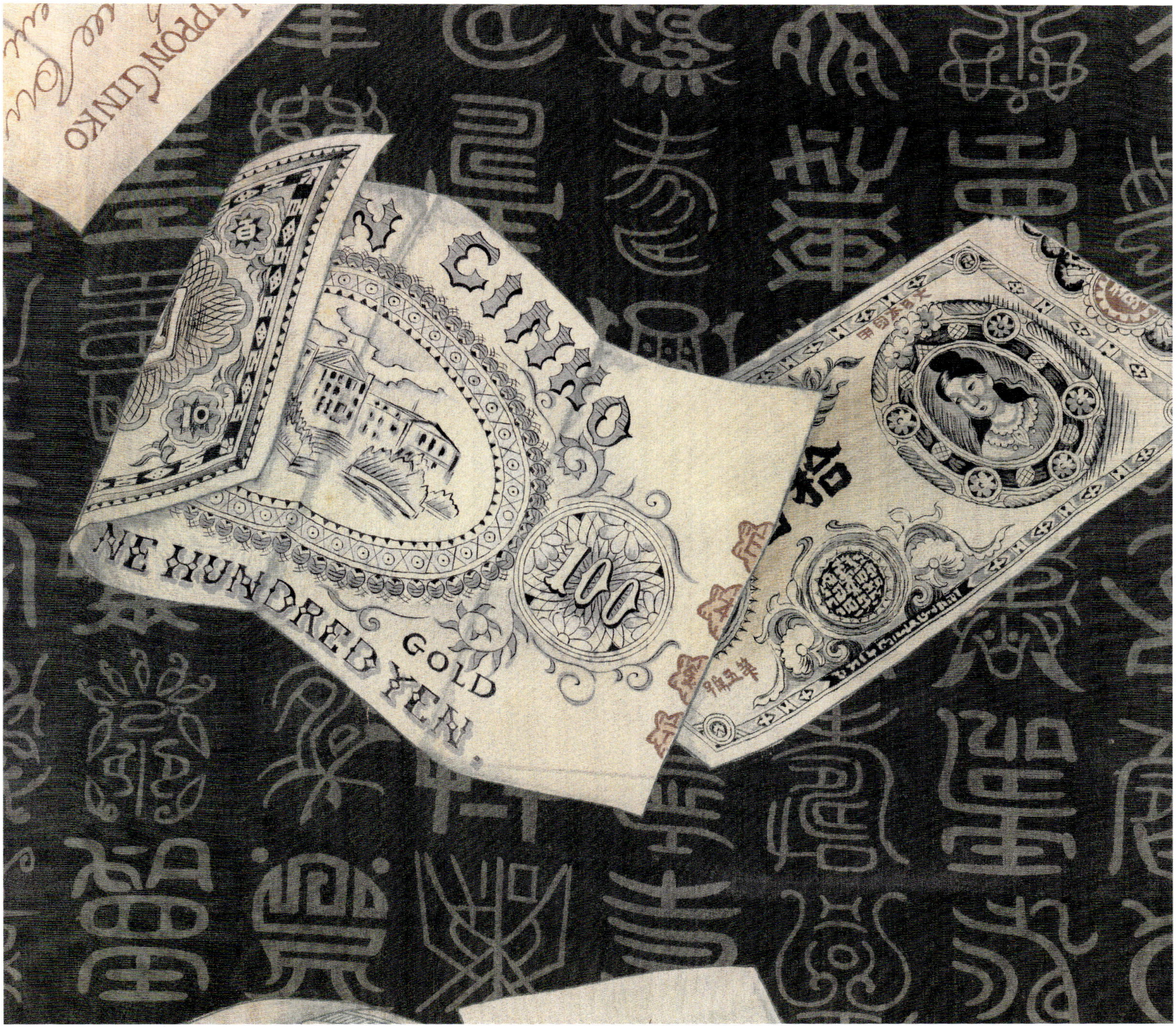

MODERNITY

Man's *haori* with a decorative lining
Paper money
Taishō–Shōwa period, early 1900s–early 1930s
Silk plain weave (outer); printed silk (lining)
51.0 × 39.0 inches (130 × 99 centimeters)
KM177

This *haori* has a silk lining printed with paper money and bank notes against a background of archaic text. Although this design may be aesthetically less interesting than other designs, it is well worth studying for historic reasons alone, as the paper money highlighted a new economic reality for Japan as it entered a changing world. The Bank of Japan (Nippon Ginko) was founded in 1882 and issued its first banknotes in 1885. The bank joined the gold standard in 1897 and phased out earlier "national" banknotes in 1899. The lining for this garment does include some of the gold standard bank notes, and it is quite possible that it was produced in the early 1900s, although the design might have been retained for use in later years as well.

MODERN ART

Man's *haori* with a decorative lining
Nudes drawn in a Western style
Taishō–early Shōwa period, early 1910s–1930
Silk plain weave *haori* (outer); *kata-yūzen* stencil-printed silk fabric (lining)
51.0 × 40.5 inches (130 × 103 centimeters)
KM178

The interior of this *haori* features a stencil-printed silk fabric that carries a design of nude women drawn in Western poses. The figures are in classical poses such as those that would be used in modeling for an art class. The models sit or stand as necessary, and in two cases appear to have been staged for a specific tableau. The fine lines drawn on the bodies of the models may be intended to look like craquelure on a painting. The hairdos vary on the women, but in general the styles seem to be closer to Taishō than Shōwa styles.

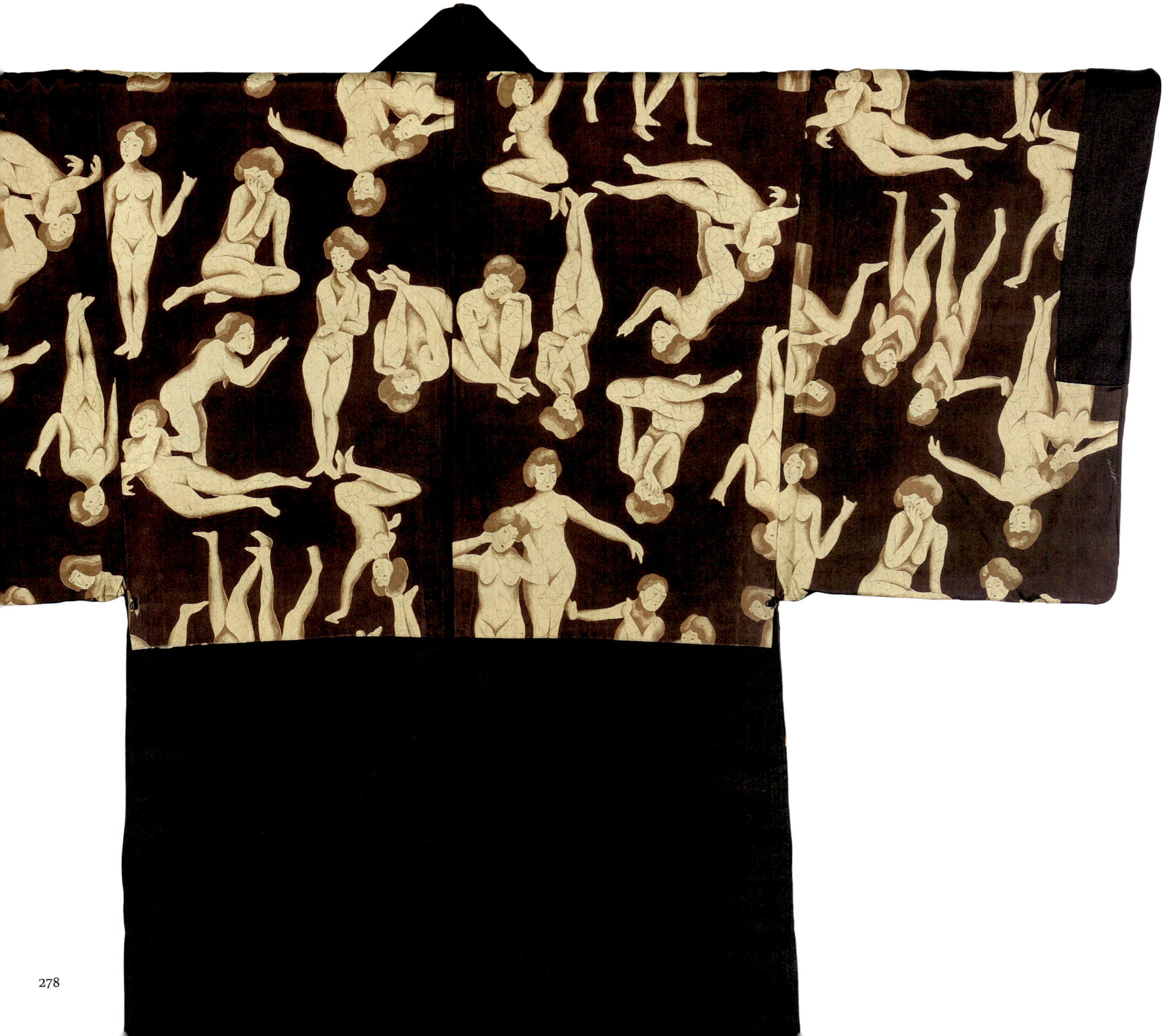

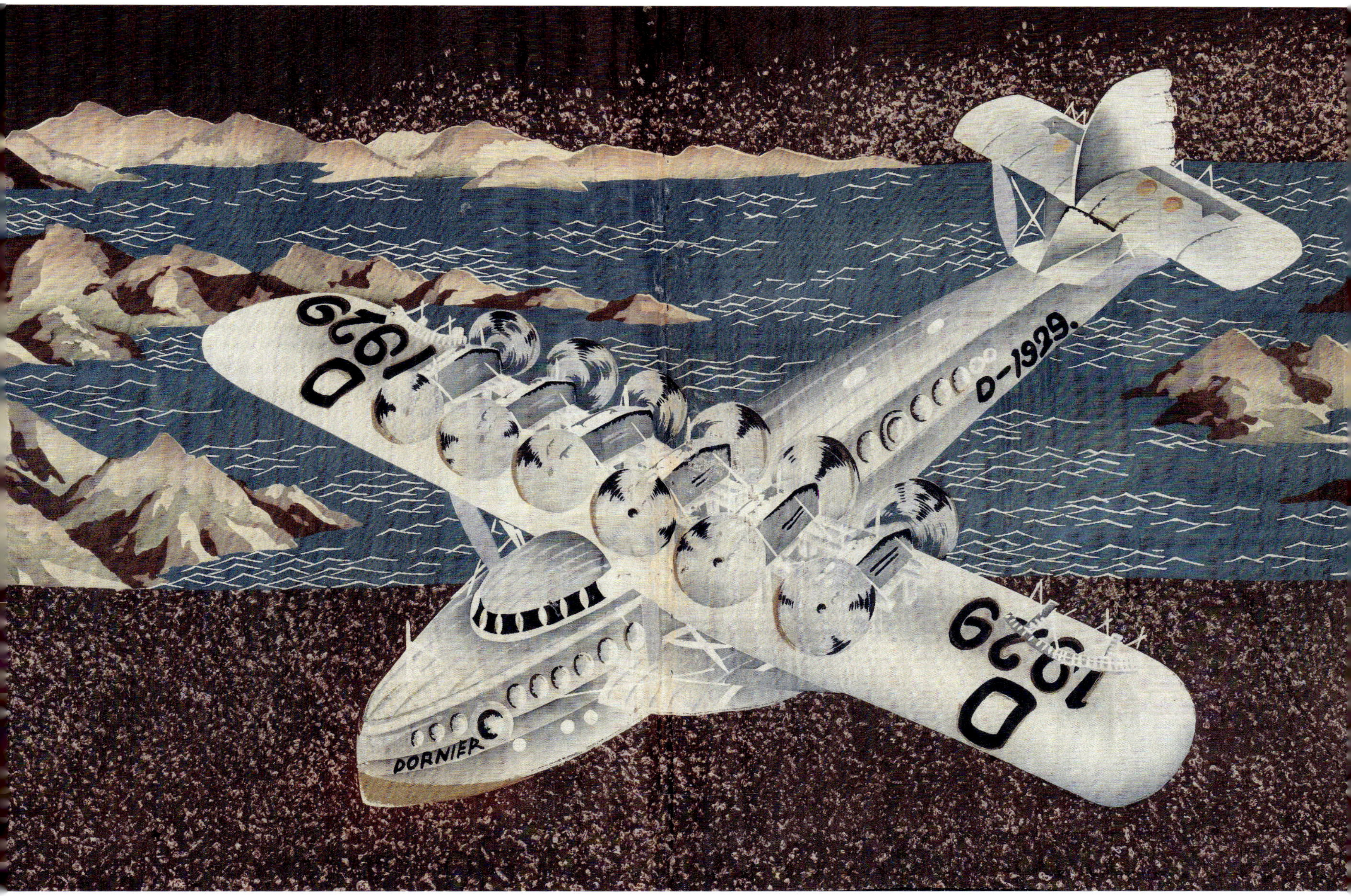

MACHINE AGE/ MODERNITY/TRAVEL

***Man's haori* with a decorative lining (*haura*)**

Marvelous flying boat

Taishō–early Shōwa period, 1929–early 1930s
Tsumugi (silk pongee) *haori* (outer); *kata-yūzen* stencil-printed silk *haura* (lining)
52.0 × 42.0 inches (132 × 107 centimeters)
KM179

The Dornier Do X was the largest, heaviest, and most powerful flying boat in the world when the Dornier Company of Germany produced it in 1929. It was a striking invention developed by Dr. Claudius Dornier, and the enthusiastic public had never seen anything like it before. At the time, the flying boat set a record for carrying the largest number of people (150) on board one flight—and also for needing the most engines and propellers on its broad wing. This stunning design for the *haura* captured the power, beauty, and mystery of this unusual flying boat.

TRAVEL/ COSMOPOLITANISM

Man's *haori* with a decorative lining (*haura*)
Sister ships at sea
Meiji–Taishō period, 1904–1919
Silk plain weave *haori* (outer); woven silk and metal threads *haura* (lining)
52.0 × 44.0 inches (132 × 112 centimeters)
KM180

This carefully woven pictorial *haura* is a wonderful example of complex weaving. The global design captures an outstanding image of the continents of the eastern hemisphere, and tiny stitches have been added to delineate the major trade routes for ships. Metallic threads were woven in to highlight the ocean waves of the panel, showcasing the sister battleships *Katori* and *Kashima*. These two ships had an important story to tell. On March 3, 1921, *Katori*, escorted by her sister ship, departed from Yokohama bound for Great Britain, carrying Crown Prince Hirohito, the first Japanese crown prince to travel abroad. As his tour progressed, Hirohito met with many celebrated European leaders, thus taking his own place as an international principal.

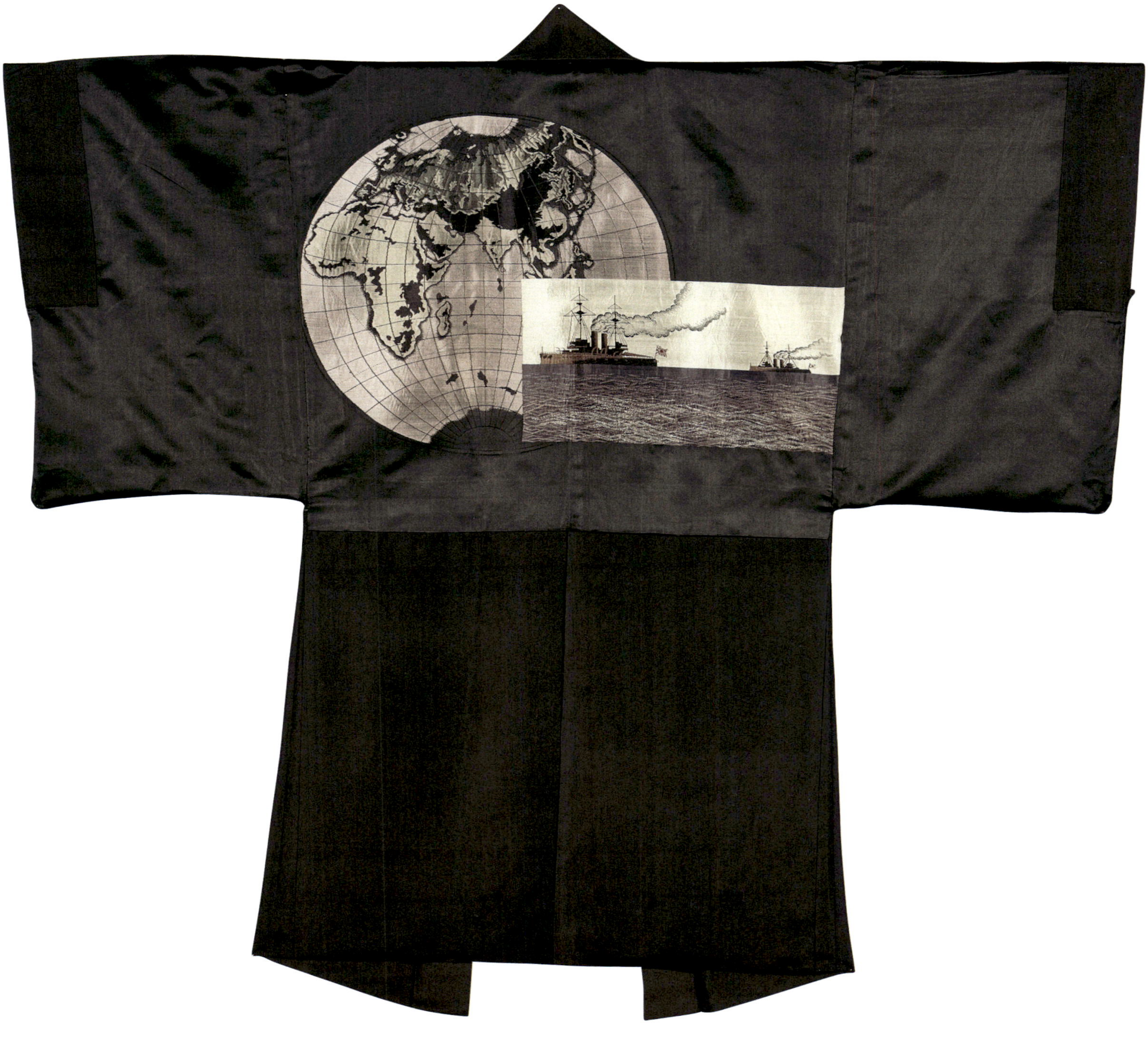

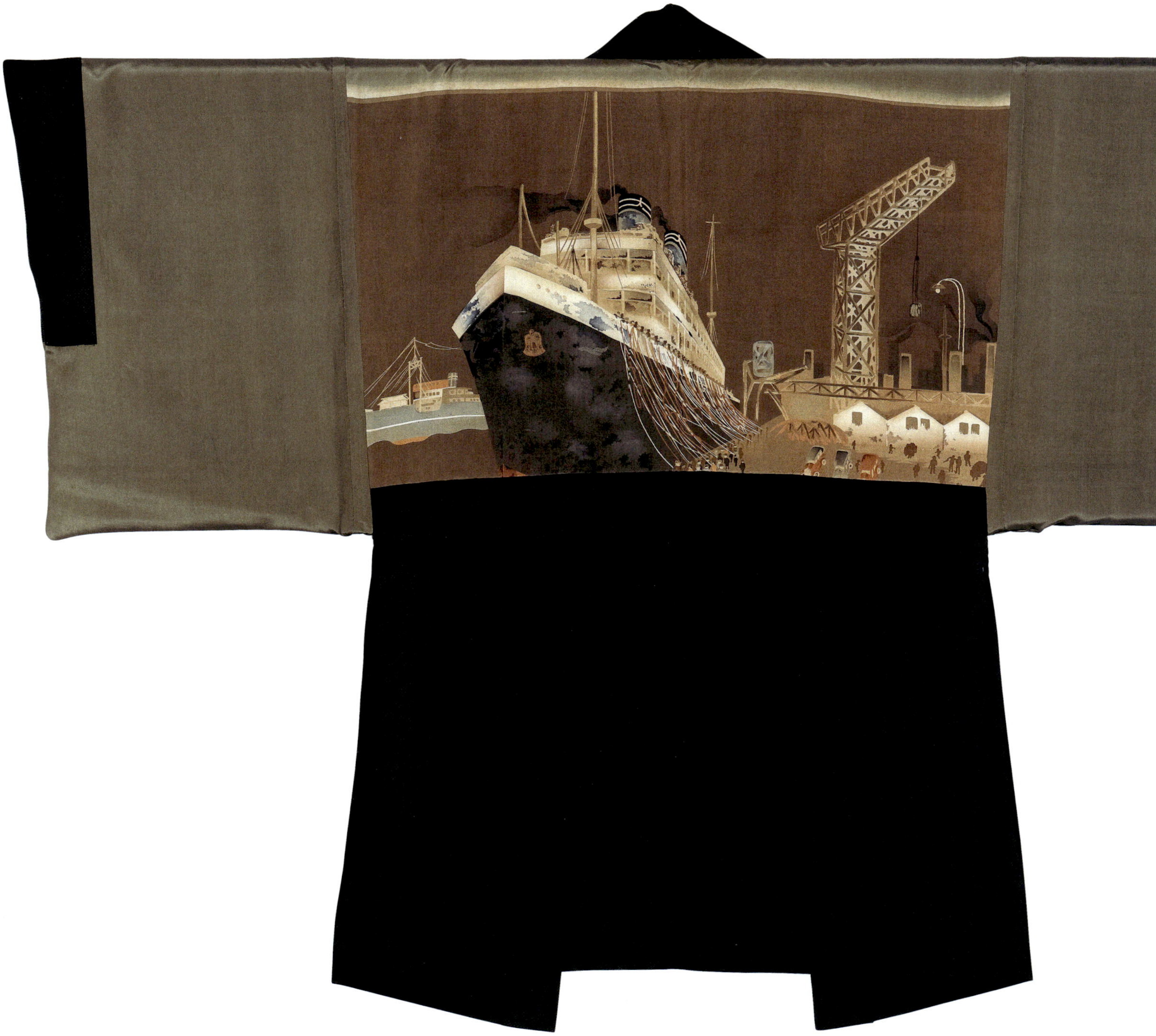

TRAVEL/MACHINE AGE

Man's *haori* with a decorative lining (*haura*)
A passenger ship ready to depart
Taishō–early Shōwa period, late 1920s–1940
Silk plain weave *haori* (outer); *kata-yūzen* stencil-printed silk *haura* (lining)
53.0 × 36.0 inches (135 × 91 centimeters)
KM181

This elegant ship is leaving for foreign shores, with passengers already aboard. The passengers throw out colorful streamers from the main deck of the ship, and the crowd on the pier enjoy capturing the ribbons, which will be celebratory mementos when their friends and colleagues are far away. This *haori* is another great design that shows the elegance of the ships of the NYK (Nippon Yusen Kaisha) Line. Although this one does not carry insignia, it is the *Asama Maru*, the ship that set a record for the fastest crossing of the Pacific Ocean on the Yokohama–San Francisco route. It is also a superb example of Japan's entry into the Machine Age.

MODERNITY

Man's *haori* with a decorative lining (*haura*)
Past and present
Taishō–early Shōwa period, late 1920s–1940
Silk plain weave *haori* (outer); *kata-yūzen* stencil-printed silk *haura* (lining)
50.0 × 40.0 inches (127 × 102 centimeters)
KM182

This garment produces an interesting mixture of past and present, with the iconic Mount Fuji placed against an endless backdrop of skyscrapers. This is a thought-provoking transition piece as Japan acknowledges a changing nation, and, in the right context, it offers the possibility for some historical discussion. The Tokyo Railroad Station appears as a vignette in front of Fuji. The primary design was *yūzen*-dyed and the shaded shadows on both Mount Fuji and the Hiroshige-like porters have been extremely carefully done, as were the sumo schedule and lunch menus from restaurants. Overall, the design indicates that an artist with superb technical skills has produced this *haura*.

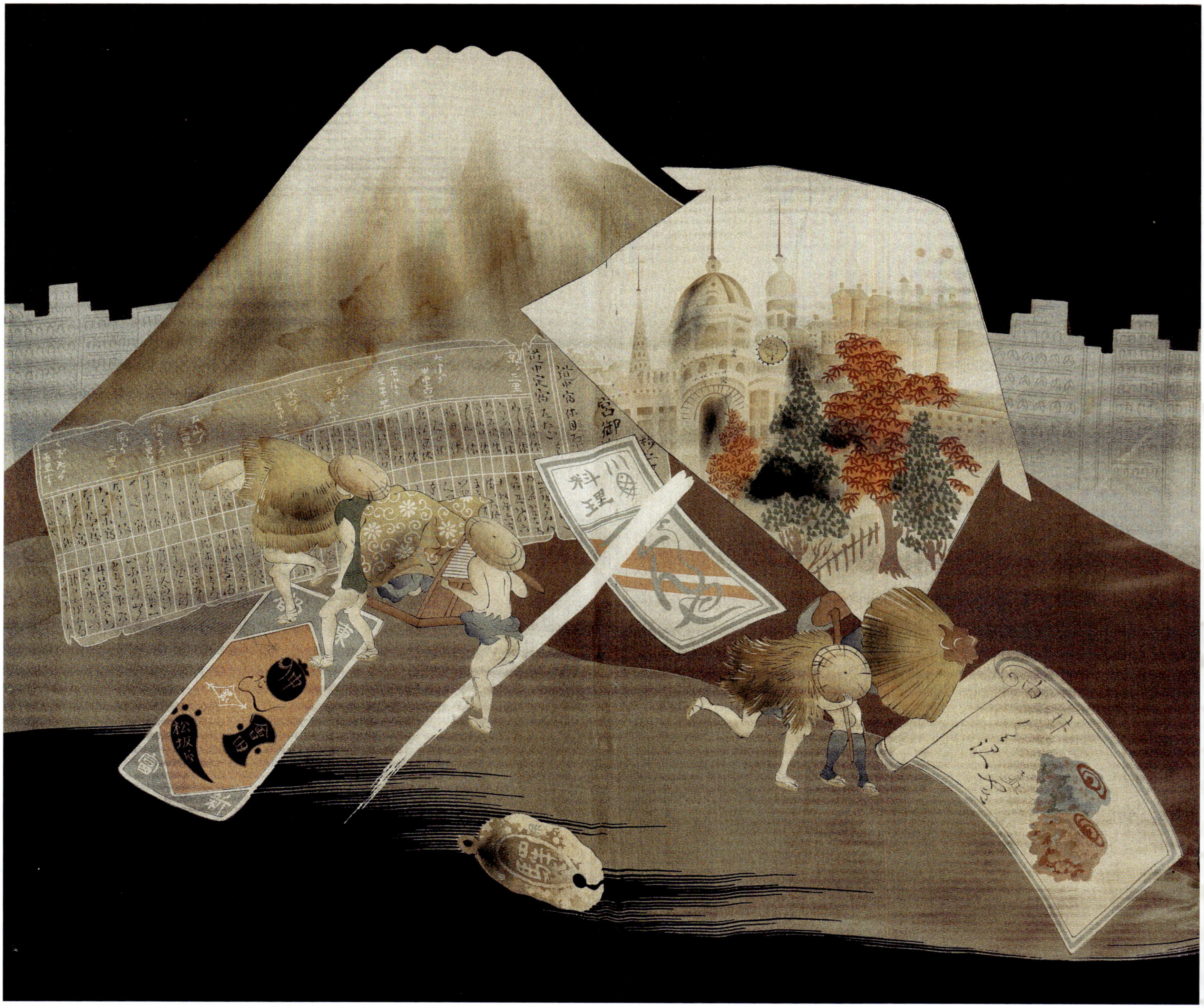

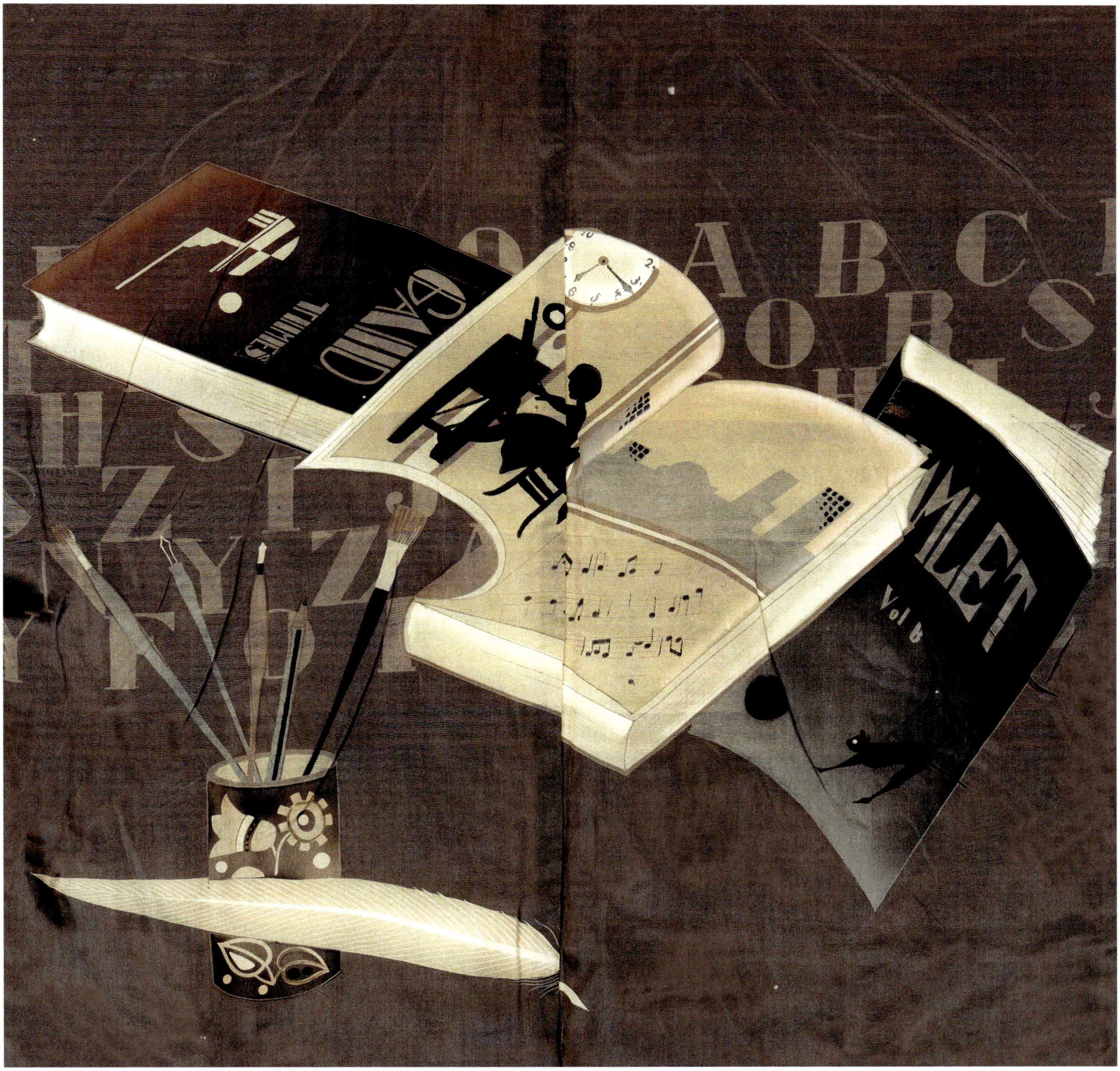

COSMOPOLITANISM/ ART

Man's *juban*
Study for a new and modern Japan
Taishō–early Shōwa period, late 1920s–1940
Kata-yūzen stencil-printed silk fabric
49.0 × 49.0 inches (124 × 124 centimeters)
KM183

This *juban* carries a great design that reflects enthusiasm for Western-style books, art, music, and travel—all signifiers of an outward-looking nation—as Japan became modernized in the 1920s and 1930s. The artist who designed the objects for this *juban* used the Western alphabet text as a background (albeit the letters are not in the proper order), and the paintbrushes placed in a decorative little pot alongside a nearby writing quill might have encouraged the *juban* owner to learn to write his Western letters, too. The bright white collar also adds a nice decorative touch to the *juban*, as does the amusing "barbell" border.

ENTERTAINMENT/ CINEMA

Woman's obi
Time for film
Taishō–early Shōwa period, late 1920s–1940
Printed wool muslin
124.0 × 11.0 inches (315 × 28 centimeters)
KM184

The design for this textile was an unusual choice for an obi, but perhaps it had captured the owner's interest for the necessary productive work required by the film projectors that were so important in reviewing the final editing and screening of movies. The projectors depicted here appear to be quite modern for their time (1930s) and probably showed many movies from three of the major production companies in the USA and Europe: Paramount Pictures (Hollywood, California), UFA (Universum-Film AG, Berlin, Germany), and Saros Film, a company thought to have been based in Europe, but which cannot be located. These names can be seen on the obi.

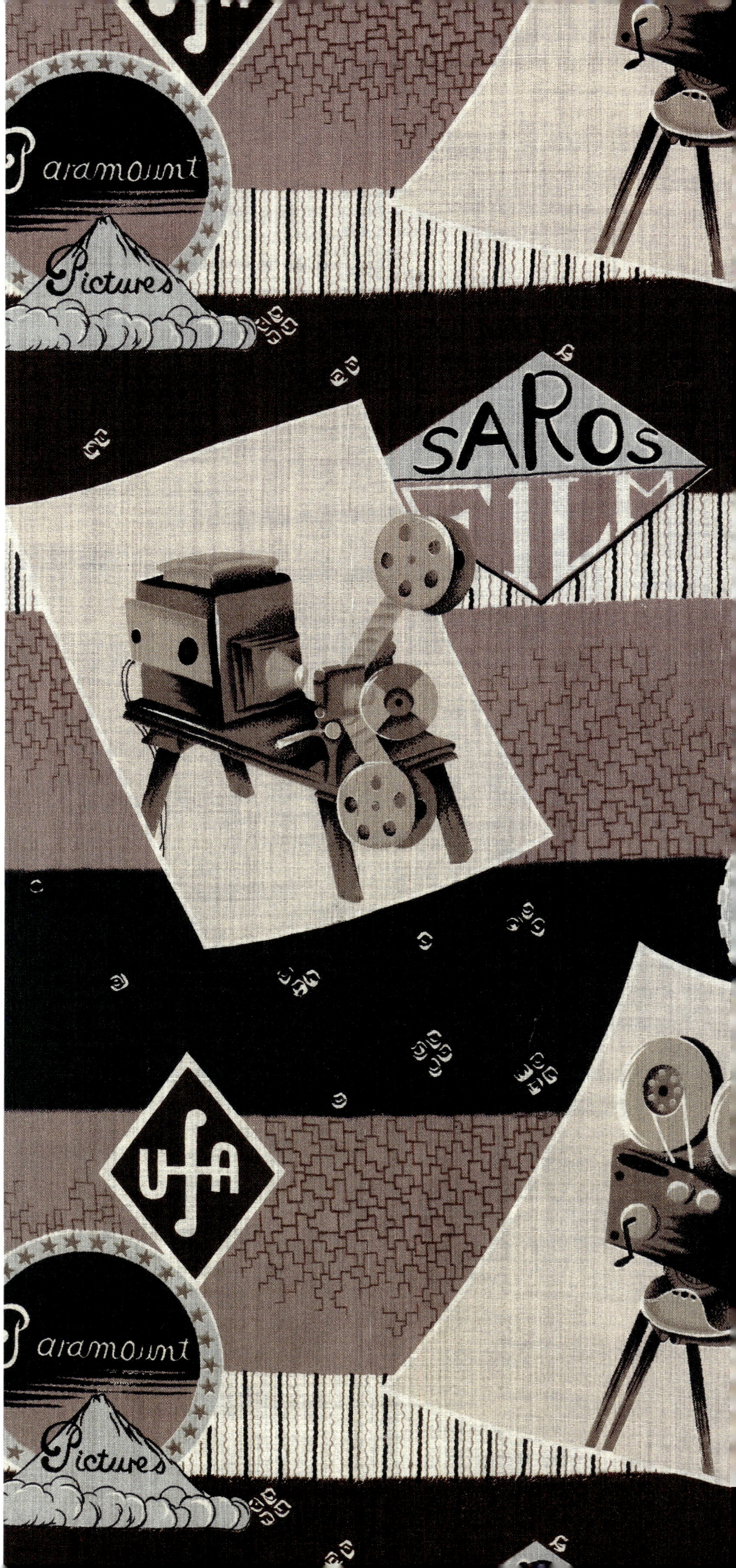

MODERNITY

***Juban* for a man**
Cigarettes, matchboxes, and a windmill ashtray
Taishō–early Shōwa period, late 1920s–1940
Kata-yūzen stencil-printed silk fabric with slubbed effect
52.0 × 51.0 inches (132 × 130 centimeters)
KM185

This *juban* offers an odd but interesting composition. This, plus additional garments in this group, shows cigarette boxes and other smoking-related paraphernalia, demonstrating how important smoking had become as a sign of modernity to the Japanese in the first decades of the 20th century. Although these new examples may seem unnecessary or redundant, the opportunity to see all these garments together is well worth taking, as each *haori* or *juban* has been given its own special features. Looking at this larger group of smoking paraphernalia gives a very strong indication of the pervasiveness of tobacco and tobacco-related goods among the general public as Japan continued to take on the trappings of modernity.

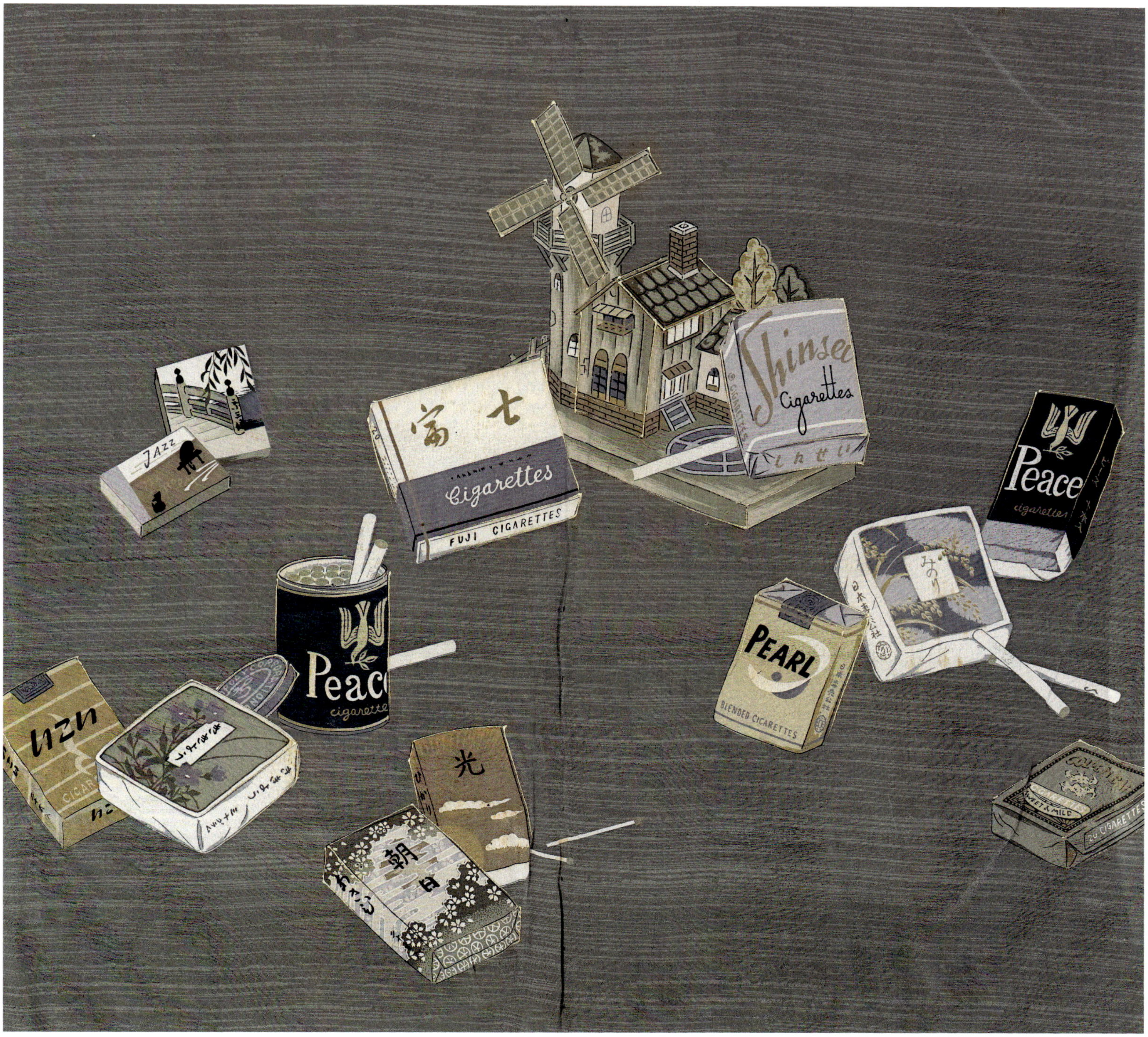

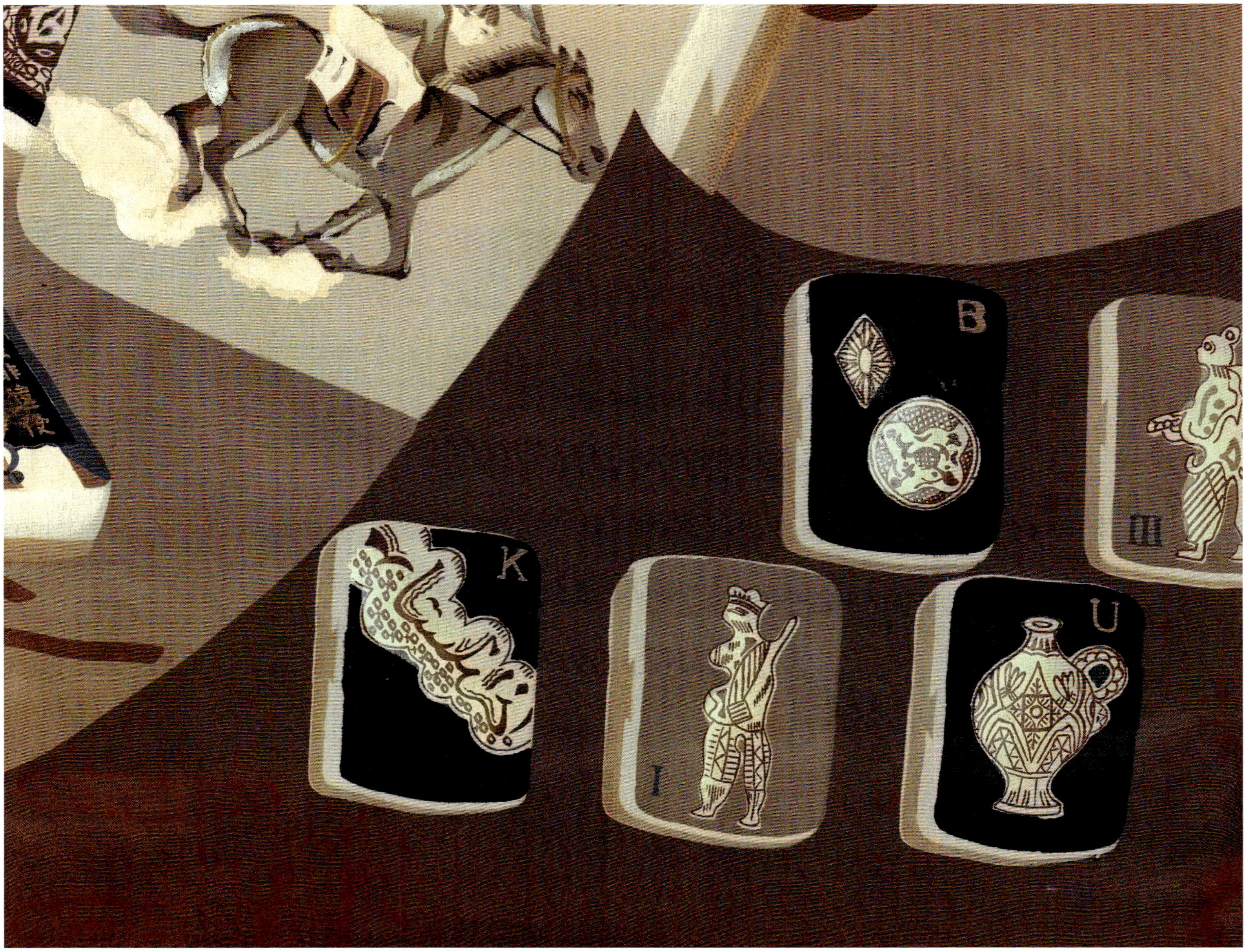

SPORTS/ ENTERTAINMENT

Man's *haori* with a decorative lining (*haura*)
Dice games with tiles and decorated boxes
Taishō–early Shōwa period, late 1920s–1940
Silk plain weave *haori* (outer); *kata-yūzen* stencil-printed silk *haura* (lining)
52.0 × 45.0 inches (132 × 114 centimeters)
KM186

This design juxtaposes tradition and modernity. The artist shows traditional pieces used in dice games (dice, tiles, sticks, boxes for tiles, and other game components). Most of the boxes and the tiles, however, have been dressed with a variety of contemporary designs that include images of various sports (rugby, baseball, and horse racing), a *moga* ("modern girl"), a baseball batter, and more. Nonetheless, not all is modern, and some tiles sport images of antiquity. This is an interesting *haura* that neatly draws together present and past.

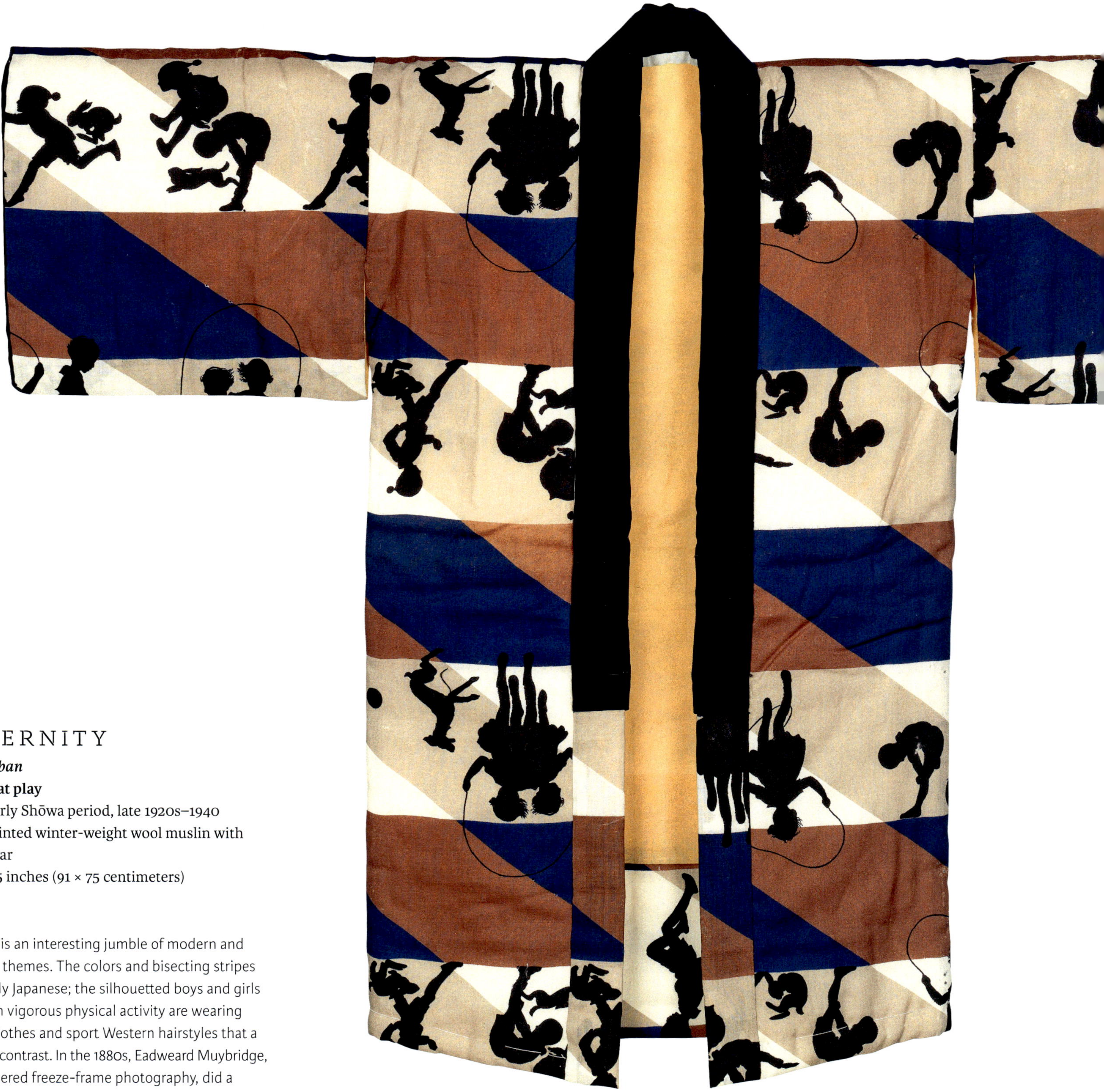

MODERNITY

Child's *juban*
Children at play
Taishō–early Shōwa period, late 1920s–1940
Stencil-printed winter-weight wool muslin with velvet collar
36.0 × 29.5 inches (91 × 75 centimeters)
KM187

This *juban* is an interesting jumble of modern and traditional themes. The colors and bisecting stripes are typically Japanese; the silhouetted boys and girls engaged in vigorous physical activity are wearing Western clothes and sport Western hairstyles that a dd a novel contrast. In the 1880s, Eadweard Muybridge, who pioneered freeze-frame photography, did a series of movement studies featuring people playing leapfrog, which may have encouraged the designer of this textile to adapt it to the activities of the children. The starkly realistic quality of the silhouettes is unusual for childrenswear, which is typically very stylized. The somersaulting rabbit may be a sly reference to Japan's beloved *Choju Jinbutsu Giga*, a 13th-century scroll that features frolicking animals.

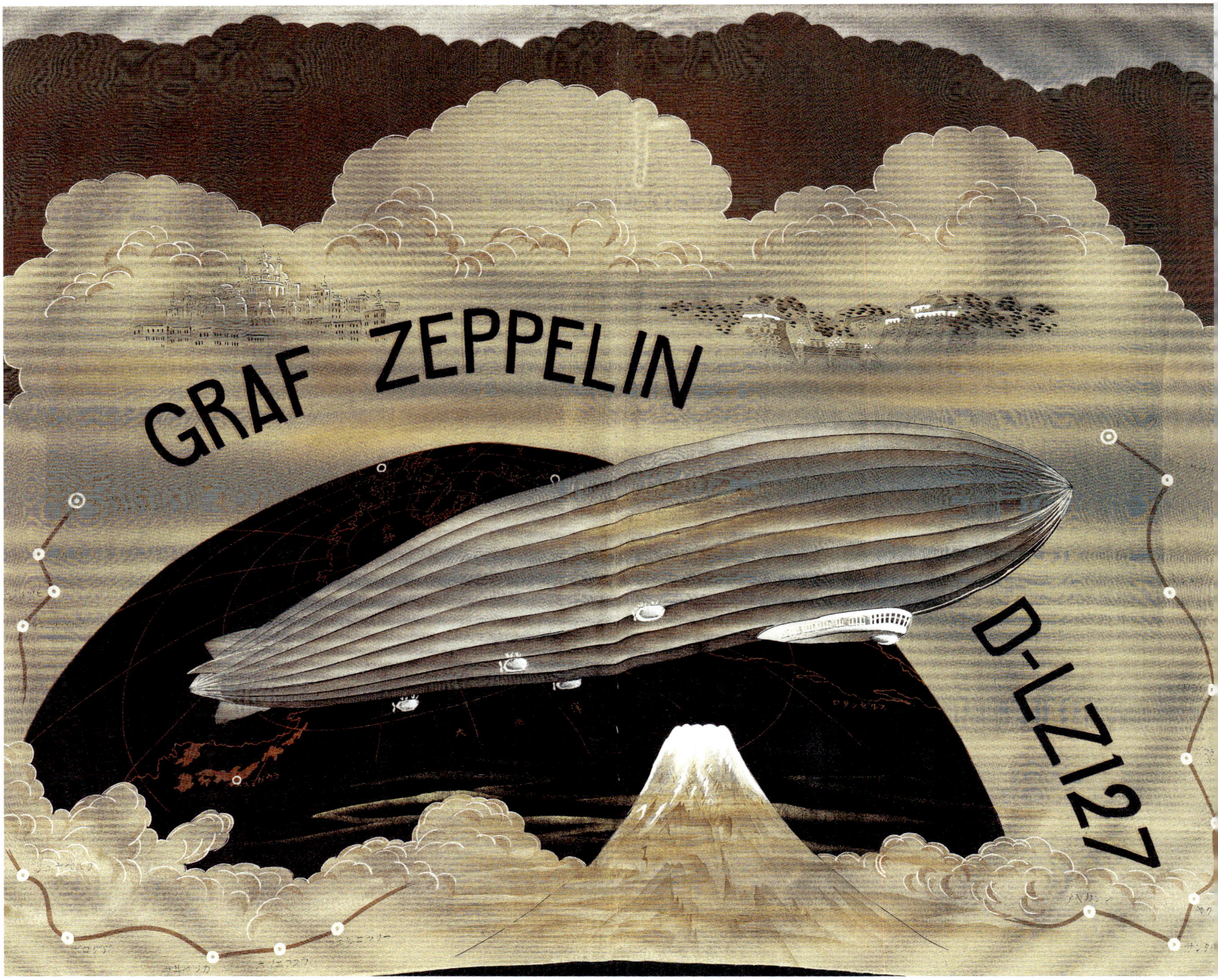

MACHINE AGE

Man's *haori* with a decorative lining (*haura*)
New modes of transport
Taishō–early Shōwa period, 1929
Silk plain weave *haori* (outer); *kata-yūzen* stencil-printed silk *haura* (lining)
51.0 × 38.0 inches (130 × 97 centimeters)
KM188

This *haori,* with its stencil-printed silk *haura* carefully designed to show the *Graf Zeppelin,* is a great addition to other Zeppelin garments. The design provided a praiseworthy road map, showing the names of the cities the *Graf Zeppelin* would fly over as this extraordinary around-the-world excursion proceeded. The elegant airship was no doubt seen by excited crowds as it passed above each city with slow grace. Passengers also gained the opportunity to see the glory of Mount Fuji as the environs of Tokyo were entered. The *Graf Zeppelin* had a five-day sojourn in Tokyo, during which Emperor Hirohito himself invited Dr. Hugo Eckener, commander of the airship, to take tea with him. Some 250,000 people also gathered to see the *Graf Zeppelin* as it remained settled in style within its moorings at the Kasumigaura Naval Air Station.

TRAVEL

Man's *haori* with a decorative lining (*haura*)
Dreaming of travel
Taishō–early Shōwa period, late 1920s–1940
Silk plain weave *haori* (outer); *kata-yūzen* stencil-printed silk *haura* (lining)
52.0 × 38.0 inches (132 × 97 centimeters)
KM189

The foreign travel theme captured in this garment has a number of intriguing elements that should encourage the owner of this *haori* to begin to look for travel brochures immediately. A black ship in the distance, waving palm trees, and camels ready to be mounted at an oasis offer mysteries that can be dwelled on in dreams, but other fantasies also await—painting a portrait, looking forward to evenings of music, song, and dance, or meeting with an unknown *moga* ("modern girl") who stands before a record disk and musical notes. The only unaccountable object in these magical travels is the American football, which leaves, perhaps, a rather puzzling mystery.

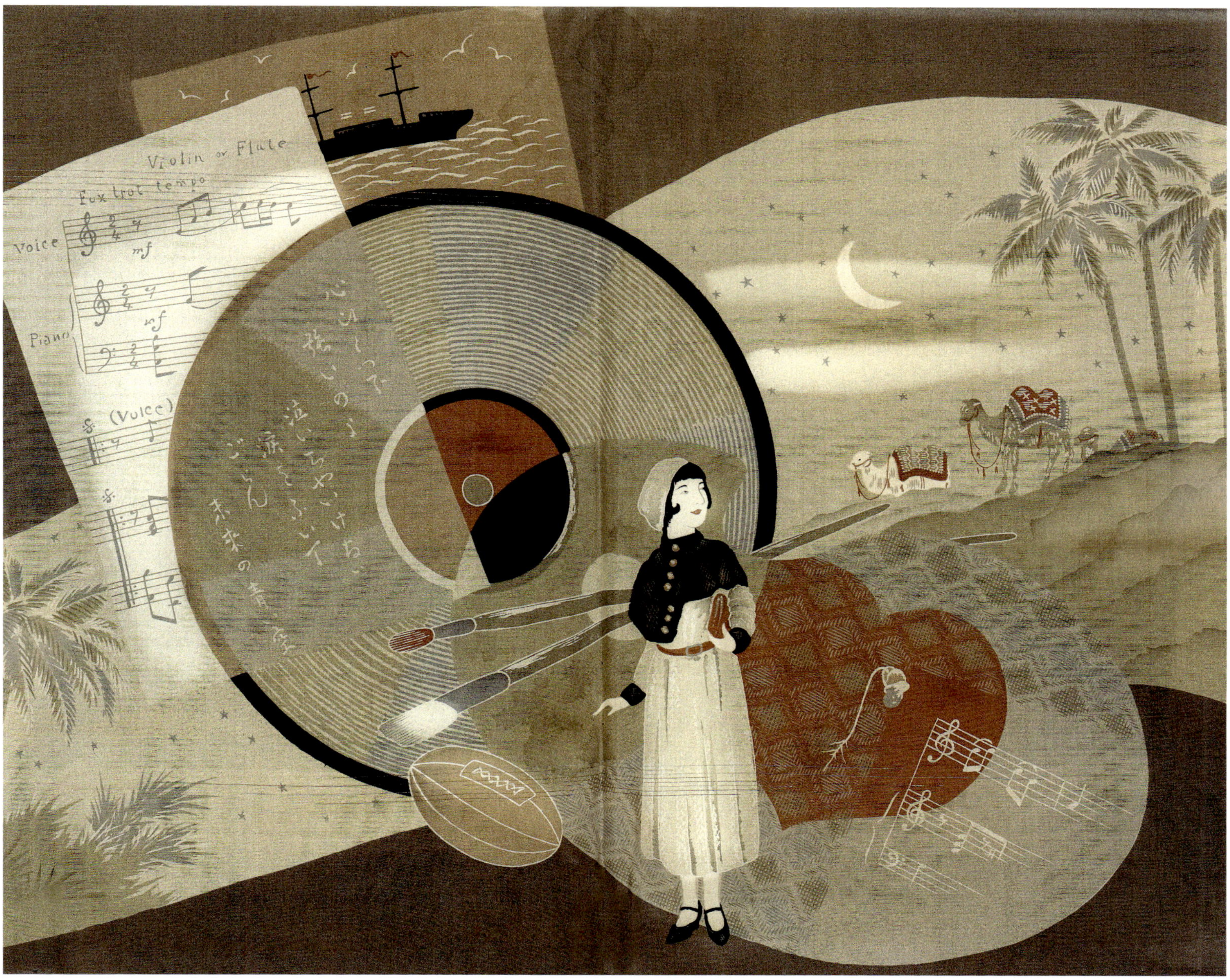

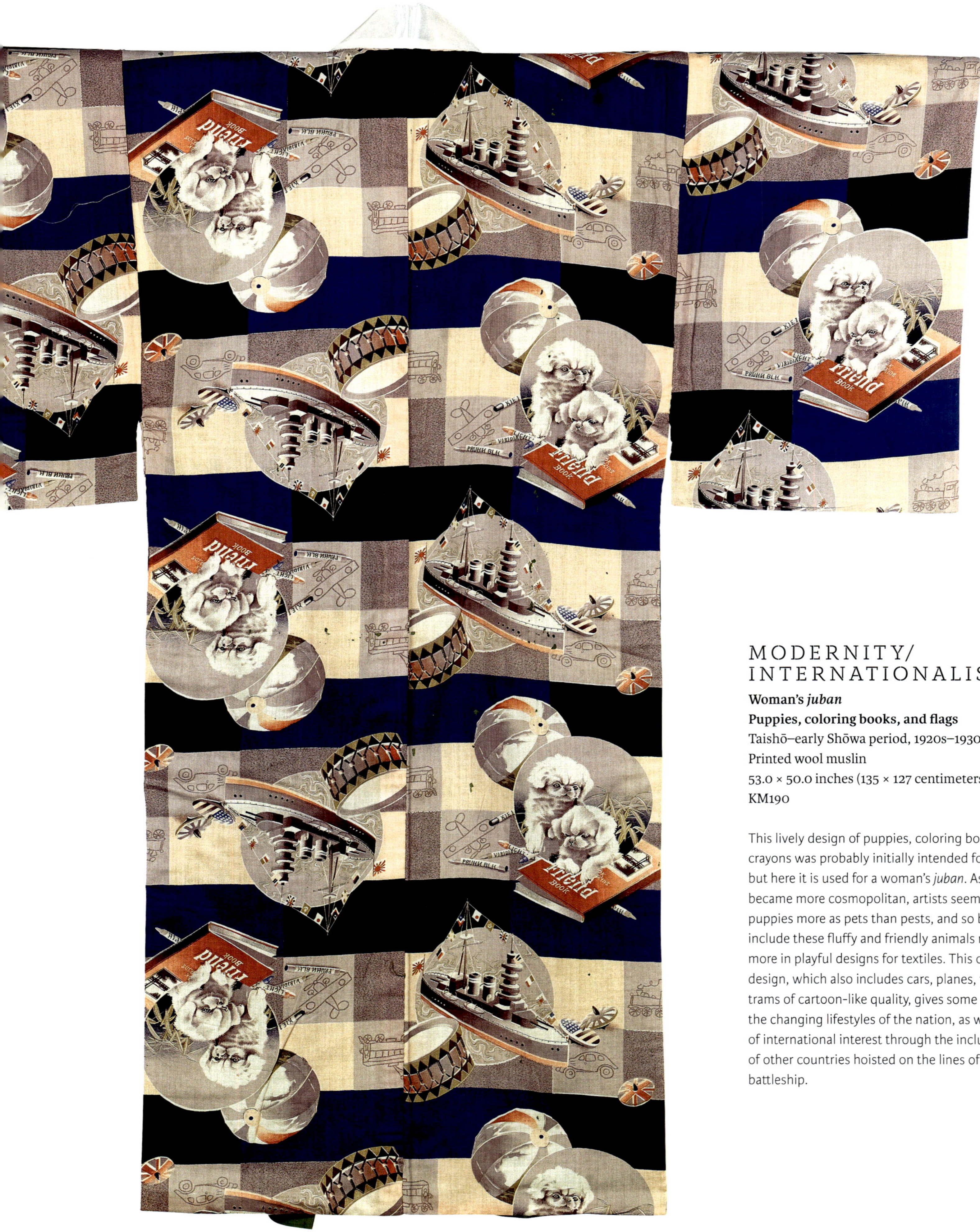

MODERNITY/ INTERNATIONALISM

Woman's *juban*
Puppies, coloring books, and flags
Taishō–early Shōwa period, 1920s–1930s
Printed wool muslin
53.0 × 50.0 inches (135 × 127 centimeters)
KM190

This lively design of puppies, coloring books, and crayons was probably initially intended for children, but here it is used for a woman's *juban*. As Japan became more cosmopolitan, artists seemed to view puppies more as pets than pests, and so began to include these fluffy and friendly animals more and more in playful designs for textiles. This overall design, which also includes cars, planes, trains, and trams of cartoon-like quality, gives some insight into the changing lifestyles of the nation, as well as a hint of international interest through the inclusion of flags of other countries hoisted on the lines of a Japanese battleship.

WINTER SPORTS

Kimono for a child
Winter sports: skiing
Taishō–early Shōwa period, late 1920s–early 1930s
Winter weight stencil-printed rayon
34.0 × 32.0 inches (86 × 81 centimeters)
KM191

The traditional background of this kimono, called *dangawari*, or alternating steps, is skillfully used by the designer to evoke the sky, snow, and earth. The skiers, zigzagging down the horizontal plane, add tension, motion, and speed to the design. Skiing was only introduced to Japan in 1911, so when this kimono was made, probably in the late 1920s or early 1930s, it would still have been very much a novelty. Skiing equipment, storage space, and transportation costs to and from a ski slope were expensive, so this little garment was meant to impart an air of the latest and most exclusive trends to its young wearer.

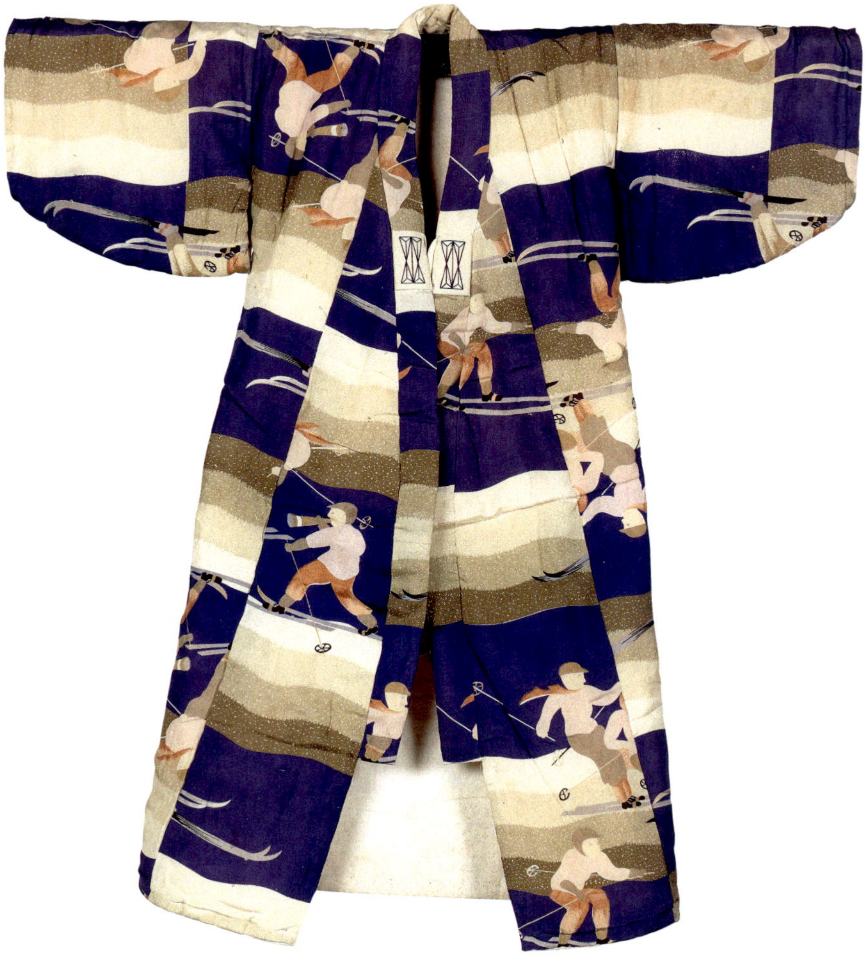

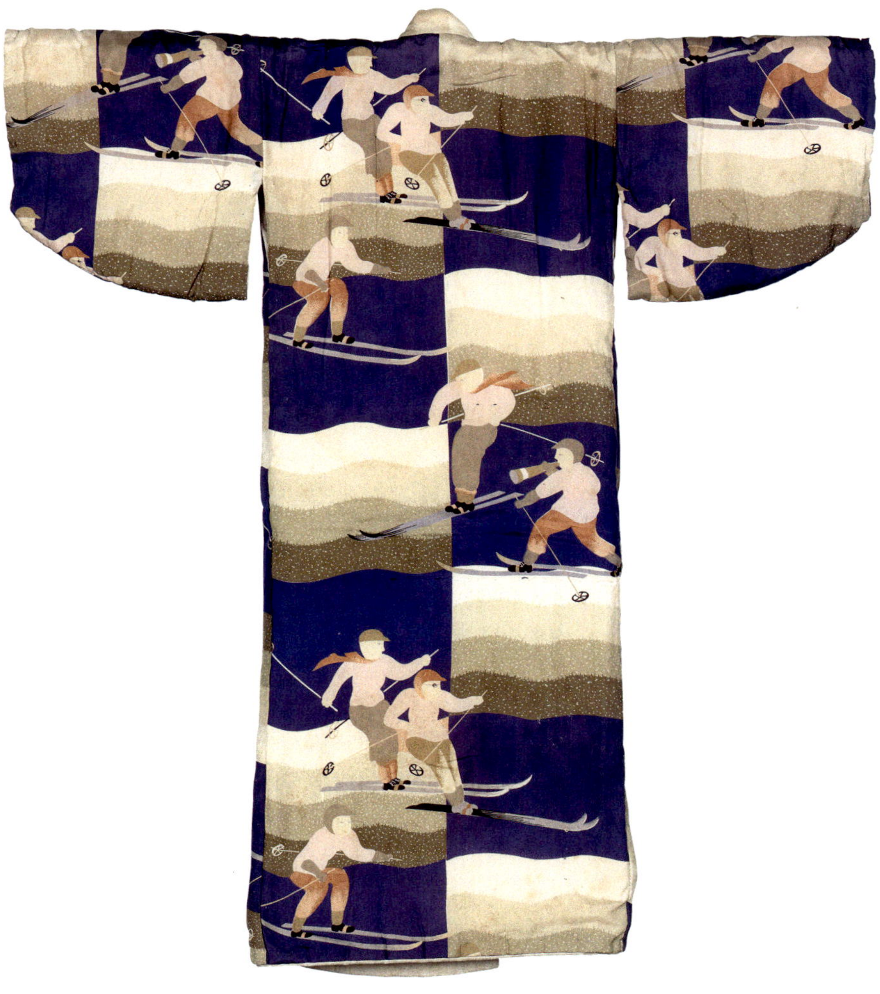

TRAVEL

Kimono for a child
Travel by ship, plane, and train
Taishō–early Shōwa period, late 1920s–early 1930s
Kata-yūzen stenciled silk
28.0 × 28.0 inches (71 × 71 centimeters)
KM192

Travel, severely restricted in Japan for more than two centuries under the shogunate, became an important element in Japan's drive toward modernization. Here, the wonders of travel are seen from a child's perspective in this infant boy's kimono. From his window on a train, a little boy dressed in Western clothes points to a sailboat, or perhaps to the airplane flying high above the majestic Mount Fuji. The gift at his feet is wrapped with pretty red and white ribbon, and the paper is stamped in Western script, probably the name of a famous department store. Perhaps the boy and the gift have traveled on the ocean liner that towers majestically above the seas, its smoking funnels a sign of its power and speed.

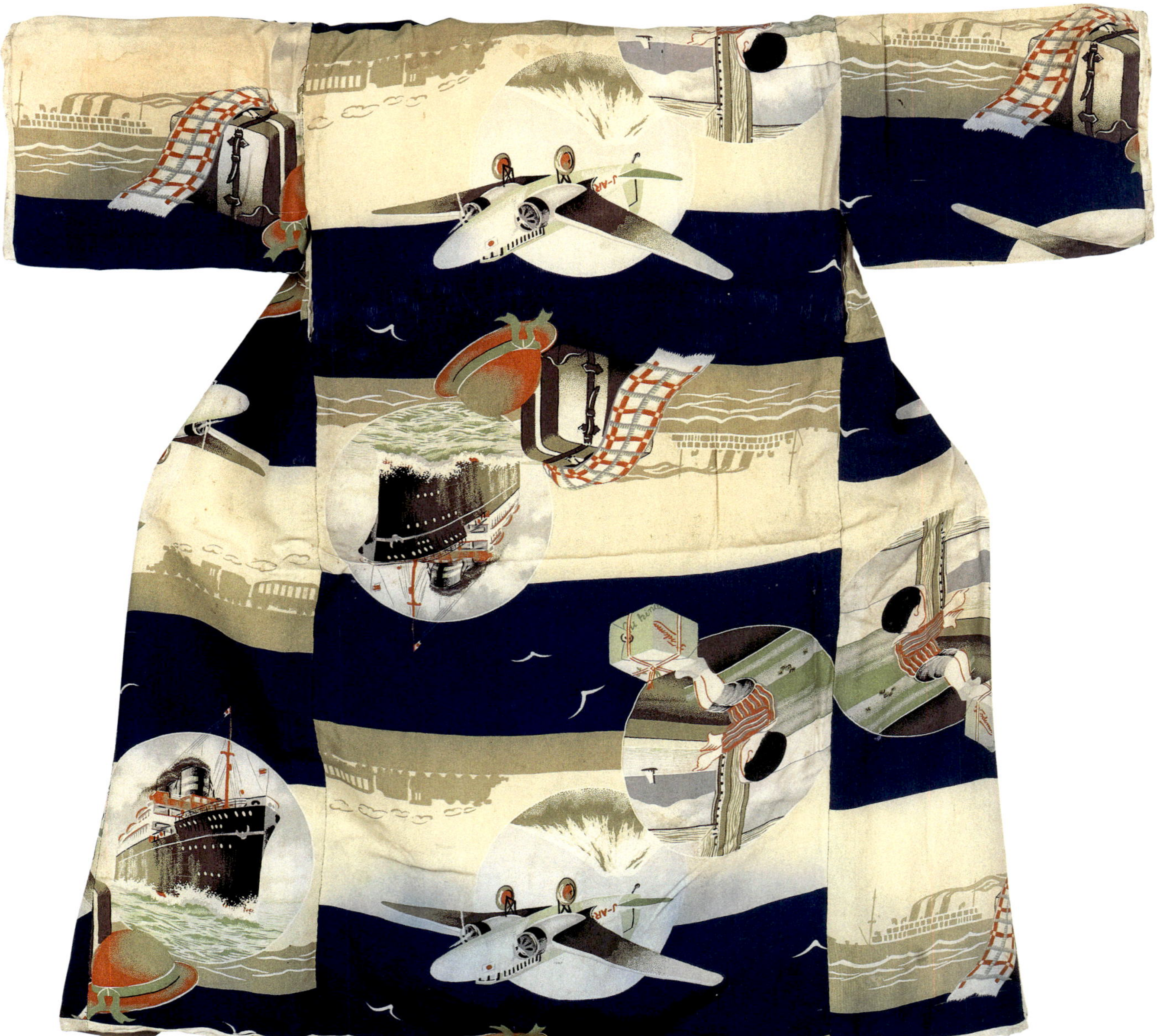

COSMOPOLITANISM/ ENTERTAINMENT

Man's *haori* with a decorative lining (*haura*)
Revue at a theatre
Taishō–early Shōwa period, 1920s–1930s
Silk plain weave *haori* (outer); *kata-yūzen* stencil-printed silk *haura* (lining)
50.0 × 41.0 inches (127 × 104 centimeters)
KM193

This is a terrific image that captures the glowing sophistication of Japan's nightlife as well as the country's growing cosmopolitanism. The artist who captured the design for this *haura* is unknown, but it is clear that his talent does wonders for textiles. The motif for this theatre brings to mind the Art Deco style of Radio City Music Hall (nicknamed the "Showcase of the Nation") in New York City. The chorus line is shown performing much like the Rockettes, an American precision dance company famous for their eye-high kicks and performances in New York City since 1932. The revue shown here adds singers, additional dancers, and an orchestra—enough to offer an audience a night of music, dance, and great entertainment.

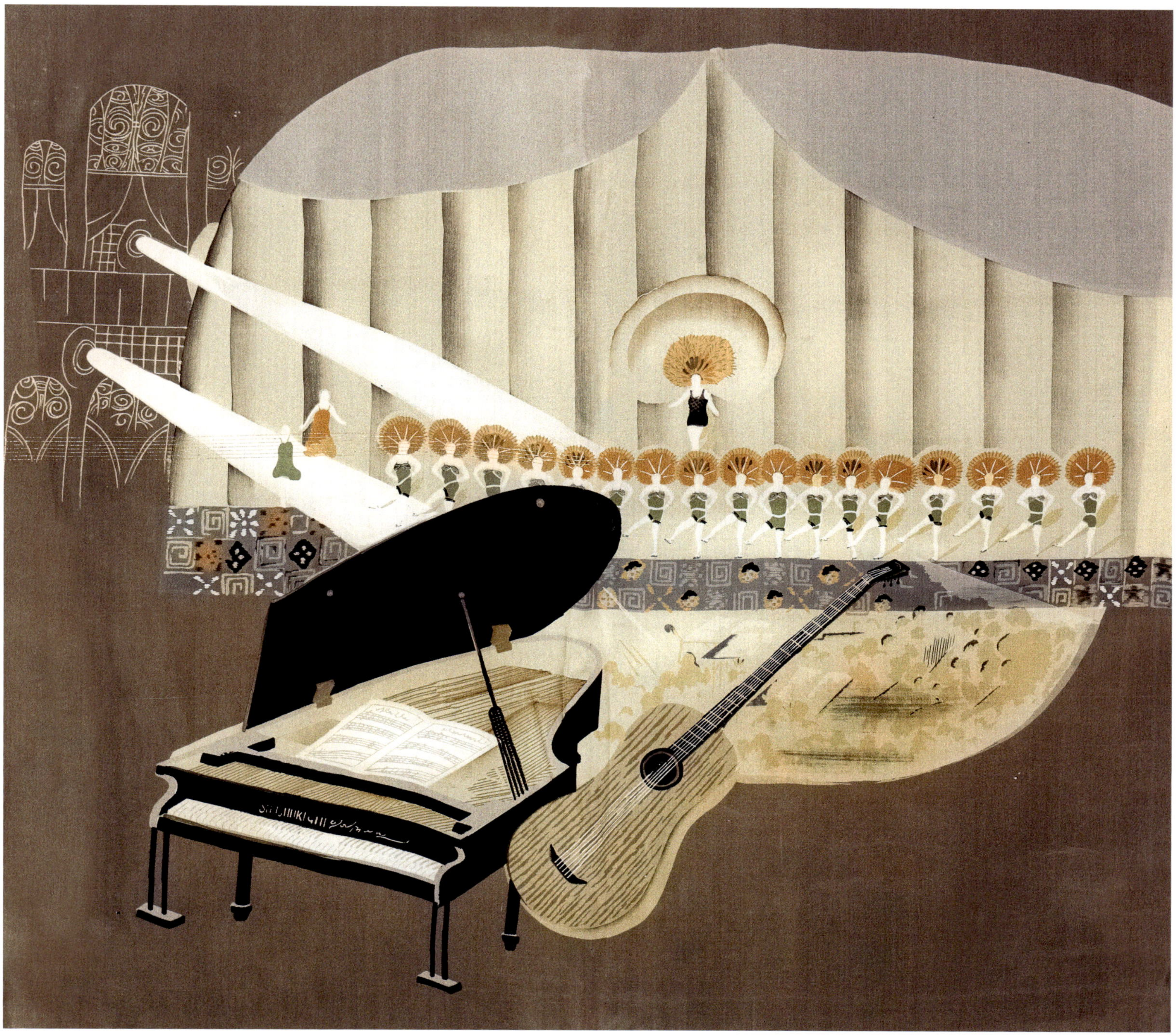

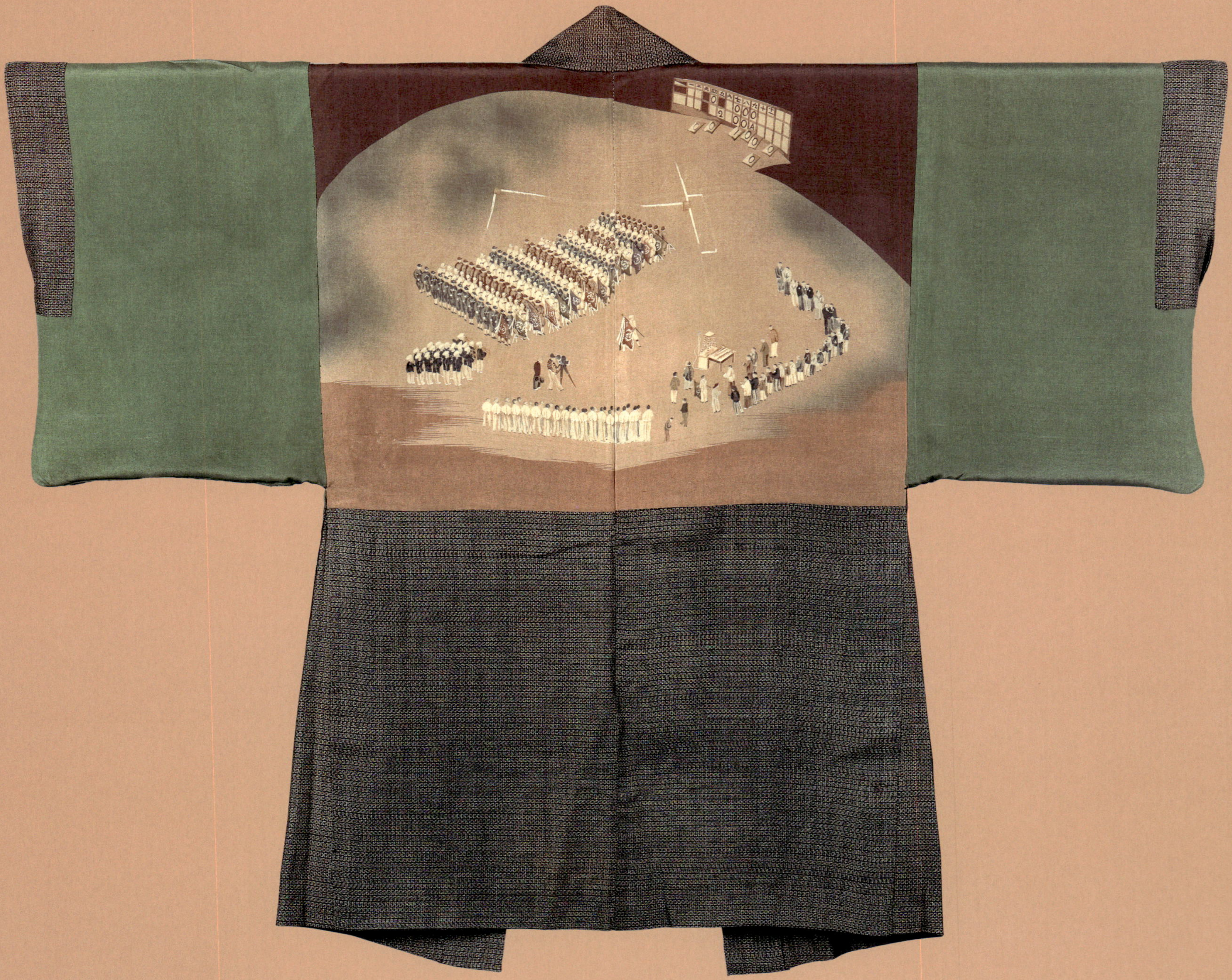

SPORTS/BASEBALL

Man's *haori* with a decorative lining (*haura*)
The 1915 Baseball Awards Ceremony
Taishō period, 1910s–1930
Silk plain weave *haori* (outer); printed silk *haura* (lining)
51.0 × 37.0 inches (130 × 94 centimeters)
KM194

Baseball was first introduced to Japan as a school sport in 1872 by Horace Wilson, an American professor who taught at an academy in Tokyo. By the early 20th century, it had become one of the most important—and popular—high-school sports in Japan. This *haori* carries an image that acknowledges a 1915 baseball awards ceremony for the winning high-school teams of the year. A cameraman on the playing field can be seen documenting this ceremony on film, which shows just how important baseball had become for boys and men alike.

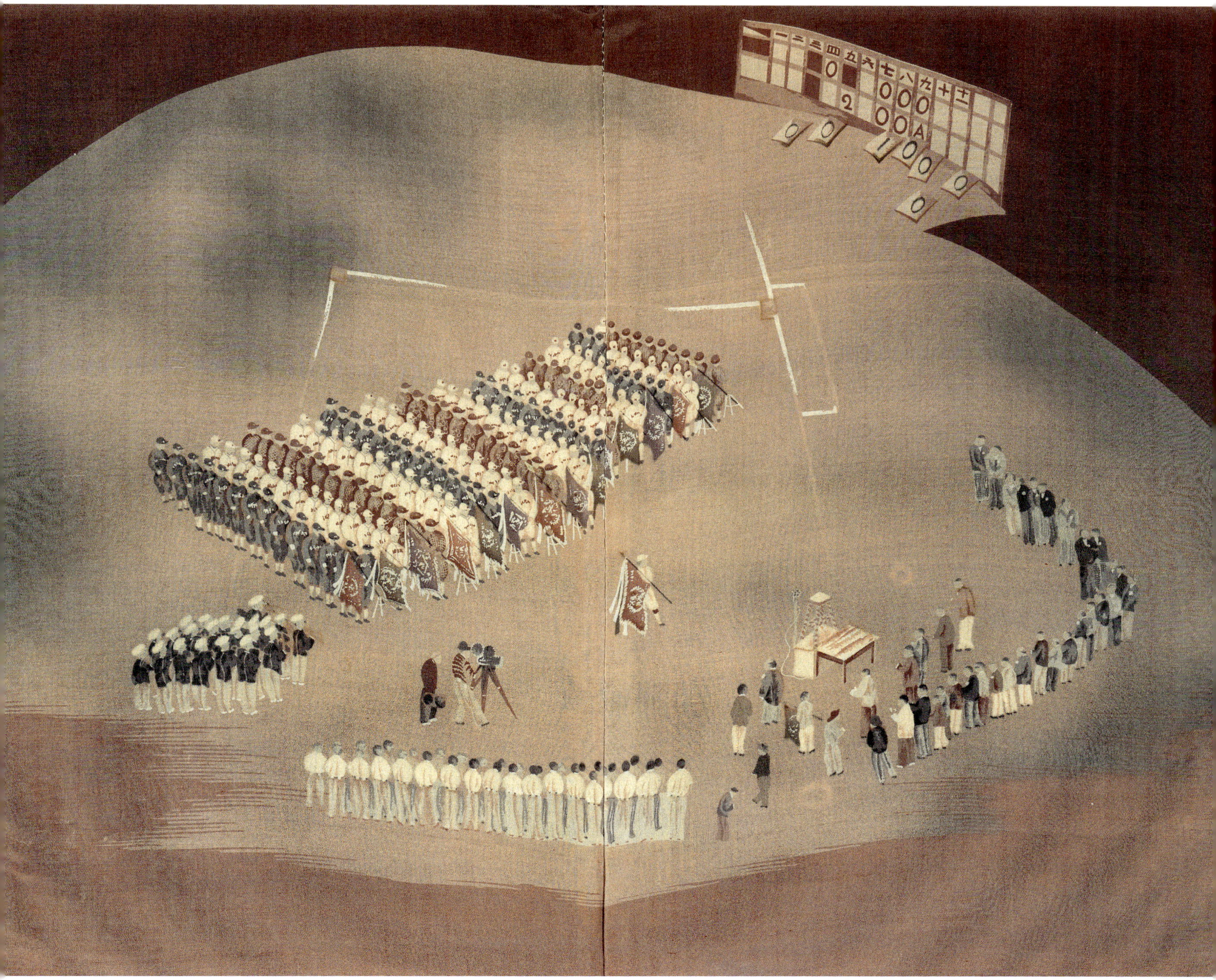

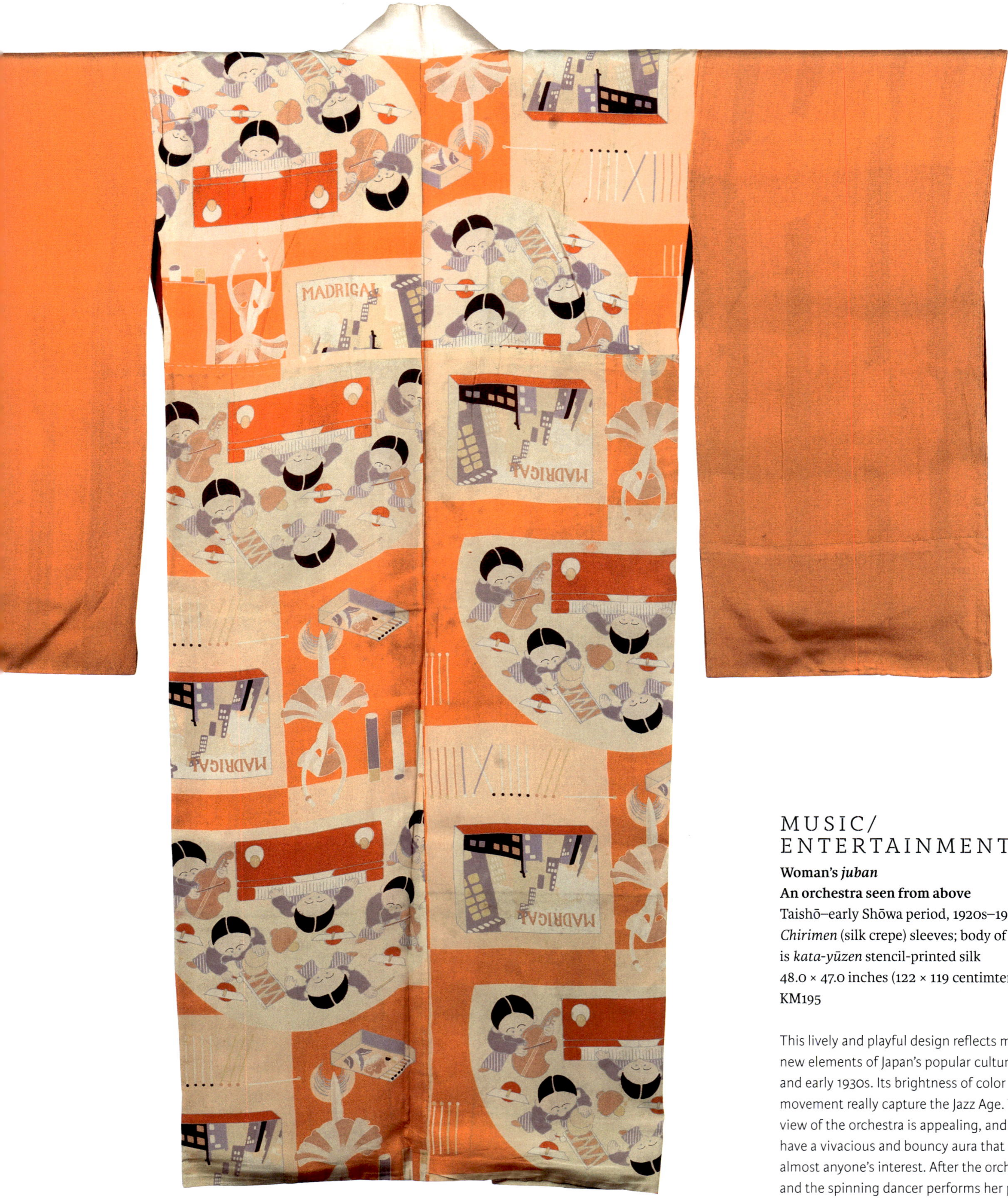

MUSIC/ ENTERTAINMENT

Woman's *juban*
An orchestra seen from above
Taishō–early Shōwa period, 1920s–1930s
Chirimen (silk crepe) sleeves; body of *juban* is *kata-yūzen* stencil-printed silk
48.0 × 47.0 inches (122 × 119 centimters)
KM195

This lively and playful design reflects many of the new elements of Japan's popular culture in the 1920s and early 1930s. Its brightness of color and sense of movement really capture the Jazz Age. The bird's eye view of the orchestra is appealing, and the players have a vivacious and bouncy aura that could capture almost anyone's interest. After the orchestra plays and the spinning dancer performs her part, a smoky environment ensues. Cigarettes and matches come out and the audience gesture with their cigarettes as they chat about the orchestra with gusto. "Madrigal" is the name of the cigarette box on the *juban*, and it might also be the orchestra's name.

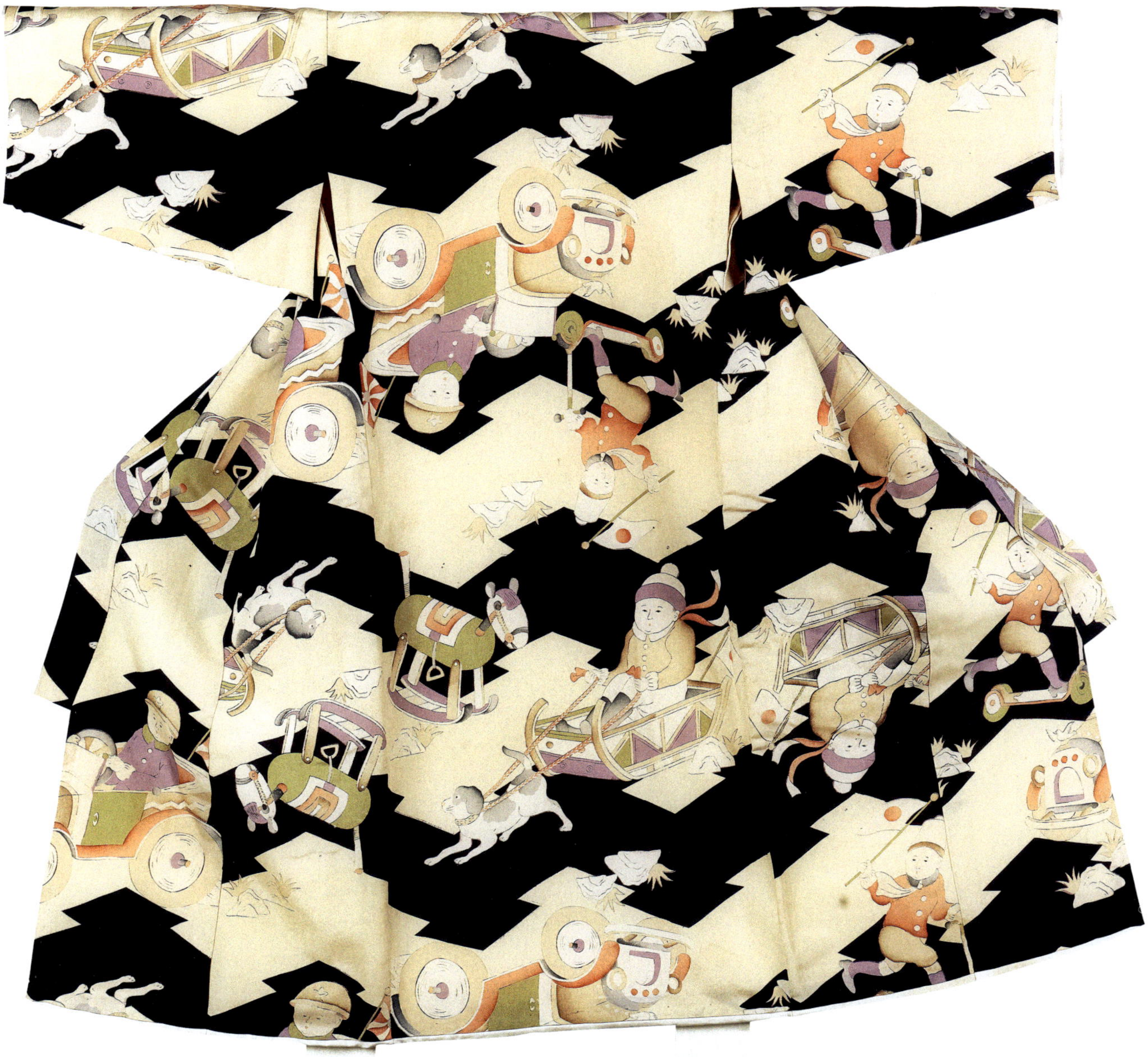

TRANSPORTATION

Kimono for a boy child
Modern transportation for boys
Taishō–early Shōwa period, 1920s–early 1930s
Kata-yūzen stenciled silk
35 × 34 inches (89 × 86 centimeters)
KM196

In Japan, the *matsukawabishi* design in horizontal stripes is associated with the military aristocracy, so this design was probably planned for boys. Even though these toy cars, sleds, hobby horses, and scooters are all clearly meant for children's use, the varieties of transportation reinforce the masculine theme while also demonstrating Japan's embrace of Western modernity. The boys here are shown in Western clothes and seem sincere about enjoying their Western playthings, which adds to the general good humor of the design. The pale colors and air-brushed style are typical of the period. The two flags that decorate the toys—Japan's national flag and the flag of the Imperial Navy—became popular design motifs after the victories in the Russo-Japanese and Sino-Japanese wars.

COSMOPOLITANISM/ TOBACCO

Man's *haori* with a decorative lining
Cigarettes galore!
Taishō–Shōwa period, 1930s–1940s
Silk plain weave *haori* (outer); *kata-yūzen* stencil-printed silk (lining)
51.0 × 41.0 inches (130 × 104 centimeters)
KM197

The Japanese government established a tobacco monopoly in the early 20th century that included manufactured tobacco products such as cigarettes, cigars, and pipes. The ostensible reason for the expansion of tobacco control was to help fund the Russo-Japanese War in 1904–05, and foreign producers were gradually pushed out to protect the domestic tobacco and cigarette industry. When Japan annexed Manchuria in 1931, cigarettes began to be produced there as well, as is documented on the silk textile used for the interior lining of this *haori*. Each of these cigarette boxes (or packets) served essentially as advertisements, reinforcing general interest in these products.

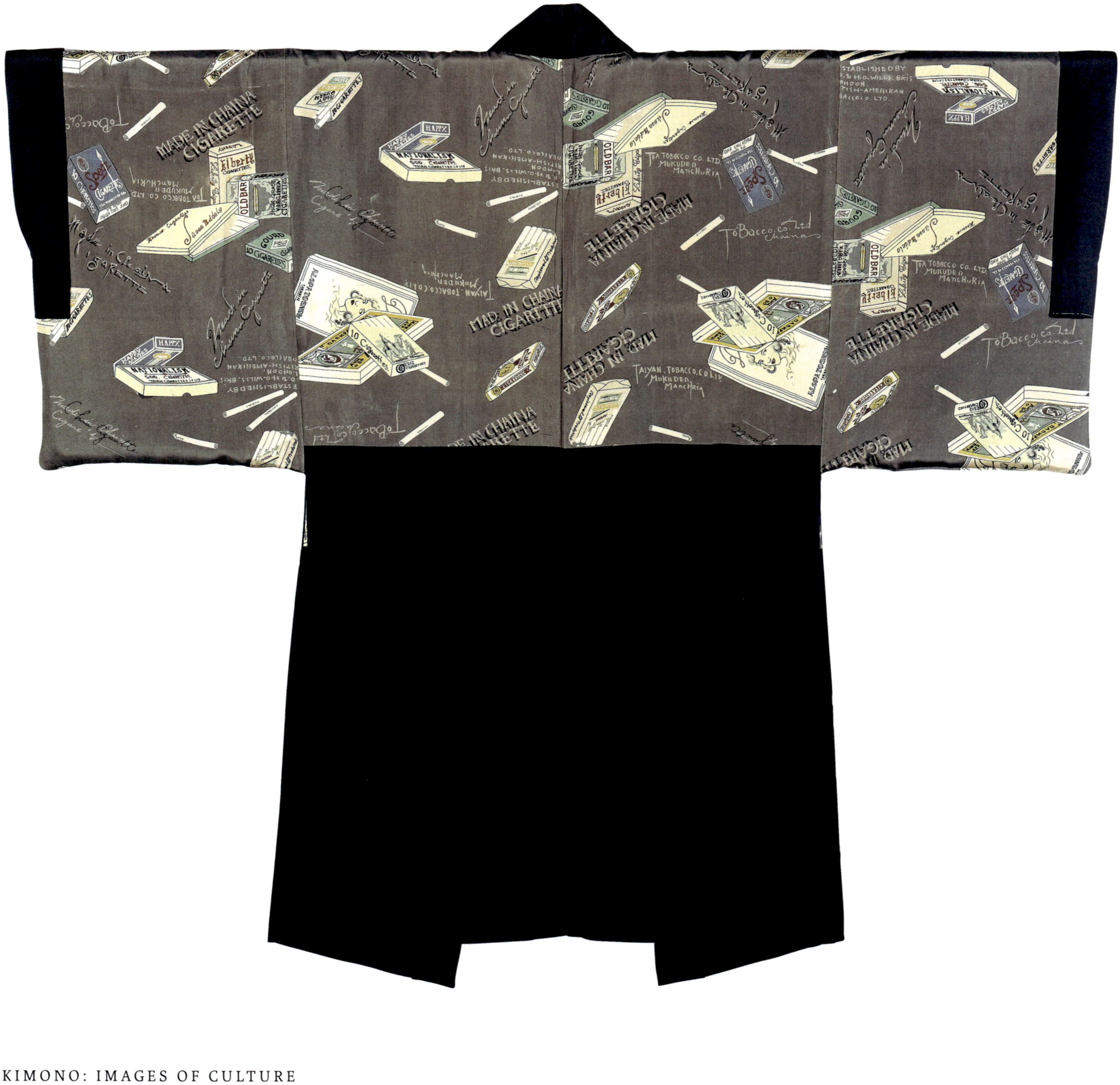

COSMOPOLITANISM/ TOBACCO

Man's *haori* with a decorative lining (*haura*)
Cigarettes and political figures
Taishō–Shōwa period, 1920s–1940s
Silk plain weave *haori* (outer); *kata-yūzen* stencil-printed silk *haura* (lining)
52.0 × 40.0 inches (132 × 102 centimeters)
KM198

The decorative *haura* in this *haori* shows off special stencil-printed cigarette boxes and packets, which sport attractive designs and text that add extra appeal for the smokers. Purchasers of these boxes would often show off the package images as they gently pulled the cigarettes from their boxes. Foreign Western cigarette companies exported and sold cigarettes to Japan, but Japan also produced their own cigarette packages—many of which were manufactured in its own new territories. The six caricatures on the *haura* are of important contemporary political figures of the time—who were quite likely to enjoy the new cigarettes at the end of their hard-working days.

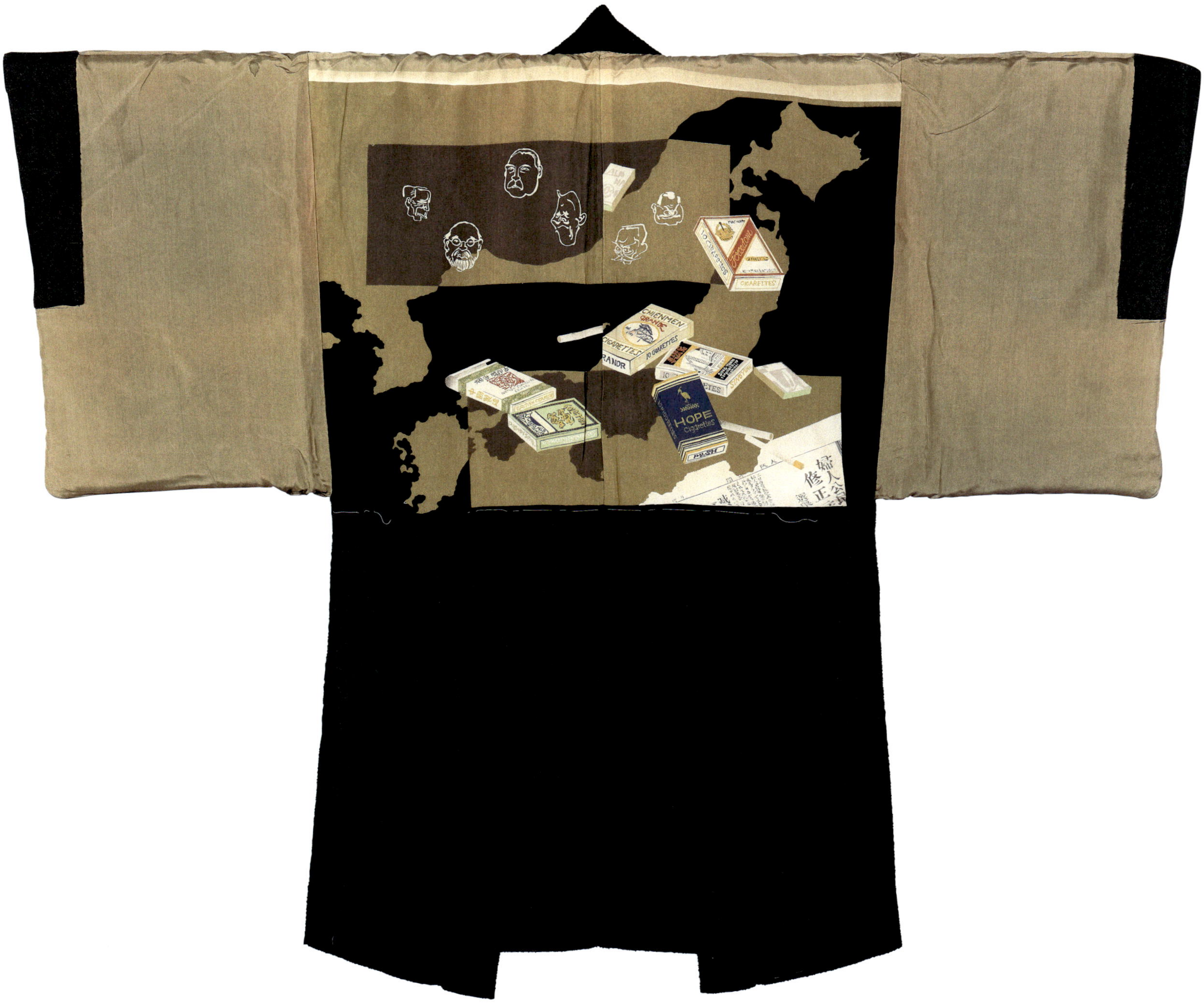

ENTERTAINMENT

***Hanjuban* (half-*juban*) for a man**
Cartoon characters: Donald Duck and friends
Shōwa period, 1930s–1940s
Striped silk (*haori* outer); printed silk lining (interior)
52.0 × 31.0 inches (132 × 79 centimeters)
KM199

This *hanjuban* was probably made as casualwear for an adult. The lining is playful and lively, and adults were likely to be as amused as children by Donald Duck's cartoon escapades. The group of cartoon animals placed on this textile are likely to have played in Donald's films between 1937 and 1942. In fact, Tootsie the penguin—who appears here with a red bowtie on his neck—appeared in the 1939 film *Donald's Penguin*. Donald Duck cartoons continued to be very popular for many more years, entertaining many people, young and old.

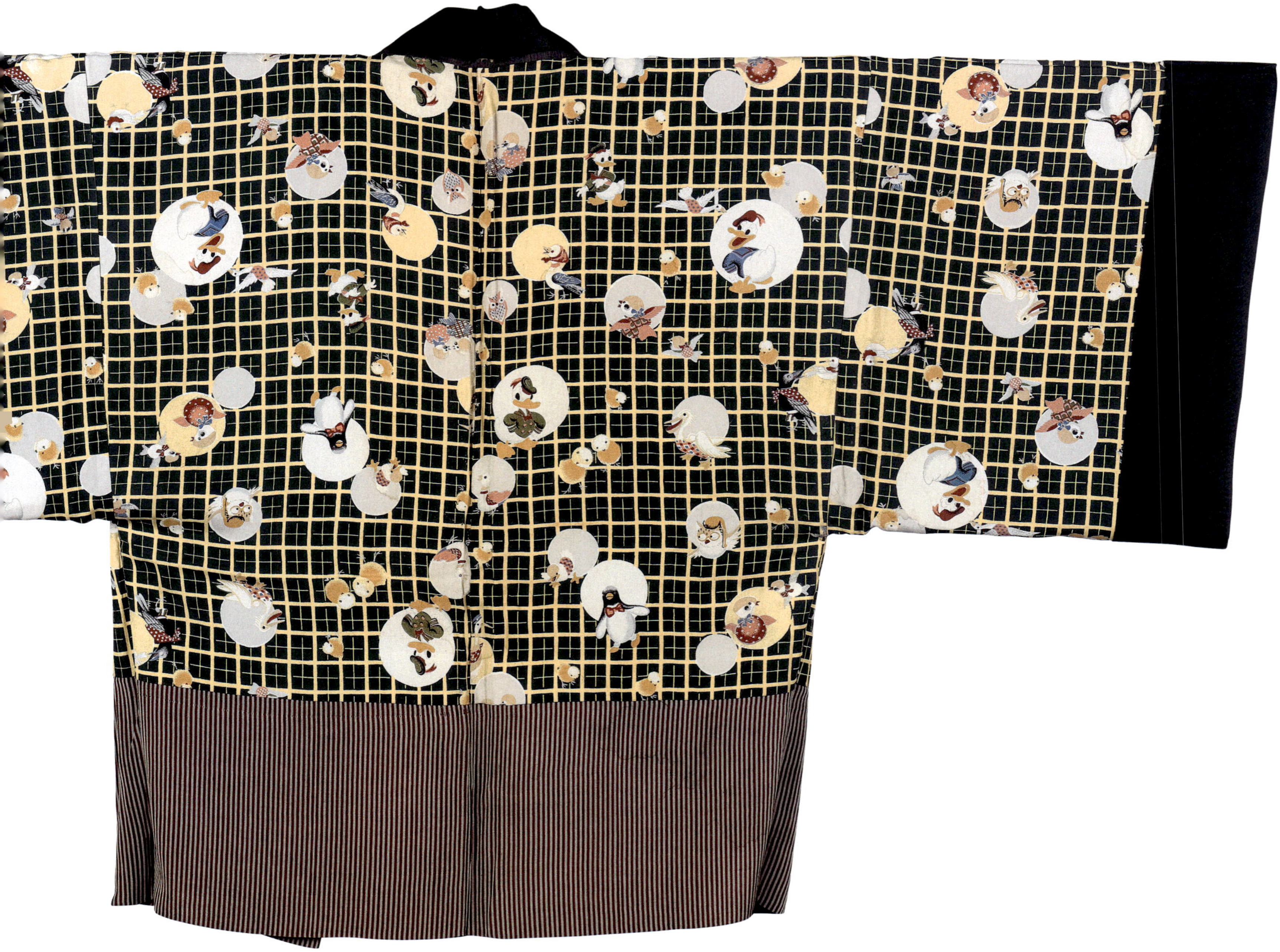

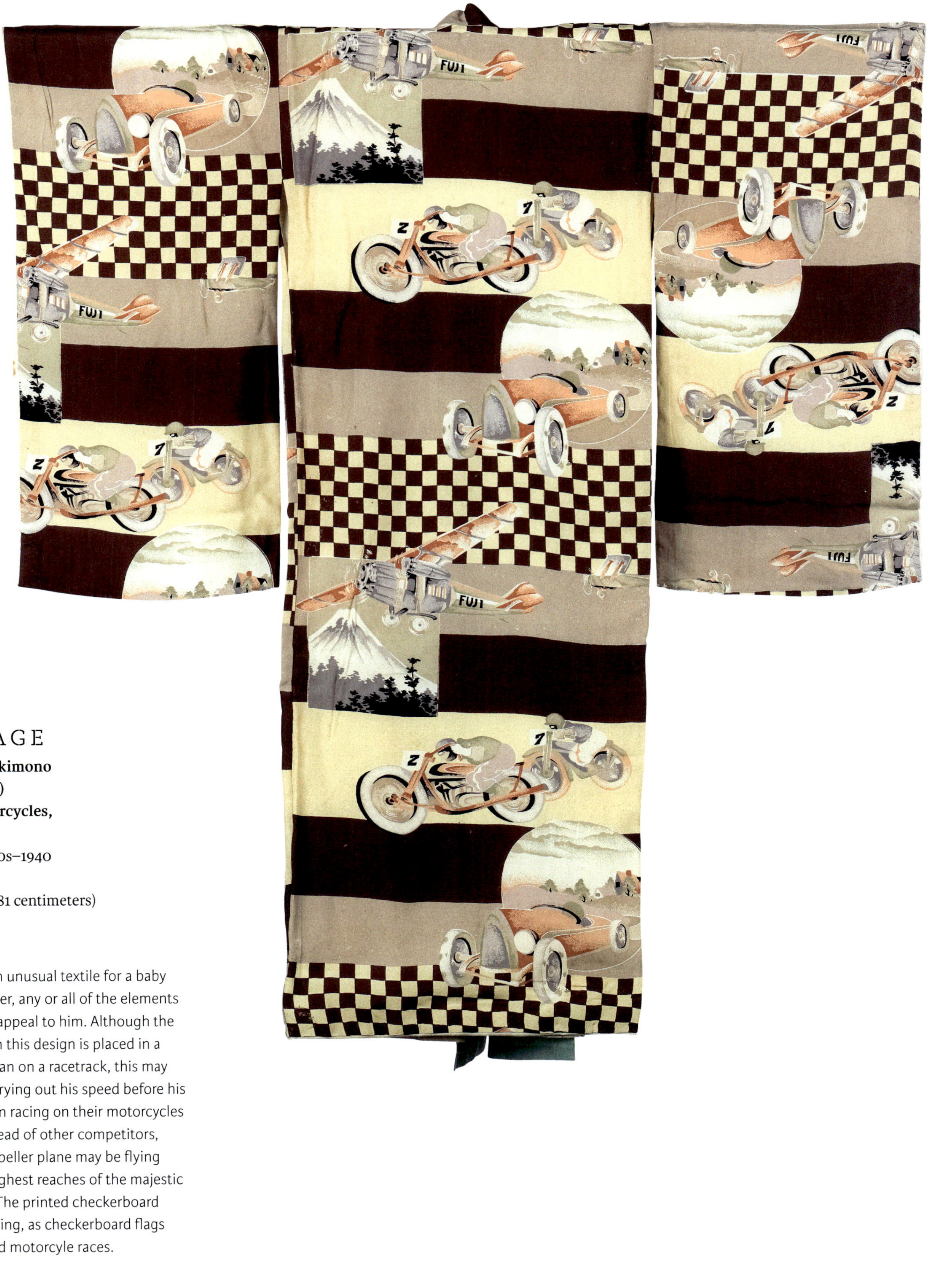

MACHINE AGE

Miyamairi **(boy child's kimono for his first shrine visit)**
Racing with cars, motorcycles, and an airplane to Fuji
Shōwa period, early 1930s–1940
Printed rayon
36.0 × 32.0 inches (91 × 81 centimeters)
KM200

This might seem to be an unusual textile for a baby boy, but, as he grows older, any or all of the elements shown here are likely to appeal to him. Although the sleek racing car shown in this design is placed in a country setting rather than on a racetrack, this may imply that the owner is trying out his speed before his race takes place. The men racing on their motorcycles can be imagined well ahead of other competitors, and the "FUJI" three-propeller plane may be flying sightseers to view the highest reaches of the majestic mountain known to all. The printed checkerboard textile serves well for racing, as checkerboard flags are used often for car and motorcyle races.

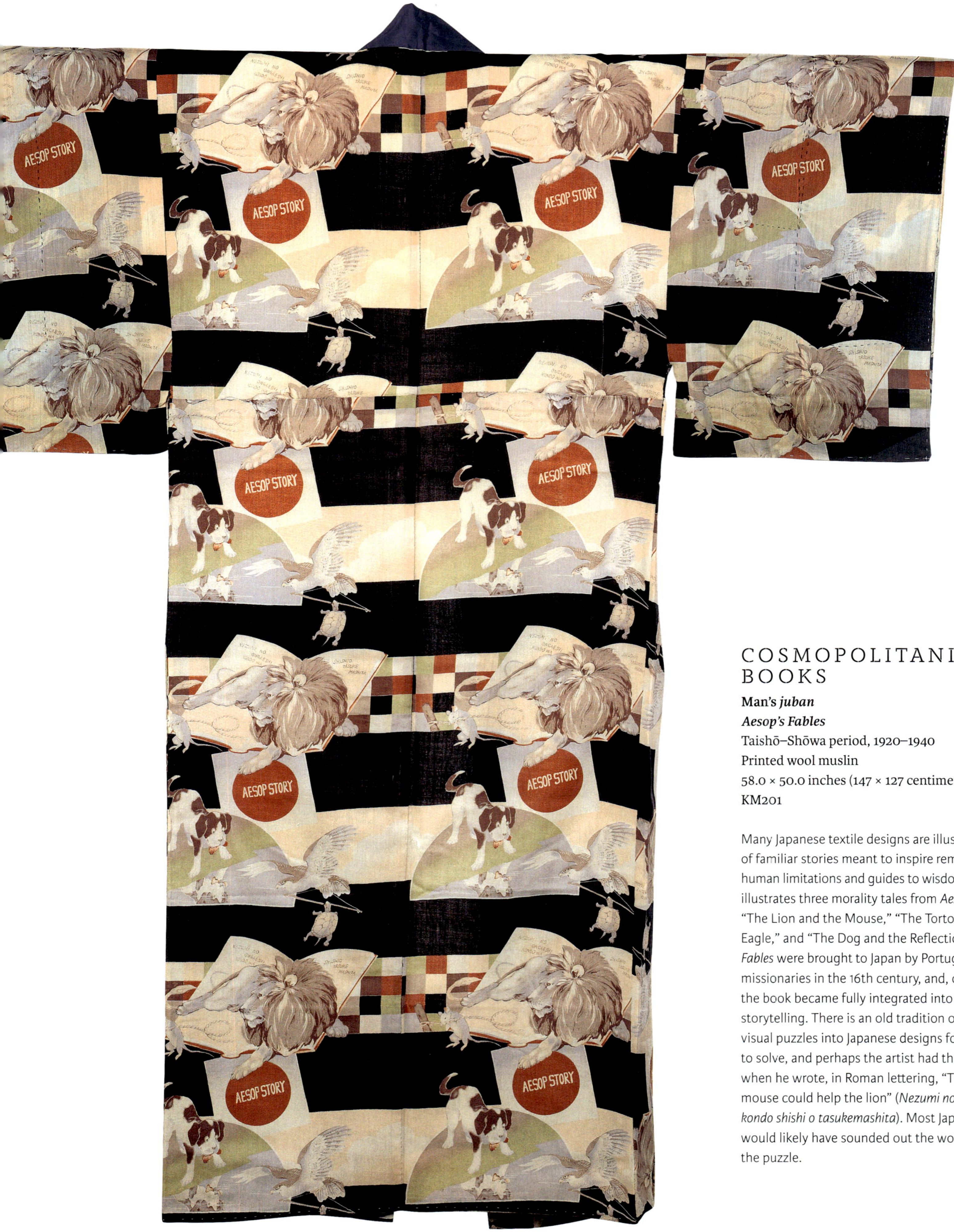

COSMOPOLITANISM: BOOKS

Man's *juban*
Aesop's Fables
Taishō–Shōwa period, 1920–1940
Printed wool muslin
58.0 × 50.0 inches (147 × 127 centimeters)
KM201

Many Japanese textile designs are illustrations of familiar stories meant to inspire reminders of human limitations and guides to wisdom. This *juban* illustrates three morality tales from *Aesop's Fables*: "The Lion and the Mouse," "The Tortoise and the Eagle," and "The Dog and the Reflection." *Aesop's Fables* were brought to Japan by Portuguese missionaries in the 16th century, and, over time, the book became fully integrated into Japanese storytelling. There is an old tradition of inserting visual puzzles into Japanese designs for the viewer to solve, and perhaps the artist had this in mind when he wrote, in Roman lettering, "This time the mouse could help the lion" (*Nezumi no ongaeshi wa kondo shishi o tasukemashita*). Most Japanese people would likely have sounded out the words in solving the puzzle.

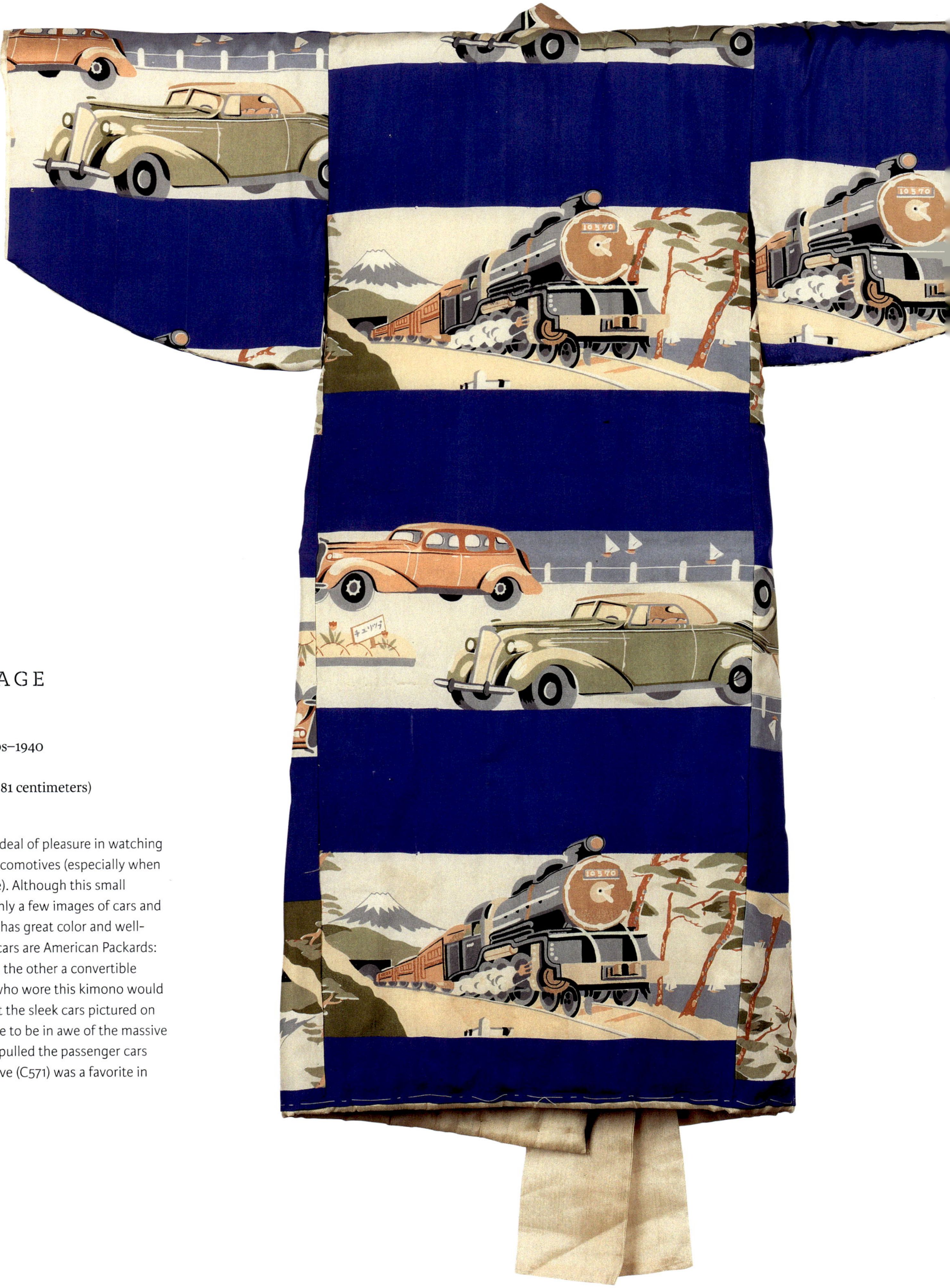

MACHINE AGE

Young boy's kimono
Favorite things
Shōwa period, late 1930s–1940
Printed silk
32.0 × 32.0 inches (81 × 81 centimeters)
KM202

Young boys find a great deal of pleasure in watching new cars and massive locomotives (especially when given a chance for a ride). Although this small garment has room for only a few images of cars and locomotives, the textile has great color and well-designed vehicles. The cars are American Packards: one is an elegant sedan, the other a convertible coupé. The young boy who wore this kimono would have smiled in delight at the sleek cars pictured on his robe, and he was sure to be in awe of the massive engine that effortlessly pulled the passenger cars behind it. This locomotive (C571) was a favorite in the late 1930s.

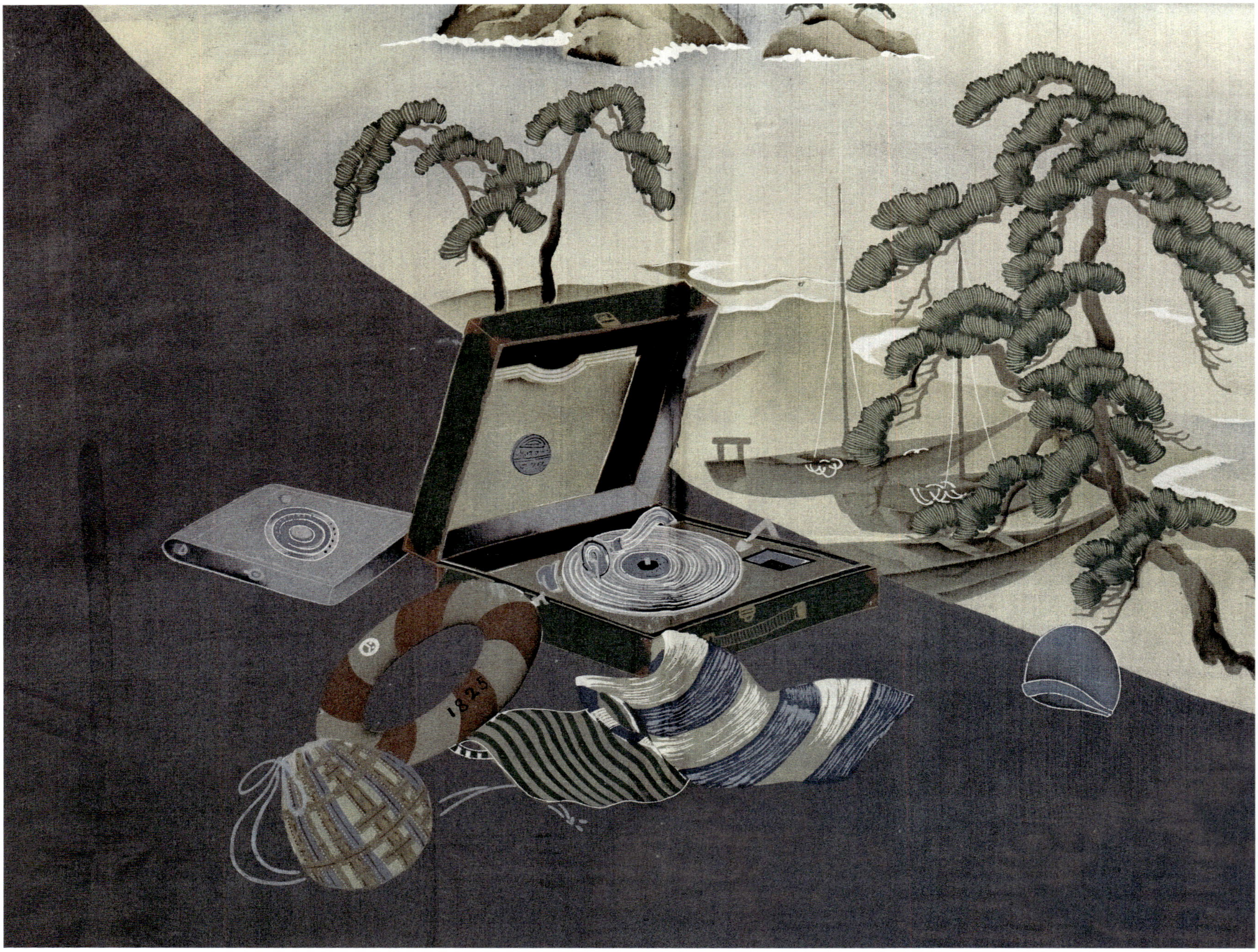

TRAVEL/MODERNITY

Man's *haori* with a decorative lining
Music on the beach
Taishō–Shōwa period, 1920s–1940
Silk plain weave *haori* (exterior); *kata-yūzen* stencil-printed fabric for *haura* (lining)
51.0 × 44.0 inches (130 × 112 centimeters)
KM203

This travel design is a delightful mystery. The objects left on the beach—a beach bag and towels, a bathing cap, a life preserver, a camera, and a record player with records—provide amusing additions to the ocean shore that also encourage the *haori* owner to make guesses as to where the lady who owns them can be found. Although another *haura* design in this book (see p. 298) has elements similar to this *haura* (travel, records and music, an island scene), the two are different enough to work as companion pieces, with the mystery beach scene central to this *haura*, and the *moga* ("modern girl") as the central feature in "Dreaming of travel."

ENTERTAINMENT/ THEATRE

Man's *haori* with a decorative lining "Two Crazy Spirits"
Late Taishō–early Shōwa period, 1920s–1930s
Silk *haori* (outer); *yūzen* dyed and hand-painted silk *haura* (lining)
51.0 × 43.0 inches (130 × 109 centimeters)
KM204

This is a wonderful and lively design for a *haura* that celebrates the cosmopolitan nightlife of 1920s Japan. Two spirited dancers perform "Two Crazy Spirits" as part of the stage show in a large, modern theatre, and an energetic group of musicians keep the entertainment lively. A narrow panel on the left shows an audience rapt with interest even as the clock marks the late hour. The stage curtain on the lower seating level carries the name Clara Bow, an American actress who rose to stardom in Hollywood films in the 1920s and was equally popular in Japan. Perhaps the inclusion of her name means that one of her movies would be shown following the stage presentations.

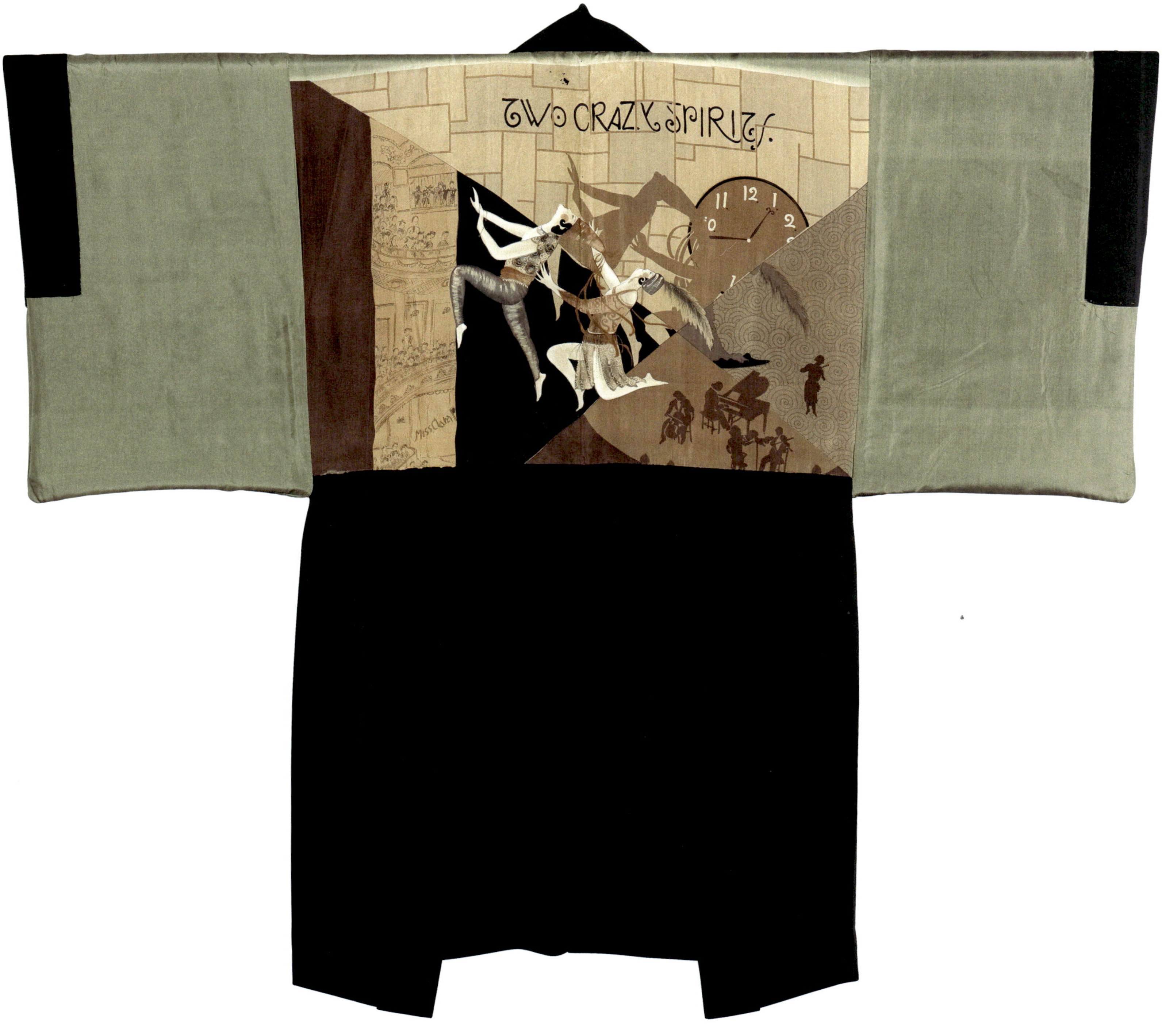

ENTERTAINMENT/ COSMOPOLITANISM

Man's *haori* with a decorative lining
Nudes posed in Western style
Taishō period, 1912–1920s
Slubbed silk (*haori* exterior); *kata-yūzen* stencil-printed rayon fabric (interior)
50.0 × 40.0 inches (127 × 102 centimeters)
KM205

The interior of this *haori* features a stencil-printed rayon fabric that carries vignettes of a nude model posed in a Western style. The images drawn in the vignettes were carefully sketched from the model, and the artist then filled in two of the backgrounds with sharply drawn parallel and cross-hatched lines for shading, which produces a strong contrast to the softer lines used for the model's figure. It is an unusual technique, but it produces an interesting study. The third pose is backed with a curtain and creates a softer feel. The three poses that the artist used seem to be following a classical style, and her hairstyle also seems to be rather classical. The vignettes are shown against a background of musical notes for interest.

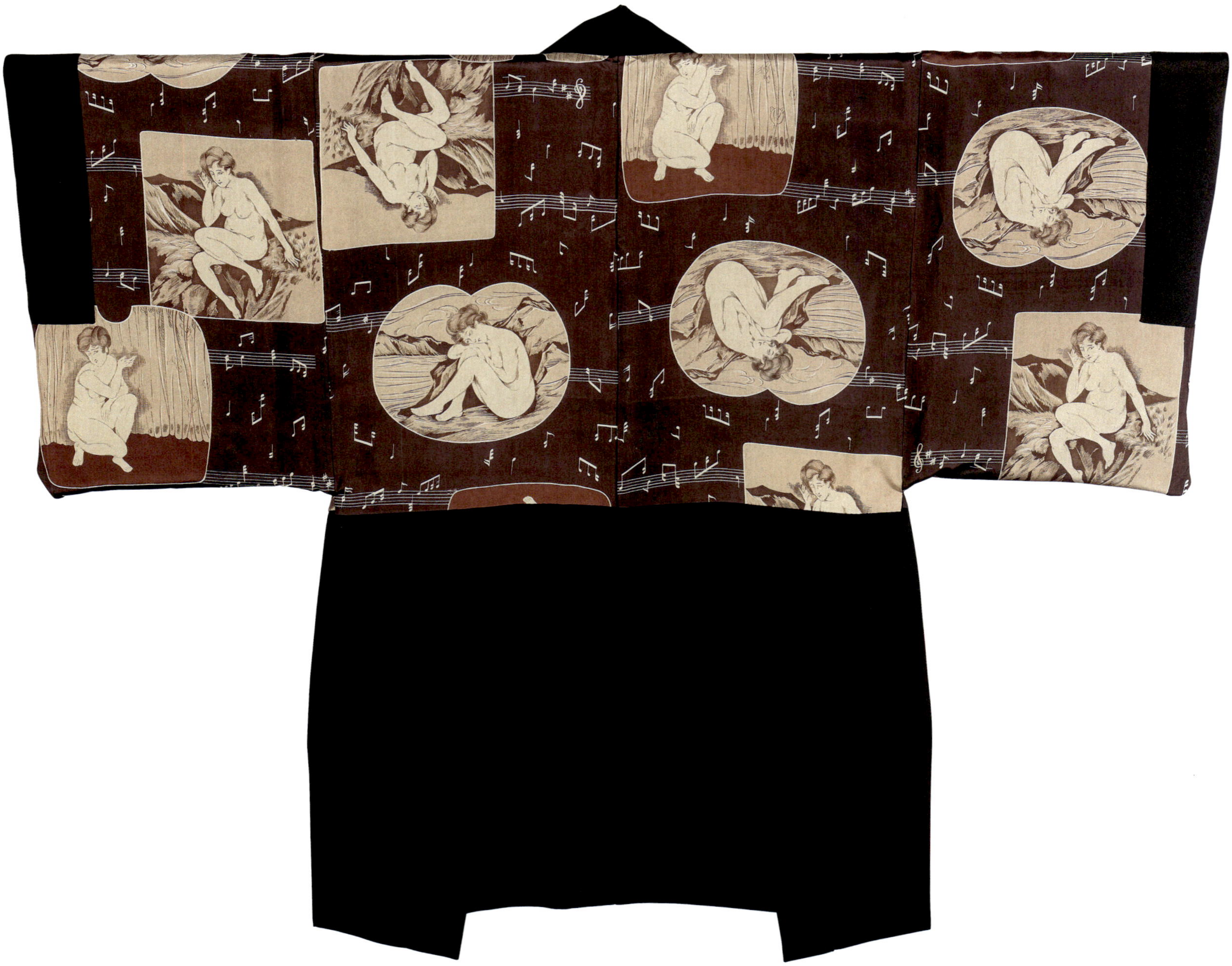

MACHINE AGE/ AIRCRAFT

Man's *haori* with a decorative lining (*haura*)
Flight around the world
Late Taishō–early Shōwa period, 1930–1940
Silk *haori* (outer); *kata-yūzen* dyed and stencil-printed silk *haura* (lining)
51.0 ×41.0 inches (130 × 104 centimeters)
KM206

Aircraft captured the Japanese imagination in the early 20th century, and flights made by adventurous aviators were frequently portrayed on men's garments, such as this *haori*. In the early 1930s, Wiley Post, an American aviator, broke two around-the-world record flights with *Winnie Mae*, a plane thought to be the most aerodynamically advanced aircraft of its time. In 1931, Post and his navigator set a record of 8 days, 15 hours, and 51 minutes—the first successful circumnavigation by a single-engine monoplane—and in 1933 he became the first person to fly solo around the world, traveling 15,596 miles in 7 days, 18 hours, and 45 minutes. The textile artist shows *Winnie Mae* circumnavigating the globe, creating a thrilling image for the *haori* owner to wear.

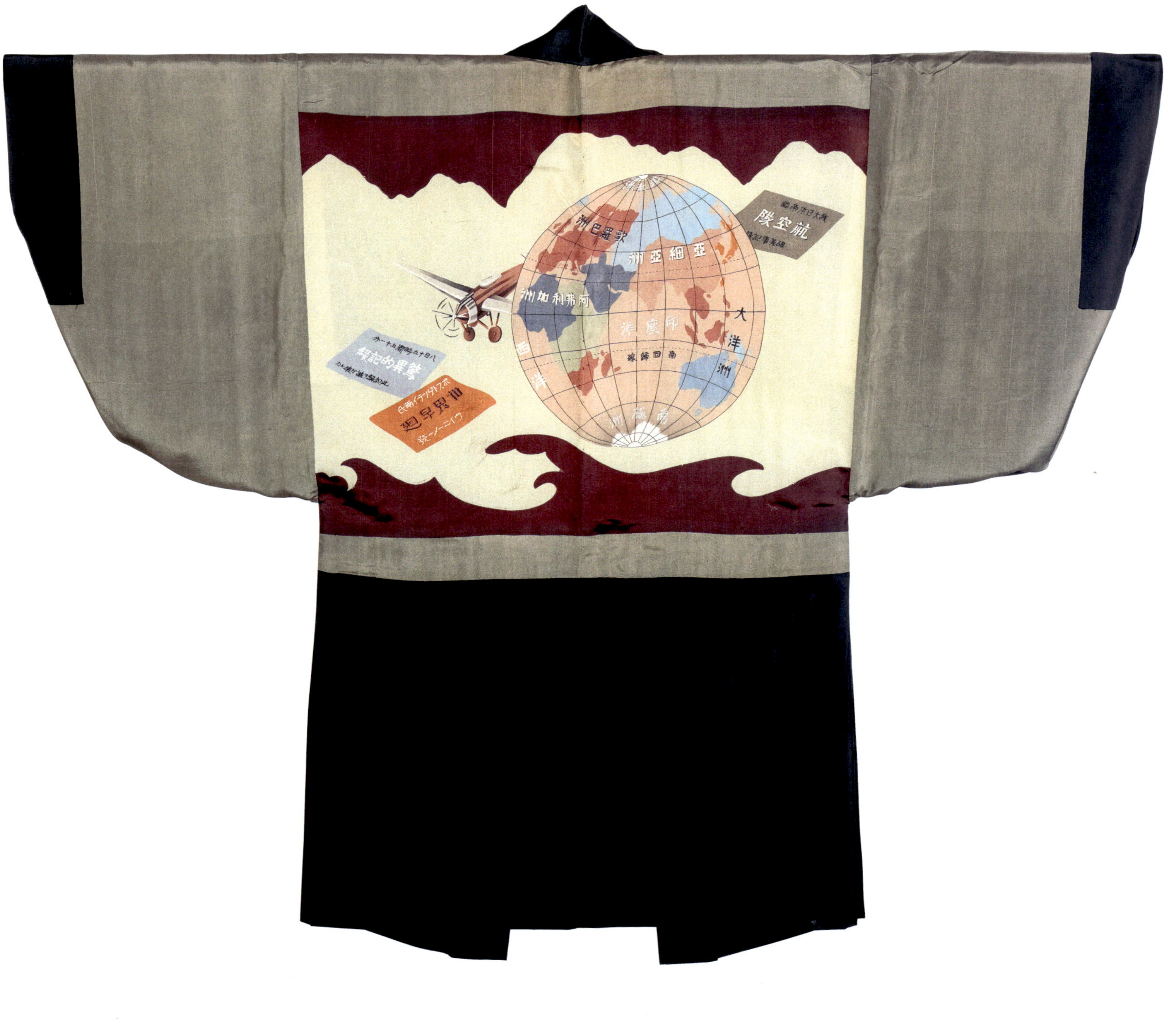

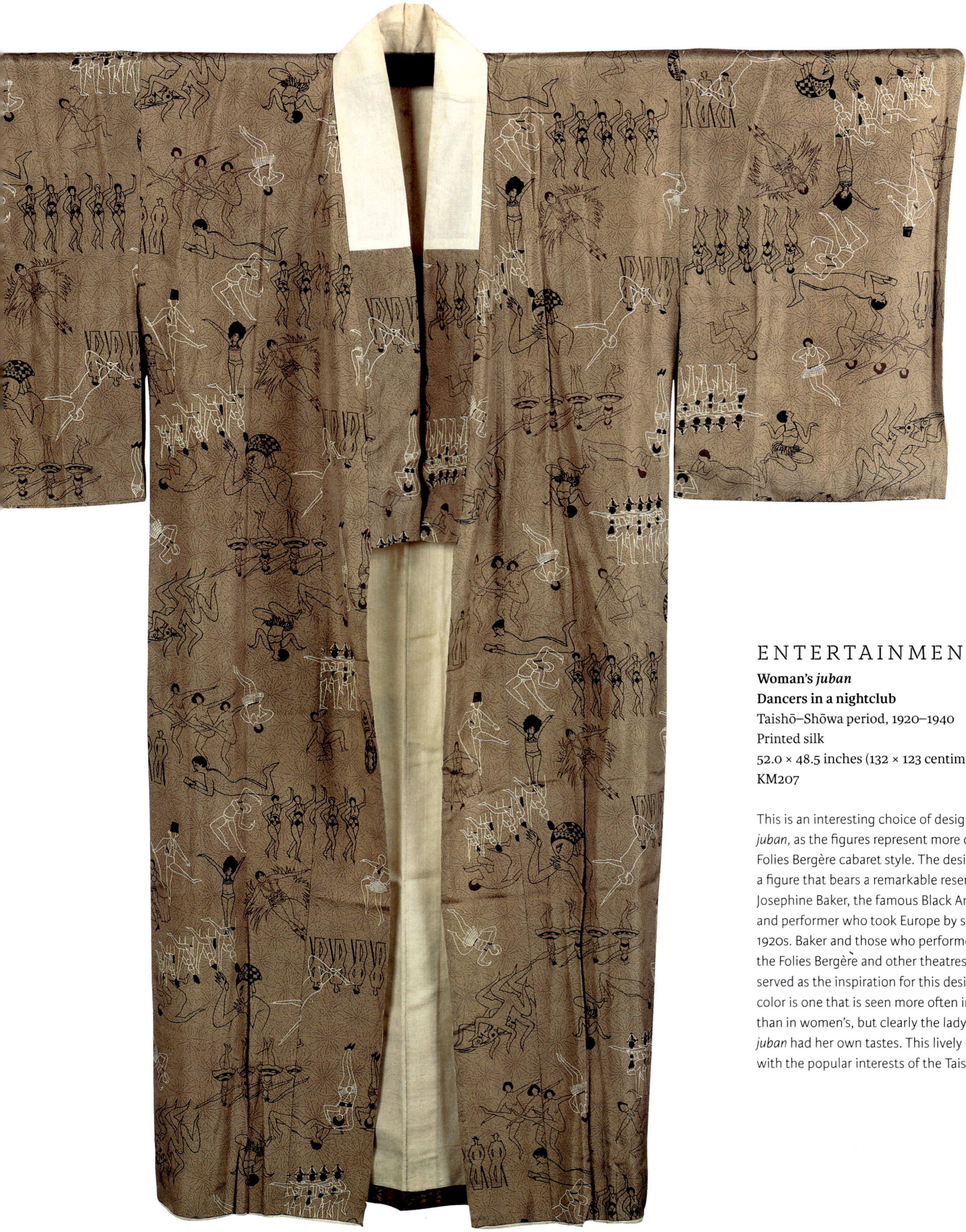

ENTERTAINMENT

Woman's *juban*
Dancers in a nightclub
Taishō–Shōwa period, 1920–1940
Printed silk
52.0 × 48.5 inches (132 × 123 centimeters)
KM207

This is an interesting choice of design for a woman's *juban*, as the figures represent more of a burlesque/ Folies Bergère cabaret style. The design includes a figure that bears a remarkable resemblance to Josephine Baker, the famous Black American dancer and performer who took Europe by storm in the 1920s. Baker and those who performed with her in the Folies Bergère and other theatres may well have served as the inspiration for this design. The subtle color is one that is seen more often in men's garments than in women's, but clearly the lady who owned this *juban* had her own tastes. This lively design fits well with the popular interests of the Taishō period.

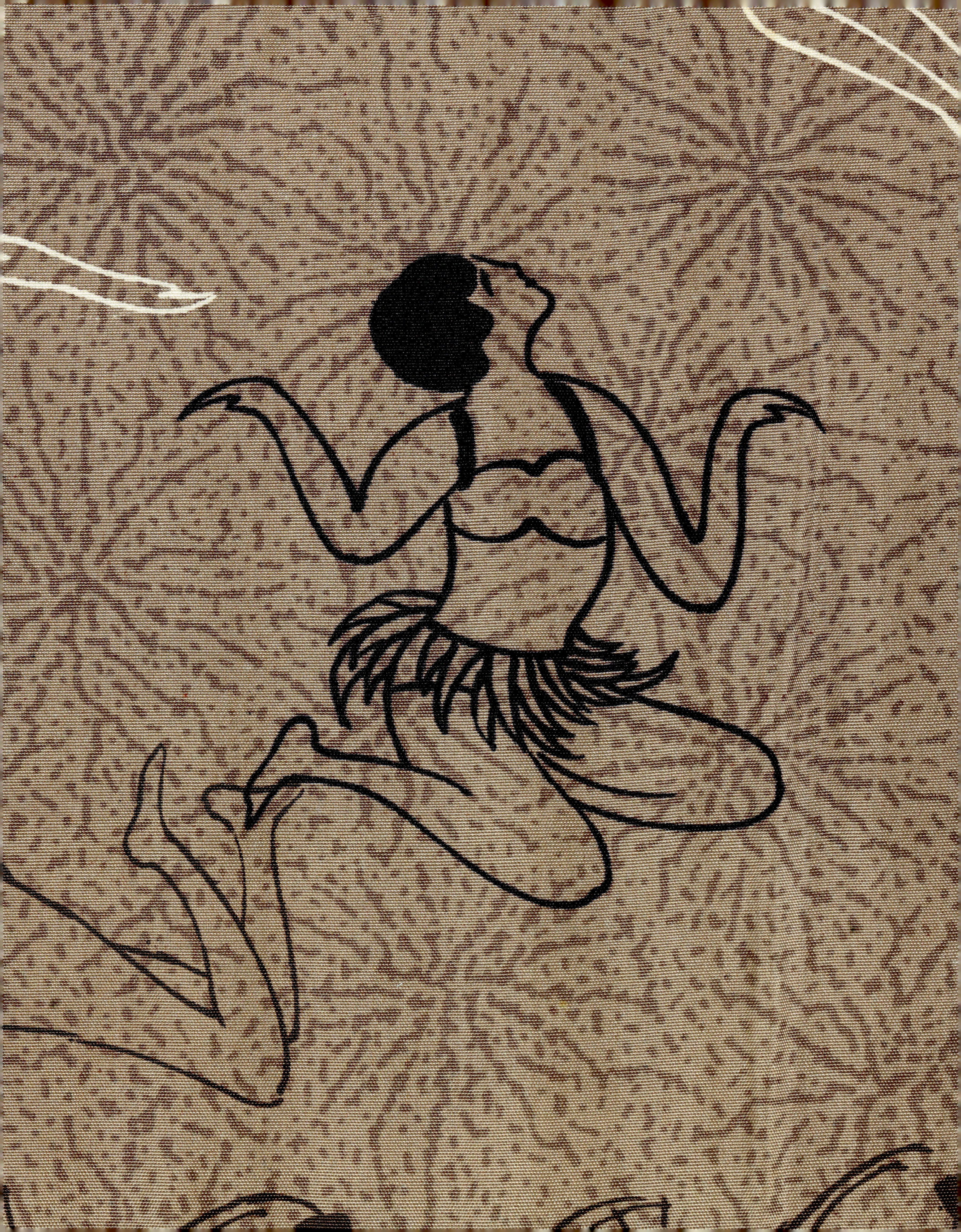

MODERNITY/ COSMOPOLITANISM

Man's *juban*
A study of love
Taishō–Shōwa period, late 1920s–1940
Silk *kata-yūzen* with stencil-printed fabric
52.8 × 51.0 inches (134 × 130 centimeters)
KM208

This design, reminiscent of modernist still lifes, offers a very eclectic group of objects for the composition. The sleeves of the *juban* carry objects of note—a glass of wine and a spoon on one sleeve, an ink bottle and feather pen on the other. At the center of the garment, a liquor bottle, matchbox, pipe, ashtray, fruit, books on sexual love, and a ship with a Grecian touch hint at a potential writer in the home. The overall design is interesting to a degree, and perhaps the objects on the table relate enough to each other for the writer to provide a coherent story.

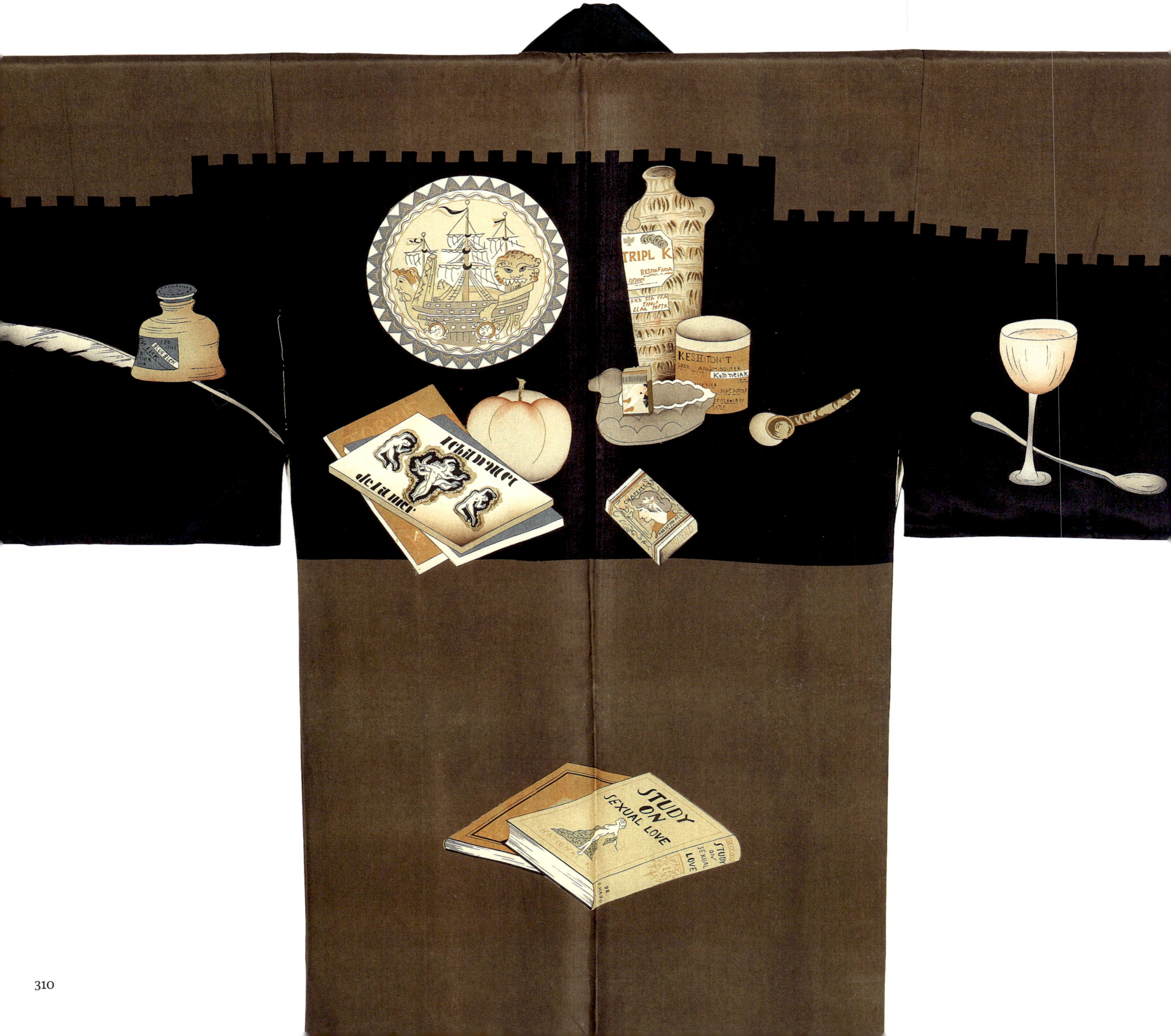

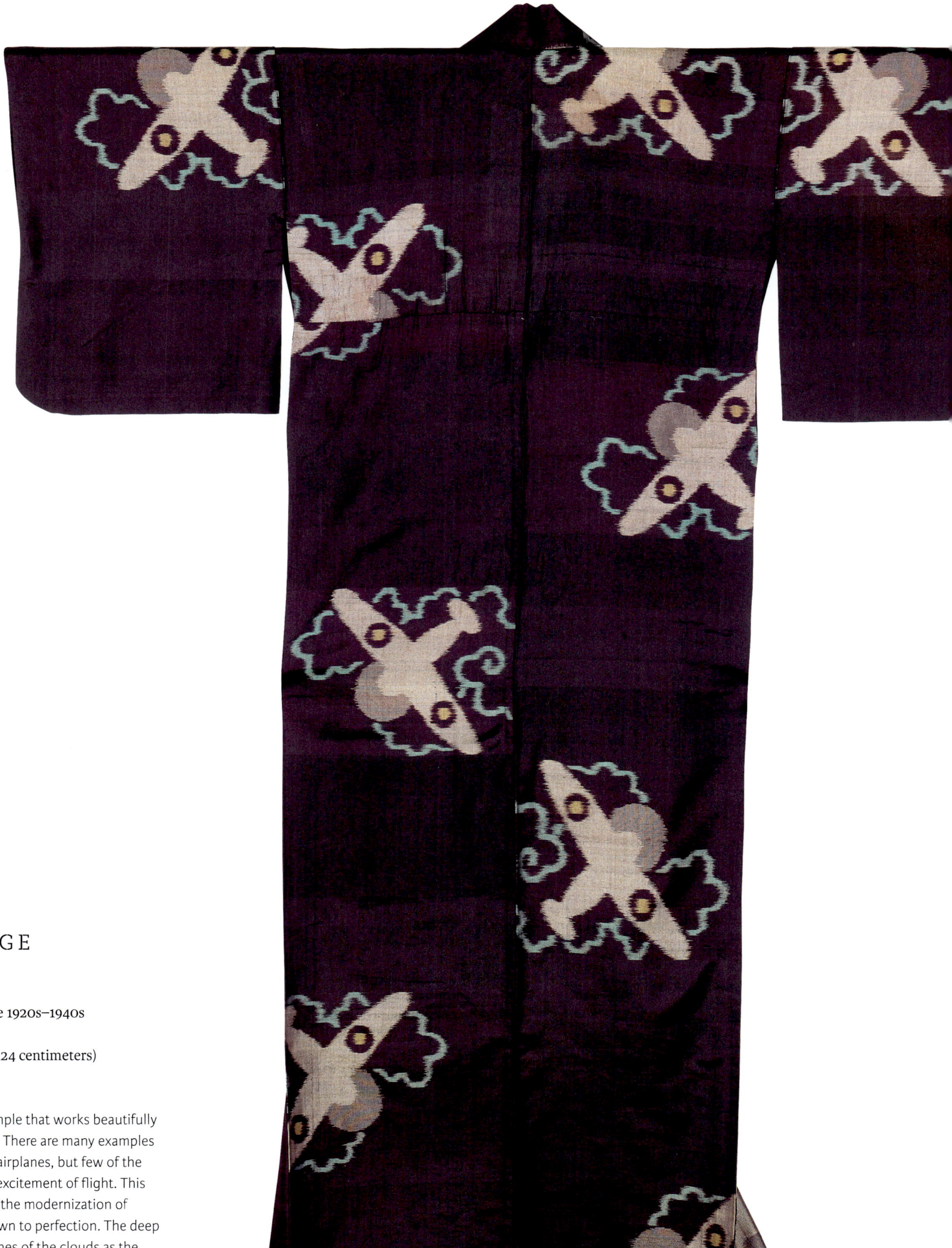

MACHINE AGE

Kimono for a woman
Airplanes in the clouds
Taishō–Shōwa period, late 1920s–1940s
Meisen silk
60.0 × 49.0 inches (152 × 124 centimeters)
KM209

This is a lovely *meisen* example that works beautifully with the garment's design. There are many examples of kimono with images of airplanes, but few of the women's capture the true excitement of flight. This is an important concept in the modernization of Japan—and this one is drawn to perfection. The deep purple highlights the outlines of the clouds as the spinning propellers on the noses of the aircraft give a halo effect. Its owner would have been very proud to wear this garment.

ENTERTAINMENT

Man's *haori*
Records for a gramophone
Taishō–early Showa period, 1910s–1930
Woven stripes (exterior); printed silk (back and front interior), silk sleeves (interior)
47.0 × 29.0 inches (119 × 74 centimeters)
KM210

The outer jacket of this man's *haori* carries a simple design of thin woven stripes of darkest blue and pale bluish grey, while the interior of the garment shows much livelier decoration in the form of Japanese records made for a gramophone. Gramophone records were printed on only one side in the last years of Meiji (around 1900), but by the Taishō years, the disks that could be played on the gramophone were two-sided. The disks shown on this garment were probably copied from real records of the early Taishō years, and the text in the background was likely taken from the music and songs on the records.

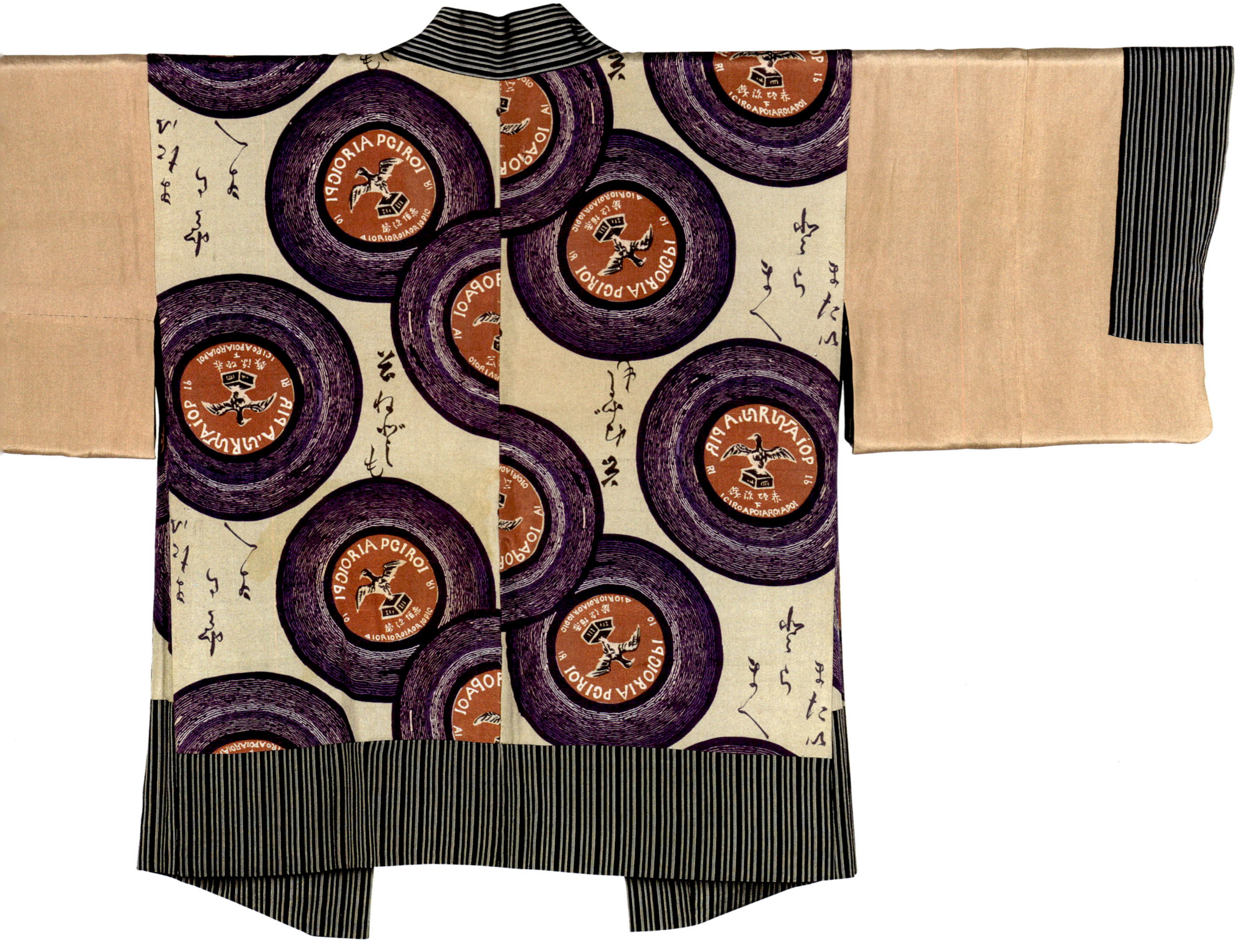

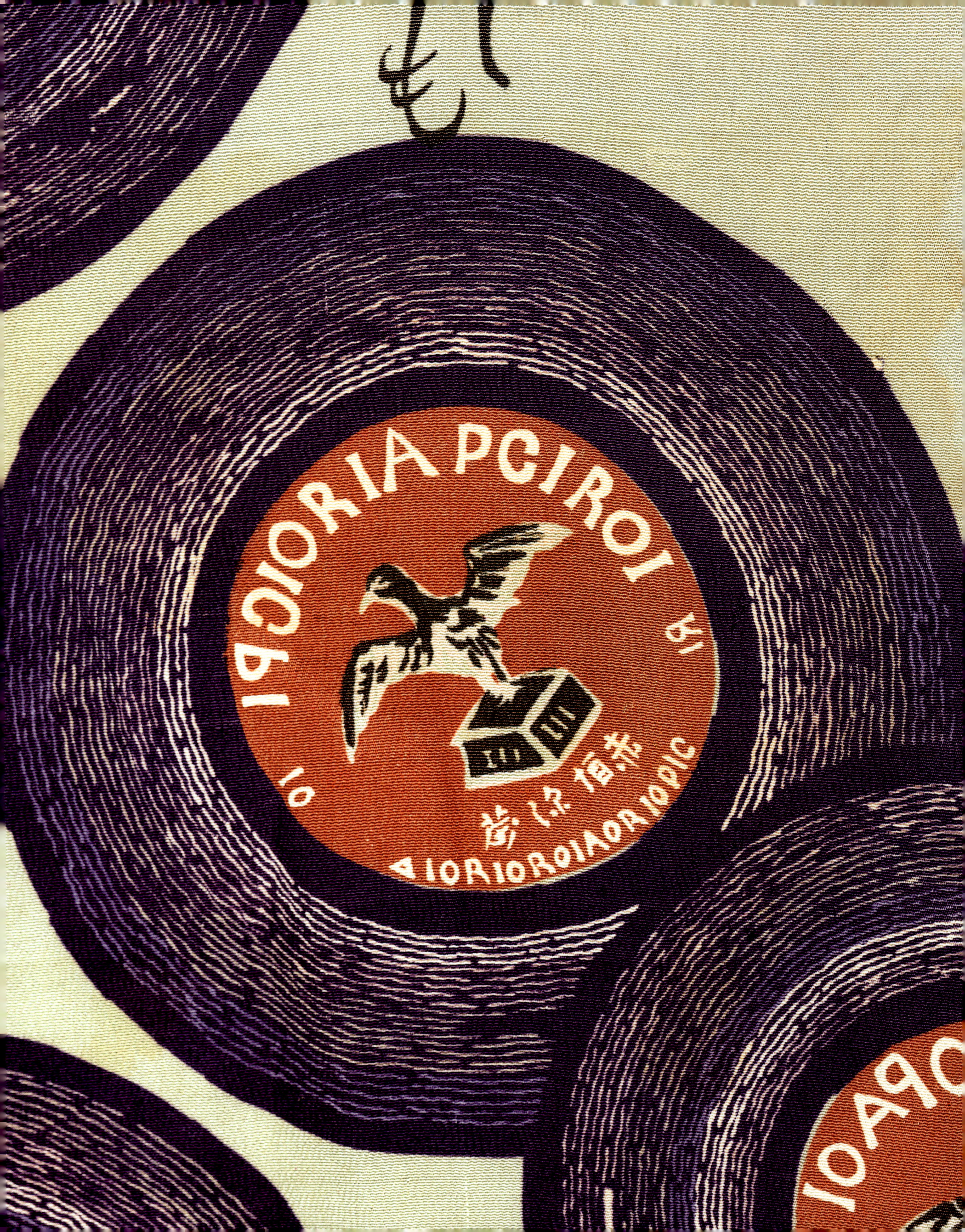

GLOSSARY OF JAPANESE TERMS

Anime – from "animation," Japanese animated films.

Asa – a general term which refers to cloth woven from bast (the inner bark of certain plants such as hemp, flax, and ramie).

Banzai – a common Japanese exclamation meaning "ten thousand years," a rallying cry for good fortune.

Bengara – derived from the Indian "Bengal," a reddish-brown pigment created from iron oxide.

Chanchanko – a sleeveless, often padded vest associated with childhood.

Chidori – plover birds.

Chikatetsu – lit. "underground iron," an unofficial Japanese term for subway, or underground railroad. See "Kokutetsu."

Chirimen – a type of silk crepe.

Dangawari – alternating color blocks.

Daruma – a traditional Japanese doll, usually round, painted red and made of papier-mâché, typically sold with eyes left intentionally white. The purchaser sets a goal or a wish and paints in the left iris. When this is completed or granted, they paint the right. Variations with both eyes filled and Daruma of different shapes are also common.

Doitsu – Germany.

E-gasuri – lit. "picture kasuri" (ikat). See "Kasuri" and "Niko-niko."

Gei – art, performance.

Gosho ningyō – lit. "palace or court dolls." Often chubby and white and, they represent hope for happiness and prosperity.

Gunshin – a god of war, military god, or war hero.

Hanjuban – half-size underkimono.

Hanten – a traditional Japanese short winter coat, padded and worn over garments. See "Tanzen."

Haori – a short hip- or thigh-length jacket worn over a kimono. See "Haura."

Haregi – formal or special-occasion kimono. Sometimes referred to as a "visiting" kimono.

Hato – a pigeon or dove.

Haura – the lining of a haori jacket. See "Haori."

Hinomaru – the national flag of Japan, also meaning "circle of the sun."

Hitotsumi – a small kimono for toddlers or babies.

Ikat – a resist dyeing technique originating in Southeast Asia, typically displaying a "blurred" finished look. See "Kasuri" and "E-gasuri."

Itajimezome – lit. "board-clamp dye." A pre-shaped resist dyeing method using carved wooden clamps.

Jinbaori – a surcoat, a short, sleeveless tunic typically worn by samurai over armor.

Jinken – artificial silk.

Ju – 寿, meaning longevity. Forms part of the name of Fukurokuju (lit. fuku, "happiness"; roku, "wealth"; and ju, "longevity"), one of the Seven Gods of Good Fortune.

Juban – overall term for undergarments worn underneath kimono. See "Nagajuban" and "Hanjuban."

Kamishibai – lit. "paper play" or "paper theatre," a form of street entertainment which featured sliding paper picture cards displayed using a wooden box, accompanied by narration.

Kasuri – a resist-dyeing method, a form of ikat dyeing. See "Ikat" and "E-gasuri."

Katabami – wood sorrel, its shape often used in family crests. See "Mon."

Kata-yūzen – stenciled yūzen. An effective and quick method of producing yūzen fabrics using paper stencils (*katagami*) for the designs. The dye is then applied using a brush directly on the fabric or using paste. See "Yūzen," "Suri-yūzen," and "Utsushi-yūzen."

Kodomogara – children's motifs.

Koi – informal name for colored variants of carp.

Kokuminfuku – Western-style national civilian uniform.

Kokutetsu – lit. "national iron," an unofficial Japanese term for overground railroad. See "Chikatetsu."

Kōshaku – an imperial rank of prince, duke, or marquis, depending on spelling.

Makinori – a technique used as part or paste-resist dyeing (yūzen) where the paste is sprinkled in small pallets to create a "mottled" or "sprinkled" effect. See "Yūzen."

Manga – Japanese printed cartoons or comics.

Matsukawabishi – lit. "bark of the pine tree," a zigzag band pattern resembling serrated lozenges.

Meisen – machine-spun silk made from lower-grade cocoons.

Miyamairi – lit. "shrine visit," a Shinto ceremony for newborn babies which involves a visit to a Shinto shrine by the family and baby for a blessing.

Mobo – lit. "modern boys," English portmanteau.

Moga – lit. "modern girls," English portmanteau.

Mon – family crest. See "Katabami."

Monpe – practical work pants typically worn by female agricultural workers became more widely used during the 1930s and 1940s due to their versatility and ease of altering.

Mosulin – transliteration of "muslin." In Japanese context refers to wool fabric, most likely derived from *mousseline de laine*, a late-19th-century French fabric of fine wool muslin.

Muso haori – "Muso" lit. "not a pair" or "only one." A haori in which there is no cutting between the interior and exterior layers. See "Haori."

Myōga – a variant of ginger, often dubbed "Japanese ginger."

Nagajuban – full-length under-kimono. See "Juban" and "Hanjuban."

Niko-niko kasuri – durable wool or cotton (and occasionally silk) textile with a printed pattern or image. Niko-niko lit. "smile" or "giggle," so a "joke" kasuri, often imitating e-gasuri. See "E-gasuri."

Ningyō – a Japanese doll.

Nippon – Japanese name for Japan.

Nisei – lit. "second generation," the children of Japanese immigrants born outside Japan.

Nobori – lit. "ascent," a Japanese vertical banner, long, narrow flags fixed to a pole.

Noshime kosode – a samurai class formal kimono, kosode being a kimono with short sleeves.

Obasan – a term denoting an older woman, an "auntie."

Obi – horizontal sash worn on the outside of a kimono.

Omishirogara – lit. "amusing" patterns in Japanese. See "Sensōgara" and "Kodomogara."

Ōshima silk – a celebrated type of silk produced in the Amami Islands (mainly Amami Ōshima) in southern Japan. It is handwoven from handspun silk yarns dyed in local mud.

Pongee – a fabric often made of silk originating in China, which bears a characteristic "slubbed" appearance of uneven texture with thick and thin threads.

Rinzu silk – a luxurious, figured, silk satin weave.

Rō silk – a loosely woven silk fabric, often with skipped lines in the weave, which create a striped, airy and sheer textile. A summer silk.

Romaji – the use of Latin script to spell Japanese words.

Samurai – a Japanese military nobility class serving under a Daimyo (feudal lord) from the late 12th century until the dissolution of the Shogunate in the late 19th century. Before the 12th century was used to denote an aristocratic warrior (bushi).

Sashiko – a type of Japanese embroidery which relies on simple, bright (typically white), run-on hand stitching, often using geometric patterns.

Semamori – a small stitched-on talisman sewn primarily into children's clothing.

Sensōgara – lit. "wartime" patterns in Japanese. See "Omoshirogara" and "Kodomogara."

Shibori – a general term for a Japanese resist-dyeing technique using binding of the fabric in various ways before applying the dye.

Shichigosan – lit. "seven-five-three," a Japanese festival for children of the titular ages, celebrating their growth.

Shinto – Japan's indigenous beliefs and practices.

Shōgunsō – a Japanese term for the arrowhead plant, lit. meaning "victorious army plant" and thus is often favoured by samurai family crests "Mon."

Suri-yūzen – a type of Kata-yūzen where stencils are used to create patterns, in this instance using a brush to dye the fabric. See "Kata-yūzen" and "Utsushi-yūzen."

Tachibana – a variety of mandarin orange native to Japan.

Takarazukushi – lit. "plethora of treasure," a decorative pattern depicting various auspicious items often associated with the Seven Gods of Good Fortune.

Tanzen – a traditional Japanese padded winter coat, a longer version of the hanten. See "Hanten."

Torii – a traditional Japanese gate, often found at the entrance to Shinto shrines, denoting an entrance to a sacred space. See "Shinto."

Tsumugi silk – a slubbed silk fabric, a variation of pongee. See "Pongee."

Ume – plum blossom.

Urushi – Japanese lacquer, used for painting and lacquerware.

Utsushi-yūzen – a type of kata-yūzen where stencils are used to create patterns, in this instance using a transfer dyeing method where the dye is mixed with paste. See "Kata-yūzen" and "Suri-yūzen."

Yamato damashii – lit. the "Japanese spirit." A term which denotes the cultural values and spirit of the Japanese people.

Yukata – an unlined, casual, and light summer kimono, used primarily for bathhouse visits or summer festivals.

Yūzen – a paste-resist dyeing method. See "Kata-yūzen," "Suri-yūzen," and "Utsushi-yūzen."

Zashiki-gei – a "parlor performance," zashiki being a special room covered in tatami mats (traditional Japanese rush-overlaid mats) usually reserved for guests. See "Gei."

NOTES

FOREWORD: WHO ARE WE NOW?
REFLECTIONS ON *OMOSHIROGARA*

1. Jacqueline M. Atkins, "Introduction," in *Wearing Propaganda: Textiles on the Home Front in Japan, Britain and the United States, 1931–1945*, Jacqueline M. Atkins, ed., London and New Haven: Yale University Press, 2005, p. 27.
2. Hiroshi Kashiwagi, "Design and War: Kimono as 'Parlor Performance' Propaganda," in *Wearing Propaganda : Textiles on the Home Front in Japan, Britain, and the United States, 1931–1945*, Atkins, ed., p. 178.
3. Steve Gdula, *Wearing History: T-Shirts from the Gay Rights Movement*, New York: Alyson Books, 2007, p. 4.
4. Michiko Suzuki, *Reading the Kimono in Twentieth-Century Japanese Literature and Film*, Honolulu: University of Hawai'i Press, 2023, p. 169.
5. Aviad E. Raz, *Riding the Black Ship: Japan and Tokyo Disneyland*, Cambridge, MA: Harvard University Press, 1999, p. 163.
6. Seigo Matsuoka, *Thousand Nights for Thousand Books* blog post, 434 night, 5 December 2001, URL: https://1000ya.isis.ne.jp/0434.html, accessed 26 February 2024. Translation author's own.
7. Suzuki, *Reading the Kimono in Twentieth-Century Japanese Literature and Film*, pp. 161–62.
8. Ibid., pp. 169–70.
9. Jacqueline M. Atkins, "Wearing Novelty," in John Dower, Anne Nishimura Morse, Jacqueline M. Atkins, and Frederic Sharf, *The Brittle Decade: Visualizing Japan in the 1930s*, Boston: Museum of Fine Arts Publications, 2012, p. 143.
10. Edward Conze, *The Psychology of Mass Propaganda* (1939), reprinted in R. N. Levine and N. H. Levine, eds, *Edward Conze's The Psychology of Mass Propaganda*, New York and London: Routledge, pp. 2–4, 6–7.
11. Isao Takahata, interview in *Animage*, 1987, translated 1994 and accessed online, archived from the original at URL: https://web.archive.org/web/20180704093747/http://ghiblicon.blogspot.com/2011/04/animerica-interviews-isao-takahata-and.html and accessed 26 February 2024.

CULTURE ON CLOTH: JAPANESE KIMONO, 1910–1950

1. This period covered the Meiji (1868–1912) and Taishō (1912–1924) eras, plus a large part of the Shōwa (1924–1960). Hirohito was the 124th emperor of Japan and ruled from December 1926 until his death in January 1989. He was Japan's longest reigning monarch.
2. Japan began initial incursions in East Asia in 1931 with the invasion and occupation of Manchuria. Its military involvement in East Asia and the Pacific continued until August 1945, a 15-year period that is often called the Asia–Pacific War.
3. Liza Crihfield Dalby, *Kimono: Fashioning Culture*, New Haven: Yale University Press, 1993), p. 67.
4. Kitamura Tetsuro, *Nihon fukushoku shojiten* (A small dictionary of Japanese clothing) Tokyo: Genryosha, 1988), p. 60. According to Kitamura, the Meiji government made Western-style uniforms compulsory for the military and also employed similar uniforms for mailmen and policemen in 1871.
5. The textile name (*mosulin*) was most likely derived from *mousseline de laine*, a late-19th-century French fabric of fine wool muslin.
6. Hiroshi Kashiwagi, "Design and War: Kimono as 'Parlor-Performance' Propaganda," in *Wearing Propaganda: Textiles on the Home Front in Japan, Britain, and the United States, 1931–1945*, Jacqueline M. Atkins, ed., New Haven: Yale University Press, 2005, p. 178.
7. *Miyamairi* ("shrine visit") is a traditional Shinto rite in Japan for newborns. Parents and grandparents bring the baby to a Shinto shrine one month after birth (31 days for boys, 33 days for girls), where the shrine priest prays for the baby's health and happiness.
8. *Yūzen* is a resist-dyeing technique that prevented dye transfer to fabric. It was perfected by Miyazaki Yūzen (1654–1736), an artist in Kyoto. Although *yūzen* has never fallen out of fashion, elegant handwoven and hand-dyed *yūzen* kimono have become extremely costly today.
9. The Imperial Diet was established by the Meiji Constitution and was first convened as the Imperial Diet in 1890. It took its current form in 1947 with the adoption of the postwar constitution.
10. The *haura* is the *haori* lining. When private parties are held, *haori* are taken off and turned inside out so the dramatic designs of the haura linings can be shown to guests at the event.
11. Mary Dusenbury, "The Art of Color," in *Beyond the Tanabata Bridge: Traditional Japanese Textiles*, William Jay Rathbun, ed., New York: Thames & Hudson in assoc. with the Seattle Art Museum, 1993, pp. 30–31.
12. Donald Keene, "Japanese Aesthetics," in *Aesthetic & Ethical Values in Japanese Culture*, Ronald McLaren, Donald Keene, and Richard Wood, Richmond, IN: Institute for Education on Japan, Earlham College, 1990, p. 27. Keene provides an extensive discussion of the "beauty of monochrome."

13 In the early to mid-Taishō era, girls at urban schools initially wore undivided *andon hakama* (a waist-to-ankle-length skirt, always red) over kimono, but schools eventually produced the sailor outfits for girls, which were considered more modern.

14. *Shichigosan* ("Seven-Five-Three" Day) is a traditional festival day in Japan for three- and seven-year-old girls and five-year-old boys. It is held annually on November 15, when the growth of young children is celebrated.

ACKNOWLEDGMENTS

I would like to offer my deepest gratitude and appreciation to several individuals without whose kind help, advice and assistance the publication of this book would not have been possible. First and foremost, to Jacqueline M. Atkins whose expert knowledge, dedication, and hard work provided us with the wonderful essays and captions which make up with book. Her continuing passion for these kimonos, which have been given so little light in both research and representation is invaluable to all of us dedicated to the study of Japanese culture and the history of fashion.

I am additionally greatly indebted to Anna Jackson for her unwavering support and advice and for always being the pillar which supports the Khalili Collections of Kimono. Her constant dedication and encouragement has been unwavering and deeply appreciated, both for our previous publication of *Kimono: The Art and Evolution of Japanese Fashion*, and in the current one, as well as her advice and assistance in curating these works.

My wholehearted appreciation also goes to Alan and Diane Marcuson, Shoji Tsumugi, Gregory Irvine, Andrew Keelan, Nahla Nassar, Dr Filippo Cervelli, Eyal Oz, Martin Brookes, and Sean Kendall, for their advice, support and knowledge in the writing and collection work which has gone into this publication, as well as a special and heartfelt thanks to Karl Bartley for his wonderful photography. To the wonderful team at Prestel Publishing for their invaluable support, Andrew Hansen, Rochelle Roberts, Agnes Perotto-Wills, and all staff involved in the creation of this publication. And to Peter Dawson and Ronja Rønning of Grade Design, and copyeditor Martha Jay.

Lastly, and most importantly, to Professor Sir Nasser David Khalili and his family for their endless dedication to collecting, preserving, exhibiting, and researching these magnificent works and innumerable others across all the Khalili Collections, and for entrusting us with the opportunity to write and bring these remarkable objects to light and share their deep dedication and love for the art and history of kimono.

Dror Elkvity
2024

INDEX

AUTHOR BIOGRAPHIES

PROFESSOR SIR NASSER DAVID KHALILI is a world-renowned scholar, collector and philanthropist. Since 1970, he has assembled eight of the world's finest and most comprehensive art collections in their field: Islamic Art (700–2000); Hajj and the Arts of Pilgrimage (700–2000); Aramaic Documents (353–324 BC); Japanese Art of the Meiji Period (1868–1912); Japanese Kimono (1700–2000); Swedish Textiles (1700–1900); Spanish Damascene Metalwork (1850–1900); and Enamels of the World (1700–2000). Together these eight collections comprise some 35,000 works and each collection is on its own merit the largest and most comprehensive in the world.

DROR ELKVITY is curator of Japanese Meiji art at the Khalili Collections.

JACQUELINE M. ATKINS is a curatorial consultant and textile historian. She is a consultant at The Kubota Kimono Collection, Itchiku Kubota Museum, and has curated for Fenimore Art Museum, New York, and the International Chodiev Foundation. She is the author of *Wearing Propaganda: Textiles on the Home Front in Japan, Britain and the United States* (Yale University Press, 2005) and *Shared Threads: Quilting Together Past and Present* (Studio, 1994).

A member of Penguin Random House Verlagsgruppe GmbH
Neumarkter Strasse 28 · 81673 Munich

Cover: Kimono for a young woman. *Gosho ningyō* (palace doll) at play, see p. 83
Back cover: Child's kimono. Trams, trains, and puppies, see p. 185
Frontispiece: *Juban* for a woman (detail). Happy Kewpies in Japanese dress, see p. 270
p. 4: Man's *haori* with a decorative lining (*haura*) (detail). Flight around the world, see p. 307

Library of Congress Control Number is available; a CIP catalogue record for this book is available from the British Library.

Editorial direction: Rochelle Roberts
Copyediting: Martha Jay
Design: Peter Dawson, Ronja Rønning, www.gradedesign.com
Production management: Corinna Pickart
Indexing: Marian Aird
Separations: Reproline Mediateam, Unterföhring
Printing and binding: Livonia print, Riga
Paper: Magno Volume

MIX
Papier | Fördert gute Waldnutzung
FSC® C002795

Penguin Random House Verlagsgruppe FSC® N001967

Printed in Latvia

ISBN 978-3-7913-7727-8

www.prestel.com

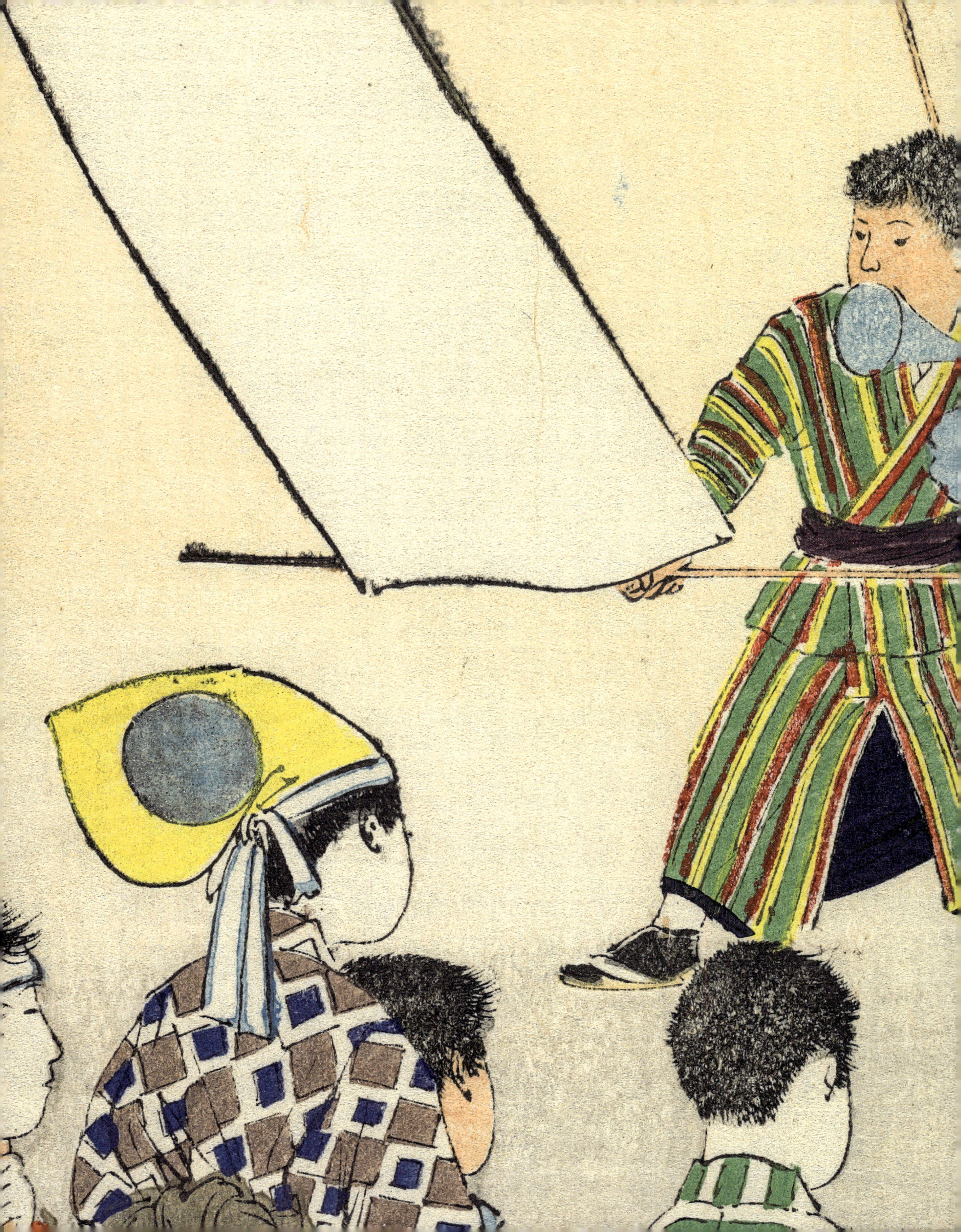